Sinister Street

SINISTER STREET

STREET

VOLUME TWO

SINISTER STREET

THE FIRST VOLUME

CONTENTS

SINISTER STREET

By *COMPTON MACKENZIE* ❧ ❧

THE SECOND VOLUME

I

LONDON: MARTIN SECKER
NUMBER FIVE JOHN STREET ADELPHI MCMXIV

BY THE SAME AUTHOR

THE PASSIONATE ELOPEMENT
CARNIVAL
SINISTER STREET : VOLUME I
GUY AND PAULINE
This novel is in preparation.

KENSINGTON RHYMES

First published November 11, 1914

VOLUME TWO

CONTAINING

III. DREAMING SPIRES

IV. ROMANTIC EDUCATION

PUBLISHER'S NOTE

SINISTER STREET: VOLUME TWO is not a sequel. It is the second and final instalment of a single novel.

The First Volume, published in September 1913, narrates Michael Fane's experience of life from earliest childhood till the time when he leaves St. James' School. His first memories are of life in Carlington Road with his sister Stella, who is however soon parted from him by her musical studies. Mrs. Fane, his mother, seems to be continually travelling, and the two children are usually left in the care of their nurse and of their governess Miss Carthew, who afterwards marries Captain Ross, uncle of Michael's great school friend Alan Merivale. Captain Ross dies in the South African War, as does also Lord Saxby : and it is only then that Mrs. Fane reveals to her children the fact that Lord Saxby was their father.

Michael's earliest religious experiences centre round a stay at Clere Abbey, where also he makes the acquaintance of the man, temporarily known as Brother Aloysius, who later re-appears at Earl's Court as Henry Meats, and by his repulsive familiarity with evil, exercises over Michael an unholy fascination.

Other school holidays Michael spends with schoolmasters in Brittany, with Alan at Eastbourne, with Stella at Compiègne, with Miss Carthew and her mother at Cobble Place, their home in Hampshire ; or wandering from London bookshops into Kensington Gardens. Here, when he is seventeen years old, he first meets Lily Haden, whom he immediately adores. But his young dream is shattered when, from the house of a neighbour and schoolfellow, Drake, he sees her in her garden kissing another boy ; and he tries to forget her in the excitement of Stella's first public concert, which takes place when he is preparing to go up to Oxford.

CONTENTS

Book Three : Dreaming Spires

Book Four : Romantic Education

Contents

BOOK THREE
DREAMING SPIRES

Bright memories of young poetic pleasure
  In free companionship, the loving stress
Of all life-beauty lull'd in studious leisure,
  When every Muse was jocund with excess
  Of fine delight and tremulous happiness;
The breath of an indolent unbridled June,
When delicate thought fell from the dreamy moon:
  But now strange care, sorrow, and grief oppress.

ROBERT BRIDGES.

Chapter I : *The First Day*

MiCHAEL felt glad to think he would start the adventure of Oxford from Paddington. The simplicity of that railway-station might faintly mitigate alarms which no amount of previous deliberation could entirely disperse. He remembered how once he had lightly seen off a Cambridge friend from Liverpool Street and, looking back at the suburban tumult of the Great Eastern Railway, he was grateful for the simplicity of Paddington.

Michael had been careful that all his heavy luggage should be sent in advance; and he had shown himself gravely exacting towards Alan in this matter of luggage, writing several times to remind him of his promise not to appear on the platform with more than a portmanteau of moderate size and a normal kit-bag. Michael hoped this precaution would prevent at any rate the porters from commenting upon the freshness of him and his friend.

"Oxford train ?" enquired a porter, as the hansom pulled up. Michael nodded, and made up his mind to show his esteem when he tipped this promethean.

"Third class ?" the porter went on. Michael mentally doubled the tip, for he had neglected to assure himself beforehand about the etiquette of class, and nothing could have suited so well his self-consciousness as this information casually yielded.

"Let me see, you didn't have any golf-clubs, did you, sir ?" asked the porter.

Michael shook his head regretfully, for as he looked

hurriedly up and down the platform in search of Alan, he perceived golf-clubs everywhere, and when at last he saw him, actually even he had a golf-bag slung over his shoulder.

"I never knew you played golf," said Michael indignantly.

"I don't. These are the governor's. He's given up playing," Alan explained.

"Are you going to play?" Michael pursued. He was feeling rather envious of the appearance of these veteran implements.

"I may have a shot," Alan admitted.

"You might have told me you were going to bring them," Michael grumbled.

"My dear old ass, I never knew I was, until the governor wanged them into my lap just as I was starting."

Michael turned aside and bought a number of papers, far too many for the short journey. Indeed, all the way they lay on the rack unregarded, while the train crossed and recrossed the silver Thames. At first he was often conscious of the other undergraduates in the compartment, who seemed to be eyeing him with a puzzled contempt; but very soon, when he perceived that this manner of looking at one's neighbour was general, he became reconciled to the attitude and ascribed it to a habit of mind rather than to the expression of any individual distaste. Then suddenly, as Michael was gazing out of the window, the pearly sky broke into spires and pinnacles and domes and towers. He caught his breath for one bewitched moment, before he busied himself with the luggage on the rack.

On the platform Michael and Alan decided to part company, as neither of them felt sure enough whether St. Mary's or Christ Church were nearer to the station to risk a joint hansom.

"Shall I come and see you this afternoon?" Michael rashly offered.

"Oh, rather," Alan agreed, and they turned away from one another to secure their cabs.

All the time that Michael was driving to St. Mary's, he was regretting he had not urged Alan to visit him first. A growing sensation of shy dread was making him vow that once safe in his own rooms at St. Mary's nothing should drag him forth again that day. What on earth would he say when he arrived at the college? Would he have to announce himself? How would he find his rooms? On these points he had pestered several Old Jacobeans now at Oxford, but none of them could remember the precise ceremonies of arrival. Michael leaned back in the hansom and cursed their inefficient memories.

Then the cab pulled up by the St. Mary's lodge, and events proceeded with unexpected rapidity. A cheerful man with red hair and a round face welcomed his luggage. The cabman was paid the double of his correct fare, and to Michael's relief drove off instantly. From a sort of glass case that filled half the interior of the lodge somebody very much like a family butler enquired richly who Michael was.

"Mr. C. M. S. Fane?" rolled out the unctuous man.

Michael nodded.

"Is there another Fane?" he asked curiously.

"No, sir," said the head porter, and the negative came out with the sound of a drawn cork. "No, sir, but I wished to hessateen if I had your initials down correct in my list. Mr. C. M. S. Fane," he went on, looking at a piece of paper. "St. Cuthbert's. Four. Two pair right. Your servant is Porcher. Your luggage has arrived, and perhaps you'll settle with me presently. Henry will show you to your rooms. Henry! St. Cuthbert's. Four. Two pair right."

The red-headed under-porter picked up Michael's bag, and Michael was preparing to follow him at once, when the

unctuous man held up a warning hand. Then he turned to
look into a large square pigeon-hole labelled Porcher.

" These letters are for you, sir," he explained pompously.
Michael took them, and in a dream followed Henry under a
great gothic gateway and along a gravel path. In a doorway numbered IV, Henry stopped and shouted ' Porcher ! '
From an echoing vault came a cry in answer, and the scout
appeared.

" One of your gentlemen arrived," said Henry. " Mr.
Fane." Then he touched his cap and retired.

" Any more luggage in the lodge, sir ? " Porcher asked.

" Not much," said Michael apologetically.

" There's a nice lot of stuff in your rooms," Porcher
informed him. " Come in yesterday morning, it did."

They were mounting the stone stairway, and on each
of the floors Michael was made mechanically aware by a
printed notice above a water-tap that no slops must be
emptied there. This prohibition stuck in his mind somehow
as the first ascetic demand of the university.

" These are your rooms, sir, and when you want me, you'll
shout, of course. I'm just unpacking Mr. Lonsdale's wine."

Michael was conscious of pale October sunlight upon the
heaped-up packing-cases ; he was conscious of the unnatural
brilliancy of the fire in the sunlight; he was conscious
that life at Oxford was conducted with much finer amenities
than life at school. Simultaneously he was aware of a
loneliness ; yet as he once more turned to survey his room,
it was a fleeting loneliness which quickly perished in the
satisfaction of a privacy that hitherto he had never possessed.
He turned into the bedroom, and looked out across the quad,
across the rectangle of vivid green grass, across the Warden's
garden with its faint gaiety of autumnal flowers and tufted
grey walls, and beyond to where the elms of the deer-park
were massed against the thin sky and the deer moved in
leisurely files about the spare sunlight.

It did not take Michael long to arrange his clothes;
and then the problem of undoing the packing-cases presented
itself. A hammer would be necessary, and a chisel. He
must shout for Porcher. Shouting in the tremulous peace
of this October morning would inevitably attract more
attention to himself than would be pleasant, and he post-
poned the summons in favour of an examination of his
letters. One after another he opened them, and every one
was the advertisement of a tailor or hairdresser or tobacconist. The tailors were the most insistent; they even
went so far as to announce that representatives would call
upon him at his pleasure. Michael made up his mind to
order his cap and gown after lunch. Lunch! How should
he obtain lunch? Where should he obtain lunch? When
should he obtain lunch? Obviously there must be some
precise manner of obtaining lunch, some ritual consecrated
by generations of St. Mary's men. The loneliness came back
triumphant, and plunged him dejectedly down into a
surprizingly deep wicker-chair. The fire crackled in the
silence, and the problem of lunch remained insoluble. The
need for Porcher's advice became more desperate. Other
freshmen before him must have depended upon their
scout's experience. He began to practise calling Porcher in
accents so low that they acquired a tender and reproachful
significance. Michael braced himself for the performance
after these choked and muffled rehearsals, and went boldly
out on to the stone landing. An almost entranced silence
held the staircase, a silence that he could not bring himself
to violate. On the door of the rooms opposite he read his
neighbour's name—*Mackintosh*. He wished he knew
whether Mackintosh were a freshman. It would be delightful to make him share the responsibility of summoning
Porcher from his task of arranging Lonsdale's wine. And
who was Lonsdale? *No slops must be emptied here! Mackintosh! Fane!* Here were three announcements hinting

at humanity in a desolation of stillness. Michael reading his own name gathered confidence and a volume of breath, leaned over the stone parapet of the landing and, losing all his courage in a sigh, decided to walk downstairs and take his chance of meeting Porcher on the way.

On the floor beneath Michael read *Bannerman* over the left-hand door and *Templeton-Collins* over the right-hand door. While he was pondering the personality and status of Templeton-Collins, presumably the gentleman himself appeared, stared at Michael very deliberately, came forward and, leaning over the parapet, yelled in a voice that combined rage, protest, disappointment and appeal with the maximum of sound : 'Porcher !' After which, Templeton-Collins again stared very deliberately at Michael and retired' into his room, while Michael hurried down to intercept the scout, hoping his dismay at Templeton-Collins' impatience would not be too great to allow him to pay a moment's attention to himself.

However, on the ground floor the silence was still unbroken, and hopelessly Michael read over the right-hand door *Amherst*, over the left-hand door *Lonsdale*. What critical moment had arrived in the unpacking of Lonsdale's wine to make the scout so heedless of Templeton-Collins' call ? Again it resounded from above, and Michael looking up involuntarily, caught the downward glance of Templeton-Collins himself.

" I say, is Porcher down there ? " the latter asked fretfully.

" I think he's unpacking Lonsdale's wine."

" Who's Lonsdale ? " demanded Templeton-Collins. " You might sing out and tell him I want him."

With this request Templeton-Collins vanished, leaving Michael in a quandary. There was only one hope of relieving the intolerable situation, he thought, which was to shout 'Porcher' from where he was standing. This he

did at the very moment the scout emerged from Lonsdale's
rooms.

" Coming, sir," said Porcher in an aggrieved voice.

" I think Mr. Templeton-Collins is calling you," Michael
explained, rather lamely he felt, since it must have been
obvious to the scout that Michael himself had been calling
him.

" And I say," he added hurriedly, " you might bring me
up a hammer or something to open my boxes, when you've
done."

Leaving Porcher to appease the outraged Templeton-
Collins, Michael retreated to the security of his own rooms,
where in a few minutes the scout appeared to raise the
question of lunch.

" Will you take commons, sir ? "

Michael looked perplexed.

" Commons is bread and cheese. Most of my gentlemen
takes commons. If you want anything extra, you go to the
kitchen and write your name down for what you want."

This sounded too difficult, and Michael gratefully chose
commons.

" Ale, sir ? "

Michael nodded. If the scout had suggested champagne,
he would have assented immediately.

Porcher set to work and undid the cases ; he also explained
where the china was kept and the wood and the coal. He
expounded the theory of roll-calls and chapels, and was
indeed so generous with information on every point of
college existence that Michael would have been glad to
retain his services for the afternoon.

" And the other men on this staircase ? " Michael asked,
" are any of them freshers ? "

" Mr. Mackintosh, Mr. Amherst, and the Honourable
Lonsdale is all freshmen. Mr. Templeton-Collins and Mr.
Bannerman is second year. Mr. Templeton-Collins had

the rooms on the ground floor last term. Very noisy gentleman. Very fond of practising with a coach-horn. And he don't improve," said Porcher meditatively.

" Do you mean on the coach-horn ? " Michael asked.

" Don't improve in the way of noise. Noise seems to regular delight him. He'd shout the head off of a deaf man. Did you bring any wine, sir ? "

Michael shook his head.

" Mr. Lonsdale's brought too much. Too much. It's easier to order it as you want it from the Junior Common Room. Anything else, sir ? "

Michael tried to think of something to detain for a while the voluble service of Porcher, but as he seemed anxious to be gone, he confessed there was nothing.

Left alone again, Michael began to unpack his pictures. Somehow those black and red scenes of Montmartre and the landscapes of the Sussex downs with a slight atmosphere of Japan seemed to him unsatisfactory in this new room, and he hung them forthwith in his bedroom. For his sitting-room he resolved to buy certain pictures that for a long time he had coveted—Mona Lisa and Primavera and Rembrandt's Knight in Armour and Mantegna's St. George. Those other relics of faded and jejune aspirations would label him too definitely. People would see them hanging on his walls and consider him a decadent. Michael did not wish to be labelled in his first term. Oxford promised too much of intellectual romance and adventure for him to set out upon his Odyssey with the stepping-stones of dead tastes hung round his neck. Oxford should be approached with a stainless curiosity. Already he felt that she would only yield her secret in return for absolute surrender. This the grave city demanded.

After his pictures Michael unpacked his books. The deep shelves set in the wall beside the fireplace looked alluring in their emptiness, but when he had set out in line all the books he possessed, they seemed a scanty and undistinguished crowd. The pirated American edition of Swinburne alone carried itself with an air: the Shelley and the Keats were really editions better suited to the glass and gloom of a seaside lodging: the school-books looked like trippers usurping the gothic grandeur of these shelves. Moreover, the space was eked out with tattered paper editions that with too much room at their disposal collapsed with an appearance of ill-favoured intoxication. Michael examined his possessions in critical discontent. They seemed to symbolize the unpleasant crudity of youth. In the familiar surroundings of childhood they had seemed on the contrary to testify to his maturity. Now at Oxford he felt most abominably young again, yet he was able to console himself with the thought that youth would be no handicap among his peers. He took down the scenes of Montmartre even from the walls of his bedroom and pushed them ignominiously out of sight under the bed.

Michael abandoned the contemplation of his possessions, and looked out of his sitting-room window at the High. There was something salutary in the jangle of the trams, in the vision of ordinary people moving unconsciously about the academic magnificence of Oxford. An undergraduate with gown wrapped carelessly round his neck flashed past on a bicycle, and Michael was discouraged by the sense of his diabolic ease. The luxury of his own rooms, the conviction of his new independence, the excitement of an undiscovered life all departed from him, and he was left with nothing but a loneliness more bitter even than when at Randell House he had first encountered school.

Porcher came in presently with lunch, and the commons of bread and cheese with the ale foaming in a silver tankard added the final touch to Michael's depression. He thought that nothing in the world could express the spirit of loneli-

ness so perfectly as a sparse lunch laid for one on a large
table. He wandered away from its melancholy invitation
into the bedroom and looked sadly down into the quad.
In every doorway stood knots of senior men talking : continually came new arrivals to hail familiarly their friends
after the vacation : scouts hurried to and fro with trays of
food : from window to window gossip, greetings, appoint-
ments were merrily shouted. Michael watched this scene
of intimate movement played against the background of
elms and grey walls. The golden fume of the October
weather transcended somehow all impermanence, and he
felt with a sudden springing of imagination that so had this
scene been played before, that so for ever would it be played
for generations to come. Yet for him as yet outside the
picture remained, fortunately less eternal, that solitary
lunch. He ate it hurriedly and as soon as he had finished
set out to find Alan at Christ Church.

Freedom came back with the elation of walking up the
High ; and in the Christ Church lodge Michael was able to
ask without a blush for Alan's rooms. The great space of
Tom quad by absorbing his self-consciousness allowed him
to feel himself an unit of the small and decorative population
that enhanced the architecture there. The scattered groups
of friends whose voices became part of the very air itself
like the wings of the pigeons and the perpetual tapping of
footsteps, the two dons treading in slow confabulation
that wide flagged terrace, even himself were here for ever.
Michael captured again in that moment the crystalized
vision of Oxford which had first been vouchsafed to him
long ago by that old print of St. Mary's tower. He turned
reluctantly away from Tom quad, and going on to seek
Alan in Meadows, by mistake found himself in Peckwater.
A tall fair undergraduate was standing alone in the centre
of the quad, cracking a whip. Suddenly Michael realized
that his father had been at Christ Church; and this tall fair

whip-cracker served for him as the symbol of his father. He must have often stood here so, cracking a whip; and Michael never came into Peckwater without recreating him so occupied on a fine autumn afternoon, whip in hand, very tall and very fair in the glinting sunlight.

Dreams faded out, when Michael ran up the staircase to Alan's rooms; but he was full-charged again with all that suppressed intellectual excitement which he had counted upon finding in Oxford, but which he had failed to find until the wide tranquility of Tom quad had given him, as it were, the benediction of the university.

" Hullo, Alan ! " he cried. " How are you getting on ? I say, why do they stick ' Mr.' in front of your name over the door ?' At St. Mary's we drop the ' Mr.' or any other sort of title. Aren't you unpacked *yet* ? You are a slacker. Look here, I want you to come out with me at once. I've got to get some more picture-wire and a gown and a picture of Mona Lisa."

" Mona how much ? " said Alan.

" La Gioconda, you ass."

" Sorry, my mistake," said Alan.

" And I saw some rattling book-shops as I came up the High," Michael went on. " What did you have for lunch ? I had bread and cheese—commons we call it at St. Mary's. I say, I think I'm glad I don't have to wear a scholar's gown."

" I'm an exhibitioner," said Alan.

" Well, it's the same thing. I like a commoner's gown best. Where did you get that tea-caddy ? I don't believe I've got one. Pretty good view from your window. Mine looks out on the High."

" Look here," asked Alan very solemnly, " where shall I hang this picture my mater gave me ? "

He displayed in a green frame The Soul's Awakening.

" Do you like it ? " Michael asked gloomily.

"I prefer these grouse by Thorburn that the governor gave me, but I like them both in a way," Alan admitted.

"I don't think it much matters where you hang it," Michael said. Then, thinking Alan looked rather hurt, he added hastily: "You see it's such a very square room that practically it might go anywhere."

"Will you have a meringue?" Alan asked, proffering a crowded plate.

"A meringue?" Michael repeated.

"We're rather famous for our meringues here," said Alan gravely. "We make them in the kitchen. I ordered a double lot in case you came in."

"You seem to have found out a good deal about Christ Church already," Michael observed.

"The House," Alan corrected. "We call it—in fact everybody calls it the House."

Michael was inclined to resent this arrogation by a college not his own of a distinct and slightly affected piece of nomenclature, and he wished he possessed enough knowledge of his own peculiar college customs to counter Alan's display.

"Well, hurry up and come out of the House," he urged. "You can't stay here unpacking all the afternoon."

"Why do you want to start buying things straight away?" Alan argued.

"Because I know what I want," Michael insisted.

"Since when?" Alan demanded. "I'm not going to buy anything for a bit."

"Come on, come on," Michael urged. He was in a hurry to enjoy the luxury of traversing the quads of Christ Church in company, of strolling down the High in company, of looking into shop windows in company, of finally defeating that first dismal loneliness with Alan and his company.

It certainly proved to be a lavish afternoon. Michael bought three straight-grained pipes so substantially silvered that they made his own old pipes take on an attenuated vulgarity. He bought an obese tobacco jar blazoned with the arms of his college and, similarly blazoned, a protuberant utensil for matches. He bought numerous ounces of those prodigally displayed mixtures of tobacco, every one of which was vouched for by the vendor as in its own way the perfect blend. He bought his cap and his gown and was measured by the tailor for a coat of Harris tweed such as everybody seemed to wear. He found the very autotype of Mona Lisa he coveted, and farther he was persuaded by the picture-dealer to buy for two guineas a signed proof of a small copperplate engraving of the Primavera. This expenditure frightened him from buying any more pictures that afternoon and seemed a violent and sudden extravagance. However, he paid a visit to the Bank where, after signing his name several times, he was presented with a cheque-book. In order to be perfectly sure he knew how to draw a cheque, he wrote one then and there, and the five sovereigns the clerk shovelled out as irreverently as if they were chocolate creams, made him feel that his new cheque-book was the purse of Fortunatus.

Michael quickly recovered from the slight feeling of guilt that the purchase of the Botticelli print had laid upon his conscience, and in order to assert his independence in the face of Alan's continuous dissuasion, he bought a hookah, a miniature five-barred gate for a pipe-rack, a mother-of-pearl cigarette-holder which he dropped on the pavement outside the shop and broke in pieces, and finally seven ties of knitted silk.

By this time Michael and Alan had reached the Oriental Café in Cornmarket Street; and since it was now five o'clock and neither of them felt inclined to accept the responsibility of inviting the other back to tea, they went into the café and ate a quantity of hot buttered toast and parti-coloured cakes. The only thing that marred their enjoyment and faintly disturbed their equanimity was the entrance of three exquisitely untidy undergraduates who stood for a moment in the doorway and surveyed first the crowded café in general, and then more particularly Michael and Alan with an expression of outraged contempt. After a prolonged stare one of them exclaimed in throaty scorn :

" Oh, god, the place is chock full of damned freshers ! "
Whereupon he and his companions strode out again.

Michael and Alan looked at each other abashed. The flavour had departed from the tea : the brilliant hues of the cakes had paled : the waitress seemed to have become suddenly critical and haughty. Michael and Alan paid their bill and went out.

" Are you coming back to my rooms ? " Michael asked. Yet secretly he half hoped that Alan would refuse. Dusk was falling, and he was anxious to be alone while the twilight wound itself about this grey city.

Alan said he wanted to finish unpacking, and Michael left him quickly, promising to meet him again to-morrow.

Michael did not wander far in that dusk of fading spires and towers, for a bookshop glowing like a jewel in the gloom of an ancient street lured him within. It was empty save for the owner, a low-voiced man with a thin pointed beard who as he stood there among his books seemed to Michael strangely in tune with his romantic surroundings, as much in tune as some old painting by Vandyck would have seemed leaning against the shelves of books.

A little wearily, almost cynically, Mr. Lampard bade Michael good evening.

" May I look round ? " Michael asked.
The bookseller nodded.
" Just come up ? " he enquired.
" To-day," Michael confessed.
" And what sort of books are you interested in ? "
" All books," said Michael.

" This set of Pater for instance," the bookseller suggested, handing Michael a volume bound in thick sea-green cloth and richly stamped with a golden monogram. " Nine volumes. Seven pounds ten, or six pounds fifteen cash." This information he added in a note of disdainful tolerance.

Michael shook his head and looked amused by the offer.

" Of course, nobody really cares for books nowadays," Mr. Lampard went on. " In the early 'nineties it was different. Then everybody cared for books."

Michael resented this slur upon the generation to which he belonged.

" Seven pounds ten," he repeated doubtfully. How well those solid sea-green volumes would become the stately book-shelves of his room.

" What college ? " asked Mr. Lampard. " St. Mary's ? Ah, there used to be some great buyers there. Let me see, Lord William Vaughan, the Marquis of Montgomery's son, was at St. Mary's, and Mr. Richard Meysey. I published his first volume of poems—of course, you've read his books. He was at St. Mary's. Then there was Mr. Chalfont and Mr. Weymouth. You've heard of The Patchbox ? I still have some copies of the first number, but they're getting very scarce. All St. Mary's men and all great book buyers. But Oxford has changed in the last few years. I really don't know why I go on selling books, or rather why I go on not selling them."

Mr. Lampard laughed and twisted his beard with fingers that were very thin and white. Outside in the darkness a footfall echoed along some entry. The sound gave to Michael a sense of communion with the past, and the ghosts of bygone loiterers were at his elbow.

" Perhaps after all I will take the Pater," he said. " Only I may not be able to pay you this term."

The bookseller smiled.

" I don't think I shall worry you. Do you know this set—

2 L

Boccaccio, Rabelais, Straparola, Masuccio, etc. Eleven guineas bound in watered silk. They'll always keep their price, and of course all the photogravures are included."

" All right. You might send them too."

Michael could not resist the swish of the watered silk as Volume One of the Decameron was put back into its vacancy. And as he hurried down to College the thought that he had spent nineteen pounds one shilling scarcely weighed against the imagination of lamplight making luminous those silken backs of faded blue and green and red and gold, against those silk markers and the consciousness that now at last he was a buyer of books, a buyer whose spirit would haunt that bookshop. He had certainly never regretted the seventeen-and-sixpence he had spent on the pirated works of Swinburne, and then he was a wretched schoolboy balanced on the top of a ladder covetous of unattainable splendours, a pitiable cipher in the accounts of Elson's bookshop. At Lampard's he was already a personality.

All that so far happened to Michael not merely in one day at Oxford, but really during his whole life was for its embarrassment nothing in comparison with the first dinner in hall. As he walked through the Cloisters and heard all about him the burble of jolly and familiar conversation, he shuddered to think what in a minute he must face. The list of freshmen, pinned up on the board in the Lodge, was a discouraging document to those isolated members of public schools other than Eton, Winchester, Harrow or Charterhouse. These four seemed to have produced all but six or seven of the freshmen. Eton alone was responsible for half the list. What chance, thought Michael, could he stand against such an impenetrable phalanx of conversation as was bound to ensue from such a preponderance? However, he was by now at the top of the steps that led up to hall, and a mild old butler was asking his name.

"You'll be at the second freshmen's table. On the right, sir. Mr. Wedderburn is at the head of your table, sir."

Michael was glad to find his table at the near end of hall, and hurriedly taking a seat, almost dived into the soup that was quickly placed before him. He did not venture to open a conversation with either of his neighbours, but stared instead at the freshman occupying the armchair at the head of the table, greatly impressed by his judicial gravity of demeanour, his neat bulk and the profundity of his voice.

"How do you become head of a table?" Michael's left-hand neighbour suddenly asked.

Michael said he really did not know.

"Because what I'm wondering," the left-hand neighbour continued, "is why they've made that ass Wedderburn head of our table."

"Why, is he an ass?" Michael enquired.

"Frightful ass," continued the left-hand neighbour whom Michael perceived to be a small round-faced youth, very fair and very pink. "Perfectly harmless, of course. Are you an Harrovian?"

Michael shook his head.

"I thought you were a cousin of my mother," said the left-hand neighbour.

Michael looked astonished.

"His name's Mackintosh. What's your name?"

Michael told him.

"My name's Lonsdale. I think we're on the same staircase—so's Mackintosh. It's a pity he's an Harrovian, but I promised my mother I'd look him up."

Then, after surveying the table, Lonsdale went on in a confidential undertone :

"I don't mind telling you that the Etonians up here are a pretty poor lot. There are two chaps from my house who are not so bad—in fact rather good eggs—but the rest! Well, look at that ass Wedderburn. He's typical."

" I think he looks rather a good sort," said Michael.

" My dear chap, he was absolutely barred. M' tutor used to like him, but really—well—I don't mind telling you, he's really an æsthete."

With this shocked condemnation, Lonsdale turned to his other neighbour and said in his jerky and somewhat mincing voice that was perfectly audible to Michael:

" I say, Tommy, this man on my right isn't half bad. I don't know where he comes from. His name's Fane."

" He's from St. James'."

" Where on earth's that ? "

" London."

" Why, I thought it was a kind of charity school," said Lonsdale. Then he turned to Michael again:

" I say, are you really from St. James' ? "

Michael replied coldly that he was.

" I say, come and have coffee with me after hall. One or two O.E.'s are coming in, but you won't mind ? "

" Why, do you want to find out something about St. James' ? " demanded Michael frowning.

" Oh, I say, don't be ratty. It's that ass Tommy. He always talks at the top of his voice."

Lonsdale, as he spoke, looked so charmingly apologetic and displayed such accomplished sang-froid that Michael forgave him immediately and promised to come to coffee.

" Good egg ! " Lonsdale exclaimed with the satisfaction of having smoothed over an awkward place. " I say," he offered, " if you'd like to meet Wedderburn, I'll ask him too. He seems to have improved since he's been up at the Varsity. Don't you think that fat man Wedderburn has improved, Tommy ? "

Tommy nodded.

" One day's done him no end of good."

" I say," Lonsdale offered, " you haven't met Fane. Mr. Fane—Mr. Grainger. I was just saying to Fane that the Etonians are a rotten lot this term."

" One or two are all right," Grainger admitted with evident reluctance.

" Well, perhaps two," Lonsdale agreed. " This dinner isn't bad, what ? "

By this time the conversation at the table had become more general, and Michael gradually realized that some of the alarm he had felt himself had certainly been felt by his companions. Now at any rate there was a perceptible relaxation of tension. Still the conversation was only general in so much as that whenever anybody spoke, the rest of the table listened. The moment the flow of his information dried up, somebody else began pumping forth instruction. These slightly nervous little lectures were delivered without any claim to authority and they came up prefaced by the third person of legendary narrative.

" They say we shall all have to interview the Warden to-morrow."

" They say on Sunday afternoon the Wagger makes the same speech to the freshers that he's made for twenty years."

" They say we ought to go head of the river this year."

" They say the freshers are expected to make a bonner on Sunday night."

" They say anyone can have commons of bread and cheese by sending out word to the buttery. It's really included in the two-and-fourpence for dinner."

" They say they charge a penny for the napkin every night."

So the information proceeded, and Michael had just thought to himself that going up to Oxford was very much like going to school again, when from the second-year tables crashed the sound of a concerted sneeze. The dons from high table looked coldly down the hall, expressing a vague,

but seemingly impotent disapproval, for immediately afterwards that sternutation shook the air a second time.

Michael thought the difference between school and
Oxford might be greater than he had supposed.

The slowest eater at the second freshmen's table had
nervously left half his savoury. Wedderburn without apparent embarrassment had received the Sub-Warden's per-
mission to rise from dinner. Lonsdale hurriedly marshalled as
many of his acquaintances as he could, and in a large and
noisy group they swarmed through the moonlight towards
his rooms.

Michael was interested by Lonsdale's sitting-room, for he
divined at once that it was typical, just a transplanted Eton
study with the addition of smoking paraphernalia. The
overmantel was plumed with small photographs of pleasant
young creatures in the gay nautical costumes of the Fourth
of June and festooned hats of Alexandra or Monarch, of the
same pleasant young creatures at an earlier and chubbier age,
of the same pleasant young creatures with pencilled moustaches and the white waistcoat of Pop. In addition to their
individual commemorations the pleasant young creatures
would appear again in house groups, in winning house
elevens, and most exquisitely of all in Eton Society. Michael
always admired the photographs of Pop, for they seemed to
him to epitomize all the traditions of all the public-schools of
England, to epitomize them moreover with something of that
immortality of captured action expressed by great Athenian
sculpture. In comparison with Pop the Harrow Philathletic
Society was a barbarous group, with all the self-consciousness
of a deliberate archaism. Besides the personal photographs in
Lonsdale's room there were studies of grouse by Thorburn;
and Michael, remembering Alan's grouse, felt in accord with
Lonsdale and with all that Lonsdale stood for. Knowing
Alan, he felt that he knew Lonsdale, and at once he became
more at ease with all his contemporaries in Lonsdale's room.

Michael looked at the coloured prints of Cecil Aldin's
pictures and made up his mind he would buy a set for Alan :
also possibly he would buy for Alan the Sir Galahad of Watts
which was rather better than The Soul's Awakening.

After Lonsdale's pictures Michael surveyed Lonsdale's
books, the brilliantly red volumes of Jorrocks, the two or
three odd volumes of the Badminton library, and the school
books tattered and ink-splashed. More interesting than such
a library were the glossy new briars, the virgin meerschaum,
the patent smoking-tables and another table evidently designed to make drinking easy, but by reason of the complexity of its machinery actually more likely to discourage
one for ever from refreshment. The rest of the space, apart
from the furniture bequeathed by the noisy Templeton-
Collins when he moved to larger rooms above, was crowded
with the freshmen whom after hall Lonsdale had so hastily
gathered together unassorted.

" I ordered coffee for sixteen," announced the host. " I
thought it would be quicker than making it in a new machine
that my sister gave me. It just makes enough for three, and
the only time I tried, it took about an hour to do that . . .
who'll drink port ? "

Michael thought the scout's prophecies about the super-
fluity of Lonsdale's wine were rather premature, for it
seemed that everybody intended to drink port.

" I believe this is supposed to be rather good port," said
Lonsdale.

" It is jolly good," several connoisseurs echoed.

" I don't know much about it myself. But my governor's
supposed to be rather a judge. He said ' this is wasted on
you and your friends, but I haven't got any bad wine to give
you.' "

Here everybody held up their glasses against the light,
took another sip and murmured their approval.

" Do you think this is a good wine, Fane ? " demanded

Lonsdale, thereby drawing so much attention to Michael
that he blushed to nearly as deep a colour as the port itself.

" I like it very much," Michael said.

" Do you like it, Wedderburn ? " asked Lonsdale, turning
to the freshman who had sat in the armchair at the head of
the second table.

" Damned good wine," pronounced Wedderburn in a
voice so rich with appreciation and so deep with judgment
that he immediately established a reputation for worldly
knowledge, and from having been slightly derided at Eton
for his artistic ambitions was ever afterwards respected and
consulted. Michael envied his air of authority, but trembled
for Wedderburn's position when he heard him reproach
Lonsdale for his lack of any good pictures.

" You might stick up one that can be looked at for more
than two seconds," Wedderburn said severely.

" What sort of picture ? " asked Lonsdale.

" Primavera, for instance," Wedderburn suggested, and
Michael's heart beat in sympathy.

" Never heard of the horse," Lonsdale answered. " Who
owned her ? "

" My god," Wedderburn rumbled, " I'll take you to buy
one to-morrow, Lonny. You deserve it after that."

" Right-O ! " Lonsdale cheerfully agreed. " Only I don't
want my room to look like the Academy, you know."

Wedderburn shook his head in benevolent contempt, and
the conversation was deflected from Lonsdale's artistic
education by a long-legged Wykehamist with crisp chestnut
hair and a thin florid face of dimpling smiles.

" Has anybody been into Venner's yet ? " he asked.

" I have," proclaimed a dumpy Etonian whose down-
curving nose hung over a perpetually open mouth. " Marjoribanks took me in just before hall. But he advised me not
to go in by myself yet awhile."

" The second-year men don't like it," agreed the long-

legged Wykehamist with a wise air. "They say one can begin
to go in occasionally in one's third term."

"What is Venner's ?" Michael asked.

"Don't you know ?" sniffed the dumpy Etonian who had
already managed to proclaim his friendship with Marjoribanks, the President of the Junior Common Room, and therefore presumably had the right to open his mouth a little
wider than usual at Michael.

"I'm not quite sure myself," said Lonsdale quickly. "I
vote that Cuffe explains."

"I'm not going to explain," Cuffe protested, and for
some minutes his mouth was tightly closed.

"Isn't it just a sort of special part of the J.C.R. ?" suggested the smiling Wykehamist, who seemed to wish to make
it pleasant for everybody, so long as he himself would not
have to admit ignorance. "Old Venables himself is a ripper.
They say he's been steward of the J.C.R. for fifty years."

"Thirty-two years," corrected Wedderburn in his voice of
most reverberant certitude. "Venner's is practically a club.
You aren't elected, but somehow you know just when you
can go in without being stared at. There's nothing in Oxford like that little office of Venner's. It's practically made
St. Mary's what it is."

All the freshmen, sipping their port and lolling back in
their new gowns, looked very reverent and very conscious of
the honour and glory of St. Mary's which they themselves
hoped soon to affirm more publicly than they could at present.
Upon their meditations sounded very loud the blast of a
coach-horn from above.

"That's Templeton-Collins," said Michael.

"Who's he ?" several demanded.

"He's the man who used to live in these rooms last year,"
said Lonsdale lightly, as if that were the most satisfactory
description for these freshmen, as indeed for all its youthful
heartlessness it was.

" Let's all yell and tell him to shut up that infernal row,"
suggested Wedderburn sternly. Already from sitting in an
armchair at the head of a table of freshmen he was acquiring an austere seniority of his own.

" To a second-year blood ? " whispered somebody in
dread surprize.

" Why not take away the coach-horn ? " Lonsdale added.

However, this the freshmen were not prepared to do,
although with unanimity they invited Templeton-Collins to
refrain from blowing it.

" Keep quiet, little boys," shouted Templeton-Collins
down the stairs.

The sixteen freshmen retreated well pleased with their
audacity, and the long-legged Wykehamist proclaimed de-
lightedly that this was going to be a hot year. " I vote we
have a bonner."

" Will you light it, Sinclair ? " asked another Wykehamist
in a cynical drawl.

" Why not ? " Sinclair retorted.

" Oh, I don't know. But you always used to be better at
theory than practice."

" How these Wykehamists love one another," laughed an
Etonian.

This implied criticism welded the four Winchester men
present in defiance of all England, and Michael was impressed by their haughty and bigoted confidence.

" Sunday night is the proper time for a bonner," said
Wedderburn. " After the first ' after.' "

" ' After ' ? " queried another.

" Oh, don't you know ? Haven't you heard ? " several
well-informed freshmen began, but Wedderburn with his
accustomed gravity assumed the burden of instruction, and
the others gave way.

" Every Sunday after hall," he explained, " people go up
to the J.C.R. and take wine and dessert. Healths are drunk,

and of course the second-year men try to make the freshers blind. Then everybody goes round to one of the large rooms in Cloisters for the ' after Common Room.' People sing and do various parlour tricks. The President of the J.C.R. gives the first ' after' of the term. The others are usually given by three or four men together. Whisky and cigars and lemon-squash. They usually last till nearly twelve. Great sport. They're much better than private wines, better for everybody. That's why we have them on Sunday night," he concluded rather vaguely.

The unwieldy bulk of sixteen freshmen was beginning to break up into bridge fours. Friendships were already in visible elaboration. The first evening had wonderfully brought them together. Something deeper than the superficial amity of chance juxtaposition at the same table was now begetting tentative confidences that would ultimately ripen to intimacies. Etonians were discovering that all Harrovians were not the dark-blue bedecked ruffians of Lords nor the aggressive boors of Etonian tradition. Harrovians were beginning to suspect that some Etonians might exist less flaccid, less deliberately lackadaisical, less odiously serene than the majority of those they had so far only encountered in summer holidays. Carthusians found that athletic prowess was going to count pleasantly in their favour. Even the Wykehamists extended a cordiality that was not positively chilling, and though they never lost an opportunity to criticize implicitly all other schools, and though their manners were so perfect that they abashed all but the more debonair Etonians, still it was evident they were sincerely trying to acknowledge a little merit, a little good-fellowship among these strange new contemporaries, however exuberantly uneducated they might appear to Wykeham's adamantine mould.

Michael did not thrust himself upon any of these miniature societies in the making, because the rather conscious efforts of diverse groups to put themselves into accord with one another made him shy and restless. Nobody yet among these freshmen seemed able to take his neighbour for granted, and Michael fancied that himself as the product of a day-school appeared to these cloistered catechumens as surprizing and disconcerting and vaguely improper as a ballet-girl or a French count. At the same time he sympathized with their bewilderment and gave them credit for their attempt not to let him think he confused their social outlook. But the obviously sustained attempt depressed him with a sense of fatigue. After all, his trousers were turned up at the bottom and the last button of his waistcoat was undone. Failure to comply with the Draconic code of dress could not be attributed to him, as mercilessly it had served to banish into despised darkness a few scholars whose trousers frayed themselves upon their insteps and whose waistcoats were ignobly buttoned to the very end.

" An Old Giggleswickian," commented someone in reference to one of these disgraced scholars, with such fanatic modishness that Michael was surprized to see he wore the crude tie of the Old Carthusians ; such inexorable scorn consorted better with the rich sobriety of the Old Wykehamist colours.

" Why, were you at school with him ? " asked Michael quickly.

" Me ? At Giggleswick ? " stammered the Carthusian.

" Why not ? " said Michael. " You seem to know all about him."

" Isn't your name Fane ? " demanded the Carthusian abruptly, and when Michael nodded, he said he remembered him at his private school.

"That'll help me along a bit, I expect," Michael prophesied.

" We were in the same form at Randell's. My name's Avery."

" I remember you," said Michael coldly. And he thought

to himself how little Avery's once stinging wit seemed to matter now. Really he thought Avery was almost attractive with his fresh complexion and deep blue eyes and girlish sensitive mouth, and when he rose to go out of Lonsdale's room, he was not sorry that Avery rose too and walked out with him into the quad.

" I say," Avery began impulsively. " Did I make an ass of myself just now ? I mean, do you think people were sick with me ? "

" What for ? "

" I mean did I sound snobbish ? " Avery pursued.

" Not more than anybody else," Michael assured him, and as he watched Avery's expression of petulant self-reproach he wondered how it was possible that once it mattered whether Avery knew he had a governess and wore combinations instead of pants and vest.

" I say, aren't you rather keen on pictures ? I heard you talking to Wedderburn. Do come up to my rooms some time. I'm in Cloisters. Are you going out ? You'll have to buck up. It's after nine."

They had reached the lodge, and Michael, nodding goodnight, was ushered out by the porter. As he reached the corner of Longwall, Tom boomed his final warning, and over the last echoing reverberation sounded here and there the lisp of footsteps in the moonlight.

Michael wandered on in meditation. From lighted windows in the High came a noise of laughter and voices that seemed to make more grave and more perdurable the spires and towers of Oxford, deepening somehow the solemnity of the black entries and the empty silver spaces before them. Michael pondered the freshmen's chatter and apprehended dimly how this magical sublunary city would convert all that effusion of naïve intolerance to her own renown. He stood still for a moment rapt in an ecstasy of submission to this austere beneficence of stone that sheltered even him, the

worshipper of one day, with the power of an immortal pride.
He wandered on and on through the liquid moonshine,
gratefully conscious of his shadow that showed him in his cap
and gown not so conspicuous an intruder as he had seemed to
himself that morning.

So for an hour he wandered in a trancéd revelry of aspirations, until at last breathlessly he turned into the tall
glooms of New College Street and Queen's Lane, where as
he walked he touched the cold stones, forgetting the world.

In the High he saw his own college washed with silver, and
the tower tremulous in the moonlight, fine-spun and frail as
a lily.

It was pleasant to nod to one or two people standing in the
lodge. It was pleasant to turn confidently under the gateway of St. Cuthbert's quad. It was pleasant to be greeted
by his own name at the entrance of his staircase. It was the
greatest contentment he had ever known to see the glowing
of his fire, and slowly to untie under the red-shaded light the
fat parcels of his newly-bought books.

Outside in the High a tram rumbled slowly·past. The
clock struck ten from St. Mary's tower. The wicker chair
creaked comfortably. The watered silk of the rich bindings
swished luxuriously. This was how Boccaccio should be read.
Michael's mind was filled with the imagination of that gay
company, secluded from the fever, telling their gay stories in
the sunlight of their garden. This was how Rabelais should
be read : the very pages seemed to glitter like wine.

Midnight chimed from St. Mary's tower. One by one the
new books went gloriously to their gothic shelves. The red
lamp was extinguished. Michael's bedroom was scented
with the breath of the October night. It was too cold to
read more than a few sentences of Pater about some splendid
bygone Florentine. Out snapped the electric light : the
room was full of moonshine, so full that the water in the
bath tub was gleaming.

Chapter II: *The First Week*

THE first two or three days were busy with interviews, initiations, addresses and all the academic panoply which Oxford brings into action against her neophytes.

First of all, the Senior Tutor, Mr. Ardle, had to be visited. He was a deaf and hostile little man whose side-whiskers and twitching eyelid and manner of exaggerated respect towards undergraduates combined to give the impression that he regarded them as objectionable discords in an otherwise justly modulated existence.

Michael in his turn went up the stairs to Mr. Ardle's room, knocked at the door and passed in at the don's bidding to where he sat sighing amid heaps of papers and statistical sheets. The glacial air of the room was somehow increased by the photographs of Swiss mountains that crowded the walls.

"Mr. ? " queried the Senior Tutor. "Oh, yes, Mr. Fane. St. James'. Your tutor will be the Dean—please sit down—the Dean, Mr. Ambrose. What school are you proposing to read ? "

"History, I imagine," said Michael. "History ! " he repeated, as Mr. Ardle blinked at him.

"Yes," said the Senior Tutor in accents of patient boredom. "But we have to consider the immediate future. I suggest Honour Moderations and Literæ Humaniores."

"I explained to you that I wanted to read History," said Michael, echoing himself involuntarily the don's tone of patient boredom.

" I have you down as coming from St. James'," snapped the Senior Tutor. " A school reputed to send out good classical scholars, I believe."

" I'm not a scholar," Michael interrupted. " And I don't intend to take Honour Mods."

" That will be for the college to decide."

" Supposing the college decided I was to read Chinese ? " Michael enquired.

" There is no need for impertinence. Well, well, for the present I have put you down for the lectures on Pass Moderations. You will attend my lectures on Cicero, Mr. Churton on the Apologia, Mr. Carder on Logic, and Mr. Vereker for Latin Prose. The weekly essay set by the Warden for freshmen you will read to your tutor Mr. Ambrose."

Then he went on to give instructions about chapels and roll-calls and dining in hall and the various regulations of the college, while the Swiss mountains stared bleakly down at the chilly interview.

" Now you'd better go and see Mr. Ambrose," said the Senior Tutor, and Michael left him. On the staircase he passed Lonsdale going up.

" What's he like ? " asked Lonsdale.

" Pretty dull," said Michael.

" Does he keep you long ? "

Michael shook his head.

" Good work," said Lonsdale cheerfully. " Because I've just bought a dog." And he whistled his way upstairs.

Michael wondered what the purchase of a dog had got to do with the Senior Tutor, but relinquished the problem on perceiving Mr. Ambrose's name on the floor below.

The Dean's room was very much like the Senior Tutor's, and the interview, save that it was made slightly more tolerable by the help of a cigarette, was of much the same chilliness owing to Michael's reiterated refusal to read Honour Moderations.

"I expected a little keenness," said Mr. Ambrose.

"I shall be keen enough when I've finished with Pass Mods," said Michael. "Though what good it will be for me to read the Pro Milone and the Apology all over again, when I read them at fifteen, I don't know."

"Then take Honour Moderations?" the Dean advised.

"I've given up classics," Michael argued, and as the cigarette was beginning to burn his fingers and the problem of disposing of it in the Dean's room seemed insoluble, he hurried out.

Lonsdale was whistling his way downstairs from his interview with Mr. Ardle.

"Hallo, Fane, what did he say to you?"

"I think all these dons are very much like schoolmasters," growled Michael resentfully.

"They can't help it," said Lonsdale. "I asked old Ardle if I could keep a dog in college, and he turned as blue as an owl. Anyone would think I'd asked him if I could breed crocodiles."

In addition to these personal interviews the freshmen had certain communal experiences to undergo. Amongst these was their formal reception into the University, when they trooped after the Senior Tutor through gothic mazes and in some beautiful and remote room received from the Vice-Chancellor a bound volume of Statuta et Decreta Universitatis. This book they carried back with them to college, where in many rooms it shared with Ruff's Guide and Soapy Sponge's Sporting Tour an intellectual oligarchy. Saturday morning was spent in meeting the Warden at the Warden's Lodgings, where they shook hands with him in nervous quartettes. Michael when he discussed this experience with his fellows fancied that the Warden's butler had left a deeper impression than the Warden himself. On Sunday afternoon, however, when they gathered in the hall to hear the annual

2 M

address of welcome and exhortation, the great moon-faced Warden shone undimmed.

"You have come to Oxford," he concluded, "some of you to hunt foxes, some of you to wear very large and very unusual overcoats, some of you to row for your college and a few of you to work. But all of you have come to Oxford to remain English gentlemen. In after life when you are ambassadors and proconsuls and members of Parliament you will never remember this little address which I have the honour now of delivering to you. That will not matter, so long as you always remember that you are St. Mary's men and the heirs of an honourable and ancient foundation."

The great moon-faced Warden beamed at them for one moment, and after thanking them for their polite attention floated out of the hall. The pictures of cardinals and princes and poets in their high golden frames seemed in the dusk faintly to nod approval. The bell was ringing for evening chapel, and the freshmen went murmurously along the cloisters to take their places, feeling rather proud that the famous quire was their quire and looking with inquisitive condescension at the visitors who sat out of sight of those candle-starred singers.

In hall that night the chief topic of conversation was the etiquette and ritual of the first J.C.R. wine.

Michael to his chagrin found himself seated next to Mackintosh, for Mackintosh, cousin though he was of the sparkish Lonsdale, was a gloomy fellow scornful of the general merriment. As somebody had quickly said, sharpening his young wit, he was more of a wet-blanket than a Mackintosh.

"I suppose you're coming to the J.C.R. ?" Michael asked.

"Why should I ? Why should I waste my time trying to keep sober for the amusement of all these fools ?"

"I expect it will be rather a rag," said Michael hopefully;

ɔut he found it tantalizing to hear farther down the table
ɲatches of conversation that heard more completely would
ɦave enlightened him on several points he had not yet
ɲastered in the ceremony of wine in the J.C.R. However,
t was useless to speculate on such subjects in the company of
ɦe lugubrious Mackintosh. So they talked instead of San-
low exercises and mountain-climbing in Cumberland, neither
ɔf which topics interested Michael very greatly.

Hall was rowdy that evening, and the dons looked petu-
antly down from high table, annoyed to think that their
distinguished visitors of Sunday evening should see so many
ɔieces of bread flung by the second-year men. The moon-
faced Warden was deflected from his intellectual revolutions
round a Swedish man of science, and sent the butler down to
whisper a remonstrance to the head of one of the second-year
ables. But no sooner had the butler again taken his place
ɔehind the Warden's chair than a number of third-year
ɲen whose table had been littered by the ammunition of
ɦeir juniors retaliated without apparent loss of dignity,
and presently both years combined to bombard the
Scholars. Meanwhile the freshmen applauded with laughter,
and thought their seniors were wonderful exemplars for
ɦe future.

After hall everybody went crowding up the narrow stairs
o the J.C.R., and now most emphatically the J.C.R. pre-
ented a cheerful sight, with the red-shaded lamps casting
such a glow that the decanters of wine stationed before the
President's place looked like a treasure of rubies. The two
ong tables were set at right angles to one another, and the
President sat near their apex. All along their shining length
at regular intervals stood great dishes of grapes richly
ɔloomed, of apples and walnuts and salted almonds and
devilled biscuits. The freshmen by instinct rushed to sit
altogether at the end of the table more remote from the
loor. As Michael looked at his contemporaries, he perceived

that of the forty odd freshmen scarcely five-and-twenty had come to this, the first J.C.R. Vaguely he realized that already two sets were manifest in the college, and he felt depressed by the dulness of those who had not come and some satisfaction with himself for coming.

The freshmen stared with awe at Marjoribanks, the President of the J.C.R., and told one another with reverence that the two men on either side of him were those famous rowing blues from New College, Permain and Strutt ; while some of them who had known these heroes at school sat anxiously unaware of their presence and spoke of them familiarly as Jack Permain and Bingey. There were several other cynosures from New College and University near the President's chair, a vivid bunch of Leander ties. There were also one or two old St. Mary's men who had descended to haunt for a swift week-end the place of their renown, and these were pointed out by knowing freshmen as unconcernedly as possible.

One by one the President released the decanters, and round and round they came. Sometimes they would be held up by an interesting conversation ; and when the sherry and the port and the burgundy were all standing idle, a shout of ' pass along the wine ' would go up, after which for a time the decanters would swing vigorously from hand to hand. Then suddenly Marjoribanks was seen to be bowing to Permain, and Permain was bowing solemnly back to his host. This was a plain token to everybody that the moment for drinking healths had arrived. A great babel of shouted names broke out at the end of the Common Room remote from the freshmen, so tremendous a din that the freshmen felt the drinking of their own healths at their end would pass unnoticed. So they drank to one another, bowing gravely after the manner of their seniors.

Michael had determined to take nothing but burgundy, and when he had exchanged sentiments with the most of his year, he congratulated himself upon the comparative steadiness of his head. Already in the case of one or two reckless mixers he noticed a difficulty in deciding how many times it was necessary to clip a cigar, an inclination to strike the wrong end of a match and a confusion between right and left when the decanters in their circulation paused before them.

After the first tumult of good wishes had died down, Marjoribanks lifted his glass, looked along to where the freshmen were sitting and shouted 'Cuffe!' Cuffe hastily lifted his glass and answering 'Marjorie!', drained his salute of acknowledgment. Then he sat back in his chair with an expression, Michael thought, very like that of an actress who has been handed a bouquet by the conductor. But Cuffe was not to be the only recipient of honour, for immediately afterwards Majoribanks sang out 'Lonsdale!' Lonsdale was at the moment trying to explain to Tommy Grainger some trick with the skin of a banana which ought to have been an orange and a wooden match which ought to have been a wax vesta. Michael, who was sitting next to him, prodded anxiously his ribs.

"What's the matter?" demanded Lonsdale indignantly. "Can't you see I'm doing a trick?"

"Marjoribanks is drinking your health," whispered Michael in an agony that Lonsdale would be passed over.

"Hurrah!" shouted Lonsdale, rising to his feet and scandalizing his fellows by his intoxicated audacity. "Where is the old ripper?" Then "Mark over!" he shouted and collapsed into Tommy Grainger's lap. Everybody laughed, and everybody, even the cynosures from New College and University, began to drink Lonsdale's health without heeltaps.

"No heelers, young Lonsdale," they called mirthfully.

Lonsdale pulled himself together, stood up, and balancing himself with one hand on Michael's shoulder replied:

" No heelers, you devils ? : No legs, you mean ! " Then he collapsed again.

Soon all the freshmen found that their healths were now being drunk, all the freshmen, that is, from Eton or Win-chester or Harrow. Michael and one or two others without old schoolfellows among the seniors remained more sober. But then suddenly a gravely indolent man with a quizzical face, who the day before in the lodge had had occasion to ask Michael some trifling piece of information, cried ' Fane ! ' raising his glass. Michael blushed, blessed his unknown ac-quaintance inwardly and drank what was possibly the sin-cerest sentiment of the evening. Other senior men hearing his name, followed suit, even the great Marjoribanks himself ; and soon Michael was very nearly as full as Lonsdale. An immense elation caressed his soul, a boundless sense of com-munal life, a conception of sublime freedom that seemed to be illimitable for ever. The wine was over. Down the narrow stone stairs everybody poured. At the foot on the right was a little office—the office of Venables, the steward of the J.C.R., the eleusinian and impenetrable sanctum of seniority called Venner's. Wine-chartered though they were, the freshmen did not venture even to peep round the corner of the door, but hurried out into the cloisters, where they walked arm-in-arm shouting.

Michael could have fancied himself at a gathering of mediæval witches. The moon temporarily clouded over by the autumnal fog made the corbels and gargoyles and sculp-tured figures above the cloisters take on a grotesque vivacity, as the vapours curled around them. The wine humming in his head : the echoing shouts of his companions : the deco-rative effect of the gowns : the chiming high above of the bells in the tower : all combined to create for Michael a nightmare of exultation. He was aware of a tremendous zest in doing nothing, and there flowed over him a conscious-ness that this existence of shout and dance along these

cloisters was really existence lived in a perpetual expression
of the finest energy. The world seemed to be going round so
much faster than usual that in order to keep up with this
new pace, it was necessary for the individual like himself to
walk faster, to talk faster, to think faster, and finally to raise
to incoherent speed every coherent faculty. Another curious
effect of the wine, for after all Michael admitted to himself
that his mental exhilaration must be due to burgundy, was
the way in which he found himself at every moment walking
beside a different person. He would scarcely have finished an
excited acceptance of Wedderburn's offer to go to-morrow
and look at some Dürer woodcuts, when he would suddenly
find himself discussing sympathetically with Lonsdale the
iniquity of the dons in refusing to let him keep his new dog
in one of the scouts' pigeon-holes in the lodge.

"After all," Lonsdale pointed out earnestly, "they're
never really full, and the dog isn't large—of course I don't
expect to keep him in a pigeon-hole when he's full grown,
but he's a puppy."

"It's absurd," Michael agreed.

"That's the word I've been looking for," Lonsdale exclaimed: "What was it again? Absurd! You see what I
say is, when one scout's box is full, move the poor little beast
into another. It isn't likely they'd all be full at the same
time. What was that word you found just now? Absurd!
That's it. It is absurd. It's absurd!"

"And anyway," Michael pointed out, "if they were all
full they could chain him to the leg of the porter's desk."

"Of course they could. I say, Fane, you're a damned
good sort," said Lonsdale. "I wish you'd come and have
lunch with me to-morrow. I don't think I've asked very
many chaps : I want to show you that dog. He's in a stable
off Holywell at present. Beastly shame! I'm not complaining, of course, but what I want to ask our dons is how would
they like to be bought by me and shut up in Holywell?"

And just when Michael had a very good answer ready, he found himself arm-in-arm with Wedderburn again, who was saying in his gravest voice that over a genuine woodcut by Dürer it was well worth taking trouble. But before Michael could disengage Wedderburn's Dürer from Lonsdale's dog, he found himself running very fast beside Tommy Grainger who was shouting:

"Five's late again! Six, you're bucketing! Bow, you're late! Two, *will* you get your belly down!"

Then Grainger stopped suddenly and asked Michael in a very solemn tone whether he knew what was the matter with the crew. Michael shook his head and watched the others steer their devious course towards him and Grainger.

"They're too drunk to row," said Grainger.

"Much too drunk," Michael agreed.

When he had pondered for a moment or two his last remark, he discovered it was extraordinarily funny. So he was seized with a paroxysm of laughter, and the more he laughed, the more he wanted to laugh. When somebody asked him what he was laughing at, he replied it was because he had left the electric light burning in his room. Several people seemed to think this just as funny as Michael thought it, and they joined him in his mirth, laughing unquenchably until Wedderburn observed severely in his deepest voice:

"Buck up, you're all drunk, and they're coming out of Venner's."

Then like some patient profound countryman he shepherded them all up to the large room on a corner staircase of Cloisters, where the 'after' was going to be held. The freshmen squeezed themselves together in a corner and were immensely entertained by the various performers, applauding with equal rapture a light comedian from Pembroke, a tenor from Corpus, a comic singer from Oriel and a mimic from professional London. They drank lemon squashes to steady themselves: they joined in choruses: they cheered and

smoked cigars and grew more and more conscious as the
evening progressed that they belonged to a great college
called St. Mary's. Their enthusiasm reached its zenith,
when the captain of the Varsity Eleven (a St. Mary's man
even as they were St. Mary's men) sang the St. Mary's song
in a voice whose gentleness of utterance and sighing modesty
in no way abashed the noisy appreciation of the audience.
It was a wonderful song, all about the triumphs of the college
on river and cricket-field, in the Schools, in Parliament and
indeed everywhere else. It had a fine rollicking chorus which
was repeated twice after each verse. And as there were about
seventeen verses, by the time the song was half over the
freshmen had learned the words and were able to sing the
final chorus with a vigour which positively detonated against
the windows and contrasted divertingly with the almost in-
audible soloist.

Last of all came Auld Lang Syne, when everybody stood
up on chairs and joined hands, seniors, second-year men and
freshmen. Auld Lang Syne ended with perhaps the noisiest
moment of all because although Lonsdale had taken several
lemon squashes to steady himself, he had not taken enough to
keep his balance through the ultimate energetic repetition,
when he collapsed headlong into a tray of syphons and
glasses, dragging with him two other freshmen. But nobody
seemed to have hurt himself, and downstairs they all rushed,
shouting and hulloaing, into the cool moonlight.

The guests from New College and University and the 'out-
of-college' men hurried home, for it was close upon midnight. In the lodge the freshmen foregathered for a few
minutes with the second-year men, and as they talked they
knew that the moment was come when they must proclaim
themselves free from the restrictions of school, and by the
kindling of a bonfire prove that they were now truly grown
up. Bundles of faggots were seized from the scouts' holes :
in the angle of St. Cuthbert's quad where the complexion

of the gravel was tanned by the numberless bonfires of past
generations the pile of wood grew taller and taller.: two or
three douches of paraffin made the mass readily inflammable:
a match was set, and with a roar the bonfire began. . From
their windows second-year men, their faces lighted by the
ascending blaze, looked down with pleasant patronage upon
the traditional pastime of their juniors.   The freshmen
danced gleefully round the pyre of their boyhood, feeding it
with faggots and sometimes daringly and ostentatiously with
chairs : the heat became intense : the smoke surged upwards,
obscuring the bland aspectful moon.   Slowly upon the group
of law-breakers fell a silence, as they stood bewitched by the
beauty of their own handiwork. The riotous preparations
and annunciatory yells had died away to an intimate murmur
of conversation. From the lodge came Shadbolt the
unctuous head-porter to survey for a moment this mighty
bonfire : conscious of their undergraduate dignity the freshmen chaffed him, until he retired with muttered protests to
summon the Dean.

   " What will the Dean do ? " asked one or two less audacious ones as they faded into various doorways, ready to
obliterate their presence as soon as authority should arrive
upon the scene.

   " What does the Dean matter ? " cried others, flinging
more faggots on to the fire until it crackled and spat and
bellowed more fiercely than ever, lighting up with its wavy
radiance the great elms beyond the Warden's garden and the
Palladian fragment of New quad whence the dons like
Georgian squires pondered their prosperity.

   Presently against the silvery space framed by the gateway
of St. Cuthbert's tower appeared the silhouette of the Dean,
lank and tall with college cap tip-tilted down on to his nose
and round his neck a gown wrapped like a shawl. Nearer he
came, and involuntarily the freshmen so lately schoolboys
took on in their attitude a certain anxiety. Somehow the

group round the bonfire had become much smaller. Somehow more windows looking upon the quad were populated with flickering watchful faces.

"Great Scott! What can Ambrose do?" demanded Lonsdale despairingly; but when at last the Dean reached the zone of the fire, there only remained about eight freshmen to ascertain his views and test his power. The Dean stood for a minute or two, silently warming his hands. In a ring the presumed leaders eyed him, talking to each other the while with slightly exaggerated carelessness.

"Well, Mr. Fane?" asked the Dean.

"Well, sir," Michael replied.

"Damned good," whispered Lonsdale ecstatically in Michael's ear. "You couldn't have said anything better. That's damned good."

Michael under the enthusiastic congratulations of Lonsdale began to feel he had indeed said something very good, but he hoped he would soon have an opportunity to say something even better.

"Enjoying yourself, Mr. Lonsdale?" enquired the Dean.

"Yes, sir. Are you?" answered Lonsdale.

"Splendid," murmured Michael.

A silence followed this exchange of courtesies. The bonfire was beginning to die down, but nobody ventured under the Dean's eye to put on more faggots. Under-porters were seen drawing near with pails of water, and though a cushion aimed from a window upset one pail, very soon the bonfire was a miserable mess of smoking ashes and the moon resumed her glory. From an upper window some second-year men chanted in a ridiculous monotone:

"The Dean—he was the Dean—he was the Dean—he was the Dean! The Dean—he was the Dean he was—the Dean he was—the Dean!!"

Mr. Ambrose did not bother to look up in the direction of the glee, but took another glance at Michael, Lonsdale,

Grainger and the other stalwarts. Then he turned away.

"Good night," Lonsdale called after the retreating figure of the tall hunched don, and not being successful in luring him back, he poured his scorn upon the defaulters safe in their rooms above.

"You are a lot of rotters. Come down and make another."

But the freshmen were not yet sufficiently hardy to do this. One by one they melted away, and Lonsdale marked his contempt for their pusillanimity by throwing two syphons and his gown into the Warden's garden. After which he invited Michael and his fellow die-hards to drink a glass of port in his rooms. Here for an hour they sat, discussing their contemporaries.

In the morning Shadbolt was asked if anybody had been hauled for last night's bonner.

"Mr. Fane, Mr. Grainger and the Honourable Lonsdale," he informed the enquirer. Together those three interviewed the Dean.

"Two guineas each," he announced after a brief homily on the foolishness and inconvenience of keeping everybody up on the first Sunday of term. "And if you feel aggrieved, you can get up a subscription among your co-lunatics to defray your expenses."

Michael, Grainger and Lonsdale sighed very movingly, and tried to look like martyrs, but they greatly enjoyed telling what had happened to the other freshmen and several second-year men. It was told, too, in a manner of elaborate nonchalance with many vows to do the same to-morrow.

Chapter III : *The First Term*

HIS first term at Oxford was for Michael less obviously a period of discovery than from his prefigurative dreams he had expected. He had certainly pictured himself in the midst of a society more intellectually varied than that in which he found himself; and all that first term became in retrospect merely a barren noisy time from which somehow after numberless tentative adjustments and developments emerged a clear view of his own relation to the college, and more particularly to his own ' year.' These trials of personality were conducted with all the help that sensitiveness could render him. But this sensitiveness when it had registered finely and accurately a few hazardous impressions was often sharp as a nettle in its action, so sharp indeed sometimes that he felt inclined to withdraw from social encounters into a solitude of books. Probably Michael would have become a recluse, if he had not decided on the impulse of the moment to put down his name for Rugby football. He was fairly successful in the first match, and afterwards Carben, the secretary of the college club, invited him to tea. This insignificant courtesy gave Michael a considerable amount of pleasure, inasmuch as it was the first occasion on which he had been invited to his rooms by a second-year man. With Carben he found about half-a-dozen other seniors and a couple of freshmen whom he did not remember to have noticed before; and the warm room, whose murmurous tinkle was suddenly hushed as he entered, affected him with a glowing hospitality.

Michael had found it so immediately easy to talk that when Carben made a general observation on the row of Sunday night's celebration, Michael proclaimed enthusiastically the excellence of the bonfire.

"Were you in that gang ?" Carben asked in a tone of contemptuous surprize.

"I was fined," Michael announced, trying to quench the note of exultation in deference to the hostility he instinctively felt he was creating.

"I say," Carben sneered, "so at last one of the ' bloods ' is going to condescend to play Rugger. Jonah," he called to the captain of the Fifteen who was lolling in muscular grandeur at the other end of the room, " we've got a college blood playing three-quarter for us."

"Good work," said Jones, with a toast-encumbered laugh. " Where is he ? "

Carben pointed to Michael who blushed rather angrily.

"No end of a blood," Carben went on. " Lights bonfires and gets fined all in his first week."

The two freshmen sniggered, and Michael made up his mind to consult Lonsdale about their doom. He was pensively damned if these two asses should laugh at him. There had already been talk of ragging one or two freshmen whose raw and mediocre bearing had offended the modish perceptions of the majority. When the proscription was on foot, Michael promised his injured pride that he would denounce them with their red wrists and their smug insignificance.

"You were at St. James', weren't you ?" asked Jones. " Did you know Mansfield ? "

"I didn't know him exactly," said Michael, " but—in fact—we thought him rather a tick."

"Thanks very much and all that," said Jones. " He was a friend of mine, but don't apologize."

There was a general laugh at Michael's expense from which Carben's guffaw survived. " Jonah was never one for moving in the best society," he said with an implication in his tone that the best society was something positively contemptible.

Michael retired from the conversation and sat silent, counting with cold dislike the constellated pimples on Carben's face. Meanwhile the others exercised their scornful wit upon the 'bloods' of the college.

"Did you hear about Fitzroy and Gingold?" Carben indignantly demanded. "Gingold was tubbing yesterday and Fitzroy was coaching. 'Can't you keep your fat little paunch down? I don't want to look at it,' said Fitzroy. That's pretty thick from a second-year man to a third-year man in front of a lot of freshers. Gingold's going to jack rowing, and he's quite right."

"Quite right," a chorus echoed.

Michael remembered Fitzroy very blithely intoxicated at the J.C.R.; he remembered, too, that Fitzroy had drunk his health. This explosion of wrath at the insult offered to Gingold's dignity irritated Michael. He felt sure that Gingold had a fat little paunch and that he thoroughly deserved to be told to keep it out of sight. Gingold was probably as offensive as Jones and Carben.

"These rowing bloods think they've bought the college," somebody was wisely propounding.

"We ought to go head of the river this year, oughtn't we?" Michael enquired with as much innocence as he could muster to veil the armed rebuke.

"Well, I think it would be a d'd good thing, if we dropped six places," Carben affirmed.

How many pimples there were, thought Michael looking at the secretary, and he felt he must make some excuse to escape from this room whose atmosphere of envy and whose castrated damns were shrouding Oxford with a dismal genteelness.

"Oh, by the way, before you go," said Carben, "you'd better let me put your name down for the Ugger."

" The what ? " Michael asked with a faint insolence.

" The Union."

Michael, occupied with the problem of adjustment, had no intention of committing himself so early to the Union and certainly not under the sponsorship of Carben.

" I don't think I'll join this term."

He ran down the stairs from Carben's rooms and stood for a moment apprehensively upon the lawn. Then sublime in the dusk he saw St. Mary's tower and, refreshed by that image of an aspiration, he shook off the memory of Carben's tea-party as if he had alighted from a crowded Sunday train and plunged immediately into deep country.

In hall that night Lonsdale asked Michael what he had been doing, and was greatly amused by his information, so much amused that he called along the table to Grainger :

" I say, Tommy, do you know we've got a Rugger rough with us ? "

Several people murmured in surprize.

" I say, have you really been playing Rugger ? "

" Well, great Scott ! " exclaimed Michael, " there's nothing very odd in that."

" But the Rugger roughs are all very bad men," Lonsdale protested.

" Some are," Michael admitted. " Still, it's a better game than Socker."

" But everybody at St. Mary's plays Socker," Lonsdale went on.

Michael felt for a while enraged against the pettiness of outlook that even the admired Lonsdale displayed. How ridiculous it was to despise Rugby football because the college was so largely composed of Etonians and Harrovians and Wykehamists and Carthusians. It was like schoolboys. And Michael abruptly realized that all of them sitting at this freshmen's table were really schoolboys. It was natural after all that with the patriotism of youth they should disdain games foreign to their traditions. This, however, was no reason for allowing Rugby to be snuffed out ignominiously.

" Anyway I shall go on playing Rugger," Michael asserted.

" Shall I have a shot ? " suggested Lonsdale.

" It's a most devilish good game," Michael earnestly avowed.

" Tommy," Lonsdale shouted, " I'm going to be a Rugger rough myself."

" I shall sconce you, young Lonsdale, if you make such a row," said Wedderburn severely.

" My god, Wedders, you are a prize ass," chuckled the offender.

Wedderburn whispered to the scout near him.

" Have you sconced me ? " Lonsdale demanded.

The head of the table nodded.

Lonsdale was put to much trouble and expense to avenge his half-crown. Finally with great care he took down all the pictures in Wedderburn's room and hung in their places gaudy texts. Also for the plaster Venus of Milo he caused to be made a miniature chest-protector. It was all very foolish, but it afforded exquisite entertainment to Lonsdale and his auxiliaries, especially when in the lodge they beheld Wedderburn's return from a dinner out of college, and when presently they visited him in his room to enjoy his displeasure.

Michael's consciousness of the sharp division in the college between two broad sections prevented him from retiring into seclusion. He continued to play Rugby football almost entirely in order to hear with a delighted irony the comments of the ' bad men ' on the ' bloods.' Yet many of these ' bad men ' he rather liked, and he would often defend them to his critical young contemporaries, although on the ' bad men ' of his own year he was as hard as the rest of the social leaders. He was content in this first term to follow loyally with other heedless ones the trend of the moment. He made few attempts to enlarge the field of his outlook by cultivating

2 N

acquaintanceship outside his own college. Even Alan he seldom
visited, since in these early days of Oxford it seemed to him
essential to move cautiously and always under the protection
of numbers. These freshmen in their first term found a
curious satisfaction in numbers. When they lunched together, they lunched in eights and twelves ; when they dined
out of college, as they sometimes did, at the Clarendon or the
Mitre or the Queen's, they gathered in the lodge almost in
the dimensions of a school-treat.

" Why do we always go about in such quantity ? " Michael
once asked Wedderburn.

" What else can we do ? " answered Wedderburn. " We
must subject each other to—I mean—we haven't got any
clubs yet. We're bound to stick together."

" Well, I'm getting rather fed up with it," said Michael.
" I feel more like a tourist than a Varsity man. Every day
we lunch and dine and take coffee and tea in great masses of
people. I'm bored to tears by half the men I go about with,
and I'm sure they're bored to tears with me. We don't talk
about anything but each other's schools and whether A is a
better chap than B, or whether C is a gentleman and if it's
true that D isn't really. I bought for my own pleasure some
rather decent books ; and every other evening about twelve
people come and read them over each other's shoulders, while
I spend my whole time blowing cigarette ash off the pictures.
And when they've all read the story of the nightingale in
the Decameron, they sit up till one o'clock discussing who of
our year is most likely to be elected president of the J.C.R.
four years from now."

But for all Michael's grumbling through that first term he
was beginning to perceive the blurred outlines of an intimate
society at Oxford which in the years to come he would remember. There was Wedderburn himself whose square-
headed solidity of demeanour and episcopal voice masked a
butterfly of a temperament that flitted from flower to flower

of artistic experiment or danced attendance upon freshmen, the honey of whose future fame he seemed always able to probe.

"I wonder if you really are the old snob you try to make yourself," said Michael. "And yet I don't think it is snobbishness. I believe it's a form of collecting. It's a throw back to primitive life in a private school. One day in your fourth year you'll give a dinner party for about twelve bloods and I shall come too and remind you just when and how and where you picked them all up before their value was perfectly obvious. Partly of course it's due to being at Eton where you had nothing to do but observe social distinction in the making and talk about Burne-Jones to your tutor."

"My dear fellow," said Wedderburn deeply, "I have these people up to my rooms because I like them."

"But it *is* convenient always to like the right people," Michael argued. "There are lots of others just as pleasant whom you don't like. For instance, Avery——"

"Avery!" Wedderburn snorted.

"He's not likely ever to be captain of the Varsity Eleven," said Michael. "But he's amusing, and he can talk about books."

"Patronizing ass," Wedderburn growled.

"That's exactly what he isn't," Michael contradicted.

"Damnable poseur," Wedderburn rumbled.

"Oh, well, so are you," said Michael.

He thought how wilfully Wedderburn would persist in misjudging Avery. Yet himself had spent most delightful hours with him. To be sure, his sensitiveness made him sharp-tongued, and he dressed rather too well. But all the Carthusians at St. Mary's dressed rather too well and carried about with them the atmosphere of a week-end in a sporting country-house owned by very rich people. This burbling prosperity would gradually trickle away, Michael thought, and he began to follow the course of Avery four years hence directed by Oxford to—to what ? To some distinguished goal of art, but whether as writer or painter or sculptor he did not know, Avery was so very versatile. Michael mentally put him on one side to decorate a conspicuous portion of the ideal edifice he dreamed of creating from his Oxford society. There was Lonsdale. Lonsdale really possessed the serene perfection of a great work of art. Michael thought to himself that almost he could bear to attend for ever Ardle's dusty lectures on Cicero in order that for ever he might hear Lonsdale admit with earnest politeness that he had not found time to glance at the text the day before, that he was indeed sorry to cause Mr. Ardle such a mortification, but that unfortunately he had left his Plato in a saddler's shop, where he had found it necessary to complain of a saddle newly made for him.

" But I am lecturing on Cicero, Mr. Lonsdale. The Pro Milone was not delivered by Plato, Mr. Lonsdale."

" What's he talking about ? " Lonsdale whispered to Michael.

" Nor was it delivered by Mr. Fane," added the Senior Tutor dryly.

Lonsdale looked at first very much alarmed by this suggestion, then seeing by the lecturer's face that something was still wrong, he assumed a puzzled expression, and finally in an attempt to relieve the situation he laughed very heartily and said : ·

" Oh, well, after all, it's very much the same." Then, as everybody else laughed very loudly, Lonsdale sat down and leaned back, pulling up his trousers in gentle self-congratulation.

" Rum old buffer," he whispered presently to Michael. " His eye gets very glassy when he looks at me. Do you think I ought to ask him to lunch ? "

Michael thought that Avery, Wedderburn and Lonsdale

might be considered to form the nucleus of the intimate ideal society which his imagination was leading him on to shape. And if that trio seemed not completely to represent the forty freshmen of St. Mary's, there might be added to the list certain others for qualities of athletic renown that combined with a charm of personality gave them the right to be set up in Michael's collection as types. There was Grainger, last year's Captain of the Boats at Eton, who would certainly row for the 'Varsity in the spring. Michael liked to sit in his rooms and watch his sprawling bulk and listen for an hour at a time to his naïve theories of life. Grainger seemed to shed rays of positive goodness, and Michael found that he exercized over this splendid piece of youth a fascination which to himself was surprizing.

"Great Scott, you are an odd chap," Grainger once ejaculated.

" Why ? "

" Why, you're a clever devil, aren't you, and you don't seem to do anything. Have I talked a lot of rot ? "

" A good deal," Michael admitted. " At least, it would be rot if I talked it, but it would be ridiculous if you talked in any other way."

" You *are* a curious chap. I can't make you out."

" Why should you ? " asked Michael. " You were never sent into this world to puzzle out things. You were sent here to sprawl across it just as you're sprawling across that sofa. When you go down, you'll go into the Egyptian Civil Service and you'll sprawl across the Sahara in exactly the same way. I rather wish I were like you. It must be quite comfortable to sit down heavily and unconcernedly on a lot of people. I can't imagine a more delightful mattress ; only I should feel them wriggling under me."

" I suppose you're a Radical. They say you are," Grainger lazily announced through puffed-out fumes of tobacco.

" I suppose I might be," said Michael, " if I wanted to

proclaim myself anything at all, but I'd much rather watch you sprawling effectively and proclaiming yourself a supporter of Conservatism. I've really very little inclination to criticize people like you. It's only in books I think you're a little boring."

Term wore on, and a pleasurable anticipation was lent to the coming vacation by a letter which Michael received from his mother.

CARLINGTON ROAD,
November 20th.

Dearest Michael,

I'm so glad you're still enjoying Oxford. I quite agree with you it would be better for me to wait a little while before I visit you, though I expect I should behave myself perfectly well. You'll be glad to hear that I've got rid of this tiresome house. I've sold it to a retired Colonel—such an objectionable old man, and I'm really so pleased he's bought it. It has been a most worrying autumn because the people next door were continually complaining of Stella's piano, and really Carlington Road has become impossible. Such an air of living next door, and whenever I look out of the window the maid is shaking a mat and looking up to see if I'm interested. We must try to settle on a new house when you're back in town. We'll stay in an hotel for awhile. Stella has had to take a studio, which I do not approve of her doing, and I cannot bear to see the piano going continually in and out of the house. There are so many things I want to talk to you about, money, and whether you would like to go to Paris during the holidays. I daresay we could find a house at some other time.

Your loving
Mother.

From Stella about the same time, Michael also received a letter.

My dear old Michael,

I seem to have made really a personal success at my concert, and I've taken a studio because the man next door—a most frightful bounder—said the noise I made went through and through his wife. As she's nearly as big round as the world, I wasn't flattered. Mother is getting very fussy and all sorts of strange women come to the house and talk about some society for dealing with Life with a capital letter. I think we're going to be rather well off, and Mother wants to live in a house she's seen in Park Street, but I want to take a house in Cheyne Walk. I hope you like Cheyne Walk, because this house has got a splendid studio in the garden and I thought with some mauve brocades it would look perfectly lovely. There's a very good panelled room that you could have, and of course the studio would be half yours. I am working at a Franck concerto. I'm being painted by rather a nice youth, at least he would be nice, if he weren't so much like a corpse. I suppose you'll condescend to ask me down to Oxford next term.

Yours ever,
Stella.

P.S.—I've come to the conclusion that mere brilliancy of execution isn't enough. Academic perfection is all very well, but I don't think I shall appear in public again until I've lived a little. I really think life is rather exciting—unless it's spelt with a capital letter.

Michael was glad that there seemed a prospect of employing his vacation in abolishing the thin red house in Carlington Road. He felt he would have found it queerly shrivelled after the spaciousness of Oxford. He was sufficiently far along in his first term to be able to feel the privilege of possessing the High, and he could think of no other word to describe the sensation of walking down that street in company with Lonsdale and Grainger and others of his friends.

Term drew to a close, and Michael determined to mark
the occasion by giving a dinner in which he thought he would
try the effect of his friends all together. Hitherto the celebrations of the freshmen had been casual entertainments arranged haphazard out of the idle chattering groups in the
lodge. This dinner was to be carefully thought out and
balanced to the extreme of nice adjustment. This terminal
dinner might, Michael thought, almost become with
him a regular function, so that people would learn to speak
with interest and respect of Fane's terminal dinners. In a
way it would be tantamount to forming a club, a club
strictly subjective, indeed so personal in character as really to
preclude the employment of the sociable world. At any rate,
putting aside all dreams of the future, Michael made up his
mind to try the effect of the first. It should be held in the
Mitre, he decided, since that would give the company an
opportunity of sailing homewards arm-in-arm along the
whole length of the High. The guests should be Avery,
Lonsdale, Wedderburn, Grainger and Alan. Yet when
Michael came to think about it, six all told seemed a beggarly
number for his first terminal dinner. Already Michael
began to think of his dinner as an established ceremony of
undergraduate society. He would like to choose a number
that should never vary every term. He knew that the guests
would change, that the place of its celebration would alter;
but he felt that some permanency must be kept, and he fixed
upon eleven as the number, ten guests and himself. For
this first dinner five more must be invited, and Michael
without much farther consideration selected five freshmen
whose athletic prowess and social amiableness drew them into
prominence. But when he had given all the invitations
Michael was a little depressed by the conventional appearance of his list. With the exception of Alan as a friend from
another college, and Avery, his list was exactly the same as
any that might have been drawn up by Grainger. As

Michael pondered it, he scented an effluence of correctness
that overpowered his individuality. However, when he sat
at the head of the table in the private room at the Mitre, and
surveyed round the table his terminal dinner party, he was
after all glad that on this occasion he had deferred to the
prejudices of what in a severe moment of self-examination
he characterized as 'snobbishness.' In this room at the
Mitre with its faded red paper and pictures of rod and gun
and steeplechase, with its two waiters whiskered and in their
garrulous subservience eloquent of Thackerayan scenes, with
its stuffed ptarmigan and snipe and glass-enshrined giant
perch, Michael felt that a more eclectic society would have
been out of place.

Only Avery's loose-fronted shirt marred the rigid convention of the group.

"*Who's* that man wearing a pie-frill ?" whispered Alan
sternly from Michael's right.

Michael looked up at him with an expression of amused
apprehension.

"Avery allows himself a little license," said Michael.
"But, Alan, he's really all right. He always wears his
trousers turned up, and if you saw him on Sunday you'd
think he was perfectly dressed. All Old Carthusians are."

But Alan still looked disapprovingly at Avery, until
Lonsdale who had met Alan several times at the House began
to talk of friends they had in common.

Michael was not altogether pleased with himself. He
wished he had put Avery on his left instead of Wedderburn.
He disliked owning to himself that he had put Avery at the
other end of the table to avoid the responsibility of listening
to the loudly voiced opinions which he felt grated upon the
others. He looked anxiously along towards Avery, who
waved a cheery hand. Michael perceived with pleasure and
faint relief that he seemed to be amusing his neighbour, a
Wykehamist called Castleton.

Michael was glad of this, for Castleton in some respects was the strongest influence in Michael's year, and his friendship would be good for Avery. Wedderburn had implied to Michael that he considered Castleton rather over-rated, but there was a superficial similarity between the two in the sort of influence they both possessed, and jealousy, if jealousy could lurk in the deep-toned and immaculate Wedderburn, might be responsible for that opinion. Michael sometimes wondered what made Castleton so redoubtable, since he was no more apparently than an athlete of ordinary ability, but Wykehamist opinion in the college was emphatic in proclaiming his solid merit, and as he seemed utterly unaware of possessing any quality at all, and as he seemed to add to every room in which he sat a serenity and security, he became each day more and more a personality impossible to neglect.

Opposite to Avery was Cuffe, and as Michael looked at Cuffe he was more than ever displeased with himself. The invitation to Cuffe was a detestable tribute to public opinion. Cuffe was a prominent freshman, and Michael had asked him for no other reason than because Cuffe would certainly have been asked to any other so representative a gathering of St. Mary's freshmen as this one might be considered. But a representative gathering of this kind was not exactly what Michael had intended to achieve with his terminal dinner. He looked at Cuffe with distaste. Then, too, in the middle of the table were Cranborne, Sterne, and Sinclair, not one of whom was there from Michael's desire to have him, but from some ridiculous tradition of his suitableness. However, it was useless to resent their presence now and, as the champagne went round, gradually Michael forgot his predilections and was content to see his first terminal dinner a success of wine and good-fellowship.

Soon Lonsdale was on his feet making a speech, and Michael sat back and smiled benignly on the company he had collected, while Lonsdale discussed their individual excellencies.

"First of all," said Lonsdale, "I want to propose the health of our distinguished friend, Mr. Merivale of Christ Church. For he's a jolly good fellow and all that. My friend Mr. Wedderburn's a jolly good fellow, too, and my friend Mr. Sterne on my centre is a jolly good fellow and a jolly good bowler and so say all of us. As for my friend Tommy Grainger—whom I will not call Mister, having known him since we were boys together—I will here say that I confidently anticipate he will get his blue next term and show the Tabs that he's a jolly good fellow. I will not mention the rest of us by name—all jolly good fellows—except our host. He's given us a good dinner and good wine and good company, which nobody can deny. So here's his health."

Then, in a phantasmagoria, in which brilliant liqueurs and a meandering procession of linked arms and the bells of Oxford and a wet night were all indistinguishably confused in one strong impression, Michael passed through his first terminal dinner.

Chapter IV : *Cheyne Walk*

THE Christmas vacation was spent in searching London for a new house. Mrs. Fane, when Carlington Road was with a sigh of relief at last abandoned, would obviously have preferred to go abroad at once and postpone the consideration of a future residence; but Michael with Stella's support prevailed upon her to take more seriously the problem of their new home.

Ultimately they fixed upon Chelsea, indeed upon that very house Stella had chosen for its large studio separated by the length of a queer little walled garden from the rest of the house. Certainly 173 Cheyne Walk was better than 64 Carlington Road, thought Michael as, leaning back against the parapet of the Embankment, he surveyed the mellow exterior in the unreal sunlight of the January noon. Empty as it was, it diffused an atmosphere of beauty and comfort, of ripe dignity and peaceful solidity. The bow windows with their half-opaque glass seemed to repulse the noise and movement of the world from the tranquil interior they so sleekly guarded. The front door with its shimmering indigo surface and fanlight and dolphin-headed knocker and on either side of the steps the flambeaux-stands of wrought iron, with the three plaster medallions and the five tall windows of the first storey all gave him much contemplative pleasure. He and his mother and Stella had in three weeks visited every feasible quarter of London and, as, Michael thought of Hampstead's leaf-haunted by-streets, of the still squares of Kensington, even of Camden Hill's sky-crowned freedom, he was sure he regretted none of them in the presence of this sedate house looking over the sun-flamed river and the crenelated line of the long Battersea shore.

Michael was waiting for Mrs. Fane, who as usual was late. Mr. Prescott was to be there to give his approval and advice, and Michael was anxious to meet this man who had evidently been a very intimate friend of his father. He saw Prescott in his mind as he had seen him years ago, an intruder upon the time-shrouded woes of childhood, and as he was trying to reconstruct the image of a florid jovial man, whose only definite impression had been made by the gold piece he had pressed into Michael's palm, a hansom pulled up at the house and someone, fair and angular with a military awkwardness, alighting from it, knocked at the door. Michael crossed the road quickly and asked if he were Mr. Prescott. Himself explained who he was and, opening the front door, led the way into the empty house. He was conscious, as he showed room after room to Prescott, that the visitor was somehow occupied less with the observation of the house than with a desire to achieve in regard to Michael himself a tentative advance towards intimacy. The January sun that sloped thin golden ladders across the echoing spaces of the bare rooms expressed for Michael something of the sensation which Prescott's attitude conveyed to him, the sensation of a benign and delicate warmth, that could most easily melt away, stretching out towards certain unused depths of his heart.

" I suppose you knew my father very well," said Michael at last, blushing as he spoke at the uninspired obviousness of the remark.

" About as well as anybody," said Prescott nervously. " Like to talk to you about him some time. Better come to dinner. Live in Albany. Have a soldier-servant and all that, you know. Must talk sometimes. Important you should know just how your affairs stand. Suppose I'm almost what you might call your guardian. Of course your

mother's a dear woman. Known her for years. Always
splendid to me. But she mustn't get too charitable."

" Do you mean to people's failings ? " Michael asked.

Michael did not ask this so much because he believed that
was what Prescott really meant as because he wished to encourage him to speak out clearly at once so that, when later
they met again, the hard shyness of preliminary encounters
would have been softened. Moreover this empty house
glinting with golden motes seemed to encourage a frankness
and directness of intercourse that made absurd these round-
about postponements of actual problems.

" Charitable to societies," Prescott explained. " I don't
want her to think she's got to endow half-a-dozen committees
with money and occupation."

" Stella's a little worried about mother's charities,"
Michael admitted.

"Awful good sort, Stella,"Prescott jerkedout. "Frightens
me devilishly. Never could stand very clever people. Oh,
I like them very much, but I always feel like a piece of furniture they want to move out of their way. Used to be in the
Welsh Guards with your father," he added vaguely.

" Did you know my father when he first met my mother?"
Michael asked directly, and by his directness tripped up
Prescott into a headlong account.

" Oh, yes, rather. I sent in my papers when he did.
Chartered a yacht and sailed all over the Mediterranean.
Good gracious, twenty years ago ! How old we're all getting.
Poor old Saxby was always anxious that no kind of——"
Prescott gibbed at the word for a moment or two—" no kind
of slur should be attached. . . . I mean, for instance, Mrs.
Fane might have had to meet the sort of women, you know,
well, what I mean is . . . there was nothing of the sort.
Saxby was a Puritan, and yet he was always a rattling good
sort. Only of course your mother was always cut off from
women's society. Couldn't be helped, but I don't want her

now to overdo it. Glad she's taken this house, though. What are you going to be ? "

Michael was saved from any declaration of his intentions by a ring at the front door, which shrilled like an alarum ,through the empty house. Soon all embarrassments were lost in his mother's graceful and elusive presence that seemed to furnish every room in turn with rich associations of leisure and tranquility, and with its fine assurance to muffle all the echoes and the emptiness. Stella, who had arrived with Mrs. Fane, was rushing from window to window, trying patterns of chintz and damask and Roman satin ; and all her notions of decoration that she flung up like released birds seemed to flutter for a while in a confusion of winged argument between her and Michael, while Mr. Prescott listened with an expression on his wrinkling forehead of admiring perplexity. But every idea would quickly be gathered in by Mrs. Fane, and when she had smoothed its ruffled doubts and fears, it would fly with greater certainty, until room by room and window by window and corner by corner the house was beautifully and sedately and appropriately arranged.

" I give full marks to Prescott," said Stella later in the afternoon to Michael. " He's like a nice horse."

" I think we ought to have had green curtains in the spare-room," said Michael.

" Why ? " demanded Stella.

And when Michael tried to discover a reason, it was difficult to find one.

" Well, why not ? " he at last very lamely replied.

There followed upon that curiously staccato conversation between Michael and Prescott in the empty house a crowded time of furnishing, while Mrs. Fane with Michael and Stella stayed at the Sloane Street Hotel, chosen by them as a convenient centre from which to direct the multitudinous activities set up by the adventure of moving. Michael, however, after the first thrills of selection had died down, must be thinking about going up again and be content to look forward on the strength of Stella's energetic promises to coming down for the Easter vacation and entering 173 Cheyne Walk as his home. .

Michael excused himself to himself for not having visited any old friends during this vacation by the business of house-hunting. Alan had been away in Switzerland with his father, but Michael felt rather guilty because he had never been near his old school nor even walked over to Notting Hill to give Viner an account of his first term. It seemed to him more important that he had corresponded with Lonsdale and Wedderburn and Avery than that he should have sought out old friends. All that Christmas vacation he was acutely conscious of the flowing past of old associations and of a sense of transition into a new life that though as yet barren of experience contained the promise of larger and worthier experiences than it now seemed possible to him could have happened in Carlington Road.

On the night before he went up Michael dined with Prescott at his rooms in the Albany. He enjoyed the evening very much. He enjoyed the darkness of the room whose life seemed to radiate from the gleaming table in its centre. He enjoyed the ghostly motions of the soldier-servant and the half-obscured vision of stern old prints on the walls of the great square room, and he enjoyed the intense silence that brooded outside the heavily curtained windows. Here in the Albany Michael was immeasurably aware of the life of London that was surging such a little distance away; but in this modish cloister he felt that the life he was aware of could never be dated, as if indeed were he to emerge into Piccadilly and behold suddenly crinolines or even powdered wigs they would not greatly surprize him. The Albany seemed to have wrung the spirit from the noisy years that swept on their course outside, to have snatched from each its heart and

n the museum of this decorous glass arcade to have preserved
t immortally, exhibiting the frozen palpitations to a sensitive
observer.

"You're not talking much," said Prescott.

"I was thinking of old plays," said Michael.

Really he was thinking of one old play to which his
mother had been called away by Prescott on a jolly evening
forgotten, whose value to himself had been calculated at
half-a-sovereign pressed into his hand. Michael wished
that the play could be going to be acted to-night and
that for half-a-sovereign he could restore to his mother that
jolly evening and that old play and his father. It seemed
to him incommunicably sad, so heavily did the Albany with
ts dead joys rest upon his imagination, that people could
not like years be frozen into a perpetual present.

"Don't often go to the theatre nowadays," said Prescott.
'When Saxby was alive"—Michael fancied that 'alive'
was substituted for something that might have hurt his
feelings—"we used to go a lot, but it's dull going alone."

"Must you go alone ?" asked Michael.

"Oh, no, of course I needn't. But I seem to be feeling
oldish. Oldish," repeated the host.

Michael felt the usurpation of his own youth, but he could
not resist asking whether Prescott thought he was at all like
his father, however sharply this might accentuate the
usurpation.

"Oh, yes, I think you are very like," said Prescott.
"Good lord, what a pity, what a pity ! Saxby was always a
great stickler for law and order, you know. He hated anything that seemed irregular or interfered with things. He
hated Radicals, for instance, and motor-cars. He had much
more brain than many people thought, but of course,"
Prescott hurriedly added, as if he wished to banish the
slightest hint of professional equipment, "of course he
always preferred to be perfectly ordinary."

2 O

".I like to be ordinary," Michael said; "but I'm not."

: "Never knew anybody at your age who was. I remember I tried to write some poetry about a man who got killed saving a child from being run over by a train," said Prescott in a tone of wise reminiscence. "You know, I think you're a very lucky chap," he added. "Here you are all provided for. In your first term at Oxford. No responsibilities except the ordinary responsibilities of an ordinary gentleman. Got a charming sister. Why, you might do anything."

"What, for example?" queried Michael.

"Oh, I don't know. There's the Diplomatic Service. But don't be in a hurry. Wait a bit. Have a good time. Your allowance is to be four hundred a year at St. Mary's. And when you're twenty-one you come into roughly seven hundred a year of your own, and ultimately you'll have at least two thousand a year. But don't be a young ass. You've been brought up quietly. You haven't *got* to cut a dash. Don't get in a mess with women, and if you do, come and tell me before you try to get out of it."

"I don't care much about women," said Michael. ": They're disappointing."

"What, already?" exclaimed Prescott, putting up his eyeglass.

Michael murmured a dark assent. The glass of champagne that owing to the attention of the soldier-servant was always brimming, the dark discreet room, and the Albany's atmosphere of passion squeezed into the mould of contemporary decorum or bound up to stand in a row of Thackeray's books, all combined to affect Michael with the idea that his life had been lived. He felt himself to belong to the period of his host, and as the rubied table glowed upon his vision more intensely, he beheld the old impressionable Michael, the nervous, the self-conscious, the sensitive slim ghost of himself receding out of sight into the gloom. Left behind was the new Michael going up to the Varsity to-

morrow morning for his second term, going up with the
assurance of finding delightful friends who would confirm
his distaste for the circumscribed past. Only a recurrent
apprehension that under the table he seemed called upon to
manage a number of extra legs, or perhaps it was only a slight
uncertainty as to which leg was crossed over the other at the
moment, made him wonder very gently whether after all
some of this easy remoteness were not due to the champagne.
The figure of his host was receding farther and farther every
moment, and his conversation reached Michael across a
shimmering inestimable space of light, while finally he was
aware of his own voice talking very rapidly and with a half-
defiant independence of precisely what he wished to say.
The evening swam past comfortably, and gradually from the
fumes of the cigar smoke the figure of Prescott leaning back
in his shadowy armchair took on once again a definite cor-
poreal existence. A clock on the mantelpiece chimed the
twelve strokes of midnight in a sort of silvery apology for
obtruding the hour. Michael came back into himself with
a start of confusion.

"I say, I must go."

Prescott and he walked along the arcade towards Albany
Courtyard.

"I say," said Michael with his foot on the step of the
hansom, "I think I must have talked an awful lot of rot
to-night."

"No, no, no, my dear boy, I've been very much interested," insisted Prescott.

And all the jingling way home Michael tried to rescue
from the labyrinth of his memory some definite conversa-
tional thread that would lead him to discover what he could
have said that might conceivably have mildly entertained his
host.

"Nothing," he finally decided.

Next morning Michael met Alan at Paddington, and they

went up to Oxford with all the rich confidence of a term's maturity. Even in the drizzle of a late January afternoon the city assumed in place of her eternal and waylaying beauty a familiarity that for Michael made her henceforth more beautiful.

After hall Avery came up to Michael's room, and while the rain dripped endlessly outside, they talked lazily of life with a more clearly assured intimacy than either of them could have contemplated the term before.

Michael spoke of the new house, of his sister Stella, of his dinner with Prescott at the Albany, almost indeed of the circumstances of his birth, so easy did it seem to talk to Avery deep in the deep chair before the blazing fire. He stopped short, however, at his account of the dinner.

"You know, I think I should like to turn ultimately into a Prescott," he affirmed. "I think I should be happy living in rooms at the Albany without ever having done a very great deal. I should like to feel I was perfectly in keeping with my rooms and my friends and my servant."

"But you wouldn't be," Avery objected, "if you thought about it."

"No, but I shouldn't think about it," Michael pointed out. "I should have steeled myself all my life not to think about it, and when your eldest son comes to see me, Maurice, and drinks a little too much champagne and talks as fast as his father used to talk, I shall know just exactly how to make him feel that after all he isn't quite the silly ass he will be inclined to think himself about the middle of his third cigar."

Michael sank farther back into the haze of his pipe and, contemplating dreamily the Mona Lisa, made up his mind that she would not become his outlook thirty years hence. Some stern old admiral with his hand on the terrestrial globe and a naval engagement in the background would better suit his mantelpiece.

" I wonder what I shall be like at fifty," he sighed.

" It depends what you do in between nineteen and fifty," said Avery. " You can't possibly settle down at the Albany as soon as you leave the Varsity. You'll have to do something."

" What, for example ? " Michael asked.

" Oh, write perhaps."

" Write ! " Michael scoffed. " Why, when I can read all these "—he pointed to his bookshelves—" and all the dozens and dozens more I intend to buy, what a fool I should be to waste my time in writing."

" Well, I intend to write," said Avery. " In fact I don't mind telling you I intend to start a paper as soon as I can."

Michael laughed.

" And you'll contribute," Avery went on eagerly.

" How much ? "

" I'm talking about articles. I shall call my paper—well, I haven't thought about the title—but I shall get a good one. It won't be like the papers of the nineties. It will be more serious. It will deal with art, of course, and literature and politics, but it won't be decadent. It will try to reflect contemporary undergraduate thought. I think it might be called The Oxford Looking-Glass."

" Yes, I expect it will be a looking-glass production," said Michael. " I should call it The World Turned Upside Down."

" I'm perfectly serious about this paper," said Avery reproachfully.

" And I'm taking you very seriously," said Michael. " That's why I won't write a line. Are you going to have illustrations ? "

" We might have one drawing. I'm not quite sure how much it costs to reproduce a drawing. But it would be fun to publish some rather advanced stuff."

" Well, as long as you don't publish drawings that look as

if the compositor had suddenly got angry with the page and thrown asterisks at it, and as long as——"

"Oh, shut up," interrupted the dreaming editor, "and don't fall into that tiresome undergraduate cynicism. It's so young."

"But I am young," Michael pointed out with careful gravity. "So are you. And, Maurice, really you know for me my own ambitions are best. I've got a great sense of responsibility, and if I were to start going through life trying to do things, I should worry myself all the time. The only chance for me is to find a sort of negative attitude to life like Prescott. You'll do lots of things. I think you're capable of them. But I'd rather watch. At least in my present mood I would. I'd give anything to feel I was a leader of men or whatever it is you are. But I'm not. I've got a sister whom you ought to meet. She's got all the positive energy in our family. I can't explain, Maurice, just exactly what I'm feeling about existence at this moment, unless I tell you more about myself than I possibly can—anyway yet awhile. I don't want to do any harm, and I don't think I could ever feel I was in a position to do any good. Look here, don't let's talk any more. I meant to dream myself into an attitude to-night, and you've made me talk like an earnest young convert."

"I think I'll go round and consult Wedderburn about this paper," said Avery excitedly.

"He thinks you're patronizing," Michael warned him.

Avery pulled up, suddenly hurt:

"Does he? I wonder why."

"But he won't, if you ask his advice about reproducing advanced drawings."

"Doesn't he like me?" persisted Avery. "I'd better not go round to his rooms."

"Don't be foolish, Maurice. Your sensitiveness is really all spoilt vanity."

When Avery had hesitatingly embarked upon his expedition to Wedderburn, Michael thought rather regretfully of his presence and wished he had been more sympathetic in his reception of the great scheme. Yet perhaps that was the best way to have begun his own scheme for not being disturbed by life. Michael thought how easily he might have had to reproach himself over Lily Haden. He had escaped once. There should be no more active exposure to frets and fevers. Looking back on his life, Michael came to the conclusion that henceforth books should give him his adventures. Actually he almost made up his mind to retire even from the observation of reality, so much had he felt, all this Christmas vacation, the dominance of Stella and so deeply had he been impressed by Prescott's attitude of inscrutable commentary.

Michael was greatly amused when two or three evenings later he strolled round to Wedderburn's rooms to find him and Maurice Avery sitting in contemplation of about twenty specimen covers of The Oxford Looking-Glass that were pinned against the wall on a piece of old lemon-coloured silk. He was greatly amused to find that the reconciling touch of the Muses had united Avery and Wedderburn in a firm friendship—so much amused indeed that he allowed himself to be nominated to serve on the obstetrical committee that was to effect the birth of this undergraduate bantling.

"Though what exactly you want me to do," protested Michael, "I don't quite know."

"We want money anyway," Avery frankly admitted. "Oh, and by the way, Michael, I've asked Goldney the Treasurer of the O.U.D.S. to put you up."

"What on earth for ? " gasped Michael.

"Oh, they'll want supers. They're doing The Merchant of Venice. Great sport. Wedders is going to join. I want him to play the Prince of Morocco."

"But are you running the Ouds as well as The Oxford Looking-Glass ?." Michael enquired gently.

-- In the end, however, he was persuaded by Avery to become a member, and not only to join himself but to persuade other St. Mary's freshmen, including Lonsdale, to join. The preliminary readings and the rehearsals certainly passed away the Lent term very well, for though Michael was not cast for a speaking part, he had the satisfaction of seeing Wedderburn and Avery play respectively the Princes of Morocco and Arragon, and of helping Lonsdale to entertain the professional actresses who came up from London to take part in the production.

"I think I ought to have played Lorenzo," said Lonsdale seriously to Michael just before the first night. "I think Miss Delacourt would have preferred to play Jessica to my Lorenzo: As it is I'm only a gondolier, an attendant and a soldier."

Michael was quite relieved when this final lament burst forth. It seemed to set Lonsdale once more securely in the ranks of the amateurs. There had been a dangerous fluency of professional terminology in 'my Lorenzo.'

"I'm only a gondolier, an attendant and a mute judge," Michael observed.

"And I don't think that ass from Oriel knows how to play Lorenzo," Lonsdale went on. "He doesn't appreciate acting with Miss Delacourt. I wonder if my governor would be very sick if I chucked the Foreign Office and went on the stage. Do you think I could act, if I had a chance ? I'm perfectly sure I could act with Miss Delacourt. Don't forget you're lunching with me to-morrow. I don't mind telling you she threw over a lunch with that ass from Oriel who's playing Lorenzo. I never heard such an idiotic voice in my life."

Such conversations coupled with requests from Wedderburn and Maurice Avery to hear them their two long speeches seemed to Michael to occupy all his leisure that term. At the same time he enjoyed the rehearsals in the lecture rooms

at Christ Church, and he enjoyed escaping sometimes to
Alan's rooms and ultimately persuading Alan to become a
gondolier, an attendant and a soldier. Moreover he met
various men from other colleges, and he began to realize
faintly thereby the individuality of each college, but most
of all perhaps the individuality of his own college, as when
Lonsdale came up to him one day with an expression of
alarm to say that he had been invited to lunch by the man
who played Launcelot Gobbo.

"Well, what of it ? " said Michael. "He probably wants
to borrow your dog."

"He says he's at Lincoln," Lonsdale stammered.

"So he is."

"Well, I don't know where Lincoln is. Have you got a
map or something of Oxford ? "

The performance of The Merchant of Venice took place
and was a great success. The annual supper of the club took
place, when various old members of theatrical appearance
came down and made speeches and told long stories about
their triumphs in earlier days. Next morning the auxiliary
ladies returned to London, and in the afternoon the disconsolate actors went down to the barges and encouraged their
various Toggers to victory.

Lonsdale forgot all about Miss Delacourt when he saw
Tommy Grainger almost swinging the St. Mary's boat into
the apprehensive stern of the only boat which stood between
them and the headship, and that evening his only lament was
that the enemy had on this occasion escaped. The Merchant of Venice with its tights and tinsel and ruffs faded out
in that Lenten week of drizzling rain, when every afternoon
Michael and Lonsdale and many others ran wildly along the
drenched towing-path beside their Togger. And when in the
end St. Mary's failed to catch the boat in front, Michael and
Lonsdale and many others felt each in his own way that after
all it had been greatly worth while to try.

Michael came down for the Easter vacation with the pleasant excitement of seeing 173 Cheyne Walk furnished and habitable. In deference to his mother's particular wish he had not invited anybody to stay with him, but he regretted he had not been more insistent when he saw each room in turn nearly twice as delightful as he had pictured it.

There was his mother's own sitting-room whose rose du Barri cushions and curtains conformed exactly to his own preconceptions, and there was Stella's bedroom very white and severe, and his own bedroom pleasantly mediæval, and the dining-room very cool and green, and the drawing-room with wallpaper of brilliant Chinese birds and in a brass cage a blue and crimson macaw blinking at the sombre Thames. Finally there was the studio to which he was eagerly escorted by Stella.

"I haven't done anything but just have it whitewashed," she said. "I wanted you to choose the scheme, as I'm going to make all the noise."

The windy March sunlight seemed to fill the great room when Michael and his sister entered it.

"But it's absolutely empty," he exclaimed, and indeed there was nothing in all that space except Stella's piano, looking now almost as small and graceful as in Carlington Road it had seemed ponderous.

"You shall decorate the room," she said. "What will you choose?"

Michael visualized rapidly for a moment, first a baronial hall with gothic chairs and skins and wrought-iron everywhere, with tapestries and blazonries and heavy gold embroideries. Then he thought of crude and amazing contrasts of barbarous reds and vivid greens and purples, with Persian rugs and a smell of joss-sticks and long low divans. Yet, even as Michael's fancy decked itself with kaleidoscopic intentions, his mind swiftly returned to the keyboard's alternations of white and black, so that in a moment exotic splendours were merged in esoteric significance.

"I don't think we want anything," he finally proclaimed. "Just two or three tall chairs and a mask of somebody—Beethoven perhaps—and black silk curtains. You see the piano wouldn't go with elaborate decorations."

So every opportunity of prodigal display was neglected, and the studio remained empty. To Michael, all that windy Eastertide, it was an infallible thrill to leave behind him the sedate Georgian house and, crossing the little walled rectangle of pallid grass, to pause and listen to the muffled sound of Stella's notes. Never had any entrance seemed to him so perfect a revelation of joy within as now when he was able to fling wide open the door of the studio and feel, while the power and glory of the sonata assailed him, that this great white room was larger even than the earth itself. Sitting upon a high-backed chair, Michael would watch the white walls melting like clouds in the sun, would see their surface turn to liquid light, and fancy in these clear melodies of Stella that he and she and the piano and the high-backed chair were in this room not more trammelled than by space itself. Alan sometimes came shyly to listen, and while Stella played and played, Michael would wonder if ever these two would make for him the union that already he was aware of coveting. Alan was rosy with the joy of life on the slopes of the world, and Stella must surely have always someone fresh and clean and straight like Alan to marvel at her.

"By Jove, she must have frightfully strong wrists and fingers," said Alan.

Just so, thought Michael, might a shepherd marvel at a lark's powerful wings.

April went her course that year with less of sweet uncertainty than usual, and Michael walked very often along the Embankment dreaming in the sunshine as day by day, almost hour by hour, the trees were greening. Chelsea appealed to his sense of past greatness. It pleased him to feel that Carlyle and Rossetti might have walked as he was walking now during some dead April of time. Moreover such heroes were not too far away. Their landscape was conceivable. People who had known them well were still alive. Swinburne and Meredith, too, had walked here, and themselves were still alive. In Carlington Road there had been none of this communion with the past. Nobody outside the contemporary residents could ever have walked along its moderately cheerful uniformity.

Michael, as he pondered the satisfaction which had come from the change of residence, began to feel a sentimental curiosity about Carlington Road and its surrounding streets. It was not yet a year since he had existed there familiarly, almost indigenously; but the combination of Oxford and Cheyne Walk made him feel a lifetime had passed since he had been so willingly transplanted. One morning late in April and just before he was going up for the summer term, he determined to pay a visit to the scenes of his childhood. It was an experience more depressing than he had imagined it would be. He was shocked by the sensation of constraint and of slightly contemptible limitation that was imposed upon his fancy by the pilgrimage. He thought to himself, as he wandered between the rows of thin red houses, that after the freedom of the river Carlington Road was purely intolerable. It did not possess the narrowness that lent a mysterious intimacy. The two rows of houses did not lean over and meet one another as houses lean over, almost seeming to gossip with one another, in ancient towns. They gave rather the impression of two mutually unattractive entities propelled into contiguity by the inexorable economy of the life around. The two rows came together solely for the purpose of crowding together a number of insignificant little families whose almost humiliating submission to the tyranny of city life was expressed pathetically by the humble flaunt-

ing of their window-boxes and in their front gardens sym-
bolically by the dingy parterres of London Pride. Michael —
wondered whether a spirit haunting the earth feels in the
perception of its former territory so much shame as he felt
now in approaching 64 Carlington Road. When he reached
the house itself, he was able to expel his sentiment for the
past with the trivial fact that the curtains of the new owner
had dispossessed the house of its personality. Only above
the door, the number in all its squat assurance was able to
convince him that this was indeed the house where he had
wrestled so long and so hardly with the problems of childhood. There too was the plane-tree that, once an object
of reproach, now certainly gave some distinction to the
threshold of this house when every area down the road
owned a lime-tree identical in age and growth.

Yet with all his distaste for 64 Carlington Road Michael
could scarcely check the impulse he had to mount the steps
and, knocking at the door, inform whomsoever should
open it that he had once lived in this very house. He
passed on, however, remembering at every corner of every
new street some bygone unimportant event which had once
occupied his whole horizon. Involuntarily he walked on
and on in a confusion of recollections, until he came to the
corner of the road where Lily Haden lived.

It was with a start of self-rebuke that he confessed to
himself that here was the ultimate object of his revisitation.
He had scarcely thought of Lily since the betrayal of his
illusions on that brazen July day when last he had seen her
in the garden behind her house. If he had thought of her
at all, she had passed through his mind like the memory, or
less even than the definite memory, like the consciousness
that never is absent of beautiful days spent splendidly in
the past. Sometimes during long railway journeys Michael
had played with himself the game of vowing to remember
an exact moment, some field or effect of clouds which the

train was rapidly passing. Yet though he knew that he had
done this a hundred times, it was always as impossible to
conjure again the vision he had vowed to remember as it
had been impossible ever to remember the exact moment of
falling asleep.

After all, however, Lily could not have taken her place
with these moments so impossible to recapture, or he would
not have come to himself with so acute a consciousness of
her former actuality here at the corner of Trelawney Road.
It was almost as uncanny as the poem of Ulalume, and
Michael found himself murmuring, 'Of my most immemorial year,' half expectant of Lily's slim form swaying
towards him, half blushful already in breathless anticipation
of the meeting.

Down the road a door opened. Michael's heart jumped
annoyingly out of control. It was indeed her door, and
whoever was coming out hesitated in the hall. Michael
went forward impulsively, but the door slammed, and a
man with a pencil behind his ear ran hurriedly down the
steps. Michael saw that the windows of the house were
covered with the names of house-agents, that several ' to
let ' boards leaned confidentially over the railings to accost
passers-by. Michael caught up the man, who was whistling off in the opposite direction, and asked him if he knew
where Mrs. Haden had gone.

" I wish I did," said the man sucking his teeth importantly. " No, sir, I'm afraid I don't. Nor nobody else."

" You mean they went away in a hurry," said Michael
shamefaced.

" Yes, sir."

" And left no address ? "

" Left nothing but a heap of tradesmen's bills in the
hall."

Michael turned aside, sorry for the ignominious end of the
Hadens, but glad somehow that the momentary temptation

to renew his friendship with the family, perhaps even his love for Lily, was so irremediably defeated.

In the sunset that night, as he and Stella sat in the drawing-room staring over the incarnadined river, Michael told his sister of his discovery.

" I'm glad you're not going to start that business again," she said. " And, Michael, do try not to fall in love for a bit, because I shall soon have such a terrible heap of difficulties that you must solve for me disinterestedly and without prejudice."

" What sort of difficulties ? " Michael demanded with eyes fixed upon her cheeks warm with the evening light.

" Oh, I don't know," she half whispered. " But let's go away together in the summer and not even take a piano."

Chapter V : *Youth's Domination*

ON May Morning, when the choir-boys of St. Mary's hymned the rising sun, Michael was able for the first time to behold the visible expression of his own mental image of Oxford's completeness, to pierce in one dazzling moment of realization the cloudy and elusive concepts which had restlessly gathered and resolved themselves in beautiful obscurity about his mind. He was granted on that occasion to hold the city, as it were, imprisoned in a crystal globe, and by the intensity of his evocation to recognize perfectly that uncapturable quintessence of human desire and human vision so supremely displayed through the merely outward glory of its repository.

All night Michael and a large party of freshmen, now scarcely to be called freshmen so much did they feel they possessed of the right to live, had sustained themselves with dressed crab and sleepy bridge-fours. During the grey hour of hinted dawn they wandered round the college, rousing from sleep such lazy contemporaries as had vowed that not all the joys and triumph of May Morning on the tower should make them keep awake during the vigil. Even so with what it contained of ability to vex other people that last hour hung a little heavily upon the enthusiasts. Slowly, however, the sky lightened: slowly the cold hues and blushes of the sun's youth, that stood as symbol for so much here in — St. Mary's, made of the east one great shell of lucent colour. The grey stones of the college lost the mysterious outlines of dawn and sharpened slowly to a rose-warmed vitality. The choir-boys gathered like twittering birds at the base of the

tower : energetic visitors came half shyly through the portal
that was to give such a sense of time's rejuvenation as never
before had they deemed possible : dons came hurrying like
great black birds in the gathering light : and at last the tired
revellers, Michael and Wedderburn, Maurice Avery and
Lonsdale and Grainger and Cuffe and Castleton and a score
besides equipped in cap and gown went scrambling and
laughing up the winding stairs to the top.

For Michael the moment of waiting for the first shaft of
the sun was scarcely to be endured : the vision of the city
below was almost too poignant during the hush of expectancy that preceded the declaration of worship. Then
flashed a silver beam in the east : the massed choir-boys
with one accord opened their mouths and sang just exactly,
Michael said to himself, like the morning stars. The rising
sun sent ray upon ray lancing over the roofs of the outspread
city until with all its spires and towers, with all its domes
and houses and still, unpopulous streets it sparkled like the
sea. The hymn was sung : the choir-boys twittered again
like sparrows and, bowing their greetings to one another,
the dons cawed gravely like rooks. The bells incredibly loud
here on the tower's top crashed out so ardently that every
stone seemed to nod in time as the tower trembled and
swayed backwards and forwards while the sun mounted
into the day.

Michael leaned over the parapet and saw the little
people busy as emmets at the base of the tower on whose —
summit, he had the right to stand. Intoxicated with
repressed adoration the undergraduates sent hurtling outwards into the air their caps, and down below the boys of
the town scrambled and fought for these trophies of May
Morning.

Michael through all the length of that May day dreamed
himself into the heart of England. He had refused
Maurice's invitation to a somewhat mannered breakfast-

2 P

party at Sandford Lasher, though when he saw the almost
defiantly jolly party ride off on bicycles from the lodge, he
was inclined to regret his refusal. He wished he had persuaded Alan, now sleeping in the stillness of the House
unmoved by May Morning celebrations, to rise early and
come with him on some daylong jaunt far afield. It was a
little dull to sit down to breakfast in the college shorn of
revellers, and for another two hours unlikely to show any
sign of life on the part of those who had declined for sleep
the excitement of eating dressed·crab and playing bridge
through the vigil. After breakfast it would still be only
about seven o'clock with a hot-eyed languor to anticipate
during the rest of the morning.· Michael almost decided to
go to bed. He turned disconsolately out of the·lodge and
walked round Cloisters, out through one of the dark entries
on to the lawns of New Quad gold-washed in the morning
stillness. It seemed incredible that no sign should remain
here of that festal life which had so lately thronged the
scene. Michael went up to the J.C.R and ate a much larger
breakfast than usual, after which, feeling refreshed, he
extracted his bicycle from the shed and at the bidding
of a momentary impulse rode out of Oxford towards
Lechlade.
· It·had been an early spring that year,·and the country
was far more typical than usual of old May‿Morning.
Michael nowadays disliked the sensation of riding a bicycle,
and though gradually the double irritation of no sleep and
a long ride unaccompanied wore·off, he was glad to see
Lechlade spire and most glad of all to find himself deep in
the grass by·the edge of the river. Lying on his back and
staring up at the slow clouds, he was glad he had refused to
attend Maurice's mannered breakfast. Soon he fell asleep,
and when he woke the morning had gone and it was time
for lunch. Michael felt magnificently at ease with the
country after his rest, and when he had eaten at the inn, he

went back to the river's bank and slept away two hours more. Then for a while in the afternoon, so richly endowed with warmth and shadows that it seemed to have stolen a summer disguise, he walked about level water-meadows very lush and vivid, painted with gay and simple flowers and holding in their green embroidered lap all England. Riding back to Oxford, Michael thought he would have tea at an inn that stood beside a dreaming ferry. He was not sure of the inn's name, and deliberately he did not ask what sweet confluence of streams here happened, whether it were Windrush or Evenlode or some other nameless tributary that was flowing into the ancestral Thames.

Michael thought he would like to stay on to dinner and ride back to Oxford by moonlight. So with dusk falling he sat in the inn garden that was faintly melodious with the plash of the river and perfumed with white stocks. A distant clock chimed the hour, and Michael, turning for one moment to salute the sunset, went into the sombre inn parlour.

At the table another undergraduate was sitting, and Michael hoped a conversation might ensue since he was attracted to this solitary inmate. His companion, however, scarcely looked up as he took his seat, but continued to stare very hard at a small piece of writing-paper on the table before him. He scarcely seemed to notice what was put on the table by the serving-maid, and he ate absently with his eyes still fixed upon his paper. Michael wondered if he were trying to solve a cypher and regretted his pre-occupation, since the longer he spent in his silent company the more keenly he felt the attraction of this strange youth with the tumbled hair and drooping lids and delicately carved countenance. At last he put away the pencil he had been chewing instead of his food, and slipped the paper into the pocket of his waistcoat. Then with an expression of curiosity so intense as to pucker up his pale forehead into numberless wrinkles the pensive undergraduate examined the food on the plate before him.

"I think it's rather cold by now," said Michael, unable to keep silence any longer in the presence of this interesting stranger.

"I was trying to alter the last line of a sonnet. If I knew you better, I'd read you the six alternative versions. But if I read them to you now, you'd think I was an affected ass," he drawled.

Michael protested he would like to hear them very much.

"They're all equally bad," the poet proclaimed gloomily. "What made you come to this inn? I didn't know that anybody else except me had ever been here. You're at the Varsity, I suppose?"

Michael with a nod announced his college.

"I'm at Balliol. At Balliol you find the youngest dons and the oldest undergraduates in Oxford."

"I think just the reverse is true of St. Mary's," Michael suggested.

"Well, certainly the youngest thing I ever met is a St. Mary's man. I refer to the ebullient Avery whom I expect you know."

"Oh, rather. In fact he's rather a friend of mine. He's keen on starting a paper just at present."

"I know. I know," said the poet. "He's asked me to be one of the forty-nine sub-editors. Are you another?"

"I was invited to be," Michael admitted. "But instead I'm going to subscribe some of the capital required. My name's Fane."

"Mine's Hazlewood. It's rather jolly to meet a person in this inn. Usually I only meet fishermen more flagrantly mendacious than anywhere else. But they've got bored with me because I always unhesitatingly go two pounds better than the biggest juggler of avoirdupois present. Have you ever thought of the romance in Troy measure? I can imagine Paris weighing the charms of Helen—no—on second thoughts I'm being forced. Don't encourage me to talk for effect. How did you come to this inn ? "

" I don't know," said Michael, wrestling as he spoke with the largest roast chicken he had ever seen. " I think I missed a turning. I've been at Lechlade all day."

" We may as well ride back together," Hazlewood proposed.

After dinner they talked and smoked for a while in the inn parlour, and then with half-a-moon high in the heavens they scudded back to Oxford. Hazlewood invited Michael — to come up to his rooms for a drink.

" Do you know many Balliol people ? " he asked.

Michael named a few acquaintances who had been the fruit of his acting in The Merchant of Venice.

" I daresay some of that push will be in my rooms. Other people use my rooms almost more than I do myself. I think they have a vague idea they're keeping a chapel, or else it's a relief from the unparagoned brutality of the college architecture."

. Hazlewood was right in his surmise, for when he and Michael reached his rooms, they seemed full of men. It was impossible to say at once how many were present because the only light was given by two gigantic wax candles that stood on either side of the fireplace in massive candlesticks of wrought iron.

" Mr. Fane of St. Mary's," said Hazlewood casually, and Michael was dimly aware of multitudinous nods of greeting and an unanimous murmur of expostulation with Hazlewood for his lateness.

" I suppose you know that this is a meeting of the Chandos, Guy ? " the chorus sighed in a climax of exasperated patience.

" Forgot all about it," said Hazlewood. " But I suppose I can bring a visitor."

Michael made a move to depart, feeling embarrassed by the implied criticism of the expostulation.

"Sit down," said Hazlewood peremptorily. "If I can't bring a visitor I resign from the Society, and the five hundred and fiftieth meeting will have to be held somewhere else. I call upon Lord Comeragh to read us his carefully prepared paper on The Catapult in Mediæval Warfare."

"Don't be an affected ass, Guy," said Comeragh. "You know you yourself are reading a paper on The Sonnet."

"Rise from the noble lord," said Hazlewood. "The first I've had in a day's fishing. I say, Fane, don't listen to this rot."

The company settled back in anticipation of the paper, while the host and reader searched desperately in the dim light for his manuscript.

Michael found the evening a delightful end to his day. He was sufficiently tired by his nocturnal vigil to be able to accept the experience without any prickings of self-consciousness and doubt as to whether this Balliol club resented his intrusion. Hazlewood's room was the most personal that so far he had seen in Oxford. It shadowed forth for Michael possibilities that in the sporting atmosphere of St. Mary's he had begun to forget. He would not have liked Tommy Grainger or Lonsdale to have rooms like this one of Hazlewood's, nor would he have exchanged the society of Grainger and Lonsdale for any other society in Oxford; but he was glad to think that Hazlewood and his rooms existed. He lay back in a deep armchair watching the candlelight flicker over the tapestries, and the shadows of the listeners in giant size upon their martial and courtly populations. He heard in half-a-dream the level voice of Hazlewood enunciating his theories in graceful singing sentences, and the occasional fizz of a replenished glass. The tobacco smoke grew thicker and thicker, curling in spirals about the emaciated loveliness of an ivory saint. The paper was over:

and before the discussion was started somebody rose and drew back the dull green curtains sown with golden fleur-de-lys. Moonbeams came slanting in and with them the freshness of the May night : more richly blue gathered the tobacco smoke : more magical became the room, and more perfectly the decorative expression of all Oxford stood for. One by one the members of the Chandos Society rose up to comment on the paper, mocking and earnest, affected and sincere, always clever, sometimes humorous, sometimes truly wise with an apologetic wisdom that was the more delightful.

Michael came to the conclusion that he liked Balliol, that most unjustly had he heard its atmosphere stigmatized as priggish. He made up his mind to examine more closely at leisure this atmosphere, so that from it he might extract the quintessential spirit. Walking with Hazlewood to the lodge, he asked him if the men he had met in his room would stand as representatives of the college.

"Yes, I should think so," said Hazlewood. "Why, are you making exhaustive researches into the social aspects of Oxford life ? It takes an American to do that really well, you know."

"But what is the essential Balliol ? " Michael demanded.

"Who could say so easily ? Perhaps it's the same sort of spirit, slightly filtered down through modern conditions, as you found in Elizabethan England."

Michael asked for a little more elaboration.

"Well, take a man connected with the legislative class, directly by birth and indirectly by opportunities, give him at least enough taste not to be ashamed of poetry, give him also enough energy not to be ashamed of football or cricket, and add a profound satisfaction with Oxford in general and Balliol in particular, and there you are."

"Will that description serve for yourself ? " Michael asked.

"For me ? Oh, great scott, no. I'm utterly deficient in proconsular ambitions."

They had reached the lodge by now, and Michael left his new friend after promising very soon to come to lunch and pursue farther his acquaintance with Balliol.

When Michael got back to college, Avery was hard at work with Wedderburn drawing up the preliminary circular of The Oxford Looking-Glass. Both the promoters insisted that Michael should listen to their announcement before he told them anything about himself or his day.

"*The Oxford Looking-Glass*," Avery began, "*is intended to reflect contemporary undergraduate thought.*"

"I prefer 'will reflect,'" Wedderburn interrupted in bass accents of positive opinion.

"I don't think it very much matters," said Michael, "as long as you don't think that 'contemporary undergraduate thought' is too pretentious. The question is whether you can see a ghost in a mirror, for a spectral appearance is just about as near as undergraduate thought ever reaches towards reality."

Neither Avery nor Wedderburn condescended to reply to his criticism, and the chief promoter went on :

"*Some of the subjects which The Oxford Looking-Glass will reflect will be Literature, Politics, Painting, Music and the Drama.*"

"I think that's a rotten sentence," Michael interrupted.

"Well, of course it will be polished," Avery irritably explained. "What Wedders and I have been trying to do all the evening is to say as simply and directly as possible what we are aiming at."

"Ah," Michael agreed smiling. "Now I'm beginning to understand."

"*It may be assumed,*" Avery went on, "*that the opinion of those who are 'knocking at the door'* (in inverted commas)——"

" I shouldn't think anybody would ever open to people standing outside a door in inverted commas," Michael observed.

" Look here, Michael," Avery and Wedderburn protested simultaneously, " will you shut up or you won't be allowed to contribute."

" Haven't you ever heard of the younger generation knocking at the door in Ibsen ? " fretfully demanded Maurice. " *That the opinion of those who are knocking at the door*," he continued defiantly, " *is not unworthy of an audience.*"

" But if they're knocking at a door," Michael objected, " they can't be reflected in a mirror ; unless it's a glass door, and if it's a glass door, they oughtn't to be knocking on it very hard. And if they don't knock hard, there isn't much point——"

" *The Editor in chief*," pursued Maurice undaunted by Michael's attempt to reduce to absurdity the claims of The Oxford Looking-Glass, " *will be M. Avery (St. Mary's) with whom will be associated C. St. C. Wedderburn (St. Mary's), C. M. S. Fane (St. Mary's), V. L. A. Townsend (B.N.C.).* I haven't asked him yet, as a matter of fact, but he's sure to join because he's very keen on Ibsen. *W. Mowbray (Univ.).* Bill Mowbray's very bucked at the scheme. He's just resigned from the Russell and joined the Canning. They say at the Union that a lot of the principal speakers are going to follow Chamberlain's lead for Protection. *N. R. Stewart (Trinity).* Nigel Stewart is most tremendously keen, and rather a good man to have, as he's had two poems taken by The Saturday Review already. *G. Hazlewood (Balliol)*——"

" That's the man I've come to talk about," said Michael. " I met him to-day."

Avery asked if Michael liked old Guy and was obviously pleased to hear he had been considered interesting. " For in his own way," said Avery solemnly, " he's about the most brilliant man in the Varsity.   I'd sooner have him under me than all the rest put together, except of course .you and Wedders,"· he added quickly. · '' I'm going to take· this prospectus round to show him ·to-morrow.   He may have some suggestions to make."

Michael joined with the Editor in supposing that Hazle-wood might have a large number of suggestions. · " And he's ,got a 'sense of humour," he added consolingly. ·

For a week or two Michael found himself deeply involved in the preliminaries of The Oxford Looking-Glass, and the necessary discussions gave many pleasant excuses for dinner parties at the O.U.D.S. or the Grid to ,which Townsend and .Stewart (both second-year men) belonged. , Vernon Townsend wished to make The Oxford Looking-Glass the organ of advanced drama ; but Avery, though he was willing for Townsend to be as advanced as he chose within the limits of the space allotted to his progressive pen, was unwilling to surrender the whole of the magazine to drama, especially since under the expanding ambitions of editorship he had come to. the conclusion he was a critic himself, and so was the more firmly disinclined to let slip the trenchant opportunity of pulverizing the four or five musical comedies that· would pass through the Oxford theatre every term. However, Townsend's demand for the drama and nothing but the drama was mitigated by his determination as a Liberal that The, Oxford .Looking-Glass should not be made the mouthpiece of the New Toryism represented by Mowbray ; and Maurice was able to recover the control of the dramatic criticism by representing to Townsend the necessity. for such unflinching exposition of Free .Trade and Palmerston Club. principles as' would balance Mowbray's torrential leadership of the Tory Democrats. " So called," Townsend bitterly observed, " because as ·he· supposed they were neither Tories·nor Democrats."

Mowbray at the end of his second year was certainly one of the personalities of undergraduate Oxford. For a year and a term he had astonished the Russell Club by the vigour of his Radicalism; and then just when they began to talk of electing him President and were looking forward to this Presidency of the Russell as an omen of his future Presidency of the Union itself, he resigned from the Russell, and figuratively marched across the road to the Canning taking with him half a dozen earnest young converts and galvanizing with new hopes and new ambitions the Oxford Tories now wilting under the strain of the Boer war. Mowbray managed to impart to any enterprize the air of a conspiracy, and Michael never saw him arrive at a meeting of The Oxford Looking-Glass without feeling they should all assume cloaks and masks and mutter with heads close together. Mowbray did indeed exist in an atmosphere of cabals, and his consent to sit upon the committee of The Oxford Looking-Glass was only a small item in his plot to overthrow Young Liberalism in Oxford. His rooms at University were always thronged with satellites, who at a word from him changed to meteors and whizzed about Oxford feverishly to outshine the equally portentous but less dazzling exhalations of Liberal opinion.

Stewart of Trinity represented an undergraduate type that perhaps had endured and would endure longer than any of the others. He would have been most in his element if he had come up in the early nineties, but yet with all his intellectual survivals he did not seem an anachronism. Perhaps it was as well that he had not come up in the nineties, since much of his obvious and youthful charm might have been buried beneath absurdities which in those reckless decadent days were carried sometimes to moral extremes that destroyed a little of the absurdity. As it was, Stewart was perhaps the most beloved member of Trinity, whether he were feeding Rugger blues on plovers' eggs or

keeping an early chapel with the expression of an earth-
bound seraph or playing tennis in the Varsity doubles or
whether, surrounded by Baudelaire and Rollinat and Rops
and Huysmans, he were composing an ode to Satan, with
two candles burning before his shrine of King Charles the
Martyr and a ramshorn of snuff and glasses of mead waiting
for casual callers.

With Townsend, Mowbray and Stewart, thought
Michael, added to Wedderburn's Pre-Raphaelitism and
staid Victorian romance, to Hazlewood's genuine inspiration,
and with Maurice Avery to whip the result into a soufflée
of exquisite superficiality, it certainly seemed as if The
Oxford Looking-Glass might run for at least a year. But
what exactly was himself doing on the committee? He
could contribute, outside money, nothing of force to help
in driving the new magazine along to success. Still, somehow he had allowed his name to appear in the preliminary
circular, and next October when the first number was published somehow he would share however indirectly in the
credit or reproach accruing. Meanwhile, there were the
mere externals of this first summer term to be enjoyed, this
summer term whose beginning he had hailed from St. Mary's
tower, this dream of youth's domination set against the grey
background of time's endurance that was itself spun of the
fabric of dreams.

Divinity and Pass Moderations would occur sometime at
the term's end, inexplicable as such a dreary interruption
seemed in these gliding river-days which only rain had power
for a brief noontide or evening to destroy. Yet, as an
admission that time flies, the candidates for Pass Mods
and Divvers attended a few sun-drowsed lectures and never
omitted to lay most tenderly underneath the cushions of
punt or canoe the text-books of their impertinent examinations. Seldom, however, did Cicero or the logical
Jevons emerge in that pool muffled from sight by trellised

boughs of white and crimson hawthorn. Seldom did
Socrates have better than a most listless audience or St. Paul
the most inaccurate geographers, when on the upper river
the punt was held against the bank by paddles fast in the
mud ; for there, as one lay at ease, the world became a world
of tall-growing grasses, and the noise of life no more than
the monotony of a river's lapping, or along the level water
meadows a faint sibilance of wind. This was the season
when supper was eaten by figures in silhouette against the
sunset, figures that afterwards drifted slowly down to
college under the tree-entangled stars and flitting assiduous
bats, with no sound all the way but the rustle of a bird's
wing in the bushes and the fizz of a lighted match dropped
idly over the side of the canoe. This was the season when
for a long while people sat talking at open windows, and
from the Warden's garden came sweetly up the scent of
May flowers.

Sometimes Michael went to the Parks to watch Alan play
in one or two of the early trial matches, and sometimes they
sat in the window of Alan's room looking out into Christ
Church meadows. Nothing that was important was ever
spoken during these dreaming nights, and if Michael tried
to bring the conversation round to Stella, Alan would always
talk of leg-drives and the problems that perpetually presented themselves to cover-point. Yet the evenings were
always to Michael in retrospect valuable, betokening a
period of perfect happiness from the lighting of the first
pipe to the eating of the last meringue.

Eights Week drew near, and Michael decided after much
deliberation that he would not ask either his mother or
Stella to take part in the festival. One of his reasons,
only very grudgingly admitted, for not inviting Stella was
his fear lest Alan might be put into the shade by certain
more brilliant friends whom he would feel bound to introduce to her. Having made up his own mind that Alan

represented the perfection of normal youth, he was unwilling
to admit dangerous competitors. Besides, though by now
he had managed to rid himself of most of his self-consciousness, he was not sure he felt equal to charging the battery
of eyes that mounted guard in the lodge. The almost
savage criticism of friends and relatives indulged in by the
freshmen's table was more than he could equably contemplate for his own mother and sister.

So Eights Week arrived with Michael unencumbered and
delightfully free to stand in the lodge and watch the
embarrassed youth, usually so debonair and self-possessed,
herding a long trail of gay sisters and cousins towards his
room where even now waited the inevitable salmon mayonnaise. Lonsdale in a moment of filial enthusiasm had
invited his father and mother and only sister to come up,
and afterwards had spent two days of lavish regret for the
rashness of the undertaking.

"After all, they can only spend the day," he sighed
hopefully to Michael. "You'll come and help me through
lunch, won't you, and we'll rush them off by the first train
possible after the first division is rowed. I was an ass to ask
them. You won't mind being bored a bit by my governor ?
I believe he's considered quite a clever man."

Michael, remembering that Lord Cleveden had been a
distinguished diplomatist, was prepared to accept his son's
estimate.

"They're arriving devilish early," said Lonsdale, coming
up to Michael's room with an anxious face on the night
before.

Ever since his fatal display of affection, he had taken
to posting, as it were, bulletins of the sad event on Michael's
door.

"Would you be frightfully bored if I asked you to come
down to the station and meet them ? It will be impossible
for me to talk to the three of them at once. I think you'd

better talk about wine to the governor. It'll buck him rather to think his port has been appreciated. Tell him how screwed we made the bobby that night when we were climbing in late from that binge on the Cher, and let down glass after glass of the governor's port from Tommy's rooms in Parsons' Quad."

Michael promised to do his best to entertain the father, and without fail to support the son at the ceremony of meeting his people next morning.

" I say, you've come frightfully early," Lonsdale exclaimed, as Lord and Lady Cleveden with his sister Sylvia alighted from the train.

" Well, we can walk round my old college," suggested Lord Cleveden cheerfully. " I scarcely ever have an opportunity to get up to Oxford nowadays."

" I say, I'm awfully sorry to let you in for this," Lonsdale whispered to Michael. " Don't encourage the governor to do too much buzzing around at the House. Tell him the mayonnaise is getting cold or something."

. Soon they arrived at Christ Church, and Michael rather enjoyed walking round with Lord Cleveden and listening to his stately anecdotes of bygone adventure in these majestic quadrangles.

" I wonder if Lord Saxby was up in your time ? " asked Michael as they stood in Peckwater.

" Yes, knew him well. In fact he was a connection of mine. Poor chap, he died in South Africa. Where did you meet him ? He never went about much."

. " Oh, I met him with a chap called Prescott," said Michael hurriedly.

" Dick Prescott ? Good gracious ! " Lord Cleveden exclaimed, " I haven't seen him for years. What an extraordinary mess poor Saxby made of his life, to be sure." .

' " Did he ? " asked Michael, well aware of the question's folly, but incapable of not asking it.

"Terrible! Terrible! But it was never a public scandal."

"Oh," gulped Michael humbly, wishful he had never asked Lord Cleveden about his father.

"I can't remember whether my old rooms were on that staircase or this one. Saxby's I think were on this, but mine surely were on that one. Let's go up and ask the present owner to let us look in," Lord Cleveden proposed, peering the while in amiable doubt at the two staircases.

"Oh no, I say, father, really, no, no," protested his son. "No, no, he may have people with him. Really."

"Ah, to be sure," Lord Cleveden agreed. "What a pity."

"And I think we ought to buzz round St. Mary's before lunch," Lonsdale announced.

"Do they make meringues here nowadays?" enquired Lord Cleveden meditatively.

"No, no," Lonsdale assured him. "They've given up since the famous cook died. Look here, we absolutely must buzz round St. Mary's. And our crème caramel is a much showier sweet than anything they've got at the House."

The tour of St. Mary's was conducted with almost incredible rapidity, because Lonsdale knew so little about his own college that he omitted everything except the J.C.R., the hall, the chapel, the buttery and the kitchen.

"Why didn't you ask Duncan Mackintosh to lunch, Arthur dear?" Lady Cleveden enquired.

"My dear mother," said Arthur, "he's quite impossible."

"But Sir Hugh Mackintosh is such a charming man," said Lady Cleveden, "and always asks us to stay with him when we're in Scotland."

"Yes, but we never are," Lonsdale pointed out. "And I'm sorry to hurt your feelings, mother, about a relation of yours, but Mackintosh is really absolutely impossible. He's the very worst type of Harrovian."

Michael felt bound to support his friend by pointing out that Mackintosh was so eccentric as to dislike enter-tainment of any kind, and urged a theory that even if he had been asked, he would certainly have declined rather offensively.

"He's not a very bonhomous lad," said Lonsdale, and — with that sentence banished Mackintosh for ever from human society.

After lunch the host supposed in a whisper to Michael that they ought to take his people out in a punt. Michael nodded agreement, and weighed down by cushions the party walked through the college to where the pleasure-craft of St. Mary's bobbed at their moorings.

Lonsdale on the river possessed essentially the grand manner, and his sister who had been ready to laugh at him gently was awed into respectful admiration. Even Lord Cleveden seemed inclined to excuse himself, if ever in one of the comprehensive and majestic indications of his opinion he disturbed however slightly the equilibrium of the punt. Lonsdale stood up in the stern and handled the un-gainly pole with the air of a Surbiton expert. His tendency — towards an early rotundity was no longer noticeable. His pink and cheerful face assumed a grave superciliousness of expression that struck with apologetic dismay the navi-gators who impeded his progress. Round his waist the rich hues of the Eton Ramblers glowed superbly.

"Thank you, sir. Do you mind letting me through, sir? Some of these toshers ought not to be trusted with a punt of — their own." This comment was for Michael and uttered in a voice of most laryngeal scorn so audible that the party of New College men involved reddened with dull fury. "Try and get along, please, sir. You're holding up the whole river, sir. I say, Michael, this is an absolute novices' com-petition."

After an hour of this slow progress Lonsdale decided

2 Q

they must go back to college for tea, an operation which required every resource of sangfroid to execute successfully. When he had landed his father and mother and sister, he announced that they must all be quick over tea and then buzz off at once to see the first division row.

"I think we shall go head to-night," Lonsdale predicted very confidentially. "I told Tommy Grainger he rowed like a caterpillar yesterday."

But after all it was not to be the joyful privilege of Lonsdale's people to see St. Mary's bump New College in front of their own barge, and afterwards to behold the victorious boat row past in triumph with the westering sun making glow more richly scarlet the cox's blazer and shine more strangely beautiful the three white lilies in his button-hole....

"Now you've just got time to catch your train," said Lonsdale when the sound of the last pistol-shots and plaudits had died away. And "Phew!" he sighed, as he and Michael walked slowly down the station-hall, "how frightfully tiring one's people are when imported in bulk."

Eights Week came to an end with the scarlet and lilies still second; and without the heartening effect of a bump-supper the candidates for Pass Mods applied themselves violently to the matter in hand. At the end of the examination, which was characterized by Lonsdale as one of the most low-down exhibitions of in-fighting he had ever witnessed, the candidates had still a week of idleness to recover from the dastardly blows they had received below their intellectual belts.

It was the time of the midsummer moon; and the fresh-men in this the last week of their state celebrated the beauty of the season with a good deal of midsummer mad-ness. Bonfires were lit for the slightest justification, and rowdy suppers were eaten in college after they had stayed on the river until midnight, rowdy suppers that demanded a great expense of energy before going to bed, in order perhaps to stave off indigestion.

On one of these merry nights towards one o'clock somebody suggested that the hour was a suitable one for the ragging of a certain Smithers who had made himself obnoxious to the modish majority not from any overt act of contumely, but for his general bearing and plebeian origin. This derided Smithers lived on the ground floor of the Palladian fragment known as New Quad. The back of New Quad looked out on the deer-park, and it was unanimously resolved to invade his rooms from the window, so that surprize and alarm would strike at the heart of Smithers.

Half-a-dozen freshmen, Avery, Lonsdale, Grainger, Cuffe, Sinclair and Michael, all rendered insensitive to the emotions of other people by the amount of champagne they had drunk, set out to harry Smithers. Michael alone possibly had a personal slight to repay, since Smithers had been one of the freshmen who had sniggered at his momentary mortification in the rooms of Carben the Rugby secretary during his first week. The others were more vaguely injured by Smithers' hitherto undisturbed existence. Avery disliked his face : Lonsdale took exception to his accent : Grainger wanted to see what he looked like : Cuffe was determined to be offensive to somebody : and Sinclair was anxious to follow the fashion.

Not even the magic of the moonlit park deterred these social avengers from their vendetta. They moved silently indeed over the filmy grass and paused to hearken when in the distance the deer stampeded in alarm before their progress, but the fixed idea of Smithers' reformation kept them to their project, and perhaps only Michael felt a slight sense of guilt in profaning this fairy calm with what he admitted to himself might very easily be regarded as a piece of stupid cruelty. Outside Smithers' open window they all stopped ; then after hoisting the first man on to the dewy

sill, one by one they climbed noiselessly into the sitting-
room of the offensive Smithers. Somebody turned on the
electric light, and they all stood half-abashed, surveying one
another in the crude glare that in contrast with the velvet
depths and silver shadows of the woodland they had traversed seemed to illuminate for one moment an unworthy
impulse in every heart.

The invaders looked round in surprize at the photographs
of what were evidently Smithers' people, photographs like
the groups in the parlours of country inns or the tender
decorations of a housemaid's mantelpiece.

"I say, look at that fringe," gurgled Avery, and forthwith he and Lonsdale collapsed on the sofa in a paroxysm of
strangled mirth.

Michael, as he gradually took in the features of Smithers'
room, began to feel very much ashamed of himself. He
recognized the poverty that stood in the background of
this splendid 'college career' of Percy or Clarence or whatever other name of feudal magnificence had been awarded
to counterbalance 'Smithers.' No doubt the champagne
in gradual reaction was over-charging him with sentiment,
but observing in turn each tribute from home that adorned
with a pathetic utility this bleak room dedicated for generations to poor scholars, Michael felt very much inclined to
detach himself from the personal ragging of Smithers and
go to bed. What seemed to him in this changed mood so
particularly sad was that on the evidence of his books
Smithers was not sustained by the ascetic glories of learning
for the sake of learning. He was evidently no classical
scholar with a future of such dignity as would compensate
for the scraping and paring of the past. To judge by his
books he was at St. Mary's to ward off the criticism of outraged Radicals by competing on behalf of the college and
the university in scientific knowledge with newer foundations like Manchester or Birmingham. Smithers was merely

an advertizement of Oxford's democratic philanthropy, and would only gain from his university a rather inferior training in chemistry at a considerably greater personal cost but with nothing else that Oxford could and did give so prodigally to others more fortunately born.

At this point in Michael's meditations Smithers woke up, and from the bedroom came a demand in startled cockney to know who was there. The reformers were just thinking about their reply, when Smithers, in a long night-gown and heavy-eyed with sleep, appeared in the doorway between his two rooms.

"Well, I'm jiggered," he gasped. "What are you fellers doing in my sitting-room?"

It happened that Cuffe at this moment chose to take down from the wall what was probably an enlarged portrait of Smithers' mother in order to examine it more closely. The son, supposing he meant to play some trick with it, sprang across the room, snatched it from Cuffe's grasp, and shouting an objurgation of his native Hackney or Bermondsey, fled through the open window into the deer-park.

Cuffe's expression of dismay was so absurd that everybody laughed very heartily; and the outburst of laughter turned away their thoughts from damaging Smithers' humble property and even from annoying any more Smithers himself with proposals for his reformation.

"I say, we can't let that poor devil run about all night in the park with that picture," said Grainger. "Let's catch him and explain we got into his rooms by mistake."

"I hope he won't throw himself into the river or anything," murmured Sinclair, anxious not to be involved in any affair that might spoil his reputation for enjoying every rag without the least reproach ever lighting upon him personally.

"I say, for goodness' sake, let's catch him," begged Michael, who had visions of being sent to explain to a weeping mother in a mean street that her son had died in defending her enlargement.

Out into the moon-washed park the pursuers tumbled, and through its verdurous deeps of giant elms they hurried in search of the outlaw.

"It's like a scene in The Merry Wives of Windsor," Michael said to Avery, and as he spoke he caught a glimpse of the white-robed Smithers, running like a young druid across a glade where the moonlight was undimmed by boughs.

He called to Smithers to go back to his rooms, but whether he went at once or huddled in some hollow tree half the night Michael never knew, for by this time the unwonted stampeding of the deer and the sound of voices in the Fellows' sacred pleasure-ground had roused the Dean who supported by the nocturnal force of the college servants was advancing against the six disturbers of the summer night. The next hour was an entrancing time of hot pursuit and swift evasion, of crackling dead branches and sudden falls in lush grass, of stealthy procedure round tree-trunks, and finally of scaling a high wall, dropping heavily down into the rose-beds of the Warden's garden and by one supreme effort of endurance going to ground in St. Cuthbert's quad.

"By Jove, that was a topping rag," puffed Lonsdale as he filled six glasses with welcome drink. "I think old Shadbolt recognized me. He said: 'It's no use you putting your coat over your 'ead, sir, because I knows you by your gait.'"

"I wonder what happened to Smithers," said Michael.

"Damned good thing if he fell into the Cher," Avery asserted. "I don't know why on earth they want to have a bounder like that at St. Mary's."

"A bounder like what?" asked Castleton, who had sloped into the room during Avery's expression of opinion.

Castleton was greeted with much fervour, and a disjointed account of the evening's rag was provided for his
entertainment.

"But why don't you let that poor devil alone?" demanded the listener.

At this time of night nobody was able to adduce any
very conclusive reason against letting Smithers alone,
although Maurice Avery insisted that men like him were
very bad for the college.

Dawn was breaking when Michael strolled round Cloisters
with Castleton, determined to probe through the medium
of Castleton's common sense and Wykehamist notions the
ethical and æsthetic rights of people like Smithers to obtain
the education Oxford was held to bestow impartially.

"After all Oxford wasn't founded to provide an expensive three years of idleness for the purpose of giving a social
cachet to people like Cuffe," Castleton pointed out.

"No, no," Michael agreed, "but no institution has ever
yet remained true to the principles of its founder. The
Franciscans, for instance, or Christianity itself. The
point surely is not whether it has evolved into something inherently worthless, but whether, however much it may have
departed from original intentions, it still serves a useful
purpose in the scheme of social order."

"Oh, I'm not grumbling at what Oxford is," Castleton
went on. "I simply suggest that the Smitherses have the
right, being in a small minority, to demand courtesy from
the majority, and after all, Oxford is serving no purpose
at all, if she cannot foster good manners in people who are
supposed to be born with a natural tendency towards good
manners. I should be the first to regret an Oxford with the
Smitherses in the majority, but I think that those Smitherses
who have fought their way in with considerable difficulty
should not go down with the sense of hatred which that poor
solitary creature must surely feel against all of us."

Michael asked Castleton if he had ever talked to him.

"No, I'm afraid I haven't. I'm afraid I'm too lazy to do much more than deplore theoretically these outbursts of rowdy superiority. Now, as I'm beginning to talk almost as priggishly as a new sub-editor of The Spectator might talk, to bed."

The birds were singing, as Michael walked back from escorting Castleton to his rooms. St. Mary's tower against the sky opening like a flower seemed to express for him a sudden aspiration of all life towards immortal beauty. In this delicate hour of daybreak all social distinctions, all prejudices and vulgarities became the base and clogging memories of the night before. He felt a sudden guilt in beholding this tranquil college under this tranquil dawn. It seemed, spread out for his solitary vision, too incommunicable a delight. And suddenly it struck him that perhaps Smithers might be standing outside the gate of this dream city, that he, too, might wish to salute the sunrise. He blushed with shame at the thought that he had been of those who rushed to drive him away from his contemplation.

Straightway when Michael reached his own door, he sat down and wrote to invite Smithers to his third terminal dinner, never pausing to reflect that so overwhelming an hospitality after such discourtesy might embarrass Smithers more than ever. Yet, after he had worried himself with this reflection when the invitation had been accepted, he fancied that Smithers sitting on his right hand next to Guy Hazlewood more charming than Michael had ever known him, seemed to enjoy the experience, and triumphantly he told himself that contrary to the doctrine of cynics quixotry was a very effective device.

Chapter VI: *Grey and Blue*

WHEN Michael, equipped with the prospect of reading at least fifty historical works in preparation for the more serious scholastic enterprize of his second year, came down for the Long Vacation, he found that somehow his mother had changed. In old days she had never lost for an instant that air of romantic mystery with which Michael as a very little boy for his own satisfaction had endowed her, and with which, as he grew older, he fancied she armed herself against the world of ordinary life. Now after a month or two of Chelsea's easy stability Mrs. Fane had put behind her the least hint of the unusual and seemed exceptionally well-suited by her surroundings. Michael at first thought that perhaps in Carlington Road to which she always came from the great world, however much apart from the great world her existence had been when she was in it, his mother had only evoked a thought of romance because the average inhabitant was lower down the ladder of the more subtly differentiated social grades than herself, and that now in Cheyne Walk against an appropriate background her personality was less conspicuous. Yet when he had been at home for a week or two he realized that indeed his mother had changed profoundly.

Michael put together the few bits of outside opinion he could muster and concluded that an almost lifelong withdrawal from the society of other women had now been replaced by an exaggerated pleasure in their company. What puzzled him most was how to account for the speed

with which she had gathered round her so many acquaintances. It was almost as if his father in addition to be-
queathing her money enough to be independent of the world
had bequeathed also enough women friends to make her
forget that she had ever stood in any other relation to
society.

"Where does mother get hold of all these women?"
Michael asked Stella irritably, when he had been trapped
into a rustling drawing-room for the whole of a hot summer
afternoon.

"Oh, they're all interested in something or other,"
Stella explained. "And mother's interested in them. I
expect, you know, she had rather a rotten time really when
she was travelling round."

"But she used always to be so vague and amusing," said
Michael, "and now she's as fussy and practical as a vicar's
wife."

"I think I know why that is," Stella theorized meditatively. "I think if I ever gave up everything for one man,
I should get to rely on him so utterly that when he wasn't
with me any sort of contact with other people would make
me vague."

"Yes, but then she would be more vague than ever now,"
Michael argued.

"No, the reaction against dependence on one person
would be bound to make her change tremendously, if, as
I think, a good deal of the vagueness came after she ran
away with father."

Michael looked rather offended by Stella's blunt reference.

"I rather wish you wouldn't talk quite so easily about
all of that," he said. "I think the best thing for you to
do is to forget it."

"Like mother, in fact," Stella pointed out. "Do you
know, Michael, I believe by this time she is entirely oblivious

of the fact that in her past there has been anything which was not perfectly ordinary, almost dull. Really by the way she worries me about the simplest little things, you'd think—however, as I know you have rather a dread of perfect frankness in your only sister, I'll shut up and say no more."

"What things?" asked Michael sharply. Stella's theories about the freedom of the artist had already worried him a good deal, and though he had laughed them aside as the extravagant affectations of a gifted child, now that, however grudgingly he must admit the fact, she was really grown up, it would never do for her without a protest from him to turn theories into practice.

"Oh, Michael," Stella laughed reprovingly. "Don't put on that professorial or priestly air or whatever you call it, because if you ever want confidences from me you'll have just to be humbly sympathetic."

Michael sternly demanded if she had been keeping up her music, which made Stella dance about the studio in tempestuous mirth.

"I don't see anything to giggle at in such a question," Michael grumbled, and simultaneously reproached himself for a method of obloquy so cheap. "Anyway, you never talk about your music now, and whatever you may say, you don't practise as much as you used. Why?"

For answer Stella sat down at the piano, and played over and over again the latest popular song until Michael walked out of the studio in a rage.

A few days later at breakfast he broached the subject of going away into the country.

"My dear boy, I'm much too busy with the Bazaar," said Mrs. Fane.

Michael sighed.

"I don't think I can possibly get away until August, and then I've half promised to go to Dinard with Mrs.

Carruthers. She has just taken up Mental Science—so interesting and quite different from Christian Science."

"I hate these mock-turtle religions," said Michael savagely.

Mrs. Fane replied that Michael must learn a little toleration in very much the same tone as she might have suggested a little Italian.

"But why don't you and Stella go away somewhere together? Stella has been quite long enough in London for the present.".

"I've got to practise hard for my next concert," said Stella looking coldly at her brother. "You and Michael are so funny, mother. You grumble at me when I don't practise all day, and yet when it's really necessary for me to work, you always suggest going away."

"I never suggested your coming away," Michael contradicted. "As a matter of fact I've been asked to join a reading-party in Cornwall, and I think I'll go."

The reading-party in question consisted besides Michael of Maurice Avery, Guy Hazlewood, Castleton and Stewart. Bill Mowbray also joined them for the first two days, but after receiving four wires in reference to the political candidature of a friend in the north of England, he decided that his presence was necessary to the triumph of Tory Democracy and left abruptly in the middle of the night with a request to forward his luggage when it arrived. When it did arrive, the reading-party sent it to await at Univ Mowbray's arrival in October, arguing that such an arrangement would save Bill and his friends much money, as he would indubitably spend during the rest of the vacation not more than forty-eight hours on the same spot.

The reading-party had rooms in a large farmhouse near the Lizard; and they spent a very delightful month bathing, golfing, cliff-climbing, cream-eating, fishing, sailing and talking. Avery and Stewart also did a certain amount of work on the first number of The Oxford Looking-Glass, work which Hazlewood amused himself by pulling to pieces.

"I'm doing an article for the O.L.G. on Cornwall," Avery announced one evening.

"What, a sort of potted guide ? " Hazlewood asked.

Maurice made haste to repudiate the suggestion.

"No, no, it's an article on the uncanny place influence of Cornwall."

"I think half of that uncanniness is due to the odd names hereabouts," Castleton observed. "The sign-posts are like incantations."

"Much more than that," Avery earnestly assured him. "It really affects me profoundly sometimes."

Hazlewood laughed.

"Oh, Maurice, not profoundly. You'll never be affected profoundly by anything," he prophesied.

Maurice clicked his thumbs impatiently.

"You always know all about everybody and me in particular, Guy, but though, as you're aware, I'm a profound materialist——"

"Maurice is plumbing the lead to-night," Hazlewood interrupted with a laugh. "He'll soon transcend all human thought."

"Here in Cornwall," Maurice pursued undaunted, "I really am affected sometimes with a sort of horror of the unknown. You'll all rag me, and you can, but though I've enjoyed myself frightfully, I don't think I shall ever come to Cornwall again."

With this announcement he puffed defiance from his pipe.

"Shut up, Maurice," Hazlewood chaffed. "You've been reading Cornish novelists—the sort of people who write about over-emotionalized young men and women acting to the moon in hut-circles or dancing with their own melodramatic Psyches on the top of a cromlech."

"Do you believe in presentiments, Guy?" Michael broke in suddenly.

"Of course I do," said Hazlewood. "And I'd believe in the inherent weirdness of Cornwall, if people in books didn't always go there to solve their problems and if Maurice weren't always so facile with the right emotion at the right moment."

"I've got a presentiment to-night," said Michael, and not wishing to say more just then, though he had been compelled against his will to admit as much, he left the rest of the party, and went up to his room.

Outside the tamarisks lisped at intervals in a faint wind that rose in small puffs and died away in long sighs. Was it a presentiment he felt or was it merely thunder in the air?

Next morning came a telegram from Stella in Paris:

join me here rather quickly.

Michael left Cornwall that afternoon, and during the length of the harassing journey to London he thought of his friends bathing all day and talking half through the intimate night, until gradually, as the train grew hotter, they stood out in his memory like cool people eternally splashed by grateful fountains. Yet at the back of all his regrets for Cornwall, Michael was thinking of Stella and wondering whether the telegram was merely due to her impetuous way or whether indeed she wanted him more than rather quickly.

It was dark when he reached London, and in the close August night the street-lamps seemed to have lost all their sparkle, seemed to glow luridly like the sinister lamps of a dream.

"I'm really awfully worried," he said aloud to himself, as through the stale city air the hansom jogged heavily along from Paddington to Charing Cross.

Michael arrived at Paris in the pale burning blue of an August morning, and arriving as he did in company with numerous cockney holiday-makers, something of the spirit of Paris was absent. The city did not express herself immediately as Paris unmistakable, but more impersonally as the great railway-station of Europe, a centre of convenience rather than the pulsing heart of pleasure. However, as soon as Michael had taken his seat in the bony fiacre and had ricocheted from corner to corner of half-a-dozen streets, Paris was herself again, with her green jalousies and gilded letterings, her prodigality of almost unvarying feminine types, those who so neatly and so gaily hurried along the pavements and those who in soiled dressing-jackets hung listlessly from upper windows.

Stella's address was near the Quai d'Orsay; and when Michael arrived he found she was living in rooms over a bookseller's shop with a view of the Seine and beyond of multitudinous roofs that in the foreground glistened to the sun like a pattern of enamel, until with distance they gradually lost all definition and became scarcely more than a woven damascene upon the irresolute horizon of city and sky.

Michael never surrendered to disillusion the first impression of his entrance that August morning. In one moment of that large untidy room looking over the city that most consciously of all cities has taken account of artists he seemed to capture the symbol of the artist's justification. Stella's chestnut hair streamed down her straight back like a warm drift of autumn leaves. She had not finished dressing yet, and the bareness of her arms seemed appropriate to that Hungarian dance she played. All the room was permeated with the smell of paint, and before an easel stood a girl in long unsmocked gown of green linen. This girl Michael had never seen, but he realized her personality as somehow inseparably associated with that hot-blooded Bacchante on whose dewy crimson mouth at the moment her brush rested. . Geranium-flowers, pierced by the slanting rays of the sun, stood on the window-sill of an inner room whose door was open. Stella did not stop to finish the dance she was playing, but jumped up to greet Michael, and in the fugitive silence that followed his introduction to her friend Clarissa Vine, he heard the murmur of ordinary life without which drowned by the lightest laugh nevertheless persisted unobtrusive and imperturbable.

Yet, for all Michael's relief at finding Stella at least superficially all right, he could not help disapproving a little of that swift change of plan which, without a word of warning to himself before the arrival of the telegram in Cornwall, had brought her from London to Paris. Nor could he repress a slight feeling of hostility towards Miss Clarissa Vine whose exuberant air did not consort well with his idea of a friend for Stella. He was certainly glad, whether he were needed or not, that he had come rather quickly. Clarie was going to paint all that morning, and Michael, who was restless after his journey, persuaded Stella to abandon music for that day and through the dancing streets of Paris come walking.

The brother and sister went silently for a while along the river's bank.

"Well," said Michael at last, "why did you wire for me?"

"I wanted you."

Stella spoke so simply and so naturally that he was inclined to ask no more questions and to accept the situation as one created merely by Stella's impetuousness. But he could not resist a little pressure and begged to know whether there were no other reason for wanting him but a fancy for his company.

Stella agreed there might be, and then suddenly she

plunged into her reasons. First she took Michael back to last autumn and a postscript she had written to a letter.

" Do you remember how I said that academic perfection was not enough for an artist, that there was also life to be lived ? "

Michael said he remembered the letter very well indeed, and asked just how she proposed to put her theory to the test.

" I told you that a youth was painting me."

" But you also said he looked like a corpse," Michael quickly interjected. " You surely haven't fallen in love with somebody who looks like a corpse ? "

" I'm not in love with his outside, but I am fascinated by his inside," Stella admitted.

Michael looked darkly for a moment, overshadowed by the thought of the fellow's presumption.

" I never yet met a painter who had very much inside," he commented.

" But then, my dearest Michael, I suppose you'll confess that your acquaintanceship with the arts as practised not talked about is rather small."

Michael looked round him and eyed all Paris with comprehensive hostility.

" And I suppose this chap is in Paris now," he said. " Well, I can't do anything. I suppose for a long time now you've been making a fool of yourself over him. What have you fetched me to Paris for ? "

He felt resentful to think that his hope of Stella and Alan falling in love with one another was to be broken up by this upstart painter whom he had never seen.

" I've certainly not been making a fool of myself," Stella flamed. " But I thought I would rather you were close at hand."

" And who's this Clarissa Vine ? " Michael indignantly demanded.

2 R

"She's the girl I travelled with to Paris."

"But I never heard of her before. All this comes of your taking that studio before we moved to Cheyne Walk."

By the token that Stella did not contradict him, Michael knew that all this had indeed come from that studio, and to show his disapproval of the studio, he began to rail at Clarissa.

"I can't bear that overblown type of girl. I suppose every night she'll sit and talk hot air till three o'clock in the morning. I shall go mad," Michael exclaimed aghast at the prospective futility of the immediate future.

Stella insisted that Clarissa was a good sort, that she had had an unhappy love-affair, that she thought nothing of men but only of her art, that she made one want to work and was therefore a valuable companion, and finally, to appease if possible Michael's mistrust of Clarie by advertizing her last advantage, Stella said that she could not stand George Ayliffe.

Michael announced that, as Miss Vine had scarcely condescended to address a single word to him in the quarter of an hour he was waiting for Stella to dress, it was impossible for him to say whether he could stand her or not, but that he was still inclined to think she was thoroughly objectionable.

"Well, to-night at our party, you shall sit next to her," Stella promised.

"Party?" interrogated Michael in dismay.

"We're having a party in our rooms to-night."

"And this fellow Ayliffe is coming, I suppose?"

She nodded.

"And I shall have to meet him?"

She nodded again very cheerfully.

They went back to fetch Clarie out to lunch, but rather decently, Michael was bound to admit, she made some excuse for not coming, so that he and Stella were able to

spend the afternoon together. It was a jolly afternoon, for
though Stella had closed her lips tightly to any more confidences, she and Michael enjoyed themselves wandering in a
lighthearted dream, grasping continually at those airy
bubbles of vitality that floated upwards sparkling from the
debonair streets.

The party at the girls' rooms that evening seemed to
Michael, almost more than he cared to admit to the side of
him conscious of being Stella's brother, a recreation of
ideal Bohemia. He knew the influence of the rich August
moon was responsible for most of the enchantment and
that the same people encountered earlier in the day in the
full glare of the sunlight would have seemed to him too
keenly aware of the effect at which they were aiming. But
to resist their appeal, coming as they did from the heart
of Paris to this long riverside room with its lamps and
shadows, was impossible. Each couple that entered seemed
to relinquish slowly on the threshold a mysterious intimacy
which set Michael's heart beating in the imagination of
what altitudes it might not have reached along the path of
romantic passions. Every young woman or young man who
entered solitary and paused in the doorway, blinking in
search of familiar faces, moved him with the respect
owed by lay worldlings to great artists. Masterpieces
brooded over the apartment, and Michael tolerated in his
present mood of unqualified admiration personalities so
pretentious, so vain, so egotistical, as would in his ordinary
temper have plunged him into speechless gloom.

Oxford after this assembly of frank opinions and incarnate enthusiasms seemed a colourless shelter for unfledged
reactionaries, a nursery of callow men in the street. Through
the open windows the ponderous and wise moon commented upon the scintillations of the outspread city whose
life reached this room in sound as emotionally melodious,
as romantically real as the sea-sound conjured by a shell.

Here were gathered people who worked always in that circumfluent inspiration, that murmur of liberty, that whisper of humanity. What could Oxford give but the bells of outworn beliefs, and the patter of aimless footsteps ? How right Stella had been to say that academic perfection was vain without the breath of life. How right she was to find in George Ayliffe someone whose artistic sympathy would urge her on to achievements impossible to attain under Alan's admiration for mere fingers and wrists.

Michael watched this favourite of his sister all through the evening. He tried to think that Ayliffe's cigarette-stained fingers were not so very unpleasant, that Ayliffe's cadaverous exterior was just a noble melancholy, that Ayliffe's high pointed head did not betray an almost insufferable self-esteem, and, what was the hardest task of all, he tried to persuade himself that Ayliffe's last portrait of Stella had not transformed his splendidly unconcerned sister into a self-conscious degenerate.

"How do you like George's picture of Stella ? "

The direct enquiry close to his ear startled Michael. He had been leaning back in his chair, listening vaguely to the hum of the guests' conversation and getting from it nothing more definite than a sense of the extraordinary ease of social intercourse under these conditions. Looking round, he saw that Clarissa Vine had come to sit next to him and he felt half-nervous of this concentrated gaze that so evidently betokened a determination to probe life and art and incidentally himself to the very roots.

" I think it's a little thin, don't you ? " said Clarie.

Michael hated to have his opinion of a painting invited; and he resented the painter's jargon that always seemed to apply equally to the subject and the medium. It was impossible to tell from Miss Vine's question whether she referred to Stella's figure or to Ayliffe's expenditure upon paint.

"I don't think it's very like Stella," Michael replied, and consoled himself for the absence of subtlety or cleverness in such an answer by the fact that at least it was a direct statement of what he thought.

"I know what you mean," said Clarissa, nodding seriously.

Michael hoped that she did. He could not conceive an affirmation of personal opinion delivered more plainly.

"You mean he's missed the other Stella," said Clarissa.

Michael bowed remotely. He told himself that contradiction or even qualified agreement would be too dangerous a proceeding with a person of Clarissa's unhumorous earnestness.

"I said so when I first saw it," cried Clarissa triumphantly. "I said, 'my god, George, you've only given us half of her.'"

Michael took a furtive glance at the portrait to see whether his initial impression of a full-length study had been correct and, finding that it was, concluded Clarissa referred to some metaphysical conception of her own.

From the amplification of this he edged away by drawing attention to the splendour of the moon.

"I know what you mean," said Clarissa. "But I like sunshine effects best."

"I wasn't really thinking about painting at that moment," Michael observed without remembering that all his mind was supposed to be occupied with it.

"You know *you're* very paintable," Clarissa went on. "I suppose you've sat to heaps of people. All the same I wish you'd let *me* paint you. I should like to bring out an aspect I daresay lots of people have never noticed."

Michael was not proof against this attack, and, despising the while his weak vanity, asked Clarissa what was the aspect.

"You're very passionate, aren't you ?" she said, shaking Michael's temperament in the thermometer of her thought.

"No, rather the reverse," said Michael, as he irritably visualized himself in a tiger-skin careering across one of Clarissa's florid canvases.

"All the same I wish you *would* sit for me," persisted Clarissa.

Michael made up his mind he must speak seriously to Stella about this friend of hers. It was really very unfair to involve him in this way with a provocative young paintress who, however clever she might be, was most obviously unsympathetic to him. What a pity Maurice Avery was not here. He would so enjoy skating on the thin ice of her thought. Yet ice was scarcely an appropriate metaphor to use in connection with her. There should be some parallel with strawberries to illustrate his notion of Clarissa, who was after all with her precious aspirations and constructive fingers a creature of the sun. Yet it was strange and rather depressing to think that English girls could never get any nearer to the Mænad than the evocation of the image of a farouche dairymaid.

All the time that Michael had been postulating these conclusions to himself, he had been mechanically shaking his head to Clarissa's request. "What can you be thinking about?" she asked, and at the moment mere inquisitiveness unbalanced the solemnity of her search for truth. Stella had gone to the piano, and someone with clumsy hair was testing the pitch of his violin. So Michael assumed the portentous reverence of a listening amateur and tried to suggest by his attitude that he was beyond the range of Clarissa's conversation. He did not know who had made the duet that was being played, nor did he greatly care, since, aside from his own participation in what it gave of unified emotion to the room, on its melodies he, as it were, voyaged from heart to heart of everyone present. There had been several moments during his talk with Clarissa when he had feared to see vanish that aureole with which

he had encircled this gathering, that halo woven by the mist
of his imagination and illuminated by the essential joy of
the company. But now, when all were fused by the power
of the music in a brilliance that actually pierced his apprehension with the sense of its positive being, Michael's
aureole gleamed with the same comparative reality. Travelling from heart to heart, he drew from each the deep-
down sweetness which justified all that was extravagant in
demeanour and dress, all that was flaunting in voice and
gesture, all that was weak in achievement and ambition.
Even Clarissa's prematurity seemed transferred from the
cause to the effect of her art, so that here and there some
strain of music was strong enough to sustain her personality
up to the very point of abandon at which her pictures aimed.
As for George Ayliffe, Michael watching him was bound to
acknowledge that, seen thus in repose with all the wandering
weaknesses of his countenance temporarily held in check
by the music, Stella's affection for him was just intelligible.
He might be said to possess now at least some of the graceful melancholy of a pierrot, and suddenly Michael divined
that Ayliffe was much more in love with Stella than she was
or ever could be in love with him. He realized that Ayliffe,
with fixed eyes sitting back and absorbing her music, was
aware of the hopelessness of his desire, aware it must be for
ever impossible for Stella to love him, as impossible as it was
for him to paint a great portrait of her. Michael was sorry
for Ayliffe because he knew that those anxious and hungry
eyes of his were losing her continually even now in complexities that could never by him be unravelled, in depths
that could never be plumbed.

More suggestive, however, than the individual listeners
were the players themselves, so essentially typical were they
of their respective instruments; and they were even
something more than typical, for they did ultimately resemble them. The violinist must himself have answered

in these harmonious wails to the lightest question addressed
to him. His whole figure had surely that very look of
obstinate surprize which belongs to a violin. The bones
in that lean body of his might have been of catgut, so much
did he play with his whole frame, so little observably with
his hands merely. As for Stella, apart from the simplicity
of her colouring, it was less easy to find physically a resemblance to the piano, and yet how well her personality consorted with one. Were she ignorant of the instrument it
would still be possible to compare her to a piano with her
character so self-contained and cool and ordered that yet,
played upon by people or circumstances, could reveal with
such decorous poignancy the emotion beneath, emotion,
however, that was always kept under control, as in a piano
the pressure or release of a pedal can swell or quell the most
expressive chord.

There was something consolatory to Michael in the way
Stella's piano part corrected the extreme yearning of the
violin. On ascending notes of the most plangent desire
the souls of the listeners were drawn far beyond the capacity of their own artistic revelation. It became almost
tragical to watch their undisciplined soaring regardless of
the height from which they must so swiftly fall. Yet when
the violin had thoughtlessly lured them to such a zenith
that had the music stopped altogether on that pole a reaction into disappointed sobs might not have been surprizing, Stella with her piano brought them back to the
normal course of their hopes, seemed to bear tenderly each
thwarted spirit down to earth and to set it back in the
lamps and shadows of this long riverside room, while with
the wistfulness of that cool accompaniment she mitigated
all the harshness of disillusion. Michael looked sharply
across at Ayliffe during this rescue and wondered how often
by Stella herself had he been just as gently treated.

The duet came to an end, and was followed by absurd

games and absurdly inadequate refreshments, until almost all together the guests departed. From the street below fainter and fainter sounded their murmurous talk, until it died away, swallowed up in the nightly whisper of the city.

Ayliffe stayed behind for a time, but he could not survive Michael's too polite 'Mr. Ayliffe' although he did not perhaps realize all the deadliness of this undergraduate insult. Clarissa went off to bed after expressing once more her wish that Michael would sit for her.

"Oh, what for? Of course he will, Clarie," cried Stella.

"Of course I won't," said Michael ruffling.

"What do you want him to sit for?" Stella persisted, paying not the least regard to Michael's objection.

"Oh, something ascetic," said Clarie, staring earnestly into space as if the pictorial idea was being dangled from the ceiling.

"Just now it was to be something passionate," Michael pointed out scornfully. He suspected Clarissa's courage in the presence of Stella's disdainful frankness.

"Ah, perhaps it will be both," Clarie promised and "Good night, most darling Stella," she murmured intensely. Then with one backward look of reproach for Michael she walked with rather self-conscious sinuousness out of the room and up to bed.

"My hat, Stella, where did you pick up that girl? She's like a performing leopard!" Michael burst out. "She's utterly stupid and utterly second-rate and she closes her eyes for effect and breathes into your face and doesn't wear stays."

"I get something out of all these queer people," Stella explained.

"New-art flower-vases, I should think," scoffed Michael. "Why on earth you wanted to fetch me from Cornwall to look after you in this crowd of idiots I can't imagine. I

may not be a great pianist in the making, and I'm jolly glad
I'm not, if it's to make one depend on the flattery of these
fools."

"You know, perfectly well that most of the evening you
enjoyed yourself very much. And you oughtn't to be
horrid about my friends. I think they're all so dreadfully
touching."

"Yes, and touched," Michael grumbled. "You're
simply playing at being in Bohemia. You'd be the first to
laugh at me, if I dressed up Alan and Maurice Avery and
half-a-dozen of my friends in velvet jackets and walked
about Paris with them, smelling of onions."

"My dear Michael," Stella argued, "do get out of
your head the notion that I dressed these people up. I
found them like that. They're not imported dolls."

"Well, you're not bound to know them. I tell you they
all hang on to you because you have money. That com-
pensates for any jealousy they might feel because you are
better at your business than any of them are at theirs."

"Rot," Stella ejaculated.

However, the argument that might have gone on endlessly
was quenched suddenly by the vision of the night seen by
Stella and Michael simultaneously. They hung over the
sill entranced and Michael was so closely held by the sorcery
of the still air that he was ready to surrender instantly his
provocative standpoint of intolerance. The contest between
prejudice and sentiment was unequal in such conditions.
No one could fail to forgive the most outrageous pretender
on such a night; no one could wish for Stella better
associates than the moonstruck company which had entered
so intangibly, had existed in reality for awhile so blatantly,
but was now again dissolved into elusive spectres of a
legendary paradise.

"I suppose what's really been the matter with me all the
evening," confessed Michael on the verge of going to bed,

" is that I've felt out of it all, not so much out of sympathy with them as acutely aware that for them I simply didn't exist. That's rather galling. Now at Oxford, supposing your friend Ayliffe were suddenly shot down amongst a lot of men in my year, he would be out of sympathy with us, and we should be out of sympathy with him, even up to the point of debagging him, but we should all be un-comfortably aware of his existence. Seriously, Stella, why did you send for me ? Not surely just to show me off to these unappreciative enthusiasts ? " ·

. " Perhaps I wanted a standard measure," Stella whispered with a gesture of disarming confidingness. " Something heavy and reliable."

" My dear girl, I'm much too much of a weathercock, or if you insist on me being heavy, let's say a pendulum. And there's nothing quite so confoundedly unreliable as either. Enough of gas. Good night."

·There followed à jolly time in Paris ; but for Michael it would have been a jollier time if he could have let him-self go with half the ridiculous pleasure he had derived from lighting bonfires in St. Cuthbert's quad or erecting a cocoa-nut shy in the Warden's garden. He was con-stantly aware of a loss of dignity which worried him con-siderably and for which he took himself to task very sternly. Finally he attributed it to one of two reasons, either that he felt a sense of constraint in Stella's presence on her account, or that his continued holding back was due to his difficulty in feeling any justification for extravagant behaviour, when he had not the slightest intention of presenting the world with the usufruct of his emotions in terms of letters or colour or sound.

" I really think I'm rather jealous of all these people," he told Stella. " They always seem to be able to go on being excited, and everything that happens to them they seem able to turn to account. Now, I can do nothing with my experience. I seize it, I enjoy it for a very short time. I begin to observe it with a warm interest, then to criticize, then to be bored by it, and finally I forget it altogether and remain just as I was before it occurred except that I never can seize the same sort of experience again. Perhaps it's being with you. Perhaps you absorb all the vitality."

Stella looked depressed by this suggestion.

"Let's go away and leave all these people," she proposed. "Let's go to Compiègne together, and we'll see if you're depressed by me then. But if you are, oh, Michael, I shan't know what to do. Only you won't be, if we're in Compiègne. It was such a success last time. In a way, you know, we really met each other there for the first time."

It was a relief to say farewell to Clarissa and her determination to produce moderately good pictures, to Ayliffe and his morbid hopes, to all that motley crowd, so pathetic and yet so completely self-satisfied. It was pleasant to arrive in Compiègne and find that Madame Regnier's house had not changed in three years, that the three old widows had not suffered from time's now slow and kindly progress, that M. Regnier still ate his food with the same noisy recklessness, that the front garden blazed with just the same vermilion of the geranium flowers.

For a week they spent industrious days of music and reading, and long mellow afternoons of provincial drowsiness that culminated in the simple pleasures of cassis and billiards at night. Michael wrote a sheaf of long letters to all his friends, amongst others to Lonsdale, who on hearing that he was at Compiègne wrote immediately to Prince Raoul de Castéra-Verduzan, an Eton contemporary, and asked him to call upon Michael. The young prince arrived one morning in a 70 h.p. car and by his visit made M. Regnier the proudest bourgeois in France. Prince Raoul who was dressed, so Stella said, as brightly as it was possible

even for a prince to dress nowadays, insisted that Michael
and his sister must become temporary members of the
Société du Sport de Compiègne. This proposal at first
they were inclined to refuse, but M. Regnier and Madame
Regnier and the three old widows were all so highly elated
at the prospect of knowing anybody belonging to this
club, and were so obviously cast down when their guests
seemed to hesitate, that Michael and Stella, more to please
the Pension Regnier than themselves, accepted Prince
Raoul's offer.

It was amusing, too, this so excessively aristocratic club
where every afternoon princesses and duchesses and the
wives of Greek financiers sat at tea or watched the tennis
and polo of their husbands and brothers and sons. Stella
and Michael played setts of tennis with Castéra-Verduzan
and the vicomte de Miramont, luxurious setts in which
there were always four little boys to pick up the balls and
at least three dozen balls to be picked up. Stella was a
great success as a tennis-player, and their sponsor introduced the brother and sister to all the languidly beautiful
women sitting at tea, and also to the over-tailored sportsmen
who were cultivating a supposedly Britannic seriousness of
attitude towards their games. Soon Michael and Stella
found themselves going out to dinner and playing bridge
and listening to much admiration of England in a Franco-
cockney accent that was the result of a foreign language
mostly acquired from grooms. With all its veneer of English
freedom, it was still a very ceremonious society, and though
money had tempered the rigidity of its forms and opinions,
there was always visible in the background of the noisiest
party Black Papalism, a dominant Army and the hope of
the Orleanist succession. Verduzan also took them for
long drives in the forest, and altogether time went by very
gaily and very swiftly, until Stella woke up to the fact that
her piano had been silent for nearly a fortnight. Verduzan

was waiting with his impatient car in the prim road outside the Pension Regnier when she made this discovery, and he looked very much mortified when she told him that to-day she really ought to practise.

"But you must come because I have to go away to-morrow," he declared.

"Ah, but I've been making such wonderful resolutions ever since the sun rose," Stella said, shaking her head. "I must work, mustn't I, Michael?"

"Oh, rot, she must come for this last time, mustn't she, Fane?"

Michael thought that once more might not spoil her execution irreparably.

"Hurrah, you can't get out of it, Miss Fane."

The car's horn tootled in grotesque exultation. Stella put on her dust-cloak of silver-grey, and in a few minutes they were racing through the forest so fast that the trees on either side winked in a continuous blur or where the forest was thinner seemed like knitting-needles to gather up folds of landscape.

After they had traversed all the wider roads at this speed, somewhere in the very heart of the forest Raoul turned sharply off along a waggoner's track over whose green ruts the car jolted abominably, but just when it would have been impossible to go on, he stopped and they all got out.

"You don't know why I've brought you here," he laughed.

Michael and Stella looked their perplexity to the great delight of the young man. "Wait a minute and you'll see," he chuckled. He was leading the way along a narrow grass-grown lane whose hedges on either side were gleaming with big blackberries.

"We shall soon be right out of the world," said Stella. "Won't that worry you, Monsieur?"

"Well, yes, it would for a very long time," replied the Prince in a tone of such wistfulness as for the moment made him seem middle-aged. "But, look," he cried, and triumphant youth returned to him once more.

The lane had ended in a forest clearing whose vivid turf was looped with a chain of small ponds blue as steel. On the farther side stood a cottage with diamonded lattices and a gabled roof and a garden full of deep crimson phlox glowing against a background of gnarled and sombre hawthorns. Cottage and clearing were set in a sweeping amphitheatre of beech-woods.

"It reminds me of Gawaine and the Green Knight," said Michael.

"I'll take you inside," Raoul offered.

They walked across the small common silently, so deeply did they feel they were trespassing on some enchantment. From the cottage chimney curled a film of smoke that gave a voiceless voice to the silence, and when as they paused in the lych-gate, Castéra-Verduzan clanged the bell, it seemed indeed the summons to waken from a spell sleepers long ago bewitched.

"Surely nobody is going to answer that bell," said Stella.

"Why, yes, of course, Ursule will open it. Ursule! Ursule!" he cried. "C'est moi, Monsieur Raoul."

The cottage door opened and, evidently much delighted, Ursule came stumping down the path. She was an old woman whose rosy face was pectinated with fine wrinkles as delicate as the pluming of a moth's wing, while everything about her dress gave the same impression of extreme fineness, though the stuff was only a black bombazine and the tippet round her shoulders was of coarse lace. When she and Raoul had talked together in rapidest French, Ursule like an old queen waved them graciously within.

They sat in the white parlour on tall chairs of black

oak amongst the sounds of ticking clocks and distant bees and a smell of sweet herbs and dryness.

"And there's a piano," cried Stella running to it. She played the Cat's Fugue of Domenico Scarlatti.

"You could practise on that piano?" Raoul anxiously enquired. "It belonged to my sister who often came here. More than any of us do. She's married now."

The sadness in Raoul's voice had made Michael suppose he was going to say his sister was dead.

"Then this divine place belongs to you?" Stella asked.

"To my sister and me. Ursule was once my nurse. Would you be my guests here, although I shall be away? For as long as you like. Ursule will look after you. Do say 'yes.'"

"Why, what else could we say?" Michael and Stella demanded simultaneously.

It was a disappointment to the Regniers when Michael and Stella came back to announce their retreat into the fast woodland, but perhaps M. Regnier found compensation in going down to his favourite café that afternoon and speaking of his guests, Monsieur and Mademoiselle Fêne, now staying with M. le prince de Castéra-Verduzan at his hunting-lodge in the forest.

Later that afternoon with their luggage and music Raoul brought Michael and Stella back to the cottage in his car, after which he said good-bye. Ursule was happy to have somebody to look after, and the cottage that had seemed so very small against the high beeches of the steep country behind was much larger when it was explored. It stretched out a rectangular wing of cool and shadowed rooms towards the forest. In this portion Ursule lived, and there was the pantry, and the kitchen embossed with copper pans, and the still-room which had garnered each flowery year in its course. Conterminous with Ursule's wing was a flagged court where a stone well-head stained with grey and orange lichen mirrored a circumscribed world. Beyond into an ancient orchard, whose last red apples ripened under the first outstretched boughs of the forest, tossed an acre of garden with runner-beans still in bloom.

. In the part of the cottage where Stella and Michael lived, besides the white parlour with the piano, there was the hall with a great hooded fireplace and long polished dining-table lined and botched by the homely meals of numberless dead banqueters; and at either end of the cottage there were two small bedrooms with frequent changing patterns in dimity and chintz, with many tinted china ornaments and holy pictures that all combined to present the likeness of two glass cases enshrining an immoderately gay confusion of flowers and fruit and birds.

Here in these ultimate September days of summer's reluctant farewell life had all the rich placidity of an apricot upon a sun-steeped wall. Michael, while Stella practised really hard, read Gregorovius' History of the Papacy; and when she stopped suddenly he would wake half-startled from the bloody horrors of the tenth century narrated laboriously with such cold (pedantry,) and hear above the first elusive silence swallows gathering on the green common, robins in their autumnal song, and down a corridor the footfalls and tinkling keys of Ursule.

It was natural that such surroundings should beget many intimate conversations between Michael and Stella, and if anything were wanting to give them a sense of perfect ease the thought that here at Compiègne three years ago they had realized one another for the first time always smoothed away the trace of shyness.

. "Whether I had come out to Paris or not," asked Michael earnestly, " there never would have been anything approaching a love-affair between you and that fellow Ayliffe ? ". He had to recur to this uneasy theme.

. " There might have been, Michael. I think that people

2 S

who like me grow to rely tremendously on themselves. require rather potty little people to play about with. It's
the same sort of pleasure one gets from eating cheap sweets
between meals. With somebody like George, one feels no
need to bother to sustain one's personality at highest pitch.
George used to be grateful for so little. He really wasn't
bad."

"But didn't you feel it was undignified to let him even
think you might fall in love with him ? I don't want to be
too objectionably fraternal, but if Ayliffe was as cheap as
you admit, you ran the risk of cheapening yourself."

"Only to other people," Stella argued, " not to myself.
My dear Michael, you've no idea what a relief it is sometimes to play on the piano a composition that is really easy—
ridiculously, fatuously easy."

"But you wouldn't choose that piece for public performance," Michael pointed out. He was beginning to
feel the grave necessity of checking Stella's extravagance.

"Surely the public you saw gathered round me in Paris
wasn't very important ? " She laughed in almost contemptuous remembrance.

"Then why did you wire for me if the whole affair was
so trivial as you make out now ? "

" I wanted a corrective," Stella explained.

"But how am I a corrective outside the fact that I'm
your brother ? And, you know, I don't believe you would
consider that relationship had much to do with my importance one way or the other."

" In fact," said Stella laughing, "what you're really
trying to do is to work the conversation round to yourself.
One reason why you're a corrective to George is that you're
a gentleman."

"There you are," cried Michael excitedly, and as if
with that word she had released a spring that was holding
back all the pent-up conclusions of some time past, he

launched forth upon the display of his latest excavation of life. "We all half apologize for using the word 'gentleman,' but we can't get on without it. People say it means nothing nowadays. Although if it ever meant anything, it should mean more nowadays than it did in the past, since every generation should add something to its value. I haven't been able to talk this out before, because you're the only person who knows what I was born and at the same time is able to understand that for me to think about my circumstances rather a lot doesn't imply any very morbid self-consciousness. *You're* all right. You have this astonishing gift which would have guaranteed you self-expression whatever you had been born. When one sees an artist up to your level, one doesn't give a damn for his ancestors or his family or his personal features apart from the security of the art's consummation. Perhaps I have a vague inclination towards art myself, but inclinations are no good without something to lean up against at the end. These people who came to your party that night in Paris are in a way much happier, or rather much more secure than me. However far they incline without support they're most of them inclining away from a top-heavy suburban life. So if they become failures, they'll always have the consolation of knowing they had either got to incline outwards or be suffocated."

Michael stopped for awhile and stared out through the cottage lattices at the stretch of common, at the steel-blue chain of ponds and the narrow portal that led to this secluded forest-world, and away down the lane to where on either side of the spraying brambles a plantation of delicate birch-trees was tinted with the diaphanous brown and gold and pale fawn of their last attiring.

"If I could only find in life itself," said Michael sighing, "a path leading to something like this cottage."

"But, meanwhile, go on," Stella urged. "Do go on

with your self-revelation. It's so fascinating to me. It's like a chord that never resolves itself, or a melody flitting in and out of a symphony."

"Something rather pathetic in fact," Michael suggested.

"Oh, no, much too elusive and independent to be pathetic," she assured him.

"My difficulty is that by natural inheritance I'm the possessor of so much I can never make use of," Michael began again. "I'm not merely discontented from a sense of envy. That trivial sort of envy doesn't enter my head. Indeed I don't think I'm ever discontented or even resentful for one moment, but if I *were* the head of a great family I should have my duties set out in a long line before me, and all my theories of what a gentleman owes to the state would be weighted down with importance, or at any rate with potential significance, whereas now——" he shrugged his shoulders.

"I don't see much difference really," Stella said. "You're not prevented from being a gentleman and proving it on a smaller scale perhaps."

"Yes, yes," Michael plunged on excitedly. "But crowds of people are doing that, and every day more and more loudly the opinion goes up that these gentlemen are accidental ornaments, rather useless, rather irritating ornaments of contemporary society. Every day brings another sneer at public schools and universities. Every new writer who commands any attention drags out the old idol of the Noble Savage and invites us to worship him. Only now the Noble Savage has been put into corduroy trousers. My theory is that a gentleman leavens the great popular mass of humanity, and however superficially useless he may seem, his existence is a pledge of the immanence of the idea. Popular education has fired thousands to prove themselves not gentlemen in the present meaning of the term, but something much finer than any gentleman we know anything about. And they are *not*, they simply and solidly are *not*. The first instinct of the gentleman is respect for the past with all it connotes of art and religion and thought. The first instinct of the educated unfit is to hate and destroy the past. Now I maintain that the average gentleman, whatever situation he is called upon to face, will deal with it more effectively than these noble savages who have been armed with weapons they don't know how to use and are therefore so much the more dangerous, since every weapon to the primitive mind is a weapon of offence. Had I been Lord Saxby instead of Michael Fane, I could have proved my theory on the grand scale, and obviously the grand scale even for a gentleman is the only scale that is any good nowadays."

" I wonder if you could," murmured Stella. " Anyway, I don't see why you shouldn't ultimately attain to the grand scale, if you begin with the small scale."

" But the small scale means just a passive existence that hurts nobody and fades out of memory at the moment of death," Michael grumbled.

" Well, if your theory of necessary ornaments is valid," Stella pointed out, " you'll find your niche."

" I shall be a sort of Prescott. That's the most I can hope for," Michael gloomily announced. " Yet after all that's pretty good."

Stella looked at him in surprize, and said that though she had known Michael liked Prescott, she had no idea he had created such an atmosphere of admiration. She was eager to find out what Michael most esteemed in him, and she plied him indeed with so many questions that he finally asked her if she did not approve of Prescott.

" Of course I approve of him. No one could accept a refusal so wonderfully without being approved. But naturally I wanted to find out your opinion of him. What

could be more interesting to a girl than to know the judgement of others on a person she might have married ? ",

Michael gazed at her, in astonishment and demanded
her reason for keeping such an extraordinary event so
secret.

"Because I didn't want to introduce an atmosphere of
curiosity into your relationship with him. You know,
Michael, that if I had told you, you would always have been
examining him when you thought he wasn't looking. And
of course I never told mother, who would have examined
him through her lorgnette whether he were looking or
not."

It seemed strange to Michael, as he and Stella sat here
with the woodland enclosing them, that she could so fear-
lessly accept or refuse what life offered. And yet he supposed the ability to do so made of her the artist she was.
Thinking of her that night, as he sat up reading in the
clock-charmed room where lately she had played him through
the dawn of the English Constitution, he told himself
that even this cottage which so essentially became them
both, was the result of Stella's appeal to Raoul de Castéra-
Verduzan, an appeal in which his own personality had
scarcely entered. Castéra-Verduzan ! Prescott ! Ayliffe !
What folly it had been for him to make his own plans for
her and Alan. Yet it had seemed so obvious and so easy
that these two should fall in love with each other. Michael
wondered whether he were specially privileged in being
able to see through to a sister's heart, whether other
brothers went blindly on without an inkling that their
sisters were loved. It was astonishing to think that the grave
Prescott had stepped so far and so rashly from his polite
seclusion as to accept the risk of ridicule for proposing to a
girl whose mother's love for a friend of his own he had
spent his life in guarding. Michael put out the lamp and,
lighting a candle, went along the corridor to bed. From the

far end he heard Stella's voice calling to him and turned back
to ask her what she wanted. She was sitting up in bed
very wide-eyed and, in that dainty room of diminutive
buds and nosegays all winking in the soft candlelight, she
seemed with her brown hair tied up with a scarlet bow
someone disproportionately large and wild, yet someone
whom for all her largeness and wildness it would still be
a joy devotedly to cherish and protect.

"Michael, I've been thinking about what you said," she
began, "and you mustn't get cranky. I wish you wouldn't
bother so much about what you're going to be. It will end
in your simply being unhappy."

"I don't really bother a great deal," Michael assured
her. "But I do feel a sort of responsibility for being a
nobody, so very definitely a nobody."

"The people who ought to have felt that responsibility
were mother and father," said Stella.

"Yes, logically," Michael agreed. "But I think father
did feel the responsibility rather heavily; and it's a sort of
loyalty I have for him which makes me so determined to
justify myself."

That night the equinoctial gales began. Stella and
Michael had only two or three walks more down the wide
glades where the fallen leaves trundled and swirled, and then
it would be time to leave this forest house. Raoul did not
manage to come back to Compiègne in time to say good-bye,
and so at the moment of departure they took leave of old
Ursule and the cottage very sadly, for it seemed, so desolate
and gusty was the October morning, that never again would
they possess for their own that magical corner of the world.

The equinoctial gales died away in a flood of rain, and
the fine weather came back. London welcomed their
return with a gracious calm. The Thames was a sheet of
trembling silver, and the distant roofs and spires and trees
of the Surrey shore no more than breath upon a glass. In

this luminous and immaterial city the house in Cheyne Walk stood out with the pleasant aspect of its demure reality, and Mrs. Fane like one of those clouded rose pastels on the walls of her room was to both of them after their absence from London for a while herself as they had known her in childhood.

"Dear children, how charming to see you looking so well. I'm not quite sure I like that very Scotch-looking skirt, darling Stella. I'm so glad you've enjoyed yourselves together. Is it a heather mixture? And I was in France too. But the trains are so oddly inconvenient. Mrs. Carruthers—most interesting! I wish, darling Stella, you would take up Mental Science. Ah, but I forgot, you have your practising."

It was time to go up to Oxford after the few days that Stella and Michael spent in making arrangements for a series of Brahms recitals in one of the smaller concert-halls. Alan met Michael on the platform at Paddington. This custom they had loyally kept up each term, although otherwise their paths seemed to be diverging.

"Good vac?" Michael asked.

"Oh, rather! I've been working at rather a tricky slow leg-break. Fifty-five wickets for 8.4 during the vac. Not bad for a dry summer. I was playing for the Tics most of the time. What did you do?"

Michael during the journey up talked mostly about Stella.

Chapter VII : *Venner's*

THE most of Michael's friends had availed themselves of the right of seniority to move into more
dignified rooms for their second year. These
'extensions of premises,' as Castleton called them, reached
the limit of expansion in the case of Lonsdale who after a
year's residence in two small ground-floor rooms of St.
Cuthbert's populous quad had acquired the largest suite of
three in Cloisters. Exalted by palatial ambitions, he spent
the first week of term in buttonholing people in the lodge,
so that after whatever irrelevant piece of chatter he had
seized upon as excuse he might wind up the conversation by
observing nonchalantly:

"Oh, I say, have you chaps toddled round to my new
rooms yet ? Rather decent. I'm quite keen on them. I've
got a dining-room now. Devilish convenient. Thought of
asking old Wedders to lay in a stock of pictures. It would
buck him up rather."

"But why do you want these barracks ?" Michael
asked.

"Oh, binges," said Lonsdale. "We ought to be able to
run some pretty useful binges here. Besides I'm thinking of
learning the bagpipes."

Wedderburn had moved into the Tudor richness of the
large gateway room in St. Cuthbert's tower. Avery had succeeded the canorous Templeton-Collins on Michael's staircase, and had brought back with him from Flanders an
alleged Rubens to which the rest of the furniture and the
honest opinions of his friends were ruthlessly sacrificed.

633

Michael alone had preferred to remain in the rooms originally awarded to him. He had a sentimental objection to denying them the full period of their participation in his own advance along the lines he had marked out for himself. As he entered them now to resume the tenure interrupted by the Long Vacation he compared their present state with the negative effect they had produced a year ago. Being anxious to arrange some decorative purchases he had made in France, Michael had ordered commons for himself alone. How intimate and personal that sparse lunch laid for one on a large table now seemed. How trimly crowded was now that inset bookcase and what imprisoned hours it could release to serve his pleasure. There was not now indeed a single book that did not recall the charmed idleness of the afternoon it commemorated. Nor was there one volume that could not conjure for him at midnight with enchantments eagerly expected all the day long.

It was a varied library this that in three terms he had managed to gather together. When he began, ornate sets like great gaudy heralds had proclaimed those later arrivals which were after all so much the more worshipful. The editions of luxury had been succeeded by the miscellanies of mere information, works that fired the loiterer to acquire them for the sake of the knowledge of human by-ways they generally so jejunely proffered. And yet perhaps it was less for their material contents that they were purchased than for the fact that in some dead publishing season more extravagant buyers had spent four or five times as much to partake of their accumulated facts and fortuitous illustrations. With Michael the passion for remainders was short-lived, and he soon pushed them ignobly out of the way, for the sake of those stately rarities that combined a decorous exterior with the finest flavour of words and a permanent value that was yet subject to mercantile elation and depression

If among these ambassadors of learning and literature was to be distinguished any predominant tone, perhaps the kindliest favour had been extended towards the more unfamiliar and fantastic quartos of the seventeenth century, those speculative compendiums of lore that though enriched by the classic Renaissance were nevertheless more truly the eclectic consummation of the Middle Ages. The base of their thought may have been unsubstantial, a mirage of philosophy, offering but a Neo-Platonic or Gnostic kaleido- scope through which to survey the universe; but so rich were their tinctures and apparels, so diverse was the pattern of their ceremonious commentary, and so sonorous was their euphony that Michael made of their reading a sanctuary where every night for awhile he dreamed upon their cadences resounding through a world of polychromatic images and recondite jewels, of spiritual maladies and minatory comets, of potions for revenge and love, of talismans to fortune, touchstones of treasure and eternal life, and strange influential herbs. Mere words came to possess Michael so perilously that under the spell of these Jacobeans he grew half contemptuous of thought less prodigally ornate. The vital ideas of the present danced by in thin-winged progress unperceived, or rather perceived as bloodless and irresolute ephemerides. When people reproached him for his wilful prejudice, he pointed out how easy it would always be to overtake the ideas of the present and how much waste of intellectual breath would be avoided by letting his three or four Oxford years account for the most immediately evanescent. Oxford seemed to him to provide an opportunity, and more than an opportunity—an inexpugnable command to wave with most reluctant hands farewell to the backward of time, around whose brink rose up more truthful dreams than those that floated indeterminate, beckoning through the mist across the wan mountains of the future.

On the walls Michael's pictures had been collected to achieve through another medium the effect of his books. Monna Lisa was there not for her lips or eyes, but rather for that labyrinth of rocks and streams behind; and since pictures seldom could be found to provide what he sought in a picture, there were very few of them in his sitting-room. One hour of the Anatomy of Melancholy or of Urn Burial could always transform the pattern of the terra-cotta wall-paper to some diagrammatic significance. Apart from the accumulation of books and pictures he had changed the room scarcely at all. Curtains and covers, chairs and tables, all preserved the character of the room itself as something that existed outside the idiosyncrasies of the transient inhabitants who read and laughed and ate and talked for so compara-tively fleeting a space of time between its four walls. With all that he had imposed of what in the opinion of his con-temporaries were eccentricities of adornment, the rooms remained, as he would observe to any critic, essentially the same as his own. Instead of college groups which marked merely by the height of the individual's waistcoat-opening the almost intolerable fugacity of their record, there were Leonardo and Blake and Frederick Walker to preserve the illusion of permanence, or at least of continuity. Instead of the bleached and desiccated ribs of momentarily current magazines cast away in sepulchral indignity, there were a hundred quartos whose calf bindings had the durableness and sober depth of walnut furniture, furniture moreover that was still in use.

Yet it was in Venner's office where Michael found the perfect fruit of time's infinitely fastidious preservation, the survival not so much of the fittest as of the most ex-pressive. Here indeed, whatever in his own rooms might affect him with the imagination of the eternal present of finite conceptions, was the embodiment of the possible truth of those moments in which at intervals he had apprehended, whether through situations or persons or places, the assurance of immortality. Great pictures, great music and most of all great literature would always remain as the most obvious pledge of man's spiritual potentiality, but these subtler intimations of momentary vision had such power to impress themselves that Michael could believe in the child Blake when he spoke of seeing God's forehead pressed against the window-panes, could believe that the soul liberated from the prison of the flesh had struggled in the very instant of her recapture to state the ineffable. To him Blake seemed the only poet who had in all his work disdained to attempt the recreation of anything but these moments of positive faith. Every other writer seemed clogged by human conceptions of grandeur. Most people, seeking the imaginative reward of their sensibility would obtain the finest thrill that Oxford could offer from the sudden sight of St. Mary's tower against a green April afterglow, or of the moon-parched High Street in frost. Michael, however, found in Venner's office, just as he had found in that old print of St. Mary's tower rather than in the tower itself, the innermost shrine of Oxford, the profoundest revelation of the shining truth round which the mysterious material of Oxford had grown through the Middle Ages.

Michael with others of his year had during the summer term ventured several times into Venner's, but the entrance of even a comparatively obscure senior had always driven them out. They had not yet enjoyed the atmosphere of security without which a club unlike an orchard never tastes sweet. Now, with the presence of a new year's freshmen and with the lordship of the college in their own hands, since to the out-of-college men age with merciless finger seemed already to be beckoning, Michael and his contemporaries in their pride of prime marched into Venner's after hall and drank their coffee.

Venner's office was one of the small ground-floor rooms

in Cloisters; but it had long ago been converted to the present use. An inner store-room, to which Venner always retired to make a cup of squash or to open a bottle of whisky, had once been the bedroom. The office itself was not luxuriously furnished, and the accommodation was small. A window-seat with a view of the college kitchens, a square table, and a couple of Windsor chairs were considered enough for the men who frequented Venner's every night after hall, and who on Sunday nights after wine in J.C.R. clustered there like a swarm of bees. Venner's own high chair stood far back in the corner behind his high sloping desk on which, always spread open, lay the great ledger of J.C.R. accounts. On the shelves above were the account books of bygone years in which were indelibly recorded the extravagances of more than thirty years of St. Mary's men. Over the fireplace was a gilt mirror of Victorian design stuck round with the fixture cards of the university and the college, with notices of grinds and musical clubs and debating societies, in fact with all the printed petty news of Oxford. A few photographs of winning crews, a book-case with stores of college stationery, a Chippendale sideboard with a glass case of priced cigars on top, and an interesting drawerful of Venner's relics above the varnished wainscot completed the furniture. The wall-paper was of that indefinite brownish yellow which one finds in the rooms of old-fashioned solicitors, and of that curious oily texture which seems to produce an impression of great age and at the same time of perfect modernity. Yet the office itself, haunted though it was by the accumulated personalities of every generation at St. Mary's, would scarcely have possessed the magical effect of fusion which it did possess, had not all these personalities endured in a perpetual present through the conservative force of Venner himself. John Venables had been Steward of the Junior Common Room for thirty-three years, but he seemed to all these young men that came within the fragrancy of his

charm to be as much an intrinsic part of the college as the
tower itself. The moon-faced Warden, the dry-voiced dons,
the deer park, the elms, the ancient doors and traceries, the
lawns and narrow entries, the groinings and the lattices, were
all subordinate in the estimation of the undergraduates to
Venner. He knew the inner history of every rag; he
realized why each man was popular or unpopular or merely
ignored; he was a treasure-house of wise counsel and kindly
advice; he held the keys of every heart. He was an old man
with florid, clean-shaven face, a pair of benignant eyes
intensely blue, a rounded nose, a gentle voice and most
inimitable laugh. Something there was in him of the old
family butler, a little more of the yeoman-farmer, a trace of
the head game-keeper, a suspicion of the trainer of horses,
but all these elements were blended to produce the effect of
someone wise and saintly and simple who could trouble himself to heal the lightest wounds and could rouse with a look
or a gesture undying affection.

With such a tutelary spirit, it was not surprizing the
freedom of Venner's should have been esteemed a privilege
that could only be conferred by the user's consciousness of
his own right. There was no formal election to Venner's:
there simply happened a moment when the St. Mary's man
entered unembarrassed that mellow office and basked in that
sunny effluence. In this ripe old room, generous and dry as
sherry wine, how pleasant it was to sit and listen to Venner's
ripe old stories: how amazingly important seemed the trivial
gossip of the college in this historic atmosphere: how much
time was apparently wasted here between eight and ten at
night, and what a thrill it always was to come into college
about half-past nine of a murky evening and stroll round
Cloisters to see if there was anybody in Venner's. It could
after all scarcely be accounted a waste of time to sit and
slowly mature in Venner's, and sometimes about half-past
nine the old man would be alone, the fire would be dying

down and during the half-hour that remained of his duty, it would be possible to peel a large apple very slowly and extract from him more of the essence of social history than could be gained from a term's reading of great historians even with all the extra lucidity imparted by a course of Mr. So-and-So's lectures.

Michael found that Venner summed up clearly for him all his own tentative essays to grasp the meaning of life. He perceived in him the finest reaction to the prejudice and nobility, the efficiency and folly of aristocratic thought. He found in him the ideal realization of his own most cherished opinions. England, and all that was most inexplicable in the spirit of England, was expressed by Venner. He was a landscape, a piece of architecture, a simple poem of England. One of Venner's applauded tricks was to attach a piece of string to the tongs for a listener to hold to his ears, while Venner struck the tongs with the poker and evoked the sound of St. Mary's chimes. But the poker and tongs were unnecessary, for in Venner's own voice was the sound of all the bells in England. Communion with this gracious, this tranquil, this mellow presence affected Michael with a sense of the calm certainty of his own life. It lulled all the discontent and all the unrest. It indicated for the remainder of his Oxford time a path, which, if it did not lead to any outburst of existence, was at least a straight path, green bordered and gay with birdsong, with here and there a sight of ancient towers and faiths, and here and there an arbour in which he and his friends could sit and talk of their hopes.

"Venner," said Lonsdale one evening, "do you remember the Bishop of Cirencester when he was up? Stebbing his name was. My mother roped him in for a teetotal riot she was inciting this vac."

"Oh, yes, I think he was rather a wild fellow," Venner began full of reminiscence. "But we'll look him up."

Down came some account-book of the later seventies, and

all the festive evenings of the Bishop, spent in the period
when undergraduates were photographed with mutton-chop
whiskers and bowler hats, lay revealed for the criticism of
his irreverent successors.

"There you are," chuckled Venner triumphantly.
"What did I say? One dozen champagne. Three bottles
of brandy. All drunk in one night, for there's another half-
dozen put down for the next day. Ah, but the men are
much quieter nowadays. Not nearly so much drinking done
in college as there used to be. Oh, I remember the Bishop—
Stebbing he was then. He put a codfish in the Dean's bed.
Oh, there was a dreadful row about it. The old Warden
kicked up such a fuss."

And, as easily as one Arabian night glides into another,
Venner glided from anecdote to anecdote of episcopal
youth.

"I thought the old boy liked the governor's port,"
laughed Lonsdale. "'What a pity everybody can't drink
in moderation,' said Gaiters. Next time he cocks his
wicked old eye at me, I shall ask him about that codfish."

"What's this they tell me about your bringing out a
magazine?" Venner enquired turning to Maurice Avery.

"Out next week, Venner," Maurice announced importantly.

"Why, whatever do you find to write about?" asked
Venner. "But I suppose it's amusing. I've often been
asked to write my own life. What an idea! As if I had any
time. I'm glad enough to go to bed when I get home,
though I always smoke a pipe first. We had two men here
once who brought out a paper. Chalfont and Weymouth.
I used to have some copies of it somewhere. They put in a
lot of skits of the college dons. The Warden was quite
annoyed. 'Most scurrilous, Venables,' he said to me I remember. 'Most scurrilous.'" Venner chuckled at the
remembrance of the Warden's indignation.

2 T

"This is going to be a very serious affair, Venner," explained somebody. "It's going to put the world quite straight again."

"Ho-ho, I suppose you're one of these Radicals," said Venner to the editor. "Dear me, how anyone can be a Radical I can't understand. I've always been a Conservative. We had a Socialist come up here to lecture once in a man's rooms—a great Radical this man was—Sir Hugh Gaston—a baronet—there's a funny thing, fancy a Radical baronet. Well, the men got to hear of this Socialist coming up and what do you think they did?" Venner chuckled in anticipatory relish. "Why, they cropped his hair down to nothing. Sir Hugh Gaston was quite upset about it, and when he made a fuss, they cut his hair too, though it was quite short already. There was a terrible rowdy set up then. The men are very much quieter nowadays."

The door opened as Venables finished his story, and Smithers came in to order rather nervously a tin of biscuits. The familiar frequenters of Venner's eyed in cold silence his entrance, his blushful wait and his hurried exit.

"That's a scholar called Smithers," Venner explained. "He's a very quiet man. I don't suppose any of you know him even by sight."

"We ragged him last term," said Michael smiling at his friends.

"He's a bounder," declared Avery obstinately.

"He hasn't much money," said Venner. "But he's a very nice fellow. You oughtn't to rag him. He's very harmless. Never speaks to anybody. He'll get a first, I expect, but there, you don't think anything of that, I know. But the dons do. The Warden often has him to dinner. I shouldn't rag him any more. He's a very sensitive fellow. His father's a carpenter. What a wonderful thing he should have a son come up to St. Mary's."

The rebuke was so gently administered that only the momentary silence betrayed its efficacy.

One day Michael brought Alan to be introduced to Venables, and it was a pleasure to see how immediately the old man appreciated Alan.

"Why ever didn't you come to St. Mary's?" asked Venner. "Just the place for you. Don't you find Christ Church a bit large? But they've got some very good land. I've often done a bit of shooting over the Christ Church farms. The Bursar knows me well. 'Pleased to see you, Mr. Venables, and I hope you'll have good sport.' That's what he said to me last time I saw him. Oh, he's a very nice man. Do they still make meringues at your place? I don't suppose you ever heard the story of the St. Mary's men who broke into Christ Church. It caused quite a stir at the time. Well, some of our men was very tipsy one night at the Bullingdon wine, and one of them left his handkerchief in the rooms of a Christ Church man, and what do you think they did? Why, when they got back to college, this man said he wasn't going to bed without his handkerchief. Did you ever hear of such a thing? So they all climbed out of St. Mary's at about two in the morning and actually climbed into Christ Church. At least they thought it was Christ Church, but it was really Pembroke. Do you know Pembroke? I don't suppose you've even been there. Our men always cheer Pembroke in the Eights—Pemmy, as they call it,—because their barge is next to us. But fancy breaking in there at night to look for a handkerchief. They woke up every man in the college, and there was a regular set-to in the quad, and the night porter at Pembroke got a most terrible black eye. The President of the J.C.R. had to send an apology, and it was all put right, but this man who lost his handkerchief, Wilberforce his name was, became a regular nuisance, because for ever afterwards, whenever he got drunk, he used to go looking for this old handkerchief. There you see, that's what comes of going to the Bullingdon wine. Are you a member of the Bullingdon ? "

" He's a cricketer, Venner," Michael explained.

" So was this fellow Wilberforce who lost his handkerchief, and what do you think ? One day when we were playing Winchester—you're not a Wykehamist, are you ?—he came out to bat so drunk that the first ball he hit, he went and ran after it himself. It caused quite a scandal. But you don't look one of that sort. Will you have a squash and a biscuit ? The men like these biscuits very much. There's been quite a run on them."

. Michael was anxious to know how deep an impression Venner had made on Alan.

" You've got nobody like him at the House ? " he asked.

Alan was bound to admit there was indeed nobody.

" He's an extraordinary chap," said Michael. " He's always different and yet he's always absolutely the same. For me he represents Oxford. When one's in his company, one feels one's with him for ever, and yet one knows that people who have gone down can feel just the same, and that people who haven't yet come up will feel just the same. You know, I do really think that what it sets out to do St. Mary's does better than any other college. And the reason of that is Venner's. It's the only successful democracy in the world."

" I shouldn't have called it a democracy," said Alan. " Everybody doesn't go there."

" But everybody can go there. It depends entirely on themselves."

" What about that fellow Smithers you were talking about ? " Alan asked. " He seems barred."

" But he won't be," Michael urged hopefully.

" He'd be happier at the House all the same," Alan said. " He'd find his own set there."

" But so he can at St. Mary's."

" Then it isn't a democracy," Alan stoutly maintained.

"I say, Alan," exclaimed Michael in surprize. "You're getting quite a logician."

"Well, you always persist in treating me like an idiot," said Alan. "But I *am* reading Honour Mods. It's a swat, but I've got to get some sort of a class."

"You'll probably get a first," said Michael.

Yet how curious it was to think of Alan, whom he still regarded as chiefly a good-looking and capable athlete, taking a first class in a school he himself had indolently passed over. Of course he would never take a first. He was too much occupied with the perfection of new leg-breaks. And what would he do after his degree, his third in greats? A third was the utmost Michael mentally allowed him in the Final Schools.

"I suppose you'll ultimately try for the Indian Civil?" Michael asked. "Do you remember when we used to lie awake talking in bed at Carlington Road? It was always going to be me who did everything intellectual; you were always the sportsman."

"I am still. Michael, I think I've got a chance of my Blue this year. If I can keep that leg-break," he added fervidly. "There's no slow right-hander of much class in the Varsity. I worked like a navvy at that leg-break last vac."

"I thought you were grinding for Mods," Michael reminded him with a smile.

"I worked like a navvy at Mods," said Alan.

"You'll be a proconsul, I really believe." Michael looked admiringly at his friend. "And do you know, Alan, in appearance you're turning into a regular viking."

"I meant to have my hair cut yesterday," said Alan in grave and reflective self-reproof.

"It's not your hair," cried Michael. "It's your whole personality. I never appreciated you until this moment."

"I think you talk more rot nowadays than you used to

talk even," said Alan. "So long, I, must go back and work."

The tall figure with the dull gold hair curling out from the green cap of Harris tweed faded away in the November fog that was travelling, in swift and smoky undulations through the Oxford streets. What a strangely attractive walk Alan had always had, and now it had gained something of determination, whether from leg-breaks or logic Michael did not know. But the result was a truer grace in the poise of his neck; a longer and more supple swing from his tapering flanks.

Michael went on up the High and stood for a moment, watching the confusion caused by the fog at Carfax, listening to the fretful tinkles of the numerous bicycles and the jangling of the trams and the shouts of the paper-boys. Then he walked down Cornmarket Street past the shops splashing through the humid coils of vapour their lights upon the townspeople, loiterers and purchasers who thronged the pavements. Undergraduates strolled along, linked arm in arm and perpetually staring. How faithfully each group resembled its forerunners and successors. All had the same fresh complexions, the same ample green coats of Harris tweed, the same grey flannel trousers. Only in the casual acknowledgments of his greeting when he recognized acquaintances was there the least variation, since some would nod or toss their heads, others would shudder with their chins, and a few would raise their arms in a fanlike gesture of social benediction. Michael turned round into the Broad, where the fog made mysterious even the tea-tray gothic of Balliol, and Trinity with its municipal ampelopsis. A spectral cabman saluted him interrogatively from the murk. A fox-terrier went yapping down the street at the heels of a don's wife hurrying back to Banbury Road. A belated paper-boy yelled, 'Varsity and Blackheath Result,' hastening towards a more profitable traffic. The fog grew denser every minute, and Michael turned round into Turl Street past many-windowed Exeter and the monastic silence of Lincoln. There was time to turn aside and visit Lampard's bookshop. There was time to buy that Glossary of Ducange which he must have, and perhaps that red and golden Dictionary of Welby Pugin which he ought to have, and ultimately, as it turned out, there was time to buy half-a-dozen more great volumes whose connection with mediæval history was not too remote to give an excuse to Michael, if excuse were needed, for their purchase. Seven o'clock chimed suddenly, and Michael hurried to college, snatched a black coat and a gown out of Venner's and just avoided the sconce for being more than a quarter of an hour late for hall.

Michael was glad he had not missed hall that night. In Lampard's alluring case of treasures he had been tempted to linger on until too late, and then to take with him two or three new books and in their entertainment to eat a solitary and meditative dinner at Buol's. But it would have been a pity to have missed hall when the electric light failed abruptly and when everybody had just helped themselves to baked potatoes. It would have been sad not to have seen the Scholars' table so splendidly wrecked or heard the volleys of laughter resounding through the darkness.

"By gad," said Lonsdale, when the light was restored and the second year leaned over their table in triumphant exhaustion. "Did you see that bad man Carben combing the potatoes out of his hair with a fork? I say, Porcher," he said to his old scout who was waiting at the table, "do bring us some baked potatoes."

"Isn't there none left?" enquired Porcher. "Mr. Lonsdale, sir, you'd better keep a bit quiet. The Sub-Warden's looking very savage—very savage indeed."

At this moment Maurice Avery came hurrying in to dinner.

"Oh, sconce him," shouted everybody. "It's nearly five-and-twenty past."

"Couldn't help it," said Maurice very importantly. "Just been seeing the first number of the O.L.G. through the press."

"By gad," said Lonsdale. "It's a way we have in the Buffs and the Forty Two'th. Look here, have we all got to buy this rotten paper of yours? What's it going to cost?"

"A shilling," said Maurice modestly.

"A bob!" cried Lonsdale. "But, my dear old ink-slinger, I can buy the five o'clock Star for a halfpenny."

Maurice had to put up with a good deal of chaff from everybody that night.

"Let's have the programme," Sinclair suggested.

The editor was so much elated at the prospect of to-morrow's great event that he rashly produced from his pocket the contents bill, which Lonsdale seized and immediately began to read out:

"THE OXFORD LOOKING-GLASS.
No. 1.
Some Reflections. By Maurice Avery.

"What are you reflecting on, Mossy?"

"Oh, politics," said Maurice lightly, "and other things."

"My god, he'll be Prime Minister next week," said Cuffe.

"*Socrates at Balliol. By Guy Hazlewood.*

"And just about where he ought to have been," commented Lonsdale. "Oh, listen to this! whoo-oop!

"*The Failure of the Modern Illustrator.*

"But wait a minute, who do you think it's by? C. St. C. Wedderburn! Jolly old Wedders! The Failure of the Modern Illustrator. Wedders! My god, I shall cat with laughing. Wedders! A bee-luddy author!"

"Sconce Mr. Lonsdale, please," said Wedderburn turning gravely to the recorder by his chair.

"What, half-a-crown for not really saying bloody?" Lonsdale protested.

That night after hall there was much to tell Venner of the successful bombardment with potatoes, and there was some chaff for Avery and Wedderburn in regard to their forthcoming magazine. Parties of out-of-college men came in after their dinner, and at half-past eight o'clock the little office was fuller than usual, with the college gossip being carried on in a helter-skelter of unceasing babble. Just when Fitzroy the Varsity bow was enunciating the glories of Wet Bobbery and the comparative obscurities of Dry Bobbery and just when all the Dry Bobs present were bowling the contrary arguments at him from every corner at once, the door opened and a freshman, as fair and floridly handsome as a young Bacchus, walked with curious tiptoe steps into the very heart of the assembly.

Fitzroy stopped short in his discourse and thrummed impatiently with clenched fists upon his inflated chest, as gorillas do. The rest of the company eyed the entrance of the new-comer in puzzled, faintly hostile silence.

"Oh, Venner," said the intruder in loftiest self-confidence and unabashed clarity of accent. "I haven't had those cigars yet."

He hadn't had his cigars yet! Confound his impudence, and what right had he to buy cigars, and what infernal assurance had led him to suppose he might stroll into Venner's in the third raw week of his uncuffed fresherdom? Who was he? What was he? Unvoiced these questions quivered in the wrathful silence.

"The boy was told to take them up, sir," said Venner. Something in Venner's manner towards this new-comer indicated to the familiars that he might have deprecated this deliberate entrance armoured in self-satisfaction

Something there was in Venner's assumption of impersonal civility which told the familiars that Venner himself recognized and sympathized with their as yet unspoken horror of tradition's breach.

"I rather want them to-night," said the new-comer, and then he surveyed slowly his seniors and even nodded to one or two of them whom presumably he had known at school. "So if the boy hasn't taken them up," he continued, "you might send up another box. Thanks very much."

He seemed to debate for a moment with himself whether he should stay, but finally decided to go. As he reached the door, he said that, by Jove, his cigarette had gone out, and "You've got a light," he added to Lonsdale who was standing nearest to him. "Thanks very much." The door of Venner's slammed behind his imperturbableness, and a sigh of pent-up stupefaction was let loose.

"Who's your young friend, Lonny?" cried one.

"He thought Lonny was the Common Room boy," cried another.

"Venner, give the cigars to Mr. Lonsdale to take up," shouted a third.

"He's very daring for a freshman," said Venner. "Very daring. I thought he was a fourth year Scholar whom I'd never seen, when he first came in the other day. Most of the freshmen are very timid at first. They think the senior men don't like their coming in too soon. And perhaps it's better for them to order what they want when I'm by myself. I can talk to them more easily that way. With all the men wanting their coffee and whiskies, I really can't attend to orders so well just after hall."

"Who is he, Venner?" demanded half-a-dozen indignant voices.

"Mr. Appleby. The Honourable George Appleby. But you ought to know him. He's an Etonian."

Several Etonians admitted they knew him, and the

Wykehamists present seized the occasion to point out the impossibility of such manners belonging to any other school.

"He's a friend of yours then ? " said Venner to Lonsdale.

"Good lord, no, Venner ! " declared Lonsdale.

"He seemed on very familiar terms with you," Venner chuckled wickedly.

Lonsdale thought very hard for two long exasperated moments and then announced with conviction that Appleby must be ragged, severely ragged this very night.

"Now don't go making a great noise," Venner advised. "The dons don't like it, and the Dean won't be in a very good temper after that potato-throwing in hall."

"He must be ragged, Venner," persisted Lonsdale inexorably. "There need be no noise, but I'm hanged if I'm going to have my cigarette taken out of my hand and used by a damned fresher. Who's coming with me to rag this man Appleby ? "

The third year men seemed to think the correction beneath their dignity, and the duty devolved naturally upon the second year men.

"I can't come," said Avery. "The O.L.G.'s coming out to-morrow."

"Look here, Mossy, if you say another word about your rotten paper, I won't buy a copy," Lonsdale vowed.

Michael offered to go with Lonsdale and at any rate assist as a spectator. He was anxious to compare the behaviour of Smithers with the behaviour of Appleby in like circumstances. Grainger offered to come if Lonny would promise to fight sixteen rounds without gloves, and in the end, he with Lonsdale, Michael, Cuffe, Sinclair and three or four others, marched up to Appleby's rooms.

Lonsdale knocked upon the door and as he opened it assumed what he probably supposed to be an expression of ferocity, though he was told afterwards he had merely looked rather more funny than usual.

" Oh, hullo, Lonsdale," said Appleby as the party entered. " Come in and have a smoke. How's your governor ? "

Lonsdale seemed to choke for breath a moment, and then sat down in a chair so deep that for the person once plunged into its recesses an offensive movement must have been extremely difficult.

" Come in, you chaps," Appleby pursued in hospitable serenity. " I don't know any of your names, but take pews, take pews. Venner hasn't sent up the cigars I ordered."

" We know," interrupted Lonsdale severely.

" But I've some pretty decent weeds here," continued Appleby without a tremor of embarrassment. " Who's for whisky ? "

" Look here, young Apple-pip, or whatever your name is, what you've got to understand is that . . ."

Appleby again interrupted Lonsdale.

" Can we make up a bridge four ? Or are you chaps not keen on cards ? "

" What you require, young Appleby," began Lonsdale.

" You've got it right this time," said Appleby encouragingly.

" What you require is to have your room bally well turned upside down."

" Oh, really ? " said Appleby with a suave assumption of interest.

" Yes," answered Lonsdale gloomily, and somehow the little affirmative that was meant to convey so much of fearful intent was so palpably unimpressive that Lonsdale turned to his companions and appealed for their more eloquent support.

" Tell him he mustn't come into Venner's and put on all that side. It's not done. He's a fresher," gasped Lonsdale obviously helpless in that absorbing chair.

"All right," agreed Appleby cheerfully. "I'll send the order up to you next time."

Immediately afterwards, though exactly how it happened Lonsdale could never properly explain, he found himself drinking Appleby's whisky and smoking one of Appleby's cigars. This seemed to kindle the spark of his resentment to flame and he sprang up.

"We ought to debag him," he cried.

Appleby was thereupon debagged; but as he made no resistance to the divestiture and as he continued to walk about trouserless and dispense hospitality without any apparent loss of dignity, the debagging had to be written down a failure. Finally he folded up his trousers and put on a dressing-gown of purple velvet, and when they left him, he was watching them descend his staircase and actually was calling after them to remind Venner about the cigars, if the office were still open.

"Hopeless," sighed Lonsdale. "The man's a hopeless ass."

"I think he had the laugh though," said Michael.

Chapter VIII : *The Oxford Looking-Glass*

ROLL-CALLS were not kept at St. Mary's with that scrupulousness of outward exterior which, in conjunction with early rising, such a discipline may have been designed primarily to secure. On the morning after the attempted adjustment of Appleby's behaviour, a raw and vaporous November morning, Michael at one minute to eight o'clock ran collarless, unbrushed, unshaven, towards the steps leading up to hall at whose head stood the Dean beside the clerkly recorder of these sorry matutinal appearances. Michael waited long enough to see his name fairly entered in the book, yawned resentfully at the Dean and started back on the taciturn journey that must culminate in the completion of his toilet. Crossing the gravel space between Cloisters and Cuther's worldly quad, he met Maurice Avery dressed finally for the day at one minute past eight o'clock. Such a phenomenon provoked him into speech.

"What on earth . . . Are you going to London ?" he gasped.

"Rather not. I'm going out to buy a copy of the O.L.G."

Michael shook his head, sighed compassionately and passed on. Twenty minutes later in Common Room he was contemplating distastefully the kedgeree which with a more hopeful appetite he had ordered on the evening before, when Maurice planked down beside his place the first number of The Oxford Looking-Glass.

" There's a misprint on page thirty-seven, line six. It ought to be 'yet' not 'but.' Otherwise I think it's a success. Do you mind reading my slashing attack on the policy of the Oxford theatre ? Or perhaps you'd better begin at the beginning and go right through the whole paper and give me your absolutely frank opinion of it as a whole. Just tell me candidly if you think my Reflections are too individual. I want the effect to be more——"

" Maurice," Michael interrupted, " do you like kedgeree ? "

" Yes, very much," Maurice answered absently. Then he plunged on again. " Also don't forget to tell me if you think that Guy's skit is too clever. And if you find any misprints I haven't noticed, mark them down. We can't alter them now of course, but I'll speak to the compositor myself. You like the colour ? I wonder whether it wouldn't have been better to have had dark blue after all. Still——"

" Well, if you like kedgeree," Michael interrupted again, " do you like it as much in the morning as you thought you were going to like it the night before ? "

" Oh, how the dickens do I know ? " exclaimed Maurice fretfully.

" Well, will you just eat my breakfast and let me know if you think I ought to have ordered eggs and bacon last night ? "

" Aren't you keen on the success of this paper ? " Maurice demanded.

" I'll tell you later on," Michael offered. " We'll lunch together quietly in my rooms, and the little mulled claret we shall drink to keep out this filthy fog will also enormously conduce to the amiableness of my judgment."

" And you won't come out with me and Nigel Stewart to watch people buying copies on their way to leckers ? " Maurice suggested in a tone of disappointment. Lonsdale arrived for breakfast at this moment, just in time to prevent

Michael's heart from being softened. The new-comer was
at once invited to remove the editor.

"Have you bought your copy of the O.L.G. yet,
Lonny ? " Maurice demanded unabashed.

"Look here, Moss Avery," said Lonsdale seriously,
" if you promise to spend the bob you screw out of me on
buying yourself some soothing syrup, I'll . . ."

But the editor rejected the frivolous attentions of his
audience, and left the J.C.R. Michael, not thinking it
very prudent to remind Lonsdale of last night's encounter
with Appleby, examined the copy of The Oxford Looking-
Glass that lay beside his plate.

It was a curious compound of priggishness and brilliance
and perspicacity and wit, this olive-green bantling so
meticulously hatched, and as Michael turned the pages and
roved idly here and there among the articles that by per-
severing exhortation had been driven into the fold by the
editor, he was bound to admit the verisimilitude of the image
of Oxford presented. Maurice might certainly be congratulated on the variety of the opinions set on record,
but whether he or that Academic Muse whose biographies
and sculptured portraits nowhere exist should be praised
for the impression of corporate unanimity that without
question was ultimately conveyed to the reader, Michael
was not sure. It was a promising fancy, this of the Academic
Muse; and Michael played with the idea of elaborating
his conception in an article for this very Looking-Glass
which she invisibly supported. The Oxford Looking-Glass
might serve her like the ægis of Pallas Athene, an ægis
that would freeze to academic stone the self-confident
chimeras of the twentieth century. Michael began to feel
that his classical analogies were enmeshing the original idea,
involving it already in complexities too manifold for him
to unravel. His ideas always fled like waking dreams at
the touch of synthesis. Perhaps Pallas Athene was herself

the Academic Muse. Well enough might the owl and the olive serve as symbols of Oxford. The owl could stand for all the grotesque pedantry, all the dismal hootings of age, all the slow deliberate sweep of the don's mind, the seclusions, the blinkings in the daylight and the unerring destruction of intellectual vermin; while the olive would speak of age and the grace and greyness of age, of age each year made young again by its harvest of youth, of sobriety sun-kindled to a radiancy of silver joy, of wisdom, peace and shelter, and Attic glories.

Michael became so nearly stifled by the net of his fancies that he almost rose from the table then and there, ambitious to take pen in hand and test the power of its sharpness to cut him free. He clearly saw the grey-eyed goddess as the personification of the spirit of the university: but suddenly all the impulse faded out in self-depreciation. Guy Hazlewood would solve the problem with his pranked-out allusiveness, would trace more featly the attributes of the Academic Muse and establish more convincingly her descent from Apollo or her identity with Athene. At least, however, he could offer the idea and if Guy made anything of it, the second number of The Oxford Looking-Glass would hold more of Michael Fane than the ten pounds he had laid on the table of its exchequer. Inspired by the zest of his own fancy, he read on deliberately.

Some Reflections. By Maurice Avery.

The editor had really succeeded in reflecting accurately the passing glance of Oxford, although perhaps the tortuous gilt of the frame with which he had tried to impart style to his mirror was more personal to Maurice Avery than general to the university. Moreover his glass would certainly never have stood a steady and protracted gaze. Still with all their faults these paragraphic reflections did show forth admirably the wit and unmatured cynicism of the various

2 U

Junior Common Rooms; did signally flash with all the illusion of an important message, did suggest a potentiality for durable criticism.

Socrates at Balliol. By Guy Hazlewood.

There was enough of Guy in his article to endear it to Michael, and there was so much of Oxford in Guy that whatever he wrote spontaneously would always enrich the magazine with that adventurous gaiety and childlike intolerance of Athene's favourites.

The Failure of the Modern Illustrator.
By C. St. C. Wedderburn.

Here was Wedders writing with more distinction than Michael would have expected, but not with all the sartorial distinction of his attire.

" Let us turn now to the illustrators of the sixties and seventies, and we shall see . . ." Wedderburn in the plural scarcely managed to convey himself into print. The neat bulk began to sprawl : the solidity became pompous : the profundity of his spoken voice was lacking to sustain so much sententiousness.

Quo Vadis? By Nigel Stewart.

Nigel's plea for the inspiration of modernity to make more vital the decorative Anglicanism whose cause he had pledged his youth to advance, was with all its predetermined logic and emphasis of rhetorical expression an appealing document. Michael did not think it would greatly serve the purpose for which it had been written, but its presence in The Oxford Looking-Glass was a guarantee that the youngest magazine was not going to ignore the force that perhaps more than any other had endowed Oxford with something that Cambridge for all ·her poets lacked. Michael himself had since he came up let the practice of religion slide, but his first fervours had not burnt themselves out so utterly as to make him despise the warmth they once had kindled. His inclination in any argument was always towards the Catholic point of view, and though he himself allowed to himself the license of agnostic speech and agnostic thought, he was always a little impatient of a sceptical nonage and very contemptuous indeed of an unbelief which had never been tried by the fire of faith. He did not think Stewart's challenge with its plaintive undercurrent of well-bred pessimism would be effective save for the personality of the writer, who revealed his formal grace notwithstanding the trumpeting of his young epigrams and the tassels of his too conspicuous style. With all the irritation of its verbal cleverness, he rejoiced to read *Quo Vadis?* and he felt in reading it that Oxford would still have silver plate to melt for a lost cause.

Under the stimulus of Nigel Stewart's article, Michael managed to finish his breakfast with an appetite. As he rose to leave the Common Room, Lonsdale emerged from the zareba of illustrated papers with which he had fortified his place at table.

"Have you been reading that thing of Mossy's ? " he asked incredulously.

Michael nodded.

"Isn't it most awful rot ? "

"Some of it," Michael assured him.

"I suppose it would be only sporting to buy a copy," sighed Lonsdale. "I suppose I ought to buzz round and buck the college up into supporting it. By Jove, I'll write and tell the governor to buy a copy. I want him to raise my allowance this year, and he'll think I'm beginning to take an interest in what he calls ' affairs.' "

Michael turned into Venner's before going back to his own rooms.

" Hullo, is that the paper ? " asked Venner. " Dear me, this looks very learned. You should tell him to put some more about sport into it—our fellows are all so dreadfully wild about sport. They'd be sure to buy it then. Going to work this morning ? That's right. I'm always advising the men to work in the morning. But bless you, they don't pay any attention to me. They only laugh and say, ' what's old Venner know about it ? ' "

Michael sitting snugly in the morning quiet of his room, leaned over to poke the fire into a blaze, eyed with satisfaction November's sodden mists against his window and settled himself back in the deep chair to The Oxford Looking-Glass.

> *Oxford Liberalism. By Vernon Townsend.*
> *A Restatement of Tory Ideals. By William Mowbray.*

These two articles Michael decided to take on trust. From their perusal he would only work himself up into a condition of irritated neutrality. Indeed he felt inclined to take all the rest of the magazine on trust. The tranquility of his own room was too seductive. Dreaming became a duty here. It was so delightful to count from where he sat the books on the shelves and to arrive each time at a different estimate of their number. It was so restful to stare up at Monna Lisa and traverse without fatigue that labyrinth of rocks and streams. His desk not yet deranged by work or correspondence possessed a monumental stability of neatness that was most soothing to contemplate. It had the restfulness of a well-composed landscape where every contour took the eye easily onward and where every tree grew just where it was needed for a moment's halt. The olive-green magazine dropped unregarded on to the floor, and there was no other book within reach. The dancing fire danced on. Far away sounded the cries of daily life. The chimes in St. Mary's tower struck without proclaiming any suggestion of time. How long these roll-call mornings were and how rapidly dream on dream piled its drowsy outline. Was there not somewhere at the other end of Oxford a lecture at eleven o'clock ? This raw morning was not suitable for lectures out of college. Was not Maurice coming to lunch ? How deliciously far off was the time for ordering lunch. He really must get out of the habit of sitting in this deep wicker-chair, until evening licensed such repose.

Some people had foolishly attended a ten o'clock lecture at St. John's. What a ludicrous idea. They had ridden miserably through the cold on their bicycles and with numb fingers were now trying to record scraps of generalization in a notebook that would inevitably be lost long before the Schools. At the same time it was rather lazy to lie back like this so early in the morning. Why was it so difficult to abandon the Sirenian creakings of this chair ? He wanted another match for his second pipe, but even the need for that was not violent enough to break the luxurious catalepsy of his present condition.

Then suddenly Maurice Avery and Nigel Stewart burst into the room, and Michael by a supreme effort plunged upwards on to his legs to receive them.

"My hat, what a frowst," exclaimed Maurice rushing to the window and letting in the mist and the noise of the High.

"We're very hearty this morning," murmured Stewart. "I heard Mass at Barney's for the success of the O.L.G."

"Nigel and I have walked down the High, round the Corn and back along the Broad and the Turl," announced Maurice. "And how many copies do you think we saw bought by people we didn't know ? "

"None," guessed Michael maliciously.

"Don't be an ass. Fifteen. Well, I've calculated that at least four times as many were being sold, while we were making our round. That's sixty, and it's not half-past ten yet. We ought to do another three hundred easily before lunch. In fact roughly I calculate we shall do five hundred and twenty before to-night. Not bad. After two thousand we shall be making money."

"Maurice bought twenty-two copies himself," said Stewart laughing, and lest he should seem to be laughing at Maurice thrust an affectionate arm through his to re-assure him.

"Well, I wanted to encourage the boys who were selling them," Maurice explained.

"They'll probably emigrate with the money they've made out of you," predicted Michael. "And what on earth are you going to do with twenty-two copies? I find this one copy of mine extraordinarily in the way."

"Oh, I shall send them to well-known literary people in town. In fact I'm going to write round and get the best-known old Oxford men to give us contributions from time to time, without payment of course. I expect they'll be rather pleased at being asked."

"Don't you think it may turn their heads?" Michael anxiously suggested. "It would be dreadful to read of the sudden death of Quiller-Couch from apoplectic pride or to hear that Hilaire Belloc or Max Beerbohm had burst with exultation in his bath."

"It's a pity you can't be funny in print," said Maurice severely. "You'd really be some use on the paper then."

"But what we've really come round to say," interposed Stewart, "is that there's an O.L.G. dinner to-night at the Grid; and then afterwards we're all going across to my digs opposite."

"And what about lunch with me?"

Both Maurice and Nigel excused themselves. Maurice

intended to spend all day at the Union. Nigel had booked himself to play fug-socker with three hearty Trindogs of Trinity.

. " But when did you join the Union ? " Michael asked the editor.

" I thought it was policy," he explained. " After all, though we laugh at it here, most of the Varsity does belong. Besides, Townsend and Bill Mowbray were both keen. You see they think the O.L.G. is going to have an influence in Varsity politics. And after all I am editor."

" You certainly are," Michael agreed. " Nothing quite so editorial was ever conceived by the overwrought brain of a disappointed female contributor."

Michael always enjoyed dining at the Grid. Of all the Oxford clubs it seemed to him to display the most completely normal undergraduate existence. Vincent's, notwithstanding its acknowledged chieftaincy, depended ultimately too much on a mechanically apostolic succession. It was an institution to be admired without affection. It had every justification for calling itself The Club without any qualifying prefix, but it produced a type too highly specialized, and was too definitely Dark Blue and Leander Pink. — In a way too, it belonged as much to Cambridge, and although violently patriotic had merged its individuality in brawn. By its substitution of co-option for election, its Olympic might was now scarcely much more than the self-deification of Roman Emperors. Vincent's was the last stronghold of muscular supremacy. Yet it was dreadfully improbable, as Michael admitted to himself, that he would have declined the offer of membership.

The O.U.D.S. was at the opposite pole from Vincent's, and if it did not offend by its reactionary encouragement of a supreme but discredited spirit, it offended even more by fostering a premature worldliness. For an Oxford club to take in The Stage and The Era was merely an exotic heresy. On the walls of its very ugly room the pictures of actors that in Garrick Street would have possessed a romantic dignity produced an effect of strain, a proclamation of mountebank-worship that differed only in degree from the photographs of actresses on the mantelpiece of a second-rate room in a second-rate college. The frequenters of the O.U.D.S. were always very definitely Oxford under-graduates, but they lacked the serenity of Oxford, and seemed already to have planted a foot in London. The big modern room over the big cheap shop was a restless place, and its pretentiousness and modernity were tinged with Thespian-ism. Scarcely ever did the Academic Muse enter the O.U.D.S., Michael thought. She must greatly dislike Thespianism with all that it connoted of mildewed statuary in an English garden. Yet it would be possible to trans-mute the O.U.D.S., he dreamed. It had the advantage of a limited membership. It might easily become a grove where Apollo and Athene could converse without quarrelling. Therefore he could continue to frequent its halls.

The Bullingdon was always delightful; the grey bowlers and the white trousers striped with vivid blue displayed its members, in their costume at least, as unchanging types, but the archaism made it a club too conservative to register much more than an effect of peculiarity. The Bullingdon had too much money, and not enough unhampered human-ity to achieve the universal. The Union on the other hand was too indiscriminate. Personality was here submerged in organization. Manchester or Birmingham could have produced a result very similar.

The Grid, perhaps for the very fact that it was primarily a dining-club, was the abode of discrete good-fellowship. Its membership was very strictly limited, and might seem to have been confined to the seven or eight colleges that considered themselves the best colleges, but any man who deserved to be a member could in the end be sure of his election. The atmosphere was neither political nor sporting nor literary, nor financial, but it was very peculiarly and very intimately the elusive atmosphere of Oxford herself. The old rooms looking out on the converging High had recently been redecorated in a very crude shade of blue. Members were grumbling at the taste of the executive, but Michael thought the unabashed ugliness was in keeping with its character. It was as if unwillingly the club released its hold upon the externals of Victorianism. Such premises could afford to be anachronistic, since the frequenters were always so finely sensitive to fashion's lightest breath. Eccentricity was not tolerated at the Grid except in the case of the half-dozen chartered personalities who were necessary to set off the correctness of the majority. The elective committee probably never made a mistake, and when somebody like Nigel Stewart was admitted, it was scrupulously ascertained beforehand that his presence would evoke affectionate amusement rather than the chill surprize with which the Grid would have greeted the entrance of someone who, however superior to the dead level of undergraduate life, lacked yet the indefinable justification for his humours.

Michael on the evening of the Looking-Glass dinner went up the narrow stairs of the club in an aroma of pleasant anticipation, which was not even momentarily dispersed by the sudden occurrence of the fact that he had forgotten to take his name off hall, and must therefore pay two shillings and fourpence to the college for a dinner he would not eat. In the Strangers' Room were waiting the typical guests of the typical members. Here and there nods were exchanged, but the general atmosphere was one of serious expectancy. In the distance the rattle of crockery told of dinners already in progress. Vernon Townsend came in soon after Michael, and as Townsend was a member,

Michael lost that trifling malaise of waiting in a club's guest-room which the undergraduate might conceal more admirably than any other class of man, but nevertheless felt acutely.

"Not here yet, I suppose," said Townsend.

It was unnecessary to mention a name. Nigel Stewart's habits were proverbial.

"Read my article?" asked Townsend.

"Splendid," Michael murmured.

"It's going to get me the Librarianship of the Union," Townsend earnestly assured Michael.

Michael was about to congratulate the sanguine author without disclosing his ignorance of the article's inside, when Bill Mowbray rushed breathlessly into the room. Everybody observed his dramatic entrance whereupon he turned round and rushed out again, pausing only for one moment to exclaim in the doorway:

"Good god, that fool will never remember!"

"See that?" asked Townsend darkly, as the Tory Democrat vanished.

Michael admitted that he undoubtedly had.

"Bill Mowbray has become a poseur," Townsend declared. "Or else he knows his ridiculous article on Toryism was too badly stashed by mine," he added.

"We shan't see him again to-night," Michael prophesied.

Townsend shrugged his shoulders.

"We shall, if he can make another effective entrance," he said a little bitterly.

Maurice Avery and Wedderburn arrived together. The combination of having just been elected to the Grid and the birth of the new paper had given Maurice such an effervescence of good spirits as even he seldom boasted. Wedderburn in contrast seemed graver, supplying in company with Maurice a solidity to the pair of them that was

undeniably beneficial to their joint impression.   They were
followed almost immediately by Guy Hazlewood who with
his long legs came sloping in as self-possessed as he always
was.   Perhaps his left eyelid drooped a little lower than it
was accustomed, and perhaps the sidelong smile that gave
him a superficial resemblance to Michael was drawn down
to a sharper point of mockery, but whatever stored-up
flashes of mood and fancy Guy had to deliver, he always
drawled them out in the same half-tired voice emphasized
by the same careless indolence of gesture.   And so this
evening he was the same Guy Hazlewood, sure of being
with his clear-cut pallor and effortless distinction of bearing, the personality that everyone would first observe in
whatever company he found himself.

"Nigel not here of course," he drawled.   "Let's have a
sweep on what he's been doing.   Five bob all round.   I say
he's just discovered Milton to be a great poet and is now
reading Lycidas to a spellbound group of the very heartiest
Trindogs in Trinity."

. "I think he saw The Perfect Flapper," said Maurice,
"and has been trying ever since to find out whether
she were a don's daughter or a theatrical bird of
passage."

"I think he's forgotten all about it," pronounced Wedderburn very deeply indeed.

"I hope he saw that ass Bill Mowbray tearing off in the
opposite direction and went to fetch him back," said
Townsend.

"I think he's saying Vespers for the week before last,"
Michael proposed as his solution.

Stewart himself came in at that moment, and in answer
to an united demand to know the reason of his lateness
embraced in that gentle and confiding air of his all the company, included them all as it were in an intimate aside, and
with the voice and demeanour of a strayed archangel

explained that the fearful velocity of a pill was responsible for his unpunctuality.

"But you're quite all right now, Nigel ? " enquired Guy. "You could almost send a testimonial ? "

"Oh, rather," murmured Nigel with tender assurance lighting up his great innocent eyes. " I expect, you know, dinner's ready." Then he plunged his arm through Guy's, and led the way towards the private dining-room he had actually not forgotten to command.

Dinner, owing to Avery's determined steering of the conversation, was eaten to the accompaniment of un- diluted shop. Never for a moment was any topic allowed to oust The Oxford Looking-Glass from discussion. Even Guy was powerless against the editor intoxicated by am- bition's fulfilment. Maurice sat in triumphant headship with only Mowbray's vacant place to qualify very slightly the completeness of his satisfaction. He hoped they all liked his scheme of inviting well-known, even celebrated old Oxford men to contribute from time to time. He flattered himself they would esteem the honour vouch- safed to them. He disclaimed the wish to monopolize the paper's criticism and nobly invited Townsend to put in their places a series of contemporary dramatists. He con- gratulated Guy upon his satiric article and assured him of his great gifts. He reproached Michael for having written nothing, and vowed that many of the books for which he had already sent a printed demand to their publishers must in the December issue be reviewed by Michael. He ar- ranged with Nigel Stewart and Wedderburn at least a dozen prospective campaigns to harry advertizers into unwilling publicity.

At nine o'clock, the staff of The Oxford Looking-Glass, reflecting now a very roseate world, marched across the High to wind up the evening in Stewart's digs. On the threshold the host paused in sudden dismay.

" Good lord, I quite forgot. There's a meeting of the De Rebus Ecclesiasticis in my digs to-night. They'll all be there, what shall I do ? "

" You can't possibly go," declared everybody.

" Mrs. Arbour," Nigel called out, hurriedly dipping into the landlady's quarters. " Mrs. Arbour."

Mrs. Arbour assured him comfortably of her existence as she emerged to confer with him in the passage.

" There may be one or two men waiting in my rooms. Will you put out syphons and whisky and explain that I shan't be coming."

" Any reason to give, sir ? " asked Mrs. Arbour.

The recalcitrant shook his seraphic head.

" No, sir," said Mrs. Arbour cheerfully, " quite so. Just say you're not coming ? Yes, sir. Oh, they'll make themselves at home without you, I'll be bound. It's not likely to be a very noisy party, is it, sir ? "

" Oh, no. It's the De Rebus Ecclesiasticis, Mrs. Arbour."

" I see, sir. Foreigners. I'll look after them."

Nigel having disposed of the pious debaters, joined his friends again, and it was decided to adjourn to Guy's digs in Holywell. Arm-in-arm the six journalists marched down the misted High. Arm-in-arm they turned into Catherine Street and arm-in-arm they walked into the Proctor outside the Ratcliffe Camera. To him they admitted their membership of the university. To him they proffered very politely their names and the names of their colleges, and with the same politeness agreed to visit him next morning. The Proctor raised his cap and with his escort faded into the fog. Arm-in-arm the six journalists continued their progress into Holywell. Guy had digs in an old house whose gabled front leaned outwards, whose oriel windows were supported by oaken beams worm-eaten and grotesquely carved. Within, a wide balustraded staircase went billowing upwards unevenly. Guy's room that he

shared with two intellectual athletes from his own college
was very large. It was panelled all round up to the ceiling,
and it contained at least a dozen very comfortable armchairs. He had imposed upon his partners his own tastes
and with that privilege had cut off electric light and gas,
so that, lit only by two Pompeian lamps, the room was very
shadowy when they all came in.

" Comeragh and Anstruther are working downstairs, I
expect," Guy explained as one by one, while his guests
waited in the dim light, he made a great illumination with
wax candles. Then he poked up the fire and set glasses
ready for anyone's need. Great armchairs were pulled
round in a semicircle : pipes were lit : the stillness and
mystery of the Oxford night crept along the ancient street,
a stillness which at regular intervals was broken by multitudinous chimes, or faintly now and then by passing footfalls.
Unexcited by argument the talk rippled in murmurous
contentment.

Michael was in no mood himself for talking, and he sat
back listening now and then, but mostly dreaming. He
thought of the conversation in that long riverside room in
Paris with its extravagance and pretentiousness. Here in
this time-haunted Holywell Street was neither. To be sure
Christianity and the soul's immortality and the future of
England and contemporary art were running the gauntlet
of youth's examination, but the Academic Muse had shown
the company her ægis, had turned everything to unpassionate stone and softened all presumption with her guarded
glances. It was extraordinary how under her guidance
every subject was stripped of obtrusive reality, how even
women, discussed never so grossly, remained untarnished ;
since they ceased to be real women, but mere abstractions
wanton or chaste in accordance with the demands of wit.
The ribaldry was Aristophanic or Rabelaisian with as little
power to offend, so much was it consecrated and refined

by immemorial usages. Michael wished that all the world could be touched by the magical freedom and equally magical restraint of the Academic Muse, and as he sat here in this ancient room, he hoped almost violently that never again would he be compelled to smirch the present clarity and steadiness of his vision.

Chapter IX : *The Lesson of Spain*

PERHAPS Michael enjoyed more than anything else during his collection of books the accumulation of as many various editions of Don Quixote as possible. He had brought up from London the fat volume illustrated by Doré over which he had fallen asleep long ago and of which owing to Nurse's disapproval he had in consequence been deprived. Half the pages still showed where they had been bent under the weight of his small body : this honourable scar and the familiar musty smell and the book's unquestionable if slightly vulgar dignity prevented Michael from banishing it from the shelf that now held so many better editions. However much the zest in Doré's illustrations had died away in the flavour of <u>Skelton</u>'s English, Michael could not abandon the big volume with what it held of childhood's first intellectual adventure. The shelf of Don Quixotes became in all his room one of the most cherished objects of contemplation. There was something in the 'Q' and the 'X' repeated on the back of volume after volume that positively gave Michael an impression in literal design of the Knight's fantastic personality. The very soul of Spain seemed to be symbolized by those sere quartos of the seventeenth century, nor was it imperceptible even that cockney rendering of <u>Smollett</u> bound in marbled boards. Staring at the row of Don Quixotes on a dull December afternoon, Michael felt overwhelmingly a desire to go to Spain himself, to drink at the source of Cervantes' mighty stream of imagination which with every year's new reading seemed to him to hold more and more

certainly all that was most vital to life's appreciation. He
no longer failed to see the humour of Don Quixote, but
even now tears came more easily than laughter, and he
regretted as poignantly as the Knight himself those times
of chivalry which with all the extravagance of their decay
were yet in essence superior to the mode that ousted them
into ignominy. Something akin to Don Quixote's impulsive
dismay Michael experienced in his own view of the twentieth
century. He felt he needed a constructive ideal of conduct
to sustain him through the long pilgrimage that must
ensue after these hushed Oxford dreams.

Term was nearly over. Michael had heard from Stella
that she was going to spend two or three months in Germany.
Her Brahms recitals, she wrote, had not been so successful
as she ought to have made them. In London she was wasting
time. Mother was continually wanting her to come to the
theatre. It seemed almost as if mother were trying to throw
her in the way of marrying Prescott. He had certainly been
very good, but she must retreat into Germany, and there
again work hard. Would not Michael come too ? Why was
he so absurdly prejudiced against Germany ? It was the
only country in which to spend Christmas.

The more Stella praised Germany, the more Michael felt
the need of going to a country as utterly different from it
as possible. He did not want to spend the vacation in
London. He did not want his mother to talk vaguely to him
of the advantage for Stella in marrying Prescott. The idea
was preposterous. He would be angry with his mother, and
he would blurt out to Prescott his dislike of such a notion.
He would thereby wound a man whom he admired and
display himself in the light of the objectionably fraternal
youth. In the dreary fog and wet murk of December the
sun-dried volumes of Cervantes spoke to him of Spain.

Maurice Avery came up to his room, fatigued with fame
and disappointed that Castleton with whom he had arranged

2 X

to go to Rome had felt at the last moment he must take his mother to Bath. To him Michael proposed Spain.

" But why not Rome ? " Maurice argued. " As I originally settled."

" Not with me," Michael pointed out. " I don't want to go to Rome now. I always feel luxuriously that there will occur the moment in my life when I shall say, ' I am ready to go to Rome. I must go to Rome.' It's a fancy of mine and nothing will induce me to spoil it by going to Rome at the wrong moment."

Maurice grumbled at him, told him he was affected, unreasonable, and even hinted Michael ought to come to Rome simply for the fact that he himself had been baulked of his intention by the absurdly filial Castleton.

" I do think mothers ought not to interfere," Maurice protested. " My mother never interferes. Even my sisters are allowed to have their own way. Why can't Mrs. Castleton go to Bath by herself ? I'm sure Castleton overdoes this ' duty ' pose. And now you won't come to Rome. Well, will you come to Florence ? "

" Yes, and be worried by you to move on to Rome the very minute we arrive there," said Michael. " No thanks. If you don't want to come to Spain I'll try to get someone else. Anyway, I don't mind going by myself."

" But what shall we do in Spain ? " asked Maurice fretfully.

Michael began to laugh.

" We can dance the fandango," he pointed out. " Or if the fandango is too hard, there always remains the bolero."

" If we went to Rome," Maurice was persisting, but Michael cut him short.

" It's absolutely useless, Mossy. I am not going to Rome."

" Then I suppose I shall have to go to Spain," said Maurice in a much injured tone.

So in the end it was settled chiefly, Michael always maintained, because Maurice found out it was advisable to travel with a passport. As not by the greatest exaggeration of insecurity could a passport be deemed necessary for Rome, Maurice decided it was an overrated city and became at once fervidly Spanish, even to the extent of saying ' gracias ' whenever the cruet was passed to him in hall. Wedderburn at the last moment thought he would like to join the expedition : so Maurice with the passport in his breast-pocket preferred to call it.

There were two or three days of packing in London, while Maurice stayed at 173 Cheyne Walk and was a great success with Mrs. Fane. The Rugby match against Cambridge was visited in a steady downpour. Wedderburn fetched his luggage, and the last dinner was eaten together at Cheyne Walk. Mrs. Fane was tenderly, if rather vaguely, solicitous for their safety.

"Dearest Michael," she said, " do be careful not to be gored by a bull. I've never been to Spain. One seems to know nothing about it. Mr. Avery, do have some more turkey. I hope you don't dreadfully dislike garlic. Such a pungent vegetable. Michael darling, why are you laughing ? Isn't it a vegetable ? Mr. Wedderburn, do have some more turkey. A friend of mine, Mrs. Carruthers, who is a great believer in Mental Science . . . Michael always laughs at me when I try to explain. . . . Hark, there is the cab, really. I hope it won't be raining in Spain. ' Rain, rain, go to Spain.' So ominous, isn't it ? Good-bye, dearest boy, and write to me at Mrs. Carruthers, High Towers, Godalming."

"I say, I know Mrs. Carruthers. She lives near us," Maurice exclaimed.

"Come on," his friends insisted. "You haven't time now to explain the complications of Surrey society."

"I'm so glad," said Mrs. Fane. "Because you'll be able to see that Michael remembers the address."

" I never forget addresses, mother," protested Michael.

" No, I know. I always think everyone is like me. Merry Christmas, and do send a post card to Stella. She was so hurt you wouldn't go to Germany."

In the drench and soak of December weather they drove off in the four-wheeler. On such a night it seemed more than ever romantic to be setting out to Spain, and all the way to Victoria Maurice tried to decide by the occasional gleam of a blurred lamp-light how many pesetas one received for an English sovereign.

The crossing to Dieppe was rough, but all memories of the discomfort were wiped out when next day they saw the Sud Express looking very long and swift and torpedo-like between the high platforms of that white drawing-room, the Gare d'Orleans. Down they went all day through France with rain speckling the windows of their compartment, past the naked poplar trees and rolling fallows until dusk fell sadly on the flooded agriculture. Dawn broke as they were leaving behind them the illimitable Landes. Westward the Atlantic clouds swept in from the Bay of Biscay, parting momentarily to reveal rifts of milky turquoise sky. Wider and wider grew the rifts, and when the train passed close to the green cliffs of St. Jean de Luz, the air was soft and fragrant : the sea was blue. At Irun they were in Spain, and Michael, as he walked up and down the platform waiting for déjeuner, watched, with a thrill of conviction that this was indeed a frontier, the red and blue toy soldiers and the black and green toy soldiers dotted about the toy landscape.

Maurice was rather annoyed that nobody demanded their passports and that every official should seem so much more anxious to examine their railway tickets, but when they reached Madrid and found that no bull-fights would be held before the spring, he began to mutter of Rome and was inclined to obliterate the Spaniards from the category of civilization, so earnestly had he applied himself by the jiggling light of the train to the mastery of all the grades from matador to banderillo.

In Seville, however, Maurice admitted he could not imagine a city more perfectly adapted to express all that he desired from life. Seville with her guitars and lemon-trees, her castanets and oranges and fans, her fountains and carnations and flashing Andalusians, was for him the city to which one day he would return and dream. Here one day he could come when seriously he began to write or paint or take up whatever destiny in art was in store for him. Here he would forget whatever blow life might hold in the future. He would send everybody he knew to Seville, notwithstanding Michael's objection that such generosity would recoil upon himself in his desire to possess somewhere on earth the opportunity of oblivion. Maurice and Wedderburn both bought Spanish cloaks and hats and went with easels to sit beside the Guadalquiver that sun-stained to the hue of its tawny banks was so contemptuous of their gentlemanly water-colours, as contemptuous as those cigarette-girls that came chattering from the tobacco-factory every noon. Michael preferred to wander over the roofs of the cathedral, until drowsed by the scent of warm stone he would sit for an hour merely conscious that the city lay below and that the sky was blue above.

After Seville they travelled to Granada, to Cadiz and Cordova and other famous cities; and in the train they went slowly through La Mancha where any windmill might indeed be mistaken for Pentapolin of the Naked Arm, and where at the stations the water-carriers even in January cried 'agua, agua,' so that already the railway-carriages seemed parched by the fierce summer sun. They travelled to Salamanca and Toledo, and last of all they went to Burgos where Maurice and Wedderburn strove in vain to draw corner after corner of the cathedral, in the dust and

shadows of whose more remote chantries Michael heard
many Masses. A realization of the power of faith was
stirred in him by these Masses that every day of every year
were said without the recognition of humanity. These
mumblings of ancient priests, these sanctus-bells that
rattled like shaken ribs, these interminable and ceremonious
shufflings were the outward expression of the force that
sustained this fabric of Burgos and had raised in Seville a
cathedral that seemed to crush like a stupendous monster
the houses scattered about in its path, insignificant as a heap
of white shells. Half of these old priests, thought Michael,
were probably puppets who did not understand even their
own cracked Latinity, yet their ministrations were almost
frightening in their efficacy: they were indeed the very
stones of Burgos made vocal.

Listening to these Masses, Michael began to regret he
had allowed all his interest in religion to peter out in the
irritation of compulsory chapel-keeping at Oxford. Here
in Burgos, he felt less the elevating power of faith than the
unrelenting and disdainful inevitableness of its endurance.
At Bournemouth, when he experienced the first thrill of
conversion, he had been exultingly aware of a personal
friendliness between himself and God. Here in Burgos he
was absorbed into the divine purpose neither against his
will nor his desire, since he was positively aware of the
impotency of his individuality to determine anything in the
presence of omnipotence. He told himself this sense of
inclusion was a sign of the outpouring once more of the
grace of God, but he wished with a half-whimsical amusement that the sensation were rather less like that of being
contemptuously swept by a broom into the main dust-heap.
Yet as on the last morning of his stay in Burgos Michael
came away from Mass, he came away curiously fortified
by his observation of the mouldy confessionals worn
down by the knees of so many penitents. That much

power of impression at least had the individual on this cathedral.

When Michael lay awake in the train going northwards he remembered very vividly the sense of subordination which in retrospect suddenly seemed to him to reveal the essential majesty of Spain. The train stopped at some French station. Their carriage was already full enough, but a bilious and fussy Frenchman insisted there was still room, and on top of him broke in a loud-voiced and assertive Englishman with a meek wife. It was intolerable. Michael, Wedderburn and Maurice displayed their most polite obstructiveness, but in the end each of them found himself upright, stiff-backed and exasperated. Michael thought regretfully of Spain, and remembered those peasants who shared their crusts, those peasants with rank skins of wine and flopping turkeys, those peasants who wrought so inimitably their cigarettes and would sit on the floor of the carriage rather than disarrange the comfort of the three English travellers. Michael went off into an uneasy sleep trying to arrange synthetically his deductions, trying to put Don Quixote and Burgos Cathedral and the grace of God and subordination and feudalism and himself into a working theory of life. And just when the theory really seemed to be shaping itself, he was woken up by the Englishman prodding his wife.

" What is it, dear ? " she murmured.

" Did you pack those collars that were in the other chest of drawers ? "

" I think so, dear."

" I wish you'd know something for a change," the husband grumbled.

The Frenchman ground his teeth in swollen sleep, exhaling himself upon the stale air of the compartment. Maurice was turning over the pages of a comic paper. Wedderburn snored. It was difficult to achieve subordination of one's personality in the presence of other personalities so insistently irritating.

Stella had not come back from Germany when Michael reached home, which was a disappointment as he had looked forward to planning with her a journey back to Spain as soon as possible. His mother during this vacation had lapsed from Mental Science into an association to prevent premature burial.

"My dearest boy, you have no idea of the numbers of people buried alive every year," she said. "I have been talking to Dick Prescott about it. I cannot understand his indifference. I intend to devote all my time to it. We are going to organize a large bazaar next season. Banging their foreheads against the coffins! It's dreadful to think of. Do be careful, Michael. I have written a long letter to Stella explaining all the precautions she ought to take. Who knows what may happen in Germany? Such an impulsive nation. At least the Kaiser is. Don't laugh, my dear boy, it's so much more serious than you think. Would you like to come with me to Mrs. Carruthers' and hear some of the statistics? Gruesome, but most instructive. At three o'clock. You needn't wait for tea, if you're busy. The lecturer is an Eurasian. Where *is* Eurasia by the by?"

Michael kissed his mother with affectionate amusement.

"Will you wear the mantilla I brought you from Spain? Look, it's as light as burnt tissue-paper."

"Dearest Michael," she murmured reproachfully, "you ought not to laugh about sacred subjects . . . I don't really see why we shouldn't have a car. We must have a consultation with Dick Prescott."

After dinner that night Michael wrapped up some stained and faded vestments he had brought for Viner and went off to see him at Notting Hill. He told himself guiltily in the hansom that it was more than a year since he had been to see old Viner, but the priest was so heartily glad

to welcome him and accepted so enthusiastically his propitiatory gifts, that he felt as much at ease as ever in the
smoke-hung room.

" Well, how's Oxford ? I was coming up last term, but I
couldn't get away. Have you been to see Sandifer yet ?
Or Pallant at Cowley, or Canon Harrowell ? "

Michael said he had not yet taken advantage of Viner's
letters of introduction to these dignitaries. He had indeed
heard Pallant preach at the church of the Cowley Fathers,
but he had thought him too much inclined to sacrifice on
the altar of empirical science.

" I hate compromise," said Michael.

" I don't think Pallant compromises, but I think he does
get hold of men by offering them Catholic doctrine in terms
of the present."

Michael shrugged his shoulders.

" This visit to Spain seems to have made you very
bigoted," Viner observed smiling.

" I haven't made up my mind one way or the other about
Christianity," Michael said. " But when I do I won't try
to include everybody, to say to every talkative young
Pragmatist with Schiller's last book in his pocket, ' come
inside, you're really one of us.' I shan't invite every callow
biologist to hear Mass just because a Cowley Dad sees
nothing in the last article on spontaneous generation that
need dismay the faithful. I'm getting rather fed up with
toleration, really : the only people with any fanaticism now
are the rationalists. It's quite exhilarating sometimes to
see the fire of disbelief glowing in the eyes of a passionate
agnostic."

" Our Lord himself was very tolerant," said Viner.

" Yes, tolerant to the weaknesses of the flesh, tolerant
to the woman taken in adultery, tolerant to the people
without wine at Cana, but he hadn't much use for people
who didn't believe just as he believed."

" Isn't it rather risky to slam the door in the face of the modern man ? "

" But, Mr. Viner," Michael protested, " you can't betray the myriads of the past because the individual of to-day finds his faith too weak to sustain him in their company, because the modern man wants to re-edit spiritual truths just as he has been able to re-edit a few physical facts that apparently stand the test of practical experiment. While men have been rolling along intoxicated by the theory of physical evolution, they may have retrograded spiritually."

" Of course, of course," the priest agreed. " By the way, your faith seems to be resisting the batterings of external progress very stoutly. I'm glad, old chap."

" I'm not sure that I have much faith, but I certainly haven't given up hope," Michael said gravely. " I think, you know, that hope, which is after all a theological virtue, has never had justice at the hands of the theologians. Oh lord, I wish earnest young believers weren't so smug and timid. Or else I wish that I didn't feel the necessity of co-ordinating my opinions and accepting Christianity as laid down by the Church. I should love to be a sort of Swedenborgian with all sorts of fanciful private beliefs. But I want to force everything within the convention. I hate Free Thought, Free Love and Free Verse, and yet I hate almost equally the stuffy people who have never contemplated the possibility of their merit. Do you ever read a paper called The Spectator ? Now I believe in what The Spectator stands for and I admire its creed enormously, but the expression of its opinions makes me spue. If only earnest young believers wouldn't treat Almighty God with the same sort of proprietary air that schoolgirls use towards a favourite mistress."

" Michael, Michael," cried Viner, " where are you taking me with your co-ordinating impulses and your Spectators and your earnest young believers ? What undergraduate paradox are you trying to wield against me ? Remember, I've been down nearly twenty years. I can no longer turn mental somersaults. I thought you implied *you* were a believer."

" Oh, no, I'm watching and hoping. And just now I'm afraid the anchor is dragging. Hope does have an anchor, doesn't she ? I'm not asking, you know, for the miracle of a direct revelation from God. The psychologists have made miracles of that sort hardly worth while. But I'm hoping with all my might to see bit by bit everything fall away except faith. Perhaps when I behold God in one of his really cynical moods . . . I'm groping in the dark after a hazy idea of subordination. That's something, you know. But I haven't found my own place in the scheme."

" You see you're very modern after all," said Viner, " with your co-ordinations and subordinations."

" But I don't want to assert myself," Michael explained. " I want to surrender myself, and I'm not going to surrender anything until I am sure by faith that I'm not merely surrendering the wastage of myself."

Michael left Viner with a sense of the pathetic sameness of the mission-priest's existence. He had known so well before he went that, because it was Monday, he would find him sitting in that armchair, smoking that pipe, reading that novel. Every other evening he would be either attending to parochial clubs in rooms of wood and corrugated iron, or his own room would be infested with boys who from year to year, from month to month never changed in general character, but always gave the same impression of shrill cockney, of boisterous familiarity, of self-satisfied election. To-morrow morning he would say Mass to the same sparse congregation of sacristan and sisters-of-mercy and devout old maids. The same red-wristed server would stump about his liturgical business in Viner's wake, and the same coffee-pot put in the same place on the same table by the same landlady would await his return. There was a dreariness about the ministrations of this Notting Hill Mission which had been absent from the atmosphere of Burgos Cathedral. No doubt superficially even at Burgos there was a sameness, but it was a glorious sameness, a sameness that approximated to eternity. Long ago had the priests learnt subordination. They had been absorbed into the omnipotence of the church against which the gates of hell could not prevail. Viner remained, however much he might have surrendered of himself to his mission-work, essentially an isolated, a pathetic individual.

As usual Michael met Alan at Paddington, and he was concerned to see that Alan looked rather pale and worried.

" What problems have you been solving this vac ? " Michael asked.

" Oh, I've been swatting like a pig for Mods," said Alan hopelessly. " You are a lucky lazy devil."

Even during the short journey to Oxford Alan furtively fingered his text-books, while he talked to Michael about a depressing January in London.

" Never mind. Perhaps you'll get your Blue next term," said Michael. " And if you aren't determined to play cricket all the Long, we'll go away and have a really sporting vac somewhere."

" If I'm ploughed," said Alan gloomily, " I've settled to become a chartered accountant."

Michael enjoyed his second Lent term. With an easy conscience he relegated Rugby football into the limbo of the past. He decided such violent exercise was no longer necessary, and he was getting to know so many people at other colleges that the cultivation of new personalities occupied all his leisure. After Maurice and Wedderburn came back from Spain, they devoted much of their time to painting, and The Oxford Looking-Glass became a very expensive business on account of the reproduction of their drawings. Moreover the circulation decreased in ratio with the increase of these drawings, and the five promoters who did not wish to practise art in the pages of their magazine convoked several meetings of protest. Finally Maurice was allowed to remain editor only on condition that he abstained from publishing any more drawings.

Nigel Stewart's meeting of the De Rebus Ecclesiasticis together with the visit to Spain induced Michael to turn his attention to that side of undergraduate life interested in religion. He went to see Canon Harrowell, and even accepted from him an invitation to a breakfast at which he met about half-a-dozen Keble men who talked about bishops. Afterwards Canon Harrowell seemed anxious to have a quiet talk with him in the library, but Michael made an excuse, not feeling inclined for self-revelation so quickly on top of six Keble men and the eggs-and-bacon. He went to see Father Pallant at Cowley, but Father Pallant appeared so disappointed that he had brought him no scientific problems to reconcile with Catholic dogma, and was moreover so contemptuous of Dom Cuthbert Manners, o.s.b. and Clere Abbey that Michael never went to see him again. He preferred old Sandifer, who with all the worldly benefits of good wine, good food and pleasant company, offered in addition his own courtly Caroline presence that added to wit and learning and trenchant theology made Michael regret he had not called upon him sooner.

Nigel Stewart took Michael to a meeting of De Rebus Ecclesiasticis, at which he met not only the six Keble men who had talked about bishops at Canon Harrowell's breakfast, but about twenty more members of the same college, all equally fervid and in his opinion equally objectionable. Michael also went with Nigel Stewart to Mass at St. Barnabas', where he saw the same Keble men all singing conspicuously and all conveying the impression that every Sunday they occupied the same place. By the end of the

term Michael's aroused interest in religion at Oxford died
out. He disliked the sensation of belonging to a particular
school of thought within an university. The ecclesiastical
people were like the ampelopsis at Trinity: they were
highly coloured, but so inappropriate to Oxford that they
seemed almost vulgar. It was ridiculous they should have to
worship in Oxford at a very ugly modern church in the
middle of very ugly modern slums, as ridiculous as it was to
call in the aid of American creepers to cover up the sins of
modern architects.

.Yet Michael was at a loss to explain to himself why the
ecclesiastical people were so obviously out of place in Oxford.
After all they were the heirs of a force which had persisted
there for many years almost in its present aspect: they
were the heirs after a fashion of the force that kept the
Royal Standard flying against the Parliament. But they
had not inherited the spirit of mediæval Oxford. They
were too self-conscious, too congregational. As individuals,
perhaps they were in tone with Oxford, but, eating bacon-
and-eggs and talking about bishops, they belonged evidently
to Keble, and Michael could not help feeling that Keble like
Mansfield and Ruskin Hall was in Oxford, but not in the
least of Oxford. The spirit of mediæval Oxford was more
typically preserved in the ordinary life of the ordinary
undergraduate: and yet it was a mistake to think of the
spirit of Oxford at any date. That spirit was dateless and
indefinable, and each new manifestation which Michael was
inclined to seize upon, even a manifestation so satisfying as
Venner's, became with the very moment that he was aware
of it as impossible to determine as a dream which leaves
nothing behind but the almost violent knowledge that it
was and exasperatingly still is.

.The revived interest lasted a very short time in its
communal aspect, and Michael retreated into his mediæval
history, still solicitous of Catholicism in so far as to support

the papacy against the Empire in the balance of his judgment,·
but no longer mingling with the Anglican adherents of the
theory, nor even indeed committing himself openly to Christianity as a general creed. Indeed his whole attitude to
religion was the result of a reactionary bias rather than of
any impulse towards constructive progression. He would
have liked to urge himself forward confidently to proclaim
his belief in Christianity, but he could acquire nothing
more positive than a gentle scepticism of the value of every
other form of thought, a gentleness that only became scornfully intolerant when provoked by ignorance or pretentious
statement.

.   Meanwhile The Oxford Looking-Glass, though inclining
officially to neither political party, was reflecting a wide-
spread interest in social reform. Michael woke up to this
phenomenon as he read through the sixth number on a
withering March day towards the end of term. Knowing
Maurice to be a chameleon who unconsciously acquired the
hue of his surroundings, Michael was sure that The Oxford
Looking-Glass by this earnest tone indicated the probable
tendency of undergraduate energy in the near future. Yet
himself, as he surveyed his acquaintances, could not perceive
in their attitude any hint of change. In St. Mary's the
debating clubs were still debating the existence of ghosts :
the essay clubs were still listening to papers that took them
along the by-ways of archæology or sport. Throughout the
university the old habit of mind persisted apparently. The
New College manner that London journalists miscalled the
Oxford manner still prevailed in the discussion of intellectual
subjects. In Balliol when any remark trembled on the edge
of a generalization, somebody in a corner would protest,
" O, shut up, fish-face," and the conversation at once
veered sharply back to golf or scandal, while the intellectual
kitten who had been playing with his mental tail would be
suddenly conscious of himself or his dignity and sit still. In

Exeter the members of the Literary Society were still called the Bloody Lits. Nothing anywhere seemed as yet to hint that the traditional flippancy of Oxford which was merely an extension of the public-school spirit was in danger of dying out. Oxford was still the apotheosis of the amateur. It was still surprizing when the Head of a House or a don or an undergraduate achieved anything in a manner that did not savour of happy chance. It was still natural to regard Cambridge as a provincial university, and to take pleasure in shocking the earnest young Cambridge man with the metropolitan humours and airy self-assurance of Oxford.

Yet The Oxford Looking-Glass reflected another spirit which Michael could not account for and the presence of which he vaguely resented.

" The O.L.G. is getting very priggish and serious and rather dull," he complained to Maurice.

" Not half so dull as it would be if I depended entirely on casual contributions," replied the editor. " I don't seem to get anything but earnestness."

" Oxford is becoming the home of living causes," sighed Michael. " That's a depressing thought. Do you really think these Rhodes Scholars from America and Australia and Germany are going to affect us ? "

" I don't know," Maurice said. " But everybody seems keen to speculate on the result."

" Why don't you take up a strong line of patronage ? Why don't you threaten these pug-nosed invaders with the thunders of the past ? " Michael demanded fiercely.

" Would it be popular ? " asked Maurice. " Personally of course I don't care one way or the other, but I don't want to let the O.L.G. in for a lot of criticism."

" You really ought to be a wonderful editor," said Michael. " You're so essentially the servant of the public."

" Well, with all your grumbles," said Maurice, " ours is the only serious paper that has had any sort of a run of late years."

" But it lacks individuality," Michael complained. " It's so damned inclusive. It's like The Daily Telegraph. It's voluminous and undistinguished. It shows the same tepid cordiality towards everything, from a man who's going to be hanged for murder to a new record at cricket. Why can't you infect it with some of the deplorable but rather delightfully juvenile indiscretion of The Daily Mail ? "

" The Daily Mail ! " Maurice scoffed.

" A man once said to me," Michael meditatively continued, " that whenever he saw a man in an empty railway compartment reading The Daily Telegraph, he always avoided it. You see he knew that man. He knew how terrible it would be to listen to him when he had finished his Telegraph. I feel rather like that about the O.L.G. But after all," he added cheerfully, " nobody does read the O.L.G. The circulation depends on the pledges of their pen sent round to their friends and relations by the casual contributors. And nobody ever meets a casual contributor. Is it true, by the way, that the fossilized remains of one were found in that great terra incognita—Queen's College ? "

But Maurice had left him, and Michael strolled down to the lodge to see if there were any letters. Shadbolt handed him an invitation to dinner from the Warden. As he opened it, Lonsdale came up with a torn replica of his own.

" I say, Michael, this is a rum sort of binge for the Wagger to give. I spotted all the notes laid out in a row by old Pumpkin-head's butler. You. Me. Tommy Grainger. Fitzroy. That ass Appleby. That worm Carben. And Smithers. There may have been some others too. I hope I don't get planted next the Pumpkinette."

" Miss Wagger may not be there," said Michael hopefully.

" But if she is, you're bound to be next her."

" I say, Shadbolt," Lonsdale demanded, " is this going to be a big squash at the Wagger's ? "

" The Warden has given me no instructions, sir, about

2 Y

carriages. And so I think we may take it for granted as it will be mostly confined to members of the college, sir. His servant tells me as the Dean is going and the Senior Tutor."

" And there won't be any does ? "

" Any what, sir ? "

" Any ladies ? "

" I expect as Miss Crackanthorpe will be present. She very rarely absconds from such proceedings," said Shadbolt, drawing every word with the sound of popping corks from the depths of his pompousness.

Michael and Lonsdale found out that to the list of guests they had established, must be added the names of Maurice, Wedderburn and two freshmen who were already favourably reported through the college as good sportsmen.

Two evenings later, at seven o'clock, Michael, Maurice, Lonsdale, Wedderburn and Grainger, bowed and starched, stood in Venner's, drinking peach-bitters sharpened by the addition of gin.

" The men have gone in to hall," said Venner. " You ought to start round to the Warden's Lodgings at ten past seven. Now don't be late. I expect you'll have a capital dinner."

" Champagne, Venner ? " asked Lonsdale.

" Oh, bound to be. Bound to be," said Venner. " The Warden knows how to give a dinner. There's no doubt of that."

" Caviare, Venner ? " asked Maurice.

" I wouldn't say for certain. But if you get an opportunity to drink any of that old hock, be sure you don't forget. It's a lovely wine. I wish we had a few dozen in the J.C.R. Now don't go and get tipsy like some of our fellows did once at a dinner given by the Warden."

" Did they, Venner ? " asked everybody greatly interested.

" It was just after the Transvaal war broke out. Only three or four years ago. There was a man called Castleton, a cousin of our Castleton, but a very different sort of man, such a rowdy fellow. He came out from the Warden's most dreadfully tipsy, and the men was taking him back to his rooms, when he saw little Barnaby, a Science don, going across New quad. He broke away from his friends and shouted out, ' there's a blasted Boer,' and before they could stop him, he'd knocked poor little Barnaby, a most nervous fellow, down in the wet grass and nearly throttled him. It was hushed up, but Castleton was never asked again you may be sure, and then soon after he volunteered for the front and died of enteric. So you see what comes of getting tipsy. Now you'd better start."

Arm-in-arm the five of them strolled through Cloisters until they came to the gothic door of the Warden's Lodgings. Up the Warden's majestic staircase they followed the butler into the Warden's gothic drawing-room where they shook hands with the great moon-faced Warden himself, and with Miss Crackanthorpe who was very much like her brother, and nearly as round on a much smaller scale. They nodded to the Dean, mentally calculating how many roll-calls they were behind, for the Dean notwithstanding the geniality of his greeting had one grey eye that seemed unable to forget it belonged to the Dean. They nodded to Mr. Ardle, the Senior Tutor, who blinked and sniffed and bowed nervously in response. Fitzroy beamed at them : Smithers doubtfully eyed them. The two freshmen reputed to be good sportsmen smiled grateful acknowledgments of their condescension. Appleby waved his hand in a gesture of such bland welcome that Lonsdale seemed to gibber with suppressed mortification and rage.

"Will you lay five to one in bobs that I don't sit next the Pumpkinette," whispered Lonsdale to Michael, as they went downstairs to dinner.

"Not a halfpenny," laughed Michael. "You will. And I shall get Ardles."

Upon the sage-green walls of the dining-room hung the portraits of three dead Wardens, and though the usual effect of family pictures was to make the living appear insignificant beside them, Michael felt that Pumpkin-head even in the presence of his three ferocious and learned forerunners had nothing to fear for his own pre-eminence. Modern life found in him a figure carved out of the persistent attributes of his office, and therefore already a symbol of the universal before his personality had been hallowed by death or had expressed itself in its ultimate form under the maturing touch of art and time. This quality in the host diffused itself through the room in such a way, that the whole dinner party gained from it a dignity and a stability which made more than usually absurd the superficial actions of eating and drinking, and the general murmur of infinitely fugacious talk.

Michael taking his first glance round the table after the preliminary shynesses of settling down, was as much thrilled by his consciousness of the eternal reality of this dinner party as he would have been if by a magical transference he could have suddenly found himself pursuing some grave task in the picture of a Dutch master. He had been to many dinners in Oxford of which commemorative photographs had been made by flashlight, and afterwards when he saw the print he could scarcely believe in his own reality, still less in that of the dinner, so ludicrously invented seemed every group. He wished now that a painter would set himself the problem of preserving by his art some of these transitory entertainments. He began to imagine himself with the commission to set on record the present occasion. He wished for the power to paint those deeper shadows in which the Warden's great round face inclined slowly now towards Fitzroy with his fair complexion and military rigour of bearing, now towards Wedderburn whose evening dress acquired from the dignity of its owner the richness of black velvet. More directly in the light of the first lamp sat

Maurice and Appleby opposite to one another, both imparting to the assemblage a charming worldliness, Maurice by his loose-fronted shirt, Appleby by the self-esteem of his restless blue eyes. The two freshmen on either side of the Dean wonderfully contrasted with his gauntness, and even more did the withered Ardles, who looked like a specimen of humanity dried as plants are dried between heavy books, contrast with the sprawling bulk of Grainger. On the other side, Michael watched with amusement Miss Crackanthorpe with shining apple-face bobbing nervously between Smithers pale and solid and domed like a great cheese, and Lonsdale cool and pink as an ice. In the background from the shadows at either end of the room the sage-green walls materialized in the lamplight: the three dead Wardens stared down at the table: and every fifteen minutes bells chimed in St. Mary's tower.

"And how is The Oxford Looking-Glass progressing, Avery?" enquired the Warden shining full upon the editor in a steady gaze. "No doubt it takes up a great deal of your valuable time?"

The Dean winked his grey decanal eye at the champagne: the Senior Tutor coughed remotely like a grasshopper: Lonsdale prodded Michael with his elbow and murmured, that ' the Wagger had laid Mossy a stymie.'

Maurice admitted the responsibility of the paper for occupying a considerable amount of his *leisure*, but consoled himself for this by the fact that certainly The Oxford Looking-Glass was progressing very well indeed.

"We don't altogether know what attitude to take up over the Rhodes Bequest," said Maurice. Then boldly he demanded from the Warden what would be the effect of these imposed scholars from America and Australia and Africa.

"The speculation is not without interest," declared the Warden. "What does Fitzroy think?"

Fitzroy threw back his shoulders as if he were going to abuse the Togger and said he thought the athletic qualifications were a mistake. " After all, sir, we don't want the Tabs,—I mean to say we don't want to beat Cambridge with the help of a lot of foreigners."

"Foreigners, Fitzroy ? Come, come, we can scarcely stigmatize Canadians as foreigners. What would become of the Imperial Idea ? "

" I think the Imperial Idea will take a lot of living up to," said Wedderburn, " when we come face to face with its practical expression. Personally I loathe Colonials except at the Earl's Court Exhibition."

" Ah, Wedderburn," said the Warden, " you are luckily young enough to be able to be particular. I with increasing age begin to suffer from that terrible disease of age— toleration."

" But the Warden is not so very old," whispered Miss Crackanthorpe to Lonsdale and Michael.

" Oh, rather not," Lonsdale murmured encouragingly.

" I think they'll wake up Oxford," announced Smithers, then, as everyone turned to hear what more he would say, Smithers seemed inclined to melt into silence, but with a sudden jerk of defiance, he hardened himself and became volubly opinionative.

" There's no doubt," he continued, " that these fellows will make the average undergrad look round him a bit." As Smithers curtailed undergraduate to the convention of a lady-novelist, a shudder ran round the dinner party. Almost the butler instead of putting ice into the champagne might have slipped it down the backs of the guests.

" In fact, what ho, she bumps," whispered Lonsdale. " Likewise pip-ip, and tootle-oo."

" Anyway he won't be able to ignore them," said Smithers.

" We hope not indeed," the Warden gravely wished. " What does Lonsdale think ? Lord Cleveden wrote to

me to say how deeply interested he was by the whole scheme
—a most appreciative letter, and your father has had a great
experience of colonial conditions."

. "Has he?" said Lonsdale. "Oh, yes, I see what you
mean. You mean when he was Governor. Oh, rather. But
I never knew him in those days." Then under his breath he
muttered to Michael. "Dive in, dive in, you rotter, I'm
getting out of my depth."

"I think Oxford will change the Rhodes Scholars much
more profoundly than the Rhodes Scholars will change
Oxford," said Michael. "At least they will if Oxford
hasn't lost anything lately. Sometimes I'm worried by
that, and then I'm not, for I do really feel that they must
be changed. Civilization must have some power, or we
should all revert."

"And are we to regard these finished oversea products
as barbarians?" asked the Warden.

"Oh, yes," said Michael earnestly. "Just as much
barbarians as any freshmen."

Everybody looked at the two freshmen on either side
of the Dean and laughed, while they laughed too and tried
to appear pleasantly flattered by the epithet.

"And what will Oxford give them?" asked the Dean
dryly. He spoke with that contempt of generalizations of
which all dons made a habit.

"Oh, I don't know," said Michael. "But vaguely I
would say that Oxford would cure them of being surprized
by themselves or of showing surprize at anybody else.
Marcus Aurelius said what I'm trying to say much better
than I ever can. Also they will gain a sense of humour, or
rather they will ripen whatever sense they already possess.
And they'll have a sense of continuity too, and perhaps,
but of course this will depend very much on their dons,
perhaps they'll take as much interest in the world as in
Australia."

" Why will that depend on their dons ? " challenged Mr. Ambrose.

" Oh, well, you know," explained Michael apologetically, " dons very often haven't much capacity for inquisitiveness. They get frightened very easily, don't they ? "

" Very true, very true," said the Warden. " But, my dear Fane, your optimism and your pessimism are both quixotic, immensely quixotic."

Later on in the quad when the undergraduate members of the dinner party discussed the evening, Maurice rallied Michael on his conversation.

" If you can talk your theories, why can't you write them ? " he complained.

" Because they'd be almost indecently diaphanous," said Michael.

" Good old Fane," said Grainger. " But, I say, you are an extraordinary chap, you know."

" He did it for me," said Lonsdale. " Pumpkin-head would have burst, if I'd let out I didn't know what part of the jolly old world my governor used to run."

Chapter X: *Stella in Oxford*

ALAN, when he met Michael at Paddington, was a great deal more cheerful then when they had gone up together for the previous term. He had managed to achieve a second class in Moderations, and he had now in view a term of cricket whose energy might fortunately be crowned with a blue. Far enough away now seemed Greats and not very alarming Plato and Aristotle at these first tentative encounters.

Michael dined with Alan at Christ Church after the Seniors' match, in which his host had secured in the second innings four wickets at a reasonable price. Alan casually nodded to one or two fellow hosts at the guest table, but did not offer to introduce Michael. All down the hall, men were coming in to dinner and going out of dinner as unconcernedly as if it had been the dining-saloon of a large hotel.

" Who is that man just sitting down ? " Michael would ask.

" I don't know," Alan would reply, and in his tone would somehow rest the implication that Michael should know better than to expect him to be aware of each individual in this very much subdivided college.

" Did you hear the hockey push broke the windows of the Socker push in Peck ? " asked one of the Christ Church hosts.

" No, really ? " answered Alan indifferently.

After hall as they walked back to Meadows, Michael tried

to point out to him that the St. Mary's method of dining in hall was superior to that of the House.

" The dinner itself is better," Alan admitted. " But I hate your system of all getting up from table at the same time. It's like school."

" But if a guest comes to St. Mary's he sits at his host's regular table. He's introduced to everybody. Why, Alan, I believe if you'd had another guest to-night, you wouldn't even have introduced me to him. He and I would have had to drink coffee in your rooms like a couple of dummies."

" Rot," said Alan. " And whom could you have wanted to meet this evening ? All the men at the guests' table were absolute ticks."

" I've never met a House man who didn't think every other House man impossible outside the four people in his own set," retorted Michael. " And yet, I suppose, you'll say it's the best college ? "

" Of course," Alan agreed.

Up in his rooms they pondered the long May day's reluctant death, while the coffee-machine bubbled and fizzed and The Soul's Awakening faintly kindled by the twilight was appropriately sentimental.

" Will you have a meringue ? " Alan asked. " I expect there's one in the cupboard."

" I'm sure there is," said Michael. " It's very unlikely that there is a single cupboard in the House without a meringue. But no, thanks, all the same."

They forsook the window-seat and pulled wicker-chairs very near to the tobacco-jar squatting upon the floor between them : they lit their pipes and sipped their coffee. For Alan the glories of the day floated before him in the smoke.

" It's a pity," he said, " Sterne missed that catch in the slips. Though of course I wasn't bowling for the slips. Five for forty-eight would have looked pretty well. Still four for forty-eight isn't so bad in an innings of 287. The point is whether they can afford to give a place to another bowler who's no earthly use as a bat. It seems a bit of a tail. I went in eighth wicket both innings. Two—first knock. Blob—second. Still four for forty-eight was certainly the best. I ought to play in the first trial match." So Alan voiced his hopes.

" Of course you will," said Michael. " And at Lord's. I think I shall ask my mother and sister up for Eights," he added.

Alan looked rather disconcerted.

" What's the matter ? " Michael asked. " You won't have to worry about them. I'll explain you're busy with cricket. Stella enquired after you in a letter this week."

During the Easter vacation Alan had stayed once or twice in Cheyne Walk, and Stella who had come back from an arduous time with music and musical people in Germany had seemed to take a slightly sharper interest in his existence.

" Give her my—er—love, when you write," said Alan very nonchalantly. " And I don't think I'd say anything about those four wickets for forty-eight. I don't fancy she's very keen on cricket. It might bore her."

No more was said about Stella that evening, and nothing indeed was said about anything except the seven or eight men competing for the three vacancies in the Varsity eleven. At about a quarter to ten Alan announced as usual that ' those men will be coming down soon for cocoa.'

" Alan, who are these mysterious creatures that come down for cocoa at ten ? " asked Michael. " And why am I never allowed to meet them ? "

" They'd bore you rather," said Alan. " They're people who live on this staircase. I don't see them any other time."

Michael thought Alan would be embarrassed if he insisted on staying, so to his friend's evident relief he got up to go.

"You House men are like a lot of old bachelors with your fads and regularities," he grumbled.

"Stay, if you like," said Alan, not very heartily. "But I warn you they're all awfully dull, and I've made a rule to go to bed at half-past ten this term."

"So long," said Michael hurriedly, and vanished.

A few days later Michael had an answer from his mother to his invitation for Eights Week.

173 CHEYNE WALK,
S.W.
May 5.

My dearest Michael,

I wish you'd asked me sooner. Now I have made arrangements to help at the Italian Peasant Jewellery Stall in this big bazaar at Westminster Hall for the Society for the Improvement of the Condition of Agricultural Labourers all over the world. I think you'd be interested. It's all about handicrafts. Weren't you reading a book by William Morris the other day? His name is mentioned a great deal always. I've been meeting so many interesting people. If Stella comes, why not ask Mrs. Ross to chaperone her? Such a capital idea. And do be nice about poor Dick Prescott. Stella is so young and impulsive. I wish she could understand how much much happier she would be married to a nice man, even though he may be a little older than herself. This tearing all over Europe cannot be good for her. And now she talks of going to Vienna and studying under somebody with a perfectly impossible name beginning with L. Not only that, but she also talks of unlearning all she has learnt and beginning all over again. This is most absurd, as I've tried to explain to her. She should have thought of this man beginning with L before. At her age to start scales and exercises again does seem ridiculous. I really dread Stella's coming of age. Who knows what she may not take it into her head to do? I can't think where she gets this

*curious vein of eccentricity. I'll write to Mrs. Ross if you like.
Stella, of course, says she can go to Oxford by herself. but that I
will not hear of, and I beg you not to encourage the idea, if she
suggests it to you.*
                    Your loving
                              Mother.

Michael thought Mrs. Ross would solve the difficulty, and
he was glad rather to relieve himself of the responsibility
of his mother at Oxford. He would have had to be so
steadily informative, and she would never have listened to a
word. Stella's view of the visit came soon after her mother's.

                              173 CHEYNE WALK,
                                        S.W.
                                    May 8.

Dear M.,
        *What's all this about Mrs. Ross chaperoning me at
Oxford? Is it necessary? At a shot I said to mother, ' No,
quite unnecessary.' But of course, if I should disgrace you by
coming alone, I won't. Isn't Mrs. Ross a little on the heavy
side? I mean wouldn't she\rather object to me smoking cigars?*

    " Great scott ! " interjaculated Michael.

*I'm going to Vienna soon to begin music all over again, so be
very charming to your only sister*
                              Stella.
    P.S.—Do crush mother over Prescott.

Michael agreed with his mother in thinking a chaperone
was absolutely necessary for Stella's visit to Oxford, and
since the threat of cigars he cordially approved of the
suggestion that Mrs. Ross should come. Moreover he
felt his former governess would approve of his own attitude
towards Oxford, and he rather looked forward to demon-
strating it to her. In the full-blooded asceticism of Oxford

Michael censured his own behaviour when he was seventeen and looked back with some dismay on the view of himself at that time as it appeared to him now. He was as much shocked by that period now as at school in his fifteenth year he had been shocked by the memory of the two horrid little girls at Eastbourne. Altogether this invitation seemed an admirable occasion to open the door once again to Mrs. Ross and to let her personality enter his mind as the sane adjudicator of whatever problems should soon present themselves. It would be jolly for Alan too, if his aunt came up and saw him playing for the Varsity in whatever cricket match was provided to relieve the tedium of too much rowing.

So finally, after one or two more protests from Stella, it was arranged that she should come up for Eights Week under the guardianship of Mrs. Ross.

Michael took care some time beforehand to incorporate a body of assistant entertainers. Lonsdale in consideration of Michael having helped him with his people for one day last year was engaged for the whole visit. Maurice was made to vow attendance for at least every other occasion. Wedderburn volunteered his services. Guy Hazlewood, who was threatened with Schools, was let off with a lunch. Nigel Stewart spoke mysteriously of a girl whose advent he expected, on which account he could not pledge himself too straightly. Rooms were taken in the High. Trains were looked out. On Saturday morning Lonsdale and Michael went down to the station to meet Mrs. Ross and Stella.

"I think it was a very bad move bringing me," said Lonsdale as they waited on the platform. "Your sister will probably think me an awful ass, and . . ."

But the train interrupted Lonsdale's self-depreciation, and he sustained himself well through the crisis of the introductions. Michael thought Mrs. Ross had never so well been suited by her background as now when tall and straight and in close-fitting grey dress she stood in the Oxford sunlight. Stella too in that flowered muslin relieved Michael instantly of the faint anxiety he had conceived lest she might appear in a Munich garb unbecoming to a reserved landscape. It was a very peculiarly feminine dress, but somehow she had never looked more like a boy, and her grey eyes, as for one moment she let them rest wide open on the city's towers and spires, were more than usually grey and pellucid.

"I say, I ordered a car to meet us," said Lonsdale. "I thought we should buzz along quicker."

"What you really thought," said Michael, "was that you would have to drive my sister in a hansom."

"Oh, no, I say, really," protested Lonsdale.

"I'm much more frightened of you than you could ever be of me," Stella declared.

"Oh no, I say, really, are you ? But I'm an awful ass, Miss Fane," said Lonsdale encouragingly. "Hallo, here's the jolly old car."

As they drove past the castle, Lonsdale informed Stella it was the county gaol, and when they reached the gaol he told her it was probably Worcester College, or more familiarly Wuggins.

"You'll only have to tell her that All Souls is the County Asylum and that Queen's is a marmalade factory, and she'll have a pretty good notion of the main points of interest in the neighbourhood," said Michael.

"He always rags me," explained Lonsdale smiling confidentially round at the visitors. "I say, isn't Alan Merivale your nephew ?" he asked Mrs. Ross. "He's playing for the Varsity against Surrey. Sent down some very hot stuff yesterday. We ought to buzz round to the Parks after lunch and watch the game for a bit."

Wedderburn, who had been superintending the preparations for lunch, met them in the lodge with a profound welcome, having managed to put at least twenty years on to his age. Lunch had been laid in Lonsdale's rooms, since he was one of the few men in college who possessed a dining-room in addition to a sitting-room. Yet, notwithstanding that Michael had invited the guests and that they were lunching in Lonsdale's rooms, to Wedderburn by all was the leadership immediately accorded.

The changeless lunch of Eights Week with its salmon mayonnaise and cold chicken and glimpses through the windows of pink and blue dresses going to and fro across the green quadrangles, with the laughter and talk and speculations upon the weather, with the overheated scout and scent of lilac and hawthorn, went its course: as fugitive a piece of mirthfulness as the dance of the mayflies over the Cher.

After lunch they walked to the Parks to watch Alan playing for the Varsity. Wedderburn, who with people to entertain feared nothing and nobody, actually went coolly into the pavilion and fetched out Alan who was already in pads, waiting to go in. Michael watched very carefully Alan's meeting with Stella, watched Alan's face fall when he saw her beside Maurice and marked how nervously he fidgeted with his gloves. There was a broken click from the field of play. It was time for Alan to go in. Michael wished very earnestly he could score a brilliant century so that Stella hearing the applause could realize how much there was in him to admire. Yet ruefully he admitted to himself the improbability of Stella realizing anything at all about the importance of cricket. However, he had scarcely done with his wishing, when he saw Alan coming gloomily back from the wicket, clean bowled by the very first ball he had received.

"Of course, you know, he isn't played for his batting," he hastened to explain to Stella.

She, however, was too deeply engaged in discussing Vienna with Maurice to pay much attention, even when

Alan sat down despondently beside them, unbuckling his pads. It was just as Michael had feared, fond though he was of Maurice.

The last Varsity player was soon out, and Wedderburn proposed an early tea in his rooms to be followed by the river. Turning into Holywell, they met Guy Hazlewood, who said without waiting to be introduced to Mrs. Ross and Stella :

" My dear people, I fall upon your necks. Suggest something for me to do that for one day and one night will let me entirely forget Schools. We can't bear our digs any longer."

" Why don't you give a party there on Monday night," suggested Wedderburn deeply.

" Let me introduce you to Mrs'sss . . . my sissss . . . Mr. H'wood," mumbled Michael in explanation of Wedderburn's proposal.

" What a charming idea," drawled Guy. " But isn't it rather a shame to ask Miss Fane to play ? Anyway, I daren't."

" Oh, no," said Stella. " I should rather like to play in Oxford."

So after a kaleidoscope of racing and a Sunday picnic on the upper river, when everybody ate as chickens drink with a pensive upward glance at the trend of the clouds, occurred Guy Hazlewood's party in Holywell, which might more truly have been called Wedderburn's party, since he at once assumed all responsibility for it.

The digs were much more crowded than anybody had expected, chiefly on account of the Balliol men invited.

" Half Basutoland seems to be here," Lonsdale whispered to Michael.

" Well, with Hazlewood, Comeragh and Anstruther, all sons of Belial, what else can you expect ? " replied Michael.

Stella had seemed likely at first to give the favour of her

2 z

attention more to Hazlewood than to anybody else, but Maurice was in a dauntless mood and, with Guy handicapped by having to pretend to assent to Wedderburn's suggestions for entertainment, he managed at last to monopolize Stella almost entirely. Alan had declined the invitation with the excuse of wanting a steady hand and eye for to-morrow. But Michael fancied there was another reason.

Stella played three times and was much applauded.

"Very sporting effort, by Jove," said Lonsdale, and this was probably the motive of most of the commendation, though there was a group of really musical people in the darkest corner who emerged between each occasion and condoled with Michael on having to hear his sister play in such inadequate surroundings.

Michael himself was less moved by Stella's playing than he had ever been. Nor was this coldness due to any anxiety for her success. He was sure enough of that in this uncritical audience.

" Do you think Stella plays as well as she did ? " he asked Mrs. Ross.

"Perhaps this evening she may be a little excited," Mrs. Ross suggested.

" Perhaps," said Michael doubtfully. " But what I mean is that, if she isn't going to advance quite definitely, there really isn't any longer an excuse for her to arrogate to herself a special code of behaviour."

"Stella says a great deal more than she does," Mrs. Ross reassured him. " You'd be surprised, as indeed I was surprised, to find how simple and childlike she really is. I think an audience is never good for her."

" But after all, her life is going to be one audience after another in quick succession," Michael pointed out.

" Gradually an audience will cease to rouse her into any violence of thought or accentuation of superficial action—

oh, Michael," Mrs. Ross exclaimed, breaking off, " what dreadfully long words you're tempting me to use, and why do you make me talk about Stella ? I'd really rather talk about you."

" Stella is becoming a problem to me," said Michael.

" And you yourself are no longer a problem to yourself ? " Mrs. Ross enquired.

" Not in the sense I was, when we last talked together."

Michael was a little embarrassed by recalling that conversation. It seemed to link him too closely for his pleasure to the behaviour which had led up to it, to be a part of himself at the time, farouche and uncontrolled.

"And all worries have passed away ? " persisted Mrs. Ross.

" Yes, yes," said Michael quickly. " For one thing," he added as if he thought he had been too abrupt, " I'm too comfortably off to worry much about anything. Boredom is the only problem I shall ever have to face. Seriously though, Mrs. Ross, I really am rather shocked when I think of myself at sixteen and seventeen." Michael was building brick by brick a bridge for Mrs. Ross to step over the chasm of three years. " I seem to see myself," he persevered, " with very untidy hair, with very loose joints, doing and saying and thinking the most impossible things. I blush now at the memory of myself, just as I should blush now with Oxford snobbishness to introduce a younger brother like myself then, say to the second-year table in hall." Michael paused for a moment, half hoping Mrs. Ross would assure him he had caricatured his former self, but as she said nothing, he continued : " When I came up to Oxford I found that the natural preparation for Oxford was not a day-school like St. James', but a boarding-school. Therefore I had to acquire in a term what most of my contemporaries had been given several years to acquire. I remember quite distinctly my father saying to my mother, ' By gad, Valèrie, he ought to go to Eton, you know,' and my mother disagreeing, ' No, no, I'm sure you were right when you said St. James'.' That's so like mother. She probably had never thought the matter out at all. She was probably perfectly vague about the difference between St. James' and Eton, but because it had been arranged so, she disliked the idea of any alteration. I'm telling you all this because, you know, you provided as it were the public-school influence for my early childhood. After you I ought to have passed on to a private school entirely different from Randell House, and then to Eton or Winchester. I'm perfectly sure I could have avoided everything that happened when I was sixteen or seventeen, if I'd not been at a London day-school."

"But is it altogether fair to ascribe everything to your school ? " asked Mrs. Ross. " Alan for instance came very successfully, as far as normality is concerned, through St. James'."

" Yes, but Alan has the natural goodness of the average young Englishman. Possibly he benefited by St. James'. Possibly at Eton, and with a prospect of money, he would have narrowed down into a mere athlete, into one of the rather objectionable bigots of the public-school theory. Now I was never perfectly normal. I might even have been called morbid and unhealthy. I should have been, if I hadn't always possessed a sort of curious lonely humour which was about twice as severe as the conscience of tradition. At the same time, I had nothing to justify my abnormality. No astounding gift of genius, I mean."

" But, Michael," interrupted Mrs. Ross, " I don't fancy the greatest geniuses in the world ever justified themselves at sixteen or seventeen."

" No, but they must have been upheld by the inner consciousness of greatness. You get that tremendously through all the despondencies of Keats' letters for instance. I have never had that. Stella absorbed all the creative and interpretative force that was going. I never have and never shall get beyond sympathy, and even the value that gives my criticism is to a certain extent destroyed by the fact that the moment I try to express myself more permanently than by mouth, I am done."

"But still, I don't see why a day-school should have militated against the development of that sympathetic and critical faculty."

"It did in this way," said Michael. "It gave me too much with which to sympathize before I could attune my sympathy to criticism. In fact I was unbalanced. Eton would have adjusted this balance. I'm sure of that, because since I've been at Oxford I find my powers of criticism so very much saner, so very much more easily economized. I mean to say, there's no wastage in futile emotions. Of course, it's partly due to being older."

"Really, Michael," Mrs. Ross protested, "if you talk like this I shall begin to regret your earlier extravagance. This dried-up self-confidence seems to me not quite normal either."

"Ah, that's only because I'm criticizing my earlier self. I really am now in a delightful state of cool judgment. Once I used to want passionately to be like everybody else. I thought that was the goal of social happiness. Then I wanted to be violently and conspicuously different from everybody else. Now I seem to be getting near the right mean between the two extremes. I'm enjoying Oxford enormously. I can't tell you how happy I am here, how many people I like. And I appreciate it so much the more because to a certain extent at first it was a struggle to find that wide normal road on which I'm strolling along now. I'm so positive that the best of Oxford is the best of England, and that the best of England is the best of humanity that I long to apply to the world the same standards we tacitly respect—we undergraduates. I believe every problem of life can be solved by the transcendency of the spirit which has transcended us up here. You remember I used to say you were like Pallas Athene? Well, just those qualities in you which made me think of that resemblance I find in Oxford. Don't ask me to say what they are, because I couldn't explain."

" I think you have a great capacity for idealization," said Mrs. Ross gravely. " I wonder how you are going to express it practically. I wonder what profession you'll choose."

" I don't suppose I shall choose a profession at all," said Michael. " There's no financial reason—at any rate—why I should."

" Well, you won't have to decide against a profession just yet," said Mrs. Ross. " And now tell me, just to gratify my curiosity, why you think Stella's playing has deteriorated —if you really think it has."

" Oh, I didn't say it had," Michael contradicted in some dismay. " I merely said that to-night it did not seem up to her level. Perhaps she was anxious. Perhaps she felt among all these undergraduates as I felt in my first week. Perhaps she's thinking what schoolboys they all are, and how infinitely youthful they appear beside those wild and worldly-wise Bohemians to whose company she has been accustomed for so long. I long to tell her that these undergraduates are really so much wiser, even if literature means Mr. Soapy Sponge's Sporting Tour, and art The Soul's Awakening, and religion putting on a bowler to go and have a hot breakfast at the O.U.D.S. after chapel, and politics the fag-ends of paternal or rather ancestral opinion, and life a hot bath and changing after a fox-hunt or a grouse-drive."

Farther conversation was stopped by Wedderburn driving everybody down to supper with pastoral exhortations in his deepest bass. Michael, after his talk with Mrs. Ross, was relieved to find himself next to Lonsdale and sheltered by a quivering rampart of jellies from more exacting company.

" These Basutos aren't so bad when you talk to them,"
said Lonsdale. Comeragh was at m'tutor's. I wonder if he
still collects bugs. I rather like that man Hazlewood. I
thought him a bit sidy at first, but he's rather keen on
fishing. I don't think much of the girl that Trinity man—
what's his name—Stewart has roped in. She looks like something left over from a needlework stall. I say, your sister
jolly well knows how to punch a piano. Topping, what ?
Mossy's been very much on the spot to-night. He and
Wedders are behaving like a couple of theatrical managers.
Why didn't Alan Merivale turn up ? I was talking to some
of the cricket push at the Club, and it doesn't look a hundred
quid to a tanner on his Blue. Bad luck. He's a very good
egg."

Michael listened vaguely to Lonsdale's babble. He was
watching the passage of the cigars and cigarettes down the
table. Thank heaven, Stella had let the cigars go by.

The party of 196 Holywell broke up. Outside in the
shadowy street of gables they stood laughing and talking
for a moment. Guy Hazlewood, Comeragh and Anstruther
looked down from the windows at their parting guests.

" It's been awfully ripping," these murmured to their
hosts. The hosts beamed down.

" We've been awfully bucked up by everything. Special
vote of thanks to Miss Fane."

" You ought all to get Firsts now," said Wedderburn.

Then he and Lonsdale and Michael and Maurice set off
with Stella and Mrs. Ross to the High Street rooms. In
different directions the rest of the party vanished on echoing
footsteps into the moon-bright spaces, into the dark and
narrow entries. Voices faint and silvery rippled along the
spell-bound airs of the May night. The echoing footsteps
died out to whispers. There was a whizzing of innumerable
clocks, and midnight began to clang.

" We must hurry," said the escort, and they ran off down

the High towards St. Mary's, reaching the lodge on the final stroke.

"Shall I come up to your rooms for a bit ?" Maurice suggested to Michael.

"I'm rather tired," objected Michael, who divined that Maurice was going to talk at great length about Stella.

He was too jealous of Alan's absence that evening to want to hear Maurice's facile enthusiasm.

Chapter XI : *Sympathy*

MRS. ROSS and Stella left Oxford two days after the party, and Michael was really glad to be relieved of the dread that Stella in order to assert her independence of personality would try to smash the glass of fashion and dint the mould of form. Really he thought the two occasions during her visit on which he liked her best and admired her most were when she was standing on the station platform. Here she was expressed by that city of spires confusing with added beauty that clear sky of Summer. Here too her personality seemed to add an appropriate foreground to the scene, to promise the interpretation that her music would give, a promise however that Michael felt she had somehow belied.

Alan dropped out of the Varsity Eleven the following week, and he was in a very gloomy mood when Michael paid him a visit of condolence.

"These hard wickets have finished me off," he sighed. "I shall take up golf, I think."

The bag of clubs he had brought up on his first day was lying covered with grey fluff under the bed.

"Oh, no, don't play golf," protested Michael, "you've got two more years to get your Blue and all your life to play golf, which is a rotten game and has ruined Varsity cricket."

"But one can be alone at golf," said Alan.

"Alone?" repeated Michael. "Why on earth should you want to play an outdoor game alone?"

"Because I get depressed sometimes," Alan explained. "What good am I ?"

Michael began to laugh.

"It's nothing to laugh at," said Alan sadly. "I've been thinking of my future. I shall never have enough money to marry. I shall never get my Blue. I shall get a fourth in Greats. Perhaps I shan't even get into the Egyptian Civil Service. I expect I shall end as a bank-clerk. Playing cricket for a suburban club on Saturday afternoons. That's all I see before me. When is Stella going to Vienna ?"

"I don't know that she is going," said Michael. "She always talks a great deal about things which don't always come off."

"I was rather surprized she seemed to like that man Avery so much," Alan said. "But I suppose he pretended to know an awful lot about music. I don't think I care for him."

"Some people don't," Michael admitted. "I think women always like him though."

"Yes, I should think they did," Alan agreed bitterly. "Sorry I'm so depressing. Have a meringue or something."

"Alan, why, are you in love with Stella ?" Michael challenged.

"What made you think I was ?" countered Alan, looking alarmed.

"It's pretty obvious," Michael said. "And curiously enough I can quite understand it. Generally of course, a brother finds it difficult to understand what other people can see in his sister, but I'm never surprized when they fall in love with Stella."

"A good many have ?" asked Alan, and his blue eyes were sharpened by a pain deeper than that of seeing a catch in the slips missed off his bowling.

Michael nodded.

"Oh, I've realized for a long time how utterly hopeless it was for me," Alan sighed. "I'm evidently going to be a failure."

"Would you care for some advice?" enquired Michael very tentatively.

"What sort of advice?" Alan asked.

Michael took this for assent and plunged in.

"Let her alone," he adjured his friend. "Let her absolutely alone. She's very young you know, and you're not very old. Let her alone for at least a year. I suggest two years. Don't see much of her, and don't let her think you care. That would interest her for a week, and really, Alan, it's not good for Stella to think that everybody falls in love with her. I don't mind about Maurice. It would do him good to be turned down."

"Would he be?" demanded Alan gloomily.

"Of course, of course . . . it seems funny to be talking to you about love . . . you used to be so very scornful about it. . . . I expect you know you'll fall in love pretty deeply now. . . . Alan, I'm frightfully keen you should marry Stella. But let her alone. Don't let her interfere with your cricket. Don't take up golf on account of her."

Michael was so much in earnest with his exhortation to Alan that he picked up a meringue and was involved in the difficulties of eating it before he was aware he was doing so. Alan began to laugh, and the heavy airs of disappointment and hopelessness were lightened.

"It's funny," said Michael, "that I should have an opportunity now of talking to you about love and cricket."

"Funny?" Alan repeated.

"Don't you remember three years ago on the river one night how I wished you would fall in love and you said something about it being bad for cricket?"

"I believe I do remember vaguely," said Alan.

Michael saw that after the explanation of his depression he wanted to let the subject drop, and since that was the very advice he had conferred upon Alan, he felt it would be unfair to tempt him to elaborate this depression merely to gratify his own pleasure in the retrospect of emotion. So Stella was not discussed again for a long while, and as she did after all go to Vienna to study a new technique, the abstention was not difficult. Michael was glad, since he had foreseen the possibility of a complication ravelled by Maurice. Her departure straightened this out, for Maurice was not inclined to gather strength from absence. Other problems more delicate of adjustment even than Stella began to arise, problems connected with the social aspects of next term.

Alan would still be in college. Scholars at Christ Church were allowed sometimes to spend even the whole of their four years in college. Michael tried in vain to persuade him to ask leave to go into digs. Alan offered his fourth year to companionship with Michael, but nothing would induce him to emerge from college sooner. And why did Michael so particularly want him ? There were surely men in his own college with whom he was intimate enough to share digs. Michael admitted there were many, but he did not tell Alan that the real reason he had been so anxious for his partnership was to have an excuse to escape from an arrangement made lightly enough with Maurice Avery in his first or second term that in their third year they should dig together. Maurice had supposed the other day that the arrangement stood, and Michael, not wishing to hurt his feelings, had supposed so too. A few days later Maurice had come along with news of rooms in Longwall. Should he engage them ? Michael said he hated Longwall as a prospective dwelling-place, and Maurice had immediately deferred to his prejudice.

It was getting unpleasantly near a final arrangement,

for the indefatigable Maurice would produce address after address, until Michael seemed bound ultimately to accept. Lonsdale and Grainger had invited him to dig with them at 202 High. Michael suggested Maurice as well, but they shook their heads. Wedderburn was already partially sharing, that is to say, though he had his own sitting-room he·was in the same house and would no doubt join in the meals. Maurice was not to be thought of. Maurice was a very good fellow but—Maurice was—but—and Michael in asking Lonsdale and Grainger why they declined his company, asked himself at the same time what were his own objections to digging with Maurice. He tried to state them in as kindly a spirit as he could, and for awhile he told himself he wished to be in digs with people who represented the broad stream of normal undergraduate life ; he accused himself in fact of snobbishness, and justified the snobbishness by applying it to undergraduate Oxford as a persistent attribute. As time went by, however, and Maurice produced rooms on rooms for Michael's choice, he began almost to dislike him, to resent the assumption of a desire to dig with him. Where was Maurice's sensitiveness that it could not react to his unexpressed hatred of the idea of living with him ? Soon it would come to the point of declaring outright that he did not want to dig with him. Such an announcement would really hurt his feelings, and Michael did not want to do that. As soon as Maurice had receded into the background of casual encountership, he would take pleasure in his company again. Meanwhile, however, it ᐧreally seemed as if Maurice were losing all his superficial attractiveness. Michael wondered why he had never before noticed how infallibly he ran after each new and petty phase of art, how vain he was too, and how untidy. It was intolerable to think of spending a year's close association with all those paint-boxes and all that modelling-wax and all those undestroyed proof-sheets of The Oxford Looking-

Glass. Finally, he had never noticed before how many cigarettes Maurice smoked and with what skill he concealed in every sort of receptacle the stained and twisted stumps that were left over. That habit would be disastrous to their friendship, and Michael knew that each fresh cigarette lighted by him would consume a trace more of the friendship, until at last he would come to the state of observing him with a cold and mute resentment. He was in this attitude of mind towards his prospective companion, when Maurice came to see him. He seemed nervous, lighting and concealing even more cigarettes than usual.

"About digs in Longwall," he began.

"I won't live in Longwall," affirmed Michael.

"Do you think you could find anybody else?"

"Why, have you got hold of some digs for three?" asked Michael hopefully. This would be a partial solution of the difficulty, as long as the third person was a tolerably good egg.

Maurice seemed embarrassed.

"No, well, as a matter of fact Castleton rather wants to dig with me. The New College man he was going to live with is going down, and he had fixed up some rather jolly digs in Longwall. He offered me a share, but of course I said I was digging with you, and there's no room for a third."

"I can go in with Tommy Grainger and Lonny," said Michael quickly.

Maurice looked much relieved.

"As long as you don't feel I've treated you badly," he began.

"That's all right," said Michael, resenting for the moment Maurice's obvious idea that he was losing something by the defection. But as soon as he could think of Maurice unlinked to himself for a year, his fondness for him began to return and his habit of perpetually smoking cigarettes was less irritating. He accepted Maurice's invitation to stay at Godalming in July with an inward amusement roused by the penitence which had prompted it.

Stella's unexpectedly prompt departure to Vienna had left Michael free to make a good many visits during the Long Vacation. He enjoyed least the visit to High Towers, because he found it hard not to be a little contemptuous of the adulation poured out upon Maurice by his father and mother and sisters. Mr. Avery was a stockbroker with a passion for keeping as young as his son. Mrs. Avery was a woman who, when her son and her husband were not with her, spoiled the dogs, and sometimes even her daughters. She was just as willing to spoil Michael, especially when his politeness led him into listening in shady corners of the tennis-lawn to Mrs. Avery's adorations of Maurice. He found Godalming oppressive with the smart suburbanity of Surrey. He disliked the facility of life there, the facile thought, the facile comfort, the facile conversation. Everything went along with a smoothness that suited the civilized landscape, the conventional picturesqueness and the tar-smeared roads. After a week Michael was summoned away by a telegram. Without a ruse he would never have escaped from this world of light-green Lovat tweeds, of fashionable — rusticity and carefully pressed trousers.

"*Dear Mrs. Avery,*" he wrote, preening himself upon the recuperative solitude of empty Cheyne Walk whence his mother had just departed to France. "*I enjoyed my visit so much, and so much wish I had not been called away on tiresome business. I hope the garden-party at the Nevilles was a great success, and that the High Towers croquet pair distinguished themselves. Please remember me to Mr. Avery.*"

"Thank heaven that's done," he sighed, and lazily turned the pages of Bradshaw to discover how to reach Wedderburn in the depths of South Wales.

The vacation went by very quickly with quiet intervals

in London between his visits, of which he enjoyed most
the fortnight at Cressingham Hall—a great Palladian house
in the heart of the broad Midlands. It was mid-August
with neither shooting nor golf to disturb the pastoral calm.
Lonsdale was trying under Lord Cleveden's remonstrances
to obtain a grasp of rural administration. So he and his
sister Sylvia with Michael drove every day in a high dogcart
to various outlying farms of the estate. Lonsdale managed
to make himself very popular, and after all as he confided
to Michael that was the main thing.

"And how's his lordship, sir?" the tenant would
enquire.

"Oh, very fit," Lonsdale would reply. "I say, Mr.
Hoggins, have you got any of that home-brewed beer on
draught? My friend Mr. Fane has heard a good deal
about it."

In a cool farm-parlour Lonsdale and Michael would toast
the health of agriculture and drink damnation to all
Radicals, while outside in the sun were Sylvia with Mrs.
Hoggins, looking at the housewife's raspberries and gooseberries.

"I envy your life," said Michael.

"A bit on the slow side, don't you think?"

"Plenty of time for thinking."

"Ah," said Lonsdale. "But then I've got no brains. I
really haven't, you know. The poor old governor's quite
worried about it."

However, when after dinner Lord Cleveden bade his son
and his guest draw up their chairs and when, as he cere-
moniously circulated the port, he delivered majestic
reminiscences of bygone celebrities and notorieties, Michael
scarcely thought that anything would ever worry him very
much, not even a dearth of partridges, still less a dearth of
brains in his only son.

"*Dear Lady Cleveden,*" he wrote when once again he sat

in the empty house in Cheyne Walk. "*London is quite impossible after Cressingham.*"

And so it was with the listless August people drooping on the Embankment, the oily river and a lack-lustre moon.

Michael was surprized at such a season to get a telegram from Prescott, inviting him to dine at the Albany. His host was jaded by the hot London weather, and the soldier-servant waited upon him with more solicitude than usual. Prescott and Michael talked of the commonplace for some time, or rather Michael talked away rather anxiously while Prescott lent him a grave attention. At last Michael's conversation exhausted itself, and for a few minutes there was silence, while Prescott betrayed his nervousness by fidgeting with the ash on his cigar. At last he burnt himself and throwing away the cigar leapt forthwith into the tide of emotion that was deepening rapidly around his solitary figure.

"Daresay your mother told you I wanted to marry Stella. Daresay Stella told you. Of course I realize it's quite absurd. Said so at once, and of course it's all over now. Phew! it's fearfully hot to-night. Always feel curiously stranded in London in August, but I suppose that's the same with most people."

Michael had an impulse to ask Prescott to come away with him, but the moment for doing so vanished in the shyness it begot, and a moment later the impulse seemed awkwardly officious. Yet by Prescott's confidence Michael felt himself committed to a participation in his existence that called for some response. But he could not with any sincerity express a regret for Stella's point of view.

"Mother was very anxious she should accept you," said Michael, and immediately he had a vision of Prescott like the puppet of an eighteenth-century novelist kneeling to receive Stella's stilted declaration of her refusal.

"Your mother was most extraordinarily gracious and

3 A

sympathetic. But of course I'm a man of fifty. I suppose you thought the idea very ridiculous."

"I don't think Stella is old enough to marry," said Michael.

"But don't you think it's better for girls to marry when they're young ?" asked Prescott, and as he leaned forward, Michael saw his eyes were very bright and his actions feverish. "I've noticed that tendencies recur in families. Time after time. I don't like this Viennese business, yet if Stella had married me I shouldn't have interfered with her," he added with a wistfulness that was out of keeping with his severely conventional appearance. "Still I should have always been in the background."

"Yes, I expect that was what she felt," said Michael.

He did not mean to be brutal, but he saw at once how deeply he had wounded Prescott, and suddenly in a panic of inability to listen any longer, he rose and said he must go.

As he was driving to Waterloo Station on the following afternoon to go down to Basingstead, he saw vaguely on the posters of the starved August journals 'Suicide of a Man About Town.' At Cobble Place newspapers were read as an afterthought, and it was not until late on the day after that above a short paragraph the headline 'Tragedy in the Albany' led him on to learn that actually Prescott was the man about town who had killed himself.

Michael's first emotion was a feeling of self-interest in being linked so closely with an event deemed sufficiently important to occupy the posters of an evening paper. For the moment the fact that he had dined with Prescott a few hours beforehand seemed a very remarkable coincidence. It was only after he had had to return to London and attend the inquest, to listen to the coroner's summing up of the evidence of depression and the perspiring jury's delivery of their verdict of temporary insanity he began to realize that in the crisis of a man's life his own words or behaviour might easily have altered the result. He was driving to Waterloo Station again in order to take up the thread of his broken visit. On the posters of the starved August journals he read now with a sharp interest 'Cat Saves Household in Whitechapel Fire.' This cat stood for him as the symbol of imaginative action. He bought the evening papers at Waterloo, and during the journey down to Hampshire read about this cat who had saved a family from an inquest's futile epigraph and even if unsuc-cessful would have been awarded the commendatory plati-tudes of the coroner.

Michael had not said by what train he would arrive, and so after the journey he was able to walk to Basingstead through lanes freshening for evening. By this time the irony of the cat's fortuitous interference was blunted, and Michael was able to see himself in clearer relation to the fact of Prescott's death. He was no longer occupied by the strange sensation of being implicated in one of the suffi-ciently conspicuous daily deaths exalted by the press to the height of a tragedy. Yet for once the press had not been so exaggerative. Prescott's life was surely a tragedy, and his death was only not a tragedy because it had violated all the canons of good-form and had falsified the stoicism of nearly fifty years. Yet why should not the stoic ideal be applied to such a death ? It was an insult to such perfect manners to suppose that a hopeless love for a girl had led him to take his life. Surely it would be kinder to ascribe it to the accumulative boredom of August in London, or possibly to a sudden realization of vulgarity creeping up to the very portals of the Albany.

Michael was rather anxious to believe in this theory, because he was beginning to reproach himself more seriously than when the cat had first obtruded a sardonic commentary on his own behaviour in having given way to the panic of wishing to listen no longer to the dead man's confidences.

With all his personal regrets it was disconcerting to think
of a man whose attitude to life had seemed so correct
making this hurried exit, an exit too that left his reputation
a prey to the public, so that his whole existence could be
soiled after death by the inquisitive grubbing of a coroner.
Prescott had always seemed secure from an humiliation
—like this. The mezzotints of stern old admirals, the soldier-
servant, the fashionable cloister in which he lived, the
profound consciousness he always betrayed of the importance
of restraint whether in morals or cravats had seemed to
combine in unrelaxing guardianship of his good-form. The
harder Michael thought about the business, the more
incredible it appeared. Himself in an earlier mood of self-
distrust had accepted Prescott as an example to whose almost
contemptuous attitude of withdrawal he might ultimately
aspire. He had often reproached himself for outlived
divergencies of thought and action, and with the example of
Prescott he had hammered into himself the possibility of
eternal freedom from their recurrence. And now he must
admit that mere austerity unless supported by a spiritual
encouragement to endure was liable at any moment to break
up pitiably into suicide. The word itself began to strike
him with all the force of its squalid associations. The fresh
dust of the Hampshire lanes became a grey miasma. Loneliness looped itself slowly round his progress so that he
hurried on with backward glances. The hazel-hedges were
sombre and monotonous and defiled here and there by the
rejected rags of a tramp. The names of familiar villages
upon the sign-posts lost their intimations of sane humanity,
and turned to horrible abstractions of the dead life of the
misshapen boot or empty matchbox at their foot. The comfortable assurance of a prosperous and unvexed country
rolling away to right and left forsook him, and only the pallid
road writhed along through the twilight. " My nerves are
in a rotten state," he told himself, and he was very glad to

see Basingstead Minor twinkling in the night below, while himself was still walking shadowless in a sickly dusk.

In the drawing-room of Cobble Place all was calm, as indeed, Michael thought, why on earth should it not be ? Mrs. Carthew's serene old age drove out the last memory of the coroner's court, and here was Mrs. Ross coming out of a circle of lamplight to greet him, and here in Cobble Place was her small son sleeping.

"You look tired and pale, Michael," said Mrs. Ross. "Why didn't you wire which train you were coming by ? I would have met you with the chaise."

"Poor fellow, of course he's tired," said Mrs. Carthew. "A most disturbing experience. Come along. Dinner will do him good."

The notion of suicide began to grow more remote from reality in this room, which had always been to Michael soft and fragrant like a great rose in whose heart, for very despair of being able ever to express in words the perfection of it, one swoons to be buried. The evening went the calm course of countless evenings at Cobble Place. Michael played at backgammon with Mrs. Carthew : Joan Carthew worked at the accounts of a parochial charity : May Carthew knitted : Mrs. Ross, reading in the lamplight, met from time to time Michael's glances with a concern that never displayed itself beyond the pitch of an unexacting sympathy. He was glad, as the others rustled to greet the ten strokes of the clock, to hear Mrs. Ross say she would stay up for awhile and keep him company.

"Unless you want to work ? " she added.

Michael shook his head.

When the others had gone to bed, he turned to her :

"Do you know, Mrs. Ross, I believe I could have prevented Prescott's death. He began to talk about Stella, and I felt embarrassed and came away."

"Oh, my dear Michael, I think you're probably accusing

yourself most unfairly. How could you have supposed the terrible sequel to your dinner ?."

" That's just it. I believe I did know."

" You thought he was going to kill himself ? "

" No, I didn't think anything so definite as that, but I had an intuition to ask him to come away with me, and I was afraid he'd think it rather cheek and, oh, Mrs. Ross, what on earth good am I ? I believe I've got the gift of understanding people, and yet I'm afraid to use it. Shall I ever learn ?"

Michael looked at Mrs. Ross in despair. He was exasperated by his own futility. He went on to rail at himself.

" The only gift I have got! And then my detestable self-consciousness wrecks the first decent chance I've had to turn it to account."

They talked for some time. At first Mrs. Ross consoled him, insisting that imagination affected by what had happened later was playing him false. Then she seemed to be trying to state an opinion which she found it difficult to state. She spoke to Michael of qualities which in the future with one quality added would show his way in the world clear and straight before him. He was puzzled to guess at what career she was hinting.

" My dear Michael, I would not tell you for anything," she affirmed.

" Why not ? "

" Why not ? Why because with all the ingenuous proclamations of your willingness to do anything that you're positive you can do better than anything else, I'm quite quite sure you're still the rather perverse Michael of old, and as I sit here talking to you I remember the time when I told you as a little boy that you would have been a Round-head in the time of the Great Rebellion. How angry you were with me. So what I think you're going to do—I almost said when you're grown up—but I mean, when you leave Oxford, I shall have to tell you after you have made up your own mind. I shall have to give myself merely the pleasure of saying, ' I knew it.' "

" I suppose really I know what you think I shall do," said Michael slowly. " But you're wrong—at least I think you're wrong. I lack the mainspring of the parson's life. Talk to me about Kenneth instead of myself. How's he getting on ? "

" Oh, he's splendid at five years old, but I want to give him something more than I ever managed to give you."

" Naturally," said Michael, smiling. " He's your son."

" Michael, would you be surprized if I told you that I thought of . . ." Mrs. Ross broke off abruptly. " No, I won't tell you yet."

" You're full of unrevealed mysteries," said Michael.

" Yes, it's bedtime for me. Good-night."

Two mornings later Michael had a letter from his mother in London. He wondered why he should be vaguely surprised by her hurried return. Surely Prescott's death could not have been a reason to bring her home.

173 CHEYNE WALK,
S.W.

My dearest Michael

I'm so dreadfully upset about poor Dick Prescott. I have so few old friends, so very few, that I can't afford to lose him. His devotion to your father was perfectly wonderful. He gave up everything to us. He remained in society just enough to be of use to your father, but he was nearly always with us. I think he was fond of me, but he worshipped him. Perhaps I was wrong in trying to encourage the idea of marrying Stella. But I console myself by saying that that had nothing to do with this idea of his to take his own life. You see, when your father died, he found himself alone. I've been so selfishly interested in re-entering life. He had no wish to do so. Michael, I can't

*write anything more about it. Perhaps, dearest boy, you
wouldn't mind giving up some of your time with the Carthews,
and will come back earlier to be with me in London for a little
time.*

Your loving

Mother.

P.S.—I hope the funeral was properly done.

Michael realized with a start the loneliness of his mother,
and in his mood of self-reproachfulness attacked himself for
having neglected her ever since the interests of Oxford had
arisen to occupy his own life so satisfyingly. He told Mrs.
Ross of the letter, and she agreed with him in thinking he
ought to go back to London at once. Michael had only time
for a very short talk with old Mrs. Carthew before the chaise
would arrive.

"There has been a fate upon this visit," said the old
lady. "And I'm sorry for it. I'd promised myself a great
many talks with you. Besides you'll miss Alan now, and he'll
be disappointed, and as for Nancy, she'll be miserable."

"But I must go," Michael said.

"Of course you must go," said Mrs. Carthew thumping
with her stick on the gravel path. "You must always think
first of your mother."

"You told me that before on this very path a long time
ago," said Michael thoughtfully. "I didn't understand so
well why at the time. Now of course," he added shyly, "I
understand everything. I used to wonder what the mystery
could be. I used to imagine all sorts of the most extraordinary things. Prisons and lunatic-asylums amongst
others."

Mrs. Carthew chuckled to herself.

"It's surprizing you didn't imagine a great deal more than
you did. How's Oxford?"

"Ripping," said Michael. "And so was your advice about Oxford. I've never forgotten. It was absolutely right."

"I always am absolutely right," said Mrs. Carthew.

The wheels of the chaise were audible ; and Michael must go at once.

"If I'm alive in two years, when you go down," said Mrs. Carthew, "I'd like to give you some advice about the world. I'm even more infallible about the world. Although I married a sailor, I'm a practical and worldly old woman."

Michael said good-bye to all the family standing by the gate of Cobble Place, to Mrs. Ross with the young Kenneth now in knickerbockers by her side and soon, thought Michael, a subject fit for speculation ; to delightful May and Joan ; to the smiling Carthew cook ; all waving to him in the sunlight with the trim cotoneaster behind them.

It gave Michael a consciousness of a new and most affectionate intimacy to find his mother alone in the house in Cheyne Walk. It was scarcely yet September, and the desolation of London all around seemed the more sharply to intagliate upon his senses the fineness of his mother's figure — set in the frame of that sedate house. They had tea together in her own room, and it struck him with a sudden surprize to see her once again in black. The room with its rose du Barri and clouded pastels sustained her beauty and to her sombre attire lent a deeper poignancy ; or perhaps it was something apart from the influence of the room, this so incontestable pathos, and was rather the effect of the imprisonment of her elusiveness by a chain whose power Michael had not suspected. Always, for nearly as many years as he could remember, when he had kissed her she had seemed to evade the statement of any positive and ordinary affection. Her personality had fluttered for a moment to his embrace and fled more than swiftly. In one moment as Michael kissed her now, the years were swept away, and he was sitting up for an extra half-hour at the seaside, while she with her face flushed by another August sunset was leaning over him. The river became the sea, and the noise of the people on the Embankment were the people walking on the promenade below. In one moment as Michael kissed her now, her embrace gave to him what it had not given during all the years between—a consciousness that he depended upon her life.

"Dearest boy," she murmured, "how good of you to come back so quickly from the Carthews."

"But I would much rather be with you," said Michael.

Indeed as he sat beside her holding her hand, he wondered to himself how he had been able to afford to miss so many opportunities of sitting like this, and immediately afterwards wondered at himself for being able to sit like this without any secret dread that he was making himself absurd by too much demonstrativeness. After all it was very easy to show emotion even to one's mother without being ridiculous.

"Poor Dicky Prescott," she said, and tears quickly blurred her great grey eyes and hung quivering on the shadowy lashes beneath. Michael held her hand closer when he saw she was beginning to cry. He felt no awe of her grief, as he had when she told him of his father's death. This simpler sorrow brought her so much nearer to him. She was speaking of Prescott's death as she might have spoken of the loss of a cherished possession, a dog perhaps or some familiar piece of jewellery.

"I shall never get used to not having him to advise me. Besides he was the only person to whom I could talk about Charles—about your father. Dicky was so bound up with all my life. So long as he was alive, I had some of the past with me."

Michael nodded with comprehending gravity of assent.

"Darling boy, I don't mean that you and darling Stella are not of course much much more deeply precious to me.

You are. But I can't help thinking of that poor dear man, and the way he and Charles used to walk up and down the 'quarter-deck, and I remember once Charles lent him a stud. It's the silly little sentimental memories like that which are so terribly upsetting when they're suddenly taken away."

Now she broke down altogether, and Michael with his arms about her, held her while she wept.

"Dearest mother, when you cry I seem to hold you very safely," he whispered. "I don't feel you'll ever again be able to escape."

She had ceased from her sobbing with a sudden shiver and catch of the breath and looked at him with frightened eyes.

"Michael, he once said that to me . . . before you were born. Before . . . on a hillside it was . . . how terribly well I remember."

Michael did not want her to speak of his father. He felt too helpless in the presence of that memory. The death of Prescott was another matter, a trivial and pathetic thing. Quickly he brought his mother back to that, until she was tired with the flowing of many tears.

Michael spent the rest of the Long Vacation with his mother in London, and gradually he made himself a companion to her. They went to theatres together, because it gave her a sentimental pleasure to think how much poor Dicky Prescott would have enjoyed this piece once upon a time. Between them was the unspoken thought of how much somebody else would have enjoyed this piece also. Michael teazed his mother lightly about her bazaars, until she told him he was turning into a second Prescott himself. He discussed seriously the problem of Stella, but he did not say a word of his hope that she would fall in love with Alan. Alan, however, who was already back in town, came to spend week-ends that were very much like the week-ends spent at Carlington Road in the past. Mrs. Fane enjoyed dining

with her son and his friend... She asked the same sort of
delightfully foolish questions about Oxford that she used
to ask about school. In October Mrs. Carruthers arrived
back in town, and by this time Mrs. Fane was ready to begin
again to flit from charity to charity, and from fad to fad.
Yet however much she seemed to become again her old
elusive exquisite self, Michael never again let her escape
entirely from the intimacy which had been created by the
sentimental shock of Prescott's death, and he went up for
his third year at Oxford with a feeling that somehow during
this vacation he had grown more sure of himself and to his
mother more precious.

"What have you done this vac?" they asked him in
Venner's on the night of reunion.

"Nothing very much," he said, and to himself he thought
less than usual in fact, and yet really in one way such a very
great deal.

Chapter XII : *202 High*

THE large room at 202 High Street which Michael shared with Grainger and Lonsdale was perhaps in the annals of university lodgings the most famous. According to tradition, the house was originally part of the palace of a cardinal. Whether it had been the habitation of ecclesiastical greatness or not, it had certainly harboured grandeur of some kind ; to this testified the two fireplaces surmounted by coats-of-arms in carved oak that enhanced this five-windowed room with a dignity which no other undergraduate lodging could claim. The house at this period was kept by a retired college-cook, who produced for dinner parties wonderful old silver which all his tenants believed to have been stolen from the kitchen of his college. The large room of 202 High gave the house its character, but there were many other rooms besides. Wedderburn, for instance, had on the third storey a sitting-room whose white panelling and Georgian grace had been occupied by generations of the transitory exquisites of art and fashion. Downstairs in the aqueous twilight created by a back-garden was the dining-room which the four of them possessed in common. As for the other lodgers, none were St. Mary's men, and their existence was only alluded to by Michael and his friends when the ex-cook charged them for these strangers' entertainments.

Michael was the first to arrive at Two Hundred and Two, and he immediately set to work to arrange in the way that pleased him best the decorative and personal adjuncts contributed by Grainger, Lonsdale and himself. For his

own library he found a fine set of cupboards which he completely filled. The books of Grainger and Lonsdale he
banished to the dining-room, where their scant numbers
competed for space on the shelves with jars of marmalade,
egg-cups and toast-racks. The inconvenience of the confusion was helpfully obviated first by the fact that their collection, or rather their accumulation, was nearly throughout in
duplicate owing to the similar literary tastes and intellectual travaux forcés of Grainger and Lonsdale, and secondly
by the fact that for a year to neither taste nor intellect was
there frequent resort. With their pictures Michael found
the same difficulty of duplication, but as there were two
fireplaces he took an ingenious delight in supporting each
fireplace with similar pictures, so that Thorburn's grouse,
Cecil Aldin's brilliant billiard-rooms, Sir Galahad and Eton
Society were to be found at either end. Elsewhere on the
spacious walls he hung his own Blakes and Frederick Walkers,
and the engraving of the morning stars singing together
he feathered with the photographic souvenirs of Lonsdale's
fagdom. As for the pictures that belonged to the ex-cook,
mostly very large photogravures of Marcus Stone such as
one sees in the corridors of theatres, these he took upstairs
and with them covered Wedderburn's white-panelled walls
after he had removed the carefully hung Dürers to the
bathroom. This transference wasted a good deal of time,
but gave him enough amusement when Wedderburn
arrived, to justify the operation. The pictures all disposed,
he called for a carpenter to hang Grainger's triumphal oars
and Lonsdale's hunting trophies of masks, pads and brushes,
and surveyed with considerable satisfaction the accumulative effect of the great room now characterized by their
joint possessions. Michael was admiring his work when
Lonsdale arrived and greeted him boisterously.

"Hullo! I say, are we all straight ? How topping !
But wait a bit. I've got something that's going to put the

jolly old lid on this jolly old room. What's the name of the joker who keeps these digs ? Macpherson ? "

He shouted from the landing to the ex-cook.

. "I say, send up the packing-case that's waiting for me downstairs."

Michael enquired what was inside.

"Wait a bit, my son," said the beaming owner. " I've got something in there that's going to make old Wedders absolutely green. I've thought this out. I told my governor I was going into digs with some of the æsthetic push and didn't want to be cut out, so he's lent me this."

"What on earth is it ? " Michael asked on a note of ambiguous welcome.

The packing-case shaped like a coffin had been set down on the floor by the ex-cook and his slave. Lonsdale was wrenching off the top.

"I had a choice between a mummy and a what d'ye call it, and I chose the what d'ye call it," said Lonsdale.

He had torn the last piece of the cover away, and lying in straw was revealed the complete armour of a Samurai.

"Rum-looking beggar. Worth twenty of those rotten statues of Wedderburn's. It was a present to the governor from somebody in the East, but as I promised not to go to dances in it, he lent it to me. Rather sporting of him, what ? Where shall we put him ? "

"I vote we hide it till this evening," suggested Michael, "and then put it in Wedder's bed. He'll think he's in the wrong room."

"Ripping !" cried Lonsdale. "In pyjamas, what ? "

That Japanese warrior never occupied the æsthetic niche that Lord Cleveden from his son's proposal may have thought he would occupy. Otherwise he played an important part in the life of Two Hundred and Two. Never did any visitor come to stay for the week-end, but Sammy, as he was soon called, was set to warm his bed. To Lonsdale,

returning home mildly drunk from Trinity Clareter or
Phœnix Wine, he was always ready to serve as a courteous
listener of his rambling account of an evening's adventures.
He was borrowed by other digs to annoy the landladies: he
went for drives in motor-cars to puzzle country-inns.
Lonsdale tried to make him into a college mascot, and he
drove in state to the St. Mary's grind on the box-seat of
the coach. He was put down on the pavement outside the
lodge with a plate for pennies and a label ' Blind' round his
neck. But Sammy's end was a sad one. He had been sent
to call on the Warden, and was last seen leaning in a despon-
dent attitude against the Warden's gothic door. Whether
the butler broke him up when Sammy fell forward on to his
toes, or whether he was imprisoned eternally in a coal-
cellar, no one knew. Lord Cleveden was informed he had
been stolen.

If Michael had tried hard to find two people in whose
company it would be more difficult to work than with any
other pair in the university, he could scarcely have chosen
better than Lonsdale and Grainger. Neither of them was
reading an Honour School, and the groups called H2 or C3
or X26, that with each term's climax they were compelled
to pass in order to acquire the degree of bachelor of arts,
produced about a week before their ordeal a state of irritable
industry, but otherwise were unheeded. Michael was not
sorry to let his own reading beyond the irreducible minimum
slide during this gay third year. He promised himself a
fourth year, when he would withdraw from this side of
Oxford life and in some cloistered digs work really hard.
Meanwhile he enjoyed 202 High as the quintessence of
youth's amenity.

Some of the most enduring impressions of Oxford were
made now, though they were not perhaps impressions that
marked any development in himself by intellectual achievements or spiritual crises. In fact at the time the impressions

seemed fleeting enough; and it was only when the third year was over, when Two Hundred and Two was dismantled of every vestige of this transient occupation that Michael in summoning these impressions from the past recaptured, often from merely pictorial recollections, as much of Oxford as was necessary to tell him how much Oxford had meant.

There were misty twilights in November when Lonsdale came back spattered with mud after a day with the Bicester or the V.W.H. At such an hour Michael, who had probably been sitting alone by the roaring fire, was always ready to fling away his book and, while Lonsdale grunted and laboured to pull off his riding-boots, to hear the tale of a great run across a great piece of country.

There was the autumn afternoon when Grainger stroked St. Mary's to victory in the Coxwainless Fours. Another oar was hung in Two Hundred and Two, and a bonfire was made in Cuther's quad to celebrate the occasion. Afterwards Grainger himself triumphantly drunk between Michael and Lonsdale was slowly persuaded along the High and put to bed, while Wedderburn prescribed in his deepest voice a dozen remedies.

There were jovial dinner parties when rowing men from Univ and New College sat gigantically round the table and ate gigantically and laughed gigantically, and were taken upstairs to Wedderburn's dim-litten room to admire his statues of Apollo, his old embroideries and his Dürer wood-cuts. These giants in their baggy blanket trousers, their brass-buttoned coats and Leander ties nearly as pink as their own faces made Wedderburn's white Apollos look almost mincing and the embroideries rather insipid. There were other dinner parties even more jovial when the Palace of Delights, otherwise 202 High, entertained the Hotel de Luxe, otherwise 230 High, the abode of Cuffe, Sterne and Sinclair, or the Chamber of Horrors, otherwise 61 Longwall, where Maurice and Castleton lived. After

dinner the guests and the hosts would march arm-in-arm
down to college and be just in time to make a tremendous
noise in Venner's, after which they would visit some of the
second-year men, and with bridge to wind up the evening
would march arm-in-arm up the High and home again.

In the Lent term there were windy afternoons with the
St. Mary's beagles, when after a long run Lonsdale and
Michael would lose the college drag and hire a dogcart in
which they would come spanking back to Oxford with the
March gale dying in their wake and the dusk gathering
fast. In the same term there was a hockey cup-match, when
St. Mary's was drawn to play an unfamiliar college on the
enemy's ground. 202 High wondered how on earth such
an out-of-the-way ground could possibly be reached, and
the end of it was that a coach was ordered in which a dozen
people drove the mile or so to the field of play, with Lonsdale blowing the horn all the way down High Street and
Cornmarket Street and the Woodstock Road.

Michael during the year at Two Hundred and Two
scarcely saw anybody who was not in the heart of the main
athletic vortex of the university. In one way his third year
was a retrogression, for he was nearer to the life of his first
year than to his second. The Oxford Looking-Glass had
created for him a society representing various interests.
This was now broken up, partly by the death of the paper,
partly by the more highly intensified existence of the
founders. Maurice certainly remained the same and was
already talking of starting another paper. But Wedderburn
was beginning to think of a degree and was looking forward
to entering his father's office and becoming in another year
a prosperous partner in a prosperous firm. Guy Hazlewood
had gone down and was away in Macedonia, trying to
fulfil a Balliol precept to mix yourself up in the affairs of
other nations or your own as much as possible. Townsend
and Mowbray thought now of nothing but of being elected

President of the Union, and as Michael was not a member and hated politics he scarcely saw them. Nigel Stewart had gone to Ely Theological College. The Oxford Looking-Glass was shattered into many pieces. Alan, however, Michael saw more often than last year, because Alan was very popular at Two Hundred and Two.

Michael more and more began to assume the opinions and the attitude of his companions. He began more and more rigidly to apply their somewhat naïve standards in his judgement of the world. He was as intolerant and contemptuous as his friends of any breach of what he almost stated to himself as the public-school tradition. Oxford was divided into Bad Men and Good Eggs. The Bad Men went up to London and womanized—some even of the worst womanized in Oxford: they dressed in a style that either by its dowdiness or its smartness stamped them: they wore college-colours round their straw-hats and for their ties: they were quiet, surreptitious, diligent, or blatantly rowdy in small sections, and at least half the colleges in the Varsity contained nothing but Bad Men. The Good Eggs went up to London and got drunk; and if they womanized no one must know anything about it. Drink was the only vice that should be enjoyed communely; in fact if it were enjoyed secretly, it transformed the victim into the very worst of Bad Men. The Good Eggs never made a mistake in dress: they only wore old school-colours or Varsity club-colours: they were bonhomous, hearty, careless and rowdy in large groups. Only the men from about eight colleges were presumed to be Good Eggs: the rest of the Varsity had to demonstrate its goodness.

Michael sometimes had misgivings about this narrowly selected paucity of Good Eggs. He never doubted that those chosen were deservedly chosen, but he did sometimes speculate whether in the masses of the Bad Men there might not be a few Good Eggs unrecognized as Eggs, un-

honoured for their Goodness. Yet whenever he made an
excursion into the midst of the Bad Men, he was always
bound to admit the refreshment of his very firm prejudice
in favour of the Good Eggs. What was so astonishing about
Good Eggery was the members' obvious equipment for citizen-
ship of the world as opposed to the provincialism of Bad
Mannery. Unquestionably it was possible to meet the most
intelligent, the most widely-read Bad Men; but intellect
and culture were swamped by their barbarous self-proclama-
tion. They suffered from an even bitterer snobbishness
than the Good Eggs. In the latter case, the snobbishness
was largely an inherited pride : with the Bad Men it was
obviously an acquired vanity. Where, however, Michael
found himself at odds with Good Eggery was in the admission to titular respect of the Christ Church blood. This
growing toleration was being conspicuously exemplified
in the attitude of St. Mary's, that most securely woven and
most intimate nest of Good Eggery.

When Michael had first come up there had been an inclination at his college to regard with as much contemptuous indifference an election to the Bullingdon as an election
to the Union. It was tacitly understood at St. Mary's
that nothing was necessary to enhance the glory of being a
St. Mary's man. Gradually, however, the preponderance
of Etonian influence outweighed the conventional self-
sufficiency of the Wykehamists, and several men in Michael's
year joined the Bullingdon, one of the earliest of these
destroyers of tradition being Lonsdale. The result of this
action was very definitely a disproportion in the individual
expenditure of members of the college. St. Mary's had
always been a college for relatively rich men, but in accordance with the spirit of the college to form itself into an
aristocratic republic, it had for long been considered bad-
form to spend more than was enough to sustain each member
of this republic on an equality with his fellows.

Now Lonsdale was so obviously a Good Egg that it did not matter when he played with equal zest roulette and polo or hunted three times a week or wore clothes of the last extreme of fashion. But Michael and Grainger were not sure they cared very much for all of Lonsdale's friends from the House. Certainly they were Etonians and members of the Bullingdon, but so many of their names were curiously familiar from the hoardings of advertizements that neither Michael nor Grainger could altogether believe in their assumption of the privilege of exclusion on the ground of inherited names.

"I think these Bullingdon bloods are rather rotters," protested Michael after an irritating evening of vacuous wealth.

"I *must* ask them in sometimes," apologized Lonsdale.

"Why ? " rumbled Wedderburn, and on his note of interrogation the Bullingdon bloods were impaled to swing unanneled.

"I don't think all this sort of thing is very good for the college," debated Grainger. "It's all very well for you, Lonny, but some of the second-year men behave rather stupidly. Personally I hate roulette at St. Mary's. As for some of the would-be fresher bloods, they're like a lot of damned cavalry subalterns."

"You can't expect the college to be handed over entirely to the rowing push," said Lonsdale.

"That's better than turning Venner's into Tattersall's," said Wedderburn.

The effect of enlarging the inclusiveness of Good Eggery was certainly to breed a suspicion that it was largely a matter of externals ; and therefore amongst the St. Mary's men who disliked the application of money as a social standard an inclination grew up to suppose that Good Eggery might be enlarged on the other side. The feeling of the college, that elusive and indefinable aroma of opinion, declared itself

⁻unmistakably in this direction, and many Bad Men became Good Eggs.

" We're all growing older," said Michael to Wedderburn in explanation of the subtle change manifesting itself. " And I suppose a little wiser. Castleton will be elected President of the J.C.R. at the end of this year. Not Tommy Grainger, although he'll be President of the O.U.B.C., not Sterne, although he'll be in the Varsity Eleven. Castleton will be elected because he never has believed and he never will believe in mere externals."

Nevertheless for all of his third year, with whatever fleeting doubts he had about the progress of St. Mary's along the lines laid down by the Good Eggery of earlier generations, Michael remained a very devoted adherent of the principle. He was able to perceive something more than mere externals in the Best Eggery. This was not merely created by money or correct habiliment or athletic virtuosity. This existed inherently in a large number of contemporary undergraduates. Through this they achieved the right to call themselves the Best. It was less an assertion of snobbishness than of faith. Good Eggery had really become a religion. It was not inconsistent with Christianity : indeed it probably derived itself from Christianity through many mailclad and muscular intercedents. Yet it shrank from anything definitely spiritual as it would have shrunk from the Salvation Army. Men who intended to be parsons were of course exceptions, but parsons were regarded as a facet of the existing social order rather than as trustees for the heirs of universal truth. Social service was encouraged by fashion, so long as it meant no more than the supporting of the College Mission in the slums of Bristol by occasional week-ends. Members of the college would play billiards in the club for dockhands under or over seventeen, would subscribe a guinea a year, and as a great concession would attend the annual report in the J.C.R.

There must however be no more extravagance in religion and social service than there should be in dress. The priestly caste of Good Eggery was represented not by the parsons, but by the schoolmasters and certain dons. The schoolmasters were the most powerful, and tried to sustain the legend common to all priestly castes that they themselves made the religion rather than that they were mere servants of an idea. Mature Good Eggs affected to laugh at the schoolmasters whose leading-strings they had severed, but an instinctive fear endured, so that in time to come Good Egglets would be handed over for the craft to mould as they had moulded their fathers. It could scarcely be denied that schoolmasters like priests were disinclined to face facts : it was indubitable that they lived an essentially artificial life : it was certain that they fostered a clod-headed bigotry, that they were tempted to regard themselves as philanthropists, that they feared dreadfully the intrusion of secular influence. It could scarcely be denied that the Schoolmasterdom of England was a priestcraft as powerful and arrogant as any which had ever been. But they were gentlemen, that is to say they shaved oftener than Neapolitan priests; they took a cold bath in the morning, which probably Calvin's ministers never did ; they were far more politely restrained than the Bacchantes and not less chaste than the Vestal Virgins. These clean and honest, if generally rather stupid gentlemen, were the wielders of that afflatus, — the public-school spirit, and so far as Michael could see at present, Good Eggs were more safe morally with that inspiration than they might have been with any other. And if a touch of mysticism were needed, it might be supplied by Freemasonry at the Apollo Lodge; while the Boy Scouts were beginning to show how admirably this public-school spirit could blow through the most unpromising material of the middle-classes.

Michael so much enjoyed the consciousness of merit

which is the supreme inducement offered by all successful religions, and more than any by Good Eggery, that he made up his mind quite finally that Good Eggery would carry him through his existence, however much it were complicated by the problem of Bad Mannery. During that year at Two Hundred and Two he grew more and more deeply convinced that to challenge any moral postulate of Good Eggery was merely contumacious self-esteem. One of the great principles of Good Eggery was that the Good Egg must only esteem himself as a valuable unit in Good Eggery. His self-esteem was entitled to rise in proportion with the distance he could run or kick or throw or hit.

Analyzed sharply, Michael admitted that Good Eggery rested on very frail foundations, and it was really surprizing with what enthusiasm it managed to sustain the Good Eggs themselves, so that apparently without either spiritual exaltation or despair, without disinterested politics or patriotism, without any deep humanity even, the Good Eggs were still so very obviously good. Certainly the suicide of Prescott made Michael wonder how much that rather ignominious surrender by such a Good Egg might have been avoided with something profounder than Good Eggery at the back of life's experience. But suicide was an accident, Michael decided, and could not be used in the arguments against the fundamental soundness of Good Eggery as the finest social nourishment in these days of a bourgeoning century.

Meanwhile at St. Mary's the Good Eggs flourished, and time went by with unexampled swiftness. In the last days of the Lent term, after St. Mary's had been defeated by Christ Church in the final of the Association Cup, Michael, Grainger and Lonsdale determined to drown woe by a triple Twenty-firster. Every contemporary Good Egg in St. Mary's and several from other colleges were invited. Forty Good Eggs groomed and polished and starched sat down at the Clarendon to celebrate this triple majority. Upon that banquet age did not lay one hesitant touch. The attainment of discretion was celebrated in what might almost have been hailed as a debauch of youthfulness. Forty Good Eggs drank forty-eight bottles of Perrier Jouet '93. They drank indeed the last four dozen gages of that superb summer stored in the J.C.R., the last four dozen lachrymatories of the 1893 sun, nor could it be said that vintage of Champagne had funeral games unworthy of its foam and fire. Forty Good Eggs went swinging out of the Clarendon about half-past nine o'clock, making almost more noise than even the Corn had ever heard. Forty Good Eggs went swinging along towards Carfax, swinging and singing, temporarily deified by the last four dozen of Perrier Jouet '93. Riotous feats were performed all down the High. Two trams were unhorsed. Hansoms were raced. Bells were rung. Forty Good Eggs, gloriously, ravishingly drunk, surged into the lodge. There was just time to see old Venner. In the quiet office was pandemonium. Good Eggs were dancing hornpipes; Good Eggs were steadying themselves with cognac; Good Eggs were gently herded out of the little office as ten o'clock chimed. "Bonner! Bonner!" the forty Good Eggs shouted and off they went not to St. Cuthbert's, but actually to the great lawn in front of New Quad. Third-year men when they did come into college roaring drunk took no half-measures of celebration. Excited freshmen and second-year men came swarming out of Cloisters, out of Parsons' Quad, out of Cuther's to support these wild seniors. What a bonfire it was! Thirty-one chairs, three tables, two doors, twelve lavatory seats, every bundle of faggots in college and George Appleby's bed. Somebody had brought Roman candles. O exquisite blue and emerald stars! Somebody else had brought Chinese crackers as big as red chimneys. O sublime din! Lonsdale was on the roof of Cloisters trying to kill a gargoyle with hurtling syphons. Michael was tossing up all by himself to decide whether he should tell the Senior Tutor or the Warden what he really thought of him. A fat welterweight, a straggler from New College, had been shorn of his coat-tails, and was plunging about like an overgrown Eton boy. With crimson faces and ruffled hair and scorched shirt-fronts the guests of the Twenty-firster acclaimed to-night as the finest tribute ever paid to years of discretion.

Next morning the three hosts paid ten guineas each to the Dean.

" I thought you people were supposed to have come of age," he said sardonically.

So incomparably slight was the hang-over from Perrier Jouet '93 that Grainger, Lonsdale and Michael smiled very cheerfully, produced their cheque-books and would, if Mr. Ambrose had not been so discouraging, have been really chatty.

After Collections of Lent term, that opportunity accepted by the college authorities to be offensive in bulk, Michael felt his historical studies were scarcely betraying such an impulse towards research as might have been expected of him at this stage. Mr. Harbottle, the History tutor, an abrupt and pleasant man with the appearance of a cat and the manners of a dog, yapped vituperations from where he sat with all the other dons in judgement along the High Table in Hall.

The Warden turned on his orbit and shone full-faced upon Michael.

" A little more work, Mr. Fane, will encourage us all. Your Collection papers have evidently planted a doubt in Mr. Harbottle's mind."

" He never does a stroke of honest work, Warden," yapped the History tutor. " If he stays up ten years he'll never get a Fourth."

" In spite of Mr. Harbottle's discouraging prophecy, we

must continue to hope, Mr. Fane, that you will obtain at least a Second next term."

"Next term!" Michael gasped. "But I was expecting to take Schools next year."

"I'm afraid," said the Warden, "that according to Mr. Ambrose the fabric of the college will scarcely survive another year of your residence. I believe I echo your views, Mr. Ambrose?"

The Dean blinked his grey eye and finally said that, possibly Mr. Fane would change next term, adding that a more immediately serious matter was a deficit of no less than seven chapels. Michael pointed out that he designed in his fourth year to go as it were into industrious solitude far away from St. Mary's.

"Are you suggesting Iffley?" enquired the Warden.

"Oh, no, not so far as that, but right away," said Michael. "Somewhere near Keble. Miles away."

"But we have to consider next term," the Warden urged. "Next term, I take it, you will still be occupied with the fashionable distractions of High Street?"

"I'll make an offer," barked Mr. Harbottle. "If he likes to do another Collection paper at the beginning of next term, and does it satisfactorily, I will withdraw my opposition, and as far as I'm concerned he can take his Schools next year."

"What luck?" asked everybody in the lodge when Michael had emerged from the ordeal.

"I had rather a hot time," said Michael. "Still, Harbottle behaved like a gentleman on the whole."

Maurice arrived in the lodge soon after Michael, and conveyed the impression that he had left the tutorial forces of the college reeling under the effect of his witty cannonade. Then Michael went off to interview the Dean in order to adjust the difficulty which had been created by the arrears of his early rising. With much generosity he admitted

the whole seven abstentions, and was willing not merely to
stay up a week to correct the deficit, but suggested that
he should spend all the Easter vacation working in Oxford.

So it fell out that Michael managed to secure his fourth
year, and in the tranquillity of that Easter vacation it
seemed to him that he began to love Oxford for the first
time with a truly intense passion and that a little learning
was the least tribute he could offer in esteem. It was strange
how suddenly history became charged with magic. Perhaps
the Academic Muse sometimes offered this inspiration,
if one spent hours alone with her. Michael was sad when the
summer term arrived in its course. So many Good Eggs
would be going down for ever after this term, and upon
Two Hundred and Two High brooded the shadow of
dissolution.

Alan again hovered on the edge of the Varsity Eleven,
but a freshman who bowled rather better the same sort of
ball came up, and it seemed improbable he would get his
Blue. However, the disappointment was evidently not so
hard for Alan to bear nowadays. He was indeed becoming
gravely interested in philosophy, and Michael was forced to
admit that he seemed to be acquiring most unexpectedly a
real intellectual grasp of life. So much the better for their
companionship next year in those rooms in St. Giles' which
Michael had already chosen.

The summer term was going by fast. It was becoming an
experience almost too fugitive to be borne, this last summer
term at Two Hundred and Two. Michael, Grainger and
Lonsdale had scarcely known how to endure some offensive
second-year men from Oriel being shown their room for
next year. They resented the thought of these Oriel men
leaning out of the window and throwing cushions at their
friends and turning to the left to keep a chapel at Oriel,
instead of scudding down to St. Mary's on the right.
Wedderburn was always the one who voiced sentimentally

the unexpressed regrets of the other three. He it was who spoke of the grime and labour of the paternal office, of Life with a capital letter as large as any lady novelist's, and of how one would remember these evenings and the leaning-out over a cushioned window-sill and the poring upon this majestic street.

"We don't realize our good luck until it's too late really," said Wedderburn seriously. "We've wasted our time, and now we've got to go."

"Well, dash it all, Wedders," said Lonsdale, "don't talk as if we were going to bolt for a train before hall. We aren't going down for three weeks yet, and jolly old Michael and jolly old Tommy aren't going down for another year."

"Lucky devils," sighed Wedderburn. "By gad, if I only had my time at the Varsity all over again."

But just when Wedderburn had by his solemnity almost managed really to impress the company with a sense of fleeting time, and when even upon Lonsdale was descending the melancholy of the deep-dyed afternoon, across the road they could see sauntering three men whom they all knew well.

"Tally-ho-ho-ho-whooop!" shouted Lonsdale.

The three men saluted thus came upstairs to the big room of Two Hundred and Two, and a bout of amiable ragging and rotting passed away the hour before dinner and restored to the big room itself the wonted air of imperishable good-fellowship.

"Lucky you lads turned up," said Lonsdale. "Old Wedders has been moping in this window-seat like a half-plucked pigeon. We're dining in hall to-night, are you?"

The new-comers were dining in hall, and so in a wide line of brilliant ties and ribbons the seven of them strolled down to college.

There were very few people in hall that night, and Venner's was pleasantly empty. Venner himself was full of anecdotes, and as they sat on the table in the middle of

the room, drinking their coffee, it seemed impossible enough
to imagine that they would not be for ever here drinking
their coffee on a fine June evening.

"Going down soon, Venner," said Wedderburn, who was
determined to make somebody sad.

"What a pity you're not taking a fourth year," said
Venner. "You ought to have read an Honour School. I
always advise the men to read for honours. The dons like
it, you know."

"Got to go and earn my living, Venner," said Wedderburn.

"That's right," said Venner cheerfully. "Then you'll
be married all the sooner, or perhaps you're not a marrying
man."

"Haven't found the right girl yet, Venner," said Wedderburn.

"Oh, there's plenty of time," chuckled Venner. "You
don't want to be thinking about girls up here. Some of our
men go getting engaged before they've gone down, and it
always messes them up in the Schools."

Maurice Avery came in while Venner was speaking. He
seemed restless and worried, and as Venner went on his
restlessness increased.

"But very few of our men have got into trouble here with
girls. We had one man once who married a widow. He
was dreadfully chaffed about it, and couldn't stand it any
longer. The men never let him alone."

"Married a widow, while he was still up ? " people asked
incredulously.

"Why, yes," said Venner. "And actually brought her
down for Eights and introduced her to the Warden on the
barge. She was a most severe-looking woman, and old
enough to be his mother. There was some trouble once at
202 High—that's where you are, isn't it ? " He turned to
Lonsdale. "But there won't be any more trouble because

Macpherson vowed he wouldn't have a servant-girl in the house again."

"I suppose that's why we have that perspiring boy," grumbled Wedderburn. "But what happened, Venner?"

"Well, the usual thing, of course. There were five of our men living there that year, and she picked out the quietest one of the lot and said it was him. He had to pay £50, and when he'd paid it all, the other four came up to him one by one and offered to pay half."

Everybody laughed, and Maurice suddenly announced that he was in a devil of a fix with a girl.

"A girl at a village near here," he explained. "There's no question of her having a baby or anything like that, you know; but her brother followed me home one night, and yesterday her father turned up. I got Castleton to talk to him. But it was damned awkward. He and old Castleton were arguing like hell in our digs."

Maurice stopped and, lighting a cigarette, looked round him as if expectant of the laughter which had hailed Venner's story. Nobody seemed to have any comment to make, and Michael felt himself blushing violently for his friend.

"Bit chilly in here to-night, Venner," said Lonsdale.

"You are a confounded lot of prigs," said Maurice angrily, and he walked out of Venner's just as Castleton came in.

"My dear old Frank Castleton," said Lonsdale immediately, "I love you very much and I think your hair is beautifully brushed, but you really must talk to our Mr. Avery very very seriously. He mustn't be allowed to make such a bee-luddy fool of himself by talking like a third-rate actor."

"What do you mean?" asked Castleton gruffly.

Lonsdale explained what Maurice had done, and Castleton looked surprized, but he would not take part in the condemnation.

" You're all friends of his in here," he pointed out. " He probably thought it was a funny story." There was just so much emphasis on the pronoun as made the critics realize that Castleton himself was really more annoyed than he had superficially appeared.

An awkwardness had arisen through the inculpation of Maurice, and everybody found they had work to do that evening. Quickly Venner's was emptied.

Michael, turning out of Cloisters to stroll for awhile on the lawns of New Quad before he gave himself to the generalizations of whatever historian he had chosen to beguile this summer night, came up to Maurice leaning over the parapet by the Cher.

" Hullo, are you going to condescend to speak to me after the brick I dropped in Venner's ? " asked Maurice bitterly.

" I wish you wouldn't be so theatrically sarcastic," complained Michael, who was half-unconsciously pursuing the simile which lately Lonsdale had found for Maurice's behaviour.

" Well, why on earth," Maurice broke out, " it should be funny when Venner tells a story about some old St. Mary's man and yet be——" he paused, evidently too vain, thought Michael a little cruelly, to stigmatize himself—" and yet be considered contrary to what is *done* when I tell a story about myself, I don't quite know, I must admit."

" It was the introduction of the personal element which made everybody feel uncomfortable," said Michael. " Venner's tale had acquired the impersonality of a legend."

" Oh, god, Michael, you do talk rot sometimes," said Maurice fretfully. " It's nothing on earth but offensive and very youthful priggishness."

" I wonder if I sounded like you," said Michael, " when I talked rather like you at about seventeen."

Maurice spluttered with rage at this, and Michael saw it would be useless to remonstrate with him reasonably. He blamed himself for being so intolerant and for not having with kindlier tact tried to point out why he had made a mistake; and yet with all his self-reproach he could not rid himself of what was something very near to active dislike of Maurice at that moment.

But Maurice went on, unperceiving.

"I hate this silly pretence up here—and particularly at St. Mary's—that nobody ever looks at a woman. It's nothing but infernal hypocrisy. Upon my soul, I'm glad I'm going down this term. I really couldn't have stood another year, playing with the fringe of existence. It seems to me, Michael, if you're sincere in this attitude of yours, you'll have a very dismal waking up from your dream. As for all the others, I don't count them. I'm sick of this schoolboy cant. Castleton's worth everybody else in this college put together. He was wonderful with that hulking fellow who came banging at the door of our digs. I wonder what you'd have done, if you'd been digging with me."

"Probably just what Castleton did," said Michael coldly. "You evidently weren't at home. Now I must go and work. So long."

He left Maurice abruptly, angry with him, angry with himself. What could have induced Maurice to make such a fool of himself in Venner's? Why hadn't he been able to perceive the difference of his confession from Venner's legendary narration which, unfettered by the reality of present emotions, had been taken under the protection of the comic spirit? The scene in retrospect appeared improbable, just as improbable in one way, just as shockingly improbable as the arrival of an angry rustic father at some Varsity digs in Longwall. And why had he made the recollection worse for himself by letting Maurice enlarge upon his indignation? It had been bad enough before, but that petulant outbreak had turned an accidental vulgarity into vulgarity itself most cruelly vocal. Back in Two Hundred

3 C

and Two, Michael heard the comments upon Maurice, and as Grainger and Lonsdale delivered their judgement, he felt they had all this time tolerated the offender merely for a certain capacity he possessed for entertainment. They spoke of him now, as one might speak of a disgraced servant.

" Oh, let Maurice drop," said Michael wearily. " It was one of those miserable aberrations from tact which can happen to anybody. I've done the same sort of thing myself. It's an involuntary spasm of bad manners, like sneezing over a crowded railway-carriage."

" Well, I suppose one must make allowances," said Grainger. "These artistic devils are always liable to breaks."

" That's right," said Michael. " Hoist the Union Jack. It's an extraordinary thing, the calm way in which an Englishman is always ready to make art responsible for everything."

Next day Maurice overtook Michael on the way to a lecture.

" I say," he began impetuously, " I made an awful fool of myself yesterday evening. What shall I do ?"

" Nothing," said Michael.

" I was really horribly worried, you know, and I think I rather jumped at the opportunity to get the beastly business off my chest, as a sort of joke."

" Come and dine at the Palace of Delights this evening," Michael invited. " And tell Frank Castleton to come."

" We can't afford to be critical during the last fortnight of jolly old Two Hundred and Two," said Michael to Lonsdale and Grainger, when they received rather gloomily at first the news of the invitation.

Maurice in the course of the evening managed to reinstate himself. He so very divertingly drew old Wedders on the subject of going down.

The last week of the summer term arrived, and really it was very depressing that so many Good Eggs were irrevocably going to be lost to the St. Mary's J.C.R.

" I think my terminal dinner this term will have to be the same as my first one," said Michael. "Only twice as large."

So they all came, Cuffe and Sterne and Sinclair and a dozen more. And just because so many of the guests were going down, not a word was said about it. The old amiable ragging and rotting went on as if the college jokes of to-night would serve for another lustrum yet, as if Two – Hundred and Two would merely be empty of these familiar faces for the short space of a vacation. Not a pipe was gone from its rack; not a picture was as yet deposed; not a hint was given of change, either by the material objects of the big room or by the merry and intimate community that now thronged it. Then the college tenor was called upon for a song, and perhaps without any intention of melancholy he sang O Moon of My Delight. Scarcely was it possible even for these Good Eggs, so rigidly conscious of each other's rigidity, not to think sentimentally for a moment how well the turning down of that empty glass applied to them. The new mood that descended upon the company expressed itself in reminiscence; and then, as if the sadness must for decency's sake be driven out, the college jester was called upon for the comic song whose hebdomadal recurrence through nine – terms had always provoked the same delirious encore. Everything was going on as usual, and at a few minutes to midnight Auld Lang Syne ought not to have been difficult. It had been sung nearly as often as the comic song, but it was shouted more fervently somehow, less in tune somehow, and the silence at its close was very acute. Twelve o'clock was sounding; the guests went hurrying out; and leaning from the windows of Two Hundred and Two, Grainger, Lonsdale, Wedderburn and Michael heard their footsteps clattering down the High.

" I suppose we'd better begin sorting out our things to-morrow," said Michael.

Chapter XIII : *Plashers Mead*

STELLA came back from Vienna for a month in the summer. Indeed she was already arrived, when Michael reached Cheyne Walk. He was rather anxious to insist directly to her that her disinclination to marry Prescott had nothing to do with his death. Michael did not feel it would be good for Stella at nineteen to believe to that extent in her power. One or two of her letters had betrayed an amount of self-interest that Michael considered unhealthy. With this idea in view, he was surprized when she made no allusion to the subject, and resented a little that he must be the one to lead up to it.

"Oh, don't let's talk of what happened nearly a year ago," protested Stella.

"You were very much excited by it at the time," Michael pointed out.

"Ah, but lots of things have happened since then."

"What sort of things?"

He disapproved of the suggestion that the suicide of a lifelong friend was a drop in the ocean of incident that swayed round Stella.

"Oh, loves and deaths and jealousies and ambitions," said she lightly. "Things do happen in Vienna. It's much more eventful than Paris. I don't know what made me come back to London. I'm missing so much fun."

This implication that he and his mother were dull company for her was really rather irritating.

"You'd better go and look up some of your Bohemian friends," he advised severely. "They're probably all hang-

ing about Chelsea still. It's not likely that any of them
is farther on with his art than he was two years ago. Who
was that bounder you were so fond of, and that girl who
painted ? Clarissa Vine, wasn't she called ? What about
her ?"

"Poor old George," said Stella. "I really must try
and get hold of him. I haven't seen Clarie for some time.
She made a fool of herself over some man."

The result of Michael's sarcastic challenge was actually
a tea-party in the big studio at 173 Cheyne Walk, which
Stella herself described as being like turning out a lumber-
room of untidy emotions.

"They're as queer as old-fashioned clothes," she said.
"But rather touching, don't you think, Michael ? Though
after all," she added pensively, "I haven't gone marching
at a very great pace along that triumphant career of mine.
I don't know that I've much reason to laugh at them. Really
in one way poor Clarie is in a better position than me. At
least she can afford to keep the man she's living with. As
for George Ayliffe, since he gave up trying to paint the girls
he was in love with, he has become ' one of our most promising realists.' "

"He looks it," said Michael sourly.

What had happened to Stella during this last year ? She
had lost nearly all her old air of detachment. Formerly a
radiance of gloriously unpassionate energy had shielded her
from any close contact with the vulgar or hectic or merely
ordinary life round her. Michael had doubted once or twice
the wisdom of smoking cigars and had feared that artistic
license of speech and action might be carried too far, but,
looking back on his earlier opinion of Stella, he realized he
had only been doubtful on his own account. He had never
really thought she ran the least danger of doing anything
more serious in its consequence than would have been enough
to involve him or his mother in a brief embarrassment.

Now, though he was at a loss to explain how he was aware of the change, she had become vulnerable. With this new aspect of her suddenly presented, he began to watch Stella with a trace of anxiety. He was worried that she seemed so restless, so steadily bored in London. He mistrusted the brightening of her eyes, when she spoke of soon going back to Vienna. Then came a week when Stella was much occupied with speculations about the Austrian post, and another week when she was perturbed by what she seemed anxious to suppose its vagaries. A hint from Michael that there was something more attractive in Vienna than a new technique of the piano made her very angry; and since she had always taken him into her confidence before, he tried to persuade himself that his suspicion was absurd and to feel tremendously at ease when Stella packed up in a hurry and went back with scarcely two days' warning of her departure to Vienna.

It was a sign of the new intimacy of relation between himself and his mother that Michael was able to approach naturally the subject of Stella's inquietude.

"My dear boy, I'm just as much worried as you are," Mrs. Fane assured him. "I suppose I ought to have been much more unpleasant than I can ever bear to make myself. No doubt I ought to have forbidden her quite definitely to go back—or perhaps I should have insisted on going back with her. Though I don't know what I would have done in Vienna. They make pastry there, don't they? I daresay there are very good tea-shops."

"I think it would have been better," said Michael firmly. Mrs. Fane turned to him with a shrug of helplessness.

"My dear boy, you know how very unpleasant Stella can be when she is crossed. Really very unpleasant indeed. Girls are so much more difficult to manage than boys. And they begin by being so easy. But after eighteen every month

brings a new problem. Their clothes, you know. And of
course their behaviour."

"It's quite obvious what's the matter," said Michael.
"Funny thing. I've never concerned myself very much with
Stella's love-affairs before, but this time she seemed less
capable of looking after herself."

"Would you like to go out to Vienna?" she suggested.

"Oh, no, really, I must go away and work. Besides I
shouldn't do any good. Nor would you," Michael added
abruptly.

"I wish Dick Prescott were alive," his mother sighed.
"Really, you know, Michael, I was shocked at Stella's
callousness over that business."

"Well, my dear mother, be fair. It wasn't anything to
do with Stella, and she has no conventional affections.
That's one comfort—you do know where you are with her.
Now, let's leave Stella alone and talk about your plans.
You're sure you don't mind my burying myself in the
country? I must work. I'm going down into Oxfordshire
with Guy Hazlewood."

Michael had met Guy the other evening in the lobby of a
theatre. He had come back from Macedonia with the intention of settling somewhere in the country. He was going to
devote himself to poetry, although he exacted Michael's
pledge not to say a word of this plan for fear that people
would accuse him of an affected withdrawal. He was
sensitive to the strenuous creed of his old college, to that
atmosphere of faint contempt which surrounded a man who
was not on the way towards administering mankind or acres.
He had not yet chosen his retreat. That would be revealed
in a flash, if his prayer were to be granted. Meanwhile why
should not Michael accompany him to some Cotswold
village? They would ride out from Oxford on bicycles and
when they had found the ideal inn, they would stay there
through August and September, prospecting the country

round. Michael was flattered by Guy's desire for his companionship. Of all the men he had known, he used to admire Guy the most. Two months with him would be a pleasure he would not care to forego, and it was easy enough to convince himself that he would be powerless to influence Stella in any direction and that anyway, whether he could or could not, it would be more serviceable for her character to win or lose her own battles.

Michael and Guy left Oxford in the mellow time of an afternoon in earliest August and rode lazily along the Cheltenham road. At nightfall, just as the stripling moon sank behind a spinney of firs that crowned the farthest visible dip of that rolling way ahead across the wold, they turned down into Wychford. The wide street of the town sloped very rapidly to a valley of intertwining streams whence the air met them still warm with the stored heat of the day, yet humid and languorous after the dry upland. On either side, as they dipped luxuriously down with their brakes gently whirring, mostly they were aware of many white hollyhocks against the grey houses that were already bloomed with dusk and often tremulous with the voyaging shadows of candlelight. At the Stag Inn they found a great vaulted parlour, a delicate roast of lamb, a salad very fragrant with mint and thyme, cream and gooseberries and ale.

" This is particularly good ale," said Guy.

" Wonderful ale," Michael echoed.

Once again they filled their pewter mugs.

" It seems to me exceptionally rich and tawny," said Guy.

" And it has a very individual tang," said Michael. " Another quart, I think, don't you ? "

" Two, almost," Guy suggested, and Michael agreed at once.

" I vote we stay here," said Guy.

" I'll wire them to send along my books to-morrow," decided Michael.

: :After supper they went on down the street and came to
the low parapet of a bridge in one of whose triangular bays
they stood, leaning over to count in the stream below the
blurred and jigging stars. Behind them in the darkness was
the melodious roar of falling, water, and close at hand the
dusty smell of ivy. Farther exploration might have broken
the spell of mystery; so in silence they pored upon the
gloom; until the rhythmic calm and contemplation were
destroyed by a belated waggon passing over the bridge
behind them. They went back to the Stag and that night
in four-posters slept soundly.

Next morning Michael and Guy went after breakfast to
visit the bridge on which they had stood in the starlight.
It managed curiously to sustain the romantic associations
with which they had endowed it on the night before. A
mighty sycamore, whose roots in their contest with the floods
had long grappled in desperate convolutions with the
shelving bank of the stream below, overshadowed the farther
end : here also at right angles was a line of gabled cottages
crumbling into ruin and much overgrown with creepers.
They may have been old almshouses, but there was no sign
of habitation, and they seemed abandoned to chattering
sparrows whose draggled nests were everywhere visible in
the ivy. Beyond on the other side of the bridge the stream
gurgled towards a sluice that was now silent; and beyond
this, grey buildings deep embowered in elms and sycamores
surrounded what was evidently a mill pool. They walked
on to where the bridge became a road that in contrast with
the massed trees all round them shone dazzlingly in the sunshine. A high grey wall bounded the easterly side; on
the west the road was bordered by a low quickset hedge —
that allowed a view of a wide valley through which the river,
having gathered once more its vagrant streams and brooks,
flowed in prodigal curves of silver as far as the eye could
follow. The hills that rose to right and left of the valley

in bald curves were at this season colourless beside the
vivider green of the water-meadows at their base, which was
generally indeterminate on account of plantations whence
at long intervals the smoke of hidden mills and cottages
ascended. When the road had traversed the width of
the valley, it trifurcated. One branch followed westward the gentle undulations of the valley; a second
ran straight up the hill, disappearing over a stark sky-line
almost marine in its hint of space beyond. The main
branch climbed the hill diagonally to the right and conveyed
a sense of adventure with the milestone which said fifty miles
to an undecipherable town.

Michael and Guy took this widest road for a while, but they
soon paused by a gate to look back at Wychford. The sun
shone high, and the beams slanting transversely through the
smoke of the chimneys in tier upon tier gave the clustered
grey roofs a superficial translucence like that of an uncut
gem. The little town built against the hill nowhere
straggled, and in its fortified economy and simplicity of
line it might have been cut on wood by a mediæval en-
graver. Higher up along the hill's ridge went rocketing
east and west the windswept highway from Oxford over the
wold to Gloucestershire. They traced its course by the
telegraph-poles whose inclinations had so long been governed
by the wind that the mechanic trunks were as much a
natural feature of the landscape as the trees, themselves
not much less lean and sparse. It was a view of such extension that roads more remote were faint scars on the hills,
and the streams of the valley narrowed ultimately to thin
blades of steel. The traffic of generations might be thought
to have converged upon this town, so much did it produce
the effect of waiting upon that hillside, so little sense did it
have of seeming to obtrude its presence upon the surroundings.

Gradually the glances of Guy and Michael came back from

the fading horizons of this wide country to concentrate
first upon the town and then upon the spire that with
glittering weather-vane rose lightly as smoke from the grey
fabric of its church, until finally they must have rested
simultaneously upon a long low house washed by one stream
and by another imprisoned within a small green island.

" It's to let," said Michael.

" I know," said Guy.

The unspoken thought that went sailing off upon the
painted board was only expressed by the eagerness with
which they stared at the proffered house.

" I might be able to take it," said Guy at last.

Michael looked at him in admiration. Such a project
conceived in his company did very definitely mark an
altogether new stage and, as it seemed to him, a somewhat
advanced stage in his relationship with the world.

They discovered the entrance immediately behind the
almshouses in the smell of whose ivy they had lingered on
the bridge last night. They passed through a wooden gateway in a high grey wall and, walking down a stained gravel
path between a number of gnarled fruit-trees trimmed as
espaliers to conform with an antique mode of ensuring
fertility, they came at last round an overgrown corner close
against the house. Seen from the hillside, it had quickly
refined itself to be for them at least the intention of that
great view, of that wide country of etched-in detail. The
just background had been given, the only background that
would have enabled them to esteem all that was offered
here in this form of stone well-ordered, grey, indigenous,
the sober crown of the valley.

Guy from the moment he saw it had determined to take
this house : his enquiries about the rent and the drains, his
discussion of the terms of the agreement, of the dampness
within, of the size of the garden were the merest conventions of the house-hunter, empty questions whose answers

really had very slight bearing on the matter in hand. Here he said to Michael he would retire: here he would live and write poetry: here life would be escorted to the tread of great verse: here an eremite of art he would show forth the austerity of his vocation.

Meanwhile Michael's books arrived, and at Guy's exhortation he worked in the orchard of Plashers Mead—so the small property of some twenty acres was called. Guy was busy all day with decorators and carpenters and masons. The old landlord had immediately surrendered his house to so enterprizing a tenant; an agreement for three years had been signed; and Guy was going to make all ready in summer that this very autumn with what furniture he had he might inhabit his own house set among these singing streams.

Michael found it a little hard to pay the keenest attention to Anson's or to Dicey's entertainment of his curiosity about the Constitution, too much did the idea of Guy's emancipation alluringly rustle as it were in the tree-tops, too much did the thought of Guy's unvexed life draw Michael away from his books. And even if he could blot out Guy's prospect, it was impossible not to follow in fancy the goldfinches to their thistle-fields remote and sunny, the goldfinches with their flighted song.

Summer passed, and Michael did not find that the amount of information he had absorbed quite outweighed a powerful impression, that was shaping in his mind, of having wasted a good deal of time in staring at trees and the funnels of light between them, in listening to the wind and the stream, to the reapers and the progress of time.

One evening in mid-September he and Guy went after supper to see how some newly painted room looked by candlelight. They sat on a couple of borrowed windsor chairs in the whitewashed room that Guy had chosen for his own. Two candles stuck on the mantelpiece burned

with motionless spearheads of gold, and showed to their
great satisfaction that by candlelight as well as by day the
green shelves freshly painted were exactly the green they
had expected. When they blew out the candles, they
realized, such a plenitude of silver light was left behind,
that the full moon of harvest was shining straight in through
the easterly bow window which overhung the stream.

"By gad, what a glorious night," sighed Guy, staring out
at the orchard. "We'll take a walk, shall we?"

They went through the orchard where the pears and
pippins were lustred by the sheen and glister of the moon.
They walked on over grass that sobbed in the dewfall
beneath their footsteps. They faded from the world into
a web of mist where trees rose suddenly like giants before
them and in the depths of whose white glooms on either
side they could hear the ceaseless munching of bullocks at
nocturnal pasturage. Then in a moment they had left the
mist behind them and stood in the heart of the valley,
watching for a while the willows jet black against the moon,
and the gleaming water at their base.

"I wish you were going to be up next term," said
Michael. "I really can hardly bear to think of you here.
You are a lucky devil."

"Why don't you come and join me?" Guy suggested.

"I wish I could. Perhaps I will after next year. And yet
what should I do? I've dreamed enough. I must decide
what I'm going to try to do at any rate. You see I'm not a
poet. Guy, you ought to start a sort of lay monastery—a
house for people to retreat into for the purpose of meditation upon their careers."

"As a matter of fact, it would be a jolly good thing if
some people did do that."

"I don't know," said Michael. "I should get caught in the
web of the meditation. I should hear the world as just now
we heard those bullocks. Guy, Wychford is a place of dreams.

You'll find that. You'll live on and on at Plashers Mead until everything about you turns into the sort of radiant unreality we've seen to-night."

The church-clock with raucous whizz and clangour sounded ten strokes.

"And time," Michael went on, "will come to mean no more than a brief disturbance of sound. Really I'm under the enchantment already. I'm beginning to wonder if life really does hold a single problem that could not be dissolved at once by this powerful moonshine."

Next day Michael said he must go back to London to-morrow since he feared that if he dallied he would never go back. Guy could not dissuade him from his resolve.

"I don't want to spoil my picture of you in this valley," Michael explained. "You know, I feel inclined to put Plashers Mead into the farthest recesses of my heart, so that whatever happens when I go down next year, it will be so securely hidden that I shall have the mere thought of it for a refuge."

"And more than the thought of it, you silly ass," Guy drawled.

They drove together to the railway station five miles away. In the sleepy September heat the slow train puffed in. Hot people with bunches of dahlias were bobbing to one another in nearly all the compartments. Michael sighed.

"Don't go," said Guy. "It's much too hot."

Michael shook his head.

"I must."

Just then a porter came up to tell Guy there were three packing-cases awaiting his disposal in the luggage-office.

"Some of my books," he shouted as the train was puffing out. Michael watched from the window Guy and the porter, the only figures among the wine-dark dahlias of the platform.

"What fun unpacking them," he thought, and leaned back regretfully to survey the placid country gliding past.

Yet even after that secluded and sublunary town where — Guy in retrospect seemed to be moving as remotely as a knight in an old tale, London, or rather the London which shows itself in the neighbourhood of great railway termini, impressed Michael with nearly as sharp a romantic strangeness, so dreadfully immemorial appeared the pale children, leaning over scabrous walls to salute the passing train. Always, as one entered London, one beheld these children haunting the backs of houses whose frontal existence as a mapped-out street was scarcely credible. To Michael they were goblins that lived only in this gulley of fetid sunlight through which the trains endlessly clanged. Riding through London in a hansom a few minutes later the people of the city became unreal to him, and only those goblin-children remained in his mind as the natural inhabitants. He drove on through the quiet streets and emerged in that space of celestial silver which was called Chelsea; but the savage roar of the train, as it had swept through those gibbering legions of children, was still in Michael's ears when the hansom pulled up before the sedate house in Cheyne Walk.

The parlourmaid showed no surprize at his unexpected arrival, and informed him casually with no more indication of human interest than would have been given by a clock striking its mechanical message of time that Miss Stella was in the studio. That he should have been unaware of his sister's arrival seemed suddenly to Michael a too intimate revelation of his personality to the parlourmaid, and he actually found himself taking the trouble to deceive this machine by an affectation of prior knowledge. He was indeed caught up and imprisoned by the coils of infinitely small complications that are created by the social stirrings of city life. The pale children seen from the train sank below the level of ordinary existence, no longer conspicuous in his memory, no longer even faintly disturbing. As for Plashers Mead and the webs of the moon, they were become the adventure of a pleasant dream. He was in fact back in town.

Michael went quickly to the studio and found Stella not playing as he hoped, but sitting listless. Then he realized how much at the very moment the parlourmaid told him of Stella's return he had feared such a return was the prelude to disaster. Almost he had it on his lips to ask abruptly what was the matter. It cost him an effort to greet her with just that amount of fraternal cordiality which would not dishonour by its demonstrativeness this studio of theirs. He was so unreasonably glad to see her back from Vienna that a gesture of weakness on her side would have made him kiss her.

"Hullo, I didn't expect to see you," was however all he said.

"Nor did I you," was what she answered.

Presently she began to give him an elaborate account of the journey from Austria, and Michael knew that exactly in proportion to its true insignificance was the care she bestowed upon its dreariness and dust.

Michael began to wish it were not exactly a quarter-of-an-hour before lunch. Such a period was too essentially consecrated to orderly ideas and London smoothness for it to admit the intrusion of anything more disturbing than the sound of a gong. What could have brought Stella back from Vienna?

"Did you come this morning?" he asked.

"Oh, no. Last night. Why?" she demanded. "Do I look as crumpled as all that?"

For Stella to imply so directly that something had happened which she had expected to change materially even her outward appearance was perhaps a sign he would soon be granted her confidence. He rather wished she would be quick with it. If he were left too long to form his own explanations, he would be handicapped at the crucial moment. Unless indeed he were imagining all this, he thought in supplement, as the lunch-gong restored by its clamour the atmosphere of measured life where nothing really happens.

After lunch Stella went up to her room : the effect of the journey, she turned round to say, still called for sleep. Michael did not see her again before dinner. She came down then, looking very much older than he had ever seen her, whether because she was dressed in oyster-grey satin or was in fact much older, Michael did not know. She grumbled at him for not putting on a dinner jacket.

"Don't look so horrified at the notion," she cried petulantly. "Can't you realize that after a year with long-haired students I want a change ? "

After dinner Michael asked her to come and play in the studio.

"Play ? " she echoed. " I'm never going to play again."

"What perfect rot you are talking," said Michael in a damnatory generalization which was intended to cover not merely all she had been saying, but even all she had been doing almost since she first announced her intention of going to Vienna.

Stella burst into tears.

"Come on, let's go to the studio," said Michael. He felt that Stella's tears were inappropriate to the dining-room. Indeed only the fact that she was wearing this evening frock of oyster-grey satin, and was therefore not altogether the invulnerable and familiar and slightly boyish Stella imprinted on his mind, prevented him from being shocked to the point of complete emotional incapacity. It seemed less of an outrage to fondle however clumsily this forlorn creature in grey satin, even though he did find himself automatically and grotesquely saying to himself 'Enter

3 D

Tilburina stark mad in white satin and the Confidante stark mad in white muslin.'

"Come along, come along," he begged her. "You must come to the studio."

Michael went on presenting the studio with such earnestness that he himself began to endow it with a positively curative influence; but when at last Stella had reached the studio, not even caring apparently whether on the way the parlourmaid saw her tears, and when she had plunged disconsolately down upon the divan, still weeping, Michael looked round at their haven with resentment. After all it was merely an ungainly bleak whitewashed room, and Stella was crying more bitterly than before.

"Look here, I say, why don't you tell me what you're crying about? You can't go on crying for ever, you know," Michael pointed out. "And when you've stopped crying, you'll feel such an ass if you haven't explained what it was all about."

"I couldn't possibly tell anybody," said Stella looking very fierce. Then suddenly she got up, and so surprizing had been her breakdown that Michael scarcely stopped to think that her attitude was rather unusually dramatic.

"But I'm damned if I *will* give up playing," she proclaimed; and, sitting down at the piano, forthwith she began to play into oblivion her weakness.

It was a very exciting piece she played, and Michael longed to ask her what it was called, but he was afraid to provoke in her any renewal of self-consciousness; so he enjoyed the fiery composition and Stella's calm with only a faint regret that he would never know its name and would never be able to ask her to play it again. When she had finished, she swung round on the stool and asked him what had happened to Lily Haden.

"I don't know—really—they've left Trelawny Road," he said feeling vaguely an unfair flank attack was being delivered.

" And you never think of her, I suppose ? " demanded Stella.

" Well, no, I don't very much."

" Yet I can remember," said Stella, " when you were absolutely miserable because she had been flirting with somebody else."

" Yes, I was very miserable," Michael admitted. " And you were rather contemptuous about it, I remember. You told me I ought to be more proud."

" And don't you realize," Stella said, " that just because I did remember what I told you, I made my effort and began to play the piano again ? "

Michael waited. He supposed that she would now take him into her confidence, but she swung round to the keyboard, and when she had finished playing she had become herself again, detached and cool and masterful. It was incredible that the wet ball of a handkerchief half-hidden by a cushion could be her handkerchief.

Michael made up his mind that Stella's unhappiness was due to a love-affair which had been wrecked either by circumstance or temperament, and he tried to persuade himself of his indignation against the unknown man. He was sensible of a desire to punch the fellow's head. With the easy exaggerations of the night-time he could picture himself fighting duels with punctilious Austrian noblemen. He went so far as mentally to indite a letter to Alan and Lonsdale requesting their secondary assistance. Then the memory of Lily began to dance before him. He forgot about Stella in speculations about Lily. Time had softened the trivial and shallow infidelity of which she had been guilty. Time with night for ally gave her slim form an ethereal charm. He had been reading this week of the great imaginative loves of the Middle Ages, and of that supple and golden-haired girl he began to weave an abstraction of passion like the Princess of Trebizond. He slept upon the evocation of her beauty just as he was setting forth upon a delicate and intangible pursuit. Next morning Michael suggested to Stella they should revisit Carlington Road.

"My god, to think we once lived here," exclaimed Stella, as they stood outside Number 64. "To me it seems absolutely impossible, but then of course I was much more away from it than you ever were."

Stella was so ferocious in her mockery of their childish haunts and habitations that Michael began to perceive her old serene contempt was become tinged with bitterness. This morning she was too straightly in possession of herself. It was illogical after last night.

"Well, thank heaven, everything does change," she murmured. "And that ugly things become even more ugly."

"Only for a time," objected Michael. "In twenty years if we visit Carlington Road we shall think how innocent and intimate and pretty it all is."

"I wasn't thinking so much of Carlington Road," said Stella. "I was really thinking of people."

"Even they become beautiful again after a time," argued Michael.

"It would take a very long time for some," said Stella coldly.

Michael had rather dreaded his mother's return, with Stella in this mood, and he was pleased when he found that his fears had been unjustifiable. Stella in fact was very gentle with her mother, as if she and not herself had suffered lately.

"I'm so glad you're back, darling Stella, and so delighted to think you aren't going to Petersburg to-morrow, because the man at Vienna whose name begins with that extraordinary letter . . . ."

"Oh, mother," Stella laughed, "the letter was quite ordinary. It was only L."

"But the name was dreadful, dear child. It always reminded one of furs. A most oppressive name. So that really you'll be in London all this winter ? "

"Yes, only I shan't play much," said Stella.

"Mrs. Carruthers is so anxious to meet you properly," Mrs. Fane said. "And Mabel Carruthers is really very nice. Poor girl! I wish you could be friends with her. She's interested in nothing her mother does."

Michael was really amazed when Stella without a shrug, without even a wink at him, promised simply to let Mrs. Carruthers 'meet her properly,' and actually betrayed as much interest in Mabel Carruthers as to enquire how old she was.

Maurice arrived at Cheyne Walk, just before Michael went up for term, to say he had taken a most wonderful studio in Grosvenor Road. He was anxious that Michael should bring his sister to see it, but Stella would not go.

"Thanks very much, my dear," she said to him, "but I've seen too much of the real thing. I'm in no mood just now for a sentimental imitation."

"I think you ought to come," said Michael. "It would be fun to see Maurice living in Grosvenor Road with all the Muses. Castleton will have such a time tidying up after them when he joins him next year."

But Stella would not go.

Chapter XIV : *99 St. Giles*

IT was strange to come up to Oxford and to find so
many of the chief figures in the college vanished. For
a week Michael felt that in a way he had no business
still to be there, so unfamiliar was the college itself in-
habited by none of his contemporaries save a few Scholars.
Very soon, however, the intimacy of the rooms in St. Giles
which he shared with Alan cured all regrets, and with a thrill
he realized that this last year was going to be of all the years
at Oxford the best, indeed perhaps of all the years of his life
the best.

College itself gave Michael a sharper sense of its entity
than he had ever gathered before. He was still sufficiently
a part of it not to feel the implicit criticism of his presence
that in a year or two, revisiting Oxford, he would feel;
and he was also far enough away from the daily round to
perceive and admire the yearly replenishment which
preserved its vigour notwithstanding the superficially
irreparable losses of each year. There were moments
when he regretted 202 High with what now seemed its
amazingly irresponsible existence, but 202 High had never
given him quite the same zest in returning to it as now
99 St. Giles could give. Nothing had ever quite equalled those
damp November dusks, when after a long walk through silent
country Michael and Alan came back to the din of Carfax
and splashed their way along the crowded and greasy
Cornmarket towards St. Giles, those damp November
dusks when they would find the tea-things glimmering in the
firelight. Buttered toast was eaten; tea was drunk; the

second-best pipe of the day was smoked to idle cracklings
of The Oxford Review and The Star; a stout, landlady
cleared away, and during the temporary disturbance
Michael pulled back the blinds and watched the darkness
and fog slowly blotting out St. John's and the alley of elm-
trees opposite, and giving to the Martyrs' Memorial and
even to Balliol a gothic and significant mystery. The room
was quiet again; the lamps and the fire glowed; Michael
and Alan, settled in deep chairs, read their History and
Philosophy; outside in the November night footsteps went
by; carts and waggons occasionally rattled; bells chimed;
outside in the November murk present life was manifesting
its continuity; here within, the battles and the glories, the
thoughts, the theories and the speculations of the past
for Michael and Alan moved across printed pages under the
rich lamplight.

Dinner dissolved the concentrated spell of two hours.
But dinner at 99 St. Giles was very delightful in the sea-
green dining-room whose decorations had survived the
departing tenant who created them. Michael and Alan
did not talk much; indeed such conversation as took place
during the meal came from the landlady. She possessed
so deft a capacity for making apparently the most barren
observations flower and fruit with intricate narrations,
that merely an enquiry as to the merit of the lemon-sole
would serve to link the occasion with an intimate revelation
of her domestic past.

After dinner Michael and Alan read on towards eleven
o'clock, at which hour Alan usually went to bed. It was
after his departure that in a way Michael enjoyed the night
most. The mediæval chronicles were put back on their
shelf; Stubbs or Lingard, Froude, Freeman, Guizot, —
Lavisse or Gregorovius were put back; round the warm and —
silent room Michael wandered uncertain for a while; and
at the end of five minutes down came Don Quixote or

Adlington's Apuleius, or Florio's Montaigne, or Lucian's
True History. The fire crumbled away to ashes and powder;
the fog stole into the room; outside was now nothing but
the chimes at their measured intervals, nothing but the
noise of them to say a city was there; at that hour Oxford
was truly austere, something more indeed than austere, for
it was neither in time nor in space, but the abstraction of a
city. Only when the lamps began to reek did Michael go
up to bed by candlelight. In his vaporous room, through
whose open window the sound of two o'clock striking came
very coldly, he could scarcely fancy himself in the present.
The effort of intense reading, whether of bygone institutions
or of past adventure, had left him in the condition of physical
freedom that saints achieve by prayer. He was aware of
nothing but a desire to stay for ever like this, half-feverish
with the triumph of tremendous concentration, to undress
in this stinging acerbity of night air, and to lie wakeful for
a long time in this world of dreaming spires.

99 St. Giles exercized just that industrious charm which
Michael had anticipated from the situation. The old house
overlooked such a wide thoroughfare that the view, while
it afforded the repose of movement, scarcely ever aroused
a petty inquisitiveness into the actions of the passers-by.
The traffic of the thoroughfare like the ships of the sea
went by merely apprehended, but not observed. The
big bay-window hung over the street like the stern-cabin of a
frigate, and as Michael sat there he had the impression
of being cut off from communication, the sense of perpetually leaving life astern. The door of 99 St. Giles did
not open directly on the street, but was reached by a
tortuous passage that ran the whole depth of the house.
This entrance helped very much the illusion of separation
from the ebb and flow of ordinary existence, and was so
suggestive of a refuge that involuntarily Michael always
hurried through it that the sooner he might set his foot

on the steep and twisted staircase inside the house. There was always an excitement in reaching this staircase again, an impulse to run swiftly up, as if this return to the sitting-room was veritably an escape from the world. Here the books sprawled everywhere. At 2c2 High they had filled the cupboards in orderly fashion. Here they overflowed in dusty cataracts, and tottered upwards in crazy escalades and tremulous piles. All the shelves were gorged with books. Moreover Michael every afternoon bought more books. The landlady held up her hands in dismay as, crunching up the paper in which they had been wrapped, he considered in perplexity their accommodation. More space was necessary, and the sea-green dining-room was awarded shelves. Here every morning after breakfast came the exiles, the dull and the disappointing books which had been banished from the sitting-room. Foot by foot the sea-green walls disappeared behind these shelves. In Lampard's bookshop Michael was certainly a personality. Lampard himself even came to tea, and sat nodding his approbation.

As for Alan, he used to stay unmoved by the invading volumes. He had stipulated at the beginning that one small bookcase should be reserved for him. Here Plato and Aristotle, Herodotus and Thucydides always had room to breathe, without ever being called upon to endure the contamination of worm-eaten bibliophily.

"Where the deuce has my Stubbs got to?" Michael would grumble, delving into the musty cascade of old plays and chap books which had temporarily obliterated the current literature of the week's work.

Alan would very serenely take down Plato from his own trim and unimpeded shelves, and his brow would already be knitted with the effort of fixing half-a-dozen abstractions before Michael had decided after a long excavation that Stubbs had somehow vanished in the by-ways of curious reading.

Yet notwithstanding the amount of time occupied by arranging and buying and finding books, Michael did manage to absorb a good deal of history, even of that history whose human nature has to be sought arduously in charters, exchequer-rolls and acts of parliament. Schools were drawing near; the dates of Kings and Emperors and Popes in their succession adorned the walls of his bedroom, so that even while he was cleaning his teeth one fact could be acquired.

Only on Sunday evenings did Michael allow himself really to re-enter the life of St. Mary's. These Sunday evenings had all the excitement of a long-interrupted reunion. To be sure Venner's was thronged with people who seemed to be taking life much too lightly; but Tommy Grainger was there, still engaged with a pass-group. People spoke hopefully of going head this year. Surely with Tommy and three other Blues in the boat, St. Mary's must go head. The conversation was so familiar that it was almost a shock to find so many of the faces altered. But Cuffe was still there with his mouth perpetually open just as wide as ever. Sterne was still there and likely, so one heard, to make no end of runs next summer. George Appleby was very much in evidence since Lonsdale's departure. George Appleby was certainly there, and Michael rather liked him and accepted an invitation to lunch. In hall the second-year men were not quite as rowdy as they used to be, and when they were rowdy, somehow to Michael and the rest of the fourth year they seemed to lack the imagination of themselves when they—but after all the only true judges of that were the Princes and Cardinals and Poets staring down from their high golden frames. The dons too at High Table might know, for there they sat, immemorial as ever.

Wine in Common Room was just the same, and it really was very jolly to be sitting between Castleton—that very

popular President of J.C.R.—and Tommy Grainger. There
certainly was a great and grave satisfaction in leading off
with a more ceremonious health drinking than had ever been
achieved in the three years past. Michael found it amusing
to catch the name of some freshman and, shouting abruptly
a salute, to behold him wriggle and blush and drink his
answer and wonder who on earth was hailing *him*. Michael
often asked himself if it really were possible he could appear
to that merry rout at the other end of J.C.R. in truly
heroic mould. He supposed, with a smile at himself for so
gross a fraud, that he really did for them pass mortal stature
and that already he had a bunch of legends dangling from
his halo. Down in Venner's after wine, Michael fancied the
shouts of the freshmen wandering round Cloisters were
more raucous than once they had seemed. Sometimes
really they were almost irritating, but the After was
capital, although the new comic song of the new college
jester lacked perhaps a little the perfect lilt of ' Father says
we're going to beat them.' Yet after all the Boer war had
been over three years now : no doubt ' Father says we're
going to beat them' would have sounded a little stale. Last
term however at Two Hundred and Two it had rung as
fresh as ever. But the singer was gone now. It was meet
his song should perish with his withdrawal from the Oxford
scene. Still the After was quite good sport, and Michael
was glad to think he and Grainger and Sterne were giving
the last After but one of this term. He bicycled back to
the digs with his head full of chatter, of clinking glasses and
catchy tunes. Nevertheless all consciousness of the evening's
merriment faded out, as he hurried up the crooked staircase
to the sitting-room where Alan, upright at the table amid
Thucydidean commentaries, was reading under the lamp's
immotionable rays, his hair glinting with what was now rare
gold.

During this autumn term neither Michael nor Alan

spoke of Stella except as an essentially third person. She
was in London; devoting so much of herself so charmingly
to her mother that Mrs. Fane nearly abandoned every other
interest in her favour. There were five Schumann recitals,
of which press notices were sent to 99 St. Giles. Michael
as he read them handed them on to Alan.

"Jolly good," said he in a tone of such conventional
praise that Michael really began to wonder whether he had
after all changed his mind instead of merely concealing
his intention. However, since conversation between these
two had been stripped to the bare bones of intercourse,
Michael could not bring himself to violate this habit of
reserve for the sake of a curiosity the gratification of which
in true friendship should never be demanded, nor even
accepted with deeper attention than the trivial news of the
day casually offered. Nor would Michael have felt it loyal
to Alan to try from Stella to extract a point of view regarding
him. Anyway, he reassured himself, nothing could be
done at present.

Towards the end of term Mrs. Ross wrote a letter to
Michael whose news was sufficiently unexpected to rouse
the two of them to a conversation of greater length than any
they had had since term began.

COBBLE PLACE,
November 30.

My dear Michael,

*You will be surprized to hear I have become a
Catholic, or I suppose I should say to you, if you still adhere to
your theories, a Roman Catholic. My reasons for this step,
apart of course from the true reason—the grace of God, were, I
think, connected a good deal with my boy. When your friend
Mr. Prescott killed himself, I felt very much the real emptiness
of such a life that on the surface was so admirable, in some
ways so enviable. I am dreadfully anxious that Kenneth—*

*he is Kenneth Michael now—I hope you won't be vexed I
should have wished him to have Michael also—well, as I
was saying—that Kenneth should grow up with all the help
that the experience of the past can give him. It has become
increasingly a matter of astonishment to me how so many
English boys manage to muddle through the crises of their
boyhood without the Sacraments. I'm afraid you'll be reading
this letter in rather a critical spirit, and perhaps resenting my
implication that you for instance have come through so many
crises without the Sacraments. But I'm not yet a good enough
theologian to argue with you about the claims of your Church.
Latterly I've felt positively alarmed by the prospect of grappling
with Kenneth's future. I have seen you struggle through, and
I know I can say win a glorious victory over one side of yourself.
But I have seen other things happen, even from where I live my
secluded life. If my husband had not been killed I might not
perhaps have felt this dread on Kenneth's account. But I like
to think that God in giving me that great sorrow has shown his
purpose by offering me this new and unimagined peace and
security and assurance. I need scarcely say I have had a rather
worrying time lately. It is strange how when love and faith
are the springs of action one must listen with greater patience
than one could listen for any lesser motive to the opinions of
other people.*

*Joan and Mary whom I've always thought of as just wrapped
up in the good works of their dear good selves, really rose in their
wrath and scorched me with the fieriest opposition. I could not
have believed they had in them to say as much in all their lives
as they said to me when I announced my intention. Nor had I
any idea they knew so many English clergymen. I believe that
to gratify them I have interviewed half the Anglican ministry.
Even a Bishop was invoked to demonstrate my apostasy. Nancy
too wrote furious letters. She was not outraged so much
theologically, but her sense of social fitness was shattered.*

My darling old mother was the only person who took my

resolve calmly. "*As long as you don't try to convert me,*"
she said, "*and don't leave incense burning about the house,*
well—you're old enough to know your own mind." *She was so*
amusing while Joan and Mary were marshalling arguments
against me. She used to sit playing '*Miss Milligan*' *with a*
cynical smile, and said, when it was all over and in spite of
everyone I had been received, that she had really enjoyed
Patience for the first time, as Joan and Mary were too busy
to prevent her from cheating.

How are you and dear old Alan getting on? Of course you can
read him this letter. I've not written to him because I fancy he
won't be very much interested. Forgive me that I did not take
you into my confidence beforehand, but I feared a controversy
with a real historian about the continuity of the Anglican church.

My love to you both at Oxford.

Your affectionate

Maud Ross.

"Great scott!" Michael exclaimed as he finished the
letter. "Alan! could you ever in your wildest dreams have
imagined that Mrs. Ross, the most inveterate Whig and
Roundhead and Orange bigot, at least whenever she used to
argue with me, would have gone over?"

"What do you mean?" Alan asked, sinking slowly to
earth from his Platonic οὐρανός. "Gone over where?"

"To Rome—become a Roman Catholic."

"Who?" gasped Alan, staggered now more than
Michael. "Mrs. Ross—Aunt Maud?"

"It's the most extraordinary thing I ever heard," said
Michael. "She—and Kenneth," he added rather maliciously, seeing that Alan's Britannic prejudice was violently
aroused. "I'll read you her letter."

Plato was shut up for the evening before Michael was
half-way through, and almost before the last sentence had
been read, Alan's wrath exploded.

" It's all very fine for her to laugh like that at Joan and Mary and Nancy," he said, colouring hotly. " But they were absolutely right and Mrs. Ross — I mean Aunt Maud——"

" I was afraid you were going to disown the relationship," Michael laughed.

" Aunt Maud is absolutely wrong. Why, my uncle would have been furious. Even if *she* became a Catholic she had no business to take Kenneth with her. The more I think of it—you know, it really is a bit thick."

" Why do you object ? " Michael asked curiously. " I never knew you thought about religion at all, except so far as occasionally to escort your mother politely to Matins, and that was after all to oblige her more than God. Besides, you're reading Greats, and I always thought that the Greats people in their fourth year abstained from anything like a definite opinion for fear of losing their First."

" I may not have a definite opinion about Christianity," said Alan. " But Catholicism is ridiculous anyway—it doesn't suit English people."

" There you're treading on the heels of the School of Modern History which you affect to despise. You really don't know, if I may say so, what could or could not suit the English people unless you know what has or has not suited them."

" Why don't you become a Catholic yourself," challenged Alan, " if you're so keen on them ? "

" For a logician," said Michael, " your conclusion is bad, being entirely unrelated to any of our premisses. Secondly, were I inclined to label myself as anything, I should be disposed to label myself as a Catholic already."

" Oh, I know that affectation," scoffed Alan.

" Well, the net result of our commentary is that you like everybody else object to Mrs. Ross changing her opinions, because you don't like it. Her position is negli-

gible, the springs of action being religious. Now if my
mother went over to Rome I should be rather bucked on
her account."

"My dear chap, if you don't mind my saying so,"
suggested Alan as apologetically as his outraged convention-
ality would allow, "your mother has always been rather
given to—er—all sorts of new cults, and it wouldn't be
so—er—noticeable in her case. But supposing Stella——".

Michael looked at him sharply.

"Supposing Stella did?" he asked.

"Oh, of course she's artistic and she's travelled and—oh,
well, I don't know—Stella's different."

At any rate, thought Michael, he was still in love with
Stella. She was evidently beyond criticism.

"You needn't worry," said Michael. "I don't think she
ever will."

"You didn't think Aunt Maud ever would," Alan pointed
out.

"And, great scott, it's still absolutely incredible,"
Michael murmured.

Although in the face of Alan's prejudice Michael had
felt very strongly that Mrs. Ross had done well by her
change of communion, or rather by her submission to a
communion, for he never could remember her as perfervid
in favour of any before, at the same time to himself he rather
regretted the step, since it destroyed for him that idea
he had kept of her as one who stood gravely holding the
balance. He dreaded a little the effect upon her of a sudden
plunge into Catholicism, just as he had felt uneasy when
eight or nine years ago Alan had first propounded the theory
of his uncle being in love with her. Michael remembered
how the suggestion had faintly shocked his conception of
Miss Carthew. It was a little disconcerting to have to justify
herself to Nancy, or indeed to anyone. It seemed to weaken
her status. Moreover his own deep-implanted notion of

' going over to Rome ' as the act of a weakling and a weather-cock was hard to allay. His own grey image of Pallas Athene seemed now to be decked with meretricious roses. He was curious to know what his mother would think about the news. Mrs. Fane received it as calmly as if he had told her Mrs. Ross had taken up palmistry; to her Catholicism was only one of the numberless fads that made life amusing. As for Stella, she did not comment on the news at all. She was too much occupied with the diversions of the autumn season. Yet Stella was careful to impress on Michael that her new mode of life had not been dictated by any experience in Vienna.

"*Don't think I'm drowning care,*" she wrote. "*I made a damned fool of myself and luckily you're almost the only person who knows anything about it. I've wiped it out as completely as a composition I've learned and played and done with. Really I find this pottering life that mother and I lead very good for my — music. I'm managing to store up a reserve of feeling. The Schumann recitals were in some ways my best effort so far. Just now I'm absolutely mad about dancing and fencing; and as mother's life is entirely devoted to the theory of physical culture at this exact moment, we're both happy.*"

Michael told Alan what Stella said about dancing and fencing, and he was therefore not surprized when Alan informed him, with the air of one who really has discovered something truly worth while, that there was a Sword club at Oxford.

"Hadn't you better join as well next term ? " he suggested. " Rather good ecker, I fancy."

" Much better than golf," said Michael.

" Oh, rather," Alan agreed in lofty innocence of any hidden allusion to his resolve of last summer.

For the Christmas vacation Michael went to Scotland, partly because he wanted to brace himself sharply for the

3 E

last two terms of his Oxford time, but more because he had
the luxurious fancy to stay in some town very remote from
Oxford, there meditating on her spires like grey and graceful
shapes of mist made perdurable for ever. Hitherto Oxford
had called him back, as to a refuge most severe, from places
whose warmth or sensuousness or gaiety was making her cold
beauty the more desirable. Now Michael wished to come
back for so nearly his ultimate visit as to a tender city of
melting outlines. Therefore to fulfil this vision of return
he refused Guy Hazlewood's invitation to Plashers Mead.
It seemed to him that no city nearer than Aberdeen would
give him the joy of charging southward in the train, back
to the moist heart of England and that wan aggregation of
immaterial domes and spires.

Aberdeen was spare and harsh enough even for Michael's
mood, and there for nearly five weeks of north-easterly
weather he worked at political economy. It was a very
profitable vacation; and that superb and frozen city of
granite indifferent to the howling North sent him back
more ready to combat the perilous dreams which like the
swathes of mist destroying with their transmutations the
visible fabric of Oxford menaced his action.

Certainly it needed the physical bracing of his sojourn
at Aberdeen to keep Michael from dreaming away utterly
his last Lent term. February was that year a month of
rains from silver skies, of rains that made Oxford melodious
with their perpetual trickling. They were rains that lured
him forth to dabble in their gentle fountains, to listen at
the window of Ninety-nine to their rippling monody, and
at night to lie awake infatuated.

Still, even with all the gutterspouts in Oxford jugging
like nightingales and with temptation from every book of
poetry to abandon history, Michael worked fairly steadily,
and when the end of term surprized him in the middle of
his industry, he looked back with astonishment at the

amount of apposite reading accomplished in what seemed, now so cruelly swift were the hours, a mere week of rain.

He obtained leave to stay up during the Easter vacation, and time might have seemed to stand still, but that Spring on these rathe mornings of wind and scudded blue sky was forward with her traceries, bringing with every morning green Summer visibly nearer. The urgency of departure less than the need for redoubled diligence in acquiring knowledge obsessed Michael all this April. Sitting in the bay-window at Ninety-nine on these luminous eves of Spring, he vexed himself with the thought of disturbing so soon his books, of violating with change the peaceful confusion achieved in two terms. The fancy haunted him that for the length of the Long Vacation 99 St. Giles would drowse under the landlady's nick-nacks brought out to replace his withdrawn treasures; that nothing would keep immortal the memory of him and Alan save their photographs in frames of almost royal ostentation. Vaguely through his mind ran the notion of becoming a don, that for ever he might stay here in Oxford, a contemplative intellectual cut off from the great world. For a week the notion ripened swiftly, and Michael worked very hard in his determination to proceed from a First to the competition for a Fellowship. The notion ripened too swiftly, however, and fell with a plump, fit for nothing, when he suddenly realized he would have to stay on in Oxford alone, since of all his friends he could see not one who would be likely in the academic cloister to accompany his meditations. With a gesture of weary contempt Michael flung Stubbs into the corner, and resolved that, come what might in the History Schools, for what remained of his time at Oxford he would enjoy the proffered anodyne.

After he had disowned his work, he took to wandering rather aimlessly about the streets; but their aspect, still unfrequented as yet by the familiar figures of term-time, made him feel sad. Guy Hazlewood was, summoned by telegram from where at Plashers Mead he was presumed to have found abiding peace. He came bicycling in from the Witney road at noon of a blue April day so richly canopied with rolling clouds that the unmatured season took on some of June's ampler dignity. After lunch they walked to Witham Woods, and Guy tried to persuade Michael to come to Wychford when the summer term was over. He was full of the plan for founding that lay monastery, that cloister for artists who wished between Oxford and the world a space unstressed by anything save ordered meditation. Michael was captured anew by the idea he had first propounded, and they talked gaily of its advantages, foreseeing, if the right people could be induced to come, a period of intense stimulation against a background of serenity. Then Guy began to talk of how day by day he was subduing words to rhyme and metre.

" And you, what would you do ?." he asked.

At once Michael realized the futility of their scheme for him.

" I should only dream away another year," he said rather sadly, " and so if you don't mind, old chap, I think I won't join you."

" Rot," Guy drawled. " I've got it all clear now in my mind. Up at seven. At breakfast we should take it in turns to read aloud great poetry. From eight to ten retire to our cells, and work at a set piece—a sonnet or six lines of prose. Ten to eleven a discussion on what we'd done. Eleven to one work at our own stuff. One o'clock lunch with some reading aloud. All the afternoon to do what we like. Dinner at seven with more reading aloud, and in the evening reading to ourselves. Not a word to be spoken after nine o'clock, and bed at eleven. After tea twice a week we might have academic discussions."

" It sounds perfect," said Michael, " if you're already

equipped with the desire to be an artist, and what is more
important if deep down in yourself you're convinced you
have the least justification for ambition. But, Guy, what
a curious chap you are. You seem to have grown so much
younger since you went down."

Guy laughed on a note of exultation that sounded
strange indeed in one whom when still at Balliol Michael
had esteemed as perhaps the most perfect contemporary
example of the undergraduate tired by the consciousness
of his own impeccable attitude. Guy had always possessed
so conspicuously that Balliol affectation of despising accentua-
tions of seriousness, of humour, of intention, of friendship,
of everything indeed except parlour rowdiness with cushions
and sofas, that Michael was almost shocked to hear the
elaborately wearied Guy declare boisterously:

"My dear chap, that is the great secret. The moment
you go down, you do grow younger."

He must be in love, thought Michael suddenly; and, so
remote was love seeming to him just now, he blushed
in the implication by his inner self of having penetrated
uninvited the secret of a friend.

Guy talked all tea-time of the project, and when they
had eaten enough bread and honey, they set out for Oxford
by way of Godstow. The generous sun was blanched by
watery clouds. A shrewd wind had risen while they sat in
the inn, and the primroses looked very wan in the shrivelled
twilight. Michael had Guy's company for a week of long
walks and snug evenings, but the real intimacy which he had
expected would be consummated by this visit never effected
itself somehow. Guy was more remote in his mood of
communal ambitions than he was at Oxford, living his
life of whimsical detachment. After he went back to
Plashers Mead Michael only missed the sound of his voice,
and was not conscious of that more violent wrench when the
intercourse of silence is broken.

— It happened that year St. Mark's Eve fell upon a Sunday,
and Michael, having been reading the poems of Keats nearly
all the afternoon, was struck by the coincidence. 'Oxford on
such an occasion was able to provide exactly the same sensation for him as Winchester had given to the poet. Michael
sat in his window-seat looking out over the broad thoroughfare of St. Giles, listening to the patter and lisp of Sabbath
footfalls, to the burden of the bells'; and as he sat there
with the city receding in the wake of his window, he was
aware more poignantly than ever of how actually in a few
weeks it would recede. The bells and the footsteps were
quiet for a while : the sun had gone : it was the vesper
stillness of evening prayer : slowly the printed page before
him faded from recognition. Already the farther corners
of the room were black, revealing from time to time, as a
tongue of flame leapt up in the grate, the golden blazonries
of the books on the walls. It was everywhere dark when the
people came out of church, and the footsteps were again
audible. Michael envied Keats the power which he had
known to preserve for ever that St. Mark's Eve of eighty
years ago in Winchester. It was exasperating that now
already the footfalls were dying away, that already their
sensation was evanescent, that he could not with the wand
of poetry forbid time to disturb this quintessential hour of
Oxford. Art alone could bewitch the present in the fashion
of that enchantress in the old fairy tale who sent long ago a
court to sleep.

What was the use of reading history unless the alchemy
of literature had transcended the facts by the immortal
presentation of them ? These charters and acts of parliament, these exchequer-rolls and raked-up records meant
nothing. Ivanhoe held more of the Middle Ages than all
of Maitland's fitting and fussing, than all of Stubbs' ponderous conclusions. The truth of Ivanhoe, the truth of the
— Ingoldsby Legends, the truth of Christabel was indeed

revealed to the human soul through the power of art to unlock for one convincing moment truth with the same directness of divine exposition as faith itself.

Now here was Oxford opening suddenly to him her heart, and he was incapable of preserving the vision. The truth would state itself to him, and as he tried to restate it, lo, it was gone. Perhaps these moments that seemed to demand expression were indeed mystical assurances of human immortality. Perhaps they were not revealed for explanation. After all, when Keats had wrought for ever in a beautiful statement the fact of a Sabbath eve, the reader could not restate why he had wrought it for ever. Art could do no more than preserve the sense of the fact : it could not resolve it in such a way that life would cease to be the baffling attempt it was on the individual's part to restate to himself his personal dreams.

Oh, this clutching at the soul by truth, how damnably instantaneous it was, how for one moment it could provoke the illusion of victory over all the muddled facts of existence : how a moment after it could leave the tantalized soul with a despairing sense of having missed by the breadth of a hair the entry into knowledge. By the way, was there not some well-reasoned psychological explanation of this physical condition ?

The sensation of St. Mark's Eve was already fled. Michael forsook the chilling window-seat and went with lighted candle to search for the psychological volume which contained a really rational explanation of what he had been trying to apprehend. He fumbled among his books for a while, but he could not find the one he wanted. Then, going to pull down the blinds, he was aware of Oxford beyond the lamplit thoroughfare, with all her spires and domes invisible in the darkness, the immutable city that neither mist nor modern architects could destroy, the immortal academy whose spirit would surely outdare the menace of these reforming Huns armed with Royal Commissions, and wither the cowardly betrayers of her civilization who, even now before the barbarian was at her gates, were cringing to him with offers to sell the half of her heritage of learning. . Michael, aware of Oxford all about him in the darkness, wished he could be a member of Convocation and make a flaming speech in defence of compulsory Greek. That happened to be the proposed surrender to modern conditions which at the moment was agitating his conservative passion.

"Thank heaven. I live when I do," he said to himself. "If it were 2000 A.D. how much more miserable I should be."

He went down to dinner and, propping The Anatomy of Melancholy against the cruet, deplored the twentieth century, but found the chicken rather particularly good.

Chapter XV : *The Last Term*

MICHAEL meant to attend the celebration of May Morning on St. Mary's tower, but when the moment came it was so difficult to get out of bed, that he was not seen in the sun's eye. This lapse of enthusiasm saddened him rather. It seemed to conjure a little cruelly the vision of speeding youth.

The last summer term was a period of tension. Michael found that notwithstanding his vow of idleness the sight of the diligence of the other men in view of Schools impelled him also to labour feverishly. He was angry with himself for his weakness, and indeed tried once or twice to join on the river the careless parties of juniors, but it was no good. The insistent Schools forbade all pleasure, and these leafy days were spent hour after hour of them at his table. Eights Week came round, and though the college went head of the river, for Michael the achievement was merely a stroke of irony. For three years he and his friends, most of whom were now fled, had waited for this moment; had counted upon this bump-supper, had planned a hundred diversions for this happy date. Michael now must attend without the majority of them, and he went in rather a critical frame of mind, for though to be sure Tommy Grainger was drunk in honour of his glorious captaincy, it was not the bump-supper of his dreams. Victory had come too late.

Tired of the howling and the horse-play, tired of the fretful fireworks, he turned into Venner's just before ten o'clock.

" Why aren't you with your friends, making a noise ? "
asked Venner.

" Ought to go home and work," Michael explained.

" But surely you can take one night off. You used
always to be well to the fore on these occasions."

" Don't feel like it, Venner."

" You mustn't work too hard, you know," said the old
man blinking kindly at him.

" Oh, it's not work, Venner. It's age.".

" Why, what a thing to say. Hark ! They're having a
rare time to-night. I don't expect the dons'll say much.
They expect a bit of noise after a bump-supper. Why ever
don't you go out and do your share ? "

Venner was ready to go home, and Michael leaving the
little office in his company paused irresolutely in Cloisters
for a moment. It was no good. He could not bring
himself to be flung into that vortex of ululation. He turned
away from its direction and walked with Venner to the
lodge.

" Don't forget to mark me down as out of college, Shadbolt," he warned the porter. " I don't want to be hauled
to-morrow morning for damage done in my absence."

The porter held up his hand in unctuous deprecation.

" There is no fear of my making a mistake, Mr. Fane. I
was observing your eggress, sir," he said pompously, " and
had it registered in my book before you spoke."

Shadbolt unlocked the door for Michael and Venner to
pass out into the High. Michael walked with Venner as
far as St. Mary's bridge, and when the old man had said
good-night and departed on his way home, he stood for
a while watching the tower in the May moonlight. He could
hear the shouts of those doing honour to the prowess of the
Eight. From time to time the sky was stained with blue
and green and red from the Roman candles. To himself
standing here now he seemed as remote from it all as the

townsfolk loitering on the bridge in the balmy night-air to
listen to the fun. Already, thought Michael, he was one
of the people, small as emmets, swarming at the base of
this slim and lovely tower. He regretted sharply now that
he had not once more, even from distant St. Giles, roused
himself to salute from the throbbing summit May Morning.
It was melancholy to stand here within the rumour of the
communal joy, but outside its participation ; and presently
he started to walk quickly back to his digs, telling himself
with dreadful warning as he went that before Schools now
remained scarcely more than a week.

Alan was in a condition of much greater anxiety even than
Michael. Michael had nothing much beyond a moral pact
with the college authorities to make him covet a good class :
to Alan it was more important, especially as he had given
up the Sudan and was intending to try for the Home Civil
Service.

" However, I've given up thinking of a First, and if I can
squeeze a Second, I shall be jolly grateful," he told Michael.

The day of Schools arrived. The Chief Examiner had
caused word to be sent round that he would insist on the
rigour of the law about black clothes. So that year many
people went back to the earlier mode of the university
examination and appeared in evening-dress. The first
four days went by with their monotony of scratching pens,
their perspiring and bedraggled women-candidates, their
tedious energy and denial of tobacco. Alan grew gloomier
and gloomier. He scarcely thought he had even escaped
being ploughed outright. For the fourth night preparatory
to the two papers on his Special Subject, Michael ordered
iced asparagus and quails in aspic, a bottle of champagne
and two quarts of cold black coffee. He sat up all night,
and went down tight-eyed and pale-faced to the final
encounter. In the afternoon he emerged, thanked heaven
it was all over and, instead of celebrating his release as he

had intended with wine and song, slept in an armchair
through the benign June evening. Alan, who had gone
to bed at his usual hour the night before, spent his time
reading the credentials of various careers offered to enterprizing young men by the Colonies. The day after, however,
nothing seemed to matter except that the purgatorial
business was done for ever, and that Oxford offered nearly
a fortnight of impregnable idleness..

This fortnight, when she was so prodigal with her beauty
and when her graciousness was a rich balm to the ordeal she
had lately exacted, was not so poignant as Michael had
expected. Indeed it was scarcely poignant at all so far as
human farewells went, though there was about it such an
underlying sadness as deepens the mellow peace of a fine
autumn day..

It seemed to Michael that in after years he would always
think of Oxford dowered so with Summer, and brooding
among her trees. Matthew Arnold had said she did not
need June for beauty's heightening. That was true. Her
beauty was not heightened now, but it was displayed with
all the grave consciousness of an unassertive renown.
Michael dreaded more the loss of this infoliated calm than
of any of the people who were enjoying its amenity. There
were indeed groups upon the lawns that next year would
not form themselves, that for ever indeed would be irremediably dispersed; but the thought of himself and other
members scattered did not move him with as much regret
as the knowledge that next year himself would have lost
the assurance that he was an organic part of this tutelary
landscape.. The society of his contemporaries was already
broken up : the end of the third year had effected that. This
farewell to Oxford herself was harder, and Michael wished
that from the very first moment of his arrival he had concentrated upon the object of a Fellowship. Such a life
would have suited him well. He would not have withered

like so many dons : he would each year have renewed his
youth in the stream of freshmen. He would have been
sympathetic, receptive, and worldly enough not to be
despised by each generation in its course. Now, since he
had not aimed at such a career, he must go. The weather
opulently fine mocked his exit.

Michael and Alan had decided to stay up for Commemoration. Stella and Mrs. Fane had been invited : Lonsdale
and Wedderburn were coming up : Maurice was bringing
his mother and sisters. For a brief carnival they would all
be reunited, and rooms would be echoing to the voices of
their rightful owners. Yet after all it would be but a
pretence of reviving their merry society. It was not a
genuine reunion this, that was requiring women to justify
it. Oxford, as Michael esteemed her, was already out of
his reach. She would be symbolized in the future by these
rooms at 99 St. Giles, and Michael made up his mind that
no intrusion of women should spoil for him their monastic
associations. He would stay here until the last day, and for
Commemoration he would try to borrow his old rooms in
college, thus fading from this wide thoroughfare without
a formal leave-taking. He would drop astern from the
bay-window whence for a time he had watched the wrack
and spume of the world drifting towards the horizon in its
wake. Himself would recede so with the world, and without him the bay-window would hold a tranquil course,
unrocked by the loss or gain of him or the transient voyagers
of each new generation. Very few eves and sunsets were
still his to enjoy from this window-seat. Already the books
were being stacked in preparation for their removal to the
studio at 173 Cheyne Walk. Dusty and derelict belongings
of him and Alan were already strewn about the landings
outside their bedrooms. Even the golf-bag of Alan's first
term, woolly now with the accumulated mildew of neglect,
had been dragged from its obscurity. Perhaps it would be

impossible to drop astern as imperceptibly as he would have
liked. Too many reminders of departure littered the rooms
with their foreboding of finality.

"I'm shore I for one am quite sorry you're going," said
the landlady. "I never wish to have a nicer norer quieter
pair of gentlemen. It's to be hoped, I'm shore, that next
term's comings-ins from St. John's will be half as nice. Yerse,
I shall be very pleased to have these coverlets—I suppose
you would call them coverlets—and you're leaving the
shelves in the dining-room? Yerse, I'm shore they'll be
as handy as anything for the cruets and what not. And so
you're going to have a dinner here to eleven gentlemen—oh,
eleven in all, yerse, I see."

It was going to be rather difficult, Michael thought,
to find exactly the ten people he wished to invite to this
last terminal dinner. Alan, Grainger and Castleton, of
course. Bill Mowbray and Vernon Townsend. And
Smithers. Certainly, he would ask Smithers. And why
not George Appleby, who was Librarian of the Union this
term, and no longer conceivable as that lackadaisical red
rag which had fluttered Lonsdale to fury? What about
the Dean? And if the Dean, why not Harbottle his
History tutor? And for the tenth place? It was really
impossible to choose from the dozen or so acquaintances
who had an equal claim upon it. He would leave the tenth
place vacant, and just to amuse his own fancy he would fill
it with the ghost of himself in the December of his first
term.

Michael, when he saw his guests gathered in the sea-
green dining-room of 99 St. Giles, knew that this last terminal
dinner was an anachronism. After all, the prime and bloom
of these eclectic entertainments had been in the two
previous years. This was not the intimate and unusual
society he had designed to gather round him as representative of his four years at the Varsity. This was merely

representative of the tragical incompleteness of Oxford. It was certainly a very urbane evening, but it was somehow not particularly distinctive of Oxford, still less of Michael's existence there. Perhaps it had been a mistake to invite the two dons. Perhaps everyone was tired under the strain of Schools. Michael was glad when the guests went and he sat alone in the window-seat with Alan.

"To-morrow, my mother and Stella are coming up," he reminded Alan. "It's rather curious my mother shouldn't have been up all the time, until I'm really down."

"Is that man Avery coming up ?" Alan asked.

Michael nodded.

"I suppose your people see a good deal of him now he's in town," said Alan, trying to look indifferent to the answer.

"Less than before he went," said Michael. "Stella's rather off studios and the Vie de Bohême."

"Oh, he has a studio ? "

"Didn't you know ? "

"I don't take very much interest in his movements," Alan loftily explained.

They smoked on for a while without speaking.

"I must go to bed," announced Alan at last.

"Not yet, not yet," Michael urged him. "I don't think you've quite realized that this is our last night in Ninety-nine."

"I've settled to stay on here during Commem Week," said Alan. "Your people are staying at the Randolph ? "

Michael nodded, wondering to himself if it were possible that Alan could really have been so far-sighted as to stay on in St. Giles for the sake of having the most obvious right to escort his mother and Stella home. "But why aren't you going into college ?" he asked.

"Oh, I thought it would be rather a fag moving in for so — short a time. Besides it's been rather ripping in these digs."

Michael looked at him gratefully. He had himself feared to voice his appreciation of this last year with Alan: he was feeling sentimental enough to dread on Alan's side a grudging assent to his enthusiasm.

"Yes, it has been awfully ripping," he agreed.

"I should like to have had another year," sighed Alan. "I think I was just beginning to get a dim sort of a notion of philosophy. I wonder how much of it is really applicable."

"To what? To God?" asked Michael.

"No, the world—the world we live in."

"I don't fancy, you know," said Michael, "that the intellectual part of Oxford is directly applicable to the world at all. What I mean to say is, that I think it can only be applied to the world through our behaviour."

"Well, of course," said Alan, "that's a truism."

Michael was rather disconcerted. The thought in his mind had seemed more worthy of expression.

"But the point is," Alan went on, "whether our philosophic education, our mental training has any effect on our behaviour. It seems to me that Oxford is just as typically Oxford whatever a man reads."

"That wasn't the case at school," said Michael. "I'm positive for instance the Modern side was definitely inferior to the Classical side—in manners and everything else. And though at Oxford other circumstances interfere to make the contrast less violent, it doesn't seem to me one gains the quintessence of the university unless one reads Greats. Even History only supplies that in the case of men exceptionally sensitive to the spirit of place. I mean to say sensitive in such a way that Oxford, quite apart from dons and undergraduates, can herself educate. I'm tremendously anxious now that Oxford should become more democratic, but I'm equally anxious that, in proportion as she offers more willingly the shelter of her learning to the people, the learning she bestows shall be more than ever rigidly un-practical, as they say."

" So you really think philosophy is directly applicable ? " said Alan.

" How Socratic you are," Michael laughed. " Perhaps the Rhodes Scholars will answer your question. I remember reading somewhere lately that it was confidently antici-pated the advent of the Rhodes Scholars would transform a provincial university into an imperial one. That may have been written by a Cambridge man bitterly aware of his own provincial university. Yet a moment's reflection should have taught him that provincialism in academic matters is possibly an advantage. Florence and Athens were provincial. Rome and London and Oxford are metro-politan—much more dangerously exposed to the metro-politan snares of superficiality and of submerged per-sonality with the corollary of vulgar display. Neither Rome nor London nor Oxford has produced her own poets. They have always been sung by the envious but happy provincials. Rome and London would have treated Shelley just as Oxford did. Cambridge would have disapproved of him, but a bourgeois dread of interference would have let him alone. As for an imperial university, the idea is ghastly. I figure something like the Imperial Institute filled with Colonials eating pemmican. The Eucalyptic Vision, it might be called."

" And you'd make a distinction between imperial and metropolitan ? " Alan asked.

" Good gracious, yes. Wouldn't you distinguish between New York and London ? Imperialism is the worst qualities of the provinces gathered up and exhibited to the world in the worst way. A metropolis takes provincialism and skims the cream. It is a disintegrating, but for itself a civilizing force. A metropolis doesn't encourage creative art by metropolitans. It ought to be engaged all the time in

3 F

trying to make the provincials appreciate what they themselves are doing."

"I think you're probably talking a good deal of rot,"
said Alan severely. "And we seem to have gone a long way
from my question."

"About the application of philosophy?"

Alan nodded.

"Dear man, as were I a Cantabrian provincial, I should
say. Dear man! Doesn't it make you shiver? It's like the
'Pleased to meet you,' of Americans and Tootingians. It's
so terribly and intrusively personal. So informative and
unrestrained, so gushing and——"

"I wish you'd answer my question," Alan grumbled,
"and call me what you like without talking about it."

"Now I've forgotten my answer," said Michael. "And
it was a wonderful answer. Oh, I remember now. Of
course your philosophy is applicable to the world. You
coming from a metropolitan university will try to infect
the world with your syllogisms. You will meet Cambridge
men much better educated than yourself, but all of them
incompetent to appreciate their own education. You will
gently banter them, trying to allay their provincial suspicion of your easy manner. You will——"

"*You* will simply not be serious," said Alan. "And so
I shall go to bed."

"My dear chap, I'm only talking like this because if I
were serious, I couldn't bear to think that to-night is almost
the end of our fourth year. It is in fact the end of
99 St. Giles."

"Well, it isn't as if we were never going to see each other
again," said Alan awkwardly.

"But it is," said Michael. "Don't you realize, even
with all your researches into philosophy, that after to-night
we shall only see each other in dreams? After to-night we
shall never again have identical interests and obligations."

" Well, anyway, I'm going to bed," said Alan, and with a good-night very typical in its curtness of many earlier ones uttered in similar accents, he went upstairs.

Michael, when he found himself alone, thought it wiser to follow him. It was melancholy to watch the moon above the empty thoroughfare, and to hear the bells echoing through the spaces of the city.

Chapter XVI : *The Last Week*

MICHAEL'S old rooms in college were lent to him for three or four days, as he had hoped they would be. The present occupant, a freshman, was not staying up for Commemoration, and though next term he would move into larger rooms for his second year, his effects had not yet been transferred. Michael found it interesting to deduce from the evidence of his books and pictures the character of the owner with whom he had merely a nodding acquaintance. On the whole he seemed to be a dull young man. The photographs of his relatives were dull : his books were dull and unkempt : his pictures were dull, narrative rather than decorative. Probably there was nothing in the room that was strictly individual, nothing that he had acquired to satisfy his own taste. Every picture had probably been brought to Oxford because its absence would not be noticed in whatever spare bedroom it had previously been hung. Every book seemed either a survival of school or the inexpensive pastime of a railway journey. The very clock on the mantelpiece, which was still drearily ticking, looked like the first prize of a consolation race, rather than the gratification of a personal choice. Michael reproached the young man for being able to spend three terms a year without an attempt to garnish decently the gothic bookshelves, without an effort to leave upon this temporary abode the impression of his lodging. He almost endowed the room itself with a capacity for criticism, feeling it must deplore three terms of such undistinguished company. Yet after all, himself had left nothing to tell of his sojourn here. Although he and the dull young freshman had both used this creaking wicker-chair, for their successors neither of them could preserve the indication of their precedence. One relic of his own occupation, however, he did find in the fragments of envelopes which he had stuck to the door on innumerable occasions to announce the time of his return. These bits of paper that straggled in a kite's tail over the oak door had evidently resisted all attempts to scrub them off. There were usually a few on every door in college, but no one had ever so extensively advertized his movements as Michael, and to see these obstinate bits of tabs gave him a real pleasure, as if they assured him of his former existence here. Each one had marked an ubiquitous hour that was recorded more indelibly than many other occasions of higher importance.

There was not, however, much time for sentimentalizing over the past, as somewhere before one o'clock his mother and Stella would arrive, and they must be met. Alan came with him to the railway-station, and it was delightful to see Wedderburn with them, and in another part of the train Maurice with his mother and sisters. They must all have lunch at the Randolph, said Wedderburn immediately. Mrs. Fane was surprized to find the Randolph such a large hotel, and told Michael that if she had known it were possible to be at all comfortable in Oxford, she would have come up to see him long before. In the middle of lunch Lonsdale appeared, having according to his own account traced Michael's movements with tremendous determination. He was introduced to Mrs. Fane, who evidently took a fancy to him. She was looking, Michael thought, most absurdly young as Lonsdale rattled away to her, himself quite unchanged by a year at Scoone's and a recent failure to enter the Foreign Office.

"I say, this is awfully sporting of you, Mrs. Fane. You know, one feels fearfully out of it, coming up like this.

Terribly old and all that. I've been mugging away for the Diplomatic and I've just made an awful 'ass of myself. So I thought I wouldn't ask my governor to come up. He's choking himself to pieces over my career at present, but I've had an awfully decent offer from a man I know who runs a motor-business, and I don't think I've got the ambassadorial manner, do you? I think I shall be much better at selling cars, don't you? I say, which balls are you going to? Because I must buzz round and see about tickets."

Lonsdale's last question seemed to demand an answer, and Mrs. Fane looked at Michael rather anxiously.

"Michael, what balls are we going to?" she enquired.

"Trinity, the House, and the Apollo," he told her.

"What house is that? and I don't think I ever heard of Apollo College. It sounds very attractive. Have I said something foolish?" Mrs. Fane looked round her, for everyone was laughing.

"The House is Christ Church, mother," said Michael, and then swiftly he remembered his father might have made that name familiar to her. If he had, she gave no sign; and Michael blushing fiercely went on quickly to explain that the Apollo was the name of the Masonic Lodge of the university. Stella and Mrs. Fane rested that afternoon, and Michael with Wedderburn, Lonsdale, and several other contemporaries spent a jolly time in St. Mary's, walking round and reviving the memories of former rags. Alan had suggested that, as he would be near the Randolph, he might as well call in and escort Mrs. Fane and Stella down to tea in Michael's rooms. Mrs. Avery with Blanche and Eileen Avery had also been invited, and there was very little space left for tea-cups. Wedderburn however, assisted by Porcher on whom alone of these familiar people time had not laid a visible finger, managed to make everybody think they had enjoyed their tea. Afterwards there was a general move to the river for a short time, but as Lonsdale said, it must be for a very short time in order that everyone might be in good form for the Trinity ball. Mrs. Fane thought she would like to stay with Michael and talk to him for a while. It was strange to see her sitting here in his old room, and to be in a way more sharply aware of her than he had ever been, as he watched her fanning herself and looking round at the furniture, while the echoes of laughter and talk died away down the stone staircase without.

" Dear Michael," she said. " I wish I'd seen this room when you lived in it properly."

He laughed.

" When I lived in it properly," he answered, " I should have been made so shy by your visit that I think you'd have hated me and the room."

" You must have been so domestic," said his mother. " Such a curious thing has happened."

" Apropos of what ? " asked Michael smiling.

" You know Dick Prescott left Stella all his money, well——"

" But, mother, I didn't know anything about it."

" It was rather vague. He left it first to some old lady whom he intended to live four or five years, but she died this week, and so Stella inherits it at once. About two thousand a year. It's all in land, and will have to be managed. Huntingdonshire, or some county nobody believes in. It's all very difficult. She must marry at once."

" But, mother, why because she is to be better off and own land in Huntingdonshire, is she to marry at once ? " asked Michael.

" To avoid fortune-hunters, odd foreign counts and people."

" But she's not twenty-one yet," he objected.

" My dearest boy, I know, I know. That's why she must marry. Don't you see, when she's of age, she'll be able to

marry whom she likes, and you know how headstrong
Stella is."

"Mother," said Michael suddenly, "supposing she
married Alan ? "

"Delightful boy," she commented.

"You mean he's too young."

"For the present, yes."

"But you wouldn't try to stop an engagement, would
you ? " he asked very earnestly.

"My dearest Michael, if two young people I were fond of
fell in love, I should be the last person to try to interfere,"
Mrs. Fane promised.

"Well, don't say anything to Alan about Stella having
more money. I think he might be sensitive about it."

"Darling Stella," she sighed. "So intoxicated with
poverty—the notion of it, I mean."

"Mother," said Michael suddenly and nervously, "you
know, don't you, that the day after to-morrow is the House
ball—the Christ Church ball ? "

"Where your father was ? " she said gently pondering
the past.

He nodded.

"I'll show you his old rooms," Michael promised.

"Darling boy," she murmured putting out her hand.
He held it very tightly for a moment.

Next day after the Trinity ball, Alan, who was very
cheerful, told Michael he thought it would be good sport to
invite everybody to tea at 99 St. Giles.

"Oh, I particularly didn't want that to happen," said
Michael taken aback.

Alan was puzzled to know his reason.

"You'll probably think me absurd," said Michael. "But
I rather wanted to keep Ninety-nine for a place that I could
remember as more than all others the very heart of Oxford,
the most intimate expression of all I have cared for up here."

"Well, so you can, still," said Alan severely. "My asking a few people there to tea won't stop you."

"All the same, I wish you wouldn't," Michael persisted. "I moved into college for Commem just to avoid taking anybody to St. Giles."

"Not even Stella?" demanded Alan.

Michael shook his head.

"Well, of course, if you don't want me to, I won't," said Alan grudgingly. "But I think you're rather ridiculous."

"I am, I know," Michael agreed. "But thanks for humouring me. Do you think Stella has altered much since she was in Vienna, and during this year in town?"

"Not a bit," Alan declared enthusiastically. "And yet in one way she has," he corrected himself. "She seems less out of one's reach."

"Or else you know better how to stretch," Michael — laughed.

"Oh, I wasn't thinking of her attitude to me," said Alan a little stiffly.

"Most generalizations come down to a particular fact," Michael answered. But he would not tease Alan too much because he really wished him to have confidence.

After the Trinity ball it seemed to Michael now not very rash to sound Stella about her point of view with regard to Alan. For this purpose he invited her to come in a canoe with him on the Cher. Yet when together they were gliding down the green tunnels of the stream, when all the warmth of June was at their service, when neither question nor answer could have cast on either more than a momentary shadow, Michael could not bring himself to approach the subject even indirectly. They discussed lazily the success of the Trinity ball, without reference to the fact that Stella had danced three-quarters of her programme with Alan. She did not even bother to say he was a good dancer, so much was the convention of indifference

demanded by the brother and sister in their progress along
this fronded stream.

That night Michael did not dance a great deal himself
at the Masonic ball. He sat with Lonsdale in the gallery,
and together they much diverted themselves with the
costumes of the Freemasons. It was really ridiculous
to see Wedderburn in a red cloak and inconvenient sword
dancing the Templars quadrille.

"I think the English are curious people," said Michael.
"How absurd that all these undergraduates should belong
to an Apollo Lodge and wear these aprons and dress up like
this. Look at Wedders!"

"Enter Second Ruffian, what?" Lonsdale chuckled.

"I suppose it does take the place of religion," Michael
ejaculated in a tone of bewilderment. "Can you see my
sister and Alan Merivale anywhere?" he added casually.

"When's that coming off?" asked Lonsdale. He had
taken to an eyeglass since he had been in London, and the
enhanced eye glittered very wisely at Michael.

"You think?"

"What? Rather! My dear old bird, I'll lay a hundred
to thirty. Look at them now."

"They're only dancing," said Michael.

"But what dancing! Beautiful action. I never saw a
pair go down so sweetly to the gate. By the way what are
you going to do now you're down?"

Michael shrugged his shoulders.

"I suppose you wouldn't like to come into the motor
business?"

"No, thanks very much," said Michael.

"Well, you must do something, you know," said Lonsdale,
letting fall his eyeglass in disapproval. "You'll find that
out in town."

Michael was engaged for the next dance to one of
Maurice's sisters. Amid the whirl of frocks, as he swung

round this pretty and insipid creature in pink crêpe-de-chine, he was dreadfully aware that neither his nor her conversation mattered at all, and that valuable time was being robbed from him to the strains of The Choristers — waltz. Really he would have preferred to leave Oxford in a manner more solemn than this, not tangled up with frills and misses and obvious music. Looking down at Blanche Avery, he almost hated her. And to-morrow there would be another ball. He must dance with her again, with her and with her sister and with a dozen more dolls like her.

Next morning, or rather next noon, for it was noon before people woke after these balls that were not over until four o'clock, Michael looked out of his bedroom window with a sudden dismay at the great elms of the deer park, deep-bosomed, verdurous, entranced beneath the June sky.

"This is the last whole day," he said, "the last day when I shall have a night at the end of it; and it's going to be absolutely wasted at a picnic with all these women."

Michael scarcely knew how to tolerate that picnic, and wondered resentfully why everybody else seemed to enjoy it so much.

"Delicious life," said his mother, as he punted her away from the tinkling crowd on the bank. "I'm not surprized you like Oxford, dear Michael."

"I like it—I liked it, I mean, very much more when it was altogether different from this sort of thing. The great point of Oxford, in fact the whole point of Oxford, is that there are no girls."

"How charmingly savage you are, dear boy," said his mother. "And how absurd to pretend you don't care for girls."

"But I don't," he asserted. "In Oxford I actually dislike them very much. They're out of place except in Banbury Road. Dons should never have been allowed to — marry. Really, mother, women in Oxford are wrong."

"Of course, I can't argue with you. But there seem to me to be a great many of them."

"Great scott, you don't think it's like this in term-time, do you ?"

"Isn't it ?" said Mrs. Fane, apparently very much sur-prized. "I thought undergraduates were so famously susceptible. I'm sure they are too."

"Do you mean to say, you really thought this Commem herd was always roaming about Oxford ?"

"Michael, your Oxford expressions are utterly un-intelligible to me."

"Don't you realize you are up here for Commem—for Commemoration ?" he asked.

"How wonderful," she said. "Don't tell me any more. It's so romantic, to be told one is 'up' for some-thing."

Michael began to laugh, and the irritation of seeing the peaceful banks of the upper river dappled with feminine forms, so that everywhere the cattle had moved away to browse in the remote corners of the meadows, vanished.

The ball at Christ Church seemed likely to be the most successful and to be the one that would remain longest in the memories of those who had taken part in this Commemo-ration. Nowhere could an arbiter of pleasure have found so perfect a site for his most elaborate entertainment. There was something very strangely romantic in this gay assembly dancing in the great hall of the House, so that along the cloisters sounded the unfamiliar noise of fiddles ; but what gave principally the quality of romance and strangeness was that beyond the music, beyond the fan-tastically brilliant hall, stretched all around the dark quad-rangles deserted now save where about their glooms dresses indeterminate as moths were here and there visible. The decrescent moon would scarcely survive the dawn, and meanwhile there would be darkness everywhere away from the golden heart of the dance in that great hall spinning with light and motion.

Alan was evidently pleased that he was being able to show Stella his own college. He wore about him an air of confidence that Michael did not remember to have seen so plainly marked before. He and Stella were dancing together all the time here at Christ Church, and Michael felt he too must dance vigorously, so that he should not find himself overlooking them. He was shy somehow of overlooking them, and when Blanche Avery and Eileen Avery and half-a-dozen more cousins and sisters of friends had been led back to their chaperones, Michael went over to his mother and invited her to walk with him in the quadrangles of Christ Church. She knew why he wanted her to walk with him, and as she took his arm gently, she pressed it to her side. He thought again how ridiculously young she seemed and how the lightness of her touch was no less than that of the ethereal Eileen or the filmy Blanche. He wished he had asked her to dance with him, but yet on second thoughts was glad he had not, since to walk with her thus along these dark cloisters, down which travelled fainter and fainter the fiddles of the Eton Boating Song, was even better than dancing. Soon they were in Peckwater, standing silent on the gravel, almost overweighted by that heavy Georgian quadrangle.

"He lived either on that staircase or that one," said Michael. "But all the staircases and all the rooms in Peck are just the same, and all the men who have lived in them for the past fifty years are just the same. The House is a wonderful place, and the type it displays best changes less easily than any other."

"I didn't know him when he lived here," she murmured.

With her hand still resting lightly upon his sleeve, Michael felt the palpitation of long stored up memories and emotions. As she stood here pensive in the darkness, the years were rolling back.

"I expect if he were alive," she went on softly, "he would wonder how time could have gone by so quickly since he was here. People always do, don't they, when they revisit places they've known in younger days? When he was here, I must have been about fifteen. Funny, severe, narrow-minded old father!"

Michael waited rather anxiously. She had never yet spoken of her life before she met his father, and he had never brought himself to ask her.

"Funny old man! He was at Cambridge—Trinity College, I think it was called."

Then she was silent for a while, and Michael knew that she was linking her father and his father in past events; but still she did not voice her thoughts, and whatever joys or miseries of that bygone time were being recalled were still wrapped up in her reserve: nor did Michael feel justified in trying to persuade her to unloose them, even here in this majestic enclosure that would have engulfed them all as soon as they were free.

"You're not cold?" he tenderly demanded.

Surely upon his arm she had shivered.

"No, but I think we'll go back to the ballroom," she sighed.

Michael felt awed when their feet grated again in movement over the gravel. Behind them in the quadrangle there were ghosts, and the noise of walking here seemed sacrilegious upon this moonless and heavy summer night. Presently however two couples came laughing into the lamplight at the corner. The sense of decorous creeds outraged by his mother's behaviour of long ago vanished in the relief that present youth gave with its laughing company and fashionable frocks. Beside such heedlessness it were vain to conjure too remorsefully the past. After all, Peckwater was a place in which young men should crack whips and shout to one another across window-boxes; here there should be no tombs. Michael and his mother went on their way to the hall, and soon the music of the waltzing filled magically the lamplit entries of the great college, luring them to come back with light hearts, so importunate was the gaiety.

Michael rather reproached himself afterwards for not trying to take advantage of his mother's inclination to yield him a more extensive confidence. He was sure Stella would not have allowed the opportunity to slip by so in a craven embarrassment; or was it rather a fine sensitiveness, an imaginative desire to let the whole of that history lie buried in whatever poor shroud romance could lend it? As he was thinking of Stella, herself came towards him over the shining floor of the ballroom emptied for the interval between two dances. How delicately flushed she was and how her grey eyes were lustred with joy of the evening, or perhaps with fortunate tidings. Michael was struck by the direct way in which she was coming towards him without bothering through self-consciousness to seem to find him unexpectedly.

" Come for a walk with me in the moonlight," she said taking his arm.

" There's no moon yet, but I'll take you for a walk."

The clock was striking two as they reached Tom quad, and the decrescent moon to contradict him was already above the roofs. They strolled over to the fountain and stood there captured by loveliness, silent themselves and listening to the talk and laughter of shimmering figures that reached them subdued and intermittent from the flagged terraces in the distance.

" I suppose," said Stella suddenly, " you're very fond of Alan ? "

" Rather, of course I am."

"So am I."

Then she blushed, and her cheeks were very crimson in the moonlight. Michael had never seen her blush like this, had never been aware before of her maidenhood that now flooded his consciousness like a bouquet of roses. Hitherto she had always been for Michael a figure untouched by human weakness. Even when last summer he had seen her break down disconsolate, he had been less shocked by her grief than by its incongruity in her. This blush gave to him his only sister as a woman.

"The trouble with Alan is that he thinks he can't marry me because I have money, whereas he will be dependent on what he earns. That's rubbish, isn't it?"

"Of course," he agreed warmly. "I'll tell him so, if you like."

"I don't think he'd pay much attention," she said. "But you know, poor old Prescott left me a lot of land."

Michael nodded.

"Well, it's got to be managed, hasn't it?"

"Of course," said Michael. "You'll want a land agent."

"Why not Alan?" she asked. "I don't want to marry somebody in the Home Civil Service. I want him to be with me all day. Wouldn't you?"

"You've not told mother?" Michael suggested cautiously.

"Not yet. I shall be twenty-one almost at once, you know."

"What's that got to do with it?"

He was determined that in Stella's behaviour there should be no reflection, however pale, of what long ago had come into the life of an undergraduate going down from Christ Church. He wished for Stella and Alan to have all the benisons of the world. "You've no right to assume that mother will object," he told her.

But Stella did not begin to speak, as she was used, of her determination to have her own way in spite of everybody.

She was a softer Stella to-night; and that alone showed to Michael how right he had been to wish with all his heart that she would fall in love with Alan.

" There he is," she cried, clapping her hands.

Michael looked up, and saw him coming across the great moonlit space, tall and fair and flushed as he should be coming like this to claim Stella. Michael punched Alan to express his pleasure, and then he quickly left them standing by the fountain close together.

3 G

Chapter XVII : *The Last Day*

AT sunrise when the stones of Oxford were the colour of lavender, a photograph was taken of those who had been dancing at the Christ Church ball; after which, their gaiety recorded, the revellers went home. Michael was relieved when Alan offered to drive his mother and Stella back to the Randolph. He was not wishing for company that morning, but rather to walk slowly down to college alone. He waited therefore to see the dancers disappear group by group round various corners, until the High was desolate and he was the only human figure under this virginal sky. In his bedroom clear and still and sweet with morning light he did not want to go to bed. The birds fluttering on the lawns, the sun sparkling with undeterrent rays of gold not yet high and fierce, and all the buildings of the college dreaming upon the bosom of this temperate morn made him too vigilant for beauty. It would be wrong to sleep away this Oxford morning. With deliberate enjoyment he changed from ruffled evening dress into flannels.

In the sitting-room Michael looked idly through the books, and glanced with dissatisfaction at the desquamating backs of the magazines. There was nothing here fit to occupy his attention at such a peerless hour. Yet he still lingered by the books. Habit was strong enough to make him feel it necessary at least to pretend to read during the hours before breakfast. Finally in desperation he pulled out one of the magazines, and as he did so a small volume bound in paper fell on to the floor. It was Manon

Lescaut, and Michael was pleased that the opportunity was given to him of reading a book he had for a long time meant to read. Moreover, if it were disappointing, this edition was so small that it would fit easily into his pocket and be no bother to carry. He wondered rather how Manon Lescaut had come into this bookshelf, and he opened it at an aquatint of ladies deject and lightly clothed—*c'est une douzaine de filles de joie*, said the inscription beneath. Here, Michael feared, was the explanation of how the Abbé Prévost found himself squeezed away between Pearson's and The Strand. Here at last was evidence in these rooms of a personal choice. Here spoke, if somewhat ignobly, the character of the purchaser. Michael slipped the small volume into his pocket and went out.

The great lawns in front of New Quad stretched for his solitary pleasure in the golden emptiness of morn. At such an hour it were vain to repine; so supreme was beauty — like this that Michael's own departure from Oxford appeared to him as unimportant as the fall of a petal unshaken by any breath of summer wind. With the air brimming to his draught and with early bees restless along the herbaceous border by the stream's parapet, Michael began to read Manon Lescaut. He would finish this small volume before breakfast, unless the fumes of the sun should drug him out of all power to award the Abbé his fast attention. The great artist was stronger than the weather, and Michael read on while the sun climbed the sky, while the noises of a new day began, while the footsteps of hurrying scouts went to and'fro.

It was half-past eight when he finished that tale of love. For a few moments he sat dazed, visualizing that dreadful waste near New Orleans where in the sand it was so easy for the star-crossed Chevalier to bury the idol of his heart.

Porcher was surprized to find Michael up and wide awake.

"You oughtn't to have gone and tired yourself like that, sir," he said reproachfully.

Michael rather resented putting back the little book among those magazines. He felt it would be almost justifiable to deprive the owner of what he so evidently did not esteem, and he wondered if, when he had cut the pages with his prurient paper-knife the purchaser had wished at the end of this most austere tale that he had not spent his money so barrenly. *C'est une douzaine de filles de joie.* It was a bitter commentary on human nature, that a mere aquatint of these poor naked creatures jolting to exile in their tumbril should extort half-a-crown from an English undergraduate to probe their history.

"Dirty-minded little beast," said Michael, as he confiscated the edition of Manon Lescaut, placing it in his suit-case. Then he went out into St. Mary's Walks, and at the end of the longest vista sat down on a garden-bench beside the Cherwell. Before him stretched the verdurous way down which he had come; beyond, taking shape among the elms, was the college; to right and left were vivid meadows where the cattle were scarcely moving, so lush was the pasturage here; and at his side ran the slow, the serpentine, the tree-green tranquil Cher.

As he sat here among the bowers of St. Mary's, the story he had just read came back to him with a double poignancy. He scarcely thought that any tale of love could purify so sharply every emotion but that of pity too profound for words. He wondered if his father had loved with such a devotion of self-destruction as had inspired des Grieux. It was strange himself should have been so greatly moved by a story of love at the moment when he was making ready to enter the world. He had not thought of love during all the time he had been up at Oxford. Now he went back in memory to the days when Lily had the power to shake his soul, even as the soul of des Grieux had been shaken in that

inn-yard of Amiens, when coming by the coach from Arras
he first beheld Manon. How trivial had been Lily's infidelity compared with Manon's: how shallow had been
his own devotion beside the Chevalier's. But the love of
des Grieux for Manon was beyond the love of ordinary
youth. The Abbé by his art had transmuted a wild infatu-
ation, a foolish passion for a wanton into something above
even the chivalry of the noblest lover of the Middle Ages.
It was beyond all tears, this tale; and the dry grief it now
exacted gave to Michael in some inexplicable way a knowledge of life more truly than any book since Don Quixote.
It was an academic tale, too: it was told within the narrow-
est confines of the most rigid form. There was not in
this narrative one illegitimate device to excite an easy
compassion in the reader: it was literature of a quality
marmoreal, and it moved as only stone can move. The
death of Manon in the wilderness haunted him even as he
sat here: almost he too could have prostrated himself in
humiliation before this tragedy.

"There is no story like it," said Michael to the sleek
river. *N'exigez point de moi que je vous décrive mes sentiments, ni que je vous rapporte mes dernières expressions.*
And it was bought by an undergraduate for half-a-crown
because he wanted to stare like the peasant-folk. *C'est une
douzaine de filles de joie.* How really promising that illus-
tration must have looked: how the coin must have itched
in his pocket: how carefully he must have weighed the
slimness of the book against his modesty: how easy it had
been to conceal behind those magazines.

But he could not sit here any longer reconstructing the
shamefaced curiosity of a dull young freshman, nor even,
with so much to arrange this last morning, could he continue
to brood upon the woes of the Chevalier des Grieux and
Manon Lescaut. It was time to go and rouse Lonsdale.
Lonsdale had slept long enough in those ground-floor

rooms of his where on the first day of the first term the inextricable Porcher had arranged his, wine.' It did not take long to drag Lonsdale out of bed.

"You slack devil, I've not been to bed at all," said Michael.

"More silly ass you," Lonsdale yawned. "Now don't annoy me while I'm dressing with your impressions of the sunrise." Michael watched him eat his breakfast, while he slowly and with the troublesome aid of his eyeglass managed to focus once again the world.

"I was going to tell you something deuced interesting about myself when you buzzed off this morning. You've heard of Queenie Molyneux—well, Queenie . . ."

"Wait a bit," Michael interrupted. "I haven't heard of Queenie Molyneux."

"Why, she's in the Pink Quartette."

Michael still looked blank, and Lonsdale adjusting his eyeglass looked at him in amazement.

"The Pink Quartette in My Mistake."

"Oh, that rotten musical comedy," said Michael. "I haven't seen it."

Lonsdale shook his head in despair, and the monocle tinkled down upon his plate. When he had wiped it clean of marmalade, he asked Michael in a compassionate voice if he *never* went to the theatre, and with a sigh returned to the subject of Queenie.

"It's the most extraordinary piece of luck. A girl that everyone in town has been running after falls in love with me. Now the question is, what ought I to do? I can't afford to keep her, and I'm not cad enough to let somebody else keep her, and use the third latchkey. My dear old chap, I don't mind telling you I'm in the deuce of a fix."

"Are you very much in love with her?" Michael asked.

"Of course I am. You don't get Queenies chucked at your head like turnips. Of course I'm frightfully keen."

"Why don't you marry her ? " Michael asked.

"What ? Marry her ? You don't seem to understand who I'm talking about. Queenie Molyneux ! She's in the Pink Quartette in My Mistake."

"Well ? "

"Well, I can't marry a chorus-girl."

"Other people have," said Michael.

"Well, yes, but—er—you know, Queenie has rather a reputation. I shouldn't be the first."

"The problem's too hard for me," said Michael.

In his heart he would have liked to push Manon Lescaut into Lonsdale's hands and bid him read that for counsel. But he could not help laughing to himself at the notion of Lonsdale wrestling with the moral of Manon Lescaut, and if the impulse had ever reached his full consciousness, it died on the instant.

"Of course, if this motor-car business is any good," Lonsdale was saying, "I might be able in a year or two to compete with elderly financiers. But my advice to you . . ."

"You asked for my advice," said Michael with a smile.

"I know I did. I know I did. But as you haven't ever been to see My Mistake—the most absolutely successful musical comedy for years—why, my dear fellow, I've been thirty-eight times ! . . . and my advice to you is ' avoid actresses.' Oh yes, I know it's difficult, I know, I know."

Lonsdale shook his head so often that the monocle fell on the floor, and his wisdom was speechless until he could find it again.

Michael left him soon afterwards, feeling rather sadly that the horizon before him was clouding over with feminine forms. Alan would soon be engaged to his sister. It was delightful, of course, but in one way it already placed a

barrier between their perfect intercourse. Maurice would
obviously soon be thinking of nothing but women. Already.
even up at Oxford a great deal of his attention had been
turned in that direction : and now Lonsdale had Queenie.
This swift severance from youth by all his friends, this
preoccupation with womanhood was likely to be depressing,
thought Michael, unless himself also fell in love. That
was very improbable, however. Love filled him with fear.
The Abbé Prévost that morning had expressed for him in
art the quintessence of what he knew with sharp prevision
love for him would mean. He felt a dread of leaving
Oxford that quite overshadowed his regret. Here was
shelter—why had he not shaped his career to stay for ever
in this cold peace ? And, after all, why should he not ? He
was independent. Why should he enter the world and call
down upon himself such troubles and torments as had
vexed his youth in London ? From the standpoint of
moral experience he had a right to stay here : and yet it
would be desolate to stay here without a vital reason,
merely to grow old on the fringe of the university. Could
he have been a Fellow, it would have been different : but
to vegetate, to dream, to linger without any power of art
to put into form even what he had experienced already,
that would inevitably breed a pernicious melancholy. On
the other hand, he might go to Plashers Mead. He might
almost make trial of art. Guy would inspire him, Guy
living his secluded existence with books above a stream.
Whatever occurred to him in the way of personal failure,
he could on his side encourage Guy. His opinion might be
valuable, for although he seemed to have no passion to
create, he was sure his judgment was good. How Guy
would appreciate Manon ; and perhaps like so many classics
he had taken it as read, nor knew yet what depths of pity,
what profundities of beauty awaited his essay.

Michael made up his mind that instead of going to

London this afternoon he would ride over to Wychford and either stay with Guy or in any case announce his speedy return to stay with him for at least the rest of the summer. Alan would escort his mother and Stella home. It would be easier for Alan that way. His mother would be so charming to him, and everything would soon be arranged. With this plan to unfold Michael hurried across to Ninety-nine. Alan was already up. Everything was packed. Michael realized he could already regard the digs without a pang for the imminence of final departure. Perhaps the Abbé — Prévost had deprived him of the capacity for a merely sentimental emotion, at any rate for the present.

Alan looked rather doubtful over Michael's proposal.

" I hate telling things in the train," he objected.

" You haven't got to tell anything in the train," Michael contradicted. " My mother is sure to invite you to dinner to-night, and you can tell her at home. It's much better for me to be out of it. I shall be back in a few days to pack up various things I shall want for Plashers Mead."

" It's a most extraordinary thing," said Alan slowly, " that the moment you think there's a chance of my marrying your sister, you drop me like a hot brick."

Michael touched his shoulder affectionately.

" I'm more pleased about you and her than about anything that has ever happened," he said earnestly. " Now are you content ? "

" Of course, I oughtn't to have spoken to her," said Alan. " I really don't know, looking back at last night, how on earth I had the cheek. I expect I said a lot of rot. I ought certainly to have waited until I was in the Home Civil."

" You must chuck that idea," said Michael. " Stella would loathe the Civil Service."

" I can't marry . . . " Alan began.

" You've got to manage her affairs. She has a tempera-

ment: She also has land." Then Michael explained about
Prescott, and so eloquent was he upon the need for Stella's
happiness that Alan began to give way.

"I always thought I should be too proud to live on a
woman," he said.

"Don't make me bring forward all my arguments over
again," Michael begged. "I'm already feeling very fagged.
You'll have all your work cut out. To manage Stella herself,
let alone her piano and let alone her land, is worth a very
handsome salary. But that's nothing to do with it. You're
in love with each other. Are you going to be selfish enough to
satisfy your own silly pride at the expense of her happiness?
I could say lots more. I could sing your praises as . . ."

"Thanks very much. You needn't bother," interrupted
Alan gruffly.

"Well, will you not be an ass?"

"I'll try."

"Otherwise I shall tell you what a perfect person you are."

"Get out," said Alan, flinging a cushion.

Michael left him and went down to the Randolph. He
found Stella already dressed and waiting impatiently in
the lobby for his arrival. His mother was not yet down.

"It's all right," he began, "I've destroyed the last
vestige of Alan's masculine vanity. Mother will be all right
—if," said Michael severely, pausing to relish the flavour
of what might be the last occasion on which he would
administer with authority a brotherly admonition, "*if*
you don't put on a lot of side and talk about being twenty-
one in a couple of months. Do you understand?"

Stella for answer flung her arms round his neck, and
Michael grew purple under the conspicuous affront she had
put upon his dignity.

"You absurd piece of pomposity," she said. "I really
adore you."

"For god's sake don't talk in that exaggerated way,"

Michael muttered. ".I hope you aren't going to make a public ass of Alan like that. He'd be rather sick."

" If you say another word," Stella threatened, " I'll clap my hands and go dancing all round this hotel."

At lunch Michael explained that he was not coming to town for a day or two, and his mother accepted his announcement with her usual gracious calm. Just before they were getting ready to enter their cab to go to the station, Michael took her aside.

, " Mother, you'll be very sympathetic, won't you ? " Then he whispered to her, fondling her arm. " They really are so much in love, but Alan will never be able to explain how much, and I swear to you he and Stella were made for each other."

" But they don't want to be married at once ? " asked Mrs. Fane in some alarm.

" Oh, not to-morrow," Michael admitted. " But don't ask them to have a year's engagement. Will you promise me ? "

" Why don't you come back to-night and talk to me about it ? " she asked.

" Because they'll be so delightful talking to you without me. I should spoil it. And don't forget—Alan is a *slow* bowler, but he gets wickets."

Michael watched with a smile his mother waving to him from the cab while still she was vaguely trying to resolve the parting metaphor he had flung at her. As soon as the cab had turned the corner, he called for his bicycle and rode off to Wychford.

He went slowly with many road-side halts, nor was there the gentlest rise up which he did not walk. It was after five o'clock when he dipped from the rolling highway down into Wychford. There were pink roses everywhere on the grey houses. As he went through the gate of Plashers Mead, he hugged himself with the thought of Guy's pleasure at seeing him so unexpectedly on this burnished afternoon of midsummer. The leaves of the old espaliers rustled crisply : they were green and glossy, and the apples, still scarcely larger than nuts, promised in the autumn when he and Guy would be together here a ruddy harvest. The house was unresponsive when he knocked at the door. He waited for a minute or two, and then he went into the stone-paved hall and up the steep stairs to the long corridor, at whose far end the framed view of the open doorway into Guy's green room glowed as vividly as if it gave upon a high-walled sunlit garden. The room itself was empty. There were only the books and a lingering smell of tobacco smoke, and through the bay-window the burble of the stream swiftly flowing. Michael looked out over the orchard and away to the far-flung horizon of the wold beyond.

Here assuredly, he told himself, was the perfect refuge. Here in this hollow waterway was peace. From here sometimes in the morning he and Guy would ride into Oxford, whence at twilight they would steal forth again and, dipping down from the bleak road, find Plashers Mead set safe in a land that was tributary only to the moon. Guy's diamond pencil, with which he was wont upon the window to inscribe mottoes, lay on the sill. Michael picked it up and scratched upon the glass : *The fresh green lap of fair King Richard's land*, setting the date below.

Then suddenly coming down past the house with the stream he saw in a canoe Guy with a girl. The canoe swept past the window and was lost round the bend, hidden immediately by reeds and overarching willows. Yet Michael had time to see the girl, to see her cheeks of frailest rose, to know she was a fairy's child and that Guy was deep in love. Although the fleet vision thrilled him with a romantic beauty, Michael was disheartened. Even here at Plashers Mead, where he had counted upon finding a cloister, the disintegration of life's progress had begun. It would be absurd for him to intrude now upon Guy. He would scarcely be welcomed now in this June weather. After all, he must go to London ; so he left behind him the long grey house and walked up the slanting hill that led to the nearest railway-station. By the gate where he and Guy had first seen Plashers Mead, he paused to throw one regret back into that hollow waterway, one regret for the long grey house on its green island circled by singing streams.

There were two hours to wait at the station before the train would arrive. He would be in London about half-past nine. Discovering a meadow pied with daisies, Michael slept in the sun.

When he woke, the grass was smelling fresh in the shadows, and the sun was westering. He went across to the station and, during the ten minutes left before his train came in, walked up and down the platform in the spangled airs of evening, past the tea-roses planted there, slim tawny buds and ivory cups dabbled with creamy flushes.

It was dark when Michael reached Paddington, and he felt depressed, wishing he had come back with the others. No doubt they would all be at the theatre. Or should he drive home and perhaps find them there ?

" Know anything about this golf-bag, Bill ? " one porter was shouting to another.

Michael went over to look at the label in case it might be Alan's bag. But it was an abandoned golf-bag belonging to no one : there were no initials even painted on the canvas. This forsaken golf-bag doubled Michael's depression, and though he had always praised Paddington as the best of railway-stations, he thought to-night it was the gloomiest in London. Then he remembered in a listless way that he had forgotten to enquire about his suit-case, which had been sent after him from Oxford to Shipcott, the station for Wychford. It must be lying there now with Manon Lescaut inside. He made arrangements to recapture it, which consummated his depression. Then he called a hansom and drove to Cheyne Walk. They had all gone to the Opera, the parlour-maid told him. Michael could not bear to stay at home to-night alone : so, getting back into the hansom, he told the man to drive to the Oxford Music--hall. It would be grimly amusing to see on the programmes there the theatrical view of St. Mary's tower.

THE END OF THE

THIRD BOOK

BOOK FOUR
ROMANTIC EDUCATION

Sancta ad vos anima atque istius inscia culpae
descendam, magnorum haud umquam indignus avorum.

VIRGIL.

For Fancy cannot live on real food :
In youth she will despise familiar joy
To dwell in mournful shades, as they grow real,
Then buildeth she of joy her fair ideal.

ROBERT BRIDGES.

Chapter I : *Ostia Ditis*

WHEN Michael reached the Oxford Music-hall he wondered why he had overspurred his fatigue to such a point. There was no possibility of pleasure here, and he would have done better to stay at home and cure with sleep what was after all a natural depression. It had been foolish to expect a sedative from contact with this unquiet assemblage. In the mass they had nothing but a mechanical existence, subject as they were to the brightness or dimness of the electrolier — that regulated their attention. Michael did not bother to buy a programme. From every podgy hand he could see dangling the lithograph of St. Mary's tower with its glazed moonlight; and he was not sufficiently aware of the glib atom who bounced about the golden dazzle of the stage to trouble about his name. He mingled with the slow pace of the men and women on the promenade. They were going backwards and forwards like flies, meeting for a moment in a quick buzz of colloquy and continuing after a momentary pause their impersonal and recurrent progress. Michael was absorbed in this ceaseless ebb and flow of motion where the sidelong glances of the women, as they brushed his elbow in the passing crowd, gave him no conviction of an individual gaze. Once or twice he diverted his steps from the stream and tried to watch in a half-hearted way the performance; but as he leaned over the plush-covered barrier a woman would sidle up to him, and he would move away in angry embarrassment from the questioning eyes under the big plumed hat. The noise of

popping corks and the chink of glasses, the whirr of the
ventilating fans, the stentorophonic orchestra, the red-
faced raucous atom on the stage combined to irritate him
beyond farther endurance; and he had just resolved to
walk seven times up and down the promenade before he
went home, when somebody cried in heartiest greeting over
his shoulder, " Hullo, Bangs ! "

Michael turned and saw Drake, and so miserable had been
the effect of the music-hall that he welcomed him almost
cordially, although he had not seen him during four years
and would probably like him rather less now than he had
liked him at school.

" *My* lord ! fancy seeing you again ! " Drake effused.

Michael found himself shaken warmly by the hand in
support of the enthusiastic recognition. After the less
accentuated cordiality of Oxford manners, it was strange
to be standing like this with clasped hands in the middle
of this undulatory crowd.

" I say, Bangs, old man, we must have a drink on this."

Drake led the way to the bar and called authoritatively
for two whiskies and a split Polly.

" Quite a little-bit-of-fluffy-all-right," he whispered to
Michael, seeming to calculate with geometrical eyes the
arcs and semicircles of the barmaid's form. She with her
nose in the air poured out the liquid, and Michael wondered
how any of it went into the glass. As a matter of fact most
of it splashed on to the bar, whence Drake presently took
his change all bedewed with alcohol and, lifting his glass,
wished Michael a jolly good chin-chin.

" 'D luck," Michael muttered in response.

" *My* lord ! " Drake began again. " Fancy meeting you
of all people. And not a bit different. I said to myself
' I'm jiggered if that isn't old Bangs,' and—well, *my* lord !
but I was surprized. Do you often come out on the
randan ? "

· " Not very often," Michael admitted. " I just happened to be alone to-night."

" Good for you, old sport. What have you been doing since you left school ? "

" I'm just down from Oxford," Michael informed him.

" Pretty good spree up there, eh ? "

" Oh, yes, rather," said Michael.

" Well, I had the chance to go," said Drake. " But it wasn't good enough. It's against you in the City, you know. Waste of time really, except of course for a parson or a schoolmaster."

" Yes, I expect it would have been rather a waste of time for you," Michael agreed.

" Oh, rotten ! So you moved from—where was it ?— Carlington Road ? "

" Yes, we moved to Cheyne Walk."

" Let's see. That's in Hampstead, isn't it ? "

" Well, it's rather nearer the river," suggested Michael. " Are you still in Trelawny Road ? "

" Yes, still in the same old hovel. My hat ! Talking of Trelawny Road, it *is* a small world. Who do you think I saw last week ? "

· " Not Lily Haden ? " Michael asked in spite of a wish not to rise so quickly to Drake's hook.

" You're right. I saw the fair Lily. But where do you think I saw her ? Bangs, old boy, I tell you I'm not a fellow who's easily surprized. But this knocked me. Of course you'll understand the Hadens flitted from Trelawny Road soon after you stopped calling. So who knows what's happened since ? I give you three guesses where I saw her."

" I hate riddles," said Michael fretfully.

· " At the Orient," said Drake solemnly. " The Orient Promenade. You could have knocked me down with a feather."

Michael stared at Drake, scarcely realizing the full implication of what he just announced. Then suddenly he grasped the horrible fact that revealed to him here in a music-hall carried a double force. His one instinct for the moment was to prevent Drake from knowing into what depths his news had plunged him.

"Has she changed?" asked Michael and could have kicked himself for the question.

"Well, of course there was a good deal of powder," said Drake. "I'm not easily shocked, but this gave me a turn. She was with a man, but even if she hadn't been, I doubt if I'd have had the nerve to talk to her. I wouldn't have known what to say. But, of course, you know, her mother was a bit rapid. That's where it is. Have another drink. You're looking quite upset."

Michael shook his head. He must go home.

"Aren't you coming up West a bit?" asked Drake in disappointment. "The night's still young."

But Michael was not to be persuaded.

"Well, don't let's lose sight of each other now we've met. What's your club? I've just joined the Primrose myself. Not a bad little place. You get a rare good one-and-sixpenny lunch. You ought to join. Or perhaps you're already suited?"

"I belong to the Bath," said Michael.

"Oh, of course, if you're suited, that's all right. But any time you want to join the Primrose just let me know and I'll put you up. The sub isn't really very much. Guinea a year."

Michael thanked him and escaped as quickly as he could. Outside even in Oxford Street the air was full of summer, and the cool people sauntering under the sapphirine sky were as welcome to his vision as if he had waked from a fever. His head was throbbing with the heat of the music-hall, and the freshness of night air was delicious. He called a hansom and told the driver to go to Blackfriars Bridge, and from there slowly along the Embankment to Cheyne Walk. For a time he leaned back in the cab, thinking of nothing, barely conscious of golden thoroughfares, of figures in silhouette against the glitter, and of the London roar rising and falling. Presently in the quiet of the shadowy cross-streets he began to appreciate what seemed the terrible importance to himself of Drake's news.

"It concerns me," he began to reiterate aloud. "It concerns me—me—me. It's useless to think that it doesn't. It concerns me."

Then a more ghastly suggestion whispered itself. How should he ever know that he was not primarily responsible? The idea came over him with sickening intensity; and upright now he saw in the cracked mirrors of the cab a face blanched, a forehead clammy with sweat, and over his shoulder like a goblin the wraith of Lily. It was horrible — to see so distorted that beautiful memory which time had etherealized out of a reality, until of her being nothing had endured but a tenuous image of earliest love. Now under the shock of her degradation he must be dragged back by this goblin to face his responsibility. He must behold again close at hand her shallow infidelity. He must assure himself of her worthlessness, hammer into his brain that from the beginning she had merely trifled with him. This must be established for the sake of his conscience. Where the devil was this driver going?

"I told you down the Embankment," Michael shouted through the trap.

"I can't go down the Embankment before I gets there, can I, sir?" the cabman asked reproachfully.

Michael closed the trap. He was abashed when he perceived they were still only in Fleet Street. Why had he gone to The Oxford to-night? Why had he spoken to Drake? Why had he not stayed at Wychford? Why had

he not returned to London with the others ?, Such regrets
were valueless. It was foredoomed that Lily should come
into his life again. Yet there was no reason why she should.
There was no reason at all., Men could, hardly be held
responsible for the fall of women, unless themselves had upon
theirsouls the guilt of betrayal or desertion. It was ridiculous
to argue that he must bother because at eighteen he had
loved her, because at eighteen he had thought she was
worthy of being loved., No doubt the Orient Promenade
was the sequel of kissing objectionable-actors in the back
gardens of West Kensington. Yet the Orient Promenade ?
That was a damnable place. The Orient Promenade ? He
remembered her kisses. Sitting in this cab, he was kissing
her now. She had ridden for hours deep in his arms. Not
Oxford could cure this relapse into the past. Every spire
and every tower had crashed to ruins around his staid conceptions, so that they too presently fell away. Four years of
plastic calm were unfashioned, and she was again beside
him. Every passing lamp lit up her face, her smouldering
eyes, her lips, her hair. The goblin took her place, the goblin
with sidelong glances, tasting of scent, powdered, pranked,
soulless, lost. What was she doing at this moment ? What
invitation glittered in her look ? Michael nearly told the
driver to turn his horse. He must reach the Orient before
the show was done. He must remonstrate with her, urge her
to go home, help her with money, plead with her, drag her
by force away from that procession. But the hansom kept
on its way. All down the Embankment, all along Grosvenor
Road the onrushing street-lamps flung their balls of light
with monotonous jugglery into the cab. To-night anyhow
it was too late to find her. He would sleep on whatever resolve he took, and in the morning perhaps the problem would
present itself in less difficult array.

Michael reached home before the others had come back
from the Opera; and suddenly he knew how tired he was.

To-day had been the longest day he could ever remember. Quickly he made up his mind to go to bed so that he would not be drawn into the discussion of the delightful engagement of Stella and Alan. He felt he could hardly face the irony of their happiness when he thought of Lily. For a while he sat at the window, staring at the water and bathing his fatigue in the balm of the generous night. Even here in London peace was possible, here where the reflected lamps in golden pagodas sprawled across the width of the river and where the glutted tide lapped and sucked the piers of the bridge, nuzzled the shelving strand and swirled in sleepy greed around the patient barges at their moorings. A momentary breeze frilled the surface of the stream, blurring the golden pagodas of light so that they jigged and glittered until the motion died away. Eastward in the sky over London hung a tawny stain that blotted out the stars.

From his window Michael grew more and more conscious of the city stirring in a malaise of inarticulate life beneath that sinister stain. He was aware of the stealthy soul of London transcending the false vision of peace before his eyes. There came creeping over him the dreadful knowledge that Lily was at this moment living beneath that London sky, imprisoned, fettered, crushed beneath that grim suffusion, that fulvid vile suffusion of the nocturnal sky. He began to spur his memory for every beautiful record of her that was stamped upon it. She was walking towards him in Kensington Gardens : not a contour of her delicate progress had been blunted by the rasp of time. Five years ago he had been the first to speak : now, must it be she who sometimes spoke first ? Seventeen she had told him had been her age, and they had kissed in the dark midway between two lamps. No doubt she had been kissed before. In that household of Trelawny Road anything else was inconceivable. The grey streets of West Kensington in terrace upon terrace stretched before him, and now as he recalled their barren stones it seemed to him there was not one corner round which he might not expect to meet her face to face. "*Michael, why do you make me love you so?*" That was her voice. It was she who had asked him that question. Never before this moment had he realized the import of her demand. Now, when it was years too late to remedy, it came out of the past like an accusation. He had answered it then with closer kisses. He had released her then like a ruffled bird, secure that to-morrow and to-morrow and to-morrow she would nestle to his arms for cherishing. And now if he thought more of her life beneath that lurid stain he would go mad; if he conjured to himself the vision of her now— had not Drake said she was powdered and painted? To this had she come. And she was here in London. Last week she had been seen. It was no nightmare. It was real, horrible and real. He must go out again at once and find her. He must not sit dreaming here, staring at the silly Thames, the smooth and imperturbable Thames. He must plunge into that phantasmagoric city; he must fly from haunt to haunt; he must drag the depths of every small hell; he must find her to-night.

Michael rose, but on the instant of his decision his mother and Stella drove up. Alan was no longer with them. He must have gone home to Richmond. How normal sounded their voices from the pavement below. Perhaps he would after all go down and greet them. They might wonder otherwise if something had happened. Looking at himself as he passed the mirror on his way down, he saw that he really was haggard. If he pleaded a headache, his countenance would bear him out. In the end he shouted to them over the balusters, and both of them wanted to come up with remedies. He would not let them. The last thing his mood desired was the tending of cool hands.

"I'm only fagged out," he told them. "I want a night's sleep."

· Yet he knew how hard it would be to fall asleep. His brain was on fire. Morning, the liquid morning of London summer, was unimaginable. He shut the door of his room and flung himself down upon the bed. Contact with the cool linen released the pent-up tears, and the fire within burnt less fiercely as he cried. His surrender to self-pity must have lasted half-an-hour. The pillow-case was drenched. His body felt battered. He seemed to have recovered from a great illness. The quiet of the room surprized him, as he looked round in a daze at the familiar objects. The cataclysm of emotion so violently expressed had left him with a sense that the force of his grief must have shaken the room as it had shaken him. But everything was quiet; everything was the same. Now that he had wept away that rending sense of powerlessness to aid her, he could examine the future more calmly. Already the numbness was going, and the need for action was beginning to make itself felt. Yet still all his impulses were in confusion. He could not attain to any clear view of his attitude.

He was not in love with her now. He was neither covetous of her kisses nor in any way of her bodily presence. To his imagination at present she appeared like one who has died. It seemed to him that he desired to bring back a corpse, that over a lifeless form he wished to lament the loss of beauty, of passion and of youth. But immediately afterwards, so constant was the impression of her as he had last known her, so utterly incapable was Drake's account to change his outward picture of her, he could not conceive the moral disintegration wrought by her shame. It seemed to him that could he be driving with her in a hansom to-night, she would lie still and fluttered in his arms, the Lily of five years ago whom now to cherish were an adorable duty.

Therefore he was in love with her. Otherwise to every prostitute in London he must be feeling the same tenderness. Yet they were of no account. Were they of no account.?!. *C'est une douzaine de filles de joie.* When he read Manon this morning—how strange! this morning he had been reading Manon at Oxford—he was moved with pity for all poor light women. And Lily was one of them.' They did not banish them to New Orleans nowadays, but she was not less an outcast. It was not because he was still in love with her that he wished to find her. It was because he had known her in the old days. He bore upon his own soul the damning weight that in the past she had said "*Michael, why do you make me love you so?*" If there was guilt, he shared the guilt. If there was shame, he was shameful. Others after him had sinned against her casually, counting their behaviour no more than a speck of dust in the garbage of human emotion with which she was already smirched. He may not have seduced her, but he had sinned against her, because while loving her he had let her soul elude him. He had made her love him. He had trifled with her sensuousness; and to say that he was too young for blame was cowardly. It was that very youth which was the sin, because under society's laws, whatever fine figure his love might seem to him to have cut, he should have known that it was a profitless love for a girl. He shared in the guilt. He partook of the shame. That was incontrovertible.

Suddenly a new aspect of the situation was painfully visible. Had not his own mother been sinned against by his father? That seemed equally incontrovertible. Prescott had known it in his heart. Prescott had said to him in the Albany on the night he killed himself that he wanted to marry Stella in order to be given the right to protect her. Prescott must always have deplored the position in which his friend's mistress had been placed. That was a hard word to use for one's mother. It seemed to hiss with scorn. No doubt his father would have married her, if Lady Saxby had divorced him. No doubt that was the salve with which he had soothed his conscience. Something was miserably wrong with our rigid divorce law, he may have said. He must have cursed it innumerable times in order to console his conscience, just as himself at eighteen had cursed youth when he could not marry Lily. His mother had been sinned against. Nothing could really alter that. It was use- less to say that the sinner had in the circumstances behaved very well, that so far as he was able he had treated her honourably. But nothing could excuse his father's initial weakness. The devotion of a lifetime could not wash out his deliberate sin against—and who was she ? Who was his mother ? Valérie . . and her father was at Trinity, Cambridge . . a clergyman . . a gentleman. And his father had taken her away, had exposed her to the calumny of the world. He had afterwards behaved chivalrously at any rate by the standards of romance. But by what small margin had his own mother escaped the doom of Lily ? All his conceptions of order and safety and custom tottered and reeled at such a thought. Surely such a realization doubled his obligation to atone by rescuing Lily, out of very thank- fulness to God that his own mother had escaped the evil which had come to her. How wretchedly puny now seemed all his own repinings. All he had gained for his own cha- — racter had been a vague dissatisfaction that he could not succeed to the earldom in order to prove the sanctity of good breeding. There had been no gratitude ; there had been nothing but a hurt conceit. The horror of Drake's news would at least cure him for ever of that pettiness. Already he felt the strength that comes from the sight of a task that must be conquered. He had been moved that morning by the tale of Manon Lescaut. This tale of Lily was in comparison with that as an earthquake to the tunnel- ling of a mole beneath a croquet-lawn. And now must he regard his father's memory with condemnation ? Must he hate him ? He must hate him indeed, unless by his own behaviour he could feel he had accepted in substitution the burden of his father's responsibility. And he had admired him so much dying out there in Africa for his country. He had resented his death for the sake of thousands more un-worthy living comfortably at home.

" All my standards are falling to pieces," thought Michael. " Heroes and heroines are all turning into cardboard. If I don't make some effort to be true to conviction, I shall turn to cardboard with the rest."

He began to pace the room in a tumult of intentions, vows and resolutions. Somehow before he slept he must shape his course. Four years had dreamed themselves away at Oxford. Unless all that education was as immaterial as the fogs of the Isis, it must provide him now with an indication of his duty. He had believed in Oxford, believed in her infallibility and glory; he had worshipped all she stood for. He had surrendered himself to her to make of him a gentle-man, and unless these four years had been a delusion, his education must bear fruit now.

Michael made up his mind suddenly, and as it seemed to him at the moment in possession of perfect calm and clarity of judgement, that he would marry Lily. He had accepted marriage as a law of his society. Well, then that law should be kept. He would test every article of the creed of an English gentleman. He would try in the fire of his purpose honour, pride, courtesy and humility. All these must come to his aid, if he were going to marry a whore. Let him stab himself with the word. Let him not blind himself with euphemisms. His friends would have no euphemisms for Lily. How Lonsdale had laughed at the idea of marrying Queenie Molyneux, and she might have been called an actress. How everybody would despise his folly. There would not be one friend who would understand. Least of all would his mother understand. It was a hard thing to do; and yet it would be comparatively easy, if he could be granted the grace of faith to sustain him. Principles were rather barren things to support the soul in a fight with convention. Principles of honour when so very personal were apt to crumple in the blast of society's principles all fiercely kindled against him. Just now he had thought of the thankfulness he owed to God. Was it more than a figure of speech, an exaggerative personification under great emotion of what most people would call chance ? At any rate here was God in a cynical mood, and the divine justice of this retributive situation seemed to hint at something beyond mere luck. And if principles were strong enough to sustain him to the onset, faith might fire him to the coronation of his self-effacement. He made up his mind clearly and calmly to marry Lily, and then he quickly fell into sleep, where as if to hearten him he saw her slim and lovely, herself again, treading for his dreams the ways of night like a gazelle.

Next morning when Michael woke, his resolve purified by sleep of feverish and hysterical promptings was fresh upon his pillow. In the fatigue and strain of the preceding night the adventure had caught a hectic glow of exaltation. Now, with the sparrows twittering and the milkman clanking and yodelling down Cheyne Walk and the young air puffing the curtains, his course acquired a simplicity in this lucid hour of deliberation, which made the future normal and even obvious. There was a great relief in this fresh following breeze after the becalmed inaction of Oxford : it seemed an augury of life's importance that so immediately on top of the Oxford dream he should find such a complete dispersion of mist and so urgent a fairway before him. The task of finding Lily might easily occupy him for some time, for a life like hers would be made up of mutable appearances and sudden strange eclipses. It might well be a year before she was seen again on the Orient Promenade. Yet it was just as likely that he would find her at once. For a moment he caught his breath in thinking of the sudden plunge which that meeting would involve. He thought

of all the arguments and all the dismay that the revelation
of his purpose would set in motion. However, the marriage
had to be. He had threshed it all out last night. But he
might reasonably hope for a brief delay. Such a hope was
no disloyalty to his determination.

Stella was already at breakfast when he came downstairs.
Michael raised his eyebrows in demand for news of her and
Alan.

"Mother was the sweetest thing imaginable," she said.
"And so we're engaged. I wanted to come and talk to you
last night, but I thought you would rather be left alone."

"I'm glad you're happy," he said gravely. "And I'm
glad you're safe."

Stella looked at him in surprise.

"I've never been anything but safe," she assured him.

"Haven't you?" he asked, looking at her and reproving
himself for the thought that this grey-eyed sister of his
could ever have exposed herself to the least likelihood of
falling into Lily's case. Yet there had been times when he
had felt alarmed for her security and happiness. There
had been that fellow Ayliffe, and more serious still there
had been that unknown influence in Vienna. Invulnerable
she might seem now in this cool dining-room on a summer
morning, but there had been times when he had doubted.

"What are you looking at?" she asked, flaunting her
imperious boyishness in his solemn countenance.

"You. Thinking you ought to be damned grateful."

"What for?"

"Everything."

"You included, I suppose," she laughed.

Still it had been rather absurd, Michael thought as he
tapped his egg, to suppose there was anything in Stella's
temperament which could ever link her to Lily. Should
he announce his quest for her approbation and sympathy?
It was difficult somehow to begin. Already a subtle change

had taken place in their relation to each other since she was engaged to. Alan.   Of course his reserve was ridiculous, but he could not bring himself to break through now. Besides in any case it were better to wait until he had found Lily again.   It would all sound very pretentiously noble in anticipation, and though she would have every right to laugh, he did not want her to laugh.   When he stood on the brink of marriage, they would none of them be able to laugh. : There was a grim satisfaction in that.

. " When does mother suggest you should be married ? " he asked.

" We more or less settled November.   Alan has given up the Civil Service.   That's my first piece of self-assertion. He's coming for me this morning, and we're going to lunch at Richmond."

" You've never met Mr. and Mrs. Merivale ? " Stella shook her head.

" Old Merivale's a ripping old boy.   Always making bad puns.   And Mrs. Merivale's a dear."

" They must both be perfect to have been the father and mother of Alan," said Stella.

" I shouldn't get too excited over him," Michael advised. " Or over yourself either. You might give me the credit of knowing all about it long before either of you."

" Darling Michael," she cried, bounding at him like a puppy.

" When you've done making an ass of yourself you might chuck me a roll."

Alan arrived soon after breakfast, and he and Michael had a few minutes together, while Stella was getting ready to go out.

" Were your people pleased ? " Michael asked.

" Oh, of course. Naturally the mater was a little nervous. She thought I seemed young.   Talked a good deal about being a little boy only yesterday and that sort of rot."

" And your governor ? "

" He supposed I was determined to steal her," said Alan
with a whimsical look of apology for the pun. " And having
worked that off he spent the rest of the evening relishing
his own joke.",

Stella came down ready to start for Richmond. Both
she and Alan were in white, and Michael said they looked
like a couple of cricketers. But he envied them as he waved
them farewell from the front-door through which the
warm day was deliciously invading the house. Their happiness sparkled on the air as visibly almost as the sunshine
winking on the river. Those Richmond days belonged
imperishably to him and Alan, yet for Alan this Saturday
would triumph over all the others before. Michael turned
back into the house rather sadly. The radiance of the
morning had been dislustred by their departure, and Michael
against his will had to be aware of the sense of exclusion
which lovers leave in their wake. He waited indoors until
his mother came down. She was solicitous for the headache of last night, and while he was with her he was not
troubled by regrets for the break-up of established intercourse. He asked himself whether he should take her into
his confidence by announcing the tale of Lily. Yet he did
not wish to give her an impression of being more straitly
bound to follow his quest than by the broadest rules of
conduct. He felt it would be easier to explain when the
marriage had taken place. How lucky for him that he was
not financially dependent. That he was not, however, laid
upon him the greater obligation. He could find, even if he
wished one, no excuse for unfulfilment.

Michael and his mother talked for a time of the engagement. She was still somewhat doubtful of Alan's youth,
when called upon to adapt itself to Stella's temperament.

" I think you're wrong there," said Michael. " Alan is

rather a rigid person in fundamentals, you know, and his youth will give just that flexibility which Stella would demand. In another five years he would have been ensconced behind an Englishman's strong but most unmanageable barrier of prejudice. I noticed so much his attitude towards Mrs. Ross when she was received into the Roman Church. I asked him what he would say if Stella went over. He maintained that she was different. I think that's a sign he'll be ready to apply imagination to her behaviour."

"Yes, but I hope he won't think that whatever she does is right," Mrs. Fane objected.

"Oh no," laughed Michael. "Imagination will always be rather an effort for Alan. Mother, would you be worried if I told you I wanted to go away for a while—I mean to say, go away and perhaps more or less not be heard of for a while ? "

"Abroad ? " she asked.

"Not necessarily abroad. I'm not going to involve myself in a dangerous undertaking ; but I'm just sufficiently tired of my very comfortable existence to wish to make an experiment. I may be away quite a short time, but I might want to be away a few months. Will you promise me not to worry yourself over my movements ? Some of the success of this undertaking will probably depend on a certain amount of freedom. You can understand, can't you, that the claims of home, however delightful, might in certain circumstances be a problem ? "

"I suppose you're taking steps to prepare my mind for something very extremely unpleasant," she said.

"Let's ascribe it all to my incurably romantic temperament," Michael suggested.

"And I'm not to worry ? "

"No, please don't."

"But when are you going away ? "

"I'm not really going away at all," Michael explained.

3 I

"But if I didn't come back to dinner one night or even the next night, would you be content to know quite positively that I hadn't been run over?"

"You're evidently going to be thoroughly eccentric. But I suppose," she added wistfully, "that after your deserted childhood I can hardly expect you to be anything else. Yet it seems so comfortable here." She was looking round at the chairs.

"I'm not proposing to go to the North Pole, you know," Michael said, "but I don't want to obey dinner-gongs."

"Very noisy and abrupt," she agreed.

Soon they were discussing all kinds of substitutions.

"Mother, what an extraordinary lot you know about noise," Michael exclaimed.

"Dearest boy, I'm on the committee of a society for the abatement of London street noises."

"So deeply occupied with reform," he said, patting her hand.

"One must do something," she smiled.

"I know," he asserted. "And therefore you'll let me ride this new hobby-horse I'm trying without thinking it bucks. Will you?"

"You know perfectly well that you will anyhow," said Mrs. Fane shaking her head.

Michael felt justified in letting the conversation end at this admission. Maurice Avery had invited him to come round to the studio in order to assist at Castleton's induction, and Michael walked along the Embankment to 422 Grosvenor Road.

The large attic which ran all the width of the Georgian house was in a state of utter confusion, in the midst of which Castleton was hard at work hammering, while Maurice climbed over chairs in eager advice, and at the Bechstein Grand a tall dark young man was playing melodies from Tchaikovsky's symphonies.

"Just trying to make this place a bit comfortable," said Castleton. "Do you know Cunningham ? " He indicated the player, and Michael bowed.

"Making it comfortable," Michael repeated. "My first impression was just the reverse. I suppose it's no good asking you people to give me lunch ? "

"Rather, of course," Maurice declared. "Castleton, it's your turn to buy lunch."

"One extraordinary thing, Michael," said Castleton, "is the way in which Maurice can always produce a mathematical reason for my doing something. You'd think he kept a ledger of all our tasks."

"We can send old Mother Wadman if you're tired," Maurice offered. Castleton however seemed to think he wanted some fresh air; so he and Cunningham went out to buy things to eat.

"I was fairly settled before old Castleton turned up," Maurice explained, "but we shall be three times as comfortable when he's finished. He's putting up divans."—

Maurice indicated with a gesture the raw material on which Castleton was at work. They were standing by the window which looked out over multitudinous roofs.

"What a great rolling sense of human life they do give," said Michael. "A sea really with telegraph poles and wires for masts and rigging, and all that washing like flotillas of small boats. And there's the lighthouse," he pointed to the campanile of Westminster Cathedral.

"The sun sets just behind your lighthouse, which is a very bad simile for anything so obscurantist as the Roman Church," said Maurice. "We're having such wonderful green dusks now. This is really a room made for a secret love-affair, you know. Such nights. Such sunny summer days. What is it Browning says ? Something about sparrows on a housetop lonely. We two were sparrows. You know 'the poem I mean. Well, no doubt soon I shall meet the

girl who's meant to share this with me.   Then I really
think I could work."

Michael nodded absently. He was wondering if an attic
like this were not the solution of what might happen to
him and Lily when they were married. Whatever bitterness
London had given her would surely be driven out by life
in a room like this with a view like this. They would be
suspended celestially above all that was worst in London,
and yet they would be most essentially and intimately part
of it. The windows of the city would come twinkling into
life as incomprehensibly as the stars. Whatever bitterness
she had guarded would vanish, because to see her in a room
like this would be to love her. How well he understood
Maurice's desire for a secret love-affair here. Nobody
wanted a girl to perfect Plashers Mead. Even Guy's fairy
child at Plashers Mead had seemed an intrusion ; but here,
to protect one's loneliness against the overpowering contemplation of the life around, love was a necessity. And
perhaps Maurice would begin to justify the ambition his
friends had for his career. It might be so. Perhaps himself
might find an inspiration in an attic high up over roofs.
It might be so. It might be so.

"What are you thinking about ? " Maurice asked.

" I was thinking you were probably right," said Michael.

Maurice looked pleasantly surprised. He was rather
accustomed to be snubbed when he told Michael of his
desire for feminine companionship.

" I don't want to get married, you know," he hastily added.

" That would depend," said Michael. " If one married
what is called an impossible person and lived up here, it
ought to be romantic enough to make marriage rather more
exciting than any silvery invitation to St. Thomas' Church
at half-past two."

" But why are you so keen about marriage ? " Maurice
demanded.

"Well, it has certain advantages," Michael pointed out.

"Not among the sparrows," said Maurice.

"Most of all among the sparrows," Michael contradicted.

He was becoming absorbed by his notion of Lily in such surroundings. It seemed to remove the last doubt he had of the wisdom or necessity of the step he proposed to take. They would be able to re-enter the world after a long retirement. For her it should be a convalescence, and for him the opportunity which Oxford denied to test academic values on the touchstone of human emotions. It was obvious that his education lacked something, though his academic education was finished. He supposed he had apprehended dimly the risk of this incompletion in Paris during that first Long Vacation. It was curious how already the quest of Lily had assumed less the attributes of a rescue than of a personal desire for the happiness of her company. No doubt he must be ready for a shock of disillusion when they did meet, but for the moment Drake's account of her on the Orient Promenade lost all significance of evil. The news had merely fired him with the impulse to find her again.

"It is really extraordinarily romantic up here," Maurice exclaimed, bursting in upon his reverie.

"Yes, I suppose that's the reason," Michael admitted.

"The reason of what ?" Maurice asked.

"Of what I was thinking," Michael said.

Maurice waited for him to explain further, but Michael was silent; and almost immediately Castleton came back with provision for lunch.

Soon after they had eaten Michael said he would leave them to their hammering. Then he went back to Cheyne Walk and, finding the house still and empty in the sunlight, he packed a kit-bag, called a hansom-cab and told the driver to go to the Seven Sisters Road.

Chapter II : *Neptune Crescent*

THE existence of the Seven Sisters Road had probably not occurred to Michael since in the hazel-coppices of Clere Abbey he had first made of it at Brother Aloysius' behest the archetype of Avernus, and yet his choice of it now for entrance to the underworld was swift as instinct. The quest of Lily was already beginning to assume the character of a deliberate withdrawal from the world in which he familiarly moved. With the instant of his resolve all that in childhood and in youth he had apprehended of the dim territory, which in London sometimes lay no farther away than the other side of the road, demanded the trial of his experience.

That he had never yet been to the Seven Sisters Road gave it a mystery; that it was not very far from Kentish Town gave it a gruesomeness, for ever since Mrs. Pearcey's blood-soaked perambulator Kentish Town had held for him a macabre significance : of the hellish portals mystery and gruesomeness were essential attributes. The drive was for a long time tediously pleasant in the June sunshine ; but when the cab had crossed the junction of the Euston Road with the Tottenham Court Road, unknown London with all its sly and labyrinthine romance lured his fancy onwards. Maple's and Shoolbred's, those outposts of shopping civilization, were left behind, and the Hampstead Road with a hint of roguery began. He was not sure what exactly made the Hampstead Road so disquieting. It was probably a mere trick of contrast between present squalor and the greenery of its end. The road itself was merely grim, but

it had a nightmare capacity for suggesting that deviation
by a foot from the thoroughfare itself would lead to obscure
calamities. Those bright yellow omnibuses in which he
had never travelled, how he remembered them from the
days of Jack the Ripper, and the horror of them skirting
the Strand by Trafalgar Square on winter dusks after the
pantomime. Even now their painted destinations affected
him with a dismay that real people could be familiar with
this sinister route.

Here was the Britannia, a terminus which had stuck in
his mind for years as situate in some grey limbo of farthest
London. Here it was, a tawdry and not very large public-
house exactly like a hundred others. Now the cab was
bearing round to the right, and presently upon an iron
railway bridge Michael read in giant letters the direction
Kentish Town behind a huge leprous hand pointing to the
left. The hansom clattered through the murk beneath,
past the dim people huddled upon the pavement, past
a wheel-barrow and the obscene skeletons and outlines of
humanity chalked upon the arches of sweating brick. Here
then was Kentish Town. It lay to the left of this bridge that
was the colour of stale blood. Michael told the driver to
stop for one moment, and he leaned forward over the apron
of the cab to survey the cross-street of swarming feculent
humanity that was presumably the entering highway. A
train roared over the bridge; a piano organ gargled its
tune; a wagon-load of iron girders drew near in a clanging
tintamar of slow progress. Michael's brief pause was
enough to make such an impression of pandemoniac din as
almost to drive out his original conception of Kentish Town
as a menacing and gruesome suburb. But just as the cab
reached the beginning of the Camden Road, he caught
sight of a slop-shop where old clothes smothered the entrance
with their mucid heaps and, just beyond, of three houses
from whose surface the stucco was peeling in great scabs

and the damp was oozing in livid arabesques and scrawls of verdigris. This group restored to Kentish Town a putative disquiet, and the impression of mere dirt and noise and exhalations of fried fish were merged in the more definite character allotted by his prefiguration.

The Camden Road was, in contrast with what had gone before, a wide and easy thoroughfare which let in the blue summer sky; and it was not for some minutes that Michael began to notice what a queerness came from the terraces that branched off on either side. The suggestion these terraces could weave extended itself to the detached houses of the main road. In the gaps between them long parallelograms of gardens could be seen joining others even longer that led up to the backs of another road behind. Sometimes it seemed that fifty gardens at once were visible, circumscribed secretive pleasure-grounds in the amount of life they could conceal, the life that could prosper and decay beneath their arbours merely for that conspiracy of gloating windows. It was impossible not to speculate upon the quality of existence in these precise enclosures; and to this the chapels of obscure sects that the cab occasionally passed afforded an indication. To these arid little tabernacles the population stole out on Sunday mornings. There would be something devilish about these reunions. Upon these pinchbeck creeds their souls must surely starve, must slowly shrink to desiccated imps. Anything more spiritually malevolent than those announcements chalked upon the black notice-board of the advent of the hebdomadal messiah, the peregrine cleric, the sacred migrant was impossible to imagine. With what apostolic cleverness would he impose himself upon these people, and how after the gravid midday meal of the Sabbath he would sit in those green arbours like a horrible Chinese fum. The cabman broke in upon Michael's fantastic depression by calling down through the trap that they were arrived at the Nag's Head and what part of Seven Sisters Road did he want.

Michael was disappointed by the Seven Sisters Road. It seemed to be merely the garish mart of a moderately poor suburban population. There was here nothing to support the diabolic legend with which under the suggestion of Brother Aloysius he had endowed it. Certainly of all the streets he had passed this afternoon there had been none less inferential of romance than this long shopping street.

" What number do you want, sir ? " the driver repeated.

" Well, really I want rooms," Michael explained. " Only this seems a bit noisy."

" Yes, it is a bit boisterous," the cabman agreed.

Michael told him to drive back along the Camden Road ; but when he began to examine the Camden Road as a prospective place of residence, it became suddenly very dull and respectable. The locked-up chapels and the quiet houses declined from ominousness into respectability, and he wondered how he had managed only a quarter of an hour ago to speculate upon the inner life they adumbrated. Nothing could be less surreptitious than those chatting nursemaids, and actually in one of the parallelograms of garden a child was throwing a scarlet ball high into the air. The cab was already nearing the iron railway bridge of Kentish Town, and Michael had certainly no wish to lodge in a noisy slum.

" Try turning off to the left," he called to the driver through the roof.

The manœuvre seemed likely to be successful, for they entered almost immediately a district of Victorian terraces, where the name of each street was cut in stone upon the first house ; and so fine and well-proportioned was each superscription that the houses' declension from gentility was the more evident and melancholy.

Michael was at last attracted to a crescent of villas

terminating an unfrequented grey street and, for the sake
of a pathetic privacy, guarded in front by a sickle-shaped
—— enclosure of grimy Portugal laurels. Neptune Crescent,
partly on account of its name and partly on account of the
peculiar vitreous tint which the stone had acquired with
age, carried a marine suggestion. The date *1805* in spidery
numerals and the iron verandahs, which even on this June
day were a mockery, helped the illusion that here was a
forgotten by-way in an old sea-port. A card advertizing
Apartments stood in the window of Number Fourteen.
Michael signalled the driver to stop: then he alighted and
rang the bell. The Crescent was strangely silent. Very
far away he could hear the whistle of a train. Close at hand
there was nothing but the jingle of the horse's harness and
the rusty mewing of a yellow cat which was wheedling its
—— lean body in and out of the railings of the falciform garden.

Soon the landlady opened the door and stood inquisitively
in the narrow passage. She was a woman of probably about
thirty-five with stubby fingers; her skin was rather moist;
but she had a good-natured expression, and perhaps when
the curl-papers were taken out from her colourless hair, and
when lace frills and common finery should soften her turgid
outlines she would be handsome in a laboured sort of way.
The discussion with Mrs. Murdoch about her vacant rooms
did not take long. Michael had made up his mind to any
horrors of dirt and discomfort, and he was really pleasantly
surprized by their appearance. As for Mrs. Murdoch, she
was evidently too much interested to know what had brought
Michael to her house to make any difficulties in the way of
his accommodation.

"Will you want dinner to-night?" she asked doubtfully.

"No, but I'd like some tea now, if you can manage it;
and I suppose you can let me have a latchkey?"

"I've got the kettle on the boil at this moment. I was
going out myself for the evening. Meeting my husband at

the Horseshoe. There's only one other lodger—Miss Carlyle. And she's in the profession."

As Mrs. Murdoch made this announcement, she looked
up at the fly-frecked ceiling, and Michael thought how extraordinarily light and meaningless her eyes were and how
curiously dim and heavy this small sitting-room was against
·the brilliancy of the external summer.

" Well then, tea when I can get it," said Mrs. Murdoch
cheerfully. " And the double-u is just next your bedroom
·on the top floor. That's all, I think."

She left him with a backward smile over her shoulder, as
if she were loath to relinquish the study of this unusual
visitor to Neptune Crescent.

Michael when he was alone examined the chairs that
were standing about the room as stiff as grenadiers in their
red rep. He stripped them of their antimacassars and pulled
the one that looked least uncomfortable close to the window.
Outside, the yellow cat was still mewing; but the cab was
gone, and down the grey street that led to Neptune Crescent
here and there sad-gaited wayfarers were visible. Two or
three sparrows were cheeping in a battered laburnum, and
all along the horizon the blue sky descending to the smoke
of London had lost its colour and had been turned to the
similitude of tarnished metal. A luxurious mournfulness
was in the view, and he leaned out over the sill scenting the
reasty London air.

It was with a sudden shock of conviction that Michael
realized he was in Neptune Crescent, Camden Town, and
that yesterday he had actually been in Oxford. And why was
he here ? The impulse which had brought him must have
lain deeper in the recesses of his character than those
quixotic resolutions roused by Drake's legend of Lily. He
would not otherwise have determined at once upon so
complete a demigration. He would have waited to test
the truth of Drake's story. His first emotional despair had

vanished with almost unaccountable ease. Certainly he wanted to be independent of the criticism of his friends until he had proved his purpose unwavering, and he might ascribe this withdrawal to a desire for a secluded and unflinching contemplation of a life that from Cheyne Walk he could never focus. But ultimately he must acknowledge that his sojourn here, following as it did straight upon his entrance into the underworld through the disappointing portals of the Seven Sisters Road, was due to that ancient lure of the shades. This experience was foredoomed from very infancy. It was designate in childish dreams to this day indelible. He could not remember any period in his life when the speculum of hidden thought had not reflected for his fear that shadow of evil which could overcast the manifestations of most ordinary existence. Those days of London fog when he had sat desolately in the pinched red house in Carlington Road; those days when on his lonely walks he had passed askance by Padua Terrace; the shouting of murders by newspaper-boys on drizzled December nights; all those dreadful intimations in childhood had procured his present idea of London. With the indestructible truth of earliest impressions they still persisted behind the outward presentation of a normal and comfortable procedure in the midst of money, friends and well-bred conventions. Nor had that speculum been merely the half-savage fancy of childhood, the endowment by the young of material things with immaterial potencies. Phantoms which had slunk by as terrors invisible to the blind eyes of grown-ups had been abominably incarnate for him. Brother Aloysius had been something more than a mere personification, and that life which the ex-monk had indicated as scarcely even below the surface, so easy was it to enter, had he not entered it that one night very easily?

Destiny, thought Michael, had stood with pointed finger beside the phantoms and the realities of the underworld.

There for him lay very easily discernible the true corollary to the four years of Oxford. They had been years of rest and refreshment, years of armament with wise and academic and well-observed theories of behaviour that would defeat the absolution of evil. It was very satisfactory to discover — definitely that he was not a Pragmatist. He had suspected all that crew of philosophers. He would bring back Lily from evil, not from any illusion of evil. He would not allow himself to disparage the problem before him by any speciousness of worldly convenience. It was imperative to meet Lily again as one who moving in the shadows meets another in the nether gloom. They had met first of all as boy and girl, as equals. Now he must not come too obviously from the world she had left behind her. Such an encounter would never give him more than at best a sentimental appeal; at worst it could have the air of a priggish reclamation, and she would for ever elude him, she with secret years within her experience. His instinct first to sever himself from his own world must have been infallible, and it was on account of that instinct that now he found himself in Neptune Crescent leaning over the window-sill and scenting the reasty London air.

And how well secluded was this room. If he met Lonsdale or Maurice or Wedderburn, it would be most fantastically amusing to evade them at the evening's end, to retreat from their company into Camden Town; into Neptune Crescent unimaginable to them; into this small room with its red rep — chairs and horsehair sofa and blobbed valances and curtains; to this small room where the dark blue wall-paper enclosed him with a matted vegetation and the picture of Belshazzar's Feast glowered above the heavy sideboard; to this small room made rich by the two thorny shells upon the mantelpiece, by the bowl of blonde goldfish in ceaseless dim circumnatation, and by those coloured pampas plumes and the bulrushes in their conch of nacreous glass.

Mrs. Murdoch came in with tea which he drank while she stood over him admiringly.

"Do you think you'll be staying long ?" she enquired.

Michael asked if she wanted the rooms for anyone else.

"No. No. I'm really very glad to let them. You'll find it nice and quiet here. There's only Miss Carlyle who's in the profession and comes in sometimes a little late. Mr. Murdoch is a chemist. But of course he hasn't got his own shop now."

She paused, and seemed to expect Michael would comment on Mr. Murdoch's loss of independence; so he said, "Of course not," nodding wisely.

"There was a bit of trouble through his being too kind-hearted to a servant-girl," said Mrs. Murdoch, looking quickly at the door and shaking her curl-papers. "Yes. Though I don't know why I'm telling you straight off as you might say. But there, I'm funny sometimes. If I take to anybody, there's nothing I won't do for them. Alf—that *is* my old man—he gets quite aggravated with me over it. So if you happen to get into conversation with him, you'd better not let on you know he used to have a shop of his own."

Michael, wondering how far off were these foreshadowed intimacies with his landlord, promised he would be very discreet, and asked where Mr. Murdoch was working now.

"In a chemist's shop. Just off of the Euston Road. You know," she said, beaming archly. "It's what you might call rather a funny place. Only he gets good money, because the boss knows he can trust him."

Michael nodded his head in solemn comprehension of Mr. Murdoch's reputation, and asked his landlady if she had such a thing as a postcard.

"Well, there. I wonder if I have. If I have, it's in the kitchen dresser, that's a sure thing. Perhaps you'd like to come down and see the kitchen ?"

Michael followed her downstairs. There were no basements in Neptune Crescent, and he was glad to think his bedroom was above his sitting-room and on the top floor. It would have been hot just above the kitchen.

" Miss Carlyle has her room here," said Mrs. Murdoch, pointing next door to the kitchen. " Nice and handy for her as she's rather late sometimes. I hate to hear anybody go creaking upstairs, I do. It makes me nervous."

The kitchen was pleasant enough and looked out upon a narrow strip of garden full of coarse plants.

" They'll be very merry and bright, won't they ? " said Mrs. Murdoch, smiling encouragement at the greenery. " It's wonderful what you can do nowadays for threepence."

Michael asked what they were.

" Why, sunflowers of course, only they want another month yet. I have them every year—yes. They're less trouble than rabbits or chickens. Now where did I see that postcard ? "

She searched the various utensils, and at last discovered the postcard stuck behind a mutilated clock.

" What *will* they bring out next ? " demanded Mrs. Murdoch surveying it with affectionate approbation. " Pretty, I call it."

A pair of lovers in black plush were sitting enlaced beneath a pink frosted moon.

" Just the thing, if you're writing to your young lady," said Mrs. Murdoch, offering it to Michael.

He accepted it with many expressions of gratitude, but when he was in his own room he laughed very much at the idea of sending it to his mother in Cheyne Walk. However, as he must write and tell her he would not be home for some time, he decided to go out and buy both writing materials and unillustrated postcards. When he came back he found Mrs. Murdoch feathered for the evening's entertainment. She gave him the latchkey, and from his window Michael

watched her progress down Neptune Crescent. Just before
her lavender dress disappeared behind the Portugal laurels
she turned round and waved to him. He wondered what
his mother would say if she knew from what curious corner
of London the news of his withdrawal would reach her to-
night.

The house was very still, and the refulgence of the afternoon light streaming into the small room fused the raw
colours to a fiery concordancy. Upon the silence sounded
presently a birdlike fidgeting, and Michael going out on to
the landing to discover what it was, caught to his surprize
the upward glance of a thin little woman in untidy pink.

"Hullao," she cried. "I never knew there was anybody
in—you did give me a turn. I've only just woke up."

Michael explained the situation, and she seemed relieved.

"I've been asleep all the afternoon," she went on. "But
it's only natural in this hot weather to go to sleep in the
afternoon if you don't go out for a walk. Why don't you
come down and talk to me while I have some tea ? "

Michael accepted the invitation with a courtesy which he
half-suspected this peaked pink little creature considered
diverting.

"You'll excuse the general untidiness," she said. "But
really in this weather anyone can't bother to put their things
away properly."

Michael assented, and looked round at the room. It certainly was untidy. The large bed was ruffled where she had
been lying down, and the soiled copy of a novelette gave it
a sort of stale slovenry. Over the foot hung an accumulation of pink clothes. On the chairs, too, there were clothes
pink and white, and the door bulged with numberless skirts.
Miss Carlyle herself wore a pink blouse whose front had
escaped the constriction of a belt. Even her face was a flat
unshaded pink, and her thin lips would scarcely have showed
save that the powder round the edges was slightly caked.

Yet there was nothing of pink's freshness and pleasant
crudity in the general effect. It was a tired, a frowzy pink
like a fondant that has lain a long while in a confectioner's —
window.

"Take a chair and make yourself at home," she invited
him. "What's your name?"

He told her 'Fane.'

"You silly thing, you don't suppose I'm going to call you
Mr. Fane, do you? What's your other name? Michael?
That's Irish, isn't it? I used to know a fellow once called
Micky Sullivan. I suppose they call you Micky at home."

He was afraid he was invariably known as Michael, and
Miss Carlyle sighed at the stiff sort of a name it was.

"Mine's Poppy," she volunteered. "That's much more
free and easy. Or I think so," she added rather doubtfully
as Michael did not immediately celebrate its license by
throwing pillows at her. "Are you really lodging here?"
she went on. "You don't look much like a pro."

Michael said that was so much the better, as he wasn't one.

"I've got you at last," cried Poppy. "You're a shop- —
walker at Russell's."

He could not help laughing very much at this, and the
queer pink room seemed to become more faded at the sound
of his merriment. Poppy looked offended by the reception
of her guess, and Michael hastened to restore her good
temper by asking questions of her.

"You're on the stage, aren't you?"

"I usually get into panto," she admitted.

"Aren't you acting now?"

"Yes, I don't think. You needn't be funny."

"I wasn't trying to be funny."

"You mind your business," she said bitterly. "And I'll
look after mine."

"There doesn't seem to be anything very rude in asking
if you're acting now," said Michael.

3 K

"Oh, shut up! As if you didn't know."

"Know what?" he repeated.

He looked so genuinely puzzled that Poppy seemed to make an effort to overcome her suspicion of his mockery.

"It's five years since I went on the game," she said.

Michael blushed violently partly on her account, partly for his own stupidity, and explained that Mrs. Murdoch had told him she was in the profession.

"Well, you didn't expect her to say 'my ground-floor front's a gay woman,' did you?"

He agreed that such an abrupt characterization would have surprized him.

"Well, I'm going out to get dinner now," she announced.

"Why don't you dine with me?" Michael suggested.

She looked at him doubtfully.

"Can you afford it?"

"I think I could manage it."

"Because if we *are* in the same house that doesn't say you've got to pay my board, does it?" she demanded proudly.

"Once in a way won't matter," Michael insisted. "And we might go on to a music-hall afterwards."

"Yes, we might, if I hadn't got to pay the woman who's looking after my kid for some clothes she's made for him," said Poppy. "And sitting with you at the Holborn all night won't do that. No, you can give me dinner and then I'll P.O. I'm not going to put on a frock even for you, because I never get off only when I'm in a coat and skirt."

Michael rose to leave the room while Poppy got ready.

"Go on, sit down. As you're going to take me out to dinner, you can talk to me while I dress as a reward."

In this faded pink room where the sun was by now shining with a splendour that made all the strewn clothes seem even more fusty and overblown, Michael could not have borne to see a live thing take shape as it were from such corruption. He made an excuse therefore of letters to be written and.

left Poppy to herself, asking to be called when she was ready.

Michael's own room upstairs had a real solidity after the ground-floor front. He wondered if it were possible that Lily was inhabiting at this moment such a room as Poppy's. It could not be. It could not be. And he realized that he had pictured Lily like Manon in the midst of luxury, craving for magnificence and moving disdainfully before gilded mirrors. This Poppy Carlyle of Neptune Crescent belonged to another circle of the underworld. Lily would be tragical, but this little peaked creature downstairs was scarcely even pathetic. Indeed she was almost grotesque with the coat and skirt that was to ensure her getting off. Of course her only chance was to attract a jaded glance by her positive plainness, her schoolma'am air, her decent unobtrusiveness. Yet she was plucky, and she had accepted the responsibility of supporting her child. There was, too, something admirable in the candour with which she had treated him. There was something friendly and birdlike about her, and he thought how when he had been first aware of her movements below he had compared them to a bird's fidgeting. There was something really appealing about the gay woman of the ground-floor front. He laughed at her description ; and then he remembered regretfully that he had allowed her to forego what might after all have been for her a pleasant evening because she must pay for some clothes the woman who was looking after her child. He could so easily have offered to give her the money. No matter, he could make amends at once and offer it to her now. It would be doubtless an unusual experience for her to come into contact with someone whose rule of life was not dictated by the brutal self-interest of those with whom her commerce must generally lie. She would serve to bring to the proof his theory that so much of the world's beastliness could be cleansed by having recourse to the natural instincts of decent behaviour without any grand effort of reformation. Nevertheless Michael did feel very philanthropic when he went down to answer Poppy's summons.

"I say," he began at once. "It was stupid of me just now not to suggest that I should find the money for your kid's clothes. Look here, we'll go to the Holborn after dinner and——" he paused. He felt a delicacy in enquiring how much exactly she might expect to lose by giving him her company—" and—er—I suppose a couple of pounds would buy something ? "

"I say, kiddie, you're a sport," she said. "Only look here, don't go and spend more than what you can afford. It isn't as if we'd met by chance as you might say."

"Oh no, I can afford two pounds," Michael assured her.

"Where shall we go ? I know a nice room which the woman lets me have for four shillings. That's not too much, is it ? "

He was touched by her eager consideration for his purse, and he stammered, trying to explain as gently as he could that the two pounds was not offered for hire.

"But, kiddie, I can't bring you back here. Not even if you do lodge here. These aren't gay rooms."

"I don't want to go anywhere with you," said Michael. "The money is a present."

"Oh, is it," she flamed out. "Then you can keep your dirty money. Thanks, I haven't come down to charity. Not yet. If I'm not good enough for you, you can keep your money. I believe you're nothing more than a dirty ponce. I've gone five years without keeping a fellow yet. And I'm not going to begin now. That's very certain. Are you going out or am I going out ? Because I don't want to be seen with you. You and your presents. Gard ! I should have to be drunk on claret and lemon before I went home with you."

Michael had nothing to say to her and so he went out,

closing the front door quickly·upon her ·rage. His first
impression when he gained the fresh air was of a fastidious
disgust. Here in the Crescent the orange lucency of the
evening shed such a glory that the discoloration of the
houses no longer spoke of miserably drawn-out decay, but
took on rather the warmth of live rock. The deepening
shadows of that passage where the little peaked creature
had spat forth her fury made him shudder with the mean and
vicious passions they now veiled. Very soon however his disgust died away. Looking back at Neptune Crescent he knew
there was not one door in all that semicircle which did not
putatively conceal secrets like those of Number Fourteen.
Like poisonous toadstools in rankness and gloom the worst
of human nature must flourish here. It was foolish to be
disgusted ; indeed already a half-aroused curiosity had taken
its place, and Michael regretted that he had not stayed to
hear what more she would have said. How far she had been
from appreciating the motives that prompted his offer of
money. Poppy's injustice began to depress him. He felt,
walking southwards to Piccadilly, an acute sense of her
failure to be grateful from his point of view. It hurt him
to find sincerity so lightly regarded. Then he realized
that it was her vanity which had been touched. *Hell knows
no fury like a woman scorned.* The ability to apply such a
famous generalization directly to himself gave. Michael
a great satisfaction. It was strange to be so familiar with
a statement, and then suddenly like this to be staggered
by its truth. He experienced a sort of pride in linking
himself on to one of the great commonplaces of rhetoric.
He need no longer feel misjudged, since Poppy had played
an universal part. In revulsion he felt sorry for her. He
hated to think how deeply her pride must have been
wounded. He could not expect her to esteem the reason
which had made him refuse her. She could have little
comprehension of fastidiousness and still less could she grasp

the existence of an abstract morality that in its practical expression must have seemed to her so insulting. That, however, did not impugn the morality, nor did it invalidate the desire to befriend her. Impulse had not really betrayed him : the mistake had been in his tactlessness, in a lack of worldly knowledge. Moreover Poppy was only an incident, and until Lily was found he had no business to turn aside. Nevertheless he had learned something this evening; he had seen proved in action a famous postulate of feminine nature, and the truth struck him with a sharpness that no academic demonstration had ever had the power to effect.

On the whole Michael was rather pleased with himself as he rode on the front seat of the omnibus down Tottenham Court Road in the cool of the evening.

At the Horseshoe he alighted and went into the saloon bar on the chance of seeing what Mr. Murdoch looked like; but there was no sign of the landlady and her husband. The saloon bar smelt very strongly of spilt stout ; and a number of men, who looked like draymen in tailcoats and top-hats, were arguing about money. He was glad to leave the tavern behind ; and in a Soho restaurant he ate a tranquil dinner, listening with much amusement to the people round him. He liked to hear each petty host assure his guests that he had brought them to a place of which very few but himself knew. All the diners under the influence of this assurance stared at one another like conspirators.

Just before nine o'clock Michael reached the Orient Palace of Varieties, and with excitement bubbling up within him notwithstanding all his efforts to stay unmoved he joined the throng of the Promenade. He looked about him at first in trepidation. Although all the way from Camden Town he had practised this meeting with Lily, now at its approach his presence of mind vanished, and he felt that to meet her suddenly without a longer preparation would lead him to make a fool of himself. However, in the first quick glance he could not see anyone who resembled her, and he withdrew to the secluded apex of the curving Promenade whence he could watch most easily the ebb and flow of the crowd. That on the stage a lady of the haute école was with a curious wooden rapidity putting a white horse through a number of tricks did not concern his attention beyond the moment. For him the Promenade was the performance. Certainly at the Orient it was a better staged affair than that weary heterogeneous mob at The Oxford. At the Orient there was an unity of effect, an individuality and a conscious equipment. At The Oxford the whole business had resembled a suburban parade. Here was a real exposition of vice like the jetty of Alexandria in olden days. Indeed so cynical was the function of the Orient Promenade that the frankness almost defeated its object, and the frequenters instead of profiting by the facilities for commerce allowed themselves to be drugged into perpetual meditation upon an attractive contingency.

Seen from this secluded corner the Promenade resembled a well-filled tank in an aquarium. The upholstery of shimmering green plush, the dim foreground, the splash of light from the bar in one corner, the gliding circumambient throng among the pillars and, displayed along the barrier, the bright-hued ladies like sea-anemones—there was nothing that spoilt the comparison. Moreover the longer Michael looked, the more nearly was the effect achieved. At intervals women whose close-fitting dresses seemed deliberately to imitate scales went by: and generally the people eyed one another with the indifferent frozen eyes of swimming fish. There was indeed something cold-blooded in the very atmosphere, and it was from this rapacious and vivid shoal of women that he was expecting Lily to materialize. Yet he was better able to imagine her in the luxury of the Orient than sleeping down the sun over a crumpled novelette in such a room as Poppy's in Camden Town.

The evening wore itself away, and the motion in that subaqueous air was restful in its continuity. Michael was relieved by the assurance that he had still a little time in which to compose himself to face the shock he knew he must ultimately expect from meeting Lily again. The evening wore itself away. The lady of the haute école was succeeded by a band of Caucasian wrestlers, by a troupe of Bolivian gymnasts, by half-a-dozen cosmopolitan ebullitions of ingenuity. The ballet went its mechanical course, and as each line of dancers grouped themselves, it was almost possible to hear the click of the kaleidoscope's shifting squares and lozenges. Michael wondered vaguely about the girls in the ballet and whether they were happy. It seemed absurd to think that down there on the stage there were eighty or ninety individuals each with a history, so little more did they seem from here than dolls. And on the Promenade where it was quite certain that every woman had a history to account for her presence there, how utterly living had quenched life. The ballet was over, and he passed out into the streets.

For a fortnight Michael came every evening to the Orient without finding Lily. They were strange evenings, these that were spent in the heart of London without meeting anyone he knew. It was no doubt by the merest chance that none of his friends saw him at the Orient, and yet he began to fancy that actually every evening he did, as it were, by some enchantment fade from the possibility of recognition. He felt as if his friends would not perceive his presence, so much would they in that circumambient throng take on the characteristics of its eternal motion. They too, he felt, irresponsive as fish, would glide backwards and forwards with the rest. Nor did Michael meet anyone whom he knew at any of the restaurants or cafés to which he went after the theatre. By the intensity of his one idea, the discovery of Lily, he cut himself off from all communion with the

life of the places he visited. He often thought that perhaps
acquaintances saw him there, that perhaps he had seemed
deliberately to avoid their greetings and for that reason
had never been hailed. Yet he was aware of seeing women
whom he had seen the night before, mostly because they
bore a superficial likeness to Lily ; and sometimes he would
be definitely conscious of a dress or a hat, perceiving it in
the same place at the same hour, but never meeting the
wearer's glance.

He did not make any attempt to be friendly with Poppy
after their unpleasant encounter, and he always tried to be
sure they would not meet in the hall or outside the front
door. That he was successful in avoiding her gave him a
still sharper sense of the ease with which it was possible to
seclude oneself from the claims of human intercourse. He
was happy in his room at Neptune Crescent, gazing out over
the sickle-shaped garden of Portugal laurels, listening in
a dream to the distant cries of railway traffic and reading
the books which every afternoon he brought back from
Charing Cross Road, so many books indeed that presently
the room in 14 Neptune Crescent came curiously to
resemble rooms in remote digs at Oxford, where poor
scholars imposed their books on surroundings they could
not afford to embellish. Mrs. Murdoch could not make
Michael out at all. She used to stand and watch him
reading, as if he were performing an intricate surgical
operation.

"I never in all my life saw anyone read like you do,"
she affirmed. "Doesn't it tire your eyes ?"

Then she would move a step nearer and spell out the
title of the book, looking sideways at it like a fat goose.

"Holy Living and Holy Dying. Ugh ! Enough to give
you the horrors, isn't it ? And only this morning they hung
that fellow at Pentonville.. This *is* Tuesday, isn't it ?"

After three or four days of trying to understand him,

Mrs. Murdoch decided that Alf must be called in to solve his peculiarity.

Mr. Alfred Murdoch was younger than Michael had expected. He could scarcely have been more than forty, and Michael had formed a preconception of an elderly chemist reduced by misfortune and misdeeds to the status of one of those individuals who with a discreet manner somewhere between a family doctor and a grocer place themselves at the service of the public in an atmosphere of antiseptics. Mr. Murdoch was not at all like this. He was a squat swarthy man with one very dark eye that stared fixedly regardless of the expression of its fellow. Michael could not make up his mind whether this eye were blind or not. He rather hoped it was, but in any case its fierce blankness was very disconcerting. Conversation between Michael and Mr. Murdoch was not very lively, and Mrs. Murdoch's adjutant inquisitiveness made Michael the more mono-syllabic whenever her husband did commit himself to a direct enquiry.

"I looked for you in the Horseshoe the other evening," said Michael finally, at a loss how in any other way to give Mr. Murdoch an impression that he took the faintest interest in his existence.

"In the Horseshoe ?" repeated Mr. Murdoch in surprize. "I never go to the Horseshoe only when a friend asks me in to have one."

Michael saw Mrs. Murdoch frowning at him and, perceiving that there was a reason why her husband must not suppose she had been to the Horseshoe on the evening of his arrival, he said he had gathered somehow, he did not exactly know where or why or when, that Mr. Murdoch was often to be found in the Horseshoe. He wished this awkward and unpleasant man would leave him and cock his rolling eye anywhere else but in his room.

"Bit of a reader, aren't you ?" enquired the chemist.

Michael admitted he read a good deal.

"Ever read Jibbon's Decline and Fall of the Roman Empire?" continued the chemist.

"Some of it."

Mr. Murdoch said in that case it was just as well he hadn't bought some volumes he'd seen on a barrow in the Caledonian Road.

"Four-and-six, with two books out in the middle," he proclaimed.

Michael could merely nod his comment, though he racked his brains to think of some remark that would betray a vestige of cordiality. Mr. Murdoch got up to retire to the kitchen. He evidently did not find his tenant sympathetic. Outside on the landing Michael heard him say to his wife: "Stuck up la-di-da sort of a ——, isn't he?"

Presently the wife came up again.

"How did you like my old man?"

"Oh, very much."

"Did you notice his eye?"

Michael said he had noticed something.

"His brother Fred did that for him."

She spoke proudly as if Fred's act had been a humane achievement. "When they were boys," she explained. "It gives him a funny look. I remember when I first met him it gave me the creeps, but I don't notice it really now. Would you believe he couldn't see an elephant with it?"

"I wondered if it were blind," said Michael.

"Blind as a leg of mutton," said Mrs. Murdoch, and still there lingered in her accents a trace of pride. Then suddenly her demeanour changed and there crept over her countenance what Michael was bound to believe to be an expression of coyness.

"Don't say anything more to Alf about the Horseshoe. You see I only gave you the idea I was meeting him, because I didn't really know you very well at the time. Of course really I'd gone to see my sister. No, without a joke, I was spending the evening with a gentleman friend."

Michael looked at her in astonishment.

"My old man wouldn't half knock me about, if he had the least suspicion. But it's someone I knew before I was married and that makes a difference, doesn't it?"

"Does your husband go out with lady friends he knew before he was married?" Michael asked, and wondered if Mrs. Murdoch would see an implied reproof.

"What?" she shrilled. "I'd like to catch him nosing after another woman. He wouldn't see a hundred elephants before I'd done with him. I'd show him."

"But why should you have freedom and not he?" Michael asked.

"Never mind about him. You let him try. You see what he'd get."

Michael did not think the argument could be carried on very profitably. So he showed signs of wanting to return to his book, and Mrs. Murdoch retired. What extraordinary standards she had, and how bitterly she was prepared to defend a convention, for after all in such a marriage the infidelity of the husband was nothing but a conventional offence: she obviously had no affection for him. The point of view became very topsyturvy in Neptune Crescent, Michael decided.

On the last evening of the fortnight during which he had regularly visited the Orient, Michael went straight back to Camden Town without waiting to scan the cafés and restaurants until half-past twelve as he usually had. This abode in Neptune Crescent was empty, and as always when that was the case the personality of the house was very vivid upon his imagination. As he turned up the gas-jet in the hall, the cramped interior with its fusty smell and its threadbare staircarpet disappearing into the upper gloom round the corner seemed to be dreadfully closing in upon

him. The old house conveyed a sense of having the power
to choke out of him every sane and orderly and decent
impulse. For a whim of tristfulness, for the luxury of
consummating the ineffable depression the house created
in him, Michael prepared to glance at every one of the five
rooms. The front door armed with the exaggerated defences
of an earlier period in building tempted him to lock and
double-lock it, to draw each bolt and to fasten the two
clanking chains. He had the fantastic notion to do this so
that Mr. and Mrs. Murdoch and Poppy might stay knocking
and ringing outside in the summer night, while himself
escaped into the sunflowers of the back garden and went
climbing over garden-wall and garden-wall to abandon this
curious mixture of salacity and respectableness, of flimsi- —
ness and solidity, this quite indefinably raffish and sinister
and yet in a way strangely cosy house. He opened gingerly
the door of the ground-floor front. He peered cautiously
in, lest Poppy should be lying on her bed. The gas-jet was
glimmering with a scarcely perceptible pinhead of blue
flame, but the light from the passage showed all her clothes
still strewn about. From the open door came out the
faint perfume of stale scent which mingled with the fusty
odour of the passage in a most subtle expression of the
house's personality. He closed the door gently. In the
silence it seemed almost as if the least percussion would
rouse the very clothes from their stupor of disuse. In the
kitchen was burning another pinhead of gas, and the light
from the passage reaching here very dimly was only just
sufficient to give all the utensils a ghostly sheen and to
show the mutilated hands at a quarter past five upon the ,
luminous face of the clock. This unreal hour added the last
touch to unreality, and when Michael went upstairs and
saw the books littering his room, even they were scarcely
sound guarantors of his own actuality. He had a certain
queasiness in opening the door of the Murdochs' bedroom,

and he was rather glad when he was confronted here by a black void whose secrecy he did not feel tempted to violate. With three or four books under his arm he went upstairs to bed. As he leaned out of the window two cats yauled and fizzed at one another among the laurels, and then scampered away into muteness. From a scintillation of coloured lights upon the horizon he could hear the scrannel sounds of the railway come thinly along the night air. Nothing else broke the silence of the nocturnal streets. Michael felt tired, and he was disappointed by his failure to find Lily. Just as he was dozing off, he remembered that his Viva Voce at Oxford was due some time this week. He must go back to Cheyne Walk to-morrow, and on this resolution he fell asleep.

Michael woke up with a start and instantly became aware that the house was full of discordant sounds. For a minute or two he lay motionless trying to connect the noise with the present, trying to separate his faculties from the inspissate air that seemed to be throttling them. He was not yet free from the confusions of sleep, and for a few seconds he could only perceive the sound almost visibly churning the clotted darkness that was stifling him. Gradually the clamour resolved itself into the voices of Mr. Murdoch, Mrs. Murdoch and Poppy at the pitch of excitement. Nothing was intelligible except the oaths that came up in a series of explosions detached from the main din. He got out of bed and lit the gas, saw that it was one o'clock, dressed himself roughly and opened the door of his room.

"Yes, my lad, you thought you was very clever."

"No, I didn't think I was clever. Now then."

"Yes! You can spend all your money on that muck. The sauce of it. In a hansom!"

Here Poppy's voice came in with a malignant piping sound.

"Muck yourself, you dirty old case-keeper."

" You call me a case-keeper ? What men have I ever let you bring back here ? "

Mrs. Murdoch's voice was swollen with wrath.

" You don't know how many men I haven't brought back. So now, you great ugly mare ! " Poppy howled.

" The only fellow you've ever brought to my house is that one-eyed —— who calls himself my husband. Mister *Mur*doch ! Mis-ter *Mur*doch ! And you get out of my house in the streets where you belong. I don't want no two-and-fours in *my* house."

" Hark at her ! " Poppy cried in a horrible screaming laugh. " Why don't you go back on the streets yourself ? Why, I can remember you as one of the old fourpenny Has-beens when I was still dressmaking ; a dirty drunken old tear that couldn't have got off with a blind tramp."

Michael punctuated each fresh taunt and accusation with a step forward to interfere ; and every time he held himself back, pondering the impossibility of extracting from these charges and countercharges any logical assignment of blame. It made him laugh to think how extraordinarily in the wrong they all three were and at the same time how they were all perfectly convinced they were right. The only factor left out of account was Mrs. Murdoch's own behaviour. He wondered rather what effect that gentleman friend would produce on the husband. He decided that he had better go back to bed until the racket subsided. Then, just as he was turning away in the midst of an outpouring of vileness far more foul than anything uttered so far, he heard what sounded like a blow. That of course could not be tolerated, and he descended to intervene.

The passage was the field of battle, and the narrow space seemed to give not only an added virulence to the fight, but also an added grotesquery. When Michael arrived at the head of the staircase, Alf had pinned his wife to the wall and was shouting to Poppy over his shoulder to get back into her own room. Poppy would go half-way, but always a new insult would occur to her, and she would return to fling it at Mrs. Murdoch, stabbing the while into its place again a hatpin which during her retreats she always half-withdrew.

As for Mrs. Murdoch, she was by now weeping hysteri-cally and occasionally making sudden forward plunges that collapsed like jelly.

Michael paused at the head of the stairs, wondering what to say. It seemed to him really rather a good thing that Alf was restraining his wife. It would be extremely unpleasant to have to separate the two women if they closed with each other. He had almost decided to retire upstairs again, when Poppy caught sight of him and at once turned her abuse in his direction.

"What's it got to do with you?" she screamed. "What's the good in you standing gaping there? We all know what *you* are. We all know what she's always going up to *your* room for."

Mrs. Murdoch was heaving and puffing and groaning, and while Alf held her, his rolling eye with fierce and meaningless stare nearly made Michael laugh. However, he managed to be serious, and he gravely advised Poppy to go to bed.

"Don't you dare try to order me about," she shrieked. "Keep your poncified ways for that fat old maggot which her husband can't hardly hold, and I don't blame him. She's about as big as a omnibus."

"Oh, you wicked woman," sobbed Mrs. Murdoch. "Oh, you mean hateful snake-in-the-grass. Oh, you filth!"

"Hold your jaw," commanded Alf. "If you don't want me to punch into you."

"All day she's in his room. Let him stand up and deny it if he can, the dirty tyke. Why don't you punch into *him*, Alf?" Poppy screamed.

Still that wobbling eye, blank and ferocious, was fixed upon vacancy.

"Let *me* look after Mrs. Murdoch I *don't* think," shouted Poppy. "And be a man, even if you can't keep your old woman out of the lodger's room. —— ——! I wouldn't half slosh his jaw in, if I was a man, the —— ——! "

It was a question for Michael either of laughing outright or of being nauseated at the oaths streaming from that little woman's thin magenta lips. He laughed. Even with her paint, she still looked so respectable. When he began to laugh, he laughed so uncontrollably that he had to hold on to the rail of the balusters until they rattled like ribs.

Michael's laughter stung the group to phrenzied action. Mrs. Murdoch spat in her husband's face, whereupon he immediately loosed his grip upon her shoulders. In a moment she and Poppy were clawing each other. Michael, though he was still laughing unquenchably, rushed downstairs to part them. He had an idea that both of the women instantly turned and attacked him. The hat-stand fell over : the scurfy front-door mat slid up and down the oil-cloth : there was a reek of stale scent and dust and spirituous breath.

At last Michael managed to secure Poppy's thin twitching arms and to hold her fast, though she was kicking him with sharp-heeled boots and he was weak with inward laughter. Mrs. Murdoch in the lull began fecklessly to gather together the strands of her disordered hair. Alf, who had gone to peep from the window of the ground-floor front in case a policeman's bull's-eye were glancing on Neptune Crescent, reappeared in the doorway.

"What a smell of gas," he exclaimed nervously.

There was indeed a smell of gas, and Michael remembered that Poppy in her struggle had grasped the bracket. She must have dislocated the lead pipe rather badly, for the light was already dimming and the gas was rushing out fast.

3 L

The tumultuous scene was allayed. Mr. Murdoch hurried to cut off the main. Poppy retired into her room, slammed and locked the door. Michael went upstairs to bed, and just as darkness descended upon the house he saw his landlady painfully trying to raise the hatstand, while with the other arm she felt aimlessly for strands of tumbled hair.

Next morning Michael was surprized to see Mrs. Murdoch enter very cheerfully with his tea; her hair that so short a time since had seemed eternally intractable had now shrivelled into subjugatory curl-papers: of last night's tear-smudged face remained no memory in this beaming countenance.

" Quite a set-out we had last night, didn't we ? " she said expansively. " But that Poppy, really, you know, she is the limit. Driving home with my old man in a hansom cab. There's a nice game to get up to. I was bound to let her have it. I couldn't have held myself in."

" I suppose you'll get rid of her now," said Michael.

" Oh, well, she's not so bad in some ways, and very quiet as a rule. She was a bit canned last night, and I suppose I'd had one or two myself. Oh, well, it wouldn't do, would it, if we never had a little enjoyment in this life ? "

She left him wondering how he would ever be able to readjust his standards to the topsyturvy standards of the underworld, the topsyturvy feuds and reconciliations, the hatreds; the loves and jealousies and fears. But to-day he must leave this looking-glass world for a time.

Mrs. Murdoch was very much upset by his departure from Neptune Crescent.

" It seems such a pity," she said. " And just as I was beginning to get used to your ways. Oh, well, we'll meet again some day, I hope, this side of the cemetery."

Michael felt some misgivings about ordering a hansom after last night, but Mrs. Murdoch went cheerfully enough to fetch one. He drove away from Neptune Crescent, waving to her where she stood in the small doorway looking very large under that rusty frail verandah. He also waved rather maliciously to Poppy, as he caught sight of her sharp nose pressed against the panes of the ground-floor front.

Chapter III : *The Café d'Orange*

MICHAEL came back to Cheyne Walk with a sense of surprize at finding that it still existed ; and when he saw the parlour-maid he half expected she would display some emotion at his reappearance. After Neptune Crescent it was almost impossible to imagine a female who was not subject to the violence of her mutable emotions. Yet her private life, the life of the alternate Sunday evening out, might be as passionate and gusty as any scene in Neptune Crescent. He looked at the tortoise-mouthed parlour-maid with a new interest, until she became waxily pink under his stare.

"Mrs. Fane is in the drawing-room, sir." It was as if she were rebuking his observation.

His mother rose from her desk when he came to greet her.

"Dearest boy, how delightful to see you again, and so thoughtful of you to send me those postcards."

If she had asked him directly where he had been, he would have told her about Neptune Crescent, and possibly even about Lily. But as she did not, he could reveal nothing of the past fortnight. It would have seemed to him like the boring recitation of a dream, which from other people was a confidence he always resented.

"Stella and Alan are in the studio," she told him.

They chatted for a while of unimportant things, and then Michael said he would go and find them. As he crossed the little quadrangle of pallid grass and heard in the distance the sound of the piano he could not keep back the thought of how utterly Alan's company had replaced his own. Not that he was jealous, not that he was not really delighted; but a period of his life was being rounded off. The laws of change were being rather ruthless just now. Both Alan and Stella were so obviously glad to see him that the fleck of bitterness vanished immediately, and he was at their service.

" Where have you been ? " Stella demanded. " We go to Richmond. We send frantic wires to you to join us on the river, and when we come back you're gone. Where have you been ? "

" I've been away," Michael answered with a certain amount of embarrassment.

" My dear old Michael, we never supposed you'd been hiding in the cistern-cupboard for a fortnight," said Stella, striking three chords of cheerful contempt.

" I believe he went back to Oxford," suggested Alan.

" I am going up to-morrow," Michael said. " When is your Viva ? "

" Next week. Where are you going to stay ? "

" In college, if I can get hold of a room."

" Bother Oxford," interrupted Stella. " We want to know where you've been this fortnight."

" You do," Alan corrected.

" I'll tell you both later on," Michael volunteered. " Just at present I suppose you won't grudge me a secret. People who are engaged to be married should show a very special altruism towards people who are not."

" Michael, I will not have you being important and carry-ing about a secret with you," Stella declared.

" You can manage either me or Alan," Michael offered. " But you simply shall not manage both of us. Personally I recommend you to break-in Alan."

With evasive banter he succeeded in postponing the reve-lation of what he was, as Stella said, up to.

" We're going in for Herefords," Alan suddenly announced without consideration for the trend of the talk. "You know. Those white-faced chaps."

Michael looked at him in astonishment.

"I was thinking about this place of Stella's in Huntingdonshire," Alan explained. "We went down to see it last week."

"Oh, Alan, why did you tell him? He doesn't deserve to be told."

"Is it decent?" Michael asked.

"Awfully decent," said Alan. "Rather large, you know."

"In fact we shall belong to the squirearchy," cried Stella, crashing down upon the piano with the first bars of Chopin's most exciting Polonaise and from the Polonaise going off into an absurd impromptu recitative.

"We shall have a dog-cart—a high and shining dog-cart—and we shall go bowling down the lanes of the county of Hunts—because in books about people who live in the county and of the county and by with or from the county dog-carts invariably bowl—we shall have a herd of Herefordshire bulls and bullocks and bullockesses—and my husband Alan with a straw in his mouth will go every morning with the bailiff to inspect their well-being—and three days every week from November to March we shall go hunting in Huntingdon—and when we aren't actually hunting in Huntingdon we shall be talking about hunting—and we shall also talk about the Primrose League and the foot-and-mouth disease and the evolutions of the new High Church Vicar—we shall . . ."

But Michael threw a cushion at her, and the recitative came to an end.

They all three talked for a long while more seriously of plans for life at Hardingham Hall.

"You know dear old Prescott requested me in his will that I would hyphen his name on to mine, whether I were married or single," said Stella. "So we shall be Mr. and Mrs. Prescott-Merivale. Alan has been very good about that, though I think he's got a dim idea it's putting on side. Stella Prescott-Merivale or The Curse of the County! And when I play I'm going to be Madame Merivale. I decline to be done out of the Madame! and everybody will pronounce it Marivahleh and I shall receive the unanimous encomia of the critical press."

"Life will be rather a rag," said Michael with approbation.

"Of course it's going to be simply wonderful. Can't you see the headlines? From Chopin to Sheep. Madame Merivale the famous Virtuosa and her Flock of Barbary Longtails."

It was all so very remote from Neptune Crescent, Michael thought. They really were going to be so ridiculously happy, these two, in their country life. And now they were talking of finding him a house close to Hardingham Hall. There must be just that small Georgian house, they vowed, where with a large garden of stately walks and a well-proportioned library of books he could stay in contented retreat. They promised him, too, that beyond the tallest cedar on the lawn a gazebo should command the widest, the greenest expanse of England ever beheld.

"It would so add to our reputation in the county of Hunts," said Stella, "if you were near by. We should feel so utterly Augustan. And of course you'd ride a nag. I'm not sure really that you wouldn't have to wear knee-breeches. I declare, Michael, that the very idea makes me feel like Jane Austen, or do I mean Dr. Johnson?"

"I should make up your mind which," Michael advised.

"But you know what I mean," she persisted. "The doctor's wife would come in to tea and tell us that her husband had dug up a mummy or whatever it was the Romans left about. And I should say, 'We must ask my brother about it. My brother, my dear Mrs. Jumble, will be sure to know. My brother knows everything.' And she would agree with a pursed-up mouth. 'Oh pray do, my dear Mrs. Prescott-Merivale. Everyone says your brother is a great scholar. It's such a pleasure to have him at the Lodge. So very distinguished, is it not?'"

"If you're supposed to be imitating Jane Austen, I may as well tell you at once that it's not a bit like it."

"But I think you ought to come and live near us," Alan solemnly put in.

"Of course, my dear, he's coming," Stella declared.

"Of course I'm not," Michael contradicted. But he was very glad they wanted him; and then he thought with a pang how little they would want him with Lily in that well-proportioned library. How little Lily would enjoy the fat and placid Huntingdon meadows. How little, too, she would care to see the blackbird swagger with twinkling rump by the shrubbery's edge or hear him scatter the leaves in shrill affright. In the quick vision that came to him of a sleek lawn possessed by birds, Michael experienced his first qualm about the wisdom of what he intended to do.

"And how about Michael's wife?" Alan asked.

Michael looked quite startled by a query so coincident with his own.

"Oh, of course we shall find someone quite perfect for him," Stella confidently prophesied.

"No, really," said Michael to hide his embarrassment. "I object. Matchmaking ought not to begin during an engagement."

Stella paid no heed to the protest, and she began to describe a lady-love who should well become the surroundings in which she intended to place him.

"I think rather a Quakerish person, don't you," Alan? Rather neat and tiny with a great sense of humour and . . ."

"In fact an admirable sick nurse," Michael interposed laughing.

· Soon he left them in the studio and went for a walk by the side of the river, thinking, as he strolled in the shade of the plane-trees, how naturally Stella would enter the sphere of English country life now that by fortune the opportunity had been given to her of following in the long line of her ancestors. That she would be able to do so seemed to Michael an additional reason why he should consider less the security of his own future, and he was vexed with himself for that fleeting disloyalty to his task.

' Michael stayed at 202 High for his Viva. He occupied Wedderburn's old white-panelled room, which he noted with relief was still sacred to the tradition of a carefully chosen decorousness. The Viva was short and irrelevant. He supposed he had obtained a comfortable third, and really it seemed of the utmost unimportance in view of what a gulf now lay between him and Oxford. However, he mustered enough interest to stay in Cheyne Walk until the lists were out, and during those ten days he made no attempt to find Lily.

Alan got a third in Greats and Michael a first in History. Michael's immediate emotion was of gladness that Alan had no reason now to feel the disappointment. Then he began to wonder how on earth he had achieved a first. Many letters of congratulation arrived; and one or two of the St. Mary's dons suggested he should try for a fellowship at All Souls. The idea occupied his fancy a good deal, for it was attractive to have anything so remote come suddenly within the region of feasibleness. He would lose nothing by trying for it, and if he succeeded what a congenial existence offered itself. With private means he would be able to divide his time between Oxford and London. There would really be nothing to mar the perfect amenity of the life that seemed to stretch before him. Since he apparently had some talent, (he certainly had not worked hard enough to obtain a first without some talent) he would prosecute the study of history. He would make himself famous in a select sort of way. He would become the authority of a minor tributary to the great stream of research. A set of very scholarly, very thorough works would testify to his reputation. There were plenty of archaic problems still to be solved. He cast a proprietary glance over the centuries, and he had almost decided to devote himself to the service of Otto I and Sylvester II, when in a moment the thought of Lily, sweeping as visibly before his mind as the ghost in an Elizabethan play, made every kind of research into the past seem a waste of resolution. He tore up the congratulatory letters and decided to let the future wait a while. This pursuit of Lily was a mad business, no doubt, but to come to grips with the present called for a certain amount of madness.

Alan remonstrated with him, when he heard that he had no intention of trying for All Souls.

" You are an extraordinary chap. You were always grumbling when you were up that you didn't know what you ought to do, and now when it's perfectly obvious you won't make the slightest attempt to do it."

" Used I to grumble ? " asked Michael.

" Well, not exactly grumble. But you were always asking theoretical questions which had no answer," said Alan severely.

" What if I told you I'd found an answer to a great many of them ? "

" Ever since I've been engaged to Stella you've found it necessary to be very mysterious. What are you playing at, Michael ? "

" It's imaginable, don't you think, that I might be making up my mind to do something which I considered more vital for me than a fellowship at All Souls ? "

" But it seems so obvious after your easy first that you should clinch it."

" I tell you it was a fluke."

" My third wasn't a fluke," said Alan. " I worked really hard for it."

" Thirds and firsts are equally unimportant in the long run," Michael argued. " You have already fitted into your place with the most complete exactitude. There's no dimension in your future that can possibly trouble you. Supposing I get this fellowship ? It will either be too big for me, in which case I shall have to be perpetually puffing out my frills and furbelows to make a pretence of filling it, or it will be too small, and I shall have to pare down my very soul in order to squeeze into it most uncomfortably."

" You'll never do anything," Alan prophesied. " Because you'll always be doubting."

" I might get rid finally of that sense of insecurity," Michael pointed out. " With all doubts and hesitations I'm perfectly convinced of one great factor in human life—the necessity to follow the impulse which lies deeper than any reason. Reason is the enemy of civilization. Reason carried to the nth power can always with absurd ease be debauched by sentiment, and sentiment is mankind's wretched little lament for disobeying impulse. Women preserve this divinity because they are irrational. The New Woman claims equality with man because she claims to be as reasonable as men. She has fixed on voting for a Member of Parliament as the medium to display her reasonableness. The franchise is to be endowed with a sacramental significance. If the New Women win, they will degrade themselves to the slavery of modern men. But of course they won't win, because God is so delightfully irrational. By the way it's worth noting that the peculiar vestment with which popular fancy has clothed the New Woman is called rational costume. You often hear of ' rationals ' as a synonym for breeches. What was I saying ? Oh, yes, about God being irrational. You never know what he'll do next. He is a dreadful problem for rationalists. That's why they have abolished him."

" You're confusing two different kinds of reason," said Alan. " What you call impulse—unless your impulse is mere madness—is what I might call reason."

" In that case I recommend you as a philosopher to set about the reconstruction of your terminology. I'm not a philosopher, and therefore I've given this vague generic name ' impulse ' to something which deserves, such a powerful and infallible and overmastering impetus does it give to conduct, a very long name indeed."

" But if you're going through life depending on impulse," Alan objected, " you'll be no better off than a weathercock. You can't discount reason in this way. You must admit that our judgements are modified by experience."

" The chief thing we learn from experience is to place upon it no reliance whatever."

" It's no good arguing with you," Alan said. " Because what you call impulse I call reason, and what you call reason I call imperfect logic."

" Alan, I can't believe you only got a third. For really, you know, your conversation is a model of the philosophic manner. Anyway, I'm not going to try to be a Fellow of All Souls and you are going to be a country squire. Let's hold on to what certainties we can."

Michael would have liked to lead him into a discussion of the problem of evil, so that he might ascertain if Alan had ever felt the intimations of evil which had haunted his own perceptions. However, he thought he had tested to the utmost that third in Greats, and therefore he refrained.

There was a discussion that evening about going away. August was already in sight and arrangements must be made quickly to avoid the burden of it in London. In the end it was arranged that Mrs. Fane and Stella and Alan should go

to Scotland, where Michael promised to join them, if he
could get away from London.

"If you can get away!" Stella scoffed. "What rot you
do talk."

But Michael was not to be teazed out of his determination
to stay where he was, and in three or four days he said good-
bye to the others northward bound, waving to them from
the steps of 173 Cheyne Walk on which already the August
sun was casting a heavy heat untempered by the stagnant
sheen of the Thames.

That evening Michael went again to the Orient Promenade; but there was no sign of Lily, and it seemed likely
that she had gone away from London for a while. After
the performance he visited the Café d'Orange in Leicester
Square. He had never been there yet, but he had often
noticed the riotous exodus at half-past twelve, and he argued
from the quality of the frequenters who stood wrangling on,
the pavement that the Café d'Orange would be a step lower
than any of the night-resorts he had so far attended. He
scarcely expected to find Lily here. Indeed he was rather
inclined to think that she was someone's mistress and that
Drake's view of her at the Orient did not argue necessarily
that she had yet sunk to the promiscuous livelihood of the
Promenade.

Downstairs at the Café d'Orange was rather more like a
corner of hell than Michael had anticipated. The tobacco-
smoke which could not rise in these subterranean airs hung
in a blue murk round the gaudy hats and vile faces, while
from the roof the electric lamps shone dazzlingly down and
made a patchwork of light and shade and colour. In a corner
left by the sweep of the stairs a quartette of unkempt
musicians in seamy tunics of beer-stained scarlet frogged
with debilitated braid were grinding out ragtime. The
noisy tune in combination with the talking and laughter,
the chink of glasses and the shouted acknowledgments of

the waiters made such a din that Michael stood for a
moment in confusion, debating the possibility of one more
person threading his way through the serried tables to a seat.

There were three arched recesses at the opposite end of
the room, and in one of these he thought he could see a
table with a vacant place. So paying no heed to the women
who hailed him on the way he moved across and sat down.
A waiter pounced upon him voraciously for orders, and
soon with an unrequired drink he was meditating upon the
scene before him in that state of curious tranquillity which
was nearly always induced by ceaseless circumfluent clamour.
Sitting in this tunnel-shaped alcove he seemed to be in
the box of a theatre whence the actions and voices of the
contemplated company had the unreality of an operatic
finale. After a time the various groups and individuals
were separated in his mind, so that in their movements he
began to take an easily transferred interest, endowing
them with pleasant or unpleasant characteristics in turn.
Round him in the alcove there were strange contrasts of
behaviour. At one table four offensive youths were showing
off with exaggerated laughter for the benefit of nobody's
attention. Behind them in the crepuscule of two broken
lamps a leaden-lidded girl, ivory white and cloying the air
with her heavy perfume, was arguing in low passionate
tones with a cold-eyed listener who with a straw was tracing
niggling hieroglyphics upon a moist surface of cigarette-ash.
In the deepest corner a girl with a high complexion and
bright eyes was making ardent love to a partially drunk
and bearded man, winking the while over her shoulder at
whomever would watch her comedy. The other places were
filled by impersonal women who sipped from their glasses
without relish and stared disdainfully at each other down
their powdered noses. At Michael's own table was a blotchy
man who alternately sucked his teeth and looked at his
watch; and immediately opposite sat a girl with a merry,

audacious and somewhat pale face of the Gallic type under
a very large and round black hat trimmed with daisies.
She was twinkling at Michael, but he would not catch her
eye, and he looked steadily over the brim of her hat towards
the raffish and rutilant assemblage beyond. Along two
sides of the wall were large mirrors painted with flowers
and bloated Naiads ; here in reflection the throng performed
its antics in numberless reduplications. Advertisements of
drink decorated the rest of the space on the walls, and at
intervals hung notices warning ladies that they must not
stay longer than twenty minutes unless accompanied by a
gentleman, that they must not move to another table unless
accompanied by a gentleman, and with a final stroke of
ironic propriety that they must not smoke unless accompanied by a gentleman. The tawdry beer hall with its
reek of alcohol and fog of tobacco-smoke, with its har-
bourage of all the flotsam of the underworld, must preserve
a fiction of polite manners.

Michael was not allowed to maintain his attitude of
disinterested commentary, for the girl in the daisied hat
presently addressed him, and he did not wish to hurt her
feelings by not replying.

"You're very silent, kiddie," she said. "I'll give you a
penny for them."

"I really wasn't thinking about anything in particular,"
said Michael. "Will you have a drink ? "

"Don't mind if I do. Alphonse ! " she shouted, tugging
at the arm of the overloaded waiter who was accomplishing
his transit. "Bring me a hot whisky-and-lemon. There's
a love."

Alphonse made the slightest sign of having heard the
request and passed on. Michael held his breath while the
girl was giving her order. He was expecting every moment
that the waiter would break over the alcove in a fountain
of glass.

".I've taken quite a fancy to whisky-and-lemon hot," she informed Michael. " You know. Anyone does, don't they ? Get a sudden fit and keep on keeping on with one drink, I mean. This'll be my sixth to-night. But I'm a long way off being drunk, kiddie. Do you like my new hat ? I reckon it'll bring me luck."

" I expect it will," Michael said.

" You are serious, aren't you ? When I first saw you I thought you was the spitting image of a fellow I know. Bert Saunders who writes about the boxing matches for Crime Illustrated. He's more of a bright-eyes than you are, though."

The whisky-and-lemon arrived, and she drank Michael's health.

, " Funny-tasting stuff when you come to think of it," she said meditatingly. " What's your name, kiddie ? "

He told her.

" Michael," she repeated. " You're a Jew then ? "

He shook his head.

" Well, kid, I suppose you know best, but Michael is a Jewish name, isn't it ? Michael ? Of course it is. I don't mind Jew fellows myself. One or two of them have been very good to me. My name's Daisy Palmer."

The conversation languished slightly, because Michael since his encounter with Poppy at Neptune Crescent was determined to be very cautious.

" You look rather French," was his most audacious sally towards the personal.

" Funny you should have said that, because my mother was a stewardess on the Calais boat. She was Belgian herself."

Again the conversation dropped.

" I'm waiting for a friend," Daisy volunteered. " She's been having a row with her fellow, and she promised to come on down to the Orange and tell me about it. Dolly

Wearne is her name. She ought to have been here by now. What's the time, kid ? "

It was after midnight and Daisy began to look round anxiously.

" I'm rather worried over Doll," she confided to Michael, " because this fellow of hers, Hungarian Dave, is a proper little tyke when he turns nasty. I said to Doll, I said to her, ' Doll, that dirty rotter you're so soft over'll swing for you before he's done. Why don't you leave him,' I said, ' and come and live along with me for a bit ? ' "

" And what did she say ? " Michael asked.

But there was no answer, for Daisy had caught sight of Dolly herself coming down the stairs, and she was now hailing her excitedly.

" Oh, doesn't she look shocking white," exclaimed Daisy. " Doll," she shouted, waving to her. " Over here, duck."

The four offensive youths near them in the alcove mimicked her in exaggerated falsetto.

" —— to you," she flung scornfully at them over her shoulder. There was a savage directness, a simple coarseness in the phrase that pleased Michael. It seemed to him that nothing except that could ever be said to these young men. Whatever else might be urged against the Café d'Orange, at least one was able to hear there a final verdict on otherwise indescribable humanity.

By this time Dolly Wearne, a rather heavy girl with a long retreating chin and flabby cheeks, had reached her friend's side. She began immediately a voluble tale.

" Oh, Daisy, I put it across him straight. I give you my word I told him off so as he could hardly look me in the face. ' You call yourself a man,' I said, ' why, you dirty little alien.' That's what I called him. I did straight, ' you dirty little—— ' "

" This is my friend," interrupted Daisy indicating Michael, who bowed. It amused him to see how in the very

3 M

middle of what was evidently going to be a breathless and desperate story both the girls could remember the convention of their profession.

"Pleased to meet you," said Dolly, offering a black kid-gloved hand with half a simper.

"What will you drink ? " asked Michael.

"Mine's a brandy-and-soda, please. 'You dirty little alien,' I said." Dolly was helter-skelter in the track of her tale again.

"Go on, did you ? And what did he say ? " asked Daisy admiringly.

"He never said nothing, my dear. What could he say ? "

"That's right," nodded Daisy wisely.

" 'For two years,' I said, ' you've let a girl keep you,' I said, ' and then you can go and give one of my rings to that Florrie. Let me get hold of her,' I said. 'I'll tear her eyes out.' 'No, you won't, now then,' he said. 'Won't I ? I will then,' and with that I just lost control of my feelings, I felt that wild . . . "

"What did you do, Doll ? " asked Daisy plying her with brandy to soothe the outraged memory.

"What did I do ? Why, I spat in his tea and came straight off down to the Orange. 'Yes,' I said, ' you can sit drinking tea while you break my heart.' Don't you ever go and have a fancy boy, Daise. Why, I was a straight girl when I first knew him. Straight—well, anyway not on the game like what I am now." Here Dolly Wearne began to weep with bitter self-compassion. "I've slaved for that fellow, and now he serves me like dirt."

"Go on. Don't cry, duck," Daisy begged. "Come home with me to-night and we can send and fetch your things away to-morrow. I wouldn't cry over him," she said fiercely. "There's no fellow worth crying over. The best of them isn't worth crying over."

The four offensive youths in the alcove began to mock Dolly's tears, and Michael who was already bitten with some of the primitive pugnacity of the underworld rose to attack them.

"Sit down," Daisy commanded. "I wouldn't mess my hands, if I was you, with such a pack of filth. Sit down, you stupid boy. You'll get us all into trouble."

Michael managed by a great effort to resume his seat, but for a minute or two he saw the beerhall through a mist of rage.

Gradually Dolly's tears ceased to flow, and after another brandy she became merely more abusive of the faithless Dave. Her cheeks swollen with crying seemed flabbier than ever and her long retreating chin expressed a lugubrious misanthropy.

"Rotten, I call it, don't you ? " said the sympathetic Daisy, appealing to Michael.

He agreed with a profound nod.

"And she's been that good to him. You wouldn't believe."

Michael thought it was rather risky to embark upon an enumeration of Dolly's virtuous acts. He feared another relapse into noisy grief.

At this moment the subject of Daisy's eulogy rose from her seat and stared very dramatically at a corner of the main portion of the beerhall.

"My God ! " she said with ominous calm.

"What is it, duck ? " asked Daisy anxiously peering.

"My God ! " Daisy repeated intensely. Then suddenly she poured forth a volley of obloquy, and with an hysterical scream caught up her glass, evidently intending to hurl it in the direction of her abuse. Daisy seized one arm : Michael gripped the other, and together they pulled her back into her chair. She was still screaming loudly, and the noise of the beerhall, hitherto scattered and variable in pitch, concentrated in a low murmur of interest. Round about them in the alcove the neighbours began to listen: the girl who had been arguing so passionately with the cold-eyed man stopped and stared; the partially drunk and bearded man collapsed into a glassy indifference, while his charmer no longer winked over her shoulder at the spectators of her wooing; the four offensive youths gaped like landed trout; even the blotchy-faced man ceased to look at his watch and confined himself to sucking steadily his teeth.

It seemed probable, Michael thought, that there was going to be rather a nasty row. Dolly would not listen to persuasion from him or her friend. She was going to attack that Florrie; she was going to mark that Florrie for life with a glass; she was going to let her see if she could come it over Doll Wearne. It would take more than Florrie to do that, yes, more than half-a-dozen Florries, it would.

The manager of the Orange had been warned, and he was already edging his way slowly towards the table. The friends of Florrie were using their best efforts to remove her from the temptation to retaliate. Though she declared loudly that nothing would make her quit the Orange, and certainly that Dolly less than anybody, she did suffer herself to be coaxed away.

Dolly, when she found her rival had retreated, burst into tears again and was immediately surrounded by a crowd of inquisitive sympathizers, which made her utterly hysterical. Michael, without knowing quite how it had happened, found that he was involved in the fortunes and enmities and friendships of a complete society. He found himself explaining to several bystanders the wrong which Dolly had been compelled to endure at the hands of Hungarian Dave. It was extraordinary how suddenly this absurd intrigue of the underworld came to seem tremendously important. He felt that all his sense of proportion was rapidly disappearing. In the middle of an excited justification of Dolly's tears he was

aware that he and his surroundings and his attitude were to
himself incredible. He was positively in a nightmare, and a
prey to the inconsequence of dreams. Or was all his life
until this moment a dream, and was this reality? One fact
alone presented itself clearly, which was the necessity to see
the miserable Dolly safely through the rest of the evening.
He felt very reliant upon Daisy who was behaving with
admirable composure, and when he asked her advice about
the course of action, he agreed at once with her that Dolly
must be persuaded into a cab and be allowed in Daisy's
rooms in Guilford Street a freedom of rage and grief that
was here, such was the propriety of the Orange, a very im-
prudent display of emotion.

" She'll be barred from coming down here," said Daisy.
" Come on, let's get her home."

" Where's that Florrie ? " screamed Dolly.

" She's gone home. So what's the use in your carrying on
so mad ? The manager's got his eye on us, Doll. Come
on, Doll, let's get on home. I tell you the manager's looking
at us. You are a silly girl."

" —— the manager," said Dolly obstinately. " Let him
look."

" Why don't you come and see if you can find Florrie outside ? " Daisy suggested.

Dolly was moved by this proposal, and presently she
agreed to vacate the Orange, much to Michael's relief, for
he was expecting every moment to see her attack the
manager with the match-stand that was fretting her fingers.
As it happened, Daisy's well-meant suggestion was very un-
lucky because Hungarian Dave, the cause of all the bother,
was standing on the pavement close to the entrance.

Daisy whispered to Michael to get a cab quickly, because
Hungarian was close at hand. He looked at him curiously,
this degraded individual in whose domestic affairs he was
now so deeply involved. A very objectionable creature he

was too, with his greasy hair and large red mouth. His cap was pulled down over the eyes, and he may have wished not to be seen ; but an instinct for his presence made Dolly turn round, and in a moment she was in the thick of the delight of telling him off for the benefit of a crowd increasing with every epithet she flung. It was useless now to attempt to get her away, and Michael and Daisy could only drag her back when she seemed inclined to attack him with finger-nails or hatpin.

"Get a cab," cried Daisy. "Never mind what she says. Get a cab, and we'll put the silly thing into it and drive off. The coppers will be here in a minute."

Michael managed to hail a hansom immediately, but when he turned back to the scene on the pavement the conditions of the dispute were entirely changed. Hungarian Dave infuriated or frightened had knocked Dolly down, and she was just staggering to her feet, when a policeman stepped into the circle.

"Come on, move along," he growled.

The bully had merged himself in the ring of onlookers, and Dolly with a cry of fury flung herself in his direction.

"Stop that, will you ? " the policeman said savagely, seizing her by the arm.

"Go on, it's a dirty shame," cried Daisy. "Why don't you take the fellow as knocked her down ? " .

Michael by this time had forced his way through the crowd, rage beating upon his brain like a great scarlet hammer.

"You infernal ass," he shouted to the constable. "Haven't you got the sense to see that this woman was attacked first ? Where is the blackguard who did it ? " he demanded of the stupid, the gross, the vilely curious press of onlookers. No one came forward to support him, and Hungarian Dave had slipped away.

"Move on, will you ? " the policeman repeated.

" Damn you," cried Michael. " Will you let go of that woman's arm ? "

The constable with a bovine density of purpose proceeded apparently to arrest the wretched Dolly, and Michael maddened by his idiocy felt that the only thing to do was to hit him as hard as he could. This he did. The constable immediately blew his whistle. Other masses of inane bulk loomed up, and Michael was barely able to control himself sufficiently not to resist all the way to Vine Street, as two of them marched him along, and four more followed with Daisy and Dolly. A spumy trail of nocturnal loiterers clung to their wake.

Next morning Michael appeared before the magistrate. He listened to the charge against him and nearly laughed aloud in court, because the whole business so much resembled the trial in Alice in Wonderland. It was not that the magistrate was quite so illogical as the King of Hearts ; but he was so obviously biassed in favour of the veracity of a London policeman, that the inconsequence of the nightmare which had begun last night was unalterably preserved. Michael, aware of the circumstances which had led up to what was being made to appear as wantonly riotous behaviour in Leicester Square, could not fail to be exasperated by the inability of the magistrate to understand his own straightforward story. He began to sympathize with the lawless population. The law could only seem to them an unintelligent machine for crushing their freedom. If the conduct of this case were a specimen of administration, it was obvious that arrest must be synonymous with condemnation. The magistrate in the first place seemed dreadfully overcome by the sorrow of beholding a young man in Michael's position in the police-court.

" I cannot help wondering when I see a young man who has had every opportunity . . . " the magistrate went on in a voice that worked on the stale air of the court like a rusty file.

"I'm not a defaulting bank-clerk," Michael interrupted. "Is it impossible for you to understand——" ...

"Don't speak to me like that. Keep quiet. I've never been spoken to like that in all my experience as a magistrate. Keep quiet."

Michael sighed in compassion for his age and stupidity.

"Are there any previous convictions against Wearne and Palmer?" the magistrate enquired. He was told that the woman Palmer had not hitherto appeared, but that Wearne had been previously fined for disorderly conduct in Shaftesbury Avenue. "Ah!" said the magistrate. "Ah!" he repeated, looking over the rim of his glasses. "And the case against the male defendant? I will take the evidence of the constable."

"Your worship, I was on duty yesterday evening at 12.25 in Leicester Square. Hearing a noise in the direction of the Caffy Dorringe and observing a crowd collect, I moved across the road to disperse it. The defendant Wearne was using obscene language to an unknown man; and wishing to get her to move on, I took hold of her arm. The male defendant also using very obscene language attempted to rescue her and struck me on the chest. I blew my whistle. . . ."

The ponderous constable with his thick red neck continued a sing-song narrative.

When Michael's turn came to refute some of the evidence against him, he merely shrugged his shoulders.

"It's really useless, you know, for me to say anything. If 'damn you' is obscene, then I was obscene. If a girl is knocked down by a bully and on rising to her feet is instantly arrested by a dunderhead in a blue uniform, and if an onlooker punches this functionary, then I did assault the constable."

"This sort of insolence won't do," said the magistrate trembling with a curious rarefied passion. "I have a very good mind to send you to prison without the option of a fine, but in consideration . . ."

Somehow or other it was made to appear a piece of extraordinary magnanimity on the part of the magistrate that Michael was only fined three guineas and costs.

"I wish to pay the fines of Miss Palmer and Miss Wearne," he announced.

Later in the morning Michael with the two girls emerged into the garish summer day. Not even yet was the illusion of a nightmare dissipated, for as he looked at his two companions feathered, frilled and bedraggled who were walking beside him, he could scarcely acknowledge even their probable reality here in the sun.

"I shan't drink hot whisky-and-lemon again in a hurry," vowed Daisy. "I knew it was going to bring me bad luck when I said it tasted so funny."

"But you said your hat was going to be lucky," Michael pointed out.

"Yes, I've been properly sucked in over that," Daisy agreed.

"Nothing ever brings me luck," grumbled Dolly resentfully.

As Michael looked at the long retreating chin and down-drawn mouth he was inclined to agree that nothing could invigorate this fatal mournfulness with the prospect of good fortune.

"I reckon I'll go home and have a good lay down," said Daisy. "Are you going to have dinner with me?" she asked turning to Dolly.

"Dinner?" echoed Dolly. "Nice time to talk to anyone about their dinner, when they've got the sick like I have! Dinner!"

They had reached Piccadilly Circus by now, and Michael wondered if he might not put them into a cab and send them back to Guilford Street. He found it embarrassing when the people slowly turned away from Swan and Edgar's window to stare instead at him and his companions.

Daisy pressed him to come back with them, but he promised he would call upon her very soon. Then he slipped into her hand the change from the second five-pound note into which the law had broken.

"Is this for us ?" she asked.

He nodded.

"You are a sport. Mind you come and see us. Come to tea. Doll's going to live with me a bit now, aren't you, Doll ?"

"I suppose so," said Doll.

Michael really admired the hospitality which was willing to shelter this lugubrious girl, and as he contemplated her looking in the sunlight like a moist handkerchief, he had a fleeting sympathy with Hungarian Dave.

When the girls had driven off, Michael recovered his ordinary appearance by visiting a barber and a hosier. The effect of the shampoo was almost to make him incredulous of the night's event, and he could not help paying a visit to the Café d'Orange, to verify the alcove in which he had sat. The entrance to the beerhall was closed, however, and he stood for a moment like a person who passes a theatre which the night before he has seen glittering. As Michael was going out of the bar, he thought he recognized a figure leaning over the counter. Yes, it was certainly Meats. He went up and tapped him on the shoulder, addressing him by name. Meats turned round with a start.

"Don't you remember me ?" asked Michael.

"Of course I do," said Meats nervously. "But for the love of Jerusalem drop calling me by that name. Here, let's go outside."

In the street Michael asked him why he had given up being Meats.

"Oh, a bit of trouble, a bit of trouble," said Meats.

"You are a strange chap," said Michael. "When I first met you it was Brother Aloysius. Then it was Meats. Now——"

"Look here," said Meats, "give over, will you? I've told you once. If you call me that again I shall leave you. Barnes is what I am now. Now don't forget."

"Come and have a drink, and tell me what you've been doing in the four years since we met," Michael suggested.

"B-a-r-n-e-s. Have you got it?"

Michael assured him that everything but Barnes as applicable to him had vanished from his mind.

"Come on then," said Barnes. "We'll go into the Afrique upstairs."

Michael fancied he had met Barnes this time in a reincarnation that was causing him a good deal of uneasiness. He had lost the knowingness which had belonged to Meats and the sheer lasciviousness which had seemed the predominant quality of Brother Aloysius. Instead, sitting opposite at the round marble table Michael saw an individual who resembled an actor out of work in the lowest grades of his profession. There was the cheesy complexion, and the over-fashioned suit of another season too much worn and faded now to flaunt itself objectionably, but with its dismoded exaggerations still conveying an air of rococo smartness; perhaps, thought Michael, these signs had always been obvious and it had merely been his own youth which had supposed a type to be an exception. Certainly Barnes could not arouse now anything but a compassionate amusement. How this figure with its grotesque indignity as of a puppet temporarily put out of action testified to his own morbid heightening of common things in the past. How incredible it seemed now that this Barnes had once been able to work upon his soul with influential doctrine.

"What have you been doing with yourself?" Michael asked again.

"Oh, hopping and popping about. I've got the rats at present."

"Where are you living?"

Barnes looked at Michael in suspicious astonishment. "What do you want to know for?" he asked.

"Mere inquisitiveness," Michael assured him. "You really needn't treat me like a detective, you know."

"My mistake," said Barnes. "But really, Fane. Let's see, that is your name? Thought it was. I don't often forget a name. No, without swank, Fane, I've been hounded off my legs lately. I'm living in Leppard Street. Pimlico way."

"I'd like to come and see you some time," said Michael.

"Here, straight, what *is* your game?" Barnes could not conceal his suspicion.

"Inquisitiveness," Michael declared again. "Also I rather want a Sancho Panza."

"Oh, of course, any little thing I can do to oblige," said Barnes very sarcastically.

It took Michael a long time to convince him that no plot was looming, but at last he persuaded him to come to 173 Cheyne Walk, and after that he knew that Barnes could not refuse to show him Leppard Street.

Chapter IV : *Leppard Street*

WHILE they were driving to Cheyne Walk, Michael extracted from Barnes an outline of his adventures since last they had met. The present narrative was probably not less cynical than the account of his life related to Michael on various occasions in the past; but perhaps because his imagination had already to some extent been fed by reality, he could no longer be shocked. He received the most sordid avowals calmly, neither blaming Barnes nor indulging himself with mental goose-flesh. Yet amid all the frankness accorded to him he could not find out why Barnes had changed his name. He was curious about this, because he could not conceive any shamelessness too outrageous for Barnes to reveal. It would be interesting to find out what could really make even him pause; no doubt ultimately, with the contrariness of the underworld, it would turn out to be something that Michael himself would consider trivial in comparison with so much of what Barnes had boasted. Anyway, whether he discovered the secret or not, it would certainly be interesting to study Barnes, since in him good and evil might at any moment display themselves as clearly as a hidden substance to a reagent flung into a seething alembic. It might perhaps be assuming too much to say that there was any good in him ; and yet Michael was unwilling to suppose that all his conversions were merely the base drugs of a disordered morality. Apart from his philosophic value, Barnes might very actually be of service in the machinery of finding Lily.

At 173 Cheyne Walk Barnes looked about him rather bitterly.

" Easy enough to behave yourself in a house like this," he commented.

Here spoke the child who imagines that grown-up people have no excuse to be anything but very good. There might be something worth pursuing in that thought. A child might consider itself chained more inseverably than one who apparently possesses the perfectiveness of free-will. Had civilization complicated too unreasonably the problem of evil ? It was a commonplace to suppose that the sense of moral responsibility increased with the opportunity of development, and yet after all was not the reverse true ?

" Why should it be easier to behave here than in Leppard Street ? " Michael asked. " I do wish you could understand it's really so much more difficult. I can't distinguish what is wrong from what is right nearly so well as you can."

" Well, in my experience, and my experience has done its bit I can tell you," said Barnes in self-satisfied parenthesis. " In my experience most of the difficulties in this world come from wanting something we haven't got. I don't care what it is—a woman or a drink or a new suit of clothes. Money'll buy any of them. Give me ten pounds a week, and I could be a bloody angel."

. " Supposing I offered you half as much for three months," suggested Michael. " Do you think you'd find life any easier while it lasted ? "

" Well, don't be silly," said Barnes. " Of course I should. If you'd walked home every night with your eyes on the gutter in case anybody had dropped a threepenny bit, you'd think it was easier. It's not a bit of good your running me down, Fane. If you were me, you'd be just the same. Those monks at the Abbey used to jaw about holy poverty. The man who first said that ought to be walking about hell with donkey's ears on his nob. What's it done for me ? I ask you. Why, it's made me so that I'd steal a farthing from one blind man to palm it off as half-a-quid on another."

"Tell me about Leppard Street," said Michael, laughing. "What's it like?"

"Well, you go and punch a few holes in a cheese rind. That's what it looks like. And then go and think yourself a rat who's lost all his teeth, and you've got what it feels like to be living in it."

"Supposing I said I'd like to try?" asked Michael. "What would you think?"

"Think? I shouldn't think two seconds. I should know you were having a game. What good's Leppard Street to you, when you can sit here bouncing up and down all day on cushions?"

"Experience," said Michael.

"Oh, rats! Nothing's experience that you haven't had to do."

"Well, I'll give you five pounds a week," Michael offered, "if you'll keep yourself free to do anything I want you to do. I shouldn't want anything very dreadful, of course," he added.

It was difficult for Michael to persuade Barnes that he was in earnest, so difficult indeed that, even when he produced five sovereigns and offered them directly to him, he had to disclose partially his reason for wishing to go to Leppard Street.

"You see, I want to find a girl," he explained.

"Well, if you go and live in Leppard Street you'll lose the best girl you've got straight off. That's all there is to it."

"You don't understand. This girl I used to know has gone wrong, and I want to find her and marry her."

It seemed to Michael that Barnes' manner changed in some scarcely definable way when he made this announcement. He pocketed the five pounds and invited Michael to come to Leppard Street whenever he liked. He was evidently no longer suspicious of his sincerity, and a perky, an almost cunning cordiality had replaced the disheartened cynicism of his former attitude. It encouraged Michael, to see how obviously his resolve had impressed Barnes. He accepted it as an augury of good hap. Involuntarily he waited for his praise; and when Barnes made no allusion to the merit of his action, he ascribed his silence to emotion. This was proving really a most delightful example of the truth of his theory. And it was clever of Barnes—it was more than clever, it was truly imaginative of him to realize without another question the need to leave for a while Cheyne Walk.

"But is there a vacant room?" Michael asked in sudden dread of disappointment.

"Look here, you'd better see the place before you decide on leaving here," Barnes advised. "It isn't a cross between Buckingham Palace and the Carlton, you know."

"I suppose it's the name that attracts me," said Michael. "It sounds ferocious."

"I don't know about the name, but old Ma Cleghorne who keeps the house is ferocious enough. Never mind." He jingled the five sovereigns.

"I'll go up and pack," said Michael. "By the way, I haven't told you yet that I was run in last night."

"Pinched?" asked Barnes. "Whatever for?"

"Drunk and disorderly in Leicester Square."

"These coppers are the limit," said Barnes emphatically. "The absolute limit. Really. They'll pinch the Archbishop of Canterbury for looking into Stagg and Mantle's window before we know where we are."

Michael left Barnes in the drawing-room, and as he turned in the doorway to see if he was at his ease, he thought the visitor and the macaw on its perch were about equally exotic.

They started immediately after lunch and, as always, the drive along the river inspired Michael with a jolly conception of the adventurousness of London. It was impossible to hear the gurgle of the high spring-tide without exulting in the movement of the stream that was washing out with

its flood all the listlessness of the hot August afternoon.
When Chelsea Bridge was left behind, the mystery of the
banks of a great river sweeping through a great city began
to be more evident. The whole character of the Embankment changed at every hundred yards. First there was that
sombre canal which, flowing under the road straight from
the Thames, reappeared between a cañon of gloomy houses
and vanished again underground not very unlike the Styx.
Then came what was apparently a large private house which
had been gutted of the tokens of humanity and filled with
monstrous wheels and cylinders and pistons, all moving perpetually and slowly with a curious absence of noise. Under
Grosvenor Road Bridge they went, the horse clattering forward and a train crashing overhead. Out again from slimy
bricks and girders dripping with the excrement of railway-
engines, they came into Grosvenor Road. They passed the
first habitations of Pimlico, two or three terraces and isolated
houses all different in character. There could scarcely be
another road in London so varied as this. Maurice had been
wise to have his studio in Grosvenor Road. From the
Houses of Parliament to Chelsea Bridge was an epitome of
London.

The hansom turned to the left up Clapperton Street, a
very wide thoroughfare of houses with heavy porticoes, a
very wide and very grey street, of a grey that almost achieved
the effect of positive colour, so insistent was it. Michael remembered that there had been a Clapperton Street murder,
and he wondered behind which of those muslin curtains the
poison had been mixed. It was a street of quite extraordinarily sinister respectableness. It brooded with a mediocre
prosperity, very wide and very grey and very silent. The
columns of the porticoes were checked off by the window of —
the cab with dull regularity, and the noise of the horse's
hoofs echoed hollowly down the empty street, to which
every evening men with black shiny bags would come hurry-

3 N

ing home. It was impossible to imagine a nursemaid lolling over a perambulator in Clapperton Street. It was impossible to imagine that anyone lived here but dried-up little men with greenish-white complexions and hatchet-shaped whiskers and gnawed moustaches, dried-up little men whose wives kept arsenic in small triangular cupboards by the bed.

"I wouldn't mind having lodgings here," said Barnes. He had caught sight of a square of cardboard at the farther end of the street. This was the outpost of an array of apartment cards, for the next street was full of them. The next street was evidently a little nearer to the period of final dilapidation; but Michael fancied that, in comparison with the middle-aged respectableness of Clapperton Street, this older and now very swiftly decaying warren of second-rate apartments was almost attractive. Street followed street, each one, as they drew nearer to Victoria Station, being a little more raffish than its predecessor, each one being a little less able to resist the corrosion of a persistently inquinating migration. Sometimes, and with a sharp effect of contrast, occurred prosperous squares; but even these, with their houses so uniformly tall and ochreous, delivered a presage of irremeable decadency.

Suddenly the long ranks of houses, which were beginning to seem endless, vanished upon the margin of a lake of railway-lines. Just before the hansom would have mounted the slope of an arcuated bridge, it swung to the right into Leppard Street, S.W. The beginning of the street ran between two high brown walls crowned with a ruching of broken glass: these guarded on one side the escarp of the railway, on the other a coal-yard. At the farther end the street swept round to an exit between two rows of squalid dwellings called Greenarbour Court, an exit, however, that was barred to vehicles by a row of blistered posts. Some fifty yards before this, the wall deviated to form a recess in which five very tall houses rose gauntly against

the sky from the very edge of the embankment. Standing
as they did upon a sort of bluff and flanked on either side
by blind walls, these habitations gave an impression of quite
exceptional height. This was emphasized by the narrow
oblong windows of which there may have been nearly
fifty. The houses were built of the same brick as the
walls, and they had deepened from yellow to the same
fuscous hue. This promontory seemed to serve as an
appendix for the draff of the neighbourhood's rubbish.
The ribs of an umbrella; a child's boot; a broken sieve;
rags of faded colour, lay here in the gutter undisturbed, the
jetsam of a deserted beach.

"Here we are," said Barnes. "Here's Leppard Street
that you've been so anxious to see."

"It looks rather exciting," Michael commented.

"Oh, it's the last act of a Drury Lane melodrama I don't
think. Exciting?" Barnes repeated. "You know, Fane,
there's something wrong with you. If you think this is
exciting, you'd go raving mad when I showed you some
of the places where I've lived. Well, here we are anyhow.
Number One—the corner house."

They walked up the steps which were gradually scaling
in widening ulcers of decay: the handle of the bell-pull
hung limply forward like a parched tongue: and the iron
railings of a basement strewn with potato parings were flaked
with rust, and here and there decapitated.

Barnes opened the door.

"We'll take your bag up to my room first, and then we'll
go downstairs and talk to Ma Cleghorne about your room,
that is if you don't change your mind when you've seen the
inside."

Michael had no time to notice Barnes' room very much.
But vaguely he saw a rickety bed with a patchwork counter-
pane and frowzy recesses masked by cheap cretonnes in
a pattern of disembowelled black and crimson fruits.

After that glimpse they went down again over the greyish stair-carpet that was worn to the very filaments. Barnes shouted to the landlady in the basement.

"She'll have a fit if she hears me calling down to her," he said to Michael. "You see, just lately I've been very anxious to avoid meeting her."

He jingled with satisfaction the sovereigns in his pocket.

They descended into the gloom that smelt of damp cloths and the stale soapiness of a sink. They peeped into the front room as they went by: here a man in shirt-sleeves was lying under the scattered sheets of a Sunday paper upon a bed that gave an effect of almost oriental luxury, so much was it overloaded with mattresses and coverlets. Indeed, the whole room seemed clogged with woolly stuffs, and the partial twilight of its subterranean position added to the impression of airlessness. It was as if these quilted chairs and heavy hairy curtains had suffocated everything else.

"That's Cleghorne," said Barnes. "I reckon he'd sleep Rip van Winkle barmy."

"What's he do?" whispered Michael, as they turned down the passage.

"He snores for a living, he does," said Barnes.

They entered the kitchen, and through the dim light Michael saw the landlady with her arms plunged into a steaming cauldron. Outside, two trains roared past in contrary directions; the utensils shivered and chinked; the ceiling was obscured by pendulous garments which exhaled a moist odorousness; on the table a chine of bacon striated by the carving-knife was black with heavy-winged flies.

"I've brought a new lodger, Mrs. Cleghorne," said Barnes.

"Have you brought your five weeks' rent owing?" she asked sourly.

He laid two pounds on the table, and Mrs. Cleghorne

immediately cheered up, if so positive an expression could be applied to a woman whose angularities seemed to forbid any display of good-will. Michael thought she looked rather like one of the withered nettles that overhung the wall of the sunken yard outside the kitchen-window.

"Well, he can have the top-floor back, or he can have the double rooms on the ground-floor which of course is unfurnished. Do you want me to come up and show you ?"

She enquired grudgingly and rubbed the palm of her hand slowly along her sharp nose as if to express a doubtful willingness.

"Perhaps Mr. Cleghorne . . ." Michael began.

"Mis-ter Cleghorne!" she interrupted scornfully, and immediately she began to dry her arms vigorously on a roller-towel which creaked continuously.

"Oh, I don't want to disturb him," said Michael.

"Disturb him!" she sneered. "Why, half Bedlam could drive through his brains in a omnibus before he'd move a little finger to trouble hisself. Yes," she shouted, "Yes!" Her voice mingling with the creak of the roller seemed to be grating the air itself, and with every word it grew more strident. "Why, the blessed house might burn before he'd even put on his boots, let alone go and show anyone upstairs, though his wife can work herself to the bone for him. Disturb him! Good job if anyone could disturb him. If I found a regiment of soldiers in the larder, he'd only grunt. Asthmatic! Yes, some people 'ud be very pleased to be asthmatic, if they could lie snorting on a bed from morning to night."

Mrs. Cleghorne's hands were dry now, and she led the way along the passage upstairs, sniffing as she passed her crapulous husband. She unlocked the door of the ground-floor rooms, and they entered. It was not an inspiriting lodging as seen thus in its emptiness, with drifts of fluff along the bare dusty boards. The unblacked grate contained some dried-up bits of orange-peel; with the last summons of the late tenant the bellrope had broken, and it now lay on the floor, like a fat worm; by the window, catching a shaft of sunlight, stood a drainpipe painted with a landscape in cobalt blue and probably once used as an umbrella-stand.

"That's all I got for two months' rent," said Mrs. Cleghorne bitterly surveying it. "And it's just about fit for my old man to go and bury his good-for-nothing lazy head in, and that's all. The bedroom's in here, of course." She opened the folding doors whose blebs of paint had been picked off up to a certain height above the floor, possibly as far as some child had been able to reach.

The bedroom was rather dustier than the sitting-room, and it was much darker owing to a number of ferns which had been glued upon the window-panes. Through this mesh could be seen the nettle-haunted square of back garden; and beyond, over a stucco wall pocked with small pebbles, a column of smoke was belching into the sky from a stationary engine on the invisible lake of railway-lines.

"Do you want to see the top-floor back?" Mrs. Cleghorne asked.

"Well, if you wouldn't mind." Michael felt bound to apologize to her, whatever was suggested.

She sighed her way upstairs, and at last flung open a door for them to enter the vacant room.

The view from here was certainly more spacious, and a great deal of the permeating depression was lightened by looking out as it were over another city across the railway, a city with streamers of smoke, and even here and there a flag flying. At the same time the room itself was less potentially endurable than the ground-floor; there was no fireplace and the few scraps of furniture were more discouraging than the positive emptiness downstairs. Michael shuddered as he looked at the gimcrack washstand through whose scanty paint the original wood was visible in long fibrous sores. He shuddered, too, at the bedstead with its pleated iron laths furred by dust and rust, and at the red mattress exuding flock like clustered maggots.

"This is furnished of course," said Mrs. Cleghorne complacently sucking a tooth. "Well, which will you have?"

"I think perhaps I'll take the ground-floor rooms. I'll have them done up."

"Oh, they're quite clean. The last people was a bit dirty. So I gave them an extra-special clear-out."

"But you wouldn't object to my doing them up?" persisted Michael.

"Oh, no, I shouldn't object," said Mrs. Cleghorne, and in her accent was the suggestion that equally she would not be likely to derive very much pleasure from the fruition of Michael's proposal.

They were going downstairs again now, and Mrs. Cleghorne was evidently beginning to acquire a conviction of her own importance, because somebody had contemplated with a certain amount of interest those two empty rooms on the ground-floor; in the gratification of her pride she was endowing them with a value and a character they did not possess.

"I've always said that properly cared for, those two rooms are worth any other two rooms in the house. And of course that's the reason I'm really compelled to charge a bit more for them. I always say to everyone right out—if you want the two best rooms in the house, why, you must pay according. They're only empty now because I've always been particular about letting them. I won't have *any*body, and that's a fact. Mr. Barnes here knows I'm really fond of those rooms."

They had re-entered them, and Mrs. Cleghorne stood with arms admiringly akimbo.

"They really are a beautiful lodging," she declared. "When would you want them from?"

"Well, as soon as I can get them done up," said Michael.

"I see. Perhaps you could explain a little more clearly just what you was thinking of doing?"

Michael gave some of his theories of decoration, while Mrs. Cleghorne waited in critical audience; as it were feeling the pulse of the apartments under the stimulus of Michael's sketch of their potentiality.

"All white?" the landlady echoed pessimistically. "That sounds very gloomy, doesn't it? More like a outhouse or a coal-cellar than a nice couple of rooms."

"Well, they couldn't look rottener than what they do at present," Barnes put in. "So if you take my advice, you'll say 'yes' and be very thankful. They'll look clean anyway."

The landlady threw back her head and surveyed Barnes like a snake about to strike.

"Rotten?" she sniffed. "I'm sure this gentleman here isn't likely to find a nicer and a cheaper pair of rooms or a more convenient and a quieter pair of rooms anywhere in Pimlico. A lot of people is very anxious to be in this neighbourhood."

Mrs. Cleghorne was much offended by Barnes' criticism, and there was a long period of dubiety before it was settled that Michael should be accepted as a tenant.

"I've never cared for white," she said in final protest. "Not since I was married."

Reminded of Mr. Cleghorne's existence in the basement, she hurried forthwith to rout him out. As she disappeared, Michael saw that she was searching in the musty folds of her skirt in order to deposit in her purse the month's rent he had paid in advance.

A couple of weeks passed while the decorators worked hard; and Michael returned from an unwilling visit to Scotland to find them ready for him. He got together a certain amount of furniture, and towards the end of August he moved into Leppard Street.

Barnes on account of the prosperity which had come to
him through Michael's money had managed to dress himself
in a series of outrageously new and fashionable suits, and on
the afternoon of his patron's arrival he strutted about the
apartments.

" Very nice," he said. " Very nice indeed. I reckon old
Ma Cleghorne ought to be very pleased with herself. Some
of these pictures are a bit too religious for me just at present,
but everyone to their own taste, that's what I always say.
To their own taste," he repeated. " Otherwise what's the
good in being given an opinion of your own ? "

Michael felt it was time to explain to Barnes more particularly his quest of Lily.

" You don't know a girl called Lily Haden ? " he asked.

" Lily Haden," said Barnes thoughtfully. " Lily Hopkins.
A great fat girl with red . . ."

" No, no," Michael interrupted. " Lily Haden. Tall.
Slim. Very fair hair. Of course she may have another name
now."

" That's it, you see," said Barnes wisely.

" Wherever she is, whatever she's doing, I must find her,"
Michael went on.

" Well, if you go about it in that spirit, you'll soon find
her," Barnes prophesied.

Michael looked at him sharply. He thought he noticed
in Barnes' manner a suggestion of humouring him. He
rather resented the way in which Barnes seemed to encourage
him as one might encourage a child.

" You understand I want to marry her ? " Michael asked
fiercely.

" That's all right, old chap. I'm not trying to stop you,
am I ? "

" But why are you talking as if I weren't in earnest ? "
Michael demanded. " When I first told you about it you
were evidently very pleased, and now you've got a sneer

which frankly I tell you I find extraordinarily objection-able."

Barnes looked much alarmed by Michael's sudden attack, and explained that he meant nothing by his remarks beyond a bit of fun.

" Is it funny to marry somebody ? " Michael demanded.

" Sometimes it's very funny to marry a tart," said Barnes.

Michael flushed. This was a directness of speech for which he was not prepared.

" But when I first told you," Michael said, " you seemed very pleased."

" I *was* very pleased to find I'd evidently struck a nice-mannered lunatic," said Barnes. " You offered me five quid a week, didn't you ? Well, you didn't offer me that to give you good advice, now did you ? "

Michael tried to conceal the mortification that was being inflicted upon him. He had been very near to making a fool of himself by supposing that his announcement had aroused admiration. Instead of admiring him, Barnes evidently re-garded him as an idiot whom it were politic to encourage on account of the money this idiot could provide. It was an humiliating discovery. The chivalry on which he congratu-lated himself had not touched a single chord in Barnes. Was it likely that in Lily herself he would find someone more responsive to what he still obstinately maintained to himself was really rather a fine impulse ? Michael began to feel half sorry for Barnes because he could not appreciate nobility of motive. It began to seem worth while trying to impose upon him the appreciation which he felt he owed. Michael was sorry for his uncultivated ideals, and he took a certain amount of pleasure in the thought of how much Barnes might benefit from a close association with himself. He did not regret the whim which had brought them to Leppard Street. Whatever else might happen, it would always be consoling to think that he would be helping

Barnes. In half a dream Michael began to build up the vision of a newer and a finer Barnes, a Barnes with sensitiveness and decent instincts, a Barnes who would forsake very willingly the sordid existence he had hitherto led in order to rise under Michael's guidance and help to a wider and better life. Michael suddenly experienced a sense of affection for Barnes, the affection of the missionary for the prospective convert. He forgave him his cynical acceptance of the five pounds a week, and he made up his mind not to refer to Lily again until Barnes should be able to esteem at its true value the step he proposed to take.

Michael looked round at the new rooms he had succeeded in creating out of the ground-floor of 1 Leppard Street. These novel surroundings would surely be strong enough to make the first impression upon Barnes. He could not fail to be influenced by this whiteness and cleanliness, so much more white and clean where everything else was dingy and vile. It was all so spare and simple that it surely must produce an effect. Barnes would see him living every day in perfect contentment with a few books and a few pictures. He must admire those cherry-red curtains and those green shelves. He must respect the cloistral air Michael had managed to import even into this warren of queer inhabitants whom as yet he had scarcely seen. It was romantic to come like this into a small secluded world which did not know him; to bring like this a fresh atmosphere into a melancholy street of human beings who lived perpetually in a social twilight. Michael's missionary affection began to extend beyond Barnes and to embrace all the people in this house. He felt a great fondness for them, a great desire to identify himself with their aspirations, so that they would be glad to think he was living in their midst. He began to feel very poignantly that his own existence hitherto had been disgracefully unprofitable both to himself and everybody else. He was grateful that destiny had brought him here to fulfil

what was plainly a purpose. But what did fate intend should
be his effect upon these people ? To what was he to lead
them ? Michael had an impulse to kneel down and pray
for knowledge. He wished that Barnes were not in this
white room. Otherwise he would surely have knelt down,
and in the peace of the afternoon sunlight he might have
resigned himself to a condition of spirit he had coveted in
vain for a very long time.

Just then there was a tap at the door, and a middle-aged
man with blinking watery eyes and a green plush smoking-cap
peeped round the corner.

"Come in," Michael cheerfully invited him.

The stranger entered in a slipshod hesitant manner. He
looked as if all his clothes were on the verge of coming off,
so much like a frayed accordion did his trousers rest upon
the carpet-slippers ; so wide a space of shirt was visible between the top of the trousers and the bottom of the waistcoat ; so utterly amorphous was his grey alpaca coat.

"What I really came down for was a match," the
stranger explained.

Michael offered him a box and with fumbling hands he
stored it away in one of his pockets.

"You don't go in for puzzles, I suppose ?" he asked tentatively. "But any time I can help. I'm the Solutionist,
you know. Don't let me keep you. Good afternoon, Mr.
Barnes. I'm worrying out this week's lot in The Golden
Penny very slowly. I've really had a sort of a headache the
last few days—a very nasty headache. Do you know anything about cricketers ?" he asked turning to Michael.
"Famous cricketers of course, that is ? For instance I
cannot think what this one can be."

He produced after much uncertainty a torn and dirty
sheet of some penny weekly.

"I've got all the others," he said to Michael. "But one
picture will often stump you like this. No joke intended."

He smiled feebly and pointed to a woman holding in one hand the letter S, in the other the letter T.

"What about Hirst ? " Michael asked.

"Hirst," repeated the Solutionist. "Her S T. That's it. That's 'it." In his excitement he began to dribble. "I'm very much obliged to you, sir. Her S T. Yes, that's it."

He began to shuffle towards the door.

"Anything you want solved at any time," he said to Michael. "I'm only just upstairs, you know, in, the room next to Mr. Barnes. I shall be most delighted to solve anything—anything !"

He vanished, and Michael smiled to think how completely some of his problems would puzzle the Solutionist.

"What's his name ? " he enquired of Barnes.

"Who ? Barmy Sid ? Sydney Carvel, as he calls himself. Yet he makes a living at it."

"At what ? " Michael asked.

"Solving those puzzles and sending solutions at so much a time. He took fifteen-and-six last week, or so he told me. You can see his advertisement in Reynolds. Barmy Sid *I* call him. He says he used to be a conjurer and take his ten pounds a week easily. But he looks to me more like one of these here soft fellows who ought to be shut up. You should see his room. All stuck over with bits of paper. Regular dust-hole, that's what it is. Did you hear what he said ? Solve anything—anything ! He hasn't solved how to earn more than ten bob a week, year in year out. Silly ——! That's what he is, barmy."

Michael's hope of entering into a close relation with all the lodgers of 1 Leppard Street was falsified. None of them except Barmy Sid once visited his rooms ; nor did he find it at all easy to strike up even a staircase acquaintance. Vaguely he became aware of the various personalities that lurked behind the four storeys of long narrow windows.

Yet so fleeting was the population, that the almost weekly arrivals and departures perpetually disorganized his attempts to observe them as individuals or to theorize upon them in the mass. No doubt Barnes himself would have left by now, had he not been sustained by Michael's subsidy; and it was always a great perplexity to Michael how Mrs. Cleghorne managed to pay the rent, since apparently half the inquilines of a night and even some of the less transient lodgers ultimately escaped owing her money.

It was a silent and a dreary house, and although children would doubtless have been a nuisance, Michael sometimes wished that the landlady's strict regulation no longer to take them in could be relaxed. All the five houses of Leppard Street seemed to be untenanted by children, which certainly added a touch to their decrepitude. In Greenarbour Court close at hand the pavements writhed with children, and occasionally small predatory bands advanced as far as Leppard Street to play in a half-hearted manner with some of the less unpromising rubbish that was mouldering there. On the steps of Number Three, two pale little girls in stammel petticoats used to sit for hours over a grocer's shop of grit and waste paper and refined mud. They apparently belonged to the basement of Number Three, for Michael often saw them disappear below at twilight. Michael thought of the children who swarmed above the walls of the embankment before Paddington Station, and he wondered what sort of a desolate appearance these five houses must present for voyagers to and from Victoria. They must surely stand up very forbidding in abandonment to those who were travelling back to their cherished dollshouses in Dulwich. From his bedroom window he could not actually see the trains, but always he could hear their shrieking and their clangour, and he looked almost with apprehension at St. Ursula in her high serene four-poster reposing tranquilly upon the white wall. Nothing except the trains could vex her sleep; for in this house was a perpetual silence. Even when Mrs. Cleghorne was vociferously arguing with her husband, the noise of her rage down in the basement among the quilts and coverlets never penetrated beyond the door at the head of the enclosing staircase, save in sounds of fury greatly minified. So silent was the house that had it not been for the variety of the smells, Michael might easily have supposed that it really was empty and that life here was indeed an illusion. The smells, however, of onions or hot blankets or machine-oil or tom-cats or dirty bicycles proclaimed emphatically that a community shared these ascending mustard-coloured walls, that human beings passed along the stale landings to frowst behind those finger-stained doors of salmon-pink. Sometimes, too, Michael emerging into the passage from his room would hear from dingy altitudes descend the noise of a door hurriedly slammed; and sometimes he would see go down the ulcerous steps in front of the house depressing women in black, or unshaven men with the debtor's wary and furtive eye. The only lodgers who seemed to be permanent were Barnes and Carvell the Solutionist. Barnes on the strength of Michael's allowance used to go up West, as he described it, every night. He used to assure Michael, when towards two o'clock of the next afternoon he extracted himself from bed, that he devoted himself with the greatest pertinacity to obtaining definite news of Lily Haden. The Solutionist occasionally visited Michael with a draggled piece of newspaper, and often he was visible in the garden attending to a couple of Belgian hares who lived in a packing-case marked Fragile among the nettles of the back-yard.

After he had spent a week or so in absorbing the atmosphere of Leppard Street, Michael felt it was time for him to move forth again at any rate into that underworld whose gaiety, however tawdry and feverish, would be welcome

after this turbid backwater. There was here the danger
of being drugged by the miasma that rose from this un-
reflecting surface. He felt inclined to renew his acquaintance with Daisy Palmer, and to hear from her the sequel
to the affair of Dolly Wearne and Hungarian Dave. He
found her card with the Guilford Street address and went
over to Bloomsbury, hoping to find her in to tea. The landlady looked surprized when he enquired for Miss Palmer.

"Oh, she's been gone this fortnight," the woman
informed him. Michael asked where she was living
now.

"I don't know, I'm sure," said the landlady, and as she
was already slowly and very unpleasantly closing the door,
Michael came away a little disconsolate. These abrupt
dematerializations of the underworld were really very
difficult to grapple with. It gave him a sense of the futility
of his search for Lily (though lately he had prosecuted it
somewhat lazily) when girls, who a month ago offered what
was presumably a permanent address, could have vanished
completely a fortnight later. Perhaps Daisy would be at
the Orange. He would take Barnes with him this evening
and ask his opinion of her and Dolly and Hungarian Dave.

The beerhall downstairs looked exactly the same as when
he had visited it a month ago. Michael could sympathize
with the affection such places roused in the hearts of their
frequenters. There was a great deal to be said for an institution that could present, day in, day out, a steady aspect to
a society whose life was spent in such extremes of elation
and despair, of prosperity and wretchedness, and whose
actual lodging was liable to be changed at any moment for
better or worse.

"Not a bad place, is it?" said Barnes, looking round in
critical approval at the prostitutes and bullies hoarded
round the tables puddly with the overflow of mineral
waters and the froth of beer.

"You really like it ?" Michael asked.

"Oh, it's cheerful," said Barnes. "And that's something nowadays."

Michael perceived Daisy before they were half-way across the room. He greeted her with particular friendliness as an individual among these hard-eyed constellations.

"Hullao !" she cried. "Wherever have you been all this time ?"

"I called at Guilford Street but you were gone."

"Oh, yes. I left there. I couldn't stand the woman there any longer. Sit down. Who's your friend ?"

Michael brought Barnes into the conversation, and suggested moving into one of the alcoves where it was easier to talk.

"No, come on, sit down here. Fritz won't like it, if we move."

Michael looked round for the protector, and she laughed.

"You silly thing. Fritz is the waiter."

Michael presently grew accustomed to being jogged in the back by everyone who passed, and so powerful was the personality of the Orange that very soon he like the rest of the crowd was able to discuss private affairs without paying any heed to the solitary smoking listeners around.

"Where's Dolly ?" he asked.

"Oh, I had to get rid of her very sharp," said Daisy. "She served me a very nasty trick after I'd been so good to her. Besides, I've taken up with a fellow. Bert Saunders. He does the boxing for Crime Illustrated."

"You told me I was like him," Michael reminded her.

"That's right. I remember now. I'm living down off Judd Street in a flat. Why don't you come round and see me there ?"

"I will," Michael promised.

3 O

" Wasn't Bert Saunders the fellow who was keeping Kitty Metcalfe ? ", asked Barnes.

. " That's right. Only he gave her the push after she hit Maudie Clive over the head with a port-wine glass in the Half Moon upstairs."

" I knew Kitty," said Barnes, shaking his head to imply that acquaintance with Kitty had involved a· wider experience than fell to most men. " What's happened to her ? "

" Oh, Gard, don't ask me," said Daisy. " She got in with a fellow who kept a fried-fish place in the Caledonian Road, and I've never even seen her since."

" And what's happened to Dolly ? " asked Michael.

" Oh, good job if that love-boy of hers does punch into her. Silly cow ! She ought to know better. Fancy going off as soft as you like with that big-mouthed five-to-two, and after I'd just given her six of my new handkerchiefs."

Michael wished he could have an opportunity of explaining to Barnes that on account of Daisy's friendship for Dolly, he and she and the cast-off had spent a night in the police-cells. He thought it would have amused him.

" Where's the Half Moon ? " he asked instead.

Daisy said it was a place in Glasshouse Street for which she had no very great affection. However, Michael was anxious to see it; and soon they left the Orange to visit the Half Moon.

It was a public-house with nothing that was demirep in its exterior; but upstairs there was a room frequented after eleven o'clock by ladies of the town. They walked up a narrow twisting staircase carpeted with bright red felt and lit by a red-shaded lamp, and found themselves in a room even more densely fumed with tobacco-smoke than downstairs at the Orange. In a corner was an electric organ which was fed with a stream of pennies and blared forth its repertory of ten tunes with maddening persistence. One of these tunes was gay enough to make the girls wish to dance, and always with its recurrence there was a certain amount of cake-walking which was immediately stopped by a commissionaire who stood in the doorway and shouted " Order, please! Quiet, please! No dancing, ladies!" To the nearest couple he always whispered that the police were outside.

Daisy, having stigmatized the Half Moon as the rottenest hole within a mile of the Dilly, proceeded to become more cheerful with every penny dropped into the slot; and finally she invited Michael to come back with her to Judd Street, as her boy had gone down to Margate to see Young Sancy, a prospective lightweight champion, who was training there.

"Anyway, you can see me home," she said. "Even if you don't come in. Besides, my flat's all right. It is, really. You know. Comfortable. He's very good to me is Bert, though he's a bit soppified. He dresses very nice and he — earns good money. Well, three pound a week. That's not so bad, is it?"

"That's all right," said Barnes. "With what you earn as well."

"There's a nerve," said Daisy. "Well, I can't stay moping indoors all the evening, can I? But he's most shocking jealous is Bert. And he calls me his pussy-cat. Puss, puss! There's a scream. He's really a bit soft, and his eyes is awful. But it's nice, so here's luck." She drained her glass. "'Do you love me, puss?' he says. Silly thing! But they think a lot of him at the office. His governor came down to see him the other morning about something he's been writing. I don't know what it was. I hate the sight of his writing. I carry on at him something dreadful, and then he says, "My pussy-cat mustn't disturb me.'"

Daisy shrieked with laughter at the recollection, and Michael who was beginning to be rather fearful for her sobriety suggested home as a good move.

"I shan't go if you don't come back with me," she declared.

Since their incarceration Michael had a tender feeling for Daisy, and he promised to accompany her. She would not go in a hansom, however; nor would she allow Barnes to make a third; and in the end she and Michael went wandering off down Shaftesbury Avenue through the warm September night.

Michael enjoyed walking with her, for she rambled on with long tales of her past that seemed the inconsequent threads of a legendary Odyssey. He flattered himself with her companionship and told himself that here at last was a demonstration of the possibility of a true friendship with a woman of that class with whom mere friendship would be more improbable than with any woman. It was really delightful to stroll with her homewards under this starlit sky of London; to wander on and on while she chattered forth her history. There had been no hint of any other relation between them; she was accepting him as a friend. He was proud as they walked through Russell Square overshadowed by the benign trees that hung down with tralucent green sprays in the lamplight; he felt a thrill in her companionship, as they dawdled along the railings of Brunswick Square in the acrid scent of the privet. It was curious to think that from the glitter and jangle of the Half Moon could rise this friendship that was giving to all the houses they passed a strange peacefulness. He fancied that here and there the windows were blinking at them in drowsy content, when the gas was extinguished by the unknown bedfarer within. Judd Street shone before them in a lane of lamps, and beyond, against the night, the gothic cliff of St. Pancras Station was indistinctly present. They turned down into

Little Quondam Street, and presently came to a red brick
house with a pretentious portico.

"Our flat's in here. Agnes House, it's called. Come in
and have one before you go home," she invited. .

Michael entered willingly. He was glad to show so quickly
his confidence in their new friendship.

Agnes House was only entitled to the distinction of a name
rather than a number because the rest of the houses in
Quondam Street were shabby, small and old. It was a new
building three storeys high, and it was already falling to
pieces, owing to work which must have been exceptionally
dishonest to give so swiftly the effect of caducity. This
collapse was more obvious because it was not dignified by the
charm of age; and Agnes House in its premature dissolution was not much more admirable than a cardboard box
which has been left out in the rain. Upon Michael it made
an impression as of something positively corrupt in itself
apart from any association with depravity: it was like a
young person with a vile disease whose condition nauseated
without arousing pity.

"Rather nice, eh ? " said Daisy as she lit the gas in the
kitchen of the flat. "Sit down. I'll get some whisky.
There's a bathroom, you know. And it's grand being on the
ground-floor. I should get the hump, if we was upstairs. I
always swore I'd never live in a flat. Well, I don't really
call them safe, do you ? Anything might happen and nothing ever be found out."

Michael as he saw the crude pink sheets of Crime Illustrated strewn about the room was not surprized that Daisy
should often get nervous when left alone. These horrors
in which fashion-plates with mangled throats lay weltering
in pools of blood could scarcely conduce to a placid loneliness, and Michael knew that she probably spent a great deal
of every day in solitude. Her life with Crime Illustrated
to fright her fancy must always be haunted by presentiments

of dread at the sound of a key in the latch. It was curious, this half childlike existence of the underworld always upon the boundaries of fear. Michael could see the villainous paper used for every kind of domestic service—to wrap up a piece of raw meat, to contain the scraps for the cat's dinner, and spread half over the kitchen table as a cloth whereon the discs of grease lay like great thunder-drops. It would be very natural, when the eyes never rested from these views of sordid violence, to expect evil everywhere. Himself, as he sat here, was already half inclined to accept the underworld's preoccupation with crime as a truer judgement of human nature than was held by a sentimental civilization, and he began to wonder whether a good deal of his own privacy had not been spent in a fool's paradise of security. The moated grange and the dark tower were harmless rococo terrors beside the maleficent commonplace of Agnes House.

"The kitchen's in a rare old mess, isn't it ? " said Daisy looking round her. "It gives Bert the rats to see it like this."

"Are you fond of him ? " Michael asked. He was anxious to display his friendly interest.

"Oh, he's all right. But I wouldn't ever get fond of *any*body. It doesn't pay with men. The more you give them, the more they think they can do as they like with you."

"I don't understand why you live with him, if he's nothing better than all right," said Michael.

"Well, I'm used to him, and he's not always in the way like some fellows are."

Michael would have liked to ask her about the beginning of her life as it was now conducted. Daisy was so essentially of the streets that it was impossible to suppose she had ever known a period of innocency. Her ancestry seemed to go back to the doxies of the eighteenth century, and beyond

them to Alsatian queans, and yet farther to the tavern
wenches of François Villon and the Chronique Scandaleuse. —
There was nothing pathetic about her; he could not
imagine her ever in a position to be wronged by a man.
She was in very fact the gay woman who was bred first from
some primordial heedlessness unchronicled. She would be a
hard subject for chivalrous treatment, so deeply would she
inevitably despise it. Nevertheless he wanted to try to
bring home to her the quality of the feeling she had inspired
in him. He was anxious to prove to her the reality of a
friendliness untainted by any thought of the relation in
which she might justifiably think he would prefer to stand.

"There's something extraordinarily attractive about
being friends," he began. "Isn't it a great relief for you
to meet someone who wishes to be nothing more than a
friend?"

"Friends," Daisy repeated. "I don't know that I think
much of friends. You don't get much out of *them*, do you?"

"Is that all anybody is for," Michael asked in disappointment. "To get something out of?"

"Well, naturally. Anyone can't live on nothing, can
they?"

"But I don't see why a friend shouldn't be as profitable
as an ephemeral . . . as a lover . . . well, what I mean is,
as a man you meet at eleven and say good-bye to next
morning. A friend could be quite as generous."

"I never knew anyone in this world give anything,
unless they wanted twice as much back in return," said
Daisy.

"Why do you suppose I gave you money the other day
and paid your fine in the police-court?" he asked, for though
he did not like it, he was so anxious to persuade her of the
feasibleness of friendship, that he could not help making
the allusion.

"I suppose you wanted to," she said.

"As a friend," he persisted.

"Oh, all right," she agreed with him lazily. "Have it your own way. I'm too sleepy to argue."

"Then we are friends?" Michael asked gravely.

"Yes. Yes. Yes. Yes. A couple of old talk-you-deads joring over a clothes-line. Get on with it, Roy—or what's your name? Michael, eh? That's right."

"Good! Now, supposing I ask your advice, will you give it to me?"

"Advice is very cheap," said Daisy.

"I used to know a girl," Michael began.

"A straight-cut?"

"Oh yes. Certainly. Oh, rather. At least in those days she was."

"I see. And now she's got a naughty little twinkle in her eye."

"Look here. Do listen seriously," Michael begged. "She isn't a straight-cut any longer."

"Well, what did I tell you? That's what I said. She's gone gay."

"I want to get her away from this life," Michael announced with such solemnity that Daisy was insulted.

"Why, what's the matter with it? You're as bad as a German ponce I knew who joined the Salvation Army. Don't you try taking me home to-night to our loving heavenly father. It gives me the sick."

"But this girl was brought up differently. She was what is called a 'lady.'"

"More shame for her then," said Daisy indignantly. "She ought to have known better."

It was curious this sense of intrusion which Lily's fall gave to one so deeply plunged. There was in Daisy's attitude something of the unionist's towards foreign blackleg labour.

"Well, you see," Michael pointed out. "As even you

have no pity for her, wouldn't it be right for me to try to get her out of the life altogether ? "

" How are you going to do it ? If she was walking about with a sunshade all day, before you sprang it on her . . ."

" I had nothing to do with it," Michael interrupted. " At least not directly."

" Well, what are you pulling your hair out over ? " she demanded in surprize.

" I feel a certain responsibility," he explained. " Go on with what you were saying."

" If she left a nice home," Daisy continued, " to live gay, she isn't going to be whistled back to Virginia the same as you would a dog. Now, is she ? "

" But I want to marry her," said Michael simply.

Daisy stared at him in commiseration for his folly.

" You must be worse than potty over her," she gasped. " Why ? "

" Why ? Why, because it doesn't pay to marry that sort of girl. She'll only do you down with some fancy fellow, and then you'll wish you hadn't been such a grass-eyes."

A blackbeetle ran quickly across the gaudy oilcloth, and Michael sitting in this scrofulous kitchen had a presentiment that Daisy was right. Sitting here, he was susceptible to the rottenness that was coeval with all creation. It called forth in him a sense of futility, so that he felt inclined to surrender his resolve to an universal pessimism. Yet in the same instant he was aware of the need for him to do something, even if his action were to carry within itself the potential destruction of more than he was setting out to accomplish.

" When do you see her ? " asked Daisy. " And what does *she* say about being married ? "

" Well, as a matter of fact I haven't seen her for nearly five years," Michael explained rather apologetically. " I'm searching for her now. I've got to find her."

" Strike me, if you aren't the funniest —— I ever met,"
Daisy exclaimed.

She leaned back in her chair and began to laugh. Her
mockery was for Michael intensified by the surroundings
through which it was echoing. The kitchen was crowded
with untidy accumulations, with half-washed plates and
dishes, with odds and ends of attire ; but the laughter
seemed to be ringing through a desert. Perhaps the illusion
of emptiness was due to the pictures nailed without frames
to the walls of the room, whose eyes watched him with
unnatural fixity ; and yet so homely was the behaviour of
the people in the pictures that by contrast suddenly they
made the kitchen seem unreal. Indeed the whole house, no
more substantial than a house in a puppet-show, betrayed its
hollowness. It became an interior very much like those
glimpses of interiors in Crime Illustrated. The slightest
effort of fancy would have shown Daisy Palmer cloven by a
hatchet, yet coquettish enough even in sanguinary death to
display lisle-thread stockings and the scolloped edge of a
white petticoat. There was nothing like this of which to
dream in Leppard Street. Death would come as slowly and
wearily thither as here he would enter sensationally.

Daisy ceased to rock herself with mirth.

" No, really," she said. " It's a shame to laugh, but you
are the limit. Only you did ask my advice, and I tell you
straight you'll be sorry if you do marry her. What's she
like, Wandering Willie ? Have some cocoa if I make it ?
Go on, do. I'll boil it on the gas-ring."

Michael was touched by her attention, and he accepted
the offer of cocoa. Then he began to describe Lily's
appearance. He could not, however much she might laugh,
keep off the object of his quest. Lily was, after all, the
only rational explanation of his present mode of life.

" She sounds a bit washed out according to your description of her," Daisy commented. " Still, everyone to their

own fancy, and if you like blue-eyed bottles of peroxide, that's your look-out."

They were drinking the cocoa she had made, and the flame of the gas-ring gave just the barren comfort that the kitchen seemed to demand. Another blackbeetle hurried over the oilcloth. A belated fly buzzed angrily against the shade of the electric light. Daisy yawned and looked up at the metal clock with its husky tick.

Suddenly there was the sound of a latchkey in the outer door. She leapt up.

"Gard, supposing that's Bert come back from Margate!"

She pushed Michael hurriedly across the passage into the front room, commanding him to keep quiet and stay in an empty curtained recess. Then she hurried back to the kitchen, leaving him in a very unpleasant frame of mind. He heard through the closed door Daisy's voice in colloquy with a deeper voice. Evidently Bert had come back; but his return had been so abrupt that he had had no time to prevent himself being placed in this ridiculous position. Would he have to stay in this recess all night? He peered out into the room, which was in a filigree of bleak shadows made by the street-lamp shining through the muslin curtains of the window. Through a desolation of undrawn blinds the houses of Little Quondam Street were visible across the road. The unused room smelt mouldy, and if Michael had ever pictured himself in the complexity of a clandestine affair, this was not at all the romantic environment he would have chosen for his drama. This was really damned annoying, and he made a step in the direction of the kitchen to put an end to the misunderstanding. Surely Saunders would have realized that his visit to Daisy was harmless: and yet would he? How stupid she had been to hustle him out of the way like this. Naturally the fellow would be suspicious now. Would that hum of conversation never stop? It reminded him of the fly which had been buzzing round the

lamp. Supposing Saunders came in here to fetch something ? Was he to hide ignominiously behind this confounded curtain, and what on earth would happen if he were
discovered ? Michael boiled with rage at the prospect of
such an indignity. Saunders would probably want to fight
him. A man who spent his life helping to produce Crime
Illustrated was no doubt deep-dyed himself in the vulgar
crudity of his material.

Ten minutes passed. Still that maddening hum of talk
rose and fell. Ten more minutes passed ; and Michael began
to estimate the difficulty of climbing out of the window into
the street. It had been delightful, this experience, until he
had entered this cursed flat. He should have parted from
Daisy on the doorstep, and then he would have carried home
with him the memory of a friendship that belonged to the
London starlight. The whole relation had been ruined by
entering this scabrous building.

He must have been here for more than an hour. It was
insufferable. He would go boldly into the kitchen and brave
Saunders' violence. Yet he could not do that because Daisy
would be involved by such a step. What could they be talking about ? It was really unreasonable for people who lived
together to sit up chatting half the night. At last he heard
the sound of an opening door ; there were footsteps in the
passage ; another door opened ; after a minute or two somebody walked out into the street. Michael had just sighed
with relief, when he heard footsteps coming back ; and the
buzz of conversation began again in a lighter timbre. This
was simply intolerable. He was evidently going to stay here
until the filigree of shadows faded in the dawn. Saunders
must have brought in a friend with him. Another half-hour
passed and Michael had reached a stage of cynicism which
disclaimed any belief in friendship. Not again would he so
easily let himself be made ridiculous. Then he became conscious of a keen desire to see this Saunders whom by the way

he was supposed to resemble. It was tantalizing to miss the opportunity of comparison.

The hum of conversation stopped. Soon afterwards Daisy came into the room and whispered that he could creep out now, but that he must not slam the front door. She would see him at the Orange to-morrow.

When they reached the passage, she called back through the kitchen :

" Bert, do you know you left the front door open ? "

Idiotically and uxoriously floated from the inner bedroom, " Did I, pussy cat ? Puss must shut it then."

Daisy dug Michael violently in the ribs to express her inward hilarity ; then suddenly she pulled him to her and kissed him roughly. In another second he was in the lamplight of Little Quondam Street. As in a nightmare it converged before him : a lean dog was routing in some garbage : a drunken man, reeling along the pavement opposite, abused him in queer disjointed obscenities without significance.

Barnes was sitting in Michael's room, when he got back to Leppard Street.

" What ho," he said sleepily. " You've been enjoying yourself with that piece then ? "

Michael regarded him angrily.

" What do you mean ? "

" Oh, chuck it, Fane. You needn't look so solemn ; she's not a bad bit of goods, either. I've heard of her before."

Michael turned away from him. He knew it would be useless to try to convince Barnes that there was nothing between him and Daisy. Moreover, if he told the true tale of the evening, he would only make himself out utterly absurd. It was a pity that an evening which had promised such a reward for his theories should now be tainted. But when Barnes had slouched upstairs to bed, Michael realized how little his insinuations had mattered. The adventure had been primarily a comic experience ; it had displayed him once more grotesquely reflected in the underworld's distorting mirror.

On the following night Michael went to the Café d'Orange, and heard Daisy's account of the wonderful way in which she had fooled Bert Saunders.

" But really you know," she said. " It did give me a turn. Fancy him coming back all of a sudden like that, and bringing in that fighting fellow. What a terrible thing, if Bert had found out you was in there and put him up to bashing your face. Oh, but Bert's all right with his pussycat."

" But why didn't you let me stay where I was ? " Michael asked. " And introduce me quite calmly. He couldn't have said anything."

" Couldn't he ? " Daisy cried. " I reckon he could then. I reckon he could have said a lot. If he hadn't, I'd have given him the chuck right away. I don't want no fellow hanging around me that hasn't got the pluck to go for anyone he finds messing about with his girl. *Couldn't* he have said anything ? "

Michael was again face to face with topsyturvydom. It really was time to meditate on the absurdity of trying to control these people of the underworld with laws and regulations and penalties which had been devised to control individuals who represented moral declension from the standards of a genteel civilization. Mrs. Murdoch, Poppy, Barnes, Daisy—they all inverted the very fabric of society. They were moral antipodeans to the magistrate or the legislator or the social reformer. They were pursuing and acting up to their own ideals of conduct : they were not fleeing or falling away from a political morality. Was it possible then to say that evil was something more than a mere failure to conform to goodness ? Was it possible to declare confidently the absolutism of evil ? In this topsyturvydom might there not be perceived a great constructive force ?

Michael pondered these questions a good deal. He had not enough evidence as yet to provide him with a synthesis ; but as he sat through the rapid darkening of the September dusks, it seemed to him that very often he was trembling upon the verge of a discovery. Leppard Street came to stand as a dark antechamber with massive curtains drawn against the light, the light which in the past he had only perceived through the chinks of impenetrable walls. Leppard Street was Dante's obscure wood of the soul ; it rustled with a thousand intimations of spiritual events. Leppard Street was dark, but Michael did not fear the gloom, because he knew that he was winning here with each new experience a small advance ; at Oxford he had merely contemplated the result of the former pilgrimages of other people. With a quickening of his ambition he told himself that the light would be visible when he married Lily, that through her salvation he would save himself.

Michael did not re-enter his own world, whose confusion of minor problems would have destroyed completely his hope to stand unperplexed before the problems of the underworld, the solution of which might help to solve the universe or at any rate his own share in the universe. He did not tell his mother or Stella where he was living, and their letters came to him at his club. They did not worry him, although Stella threatened a terrible punishment if he did not appear in their midst in time to give her away in November. This he promised to do in spite of everything. He was faithful to his search for Lily, and he even went so far as to call upon Drake to ask if he had ever seen her since that night at the Orient. But he had not. Michael did not vex himself over the failure to discover Lily's whereabouts. Having placed himself at the nod of destiny, he was content to believe that if he never found her he must be content to look elsewhere for the expression of himself. September became October. It would be six years this

month since first they met, and she was twenty-two now.
Could seventeen be captured anew?

One afternoon from his window Michael was pondering
the etiolated season whose ghostliness was more apparent
in Leppard Street, because no fall of leaves marked
material decline. Hurrying along the brindled walls from
the direction of Greenarbour Court was a parson whose
walk was perfectly familiar, though he could not affix it
to any person he knew. Yes, he could. It was Chator's,
the dear, the pious and the bubbling Chator's; and how
absurdly the same as it used to be along the corridors of
St. James'. Michael rushed out to meet him, and had
seized and shaken his hand before Chator recognized him.
When he did, however, he was twice as much excited as
Michael, and spluttered forth a fountain of questions
about his progress during these years with a great deal of
information about his own. He came in eagerly at Michael's
invitation, and so much had he still to ask and tell that it
was a long time before he wanted to know what had brought
Michael to Leppard Street.

"How extraordinary to find you here, my dear fellow.
This isn't my district, you know. But the Senior Curate is
ill. Greenarbour Court! I say, what a dreadful slum!"
Chator looked very intensely at Michael, as if he expected
he would offer to raze it to the ground immediately. "I
never realized we had anything quite so bad in the parish.
But what really is extraordinary about running across you
like this is that a man who's just come to us from Ely was
talking about you only yesterday. My goodness, how . . ."

"It's no larger than a grain of sand," Michael interrupted
quickly.

"What is?" asked Chator with his familiar expression
of perplexity at Michael.

"You were going to comment on the size of the world,
weren't you?"

".I suppose you'll rag me just as much as ever, you old brute.". Chator was beaming with delight.at the prospect. ".But seriously, this man Stewart—Nigel Stewart. I think he was at Trinity, Oxford. You do know him ? "

" Nigel isn't here too ? " Michael exclaimed.

. " He's our deacon."

" Oh, how priceless you'll both be in the pulpit," said Michael. " And to-morrow's Sunday. Which of you will be preaching at Mass ? "

: " My dear fellow, the Vicar always preaches at Mass. I shall be preaching at Evening Prayer. Why don't you come to supper in the Clergy House afterwards ? "

·· " How do you like your Vicar ? "

" Oh, very sound, very sound," said Chator shaking his head.

" Does he take the Ablutions at the right moment ? " asked Michael twinkling.

".Oh, yes. Oh, yes. He's very sound. Quite all right. I was afraid at first he was going to be a leetle High Church. But he's not. Not a bit. We had a procession this June on Corpus Christi. The people liked it. And of course we've got the children."

They talked for an hour of old friends, of Viner, of Dom Cuthbert and Clere Abbey and schooldays, until at last Chator had to be going.

" You will come on Sunday ? "

" Of course. But what's the name of your church ? "

·" My dear fellow, that shows you haven't .heard your parochial Mass," said Chator with mock seriousness. " St. Chad's is our church."

" It sounds as if you had a saintly fish for Patron," said Michael.

" I say, steady. Steady. St. Chad, you know, of Lich-field."

, Michael laughed loudly.

3 P

"My dear old Chator, you are just as inimitable as ever. You haven't changed a bit. Well, St. Chad's—Sunday."

From the window he watched Chator hurrying along beside the brindled walls. He thought how every excited step he took showed him to be bubbling over with the joy of telling Nigel Stewart of such a coincidence in the district of the Senior Curate.

Michael suggested to Barnes that he should come with him to church on Sunday, and Barnes, who evidently thought his salary demanded deference to Michael's wishes, made no objection. It was an October evening through which a wintry rawness had already penetrated, and the interior of St. Chad's with its smell of people and warm wax and stale incense was significant of comfort and shelter. The church, a dreary Byzantine edifice, was nevertheless a very essential piece of London, being built of the yellow bricks whose texture and colour more than that of any other material adapt themselves to the grime of the city. Nothing deliberately beautiful would have had power here. These people who sat thawing in a stupor of waiting felt at home. They were submerged in London streets, and their church was as deeply engulfed as themselves. The Stations of the Cross did not seem much more strange here than the lithographs in their own kitchens, and the raucous drone of Gregorians was familiar music.

As the Office proceeded, Michael glanced from time to time towards his companion. At first Barnes had kept an expression of injured boredom, but with each chant he seemed less able to resist the habits of the past. Michael felt bound to ascribe to habit his compliance with the forms and ceremonies, for it was scarcely conceivable that he could any longer be moved by the appeal of a sensuous worship, still less by the craving of his soul for God.

Chator's discourse was a simple one delivered with all the spluttering simplicity he could bring to it. Michael was not

sure of the effect upon the congregation, but himself found
it moving in a gently pathetic way. The sermon had the
naïve obviousness and the sweet seriousness of a child telling
a long tale of imaginary adventure. It was easy to see that
Chator had never known from the moment of his Ordina-
tion, or indeed from the moment he began to suppose he
was thinking for himself, a single doubt of the absolute truth
of his religion, still less of its expediency. Michael wondered
again what effect the sermon was having upon the congregation, which was sitting all round him woodenly in a sort
of browse. Did one sentence reach it, or was the whole
business of the sermon merely an excuse to sit here basking
in the stuffiness of the homely church ? Michael turned a
sidelong look at Barnes. Tears were in his eyes, and he was
staring into the gloom of the dingy apse with its tessellations —
of dull gold. This was disconcerting to Michael's opinion
of the sermon, for Chator could not be shaking Barnes by
his eloquence : these splutterings of dogma were surely
not able to rouse one so deep in the quagmire of his own
corruption. Must he confess that a positive sanctity abode
in this church ? He would be glad to believe it did ; he
would be glad to imagine that an imperishable temple of
truth was posited among these perishable streets.

The sermon was over, and as the congregation rose to sing
the hymn, Michael was aware, he could not have said how,
that these people pouring forth this sacred jingle were all
very weary. They had come here to rest from the fatigue
of dulness, and in a moment now the chill vapours of the
autumn night would wreathe themselves round their
journey home. Sunday was a day of pause when the people
of the city had leisure to sigh out their weariness : it was
no shutting of theatres or shops that made it sad. This
congregation was composed of weaklings fit for neither
good nor evil; and every Sunday night they were gathered
together for a little while in the smell of warm wax and

incense. Now already they were trooping out into the frore evening; their footsteps would shuffle for a space over the dark pavements; a few would have pickled cabbage and cheese for supper, a few would not; such was life in this limbo between Hell and Heaven. Barnes, however, was not to be judged with the bulk of the congregation: another reason must be found for the influence of Evening Prayer or Chator's words upon him.

"Did you like the sermon?" Michael asked in the porch.

"I didn't listen to a word of it," said Barnes emphatically.

"Oh, really? I thought you were interested. You seemed interested," said Michael.

"I was thinking what a mug I'd been not to back The Clown for the Cesarewitch. I had the tip. You know, Fane, I'll tell you what it is. I'm not used to money, and that's a fact. I don't know how to spend it. I'm afraid of it. So bang it all goes on drinks."

"I thought you enjoyed the service," said Michael.

"Oh, I'm used to services. You know. On and off I've done a lot of churchifying, I have. It would take something more than that fellow preaching to curdle me up. I've gone through it. Religion, love, and measles; they're all about the same. I don't reckon anybody gets them more than once properly."

Michael told Barnes he was going on to supper at the Clergy House, and though he had intended to invite him to come as well, he was so much irritated by his unconscious deception that he let him go off, and went back into the empty church to wait for Chator and Nigel Stewart. What puzzled Michael most about Barnes was how himself had ever managed to be impressed by his unusual wickedness. As he beheld him nowadays, a mean and common little squirt of exceptional beastliness really, he was amazed to think that once he had endowed him with almost diabolical powers. He remembered to this day the gleam in Brother

Aloysius' blue eyes when he was gathering the blackberries by that hazel coppice. Perhaps it had been the monkish habit, which by contrast with his expression had made him seem almost supernaturally evil; and yet when he met him again at Earl's Court he had been kindled by those blue eyes. Henry Meats had been very much like Henry Barnes; but where was now that lambent flame in the eyes ? — He had looked at them many times lately, but they had always been cold and unintelligent as a doll's.

"I really must have been mad when I was young," Michael said to himself. "And yet other people have preserved the influence they used to have over me. Other people haven't changed. Why should he ? I wonder whether it was always myself I saw in him: my own evil genius ? "

Chator came to fetch him while he was worrying over Barnes' lapse into unimportance, and together they passed through the sacristy into the Clergy House.

Nigel Stewart's room, which they visited in the minutes before supper, had changed very little from his digs in the High. Ely had added a picture or two; that was all. Nor had Nigel changed, except that his clerical attire made him more seraphic than ever. While he and Michael chattered of Oxford friends, Chator stood with his back to the fire beaming at the reunion which he felt he had brought about: his biretta at a military angle gave him a look of knowing benevolence.

The bell sounded for supper, and they went along corridors hung with Arundel prints and faded photographs of — cathedrals, until they came to a brightly lit room where it seemed that quite twenty people were going to sit down at the trestle-table. Michael was introduced to the Vicar and two more curates, and also to a dozen church workers who made the same sort of jokes about whatever dish they were helping. Also he met that walrus-like man who

whether as organist or ceremonarius or treasurer of club
accounts or vicar's churchwarden is always to be found
attached to the clergy. Michael sat next to him, as it
happened, and found he had a deep voice and was unable
to get nearer to ' th ' than ' v.'

"We're raver finking," he confided to Michael over a
high-heaped plate, " of starting Benediction, vis year."

" That will be wonderful," said Michael politely.

" Yes, it ought to annoy ver poor old Bishop raver."

The walrus-like man chuckled and bent over his food with
a relish stimulated by such a prospect. After supper the
two curates carried off their favourites upstairs to their own
rooms; and as Chator, Stewart and Michael were determined
to spend the evening together, the Vicar was left with
rather more people than usual to smoke his cigarettes.

"I envy you people," said Michael, as the three of them
sank down into deep wicker chairs. " I envy this power you
have to bring Oxford—or Cambridge—into London. For
it is the same spirit in terms of action, isn't it ? And you're
free from the thought which must often worry dons that
perhaps they are having a very good time without doing
very much to deserve it."

"We work hard in this parish," spluttered Chator. " Oh,
rather. Very hard."

" That's what I say. You have the true peace that thrives
on activity," said Michael. " But at the same time, what
I'm rather anxious to know is how nearly you touch the real
sinners."

Stewart and Chator looked at one another across his
chair.

" How much do we, brother ? " asked Stewart.

" No, really," protested Michael. " My dear Nigel, I
can't have you being so affected. Brother! You must
give up being archaic now that you're a pale young curate."

" What do you call the real sinners ? " asked Chator.

"You saw our congregation to-night. All poor, of course."

"Shall I say frankly what I think?" Michael asked.

The other two nodded.

"I'm not sure if that congregation is worth a very great deal. I'm not trying to be offensive, so listen to me patiently. That congregation would come whatever you did. They came not because they wanted to worship God or because they desired the forgiveness of their sins, nor even because they think that going to church is a good habit. No, they came in a sort of sad drift of aimlessness; they came in out of the dreariness of their lives to sit for a little while in the glow that a church like yours can always provide. They went out again with a vague memory of comfort, material comfort, I mean; but they took away with them nothing that would kindle a flame to light up the grey week-days. Do you know, I fancy that when these picture-theatres become more common, as they will, most of your people will get from them just the same sensation of warmth and material comfort. Obviously if this is a true observation on my part, your people regard church from a merely negative attitude. That isn't enough, as you'll admit."

"But it's not fair to judge by the evening congregation," Chator burst out. "You must remember that we get quite a different crowd at Mass."

"But do you get the real sinners?" Michael repeated.

"My dear Michael, what does this inquisition forebode?" said Stewart. "You're becoming wrapped in mystery. You're found in Leppard Street for no reason that I've yet heard. And now you attack us in this unkind way."

"I'm not attacking you," Michael said. "I'm trying to extract from you a point of view. Lately it happens that I've found myself in the company of a certain class, well— the company of bullies and prostitutes. You must have lots of them in this parish. Do you get hold of them? I don't believe you do, because the chief thing which has struck me is the utter remoteness of the Church or indeed of any kind of religion from the life of that class. And their standards are upside-down—actually upside-down. They're handed over entirely to the powers of darkness. Now, as far as I can see, the Devil—or whatever you choose to call him—only cares about people who are worth his while. He hands the others over to anybody that likes to deal with them. Equally I would say that God is a little contemptuous of the poor intermediates. The Church, however, in these hard times for religion is glad to get hold even of them, and this miserable spirit of mediocrity runs through the whole organization. The bishops are moderate; the successful parsons are moderate; and the flock is moderate. To come back to the sinners. You know, they *would* be worth getting. You've no idea what a force they would raise. And now, all their industry, all their ingenuity, all their vitality is devoted to the service of evil."

Chator could contain himself no longer.

"My dear fellow, you don't understand how impossible it is to get in touch with the people you're talking about. They elude one. Of course, we should rejoice to get them. But they're impossible."

"Christ moved among sinners," said Michael.

"It's not because we don't long to move among them," Chator spluttered in exasperation. "We would give anything to move among them. But we can't. I don't know why. But they won't relax any of their barriers. They're notoriously difficult."

"Then it all comes down to a 'no' in answer to my question," said Michael. "You don't get the real sinners. That's what's the matter with St. Chad's—until you can compel the sinner to come in, you'll stay in a spiritual backwater."

"If you were a priest," said Chator, "you'd realize our handicap better."

"No doubt," Michael agreed. "But don't forget that the Salvation Army gets hold of sinners. In fact I'll wager that nine out of ten of the people with whom I've been in contact lately would only understand by religion the Salvation Army. Personally I loathe the Salvation Army. I think it is almost a more disruptive organization than anything else in the world. But at least it is alive; it's not suet like most of the Dissenting Sects or a rather rich and heavy plum-pudding like the greater part of the Church of England. It's a maddening and atrociously bad and cheap alcohol, but it does enflame. I tell you, my dear old Chator and my dear old Nigel, you have the greatest opportunity imaginable for energy, for living and bringing life to others, if only you'll not sit down and be content because you've got the children and can fill the church for Evening Prayer with that colourless, dreary, dreadfully sorrowful crowd I saw to-night."

Michael leaned back in his chair; the fire crackled above the silence; and outside, the disheartened quiet of the Sabbath was brooding. Chator was the first to speak.

"Some of what you say may be true, but the rest of it is a mere muddle of heresies and misconceptions and misstatements. It's absolute blasphemy to say that God is contemptuous of what you called the intermediates, and you apparently believe that evil is only misdirected good. You apparently think that your harlots and bullies are better for being more actively harmful."

"No, no," Michael corrected. "You didn't follow my argument. As a matter of fact I believe in the absolutism of evil the more, the more I see of evil men and women. What I meant was that in proportion to the harm they have power to effect would be the inspiration and advantage of turning their abilities towards good. But cut out all theological questions and confess that the Church has failed with the class I speak of."

The argument swayed backwards and forwards for a long time, without reaching a conclusion.

"You can't have friars nowadays," said Chator in response to Michael's last expression of ambition. "Conditions have changed."

"Conditions had changed when St. Francis of Assisi tried to revive an absolute Christianity," Michael pointed out. "Conditions had changed when the Incarnation took place. Pontius Pilate, Caiaphas, Judas, and a host of contemporaries must have tried to point that out. Materialists are always peculiarly sensitive to the change of external conditions. Do you believe in Christ?"

"Don't try to be objectionable, my dear fellow," said Chator, getting very red.

"Well, if you do," persisted Michael, "if you accept the Gospels, it is utterly absurd for you as a Christian priest to make 'change of conditions' an excuse for having failed to rescue the sinners of your parish."

"Michael," said Stewart, intervening on account of Chator's obviously rising anger, "why are you living in Leppard Street? What fiery mission are you upon? I believe you're getting too much wrapped up in private fads and fancies. Why don't you come and work for us at St. Chad's?"

"He's one of those clever people who can always criticize with intense fervour," said Chator bitterly. He was still very red and ruffled, and Michael felt rather penitent.

"I wish I *could* work here. Chator, do forgive me for being so offensive. I really have no right to criticize, because my own vice is inability to do anything in company with other people. The very sight of workers in co-operation freezes me into apathy. If I were a priest, I should probably feel like you that the children were the most important. Have either of you ever heard of anybody whose faith was confirmed by the realization of evil? Usually, it's the other way about, isn't it? I've met many unbelievers who first began to doubt, because the problem of evil upset their notions of divine efficiency. Chator, you have forgiven me, haven't you?"

"I ought to have realized that you didn't mean half you were saying," said Chator.

Michael smiled. Should he start the argument again by insisting that he had meant even twice as much as he had said? In the end, however, he let Chator believe in his exaggeration, and they parted good friends.

Nigel Stewart came often to see him during the next fortnight, and he was very anxious to find out why Michael was living in Leppard Street. Michael would not tell him, however, but instead he introduced him to Barnes who with money in his pocket was very independent and gave no sign of his boasted ability to circumvent parsons financially. No doubt, however, when he was thrown back on his own resources, he would benefit greatly by this acquaintance. Stewart had a theory that Michael had shut himself in Leppard Street to test the personality of Satan, and he used to insist that Michael performed all kinds of magical experiments in his solitude there. Having himself been a Satanist on several occasions at Oxford, he felt less than Chator would have done the daring of discussing Baudelaire and Huysmans. Deacon though he was, Nigel was still an undergraduate, nor did it seem probable that he would ever cease to be one. He tried to thrill Michael with some of his own diabolic experiences, but Michael was a little contemptuous and told him that his devil was merely a figure of academic naughtiness.

"All that kind of subjective wickedness is nothing at all," said Michael. "At the worst it can only unbalance your judgment. I passed through it at the age of sixteen."

"You must have been horribly precocious," said Nigel disapprovingly.

"Oh, not more-so than anyone who has freedom to develop. I should give up subjective encounters with evil, if I were you. You'll be telling me soon that you've been pinched by demons like an Egyptian eremite."

Nigel gave the impression of rather deploring the lack of such an experience, and Michael laughed:

"Go and see Maurice Avery in Grosvenor Road. He's just the person you ought to convert. Nothing could be easier than to turn Mossy into an æsthetic Christian. Would that satisfy your zeal?"

"I really think you *are* growing very offensive," said Nigel.

"No, I'm not. I'm illustrating a point. Your encounters with evil and Maurice's encounters with religion would match each other. Both would have a very wide, but also a very superficial area."

November had arrived, and Michael reappeared in Cheyne Walk to assist at Stella's wedding. He paid no attention to the scorn she flung at his affected mode of life, and he successfully resisted her most carefully planned sallies of curiosity:

"What you have to do at present is to keep your own head, not mine. Think of the responsibilities of marriage and let me alone. I'll tell you quite enough when the moment comes for telling."

"Michael, you're getting dreadfully obstinate," Stella declared. "I remember when I could get a secret out of you in no time."

"It's not I who am obstinate," said Michael. "It's you who are utterly spoilt by the lovelorn Alan."

Michael and Alan went for a long walk in Richmond Park on the day before the wedding. It was a limpid day at the shutting-in of St. Martin's summer, and to Michael it seemed like the ghost of one of those June Saturdays of eight years ago. Time had faded that warmer blue to a wintry turquoise, but there was enough of summer's image in this wraith of a day to render very poignantly to him the past. He wondered if Alan were thinking of the afternoons when they had sent the sun down from Richmond Hill. That evening before the examinations of a summer term recurred to him now more insistently than any of those dead days.

> *Thick as autumnal leaves that strew the brooks*
> *In Vallombrosa.*

Now the leaves were lying brown and dewy in the Richmond thickets. Then it was a summer evening of foliage in the prime. He wished he could remember the lines of Virgil which had matched the Milton. He used to know them so well :

> *Matres atque viri defunctaque corpora vita*
> *Magnanimum heroum, pueri innuptæque puellæ.*

There were two complete hexameters, but all that remained in his memory of the rest were two or three disjointed phrases :

> *Lapsa cadunt folia . . . ubi frigidus annus . . . et . . .*
> *terris apricis.*

. Even at fourteen he had been able to respond to the melancholy of these lines ; really, he had been rather an extraordinary boy. The sensation of other times which was evoked by walking like this in Richmond Park would soon be too strong for him any longer not to speak of it. Yet because those dead summer days seemed now to belong to the mystery of youth, to the still unexpressed and inviolate heart of a period that was for ever overpast, Michael could not bring himself to destroy their sanctity with sentimental reminiscence. However, there had been comedy and absurdity also, perhaps rather more fit for exhumation now than those deeper moments.

"Do you remember the wedding of Mrs. Ross?" he asked.

"Rather," said Alan, and they both smiled.

"Do you remember when you first called her Aunt Maud, and we both burst out laughing and had to rush out of the room?"

"Rather," said Alan. "Boys *are* ridiculous, aren't they?"

"Supposing we both laugh like that when Stella is first called Mrs. Merivale?" Michael queried.

"I shall be in much too much of a self-conscious funk to laugh at anything," said Alan.

"And yet do you realize that we're only talking of eight years ago? Nothing at all really. Six years less than we had already lived at the time when that wedding took place."

To Alan upon the verge of the most important action of his life Michael's calculation seemed very profound indeed, and they both walked on in silence, meditating upon the revelation it afforded of a fugitive mortality.

"You'll be writing epitaphs next," said Alan in rather an aggrieved voice. He had evidently traversed the swift years of the future during the silence.

"At any rate," Michael said, "you can congratulate yourself upon not having wasted time."

"My god," cried Alan, stopping suddenly, "I believe I'm the luckiest man alive."

"I thought you'd found a sovereign," said Michael. He had never heard Alan come so near to emotional expression and, knowing that a moment later Alan would be blushing at his want of reserve, he loyally covered up with a joke the confusion that must ensue.

Very few people came to the wedding, for Stella had insisted that as none of her girl friends were reputable enough to be bridesmaids, she must do without them. Mrs. Ross came, however, and she brought with her Kenneth to be a solemn and freckled and carroty page. She was very anxious that Michael should come back after the wedding to Cobble Place, but he said he would rather wait until after Christmas. Nancy came, and Michael tried to remember if he had once seriously contemplated marrying her. How well he remembered her in short skirts, and here she was a woman of thirty with a brusque jolly manner and gold pince-nez.

"You *are* a brute always to avoid my visits at Cobble Place," grumbled Nancy. "Do you realize we haven't met for years ?"

"You're such a woman of affairs," said Michael.

"Well, do let's try to meet next time. I say, don't you think Maud looks terribly ill since she became a Romanist ?"

Michael looked across to where Mrs. Ross was standing.

"I think she's looking rather well."

"Absolute destruction of individuality, you know," said Nancy shaking her head. "I was awfully sick about that business. However, I must admit that she hasn't forced her religion down our throats."

"Did you expect an auto-da-fé in the middle of the lawn?" he asked. She thumped him on the shoulder :

"Silly ass ! Don't you try to rag me."

They had a jolly talk, but Michael was glad he had not married her at eight years old. He decided that by now he would probably have regretted the step.

Michael managed to get two or three minutes alone with Stella after the ceremony.

"Well, Mrs. Prescott-Merivale ?"

"You've admitted I'm a married woman," she exclaimed.

"Now surely you can tell me what you've been doing since August and where you've been."

" I thought very fondly that you were without the curiosity of every woman," said Michael. ".Alas, you are not."

"Michael, you're perfectly horrid to me."

"Don't be too much the young wife," he advised with mocking earnestness.

" I won't listen to anything you say, until I know where you've been. Of course if I hadn't been so busy, I could easily have found you out."

"Not even can you sting me into the revelation of my hiding-place," Michael laughed.

"You shan't stay with us at Hardingham unless you tell me."

"By the time you come back from your honeymoon, I may have wonderful news," said Michael. "Oh, and by the way, where are you going for your honeymoon ? It sounds absurd to ask such a question at this hour, but I've never heard."

"We're going to Compiègne," said Stella. "I wrote to little Castéra-Verduzan, and he's lent us the cottage where you and I stayed."

That choice of Stella's seemed to mark more decisively than anything she had said or done his own second place in her thoughts nowadays.

When the bride and bridegroom were gone, Michael sat with his mother talking.

"I had arranged to go to the South of France with Mrs. Carruthers," she told him. "But if you're going to be here, I could put her off."

Michael felt rather guilty. He had not considered his mother's loneliness, and he had meant to return at once to Leppard Street.

"No, no, I'm going away again," he told her.

" Just as you like, dearest boy."

" You're glad about Stella ? "

" Very glad."

" And you like Alan ? "

" Of course.   Charming—charming." ·

·The firelight danced in opals on the window-panes, and the macaw who had been brought up to Mrs. Fane's sitting-room out of the way of the wedding-guests sharpened his beak on the perch.

 "" It's really quite chilly this afternoon," said Mrs. Fane.

" Yes, there's a good deal of mist along the river," said Michael. · " A pity that the fine weather should have broken up.   It may be rather dreary in the forest."

" Why did they go to a forest ? " she asked.   " So like Stella to choose a forest in November.   Most unpractical. Still, when one is young and in love, one doesn't notice the mud."

Next day Mrs. Fane went off to the South of France, and Michael went back to Leppard Street.

Chapter V : *The Innermost Circle*

NOVEMBER fogs began soon after Michael returned to Leppard Street, and these fuliginous days could cast their own peculiar spell. To enter the house at dusk was to stand for a moment choking in blackness; and, even when the gas flared and whistled through a sickly nebula, it only made more vast the lightless vapours above, so that the interior seemed at first not a place of shelter, but a mirage of the streets that would presently dissolve in the drifting fog. These nights made Pimlico magical for walking. Distance was obliterated; time was abolished; life was disembodied. He never tired of wandering up and down the Vauxhall Bridge Road where the trams came trafficking like strange ships, so unfamiliar did they seem here beside the dumpy horse-omnibuses.

One evening when the fog was not very dense Michael went up to Piccadilly. Here the lamps were strong enough to shine through the murk with a golden softness that made the Circus like a landscape seen in a dying fire. Michael could not bear to withdraw from this glow in which every human countenance was idealized as by amber limes in a theatre. At the O.U.D.S. performance of The Merchant of Venice they had been given a sunset like this on the Rialto. It would be jolly to meet somebody from Oxford to-night—Lonsdale for instance. He looked round half-expectant of recognition; but there was only the shifting crowd about him. How were Stella and Alan getting on at Compiègne ? Probably they were having clear blue days there, and in the forest would be a smell of wood fires. With such unrelated thoughts Michael strolled round Piccadilly, sometimes in a wider revolution turning up the darker side-streets, but always ultimately returning to the Island in the middle. Here he would stand in a dream, watching the omnibuses go East and West and South and North. The crowd grew stronger, for the people were coming out of the theatres. Should he go to the Orange and talk to Daisy? Should he call a hansom and drive home? Bewitched as by the spinning of a polychromatic top, he could not leave the Island. They were coming out of the Orient now, and he watched the women emerge one by one. Their ankles all looked so white and frail under the opera-cloaks puffed out with swansdown; and they all of them walked to their carriages with the same knock-kneed little steps. Soon he must begin to frequent the Orient again.

Suddenly Michael felt himself seized with the powerless excitement of a nightmare. There in black, strolling nonchalantly across the pavement to a hansom, was Lily! She was with another girl. Then Drake's story had been true. Michael realized that gradually all this time he had been slowly beginning to doubt whether Drake had ever seen her. Lily had become like a princess in a fairy tale. Now she was here! He threw off the stupefaction that was paralyzing him, and started to cross the road. A wave of traffic swept up and he was driven back. When the stream had passed, Lily was gone. In a rage with his silly indecision he set out to walk back to Pimlico. The fog had lifted entirely, and there was frost in the air.

Michael walked very quickly because it seemed the only way to wear out his chagrin. How idiotic it had been to let himself be caught like that. Supposing she did not visit the Orient again for a long time? It would serve him right. Oh, why had he not managed to get in front of those vehicles in time? He and she might have been driving together now; instead of which he was stamping his way along this dull dark pavement. How tall she had seemed, how beautiful in her black frock. At last he knew why all this time women had left him cold. He loved her still. What nonsense it had been for him to think he wanted to marry her in order to rescue her. What priggish insolence. He loved her still: he loved her now: he loved her: he loved her! The railings of Green Park rattled to his stick. He loved her more passionately because the ghost of her whom he had thought of with romantic embellishment all these years was but a caricature of her reality. That image of gossamer which had floated through his dreams was become nothing, now that again he had seen herself with her tall neck and the aureole of her hair and the delicate poise of her as she waited among those knock-kneed women on the pavement. He brought his stick crashing down upon a bin of gravel by the kerb that it might clang forth his rage. In what direction had she driven away? Even that he did not know. She might have driven past this very lamp-post a few minutes back.

Here was Hyde Park Corner. In London it was overwhelming to speculate upon a hansom's progress. Here already were main roads branching, and these in their turn would branch, and others after them until the imagination was baffled. Waste of time. Waste of time. He would not picture her in any quarter of London. But never one night should elapse without his waiting for her at the Orient. Where was she now? He would put her from his mind until they met. Supposing that round the corner of that wall she were waiting, because the cab-horse had slipped. How she would turn towards him in her black dress. "I saw you outside the Orient," he would say. She should know immediately that he was not deceived about her life. So vividly had he conjured the scene that when he rounded the wall on his way down Buckingham Palace Road, he was disappointed to see no cab, no Lily standing perplexed; merely a tabid woman clothed in a cobweb of crape, asleep over her

tray of matches and huddled against the wall of the King's
garden. He put a sixpence among her match-boxes, and
wondered of what were her dark dreams. The stars were
blue as steel in the moonless sky above the arc-lamps; and
a cold parching wind had sprung up. Michael deviated
from the nearest way to Leppard Street, and walked on
quickly into the heart of Pimlico. This kind of clear-cut
air suited the architecture of the ashen streets. One after
another they stretched before him with their dim chequers
of doors and windows. Sometimes, where they were inter-
sected by wider thoroughfares, an arc-lamp fizzed above the
shape of a solitary policeman, and the corner houses stood
out sharper and more cadaverous. And always in contrast
with these necropolitan streets, these masks of human dwellings, were Michael's own thoughts thronged with fancies
of himself and Lily.

It was nearly one o'clock when he walked over the arcuated
bridge across the lake of railway-lines and turned the corner
into Leppard Street. From the opposite pavement a
woman's figure stepped quickly towards him out of a circle
of lamplight. The sudden shadow lanced across the road
made him start. Perhaps she noticed him jump, for she
stopped at once and stared at him owlishly. He felt sick for
a moment, and yet he could not, from an absurd compassion
for her, do as he would have liked and run.

"Where are you off to in such a hurry?" he heard her
say.

It was too late to avoid her now. He only had two sovereigns in his pocket. It would be ridiculous and cowardly
to escape by offering her one of them. He had given his
last silver coin to the match-seller. Yet it would have been
just as cowardly to have offered her that. He pitied the
degradation that prompted her so casual question; the
diffidence in her tones marked the fear of answering brutality
which must always haunt her. Now that she was close to

him, he no longer dreaded her. She was not an ancient drab, a dreadful old woman with black cotton gloves, as at first he had shuddered to suppose her. If those raddled smears and that deathly blanch of coarse powder were cleared from her cheeks, there would be nothing to attract or repel : she would scarcely become even an individual in the multitude of weary London women.

"Where are you off to, dearie, in such a hurry ?" she repeated.

"Home. I'm going home," he said.

"Let's walk a bit of the way together."

He could say nothing to her, and if he hurried on, he would hear her voice whining after him like a cat in a yard. He did not wish to let her know where he was living; for every evening he would expect to see her materialize from a quivering circle of lamplight so close to Leppard Street.

"Why don't you come back with me ? I live quite near here," she murmured. "Go on. You look as if you wanted someone to make a fuss of you."

Already they were beside the five houses that rose jet-black against the star-encrusted sky.

"Come on, dear. I live in the corner house."

Michael looked at her in astonishment and she mistaking his scrutiny smiled in pitiable allurement. He felt as if a marionette were blandishing him. The woman evidently thought he was considering the question of money, and she sidled close up to him.

"Go on, dear, you've got some money with you ?"

"It's not that," said Michael. "I don't want to come in with you."

Yet he knew that he must enter Number One with her in order to find in what secret room she lived. And to-morrow morning he would leave the house for ever, since it would be unimaginable to stay there longer with the consciousness that perhaps they were creatures like this, who slammed the doors in passages far upstairs. He would not sleep comfortably again with the sense that women like this were creeping about the stairs like spiders. He must probe her existence, and he put his foot on the steps of the front-door.

"Not that door," she said. "Down here."

She pushed back the gate of the area steps, and led the way down into the basement. It was incredible that she could live on the same floor as the Cleghornes. Yet obviously she did.

"Don't make a noise," she whispered. "Because the woman who keeps the house sleeps down here."

She opened the back-door, and he followed her into the frowsty passage. When the door was closed behind them, the blackness was absolute.

"Got a vesta with you?" she whispered.

Michael felt her hands pawing him, and he shrank back against the greasy wall.

"Here you are. Here you are."

The match flamed, but went out before he could light the nodulous candle she proffered. In the darkness he felt her spongy lips upon his cheek, but disengaging himself from her assiduousness, he managed to light the candle. They went along the corridor past the front room where Cleghorne snored the day away; past the kitchen whose open door exhaled an odorous breath of habitation; and through a stone pantry. Then she led him down three steps and up another, unlocked a rickety door and welcomed him.

"I'm quite on my own, you see," she said in a voice of tentative satisfaction.

Michael looked round at the room which was small and smelt very damp. The ceiling sloped to a window closely curtained with the cretonne of black and crimson fruits — which Michael recognized as the same stuff he had seen in Barnes' room above. He tried to recall how much of this room he could see from his bedroom window, and he connected it in his mind with a projecting roof of cracked slates which he had often noticed. The action of the rain on the plaster had made it look like a map of the moon in relief. The furniture consisted of a bed, a washstand and a light blue chest. There was also a narrow shelf on which was a lamp with a reflector of corrugated tin, a bald powder-puff and two boot-buttons. The woman lit the lamp, and as she stooped to look at the jagged flame, Michael saw that her hair was as iridescent as oil on a canal, with what remained of henna and peroxide.

"That's more cheerful. Though I must say it's a pity they haven't put the gas in here. Oh, don't sit on that old box. It makes you look such a stranger."

Michael said he had a great fondness for sitting on something that was hard; but he thought how absurd he must appear sitting like this on a pale blue chest next to a washstand.

"Are you looking at my cat?" she asked.

"What cat?"

"He's under the bed, I'll be bound."

She called and a small black cat came out.

"Isn't he lovely? But, fancy, he's afraid of men. He always gets under the bed like that."

Michael felt he ought to make up to the cat what his cordiality had lacked towards the mistress, and he paid so much attention to it that finally the animal lost all fear and jumped upon his knee.

"Well there!" the woman exclaimed. "Did you ever? I've never seen him do that before. He knows you're a gentleman. Oh, yes, they know. His mother ran away. But she comes to see me sometimes and always looks very well, so she's got a good home. But *he* isn't stinted. Oh, no. He gets his milk every day. What I say is, if you're going to have animals, look after them."

Michael nodded agreement.

"Because to my mind," she went on, "a great many animals are better than human beings."

"Oh, yes, I think they probably are," said Michael.

"Poor Peter," she crooned. "I wouldn't starve you, would I?"

The cat left Michael and went and sat beside her on the bed.

"Why do you call it Peter?" he asked. The name savoured rather of the deliberate novelist.

"After my boy."

"Your boy?" he echoed.

"Oh, he's a fine boy, and a good boy." The mention of her son stiffened the woman into a fleeting dignity.

"I suppose he's about twelve?" Michael asked. Her age had puzzled him.

"Well, thirteen really. Of course, you see, I'm a little older than what I look." As she looked about forty-five, Michael thought that the converse was more probable.

"He's not living with you?"

"Oh, no, certainly not. Why, I wouldn't have him here for anything—not ever. Oh, no, he's at school with the Jesuits. He's to go in the Civil Service. I lived with his father for many years—in fact from the time I was sixteen. His father was a Frenchman. A silk-merchant he was. He's been dead about six years now."

"I suppose he left money to provide for the boy."

"Oh, no! No, he left nothing. Well, you see, silk merchants weren't what they used to be, when he died; and before that his business was always falling off bit by bit. No, the Jesuits took him. Of course I'm a Catholic myself."

As she made her profession of faith, he saw hanging from the knob of the bed a rosary. With whatever repulsion, with whatever curiosity he had entered, Michael now sat here on the pale blue chest in perfect humility of spirit.

" I suppose you don't care for this life ? " he asked after a short silence.

" Well, no, I do not. It's not at all what I should call a refined way of living, and often it's really very unpleasant."

Somehow their relation had entirely changed, and Michael found himself discussing her career as if he were talking to an old maid about her health.

" For one thing," she continued, " the police are very rough with one, and if anyone doesn't behave just as they'd like for them to behave, they make it very awkward. They really take it out of anyone. That isn't right, is it ? It's really not as it should be, I don't think."

Michael thought of the police in Leicester Square.

" It's damnable," he growled. " And I suppose you have to put up with a good deal from some of the men ? "

" Undoubtedly," she said shaking her head, and becoming every moment more and more like a spinster who kept a stationer's shop in a provincial town. " Undoubtedly. Well, for one thing, I'm at anyone's mercy in here. Of course if I called out, I might be heard and I might not. Really if it wasn't for the woman who keeps the house being always so anxious for her rent, I might be murdered any time and stay in here for days without anyone knowing about it. Last Wednesday—or was it Thursday—time goes by so fast, it seems hardly worth while to count the days, does it ? One day last week I did what I've never done before : I accepted six shillings. Well, it was late and what with one thing and another I wanted the money. Will you believe it, I very carefully as I thought hid it safe away in my bag and this man—a very rough sort of a man he was, I'm not surprized poor Peter runs away from them—I heard him walking about the room when I woke up in the middle of the night. And will you believe it, he'd gone to my bag and taken out his six shillings, as well as fourpence-halfpenny of my own which was all I had at the moment. He was really out of the house and gone in a flash, as they say. I wouldn't be surprized if he makes a regular trade of it with women like myself. Well now, you can't say a man like that is any better than my cat. I was very angry about it, but anyone soon forgets. Though I will say it was a warning."

"I suppose you'd be glad to give up the life ?" said Michael, and as he asked the question, it seemed to him in this room and in the presence of this woman a very futile one.

"Oh, I should be glad to give it up. Yes. You see, as I say, I'm really at anyone's mercy in here. But really what else could I do ? You see, in one way, the harm's done."

Michael looked at her tarnished hair ; at her baggy cheeks raddled and powdered ; at the clumsy black upon her lashes that made so much the more obvious the pleated lids beneath; at her neck already flaccid; and at her dress plumped out like an ill-stuffed pillow to conceal the arid flesh beneath. It certainly seemed as if the harm had been done.

"You see," she went on, "though I have to put up with a great deal, it's only to be expected after all. Now I was very severely brought up by my father, and my mother being —well, it's no use to mince matters as they say—my mother really was a saint. Then of course after this occurred with the Frenchman I told you about—that really was a downward step, though at the time I was happy and though he was always very good to me from the beginning to the end. Still, I'm used to refinement, and I have a great deal to put up with here in this house. Not that I dislike the woman who keeps it. But having paid my rent regular—eight-and-six, that is . . ."

"Quite enough too," said Michael looking up at the ceiling that was so like the scarred surface of the moon.

"You're right. It is enough. It is quite enough. But still I'm my own mistress. No one interferes with me. At

the same time I don't interfere with anybody else. I have
the right to use the kitchen for my cooking, but really
Mrs. Cleghorne—that is the woman who keeps the house—
really she is not a clean cook, and very often my stomach
is so turned that I go all day with only a cup of tea."

Michael was grateful to the impulse which had led him
to cook his own breakfast on a chafing-dish.

"I interrupted you," he said. "You were going to tell
me something about Mrs. Cleghorne."

"Well, you must know, I had a friend who was very good
to me, and this seemed to annoy her. Perhaps she disliked
the independence it gave me. Well, she really caused a row
between us by telling me she'd seen him going round drinking with another woman. Now that isn't a nice thing to do,
is it? One doesn't want to go round drinking in public-
houses. It looks so bad. I spoke to him about it a bit sharp,
and we've fallen out over it. In fact I haven't seen him for
some months. Still I shouldn't complain, but just lately what
with one thing and another I had some extras to get for my
boy which was highly necessary, you'll understand—well, as
I was saying—what with one thing and another my rent *has*
been a little bit behind. Still after you've paid regular for
close on two years, you expect a little consideration."

"Have you lived in this burrow for two years?" Michael
asked in amazement.

"In the week before Christmas it'll be two years. Yes.
Not that Mrs. Cleghorne herself has been so nasty, but
she lets her mother come round here and abuse me. Her
mother's an old woman, you'll understand, and her language
—well, really it has sometimes made me feel sick." She put
her hand up to her face with a gesture of disgust. "She
stands in that doorway and bullies me until I'm ashamed to
sit on this bed and stand it. I really am. You'd hardly believe there was such things to say to anyone. I think I have
a right to feel aggravated and I've made up my mind she

isn't going to do it again. I'm not going to *have* it." She was nodding at Michael with such energetic affirmation that the springs of the bed creaked.

" The mother doesn't live here ? " he asked.

" Oh, no, she simply comes here for the purpose of bullying me. But I'm not going to let it occur again. I don't consider I've been well treated. If I'd spent the money on gin, I shouldn't so much object to what the old woman calls me, for I don't say my life isn't a bit of a struggle. But there's so many things to use up the money, when I've got what's wanted for my boy, and paid the policeman on this beat his half-crown which he expects, and tried to keep myself looking a little bit smart—really I have to buy something occasionally or where should I be ?—and I never waste money on clothes for clothes' sake as they say—well, after that it's none so easy to find eight-and-six for the week's rent and buy myself a bit of food and the cat's milk."

Michael had nothing to say in commentary. It seemed to him that even by living above this woman he shared in the responsibility for her wretchedness.

" I hope your boy will turn out well," he ventured at last.

" Oh, he's a good boy, he really is. And I have had hopes that perhaps the Fathers will make him a Brother. I should really prefer that to his being in the Civil Service."

" Or even a priest," Michael suggested.

" Well, you see, he wasn't born in wedlock. Would that make a difference ? "

" I don't think so," said Michael gently. " Oh, no, I hope that wouldn't make a difference."

He was finding the imagination of this woman's life too poignant, and he rose from the light blue chest to bid her good-bye. He begged inwardly that she would not attempt to remind him of the relation in which she had expected to stand to him. He feared to wound her, but he would have to repulse her or go mad if she came near him. He plunged

down into his pocket for the two sovereigns. Half of this
money he had thought an exaggerated and cowardly bribe
to buy off her importunity when she had stood in the circle
of lamplight, owlishly staring. Now he wished he had five
times as much. His pocket was empty! He felt quickly and
hopelessly in his other pockets. He could not find the gold.
She must have robbed him. He looked at her reproachfully.
Was that the thief's and liar's film glazing her eyes as they
stared straight into his own? Was it impossible to believe
that he had pulled the sovereigns out of his pocket, when
nervously he had first seen her. But she had pawed him
with her hands in the black passage, and if the money had
fallen on the road, he must have heard it. He ought to tax
her with the unjust theft; he ought to tell her that what
she had taken he had meant to give her. And yet supposing
she had not taken the money? She had said the cat recognized him as a gentleman. Supposing she had not taken
the sovereigns, he would add by his accusation another stone
to the weight she bore. And if she had taken them, why not?
The cat was not at hand to warn her that he was to be
trusted. She had not wanted the money for herself. She
had been preyed upon, and had learnt to prey upon others
in self-defence.

"I find I haven't any money with me," said Michael looking at her.

"That doesn't matter. I've really quite enjoyed our
little talk."

"But I'll send you some more," he promised.

"No, it doesn't matter. I haven't done anything to have
you send your money for. I expect when you saw me in the
light, you didn't think I was really quite your style. Of
course I've really come down. It's no use denying it. I'm
not what I was."

If she had robbed him, she wanted nothing more from
him. If she had robbed him, it was because in the humility

of her degradation she had feared to see him shrink from her in disgust."

"I shall send you some money for your boy," he said in the darkness by the door.

"No, it doesn't matter." ·

"What's your name?"

"Well, I'm known here as Mrs. Smith." Doubtfully she whispered as the cold air came in through the open door: "I don't expect you'd care about giving me a kiss."

·Michael had never known anything in his life so difficult to do, but he kissed her cold and flaccid cheek and hurried up the area steps.

When he stood again upon the pavement in the menace of the five black houses of Leppard Street, Michael felt that he never again could endure to return to them at night, nor ever again in the day perceive their fifty windows inscrutable as water. Yet he must walk for a while in the stinging northerly air before he went back to his rooms; he must try to rid himself of the oppression which now lay so heavily upon him; he must be braced even by this lugubrious night of Pimlico before he could encounter again the permeating fug of Leppard Street. He walked as far as the corner, and saw in silhouette upon the bridge a solitary policeman thudding his chest for warmth. In this abominable desert of lamps he should have seemed a symbol of comfort; but Michael with the knowledge of the power he wielded over the unfortunates beheld him now as the brutish servant of a dominating class. He was after all very much like a dressed-up gorilla, as he stood there thudding his chest in the haggard lamplight.

Michael turned and went back to his rooms.

He stared at the picture of St. Ursula on the white wall, and suddenly in a fit of rage he plucked it from the hook and ground it face downwards upon his writing-table. It seemed to him almost monstrous that anything so serene should be allowed any longer to exist. Immediately afterwards he thought that his action had been melodramatic, and shamefacedly he put away the broken picture in a drawer.

Lily was in London : and Mrs. Smith was beneath him in this house. In twenty years Lily might be sunk in such a pit, unless he were quick to save her now. All through the night he kept waking up with the fancy that he could hear the rosary rattling in that den beneath; and every time he knew it was only the sound of the broken hasp on his window rattling in the wind.

Chapter VI : *Tinderbox Lane*

NEXT morning, when he woke, Michael made up his mind to leave Leppard Street finally in the course of this day. He could not bear the thought that he would only have to lean out of his window to see the actual roof which covered that unforgettable den beneath him. He wondered what would be the best thing to do with the furniture. It might be worth while to install Barnes in these rooms and pay his rent for some months instead of the salary which, now that Lily had been seen, was no longer a justifiable expenditure. He certainly would prefer that Barnes should never meet Lily now, and he regretted he had revealed her name. Still he had a sort of affection for Barnes which precluded the notion of deserting him altogether. These rooms, with their simple and unmuffled furniture, their green shelves and narrow white bed, would be good for his character. He would also leave a few chosen books behind, and he would write and ask Nigel Stewart to visit here from time to time. Michael dressed himself and went upstairs to interview Barnes where he lay beneath a heap of bedclothes.

"Oh, I daresay I could make the rooms look all right," said Barnes. "But what about coal ?"

"I shall pay for coal and light as well as the rent."

"I thought you'd find it a bit dismal here," said Barnes knowingly. "I wonder you've stuck it out as long as you have."

"After February," Michael said, "I may want to come to some other arrangement ; but you can count on being here till then. Of course you understand that when the three months are up, I shan't be able to allow you five pounds a week any longer."

" No, I never supposed you would," said Barnes in a tone of resignation.

Michael hesitated whether to speak to him about Mrs. Smith or not : however, probably he was aware of her existence already, and it could do no harm to mention it.

" Did you know that there was a woman living down in the basement here ? " he asked.

" I didn't know there was one here ; but it's not a very rare occurrence in this part of London, nor any other part of London, if it comes to that."

" If you hear any row going on down there," said Michael, " you had better interfere at once."

" Who with ? " Barnes enquired indignantly.

" With the row," said Michael. " If the woman is being badly treated on account of money she owes, you must let me know immediately."

" Well, I'm not in the old tear's secret, am I ? " asked Barnes in an injured tone. " You can't expect me to go routing about after every old fly-by-night stuck in a basement."

" I'm particularly anxious to know that she is all right," Michael insisted.

" Oh well, of course, if she's a friend of yours, Fane, that's another matter. If it's any little thing to oblige *you*, why certainly I'll do it."

Michael said goodbye and left him in bed. Then he called in to see the Solutionist, who was also in bed.

" I've got a commission for you," said Michael.

The Solutionist's watery eyes brightened faintly.

" You're fond of animals, aren't you ? " Michael went on. " I see you feeding your Belgian hares. Well, I'm interested in a cat who appreciated my point of view. I want you to

see that this cat has a quart of milk left for her outside
Mrs. Smith's door every morning. Mrs. Smith lives in the
basement. You must explain to her that you are fond
of animals; but you mustn't mention me. Here's a cheque
for five pounds. Spend half this on the cat and the other
half on your rabbits."

The Solutionist held the cheque between his tremulous
fingers.

"I couldn't cash this nowadays," he said helplessly.
"And get a quart of milk for a cat? Why, the thing
would burst."

"All right. I'll send you postal orders," said Michael.
"Now I'm going away for a bit. Never mind if a quart is
too much. I want that amount left every day. You'll do
what I ask? And you'll promise not to say a word about
me?"

The Solutionist promised, and Michael left him looking
more completely puzzled than he had ever seen him.

Michael could not bring himself to the point either of
going down into the basement or of calling to Mrs. Cleghorne from the entrance to her cave; and as the bell-pull
in his room had never been mended, he did not know how
to reach her. The existence of Mrs. Smith had dreadfully
complicated the mechanism of Number One. He ought to
have made Barnes get out of bed and fetch her. By good
luck Michael saw from his window the landlady standing at
the top of the area steps. He ran out and asked her to come
and speak to him.

"I see," she said. "Mr. Barnes is to have your rooms,
and you're paying in advance up to February. Oh, and his
coal and his gas as well? I see. Well, that you can settle
month by month. Through me? Oh, yes."

Mrs. Cleghorne was in a very good temper this morning.
Michael could not help wondering if Mrs. Smith had paid
some arrears of her rent.

"Do you think Mr. Cleghorne would go and fetch me a hansom?" Michael asked.

"He's still in his bed, but I'll go myself."

This cheerfulness was really extraordinary; and Michael was flattered. Already he was beginning to feel some of the deference mixed with hate which throughout the underworld was felt towards landladies. Her condescension struck him with the sense of a peculiar favour, as if it were being bestowed from a superior height.

Michael packed up his kitbags and turned for a last look at the white rooms in Leppard Street. Suddenly it struck him that he would take with him one or two of the pictures and present them to Maurice's studio in Grosvenor Road. Monna Lisa should go there, and the Prince of Orange whom himself was supposed to resemble slightly, and Don Baltazar on his big horse. They should be the contribution which he had been intending for some time to pay to that household. The cab was at the door, and presently Michael drove away from Leppard Street.

As soon as he was in the hansom he felt he could begin to think of Lily again, and though he knew that probably he was going to suffer a good deal when they met, he nevertheless thought of her now with elation. It had not seemed to be so sparkling a morning in Leppard Street; but driving towards Maurice's studio along the banks of the river, Michael thought it was the most crystalline morning he had ever known.

"I've brought you these pictures," he explained to Maurice, and let the gift account for his own long disappearance from communion with his friends. "They're pretty hackneyed, but I think it's rather good for you to have a few hackneyed things amid the riot of originality here. What are you doing, Mossy?"

"Well, I'm rather hoping to get a job as dramatic critic on The Point of View."

·· " You haven't met your lady-love yet ? "

" No, rather not, worse luck. Still there's plenty of time.· What about you ? ". Maurice asked the question indiffer- ently. He regarded his friend as a stone where women were concerned.

" I've seen her," said Michael. He simply had to give himself the pleasure of announcing so much.

" By Jove, have you really ? You've actually found your fate ? " Maurice was evidently very much excited by Michael's lapse into humanity ; he had been snubbed so often when he had rhapsodized over girls. " What's she like ? " ·

" I haven't spoken to her yet. I've only seen her in the distance."

" And you've really fallen in love ? I say, do stay and have lunch with me here. Castleton isn't coming back from the Temple until after tea."

Michael would have liked to sit at the window and talk of Lily, while he stared out over the sea of roofs under one of which at this very moment herself might be looking in his direction. However, he thought if he once began to talk about Lily to Maurice, he would tell him too much, and he might regret that afterwards. Yet he could not resist saying that she was tall and fair and slim. Such epithets might be applied to many girls, and it was only for himself that in this case they had all the thrilling significance they did.

" I like fair girls best," Maurice agreed. " But most fair girls are dolls. If I met one who wasn't, I should be hope- lessly in love with her."

" Perhaps you will," Michael said. Since he had seen Lily he felt very generous, and even more than generosity he felt that he actually had the power to offer to Maurice dozens of fair girls from whom he could choose his own ideal. Really he must not stay a moment longer in the studio, or he would be blurting out the whole tale of Lily ; and were she to be his, he must hold secrets about her that could never be unfolded.

"I really must bolt off," he declared. "I've got a cab waiting."

Michael drove along to Cheyne Walk, and when he reached home, it caused the parlourmaid not a flicker to receive him and to take his luggage and enquire what should be obtained for his lunch.

"Life's really too easy in this house," he thought. "It's so impossible to surprize the servants here that one would give up trying ultimately. I suppose that will be the beginning of settling down. At this rate I shall settle down much too soon. Yes, life is too easy here."

Michael went to the Orient that night certain that he would meet Lily at once, so much since he left Leppard Street had the imagination of her raced backwards and forwards in his brain. Everything that would have made their meeting painful in such surroundings was forgotten in the joyful prospect at hand. The amount they would have to talk about was really tremendous. Love had destroyed time so completely that Lily was to be exactly the same as when first he had met her in Kensington Gardens. However, her appearance on the pavement outside the theatre had made such a vivid new impression that Michael did pay as much attention to lapsing time as to visualize her now in that black dress. Otherwise he was himself again of six years ago, with only the delightful difference that he was now independent and could carry her forthwith into marriage. The knowledge that from a material point of view he could do this filled him with a magnificent consciousness of life's plenitude. So far, all his experiments in living had been bounded by ignorance or credulity on his own side, and on the side of other people by their unsuitableness for experiments. Certainly he had made discoveries, but they might better be called disillusionments. Now here was Lily

who would give him herself to discover, who would open
for him, not a looking-glass world in which human nature reflected itself in endless reduplications of perversity, but a
world such as lovers only know, wherein the greatest deeps
are themselves. Michael scarcely bothered to worry himself
with the thought that Lily had embarked upon her own discoveries apart from him ; she had been bewitched again by
his romantic spells into the innocent girl of seventeen. All
his hopes, all his quixotry, all his capacity for idealization,
all his prejudice and impulsiveness converged upon her.
Whatever had lately happened to spoil his theory of behaviour was discounted ; and even the very theory fell to
pieces in this intoxication of happiness.

With so much therefore to make him buoyant, it was depressing to visit the Orient that evening without a glimpse
of Lily. The disappointment threw Michael very unpleasantly back into those evenings when he had come here
regularly and had always been haunted by the dread that,
when he did see her, his resolve would collapse in the presence
of a new Lily wrought upon by man and not made more
lovable thereby. The vision of her last night (it was only
last night) had swept him aloft ; the queer adventure with
the woman in the basement had exalted him still higher upon
his determination ; his flight from Leppard Street and his
return to Cheyne Walk had helped to strengthen his hope-
fulness. Now he had returned to this circumambient crowd,
looking round as each new-comer came up the steps, and all
the while horribly aware that this evening Lily was not
coming to the Orient. He had never been upset like this
since his resolve was taken. The glimpse of her last night
had made him very impatient, and he reviled himself again
for having been such a fool as to let her escape. He fell in
a rage with his immobility here in London. He demanded
why it was not possible to swirl in widening circles round the
city until he found her. He was no longer content to remain

in this aquarium, stuck like a mollusc to the side of the tank. He wanted to see her again. He was fretful for her slow contemptuous walk and her debonair smile. He wanted to see her again. Already this quest was becoming the true torment of love. Every single other person in sight was a dreary automaton in whom he took no trace of interest. Every movement, every laugh, every shadow made him repine at its uselessness to him. All those years at Oxford of dreams and hesitations had let him store up within himself a very fury of love. He had been living falsely all this time : there had never been one dull hour which could not have been enchanted by her to the most glorious hour imaginable. He had realized that when he saw her last night ; he had realized all the waste, all the deadness, all the idiotic philosophy and impotence of these years without her. How the fancy of her vexed him now ; how easily could he in his frustration knock down the individuals of this senseless restless crowd, one after another, like the dummies of humanity they were.

The last tableau of the ballet had dissolved behind the falling curtain. Lily was not here to-night, and he hurried out into Piccadilly. She must be somewhere close at hand. It was impossible for her to come casually like that to the Orient and afterwards to disappear for weeks. Or was she a man's mistress, the mistress of a man of forty ? He could picture him. He would be a stockbroker, the sort of man whom one saw in first-class railway carriages travelling up to town in the morning and reading The Financial Times. He would wear a hideous orchid in his buttonhole and take her to Brighton for week-ends. He knew just the shade of bluish pink that his cheeks were ; and the way his neck looked against his collar ; the shape of his moustache, the smell of his cigar, and his handicap at golf.

It was impossible that Lily could be the mistress of a man like that. Last night she had come out of the Orient with a girl. Obviously they must at this moment be somewhere near Piccadilly. Michael rushed along as wildly as a cat running after its tail. He entered restaurant after restaurant, café after café, standing in the doorways and staring at the tables one after another. The swinging doors would often hit him, as people came in; the drinkers or the diners would often laugh at his frown and his pale eager gaze; often the manager would hurry up and ask what he could do for him, evidently suspecting the irruption of a lunatic.

Michael's behaviour in the street was even more noticeable. He often ricocheted from the inside to the outside of the pavement to get a nearer view of a passing hansom whose occupant had faintly resembled Lily. He mounted omnibuses going in all sorts of strange directions, because he fancied for an instant that he had caught a glimpse of Lily among the passengers. It was closing-time before he thought he had been searching for five minutes; and when the lights were dimmed, he walked up and down Regent Street, up and down Piccadilly, up and down Coventry Street, hurrying time after time to pursue a walk that might have been hers.

By one o'clock Piccadilly was nearly empty, and it was an insult to suppose that Lily would be found among these furtive women with their waylaying eyes in the gloom. Michael went back tired out to Cheyne Walk. On the following night he visited the Orient again and afterwards searched every likely and unlikely place in the neighbourhood of the heart of pleasure. He went also to the Empire and to the Alhambra; sometimes hurrying from one to the other twice in the evening, when panics that he was missing Lily overtook him. He met Lonsdale one night at the Empire, and Lonsdale took him to several night-clubs which gave a great zest to Michael's search; for he became a member of them himself, and so possessed every night another hour or more before he had to give up hope of finding her.

Mrs. Fane wrote to him from Cannes to say she thought that, as she was greatly enjoying herself on the Riviera, she would not come home for Christmas. Michael was relieved by her letter, because he had felt qualms about deserting her, and he would have found it difficult, impossible really, to go away so far from London and Lily.

Guy wrote to him several times, urging him to come and stay at Plashers Mead. Finally he went there for a week-end; and Guy spent the whole time rushing in and out of the house on the chance of meeting Pauline Grey, the girl whom Michael had seen with him in the canoe last summer. Guy explained the complications of his engagement to Pauline; how it seemed he would soon have to choose between love and art; how restrictions were continually being put upon their meeting each other; and how violently difficult life was becoming here at Plashers Mead, where Michael had prophesied such abundant ease. Michael was very sympathetic and when he met Pauline on a soft December morning, he did think she was beautiful and very much like the wild rose that Guy had taken as the symbol of her. She seemed such a fairy child that he could not imagine problems of conduct in which she could be involved. Nevertheless it was impossible not to feel that over Plashers Mead brooded a sense of tragedy: and yet it seemed ridiculous to compare Guy's difficulties with his own.

For Christmas Michael went down to Hardingham, where Stella and Alan had by this time settled down in their fat country. He was delighted to see how much the squire Alan was already become; and there was certainly something very attractive in these two young people moving about that grave Georgian house. The house itself was of red brick and stood at the end of an avenue of oaks in a park of about two hundred acres. That it could ever have not been there ; that ever those lawns had been defaced by builder's rubbish was now inconceivable. So too within, Michael could not realize that anybody else but Stella and Alan had ever stood in this drawing-room, looking out of the tall windows whose sills scarcely rose above the level of the grass outside ; that anyone else but Stella and Alan had ever laughed in this solemn library with its pilasters and calf-bound volumes and terrestrial globe ; that anyone else but Stella and Alan had ever sat at dinner under the eyes of those bag-wigged squires, that long-nosed Light Dragoon, or that girl in her chip hat, holding a bunch of cherries.

"No doubt you've got a keen scent for tradition," said Michael to Stella. "But really you have been able to get into the manner surprizingly fast. These cocker-spaniels for instance who follow you both round, and the deerhound on the steps of the terrace—Stella, I'm afraid the concert platform has taught you the value of effect ; and where do hounds meet to-morrow ? "

"We're simply loving it here," Stella said. "But I think the piano is feeling a little bit out of his element. He's stiff with being on his best behaviour."

"I'm hoping to get rather a good pitch in Six Ash field," said Alan. "I'll show it to you to-morrow morning."

· The butler came in with news of callers :

"The Countess of Stilton and Lady Anne Varley."

"Oh, damn," Stella exclaimed when the butler had retired. "I really don't think people ought to call just before Christmas. However, you've both got to come in and be polite."

Michael managed to squeeze himself into a corner of the drawing-room, whence he could watch Lady Stilton and her daughter talking to Mr. and Mrs. Prescott-Merivale.

"We ought not to have bothered you in this busy week before Christmas, but my husband has been so ill in Marien-bad, ever since the summer really, that we only got home a fortnight ago. So very trying. And I've been longing to meet you. Poor Dick Prescott was a great friend of ours."

Michael had a sudden intuition that Prescott had bequeathed Stella's interests to Lady Stilton who probably knew all about her. He wondered if Stella had guessed this.

"And Anne heard you play at King's Hall. Didn't you, Anne dear ?"

Lady Anne nodded and blushed.

"That child is going to worship Stella," Michael thought.

"We're hoping you will all be able to come and dine with us for Twelfth Night. My husband is so fond of keeping up old English festivals. Mr. Fane, you'll still be at Hardingham, I hope, so that we may have the pleasure of seeing you as well ?"

Michael said he was afraid he would have to be back in town.

"What absolute rot !" Stella cried. "Of course you'll be here."

But Michael insisted that he would be gone.

"They tell us you've been buying Herefords, Mr. Merivale. My husband was so much interested and is so much looking forward to seeing your stock ; but at present he must not drive far. I've also heard of you from my youngest boy who went up to Christ Church last October year. He is very much excited to think that Hardingham is going to have such a famous—what is it called, Anne ?—some kind of a bowler."

"A googlie bowler, I expect you mean, mother," said Lady Anne.

"Wasn't he in the Eton eleven ?" asked Alan.

"Well, no. Something happened to oust him at the last moment," said Lady Stilton. "Possibly a superior player."

".Oh, no, mother," Lady Anne indignantly declared. "He would have played for certain against Harrow, if he hadn't sprained his ankle at the nets the week before."

"I do hope you'll let him come and see you this vacation," Lady Stilton said.

"Oh, rather. I shall be awfully keen to talk about the cricket round here," Alan replied. "I'm just planning out a new pitch now."

"How delightful all this is," thought Michael with visions of summer evenings.

Soon Lady Stilton and her daughter went away, having plainly been a great success with Mr. and Mrs. Prescott-Merivale.

".Of course, *you*'ve got to marry Anne," said Stella to Michael, as soon as they were comfortably round the great fire in the library.

"Alan," Michael appealed, "is it impossible for you to nip now for ever this bud of matchmaking ? "

"I think it's rather a good idea," said Alan. "I knew young Varley by sight. He's a very sound bat."

"I shan't come here again," Michael threatened, "until you've dissolved this alliance of mutual admiration. Instead of agreeing with Stella to marry me, to every girl you meet, why don't you devote yourself to the task of making Huntingdon a first-class county in cricket ? Stella might captain the team."

Time passed very pleasantly with long walks and rides and drives, with long evenings of cut-throat bridge and Schumann ; but on New Year's morning Michael said he must go back to London. Nor would he let himself be deterred by Stella's gibes.

"I admit you're as happy as you can be," he said. "Now surely you, after so much generosity on my side, will admit that I may know almost as well as yourselves how to make myself happy, though not yet married."

" Michael, you're having an affair with some girl," Stella said accusingly.

He shook his head.

" Swear ? "

" By everything I believe in, I vow I'm not having an affair with any girl. I wish I were."

His luggage was in the hall, and the dogcart was waiting. At King's Cross he found a taxi, which was so difficult to do in those days that it made him hail the achievement as a good omen for the New Year.

Near South Kensington Station he caught sight of a poster advertizing a carnival in the neighbourhood : he thought it looked rather attractive with the bright colours glowing into the grey January day. Later on in the afternoon, when he went to his tobacconist's in the King's Road, he saw the poster again and read that to-night at Redcliffe Hall, Fulham Road, would take place a Grand Carnival and Masked Ball for the benefit of some orphanage connected with licensed victualling. Tickets were on sale in various public-houses of the neighbourhood, at seven and sixpence for gentlemen and five shillings for ladies.

" Ought to be very good," commented the tobacconist. " Well, we want a bit of brightening up nowadays down this way, and that's a fact. Why, I can remember Cremorne Gardens. Tut-tut ! Bless my soul. Yes, and the old World's End. That's going back into the 'seventies, that is. And it seems only yesterday."

" I rather wish I'd got a ticket," said Michael.

" Why not let me get you one, sir, and send it round to Cheyne Walk ? I suppose you'd like one for a lady as well ? "

" No, I'll have two men's tickets."

Michael had a vague notion of getting Maurice or Lonsdale to accompany him, and he went off immediately to 422 Grosvenor Road; but the studio was deserted. Nor was he successful in finding Lonsdale. Nobody seemed to have

finished his holidays yet. It would be rather boring to go
alone, he thought ; but when he found the tickets waiting
for him, they seemed to promise a jolly evening, even if he
did no more than watch other people enjoying themselves.
No doubt there would be plenty of spectators without masks
like himself, and in ordinary evening-dress. So about half-
past nine Michael set off alone to the carnival.

Redcliffe Hall, viewed from the outside in the January
fog which was deepening over the city, seemed the last place
in the world likely to contain a carnival. It was one of
those dismal gothic edifices which, having passed through
ecclesiastical and municipal hands with equal loss to both,
awaits a suitable moment for destruction before it rises
again in a phœnix of new flats. However, the awning hung
with Japanese lanterns that ran from the edge of the kerb
up to the entrance made it now not positively forbidding.

Michael went up to the gallery and watched the crowd
of dancers. Many of the fancy dresses had a very homely
look, but there were also professional equipments from
costumiers and a very few really beautiful inventions. The
medley of colours, the motion of the dance, the sound of the
music, the streamers of bunting and the ribbons fluttering
round the Maypole in the middle of the room, all combined
to give Michael an illusion of a very jocund assemblage.
There were plenty of men dancing without masks, which
was rather a pity, as their dull ordinary faces halted abruptly
the play of fancy. On second thoughts he was glad such
revellers were allowed upon the floor, since as the scene
gradually began to affect him he felt it might be amusing
for himself to dance once or twice before the evening
ended. With this notion in view he began to follow more
particularly the progress of different girls, balancing their
charms one against another, and always deriving a good deal
of pleasure from the reflection that, while at this moment
they did not know of his existence, in an hour's time he

might have entered their lives. This thought did give a romantic zest to an entertainment which would otherwise have been quite cut off from his appreciation.

Suddenly Michael's heart began to quicken: the blood came in rushes and swift recessions that made him feel cold and sick. Two girls walking away from him along the side of the hall—those two pierrettes in black—that one with the pale blue pompons was Lily! Why didn't she turn round? It must be Lily. The figure, the walk, the hair were hers. The pierrettes turned, but as they were masked, Michael could still not be sure if one were Lily. They were dancing together now. It must be Lily. He leaned over the rail of the gallery to watch them sweep round below him, so that he might listen if by chance above the noise Lily's languorous voice could reach him. Michael became almost positive that it was she. There could not be another girl to seem so like her. He hurried down from the gallery and stood in the entrance to the ball-room. Where were they now? They were coming towards him: the other pierrette with the rose pompons said something as they passed. It could only be Lily who bowed her head like that in lazy assent. It was Lily! Should he call out to her, when next they passed him? If it were not Lily, what a fool he would look. If it were not Lily, it would not matter what he looked, for the disappointment would outweigh everything else. They were going up the room again. They were turning the corner again. They were sweeping towards him again. They were passing him again. He called 'Lily! Lily!' in a voice sharp with eagerness. Neither girl gave a sign of attention. It was not she after all. Yet his voice might have been drowned in the noise of the dance. He would call again; but again they passed him by unheeding. The dance was over. They had stopped at the other end of the room. He pressed forward against the egress of the dancers. He pressed forward roughly, and once or twice he heard grumbling murmurs because he had deranged a difficult piece of costumery. He was conscious of angry masks regarding him; and then he was free of the crowd, and before him, talking together under a canopy of holly, were the two pierrettes. The musicians sat among the palms looking at him as they rested upon their instruments. Michael felt that his voice was going to refuse to utter her name.

"Lily! Lily!"

The pierrette with the pale blue pompons turned at the sound of his voice. Why did she not step forward to greet him, if indeed she were Lily? She was, she was Lily: the other pierrette had turned to see what she was going to do.

"I say, how on earth did you recognize me?" Lily murmured, raising her mask and looking at Michael with her smile that was so debonair and tender, so scornful and so passionate.

"I saw you in November coming out of the Orient. I tried to get across the road to speak to you, but you'd gone before I could manage it. Where have you been all these years? Once I went to Trelawny Road, but the house was empty." He could not tell her that Drake had been the first to bring him news of her.

"It's years since I was there," said Lily. "Years and years." She turned to call her friend, and the pierrette with the rose pompons came closer to be introduced.

"Miss Sylvia Scarlett: Mr. Michael Fane. Aren't I good to remember your name quite correctly?" Michael thought that her mouth for a moment was utterly scornful. "What made you come here? Have you got a friend with you?"

Michael explained that he was alone and that his visit here was an accident.

"Why did *you* come?" he asked.

"Oh, something to do," said Lily. "We live near here."

3 S

" So do I," said Michael hastily.

" Do you ? " Her eyebrows went up in what he imagined was an expression of rather cruel interrogation. " This is a silly sort of a show. Still even Covent Garden is dull now."

Michael thought what a fool he had been not to include Covent Garden in his search. How well he might have known she would go there.

" Where's Doris ? " he asked.

Lily shrugged her shoulders.

" I never see anything of her nowadays. She married an actor. I don't often get letters from home, do I, Sylvia ? "

The pierrette with rose pompons, who ever since her introduction had still been standing outside the conversation, now raised her mask. Michael liked her face. She had merry eyes, and a wide nose rather Slavonic. Next to Lily she seemed almost dumpy.

" Letters, my dear," she exclaimed in a very deep voice. " Who wants letters ? "

The music of a waltz was beginning, and Michael asked Lily if she would dance with him. She looked at Sylvia :

" I don't think . . ."

" Oh, what rot, Lily. Of course you can dance."

Michael gave her a grateful smile.

In a moment Lily had lowered her mask, and they were waltzing together.

" My gad, how gloriously you waltz," he whispered. " Did we ever dance together five years ago ? "

She shrugged her shoulders, and he felt the faint movement tremble through the imponderable form he held.

" Lily, I've been looking for you since June," he sighed.

" You're breaking step," she said. Though her mask was down, Michael was sure that she was frowning at him.

" Lily, why are you so cold with me ? Have you forgotten ? "

" What ? "

" Why, everything ! " Michael gasped.

" You're absolutely out of time now," she said sternly.

They waltzed for a while in silence, and Michael felt like a midge spinning upon a dazzle.

"Do you remember when we met in Kensington Gardens ? " he ventured. " I remember you had black pompons on your shoes then, and now you have pale blue pompons on your dress."

' She was not answering him.

· " It's funny you should still be living near me," he went on. " I suppose you're angry with me because I suddenly never saw you again. That was partly your mother's fault."

. She looked at him in faint perplexity, swaying to the melody of the waltz. Michael thought he had blundered in betraying himself as so obviously lovestruck now. He must be seeming to her like that absurd and sentimental boy of five years ago. Perhaps she was despising him, for she could compare him with other men. Ejaculations of wonder at her beauty would no longer serve, with all the experience she might bring to mock them. She was smiling at him now, and the mask she wore made the smile seem a sneer. He grew so angry with her suddenly that almost he stopped in the swing of the dance to shake her.

" But it was much more your fault," he said savagely. " Do you remember Drake ? "

She shook her head : then she corrected herself.

" Oh, yes. Arthur Drake who lived next door to us."

" Well, I saw you in the garden from his window. You were being kissed by some terrible bounder. That was jolly for me. Why did you do that ? Couldn't you say ' no ' ? Were you too lazy ? "

· Michael thought she moved closer to him as they danced.

· " Answer me, will you ; answer me, I say. Were you too

lazy to resist or did you enjoy being cheapened by that insufferable brute you were flirting with ? "

Michael in his rage of remembrance twisted her hand. But she made no gesture, nor uttered any sound of pain. Instead she sank closer to his arms, and as the dance rolled on, he told himself triumphantly that, while she was with him, she was his again.

What did the past matter ?

" Ah, Lily, you love me still. I'll ask no more questions. Am I out of step ? "

" No, not now," she whispered, and he saw that her face was pale with the swoon of their dancing.

" Take off that silly mask," he commanded. " Take it off and give it to me. I can hold you with one arm."

She obeyed him, and with a tremendous exultation he swung her round, as if indeed he were carrying her to the edge of the world. The mask no longer veiled her face ; her eyelids drooped clouding her eyes ; her lips were parted : she was now dead white. Michael crooked her left arm until he could touch her shoulder.

" Look at me. Look at me. The dance will soon be over."

She opened her eyes, and into their depths of dusky blue he danced and danced until, waking with the end of the music, he found himself and Lily close to Sylvia Scarlett, who was laughing at them where she stood in the corner of the room under a canopy of holly.

Lily was for the rest of the evening herself as Michael had always known her. She had always been superficially indifferent to anything that was happening round her, and she behaved at this carnival as if it were a street full of dull people among whom by chance she was walking. Nor with her companions was she much more alert, though when she danced with Michael her indifference became a passionate languor. Soon after midnight both the girls

declared they were tired of the Redcliffe Hall, and they asked
Michael to escort them home. He was going to fetch a
cab, but they stopped him, saying that Tinderbox Lane
where they lived was only a little way along on the other
side of the Fulham Road. The fog was very dense when
they came out, and Michael took the girls' arms with a
delicious sense of intimacy, with a feeling too of extraordinary freedom from the world, as if they were all three
embarked upon an adventure in this eclipse of fog. He had
packed their shoes deep down in the pockets of his overcoat,
and with the possession of their shoes he had a sensation
of possessing the wearers of them. The fog was denser and
denser : they paused upon the edge of the kerb, listening
for oncoming traffic. A distant omnibus was lumbering
far down the Fulham Road. Michael caught their arms
close, and the three of them seemed to sail across to the
opposite pavement. He had nothing to say because he was
so happy, and Lily had nothing to say because she talked now
no more than she used to talk. So it was Sylvia who had to
carry on the conversation, and since most of this consisted
of questions to Lily and Michael about their former friendship, which neither Lily or Michael answered, even Sylvia
was discouraged at last ; and they walked on silently through
the fog, Michael clasping the girls close to him and
watching all the time Lily's hand holding up her big black
cloak.

"Here we are, you two dreamers," said Sylvia pulling
them to a stop by a narrow turning which led straight from
the pavement unexpectedly, without any dip down into a
road.

"Through here ? How fascinating," said Michael.

They passed between two posts, and in another three
minutes stopped in front of a door set in a wall.

"I've got the key," said Sylvia, and she unlocked the
door.

" But this is extraordinary," Michael exclaimed. " Aren't we walking through a garden ? "

" Yes, it's quite a long garden," Sylvia informed him. There was a smell of damp earth here that sweetened the harshness of the fog, and Michael thought that he had never imagined anything so romantic as following Lily in single file along the narrow gravel path of a mysterious garden like this. There must have been thirty yards of path, before they walked up the steps of what seemed to be a sort of balcony.

" She's downstairs," said Sylvia, tapping upon a glass door with the key. A woman's figure appeared with an orange-shaded lamp in the passage.

" Open quickly, Mrs. Gainsborough. We're frozen," Sylvia called. As the woman opened the door, Sylvia went on in her deep voice :

" We've brought an old friend of Lily's back from the dance. It wasn't really worth going to. Oh, I oughtn't to have said that, ought I ? " she laughed, turning round to Michael. " Come in and get warm. This is Mrs. Gainsborough, who's the queen of cards."

" Get along with you, you great saucy thing," said Mrs. Gainsborough, laughing.

She was a woman of enormous size with a triplication of chins. Her crimson cheeks shone with the same glister as her black dress ; and her black hair, so black that it must have been dyed, was parted in the middle and lay in a chignon upon her neck. She seemed all the larger, sitting in this small room full of Victorian finery, and Michael was amused to hear her address Sylvia as ' great.'

" We want something to eat and something to drink, you lovely old mountain," Sylvia said.

Mrs. Gainsborough doubled herself up and smacked her knees in a tempest of wheezy laughter.

" Sit here, you terrors, while I get the cloth on the

dining-room table," and out she went, her laughter dying in sibilations along the diminutive corridor. Lily had flung herself down in an armchair near the fire. Behind her stood a small mahogany table on which was a glass case of humming-birds; by her elbow on the wall was a white china bell coronated with a filigree of gilt, and by chance the antimacassar on the chair was of Berlin wool chequered black and blue. She in her pierrette's dress of black with light blue pompons looked strangely remote from present time in that setting. Michael could not connect this secluded house with anything which had made an impression upon him during his experience of the underworld. Here was nothing that was not cosy and old-fashioned; here was no sign of decay whether in the fabric of the house or in the attitude of the people living there. This small square room with the heavy furniture that occupied so much of the space had no demirep demeanour. That — horsehair sofa with lyre-shaped sides and back of floriated wood; that brass birdcage hanging in the window against the curtains of maroon serge; those cabinets in miniature, some lacquered, some of plain wood with tiny drop-handles of brass; those black chairs with seats of gilded cane; those trays with marquetry in mother-of-pearl of wreaths and rivulets and parrots; that table-cloth like a dish of black Sèvres; those simpering steel engravings; — —there was nothing that did not bespeak the sobriety of the Victorian prime here miraculously preserved. Lily and Sylvia in such dresses belonged to a period of fantasy; Mrs. Gainsborough was in keeping with her furniture; and Michael, as he looked at himself in the glass overmantel, did not think that he was seeming very intrusive.

"Whose are these rooms?" he asked. Lily was adorable, but he did not believe they were her creation or discovery.

"I found them," said Sylvia. "The old girl who owns the house is bad, but beautiful. Aren't you, you most astonishing but attractive mammoth?" This was addressed to Mrs. Gainsborough who was at the moment panting into the room for some accessory to the dining-table.

"Get along with you," the landlady chuckled. "Now don't go to sleep, Lily. Your supper is just on ready." She went puffing from the room in busy mirthfulness.

"She's one of the best," said Sylvia. "This house was given to her by an old General who died about two years ago. You can see the painting of him up in her bedroom as a dare-devil hussar with drooping whiskers. She was a gay contemporary of the Albert Memorial. You know. Argyle Rooms and Cremorne. With the Haymarket as the centre of naughtiness."

It was funny, Michael thought, that his tobacconist should have mentioned Cremorne only this afternoon. That he had done so affected him more sharply now with a sense of the appropriateness of this house in Tinderbox Lane. Appropriateness to what? Perhaps merely to the mood of this foggy night.

"Supper! Supper!" Mrs. Gainsborough was crying.

It was dismaying for Michael to think that he had not kissed Lily yet, and he wished that Sylvia would hurry ahead into the other room and give him an opportunity. He wanted to pull her gently from that chair, up from that chair into his arms. But Sylvia was the one who did so, and she kissed Lily half fiercely, leaving Michael disconsolately to follow them across the passage.

It was jolly to see Mrs. Gainsborough sitting at the head of the table with the orange-shaded lamp throwing warm rays upon her countenance. That it was near the chilly hour of one, with a cold thick fog outside, was inconceivable when he looked at that cheery great porpoise of a woman unscrewing bottles of India Pale Ale.

Michael did not want the questions about him and Lily

to begin again. So he turned the conversation upon a more
remote past.

"Oh, my eye, my eye," laughed Sylvia. "To think that
Aunt Enormous was once in the ballet at the Opera."

"How dare you laugh at me? Whoof!" Mrs. Gainsborough gave a sort of muffled bark as her arm pounced out
to grab Sylvia. The two of them frisked with each other
absurdly, while Lily sat with wide-open blue eyes, so graceful
even in that stiff chair close up to the table, that Michael
was in an ecstasy of admiration, and marvelled gratefully
at the New Year's Day which could so change his fortune.

"Were you in the ballet?" he asked.

"Certainly I was, though this great teazing thing beside
me would like to make out that when I was eighteen I
looked just as I do now."

"Show the kind gentleman your picture," said Sylvia.
"She wears it round her neck in a locket, the vain old
mountebank."

Mrs. Gainsborough opened a gold locket, and Michael
looked at a rosy young woman in a pork-pie hat.

"That's myself," said Mrs. Gainsborough sentimentally.
"Well, and I always loved being young better than anything or anybody, so why shouldn't I wear next my own
heart myself as I used to be?"

"But show him the others," Sylvia demanded.

Mrs. Gainsborough fetched from a desk two daguerreo-
types in stained morocco cases lined with faded puce velvet.
By tilting their surfaces against the light could be seen
the shadow of a portrait's wraith: a girl appearing
in pantalettes and tartan frock; a ballerina glimmering,
with points of faint celeste for eyes, and for cheeks the
evanescence of a ghostly bloom.

"Oh, look at her," cried Sylvia. "In her beautiful
pantalettes!"

"Hold your tongue, you!"

They started again with their sparring and mock encounters, which lasted on and off until supper was over. Then they all went back to the other room and sat round the fire.

"Tell us about the General," said Sylvia.

"Go on, as if you hadn't heard a score of times all I've got to tell about the General—though you know I hate him to be called that. He'll always be the Captain to me."

Soon afterward, notwithstanding her first refusal, Mrs. Gainsborough embarked upon tales of gay days in the 'sixties and 'seventies. It was astonishing to think that this room in which they were sitting could scarcely have changed since then.

"The dear Captain! He bought this house for me in 1869 before I was twenty, and I've lived in it ever since. Ah, dear! many's the summer daybreak we've walked back here after dancing all night at Cremorne. Such lovely lights and fireworks. Earl's Court is nothing to Cremorne. Fancy their pulling it down as they did. But perhaps it's as well it went, as all the old faces have gone. It would have given me the dismals to be going there now without my Captain."

She went on with old tales of London, tales that had in them the very smoke and grime of the city.

"Who knows what's going to happen when the clock strikes twelve?" she said shaking her head. "So enjoy yourselves while you can. That's my motto. And if there's a hereafter, which good God forbid, I should be very aggravated to find myself waltzing around as fat and funny as I am now."

The old pagan, who had mellowed slowly with her house for company, seemed to sit here hugging the old friend; and as she told her tales it was difficult not to think she was playing hostess to the spirits of her youth, to ghostly Dundrearies and spectral belles with oval faces. Michael could have listened all night to her reminiscences of dead singers and dead dancers, of gay women become dust and of rakes reformed, of beauties that were now hags and of handsome young subalterns grown parched and liverish. Sylvia egged her on from story to story, and Lily lay languidly back in her chair. It must be after two o'clock, and Michael rose to go.

"We'll have one song," cried Sylvia, and she pulled Mrs. Gainsborough to the piano. The top of the instrument was hidden by stacked-up albums, and the front of it was of fretted walnut-wood across a pleating of claret-coloured silk.

Mrs. Gainsborough, pounding with her fat fingers the keys that seemed in comparison so frail and old, sang in a wheezy pipe of a voice: *The Captain with his Whiskers took a Sly Glance at Me.*

"But you only get me to do it, so as you can have a good laugh at me behind my back," she declared, swinging round upon the stool to face Sylvia when she had finished.

"Nothing of the sort, you fat old darling. We do it because we like it."

"Bless your heart, my dearie." She laid a hand on Sylvia's for an instant. Michael thanked Mrs. Gainsborough for the entertainment, and asked Sylvia if she thought he might come round to-morrow and take Lily and her out to lunch.

"We can lunch to-morrow, can't we?" Sylvia asked tugging at Lily's arm, for she was now fast asleep.

"Is Michael going? Yes, we can lunch with him to-morrow," Lily yawned.

He promised to call for them about midday. It seemed ridiculous to shake hands so formally with Lily, and he hoped she would suggest that the outside door was difficult to open. Alas, it was Sylvia who came to speed his departure.

The fog was welcome to Michael for his going home. At this hour of the night there was not a sound of anything, and he could walk on, dreaming undisturbed. He supposed he would arrive ultimately at Cheyne Walk. But he did not care. He would have been content to fill the long winter night with his fancies. Plunging his hands down into the pockets of his overcoat, he discovered that he had forgotten to take out the girls' shoes, and what company they were through the gloom! It was a most fascinating experience, to wander along holding these silky slippers which had twinkled through the evening of this night. Not a cab-horse blew a frosty breath by the kerb; not a policeman loomed; nor passer-by nor cat offended his isolation. The London night belonged to him; his only were the footsteps echoing back from the invisible houses on either side; and the golden room in Tinderbox Lane was never more than a few yards in front.

He had found Lily at last, and he held her shoes for a token of his good luck. Let no one tell him again that destiny was a fable. Nothing was ever more deliberately foredoomed than the meeting at that carnival. Michael was so grateful to his tobacconist that he determined to buy all sorts of extravagant pipes and cigarette-holders he had fingered vaguely from time to time in the shop. For a while Lily's discovery was coloured with such a glamour that Michael did not analyze the situation in which he had found her. Walking back to Chelsea through the fog he was bemused by the romantic memory of her which was travelling along with his thoughts. He could hold very tightly her shoes: he could almost embrace the phantom of her beauty that curled upon the vapours round each lamp: he was intoxicated merely by the sound of the street where she lived.

"Tinderbox Lane! Tinderbox Lane! Tinderbox Lane!"

He sang it in triumph, remembering how only this morning he had sighed to himself, as he chased the telegraph-wires up and down the window of the railway-carriage: " Where is she ? Where is she ? Where is she ? "

" Tinderbox Lane !   Tinderbox Lane ! Tinderbox Lane ! " he chanted at the fog, and throwing a slipper into the air, he caught it and ran on ridiculously until he bumped into a policeman standing by the corner.

" I'm awfully sorry, constable."

" Feeling a bit happy, sir, aren't you ? "

" Frightfully happy. I say, by the by, happy new year, constable. Drink my health when you're off duty."

He pressed half-a-crown into the policeman's hand, and as he left the stolid form behind him in the fog, he remembered that half-a-crown was the weekly blackmail paid by Mrs. Smith of Leppard Street. He was on the Embankment now, and the fog had lifted so that he saw the black river flowing sullenly through the night. The plane-trees dripped with monotonous beads of dankness. The fog was become a mist here, a frore whitish mist that saturated him with a malignant chill. Michael was glad to find himself looking at the dolphin-headed knocker of 173 Cheyne Walk. The effect of being in his own bedroom again, even though the girls' shoes lay fantastically upon the floor, was at first to make him believe that Tinderbox Lane might have been a dream, and after that, because he knew it was not a dream, to wonder about it.

Yet not even now in this austere and icy bedroom of his own could Michael feel that there was anything really wrong about that small house. It still preserved for him an illusion of sobriety and stability, almost of primness, yet of being rich with a demure gaiety. Mrs. Gainsborough, however, was scarcely a chaperone. Nor was she very demure. And who was Sylvia ? And what was Lily doing there ? It would have been mysterious, that household, in any case, but was it necessary to assume that there was anything wrong? Sylvia was obviously a girl of high spirits. He had asked her no questions about herself. She might be on the stage. For fun, or perhaps because of their landlady's kindling stories, Sylvia might have persuaded Lily to come once or twice to the Orient. It did not follow that there was anything wrong. There had been nothing wrong in that carnival. Michael's heart leapt with the fancy that he was not too late. That would indeed crown this romantic night; and picking up Lily's shoe, he held it for a while, wondering about its secrets.

In the morning the fog had turned to a drench of dull January rain; but Michael greeted the outlook as cheerfully as if it had been perfect May weather. He went first to a post office to send off the money he had promised to Mrs. Smith and the Solutionist. After this discharge of business he felt more cheerful than ever, and as if to capture the final touch of fantasy necessary to bewitch yesterday night, he suddenly realized, when he was hurrying along Fulham Road in the rain, that he had no idea of the number of Mrs. Gainsborough's house. He also began to wonder if there really could be such a place as Tinderbox Lane, and as he walked on without discovering any indication of its existence, he wondered if Sylvia had invented the name, so that he might never find her and Lily again. It was an uneasy thought, for without a number and without a name—but just as he was planning an elaborate way to discover the real name of the street, he saw in front of him Tinderbox Lane enamelled in the ordinary characters of municipal direction. Here were the two posts: here was the narrow entrance. The rumble of the traffic grew fainter. On one side was a high blank wall; on the other a row of two-storied houses. They were naturally dwellings of the poorer classes, but at intervals a painter had acquired one, and had painted it white or

affixed green shutters with heart-shaped openings. The
width of the pavement varied continually, but generally
at the beginning it was very narrow. Later on, however, it
became wide enough to allow trees to be planted down the
middle. Beyond this part was a block of new flats round
which Tinderbox Lane narrowed again to a mere alley
looking now rather dank and gloomy in the rain. Michael
could not remember from last night in the fog either the
trees or the flats. The door of Lily's lodging had been set
in a wall: here on one side was certainly a wall, but never
a door to relieve the grimy blankness. He began to feel
discouraged, and he walked round into the narrow alley
behind the flats. Here were doors in the wall at last, and
Michael examined each of them in turn. Two were dark
blue: one was green: one was brown. 74: 75: 76: 77.
He chose 77 because it was farthest away from the flats.
After a very long wait, an old woman holding over herself
a very large umbrella opened it.

"Mrs. Gainsborough . . . ?" Michael began.

But the old woman had slammed the door before he
could finish his enquiry.

Michael rang the bell of 76, and again he waited a long
time. At last the door was opened, and to his relief he saw
Mrs. Gainsborough herself under a green and much larger
umbrella than the old woman's next door.

"I've come to take the girls out to lunch."

"That's a good boy," she wheezed. "The dearies will
be glad to get out and enjoy themselves a bit. Here's a
day. This would have suited Noah, wouldn't it ?"

She was leading the way up the gravel path, and Michael
saw that in the garden-beds there were actually Christmas
roses in bloom. The house itself was covered with a mat of
Virginia creeper and jasmine, and the astonishing rusticity
of it was not at all diminished by the pretentious grey
houses of the next road which towered above it behind, nor

even in front by the flats with their eruption of windows.
These houses with doors in their garden-walls probably all
belonged to individuals, and for that reason they had
escaped being overwhelmed by the development of the
neighbourhood twenty years ago. Their four long gardens
in a row must be a bower of greenery in summer, and it was
sad to think that the flats opposite were no doubt due to the
death of someone who had owned a similar house and
garden.

Michael remembered the balcony in front with steps on
either side. Underneath this he now saw that there was
another entrance, evidently to the kitchen. Two fairly
large trees were planted in the grass that ran up to the
house on either side of the balcony.

"Those are my mulberries," said Mrs. Gainsborough.
"This is called Mulberry Cottage. I've been meaning to
have the name painted on the outside door for nearly forty
years, but I always forget. There's a character to give
myself. Ah, dear me! The Captain loved his mulberries.
But you ought to see this in the springtime. Well, my
flowers are really remarkable. But there, it's not to be
wondered at. M' father was a nursery gardener."

She looked round at Michael and winked broadly. He
could not think why. Possibly it was a comic association
in her mind with the behaviour of the Captain in carrying
her off from such a home.

"The Duke of Fulham to see you, girls," she wheezed
at the door of the sitting-room and, giving Michael a push,
retreated with volleys of bronchial laughter. The girls
were sitting in front of the fire. Lily was pretending to
trim a hat : Sylvia was reading, but she flung her book
down as Michael entered. He had the curiosity to look at
the title and found it was the Contes Drôlatiques of Balzac.
An unusual girl, he thought : but his eyes were all for Lily,
and because he could not kiss her, he felt shy and stupid.

However, the shoes, which he now restored, supplied an immediate topic, and he was soon perfectly at ease again. Presently the girls left him to get ready to go out, and he sat thinking of Lily, while the canary chirped in the brass cage. The silence here was very like the country. London was a thousand miles away and he could hear Lily and Sylvia moving about overhead. Less and less did he think there could be anything wrong with Mulberry Cottage. Yet the apparent security was going to make it rather difficult to take Lily away. Certainly he could ask her to marry him at once; but she might not want to marry him at once. The discovery of her in this pleasant house with a jolly friend was spoiling the grand swoop of rescue which he had planned. She would not presumably be escaping from a situation she abhorred. It was difficult to approach Lily here. Was it Sylvia who was making it difficult? He must talk to Sylvia and explain that he had no predatory intentions. She would surely be glad that he wanted to marry Lily. Or would she not? Michael jumped up and tinkled the lustres on the mantelshelf. 'Sweet,' said the canary in the brass cage: the rain sizzled without. Faintly pervading this small square room was the malaise of someone's jealousy. The tentative solution that was propounding itself did not come from his own impression of Sylvia, but it seemed positively to be an emanation from the four walls of the room which in the stillness was able to force its reality upon him. 'Sweet,' said the canary: the lustres stopped their tinkling: the rain sizzled steadily outside.

Lunch at Kettner's was a great success. At least Michael thought it was a great success, because Lily looked exquisite against the bronzy walls, and her hair on this dull day seemed not to lack sunlight, but rather to give to the atmosphere a thought of the sun, the rare and wintry sun. Sylvia talked a great deal in her deep voice, and he was

3 T

conscious that the other people in the restaurant were turning round to envy their table.

The longer that Michael was in the company of Lily and Sylvia, the less he was able to ask the direct questions that would have been comparatively easy at the beginning. Sylvia, by the capacity she displayed of appreciating worldliness without ever appearing worldly herself, made it impossible for him to risk her contempt by a stupid question. She was not on the stage; so much he had discovered. She and Lily had apparently a number of men friends. That fact would have been disquieting, but that Sylvia talked of them with such a really tomboyish zest as made it impossible to suppose they represented more than what they were superficially, the companions of jolly days on the river and at race-meetings, of jolly evenings at theatres and balls. Quite definitely Michael was able to assure himself that out of the host of allusions there was not one which pointed to any man favoured above the rest. He was able to be positive that Lily and Sylvia were independent. Yet Lily had no private allowance or means. It must be Sylvia who was helping her. Perhaps Sylvia was always strict, and perhaps all these friends were by her held at arm's length from Lily, as he felt himself being held now. Her attitude might have nothing to do with jealousy. But Sylvia was not strict in her conversation; she was, indeed, exceptionally free. That might be a good sign. A girl who read the Contes Drôlatiques might easily read Rabelais himself, and a girl who read Rabelais would be inviolable. Michael, when Sylvia had said something particularly broad, used to look away from Lily; and yet he knew he need not have bothered, for Lily was always outside the conversation; always under a spell of silence and remoteness. Of what was she for ever thinking? There were looking-glasses upon the bronzy walls.

For a fortnight Michael came every day to Tinderbox

Lane and took the girls out; but for the whole of that
fortnight he never managed to be alone with Lily. Then
one day Sylvia was not there when he called. To find Lily
like this after a tantalizing fortnight was like being in a room
heavily perfumed with flowers. It seemed to stifle his
initiative, so that for a few minutes he sat coldly and awkwardly by the window.

"We're alone," he managed to say at last.

"Sylvia's gone to Brighton. She didn't want to go a
bit."

"Bother Sylvia! Lily, we haven't kissed for five years."

He stumbled across to take her in his arms; and as he held
her to him, it was a rose falling to pieces, so did she melt
upon his passion. He heard her sigh; a coal slipped in
the grate; the canary hopped from perch to perch. These
small sounds but wrapped him more closely in the trance
of silence.

"Lily, you will marry me, won't you? Very soon? At
once?"

Michael was kneeling beside her chair, and she was
looking down at him from clouded eyes still passionate.
Marriage was an intrusion upon the remoteness where
they brooded; and he, ravished by their flamy blue
relucency, could not care whether she answered him or
not. This was such a contentment of desire that the
future with the visible shapes of action it tried to display
was unheeded, while now she stirred in his arms. She was
his, and so for an hour she stayed, immortal, and yet most
poignantly the prisoner of time. Michael, with all that he
had dreaded at the back of his mind he would have to face
in her condition, scarcely knew how to celebrate this reward
of his tenacity. This tranquillity of caresses, this slow
fondling of her wrist were a lullaby to his fears. It was the
very rhapsody of his intention to kneel beside her, murmuring huskily the little words of love. He would have married

her wherever and whatever he found her, but the relief was overwhelming. He had thought of a beautiful thing ruined; he had foreshadowed glooms and tragic colloquies; he had desperately hoped his devotion might be granted at least the virtue of a balm. Instead, he found this ivory girl, this loveliness of rose and coral within his arms. So many times she had eluded him in dreams upon the midway of the night, and so often in dreams he had held her for kisses that were robbed from him by the sunlight of the morning, that he scarcely could believe he held her now, now when her hair was thistledown upon his cheeks, when her mouth was a butterfly. He shuddered to think how soon this airy beauty must have perished; and even now what was she ? A shred of goldleaf on his open hand, pliant, but fugitive at a breath, and destructible in a moment of adversity.

Always in their youth, when they had sat imparadised, Michael had been aware of the vulgar Haden household in the background. Now here she was placed in exactly the room where he would have wished to find her, though he would scarcely desire to maintain her in such a setting. He could picture her at not so distant a time in wonderful rooms, about whose slim furniture she would move in delicate and languorous promenades. This room pleased him, because it was the one from which he would have wished to take her into the misty grandeurs he imagined for her lodging. It was a room he would always regard with affection, thinking of the canary in the brass cage and the Christmas roses blowing in the garden and the low sounds of Mrs. Gainsborough busy in her kitchen underneath. — Tinderbox Lane ! It was an epithalamium in itself; and as for Mulberry Cottage, it had been carried here by the fat pink loves painted on the ceiling of that Cremorne arbour in which the Captain had first imagined his gift.

So with fantastic thoughts and perfect kisses, perfect, but yet ineffably vain because they expressed so little of what Michael would have had them express, the hour passed.

" We must talk of practical things," he declared, rising from his knees.

" You always want to talk," Lily pouted.

" I want to marry you. Do you want to marry me ? "

" Yes, but it's so difficult to do things quickly."

" We'll be married in a month. We'll be married on St. Valentine's Day," Michael announced.

" It's so wet now to think of weddings." She looked peevishly out of the window.

" You haven't got to think about it. You've got to do it."

" And it's so dull," she objected. " Sylvia says it's appallingly dull. And she's been married."

" What has Sylvia got to do with it ? " he demanded.

" Oh, well, she's been awfully sweet to me. After all, when mother died, what was I to do ? I couldn't bear Doris any more. She always gets on my nerves. Anyway, don't let's talk about marriage now. In the summer I shall feel more cheerful. I hate this weather."

" But look here," he persisted. " Are you in love with me ? "

She nodded, yet too doubtfully to please him.

" Well, if you're not in love with me . . ."

" Oh, I am, I am. Don't shout so, Michael. If I wasn't awfully fond of you, I shouldn't have made Sylvia ask you to come back. She hates men coming here."

" Are you Sylvia's servant ? " said Michael in exasperation.

" Don't be stupid. Of course not."

" It's ridiculous," he grumbled, " to quote her with every sentence."

" Why you couldn't have stayed where you were,"
said Lily fretfully, " I don't know. It was lovely sitting
by the fire and being kissed. If you're so much in love with
me, I wonder you wanted to get up."

" So we're not to talk any more about marriage ? "

After all, he told himself, it was unreasonable of him to
suppose that Lily was likely to be as impulsive as himself.
Her temperament was not the same. She did not mean to
discourage him.

" Don't let's talk about anything," said Lily. He could
not stand aloof from the arms she held wide open.

Sylvia would not be coming back for at least three days,
and Michael spent all his time with Lily. He thought that
Mrs. Gainsborough looked approvingly upon their love ;
at any rate she never worried them. The weather was
steadily unpleasant, and though he took Lily out to lunch,
it never seemed worth while to stay away from Tinderbox
Lane very long. One night, however, they went to the
Palace, and afterwards, when he asked her where she would
like to go, she suggested Verrey's. Michael had never
been there before and he was rather jealous that Lily should
seem to know it so well. However, he liked to see her sitting
in what he told himself was the only café in London which
had escaped the cheapening of popularity and had kept its
old air of the Third Empire.

As Lily was stirring her lemon-squash, her languid fore-
arm looked very white swaying from the sombre mufflings
of her cloak. Something in her self-possession, a momentary
hardness and disdain, made Michael suddenly suspicious.

" Do you enjoy Covent Garden balls ? " he asked.

She shrugged her shoulders.

" It depends who we go with. Often I don't care for
them much. And the girls you see there are frightfully
common."

He could not bring himself to ask her straight out what

he feared. If it were so, let it rest unrevealed. The knowledge would make no difference to his resolution. People began to come into the Café, shaking the wet from their shoulders; and the noise of the rain was audible above the conversation.

"I wish we could have had one fine day together," said Michael regretfully. "Do you remember when we used to go for long walks in the winter?"

"I must have been very fond of you," Lily laughed. "I don't think you could make me walk like that now."

"Aren't you so fond of me now?" he asked reproachfully.

"You ought to know," she whispered.

All the way home the raindrops were flashing in the road like bayonets, and her cheeks were dabbled with the wet.

"Shall I come in?" Michael asked, as he waited by the door in the wall.

"Yes, come in and have something to drink, of course."

He was stabbed by the ease of her invitation.

"Do you ask all these friends of yours to come in and have a drink after midnight?"

"I told you that Sylvia doesn't like me to," she said.

"But you would, if she didn't mind?" Michael went on, torturing himself.

"How fond you are of 'ifs,'" she answered. "I can't bother to think about 'ifs' myself."

If only he had the pluck to avoid allusions and come at once to grips with truth. Sharply he advised himself to let the truth alone. Already he was feeling the influence of Lily's attitude. He wondered if, when he married her, all his activity would swoon upon Calypso like this. It was — as easy to dream life away in the contemplation of a beautiful woman as in the meditation of the Oxford landscape.

"Happiness makes me inactive," said Michael to himself.

"So of course I shall never really be happy. What a paradox."

He would not take off his overcoat. He was feeling afraid of a surrender to-night.

"I'm glad I didn't suggest staying late," he thought, as he walked away down the dripping garden path. "I should have been mad with unreasonable suspicions, if she had said 'yes.'"

Sylvia came back next day, and though Michael still liked her very much, he was certain now of her hostility to him. He was conscious of malice in the air, when she said to Lily that Jack wanted them to have dinner with him to-night and go afterwards to some dance at Richmond. Michael was furious that Lily should be invited to Richmond, and yet until she had promised to marry him how could he combat Sylvia's influence? And who was Jack? And with whom had Sylvia been to Brighton?

The day after the dance, Michael came round about twelve o'clock as usual, but when he reached the sitting-room only Sylvia was before the fire.

"Lily isn't down yet," she told him.

He was aware of a breathlessness in the atmosphere, and he knew that he and Sylvia were shortly going to clash.

"Jolly dance?" he asked.

She shrugged her shoulders, and there was a long pause.

"Will Lily be dressed soon? I rather want to take her out." Michael flung down his challenge.

"She's been talking to me about what you said yesterday," Sylvia began.

Michael could not help liking her more and more, although her countenance was set against him. He could not help admiring that out-thrust underlip and those wide-set, deep and bitter brown eyes.

"When do you propose to marry her?" Sylvia went on.

"As soon as possible," he said coolly.

" Which of us do you think has the greater influence over her ? " she demanded.

" I really don't know. You have rather an advantage over me in that respect."

" I'm glad you admit that," interrupted Sylvia with sarcastic chill.

" You have personality. You've probably been very kind to Lily. You're cleverer than she is. You're with her all the time. I've only quite suddenly come into her life again."

" I'm glad you think you've managed to do that," she said glowering.

More and more, Michael thought, with her wide-set eyes was she like a cat crouching by the fire.

" Just because I had to go away for three days and you had an opportunity to be alone with Lily, you now think you've come into her life. My god, you're like some damned fool in a novel."

" A novel by whom ? " Michael asked. Partly he was trying to score off Sylvia, but at the same time he was sincerely curious to know, for he never could resist the amplification of a comparison.

" Oh, any inkslinger with a brain of pulp," she answered savagely.

He bowed.

" I suppose you're suffering from the virus of sentimental redemption ? " she sneered.

Michael was rather startled by her divination.

" What should I redeem her from ? "

" I thought you boasted of knowing Lily six years ago ? "

" I don't know that I boasted of it," he replied in rather an injured tone. " But I did know her—very well."

" Couldn't you foresee what she was bound to become ?

Personally I should have said that Lily's future must have been obvious from the time she was five years old.. Certainly at seventeen it must have been. You got out of her life then : what the hell's your object in coming into it again now, as you call it, unless you're a sentimentalist ? People don't let passion lapse for six years and pick up the broken thread without the help of sentiment."

Michael in the middle of the increasing tension of the conversation was able to stop for a moment and ask himself if this by chance were true. He was standing by the mantelpiece and tinkling the lustres. Sylvia looked up at him irritably, and he silenced them at once.

" Sentiment about what ? " he asked, taking the chair opposite hers.

" You think Lily's a tart, don't you ? And you think I am, don't you ? "

He frowned at the brutality of the expression.

" I did think so," he said. " But of course I've changed my mind since I've seen something of you."

" Oh of course you've changed your mind, have you ? " she laughed contemptuously. " And what made you do that ? My visit to Brighton ? "

" Even if *you* are," said Michael hotly, " I needn't believe that Lily is. And even if she is, it makes no difference to my wanting to marry her."

" Sentimentalist," she jeered. " Damned sugar-and-water sentimentalist."

" Your sneers don't particularly affect me, you know," he said politely.

" Oh, for god's sake, be less the well-brought-up little gentleman. Cut out the undergraduate. You fool, I was married to an Oxford man. And I'm sitting here now with the glorious knowledge that I'm a perpetual bugbear to his good form."

" Because you made a hash of marriage," Michael

pointed out, "it doesn't follow that I'm not to marry Lily. I can't understand your objections."

"Listen. You couldn't make her happy. You couldn't make her any happier than the dozens of men who want to be fond of her for a short time without accepting the responsibility of marriage. Do you think I let any one of those dozens touch her? Not one, if I can get the money myself. And I usually can. Well, why should I stand aside now and let you carry her off, even though you do want to marry her? I could argue against it on your side by telling you that you have no chance of keeping Lily faithful to you. Can't you see that she has no moral energy? Can't you see that she's vain and empty-headed? Can't you see that? But why should I argue with you for your benefit? I don't care a damn about your side in the matter."

"What exactly do you care about?" Michael asked. "If Lily is what you say, I should have thought you'd be glad to be rid of her. After all, I'm not proposing to do her any wrong."

"Oh, to the devil with your right and wrong!" Sylvia cried. "Man can only wrong woman, when he owns her, and if this marriage is going to be a success, you'll have to own Lily. That's what I rebel against—the ownership of women. It makes me mad."

"Yes, it seems to," Michael put in. He was beginning to be in a rage with Sylvia's unreasonableness. "If it comes to ownership," he went on angrily, "I should have thought that handing her over to the highest bidder time after time would be the real way to make her the pitiable slave of man."

"Why?" challenged Sylvia. "You sentimental ass, can't you understand that she treats them as I treat them, like the swine they are. She's free. I'm free."

"You're not at all free," Michael indignantly contradicted. "You're bound hand and foot by the lust of wealthy brutes. If you read a few less elaborately clever books, and thought a few simpler thoughts, you'd be a good deal happier."

" I don't want to be happier."

" Oh, I think you're merely hysterical," he said disdain-fully. " But after all, your opinions about yourself don't matter to me. Only I can't see what right you have to apply them to Lily ; and even if you have the right, I don't grasp your reason for wanting to."

" When I met Lily first," said Sylvia, " she had joined the chorus of a touring company in which I was. Her mother had just died, and I'd just run away from my husband. I thought her the most beautiful thing I'd ever seen. That's three years ago. Is she beautiful still ? "

" Of course she is," said Michael.

" Well, it's I who have kept her beautiful. I've kept her free also. If sometimes I've let her have affairs with men, I've taken care that they were with men who could do her no harm, for whom she had no sort of . . ."

" Look here," Michael burst in, " I'm sick of this conver-sation. You're talking like a criminal lunatic. I tell you I'm going to marry her whatever you think."

" I say you won't, and you shan't," Sylvia declared.

The deadlock had been reached, and they sat there on either side of the fire, glaring at each other.

" The extraordinary thing is," said Michael at last, " I thought you had a sense of humour when I first met you. And another extraordinary thing is that I still like you very much. Which probably rather annoys you. But I can't help saying it."

" The opinions of sentimentalists don't interest me one way or the other," Sylvia snapped.

" Will you answer one question ? Will you tell me why you were so pleasant on the evening we met ? "

" I really can't bother to go back as far as that."

" You weren't jealous *then*," Michael persisted.

" Who says I'm jealous now ? " she cried.

" I do. What do you think you are, unless you're jealous ? When is Lily coming down ? "

" She isn't coming down until you've gone."

" Then I shall go and call her."

" She's not in London."

" I don't believe you."

A second deadlock was reached. Finally Michael decided to give Sylvia the pleasure of supposing that he was beaten for the moment. He congratulated himself upon the cunning of such a move. She was obviously going to be rather difficult to circumvent.

On the steps of the balcony he turned to her :

" You hate me because I love Lily, and you hate me twice as much because Lily loves me."

" It's not true," Sylvia declared. " It's not true. She doesn't love you, and what right have you to love her ? "

She tossed back her mane of brown hair, biting her nails.

" What college was your husband at ? " Michael suddenly enquired.

" Balliol."

" I wonder if I knew him."

" Oh, no. He was older than you."

It was satisfactory, Michael thought as he walked down Tinderbox Lane, that the conversation had ended normally. At least he had effected so much. She had really been rather wonderful, that strange Sylvia. He would very much like to pit her against Stella. It was satisfactory to have his doubts allayed : notwithstanding her present opposition, he felt that he did owe Sylvia a good deal. But it would be absurd to let Lily continue in such a life : women always quarrelled ultimately, and if Sylvia were to leave her, her fall would be rapid and probably irredeemable. Besides, he wanted her for himself. She was to him no less than to

Sylvia the most beautiful thing in the world. He did not want to marry a clever woman : he would be much more content with Lily, from whom there could be no reaction upon his nerves. Somehow all his theories of behaviour were being referred back to his own desires. It was useless to pretend any longer that his pursuit had been quixotry. Even if it had seemed so on that night when he first heard the news of Lily from Drake, the impulse at the back of his resolve had been his passion for her. When he looked back at his behaviour lately, a good deal of it seemed to have been dictated by self-gratification. He remembered how deeply hurt he had felt by Poppy's treatment of what he had supposed his chivalry. In retrospect his chivalry was seeming uncommonly like self-satisfaction. His friendship for Daisy ; for Barnes ; for the underworld ; it had been nothing but self-satisfaction. Very well, then. If self was to be the touchstone in future, he could face that standard as easily as any other. By the time he had reached the end of Tinderbox Lane Michael was convinced of his profound cynicism. He felt truly obliged to Sylvia for curing him of sentiment. He had so often inveighed against sentiment as the spring of human action, that he was most sincerely grateful for the proof of his own sentimental bias. He would go to Sylvia to-morrow and say frankly that he did not care a bit what Lily had been, was now or would be ; he wanted her. She was something beautiful which he coveted. For the possession of her he was ready to struggle. He would declare war upon Sylvia as upon a rival. She should be rather surprized to-morrow morning, Michael thought, congratulating himself upon this new and ruthless policy.

On the next morning, however, all Michael's plans for his future behaviour were knocked askew by being unable to get into Mulberry Cottage. His brutal frankness ; his cynical egotism ; his cold resolution, were ignominiously repulsed by a fast-closed door. Ringing a bell at intervals of a minute was a very undignified substitute for the position he had imagined himself taking up in that small square room. This errand-boy who stood at his elbow, gazing with such rapt interest at his ringing of the bell, was by no means the audience he had pictured.

"Does it amuse you to watch a bell being rung ? " Michael asked.

The errand boy shook his head.

"Well, why do you do it ? "

"I wasn't," said the errand-boy.

"What are you doing, then ? "

"Nothing."

Michael could not grapple with the errand-boy, and he retired from Tinderbox Lane until after lunch. He rang again, but he could get no answer to his ringing. At intervals until midnight he came back, but there was never an answer all the time. He went home and wrote to Sylvia :

173 CHEYNE WALK,
S.W.

Dear Sylvia,

    If you aren't afraid of being beaten, why are you afraid to let me see Lily ?

I dare you to let me see her. Be sporting.

Yours,
M. F.

To Lily he wrote :

Darling,

    Meet me outside South Kensington Station any time from twelve to three.

Michael

Alone of course.

Next day he waited three hours and a half for Lily, but she did not come. All the time he spent in a second-hand bookshop with one eye on the street. When he got home, he found a note from Sylvia.

Come to-morrow at twelve.

S. S.

Michael crumpled up the note and flung it triumphantly into the waste-paper-basket.

"I thought I should sting you into giving way," he exclaimed.

Mrs. Gainsborough opened the door to him, when he arrived.

"They've gone away, the demons," was what she said.

Michael was conscious of the garden rimed with hoar-frost stretching behind her in a vista; and as he stared at this silver sparkling desert he realized that Sylvia had inflicted upon him a crushing humiliation.

"Where have they gone?" he asked blankly.

"Oh, they never tell me where they get to. But they took their luggage. There's a note for you from Sylvia. Come in, and I'll give it to you."

Michael followed her drearily along the gravel path.

"We shall be having the snowdrops before we know where we are," Mrs. Gainsborough said.

"Very soon," he agreed. He would have assented if she had foretold begonias to-morrow morning.

In the sitting-room Michael saw Sylvia's note, a bleak little envelope waiting for him on that table-cloth. Mrs. Gainsborough left him to read it alone. The old silence of the room haunted him again now, the silence that was so much intensified by the canary hopping about his cage. Almost he decided to throw the letter unread into the fire.

From every corner of the room the message of Sylvia's hostility was stretching out towards him. 'Sweet,' said the canary. Michael tore open the envelope and read :—

Perhaps you'll admit that my influence is as strong as yours. You'd much better give her up. In a way I'm rather sorry for you, but not enough to make me hand over Lily to you. Do realize, my dear young thing, that you aren't even beginning to understand women. I admit that there's precious little to understand in Lily. And for that very reason, when even you begin to see through her beauty, you'll hate her. Now I hate to think of this happening. She's a thousand times better off with me than she ever could be with you. Perhaps my maternal instinct has gone off the lines a bit and fixed itself on Lily. And yet I don't think it's anything so sickly as sentimental mothering. No, I believe I just like to sit and look at her. Lily's rather cross with me for taking her away from 'such a nice boy.' Does that please you? And doesn't it exactly describe you? However, I won't crow. Don't break the lustres, when you read this. They belong to Fatty. What I suggest for you is a walk in Kensington Gardens to the refrain of " Blast the whole bloody world." Now look shocked, my little Vandyck. S. S.

Michael tore the letter up. He did not want to read and re-read it for the rest of the day. His eyelids were pricking unpleasantly, and he went out to find Mrs. Gainsborough. He was really sensitive that even a room should witness such a discomfiture. The landlady was downstairs in the kitchen, where he had not yet been. In this room of copper pots and pans, with only the garden in view, she might have been a farmer's wife.

" Sit down," she said. " And make yourself at home."

" Will you sit down ? " Michael asked.

" Oh, well, yes, if it's any pleasure to you." She took off

3 U

her apron and seated herself, smoothing the bombasine skirt over her knees.

A tabby cat purred between them; a kettle was singing; and there was a smell of allspice.

"You really don't know where the girls have gone?" Michael began.

"No more than you do," she assured him. "But that Sylvia is really a Turk."

"I suppose Lily didn't tell you that I used to know her six years ago?" he asked.

"Oh, yes, she talked about you a lot. A good deal more than Miss Sylvia liked, that's a sure thing."

"Well, do you think it's fair for Sylvia to carry her off like this? I want to marry Lily, Mrs. Gainsborough."

"There, only fancy what a daring that Sylvia has. She's a nice girl and very high-spirited, but she *is* a Miss Dictatorial."

Michael felt encouraged by Mrs. Gainsborough's attitude, and he made up his mind to throw himself upon her mercy. Sentiment would be his only weapon, and he found some irony in the reflection that he had set out this morning to be a brutal cynic in his treatment of the situation.

"Do you think it's fair to try to prevent Lily from marrying me? You know as well as I do that the life she's leading now isn't going to be the best life possible for her. You're a woman of the world, Mrs. Gainsborough . . ."

"I was once," she corrected. "And a very naughty world it was too."

"You were glad, weren't you, when the Captain brought you to this house? You were glad to feel secure? You would have married him?"

"No, I wouldn't marry him. I preferred to be as I am. Still that's nothing for Lily to go by. She's more suited for marriage than what I was."

" Don't you think," Michael went on eagerly, " that if after six years I'm longing to marry her, I ought to marry her ? I know that she might be much worse off than she is, but equally she might be much better off. Look here, Mrs. Gainsborough, it's up to you. You've got to make it possible for me to see her. You've got to."

" But if I do anything like that," said Mrs. Gainsborough, " it means I have an unpleasantness with Sylvia. That girl's a regular heathen when she turns nasty. I should be left all alone in my little house. And what with Spring coming on and all, and the flowers looking so nice in the garden, I should feel very much the square peg in the round hole."

" Lily and I would come and see you," he promised. " And I don't think Sylvia would leave you. She'd never find another house like Mulberry Cottage or another land-lady like you."

" Yes, I daresay, but you can't tell these things. Once she's in her tantrums, there's no saying what will happen. And besides, I don't know what you want me to do."

" I want you to send me word the first moment that Lily's alone for an hour ; and when I ring, do answer the bell."

" Now that wasn't my fault yesterday," said Mrs. Gains-borough. " Really I thought we should have the fire-escape in. The way you nagged at that poor bell ! It was really chronic. But would she let me so much as speak to you, even with the door only on the jar ? Certainly not ! And all the time she was snapping round the house like a young crocodile. And yet I'm really fond of that girl. Well, when the Captain died, she was a daughter to me. Oh, she was, she was really a daughter to me. Well, you see, his sister invited me to the funeral, which I thought was very nice, her being an old maid and very strict. Now, I hardly liked to put on a widow's cap and yet I hardly didn't like to. But Sylvia, she said not on any account, and I was very glad I didn't, because there was a lot of persons there very stand-offish, and I should have been at my wits to know whatever I was going to say."

"Look here," said Michael. "When the Captain gave you this house, he loved you. You were young, weren't you? You were young and beautiful? Well, would you like to think your house was going to be used to separate two people very much in love with each other? You can say I climbed over the wall. You can make any excuse you like to Sylvia. But, Mrs. Gainsborough, do, do let me know when Lily is going to be alone. If she doesn't want to come away with me, it will be my fault, and that will be the end of it. If only you'll help me at the beginning. Will you? Will you promise to help me?"

"I never could resist a man," sighed Mrs. Gainsborough with resignation. "There's a character! Oh, well, it's my own and no one else's, that's one good job."

Michael had to wait until February was nearly over before he heard from her. It had been very difficult to remain quietly at Cheyne Walk, but he knew that if he were to show any sign of activity, Sylvia would carry Lily off again.

"A person to see you, sir," said the tortoise-mouthed parlourmaid.

Michael found Mrs. Gainsborough sitting in the hall. She was wearing a bonnet tied with very bright cerise ribbons.

"They've had a rumpus, the pair of them, this afternoon. And Sylvia's gone off in the sulks. I really was quite aggravated with her. Oh, she's a wilful spitfire, that girl, sometimes. She really is."

Michael was coming away without a coat or hat, and Mrs. Gainsborough stopped him.

"Now don't behave like a silly. Dress yourself properly and don't make me run. I'm getting stout, you know," she protested.

" We'll get a hansom."

" What, ride in a hansom ? Never ! A four-wheeler if you *like*."

It was difficult to find a four-wheeler, and Michael was nearly mad with impatience.

" Now don't upset yourself. Sylvia won't be back tonight, and there's no need to tug at me as if I was a cork in a bottle. People will think we're a walking poppy-show, if you don't act more quiet. They're all turning round to stare at us."

A four-wheeler appeared presently, and very soon they were walking down Tinderbox Lane. Michael felt rather like a little boy out with his nurse, as he kept turning back to exhort Mrs. Gainsborough to come more quickly. She grew more and more red in the face, and so wheezy that he was afraid something would happen to her, and for a few yards made no attempt to hurry her along. At last they reached Mulberry Cottage.

" Supposing Sylvia has come back ! " he said.

" I keep on telling you she's gone away for the night. Now get on indoors with you. You've nearly been my death."

"I say, you don't know how grateful I am to you," Michael exclaimed, turning round and grasping her fat hands.

Mrs. Gainsborough shouted upstairs to Lily as loudly as her breathlessness would permit :

" I've brought you back that surprize packet I promised."

Then she vanished, and Michael waited for Lily at the foot of the stairs. She came down very soon, looking very straight and slim in her philamot frock of Chinese crape that so well became her. Soon she was in his arms and glad enough to be petted after Sylvia's rages.

" Lily, how can you bear to let Sylvia manage you like this ? It's absolutely intolerable."

" She's been horrid to me to-day," said Lily resentfully.

"Well, why do you put up with it?"

"Oh, I don't know. I hate always squabbling. It's much easier to give way to her, and usually I don't much mind."

"You don't much mind whether we're married!" Michael exclaimed. "How can you let Sylvia persuade you against marriage? Darling girl, if you marry me you shall do just as you like. I simply want you to look beautiful. You'd be happy married to me,—you really would."

"Sylvia says marriage is appallingly dull, and my mother and father didn't get on, and Doris doesn't get on with the man she's married to. In fact everybody seems to hate it."

"Do you hate me?" Michael demanded.

"No, I think you're awfully sweet."

"Well, why don't you marry me? You'll have plenty of money and nothing to bother about. I think you'd thoroughly enjoy being married."

For an instant, as he argued with her, Michael wavered in his resolve. For an instant it seemed after all impossible to marry this girl. A chill came over him, but he shook it off, and he saw only her loveliness, the eyes sullen with thoughts of Sylvia, the lips pouting at the remembrance of a tyranny. And again as he watched her beauty, the bitter thought crossed his mind that it would be easier to possess her without marriage. Then he thought of her at seventeen. "*Michael, why do you make me love you so?*" Was that the last protest she ever made against the thraldom of passion? If it was, the blame must primarily be his, since he had not heeded her reproach.

"Lily," he cried catching her to him, "you're coming away with me now."

He kissed her a hundred times.

"Now! Now! Do you hear me?"

She surrendered to his will, and as he held her Michael thought grimly what an absurd paradox it was, that in order to make her consent to marry him, he like the others must play upon the baser side of her yielding nature. There were difficulties of packing and of choosing frocks and hats, but Michael had his way through them all.

"Quite an elopement," Mrs. Gainsborough proclaimed.

"A very virtuous elopement," said Michael with a laugh.

"Oh, but shan't I catch it when that Hottentot comes back!"

"Well, it's Sylvia's fault," said Lily fretfully. "She shouldn't worry me all the time to know whether I like her better than anyone else in the world."

The man arrived with a truck for the luggage.

"Where are you going?" Mrs. Gainsborough asked. "I declare you're like two babes in the wood."

"To my sister's in Huntingdonshire," said Michael, and he wrote out the address.

"Oh, in the country! Well, Summer'll be on us before we know where we are. I declare my snowdrops are quite finished."

"Is your sister pretty?" Lily asked, as they were driving to King's Cross.

"She's handsome," said Michael. "You'll like her, I think. And her husband was a great friend of mine. By the way I must send a wire to say we're coming."

Chapter VII : *The Gate of Ivory*

IT was only when he was sitting opposite to Lily in a first-class compartment that Michael began to wonder if their sudden arrival would create a kind of consternation at Hardingham. He managed to reassure himself when he looked at her. The telegram might have puzzled Stella, but in meeting Lily she would understand his action. Nevertheless he felt a little anxious when he saw the Hardingham brougham waiting outside the little station. The cold drive of four miles through the still, misty evening gave him too long to meditate the consequences of his action. Impulse was very visibly on trial, and he began to fear a little Stella's judgment of it. The carriage-lamps splashed the hedgerows monotonously, and the horses' breath curled round the rigid form of the coachman. Trees, hedges, gates, signposts went past in the blackness and chill. Michael drew Lily close and asked in a whisper if she were happy.

"It makes me sleepy driving like this," she murmured. Her head was on his shoulder; the astrakhan collar was silky to his chin. So she travelled until they reached the gates of the park : then Michael woke her up.

There was not time to do much but dress quickly for dinner when they arrived, though Michael watched Stella's glances rather anxiously.

Lily put on a chiffon frock of aquamarine, and though she looked beautiful in it, he wished she had worn black : this frock made her seem a little theatrical, he ·fancied ; or was it the effect of her against the stern dining-room, and nothing whatever to do with the frock ? Stella, too, whom he had always considered a personality of some extravagance, seemed to have grown suddenly very stiff and conventional. It used always to be himself who criticized people : Stella had always been rather too lenient. Perhaps it was being married to Alan; or was Lily the reason ? Yet superficially everything seemed to be going all right, especially when he consoled himself by remembering the abruptness of Lily's introduction. After dinner Stella took Lily away with her into the drawing-room and left Michael with Alan. Michael tried to feel that this was what he had expected would happen; but he could not drive away the consciousness of a new formality brooding over Hardingham. It was annoying, too, the way in which Alan seemed deliberately to avoid any reference to Lily. He would not even remind Michael of the evening at the Drury Lane pantomime, when he had met her five or six years ago. Perhaps he had forgotten driving home in a cab with her sister on that occasion. Michael grew exasperated by his talk about cricket pitches ; and yet he could not bring himself to ask right out what Alan thought of her, because it would have impinged upon his pride to do so. In about ten minutes they heard the sound of the piano, and tacitly they agreed to forego the intimacy of drinking port together any longer.

Stella closed the piano with a slam when they came into the drawing-room, and asked Lily if she would like some bridge.

" Oh, no. I hate playing cards. But you play."

It was for Michael a nervous evening. He was perpetually on guard for hostile criticism ; he was terribly anxious that Lily should make a good impression. Everything seemed to go wrong. Games were begun and ended almost in the same breath. Finally he managed to find a song that Lily thought she remembered, and Stella played her accompaniment very aggressively, Michael fancied ; for by this time he regarded the slightest movement on her part or Alan's as an implication of disapproval. Lily was tired, luckily, and was ready to go to bed early.

When Stella came down again, Michael felt he ought to supplement the few details of his telegram, and it began to seem almost impossible to explain reasonably his arrival here with Lily. An account of Tinderbox Lane would sound fantastic : a hint of Lily's life would be fatal. He found himself enmeshed in a vague tale of having found her very hard up and of wishing to get her away from the influence of a rather depressing home. It sounded very unconvincing as he told it, but he hoped that the declaration of his intention to marry her at once would smother everything else in a great surprize.

" Of course, that's what I imagined you were thinking of doing," said Stella. " So you've made up your quarrel of five years ago ? "

" When are you going to get married ? " Alan asked.

" Well, I hoped you'd be able to have us here for a week or so, or at any rate Lily, while I go up to town and find a place for us to live."

" Oh, of course, she can stay here," said Stella.

" Oh, rather, of course," Alan echoed.

Next morning it rained hard, and Michael thought he saw Stella making signs of dissent when at breakfast Alan proposed taking him over to a farm a couple of miles away. He was furious to think that Stella was objecting to being left alone with Lily, and he retired to the billiard-room where he spent half-an-hour playing a game with himself between spot and plain, a game which produced long breaks that seemed quite unremarkable, so profound was the trance of vexation in which he was plunged.

A fortnight passed, through the whole of which Alan never once referred to Lily ; and, as Michael was always too proud to make the first advance towards the topic, he felt that his friendship with Alan was being slowly chipped away. He knew that Stella, on the other hand, was rather anxious to talk to him, but perversely he avoided giving her any opportunity. As for Lily, she seemed perfectly happy doing nothing and saying very little. Obviously, however, this sort of existence under the shadow of disapproval could not continue much longer, and Michael determined to come to grips with the situation. Therefore, one morning of strong easterly wind when Lily wanted to stay indoors, he proposed a walk to Stella.

They crossed three or four fields in complete silence, the dogs scampering to right and left, the gale crimsoning their cheeks.

"I don't think I care much for this country of yours," said Michael at last. "It's flat and cold and damp. Why on earth you ever thought I should care to live here, I don't know."

"There's a wood about a quarter of a mile farther on. We can get out of the wind there."

Michael resented Stella's pleasantness. He wanted her to be angry and so launch him easily upon the grievances he had been storing up for a fortnight.

"I hate badly trained dogs," he grumbled when Stella turned round to whistle vainly for one of the spaniels.

"So do I," she agreed.

It was really unfair of her to effect a deadlock by being perpetually and unexpectedly polite. He would try being gracious himself: it was easier in the shelter of the wood.

"I don't think I've properly thanked you for having us to stay down here," he began.

Stella stopped dead in the middle of the glade :

"Look here, do you want me to talk about this business ? " she demanded.

Her use of the word ' business ' annoyed him : it crystallized all the offensiveness, as he was now calling it to himself, of her sisterly attitude these two weeks.

"I shall be delighted to talk about this 'business.' Though why you should refer to my engagement as if a hot-water pipe had burst, I don't quite know."

"Do you want me to speak out frankly—to say exactly what I think of you and Lily and of your marrying her? You won't like it, and I won't do it unless you ask me."

"Go on," said Michael gloomily. Stella had gathered the dogs round her again, and in this glade she appeared to Michael as a severe Artemis with her short tweed skirt and her golf-coat swinging from her shoulders like a chlamys. These oaks were hers: the starry moss was hers: the anemones flushing and silvering to the ground wind, they were all hers. It suddenly struck him as monstrously unfair that Stella should be able to criticize Lily. Here she stood on her own land for ever secure against the smallest ills that could come to the other girl; and, with this consciousness of a strength behind her, already she was conveying that rustic haughtiness of England. Michael loved her, this cool and indomitable mistress of Hardingham; but while he loved her, almost he hated her for the power she had to look down on Lily. Michael wished he had Sylvia with him. That would have been a royal battle in this wood. Stella with her dogs and trees behind her, with her green acres all round her and the very wind fighting for her, might yet have found it difficult to discomfit Sylvia.

"Go on, I'm waiting for you to begin," Michael repeated.

"Straight off, then," she said, "I may as well tell you that this marriage is impossible. I don't know where you found her again, and I don't care. It wouldn't make the slightest difference to me what she had been, if I thought she had a chance of ever being anything else. But, Michael, she's flabby. You'll hate me for saying so, but she is, she really is! In a year you'll admit that; you'll see her growing older

and flabbier, more and more vain ; emptier and emptier, if
that's possible. Even her beauty won't last. These very
fair girls fall to pieces like moth-eaten dolls. I've tried to
find something in her during this fortnight. I've tried and
tried ; but there's nothing. You may be in love with her
now, though I don't believe you are. I think it's all a piece
of sentimentalism. I've often teazed you about getting
married, but please don't suppose that I haven't realized
how almost impossible it would be, ever to find a woman that
would stand the wear and tear of your idealism. I'm prepared to bet that behind your determination to marry this
girl there's a reason, a lovely, unpractical, idealistic reason.
Isn't there ? You've been away with her for a week-end
and have tortured yourself into a theory of reparation. Is
that it ? Or you've fallen in love with the notion of yourself in love at eighteen. Oh, you can't marry her, you
foolish old darling."

"Your oratory would be more effective, if you wouldn't
keep whistling to that infernal dog," said Michael. "If
this marriage is so terrible, I should have thought you'd
have forgotten there were such animals as cocker-spaniels. It's
rubbish for you to say you've tried to find something in Lily.
You haven't made the slightest attempt. You've criticized
her from the moment she entered the house. You're sunk
deep already in the horrible selfishness of being happy. A
happy marriage is the most devastating joint egotism in the
world. Damn it, Stella, when you were making a fool of
yourself with half the men in Europe, I didn't talk as
you've been talking to me."

"No, you were always very cautiously fraternal," said
Stella. "Ah, no, I won't say bitter things, for, Michael, I
adore you ; and I'll break my heart if you marry this
girl."

"You won't do anything of the kind," he contradicted.
"You'll be whistling to spaniels all the time."

" Michael, it's really unkind of you to try and make me laugh, when I'm feeling so wretched about you."

" It's all very fine for you to sneer at Lily," said Michael. " But I can remember your coming back from Vienna and crying all day in your room over some man who'd made a fool of you. *You* looked pretty flabby then."

" How dare you remind me of that ? " Stella cried in a fury. " How dare you ? How dare you ? "

" You brought it on yourself," said Michael coldly.

" You're going to pieces already under the influence of that girl. Marry her, then ! But don't come to me for sympathy, when she's forced you to drag yourself through the divorce-court."

" No, I shall take care not to come to you for anything ever again," said Michael bitterly. " Unless it's for advice when I want to buy a spaniel."

They had turned again in the direction of the Hall, and over the windy fields they walked silently. Michael was angry with himself for having referred to that Vienna time. After all, it had been the only occasion on which he had seen Stella betray a hint of weakness ; besides, she had always treated him generously in the matter of confidences. He looked sidelong at her, but she walked on steadily, and he wondered if she would tell Alan that they had been nearer to quarrelling than so far they had ever been. Perhaps this sort of thing was inevitable with marriage. Chains of sympathy and affection forged to last eternally were smashed by marriage in a moment. He had heard nothing said about Stella's music lately. Was that also to vanish on account of marriage ? The sooner he and Lily left Hardingham, the better. He supposed he ought to suggest going immediately. But Lily would be a problem until he could find a place for her to live, and someone to chaperon her. They would be married next month, and he would take her abroad. He would be able to see her at last in some of the places where in days gone by he had dreamed of seeing her.

" I suppose you wouldn't object to keeping Lily here two or three days more, while I find a place in town ? " said Michael. It only struck him when the request was out how much it sounded like asking for a favour. Stella would despise him more than ever.

_ " Michael," Stella exclaimed, turning round and stopping in his path. " Once more I beg you to give up this idea of marriage. Surely you can realize how deeply I feel about it, when even after what you said I'm willing actually to plead with you. It's intolerable to think of you tied to her ! "

" It's too late," said Michael. " I must marry her. Not for any reasons that the world would consider reasons," he went on. " But because I want to marry her. The least you can do for me is to pretend to support me before the world."

" I won't, I won't, I won't. It's all wrong. She's all wrong. Her people are all wrong. Why, even Alan remembers them as dreadful, and you know how casual he is about people he doesn't like. He usually flings them out of his mind at once."

" Oh, Alan's amazing in every way," said Michael. He longed to say that he and Lily would go by the first train possible, but he dreaded so much the effect of bringing her back to London without any definite place to which she could go, that he was willing to leave her here for a few days, if she would stay. He hated himself for doing this, but the problems of marriage and Lily were growing unwieldy. He wished now that he had asked his mother to come back, so that he could have taken Lily to Cheyne Walk. It was stupid to let himself be caught unprepared like this. After all, perhaps it would be a good thing to leave Lily and Stella together for a bit. As he was going to marry her and as he could not face the possibility of quarrelling with Stella finally, it would be better to pocket his pride.

Suddenly Stella caught hold of his arm.

"Look here," she said. "You absurd old Quixote, listen. I'm going to do all in my power to stop your marrying Lily. But meanwhile go up to town and leave her here. I promise to declare a truce of a fortnight, if you'll promise me not to marry her until the middle of April. By a truce I mean that I'll be charming to her and take no steps to influence her to give you up. But after the fortnight it must be war, even if you win in the end and marry her."

"Does that mean we should cease to be on speaking terms?"

"Oh, no, of course, as a matter of fact, if you marry her, I suppose we shall all settle down together and be great friends, until she lands you in the divorce-court with half-a-dozen co-respondents. Then you'll come and live with us at Hardingham, a confirmed cynic and the despair of all the eligible young women in the neighbourhood."

"I wish you wouldn't talk like that about Lily," said Michael frowning.

"The truce has begun," Stella declared. "For a fortnight I'll be an angel."

Just before dusk was falling, the gale died away; and Michael persuaded Lily to come for a walk with him. Almost unconsciously he took her to the wood where he and Stella had talked so angrily in the morning. Chaffinches flashed their silver wings about them in the fading light.

"Lily, you look adorable in this glade," he told her. "I believe, if you were a little way off from me, I should think you were a birch-tree."

The wood was rosy brown and purple. Every object had taken on rich deeps of quality and colour reflected from the March twilight. The body of the missel-thrush, flinging his song from the bare oak-bough into the ragged sky, flickered with a magical sublucency. Michael found some primroses and brought them to Lily.

"These are for you, you tall tall primrose of a girl. Listen, will you let me leave you for a very few days so that I can find the house you're going to live in. Will you not be lonely ? "

" I like to have you with me always," she murmured.

He was intoxicated by so close an avowal of love from lips that were usually mute.

"We shall be married in a month," he cried. "Can you smell violets ? "

" Something sweet I smell."

But it was getting too dusky in the coppice to find these violets themselves twilight-hued, and they turned homeward across the open fields. Birds were flying to the coverts, linnets mostly in twittering companies.

"These eves of early Spring are like swords," Michael exclaimed.

"Like what ? " Lily asked, smiling at his exaggeration.

"Like swords. They seem to cut one through and through with their sharpness and sweetness."

"Oh, you mean it's cold," she said. "Take my arm."

"Well, I meant rather more than that, really," Michael laughed. But because she had offered him her arm he forgot at once how far she had been from following his thoughts.

Michael went up to London after dinner. He left Lily curled up before the fire presumably quite content to stay at Hardingham.

"Not more than a fortnight, mind," were Stella's last words.

He went to see Maurice next morning to get the benefit of his advice about possible places in which to live. Maurice was in his element.

3 X

" Of course there really are very few good places. Cheyne Walk and Grosvenor Road, the Albany, parts of Hampstead and Campden Hill, Kensington Square, one or two streets near the Regent's Canal, Adelphi Terrace, the Inns of Court and Westminster. Otherwise London is impossible. But you're living in Cheyne Walk now. Why do you want to move from there ? "

Michael made up his mind to take Maurice into his confidence. He supposed that of all his friends he would be as likely as any to be sympathetic. Maurice was delighted by his description of Lily, so much delighted, that he accepted her as a fact without wanting to know who she was or where Michael had met her.

" By Jove, I must hurry up and find my girl. But I don't think I'm desperately keen to get married yet. I vote for a house near the Canal, if we can find the right one."

That afternoon they set out.

They changed their minds and went to Hampstead first, where Maurice was very anxious to take a large Georgian house with a garden of about fifteen acres. He offered to move himself and Castleton from Grosvenor Road in order to occupy one of the floors, and he was convinced that the stable would be very useful if they wanted to start a printing-press.

" Yes, but we don't want to start a printing-press," Michael objected. " And really, Mossy, I think twenty-three bedrooms more than one servant can manage."

It was with great reluctance that Maurice gave up the idea of this house, and he was so much depressed by the prospect of considering anything less huge that he declared Hampstead was impossible, and they went off to Regent's Park.

" I don't think you're likely to find anything so good as that house," Maurice said gloomily. " In fact I know you won't. I wish I could afford to take it myself. I should, ike a shot. Castleton could be at the Temple just as soon from there."

"I don't see why he should bother about the Temple," said Michael. "That house was rather bigger."

"You'll never find another house like it," Maurice prophesied. "Look at this neighbourhood we're driving through now. Impossible to live here!"

They were in the Hampstead Road.

"I haven't any intention of doing so," Michael laughed. "But there remains the neighbourhood of the canal, the neighbourhood you originally suggested. Hampstead was an afterthought."

"Wonderful house!" Maurice sighed. "I shall always regret you didn't take it."

However, when they had paid off the cab, he became interested by the new prospect; and they wandered for a while, peering through fantastic railings at houses upon the steep banks of the canal, houses that seemed to have been stained to a sad green by the laurels planted close around them. Nothing feasible for a lodging was discovered near Regent's Park; and they crossed St. John's Wood and Maida Vale, walking on until they reached a point where at the confluence of two branches the canal became a large triangular sheet of water. Occupying the whole length of the base of this triangle and almost level with the water stood the garden of a very large square house.

"There's a curious place," said Michael. "How on earth does one get at it?"

They followed the road, which was considerably higher than the level of the canal, and found that the front door was reached by an entrance down a flight of steps.

"Ararat House," Michael read.

"Flat to let," Maurice read.

"I think this looks rather promising," said Michael.

It was an extraordinary pile, built in some Palladian

nightmare. A portico of dull crimson columns ran round three sides of the house, under a frieze of bearded masks. The windows were all very large, and so irregularly placed as completely to destroy the classic illusion. The stucco had been painted a colour that was neither pink nor cream nor buff, but a mixture of all three ; and every bit of space left by the windows was filled with banderoles of illegible inscriptions and with plaster garlands, horns, lyres, urns and Grecian helmets. There must have been half an acre of garden round it, a wilderness of shrubs and rank grass with here and there a dislustred conservatory. The house would have seemed uninhabitable save for the announcement of the flat to be let, which was painted on a board roped to one of the columns.

They descended the steps and pressed a bell marked Housekeeper. Yes, there was a flat to let on the ground-floor, in fact the whole of the ground-floor with the exception of this part of the hall and the rooms on either side. The housekeeper threw her apron over her shoulder like a plaid and unlocked a door in a wooden partition, that divided the flat called Number One from the rest of Ararat House.

They passed through and examined the two gaunt bed-rooms : one of them had an alcove, which pleased Michael very much. He decided that without much difficulty it could be made to resemble a Carpaccio interior. The dining-room was decorated with Spanish leather, and must have been very brilliantly lit by the late tenants, for every-where from the ceiling and walls electric wires protruded like asps. There was also a murky kitchen ; and finally the housekeeper led the way through double doors into the drawing-room.

As soon as he had stepped inside, Michael was sure that he and Lily must live here.

It was a room that recalled at the first glance one of those

gigantic saloons in ancient Venetian palaces ; but as he looked
about him he decided that any assignment in known
topography was absurd. It was a room at once for Werther,
for Taglioni, for the nocturnes of Chopin and the cameos —
of Théophile Gautier. Beckford might have filled it with —
orient gewgaws ; Barbey d'Aurevilly could have strutted —
here ; and in a corner Villiers de l'Isle Adam might have sat —
fiercely. The room was a tatterdemalion rococo barbarized
more completely by gothic embellishments that nevertheless gave it the atmosphere of the fantasts with whom —
Michael had identified it.

"But this is like a scene in a pantomime," Maurice
exclaimed.

It was indeed like a scene in a pantomime, and a pro-
scenium was wanted to frame suitably the effect of those
fluted pillars that supported the ceiling with their groined —
arches. The traceries of the latter were gilded, and the —
spaces between were painted with florid groups of nymphs
and cornucopias. At either end of the room were large
fireplaces fructuated with marble pears and melons, and the
floor was a parquet of black and yellow lozenges.

"It's hideous," Maurice exclaimed.

The housekeeper stood aside, watching impersonally.

"Hideous but rather fascinating," Michael said. "Look
at the queer melancholy light, and look at the view."

It was after all the view which gave the character of
romance to the room. Eight French windows, whose
shutters one by one the housekeeper had opened while
they were talking, admitted a light that was much subdued
by the sprays of glossy evergreen outside. Seen through
their leaves the garden appeared to be a green twilight
in which the statues and baskets of chipped and discoloured
stone had an air of overthrown magnificence. The housekeeper opened one of the windows, and they walked out into
the wilderness, where ferns were growing on rockeries of

slag and old tree-stumps ; where the paths were smeared with bright green slime, with moss and sodden vegetation. They came to a wider path running by the bank of the canal ; and pausing here, they pondered the sheet of dead water where two swans were gliding slowly round an islet and where the reflections of the houses beyond lay still and deep everywhere along the edge. The distant cries of London floated sharply down the air ; smuts were falling perpetually ; the bitter March air diffused in a dull sparkle tasted of the city's breath :: the circling of the swans round their islet made everything else the more immotionable.....

"In summer this will be wonderful," Michael predicted.

"On summer nights those swans will be swimming about among the stars," Maurice said.

"Except that they'll probably have retired to bed," Michael pointed out.

"I wonder if they build their nests on chimney-tops like storks," Maurice laughed.

"Let's ask the housekeeper," Michael said solemnly.

They went back into the drawing-room, and more than ever did it seem exactly the room one would expect to enter after pondering that dead water without.

"Who lives in the other flats ?" Michael enquired of the housekeeper.

"There's four others," she began. "Up above there's Colonel and Mrs. . . ."

"I see," Michael interrupted. "Just ordinary people. Do they ever go out ? Or do they sit and peer at the water all day from behind strange curtains ?"

The housekeeper stared at him.

"They play tennis and croquet a good deal in the summer, sir. The courts is on the other side of the house. Mr. Gartside is the gentleman to see about the flat."

She gave Michael the address, and that afternoon he settled to take Number One, Ararat House.

.! " It absolutely was made to set her off," he told Maurice.
" You wait till I've furnished it as it ought to be furnished."

¡ ." And we'll have amazing fêtes aqueuses in the summer," —
Maurice declared. " We'll buy a barge and—why of course
—the canal flows into the Thames at Grosvenor Road."

· ." Underground—like the Styx," said Michael nodding.

. ." Of course it's going to be wonderful. We must never
·visit each other except by water."

"Like splendid dead Venetians," said Michael.

¡' The fortnight of Lily's stay at Hardingham was spent by
him and Maurice in a fever of decoration. Michael bought
oval mirrors of Venetian glass ; oblong mirrors crowned
with gilt griffins and scallops ; small round mirrors in
frames of porcelain garlanded with flowerbuds ; so many
mirrors that the room became even more mysteriously vast.
The walls were hung with brocades of gold and philamot —
and pomona green. There were slim settees the colour of —
ivory, with cushions of primrose and lemon satin, of cinna-
mon and canary citron and worn russet silks. Over the
parquet was a great grey Aubusson carpet with a design —
of monstrous roses as deep as damsons or burgundy ; and
from the ceiling hung two chandeliers of cut glass.

¡.!" You know," said Maurice seriously, " she'll have to be
very beautiful to carry this off."

. ." She is very beautiful," said Michael. " And there's
room for her to walk about here. She'll move about this
room as wonderfully as those swans upon the canal." · ·

¡· " Michael, what's happened to you ? You're becoming
as eccentric as 'me."· Maurice looked at him rather
jealously.· " And, I say, do you really want me to come with
you to King's Cross to-morrow afternoon ? "

· Michael nodded.

. ." After you've helped to gather together this room, you
deserve to see the person we've done it for." ·   · ·

"Yes, but look here. Who's going to stay in the flat

with her ? ┆ You can't leave her alone until you're married. As you told me the story, it sounded very romantic ; but if she's going to be your wife, you've got to guard her reputation."

Michael had never given Maurice more than a slight elaboration of the tale which had served for Stella ; and he thought how much more romantic Maurice would consider the affair if he knew the whole truth. He felt inclined to tell him, but he doubted his ability to keep it to himself.

"I thought of getting hold of some elderly woman," he said.

"That's all very well, but you ought to have been doing it all this time."

"You don't know anybody ?"

"I ? Great scott, no ! "

They were walking towards Chelsea, and presently Maurice had to leave him for an appointment.

"To-morrow afternoon then at King's Cross," he said, and jumped on an omnibus.

Michael walked along in a quandary. Whom on earth could he get to stay with Lily ? Would it not be better to marry at once ? But that would involve breaking his promise to Stella. If he asked Mrs. Gainsborough, it would mean Sylvia knowing where Lily was. If on the other hand he should employ a strange woman, Lily might dislike her. Could he ask Mrs. Ross to come up to town ? No, of course, that was absurd. It looked as if he would have to ask Mrs. Gainsborough. Or why not ask Sylvia herself ? In that case why establish Lily at Ararat House before they were married ? This marriage had seemed so very easy an achievement ; but slowly it was turning into an insoluble complex. He might sound Sylvia upon her attitude. It would enormously simplify everything if she would consent ; and if she consented she would, he believed, play fair with him. The longer Michael thought about it the more it

seemed the safest course to call in Sylvia's aid. He was
almost hailing a hansom to go to Tinderbox Lane, when he
realized how foolish it would be not to try to sever Lily
completely from the life she had been leading in Sylvia's
company. Not even ought he to expose her to the beaming
laxity of Mrs. Gainsborough.

Michael had reached Notting Hill Gate, and, still pondering the problem which had destroyed half the pleasure of
the enterprize, he caught sight of a Registry for servants.
Why not employ two servants, two of the automatons who
simplified life as it was simplified in Cheyne Walk ? Then
he remembered that he had forgotten to make any attempt
to equip the kitchen. Surely Lily would be able to help
with that. He entered the Registry and interviewed a
severe woman wearing glasses, who read in a sing-song the
virtues of a procession of various automatons seeking
situations as cooks and housemaids.

"What wages do you wish to give ? "

"Oh, the usual wages," Michael said. " But I rather want
these servants to-day."

He made an appointment to interview half-a-dozen after
lunch. He chose the first two that presented themselves,
and told them to come round to Ararat House. Here he
threw himself on their mercy and begged them to make a
list of what was wanted in the kitchen. They gave notice
on the spot, and Michael rushed off to the Registry again.
To the severe woman in glasses he explained the outlines
of the situation and made her promise to suit him by
to-morrow at midday. She suggested a capable housekeeper; and next morning, a hard-featured, handsome
woman very well dressed in the fashion of about 1892
arrived at Ararat House. She undertook to find someone
to help, and also to procure at once the absolute necessities
for the kitchen. Miss Harper was a great relief to Michael,
though he did not think he liked her very much ; and he

made up his mind to get rid of her, as soon as some sort of domestic comfort was perceptible. Lily would arrive about four o'clock, and he drove off to King's Cross to meet her. He felt greatly excited by the prospect of introducing her to Maurice, who for a wonder was punctually waiting for him on the platform.

Lily evidently liked Maurice, and Michael was rather disappointed when he said he could not come back with them to assist at the first entry into Ararat House. Maurice had certainly given him to understand that he was free this afternoon.

"Look in at Grosvenor Road on your way home to-night," said Maurice. "Or will you be very late?"

"Oh, no, I shan't be late," Michael answered flushing. He had a notion that Maurice was implying a suspicion of him by his invitation. It seemed as if he were testing his behaviour.

Lily liked the rooms; and although she thought the Carpaccio bedroom was a little bare, it was soon strewn with her clothes, and made thereby inhabitable.

"And of course," said Michael, "you've got to buy lots and lots of clothes this fortnight. How much do you want to spend? Two hundred—three hundred pounds?"

The idea of buying clothes on such a scale of extravagance seemed to delight her, and she kissed him, he thought almost for the first time, in mere affection without a trace of passion. Michael felt happy that he had so much money for her to spend, and he was glad that no one had been given authority to interfere with his capital. There flashed through his mind a comparison of himself with the Chevalier des Grieux, and remembering how soon that money had come to an end, he was glad that Lily would not be exposed to the temptation which had ruined Manon.

"And do you like Miss Harper?" he enquired.

"Yes, she seems all right."

They went out to dine in town, and came back about eleven to find the flat looking wonderfully settled. Michael confessed how much he had forgotten to order, but Lily talked of her dresses and took no interest in household affairs.

"I think I ought to go now," said Michael.

"Oh, no, stay a little longer."

But he would not, feeling the violent necessity to impress upon her as much as possible, during this fortnight before they were married, how important were the conventions of life, even when it was going to be lived in so strange a place as Ararat House.

"Oh, you're going now?" said Miss Harper, looking at him rather curiously.

"I shall be round in the morning. You'll finish making the lists of what you still want?"

Michael felt very deeply plunged into domestic arrangements, as he drove to Grosvenor Road.

Maurice was sitting up for him, but Castleton had gone to bed.

"Look here, old chap," Maurice began at once, "you can't possibly marry that girl."

Michael frowned:

"You too?"

"I know all about her," Maurice went on. "I've never actually met her, but I recognized her at once. Even if you did know her people five years ago, you ought to have taken care to find out what had happened in between. As a matter of fact I happen to know a man who's had an affair with her—a painter called Walker. Ronnie Walker. He's often up here. You're bound to meet him some time."

"Not at all, if I never come here again," said Michael in a cold rage.

"It's no use for you to be angry with me," said Maurice. "I should be a rotten friend, if I didn't warn you."

"Oh, go to hell," said Michael, and he marched out of the studio.

Maurice came on the landing and called, begging him to come up and not to be so hasty, but Michael paid no attention.

"So much for 422 Grosvenor Road," he said, slamming the big front door behind him. He heard Maurice calling to him from the window, but he walked on without turning his head.

It was a miserable coincidence that one of his friends should know about her. It was a disappointment, but it could not be helped. If Maurice chattered about a disastrous marriage, why, other friends would have to be dropped in the same way. After all, he had been aware from the first moment of his resolve that this sort of thing was bound to happen. It left him curiously indifferent.

A week passed. There were hundreds of daffodils blooming in the garden round Ararat House; and April bringing an unexpected halcyon was the very April of the poets whose verses haunted that great rococo room. Every day Michael went with Lily to dressmakers and worshipped her taste. Every day he bought her old pieces of jewellery, old fans or old silver, or pots of purple hyacinths. He was just conscious that it was London and the prime of the Spring; but mostly he lived in the enchantment of her presence. Often they walked up and down the still deserted garden, by the edge of the canal. The swans used to glide nearer to them, waiting for bread to be thrown; and Lily would stand with her hair in a stream of sunlight and her arms moving languidly like the necks of the birds she was feeding. Nor was she less graceful in the long luminous dusks under the young moon and the yellow evening star that were shining upon them as they walked by the edge of the water.

For a week Michael lived in a city that was become a

mere background to the swoons and fevers of love. He knew that round him houses blinked in the night and that chimney-smoke curled upwards in the morning; that people paced the streets; that there was a thunder of far-off traffic; that London was possessed by April. But the heart of life was in this room, when the candles were lit in the chandeliers and he could see a hundred Lilies in the mirrors. It seemed wrong to leave her at midnight, to leave that room so perilously golden with the golden stuffs and candle-flames. It seemed unfair to surprize Miss Harper by going away at midnight, when so easily he could have stayed. Yet every night he went away, however hard it was to leave Lily in her black dress, to leave in the mirrors those hundred Lilies that drowsily were not forbidding him to stay. Or when she stood under the portico sleepily resting in his arms, it was difficult to let her turn back alone. How close were their kisses wrapped in that velvet moonlessness. This was no London that he knew, this scented city of Spring, this tropic gloom, this mad innominate cavern that engorged them. The very stars — were melting in the water of the canal: the earth bedewed with fevers of the Spring was warm as blood: why should he forsake her each night of this week? Yet every midnight when the heavy clocks buzzed and clamoured, Michael left her, saying that May would come, and June, and another April when she would have been his a year.

.. The weather veered back in the second week of the fortnight to rawness and wet. Yet it made no difference to Michael; for he was finding these days spent with Lily so full of romance that weather was forgotten. They could not walk in the garden and watch the swans: of nothing else did the weather deprive him.

.. Two days before the marriage was to take place, Mrs. Fane arrived back from the South of France. Michael was glad to see her, for he was so deeply infatuated with Lily that his first emotion was of pleasure in the thought of being able now to bring her to see his mother, and of taking his mother to see her in Ararat House among those chandeliers and mirrors.

"Why didn't you wire me to say you were coming?" he asked.

"I came because Stella wrote to me."

Michael frowned, and his mother went on:

"It wasn't very thoughtful of you to let me know about your marriage through her. I think you might have managed to write to me about it yourself."

Michael had been so much wrapped up in his arrangements, and apart from them so utterly engrossed in his secluded life with Lily during the past ten days, that it came upon him with a shock to realize that his mother might be justified in thinking that he had treated her very inconsiderately.

"I'm sorry. It was wrong of me," he admitted. "But life has been such a whirl lately that I've somehow taken for granted the obvious courtesies. Besides, Stella was so very unfair to Lily that it rather choked me off taking anybody else into my confidence. And, mother, why do you begin on the subject at once, before you've even taken your things off?"

She flung back her furs and regarded him tragically.

"Michael, how can you dare to think of such trivialities when you are standing at the edge of this terrible step?"

"Oh, I think I'm perfectly level-headed," he said, "even on the brink of disaster."

"Such a dreadful journey from Cannes. I wish I'd come back in March as I meant to. But Mrs. Carruthers was ill, and I couldn't very well leave her. She's always nervous in lifts, and hates the central-heating. I did not sleep a moment, and a most objectionable couple of Germans in the next compartment of the wagons-lits used all the water in the washing-place. So very annoying, for one never expects foreigners to think about washing. Oh, yes, a dreadful night and all because of you, and now you ask most cruelly why I don't take my things off.",

"There wasn't any need for you to worry yourself," he said hotly. "Stella had no business to scare you with her prejudices."

"Prejudices!" his mother repeated. "Prejudice is a very mild word for what she feels about this dreadful girl you want to marry."

"But it is prejudice," Michael insisted. "She knows nothing against her."

"She knows a great deal."

"How?" he demanded incredulously.

"You'd better read her letter to me. And I really must go and take off these furs. It's stifling in London. So very much hotter than the Riviera."

Mrs. Fane left him with Stella's letter.

LONG'S HOTEL.

April 9.

Darling Mother,

When you get this you must come at once to London. You are the only person who can save Michael from marrying the most impossible creature imaginable. He had a stupid love-affair with her, when he was eighteen; and I think she treated him badly even then—I remember his being very upset about it in the summer before my first concert. Apparently he re-discovered her this winter, and for some reason or other wants to marry her now. He brought her down to Hardingham, and I saw then that she was a minx. Alan remembers her mother as a dreadful woman who tried to make love to him. Imagine Alan at eighteen being pursued.

Of course I tackled Michael about her, and we had rather a row about it. We kept her at Hardingham for a month (a fort-night by herself), and we were bored to death by her. She had nothing to say, and nothing to do except look at herself in the glass. I had declared war on the marriage from the moment she left, but I had only a fortnight to stop it. I was rather in a difficulty because I knew nothing definite against her, though I was sure that if she wasn't a bad ot already, she would be later on. I wrote first of all to Maurice Avery, who told me that she'd had a not at all reputable affair with a painter friend of his. It seems, however, that he had already spoken to Michael about this and that Michael walked out of the house in a rage. Then I came up to town with Alan and saw Wedderburn, who knew nothing about her and hadn't seen Michael for months. Then we got hold of Lonsdale. He has apparently met her at Covent Garden, and I'm perfectly sure that he has actually been away with her himself. Though of course he was much too polite to tell me so. He was absolutely horrified when he heard about her and Michael. I asked him to tell Michael anything he knew against her, but he didn't see how he could. He said he wouldn't have the heart. I told him it was his duty, but he said he wouldn't be able to bear the sight of Michael's face when he told him. Of course the poor darling knows nothing about her. You must come at once to London and talk to him yourself. You've no time to lose. I'll meet you if you send me a wire. I've no influence over Michael any more. You're the only person who can stop it. He's so sweet about her. She's rather lovely to look at, I must say. Lots of love from Alan and from me.

> Your loving
> Stella.

Michael was touched by Lonsdale's attitude. It showed, he thought, an exquisite sensitiveness, and he was grateful for it. Stella had certainly been very active: but he had foreseen all of this. Nothing was going to alter his determination. He waited gloomily for his mother to come down. Of all antagonists she would be the hardest to combat in argu-

ment, because he was debarred from referring to so much
that had weighed heavily with him in his decision. His
mother was upstairs such a very short time that Michael
realized with a smile how deeply she must have been moved.
Nothing but this marriage of his had ever brought her downstairs so rapidly from taking off her things.

" Have you read Stella's letter ? " she asked.

- He nodded.

" Well, of course you see that the whole business must be
stopped at once. It's dreadful for you to hear all these
things, and I know you must be suffering, dearest boy ; but
you ought to be obliged to Stella and not resent her interference."

" I see that you feel bound to apologize for her," Michael
observed.

" Now, that is so bitter."

He shrugged his shoulders.

" I feel rather bitter that she should come charging up
to town to find out things I know already."

" Michael ! You knew about Lonsdale ? "

" I didn't know about him in particular, but I knew that
there had been people. That's one of the reasons I'm going
to marry her."

" But you'll lose all your friends. It would be impossible
for you to go on knowing Lonsdale for instance."

" Marriage seems to destroy friendships in any case,"
Michael said. " You couldn't have a better example of that
than Stella and Alan. I daresay I shall be able to make new
friends."

" But, darling boy," she said pleadingly, " your position
will be so terribly ambiguous. Here you are with everything
that you can possibly want, with any career you choose open
to you. And you let yourself be dragged down by this
horrible creature ! "

" Mother, believe me, you're getting a very distorted idea

3 Y

of Lily. She's beautiful, you know; and if she's not so clever as Stella, I'm rather glad of it. I don't think I want a clever wife. At any rate she hasn't committed the sin of being common. She won't disgrace you outwardly, and if Stella hadn't gone round raking up all this abominable information about her, you would have liked her very much."

"My dearest boy, you are very young, but you surely aren't too young to know that it's impossible to marry a woman whose past is not without reproach."

"But, mother, you . . ." he stopped himself abruptly, and looked out of the window in embarrassment. Yet his mother seemed quite unconscious that she was using a weapon which could be turned against herself.

"Will nothing persuade you? Oh, why did Dick Prescott kill himself? I knew at the time that something like this would happen. You won't marry her, you won't, will you?"

"Yes, mother. I'm going to," he said coldly.

"But why so impetuously?" she asked. "Why won't you wait a little time?"

"There's no object in waiting while Stella rakes up a few more facts."

"If only your father were alive!" she exclaimed. "It would have shocked him so inexpressibly."

"He felt so strongly the unwisdom of marriage, didn't he?" Michael said, and wished he could have bitten his tongue out.

She had risen from her chair, and seemed to tower above him in tragical and heroic dignity of reproach:

"I could never have believed you would say such a thing to me."

"I'm awfully sorry," he murmured. "It was inexcusable."

"Michael," she pleaded, coming to him sorrowfully, "won't you give up this marriage?"

He was touched by her manner so gently despairing after his sneer.

" Mother, I must keep faith with myself."

" Only with yourself ? Then she doesn't care for you ? And you're not thinking of *her* ? "

" Of course she cares for me."

" But she'd get over it almost at once ? "

" Perhaps," he admitted.

" Do you trust her ? Do you believe she will be able to be a good woman ? "

" That will be my look-out," he said impatiently. " If she fails, it will be my fault. It's always the man's fault. Always."

" Very well," said his mother resignedly. " I can say no more, can I ? You must do as you like."

The sudden withdrawal of her opposition softened him as nothing else would have done. He compared the sweetness of her resignation with his own sneer of a minute ago. He felt anxious to do something that would show his penitence. " Mother, I hate to wound you. But I must be true to what I have worked out for myself. I must marry Lily. Apart from a mad love I have for her, there is a deeper cause, a reason that's bound up with my whole theory of behaviour, my whole attitude towards existence. I could not back out of this marriage."

" Is all your chivalry to be devoted to the service of Lily ? " she asked.

He felt grateful to her for the name. When his mother no longer called her ' this girl,' half his resentment fled. The situation concerned the happiness of human beings again ; there were no longer prejudices or abstractions of morality to obscure it.

" Not at all, mother. I would do anything for you."

" Except not marry her."

" That wouldn't be a sacrifice worth making," he argued.

" Because if I did that I should destroy myself to myself, and what was left of me wouldn't be a complete Michael. It wouldn't be your son."

" Will you postpone your marriage, say for three months?"

He hesitated. How could he refuse her this ?

" Not merely for your own sake," she urged ; " but for all our sakes. We shall all see things more clearly and pleasantly, perhaps, in three months' time."

He was conquered by the implication of justice for Lily.

" I won't marry her for three months," he promised.

" And you know, darling boy, the dreadful thing is that I very nearly missed the train owing to the idiocy of the head-porter at the hotel."

She was smiling through her tears, and very soon she became her stately self again.

Michael went at once to Ararat House, and told Lily that he had promised his mother to put off their marriage for three months. She pouted over her frocks.

" I wish you'd settled that before. What good will all these dresses be now ? "

" You shall have as many more as you want. But will you be happy here without me ? "

" Without you ? Why are you going away ? "

" Because I must, Lily. Because . . . oh, dearest girl, can't you see that I'm too passionately in love with you to be able to see you every day and every night as I have been all this fortnight."

" If you want to go away, of course you must, but I shall be rather dull, shan't I ? "

" And shan't I ? " he asked.

She looked at him.

" Perhaps."

" I shall write every day to you and you must write to me."

He held her close and kissed her. Then he hurried away.

Now that he had made the sacrifice to please his mother

he was angry with himself for having done so. He felt that during this coming time of trial he could not bear to see either his mother or Stella. He must be married and fulfil his destiny, and after that all would be well. He was enraged with his weakness, wondering where he could go to avoid the people who had brought it about.

Suddenly Michael thought he would like to see Clere Abbey again, and he turned into Paddington Station to find out if there were a train that would take him down into Berkshire at once.

Chapter VIII : *Seeds of Pomegranate*

IT was almost dark when Michael reached the little station at the foot of the Downs. He was half inclined to put up at the village inn and arrive at the Abbey in the morning; but he was feeling depressed by the alteration of his plans, and longed to withdraw immediately into the monastic peace. He had bought what he needed for the couple of nights before any luggage could reach him, and he thought that with so little to carry he might as well walk the six miles to the Abbey. He asked when the moon would be up.

"Oh, not much before half-past nine, sir," the porter said.

Michael suddenly remembered that to-morrow was Easter Sunday and, thinking it would be as well not to arrive too late in case there should be a number of guests, he managed to get hold of a cart. The wind blew very freshly as they slowly climbed the Downs, and the man who was driving him was very voluble on the subject of the large additions which had been made to the Abbey buildings during the last few years.

"They've put up a grand sort of a lodge—Gatehouse, so some do call it. A bit after the style of the Tower of London, I've heard some say."

Michael was glad to think that Dom Cuthbert's plans seemed to be coming to perfection in their course. How long was it since he and Chator were here? Eight or nine years; now Chator was a priest, and himself had done nothing.

The Abbey Gatehouse was majestic in the darkness, and the driver pealed the great bell with a portentous clangour. Michael recognized the pock-marked brother who opened the door ; but he could not remember his name. He felt it would be rather absurd to ask the monk if he recognized him by this wavering lanthorn-light.

" Is the Reverend—is Dom Cuthbert at the Abbey now ? " he asked. " You don't remember me, I expect ? Michael Fane. I stayed here one Autumn eight or nine years ago."

The monk held up the lanthorn and stared at him.

" The Reverend Father is in the Guest Room now," said Brother Ambrose. Michael had suddenly recalled his name.

" Do you think I shall be able to stay here to-night ? Or have you a lot of guests for Easter ? "

" We can always find room," said Brother Ambrose. Michael dismissed his driver and followed the monk along the drive.

Dom Cuthbert knew him at once and seemed very glad that he had come to the Abbey.

" You can have a cell in the Gatehouse. Our new Gate-house. It's copied from the one at Cerne Abbas in Dorset-shire. Very beautiful. Very beautiful."

Michael was introduced to the three or four guests, all types of ecclesiastical laymen, who had been talking with the Abbot. The Compline bell rang almost at once, and the Office was still held in the little chapel of mud and laths built by the hands of the monks.

> *Keep me as the apple of an eye.*
> *Hide me in the shadow of thy wing.*

Here was worship unhampered by problems of social behaviour : here was peace.

Lying awake that night in his cell ; watching the lattices very luminous in the moonlight ; hearing the April wind in the hazel coppice, Michael tried to reach a perspective of his life these nine months since Oxford, but sleep came to him and pacified all confusions. He went to Mass next morning, but did not make his Communion, because he had a feeling that he could only have done so under false pretences. There was no reason why he should have felt thus, he assured himself; but this morning there had fallen upon him at the moment a dismaying chill. He went for a walk on the Downs, over the great green spaces that marked no season save in the change of the small flowers blowing in their turf. He wondered if he would be able to find the stones he had erected that July day when he first came here with Chator. He found what, as far as he could remember, was the place; and he also found a group of stones that might have been the ruins of his little monument. More remarkable than old stones now seemed to him a Pasque anemone coloured a sharp cold violet. It curiously reminded him of the evening in March when he had walked with Lily in the wood at Hardingham.

The peace of last night vanished in a dread of the future : Michael's partial surrender to his mother cut at his destiny with ominous stroke. He was in a turmoil of uncertainty, and afraid to find himself out here on these Downs with so little achieved behind him in the city. He hurried back to the Abbey and wrote a wild letter to Lily, declaring his sorrow for leaving her, urging her to be patient, protesting a feverish adoration. He wrote also to Miss Harper a hundred directions for Lily's entertainment while he was away. He wrote to Nigel Stewart begging him to look after Barnes. All the time he had a sense of being pursued and haunted; an intolerable idea that he was the quarry of an evil chase. He could not stay at the Abbey any longer : he was being rejected by the spirit of the place.

Dom Cuthbert was disappointed when he said he must go.

" Stay at least to-night," he urged, and Michael gave way.

He did not sleep at all that night. The alabaster image of the Blessed Virgin kept turning to a paper thing, kept nodding at him like a zany. He seemed to hear the Gate- . house bell clanging hour after hour. He felt more deeply sunk in darkness than ever in Leppard Street. At daybreak he dressed and fled through the woods, trampling under foot the primroses limp with dew. He hurried faster and faster across the Downs; and when the sun was up, he was standing on the platform of the railway station. To-day he ought to have married Lily.

At Paddington, notwithstanding all that he had suffered in the parting, unaccountably to himself he did not want to turn in the direction of Ararat House. It puzzled him that he should drive so calmly to Cheyne Walk.

" I think my temperature must have been a point or two up last night," was the explanation he gave himself of what already seemed mere sleeplessness.

Michael found his mother very much worried by his disappearance; she had assumed that he had broken his promise. He consoled her, but excused himself from staying with her in town.

" You mustn't ask too much of me," he said.

" No, no, dearest boy, I'm glad for you to go away, but where will you go ? "

He thought he would pay an overdue visit to Cobble Place.

Mrs. Ross and Mrs. Carthew were delighted to see him, and he felt as he always felt at Cobble Place the persistent tranquillity which not the greatest inquietude of spirit could long withstand. It was now nearly three years since he had been here, and he was surprized to see how very old Mrs. Carthew had grown in that time. This and the active presence of Kenneth, now a jolly boy of nine, were the only changes in the aspect of the household. Michael enjoyed himself in firing Kenneth with a passion for birds' eggs and butterflies, and they went long walks together and made expeditions in the canoe.

Yet every day when Michael sat down to write to Lily, he almost wrote to say he was coming to London as soon as his letter. Her letters to him written in a sprawling girlish hand were always very much alike.

1 Ararat House,

Island Road, W.

My dear,

Come back soon. I'm getting bored. Mrs. Harper isn't bad. Can't write a long letter because this nib is awful. Kisses.

Your loving

Lily.

This would stand for any of them.

May month had come in : Michael and Kenneth were finding whitethroats' nests in the nettle-beds of the paddock, before a word to Mrs. Ross was said about the marriage.

" Stella has written to me about it," she told him.

They were sitting in the straggling wind-frayed orchard beyond the stream : lambs were leaping : apple-blossom stippled the grass : Kenneth was chasing Orange Tips up the slope towards Grogg's Folly.

" Stella has been very busy all round," said Michael. " I suppose according to her I'm going to marry an impossible creature. Creature is as far as she usually gets in particular description of Lily."

" She certainly wasn't very complimentary about your choice," Mrs. Ross admitted.

" I wish somebody could understand that it doesn't necessarily mean that I'm mad because I'm going to marry a beautiful girl who isn't very clever."

" But I gathered from Stella," Mrs. Ross said, " that her past . . . Michael, you must be very tolerant of me if I upset you, because we happen to be sitting just where I was stupid and unsympathetic once before. You see what an impression that made on me. I actually remember the very place."

" She probably has done things in the past," said Michael. " But she's scarcely twenty-three yet, and I love her. Her past becomes a trifle. Besides, I was in love with her six years ago, and I—well, six years ago I was rather thoughtless very often. I don't want you to think that I'm going to marry her now from any sense of duty. I love her. At the same time when people argue that she's not the correct young Miss they apparently expect me to marry, I'm left unmoved. Pasts belong to men as well as to women."

Mrs. Ross nodded slowly. Kenneth came rushing up, shouting that he had caught a frightfully rare butterfly. Michael looked at it :

" A female Orange Tip," was the verdict.

" But isn't that frightfully rare ? "

Michael shook his head.

" No rarer than the males ; but you don't notice them, that's all."

Kenneth retired to find some more.

" And you're sure you'll be happy with her ? " Mrs. Ross asked.

" As sure as I am that I shall be happy with anybody. I ought to be married to her by now. This delay that I've so weakly allowed isn't going to effect much."

Michael sighed. He had meant to be in Provence this month of May.

" But the delay can't do any harm," Mrs. Ross pointed out. " At any rate it will enable you to feel more sure of yourself, and more sure of her too."

" I don't know," said Michael doubtfully. " My theory has always been that if a thing's worth doing at all, it's worth doing at once."

"And after you're married," she asked, "what are you going to do? Just lead a lazy life?"

"Oh, no, I suppose I shall find some occupation that will keep me out of mischief."

"That sounds a little cynical. Ah, well, I suppose it is a disappointment to me."

"What's a disappointment?"

"I've hoped and prayed so much lately that you would have a vocation. . . ."

"A priest," he interrupted quickly. "It's no good, Mrs. Ross. I have thought of being one, but I'm always put off by the professional side of it. And there are ways of doing what a priest does without being one."

"Of course, I can't agree with you there," she said.

"Well, apart from the sacraments I mean. Lately I've seen something of the underworld, and I shall think of some way of being useful down there. Already I believe I've done a bit."

They talked of the problems of the underworld, and Michael was encouraged by what he fancied was a much greater breadth in her point of view nowadays to speak of things that formerly would have made her grey eyes harden in fastidious disapproval.

"I feel happier about you since this talk," she said. "As long as you won't be content to let your great gift of humanity be wasted, as long as you won't be content to think that in marrying your Lily you have done with all your obligations."

"Oh, no, I shan't feel that. In fact I shall be all the more anxious to justify myself."

Kenneth came back to importune Michael for a walk as far as Grogg's Folly.

"It's such fun for Kenneth to have you here," Mrs. Ross exclaimed. "I've never seen him so boisterously happy."

" I used to enjoy myself here just as much as he does,"
said Michael. " Though perhaps I didn't show it. I
always think of myself as rather a dreary little beast when
I was a kid."

" On the contrary you were a most attractive boy, such
a wide-eyed little boy," said Mrs. Ross softly looking back
into time. " I've seldom seen you so happy as just before
I blew out your candle the first night of your first stay
here."

" I say, do come up the hill," interrupted Kenneth
despairingly.

" A thousand apologies, my lord," said Michael. " We'll
go now."

They did not stop until they reached the tower on the
summit.

" When I was your age," Michael told him, " I used to
think that I could see the whole of England from here."

" Could you really ? " said Kenneth in admiration.
" Could you see any of France too ? "

" I expect so," Michael answered. " I expect really I
thought I could see the whole world. Kenneth, what are
you going to be when you grow up ? A soldier ? "

" Yes, if I can—or what is a philosopher ? "

" A philosopher philosophizes."

" Does he really ? Is that a difficult thing to do, to
philosopherize ? "

" Yes, it's almost harder to do than to pronounce."

Soon they were tearing down the hill, frightening the
larks to right and left of their progress.

The weather grew warmer every day, and at last
Mrs. Carthew came out in a wheel-chair to see the long-
spurred columbines, claret and gold, watchet, rose and white. —

" Really quite a display," she said to Michael. " And
so you're to get married ? "

He nodded.

"What for?" the old lady demanded, looking at him over her spectacles.

"Well, principally because I want to," Michael answered after a short pause.

"The best reason," she agreed. "But in your case insufficient, and I'll tell you why—you aren't old enough yet to know what you do want."

"Twenty-three," Michael reminded her.

"Twenty-fiddlesticks," she snapped. "And isn't there a good deal of opposition?"

"A good deal."

"And no doubt you feel a fine romantical heroical young fellow?"

"Not particularly."

"Well, I'm not going to argue against your marrying her," said Mrs. Carthew. "Because I know quite well that the more I proved you to be wrong, the more you'd be determined to prove *I* was. But I can give you advice about marriage, because I've been married and you haven't. Is she dark? If she's dark, be very cold for a year, and if she doesn't leave you in that time, she'll adore you for the rest of her life."

"But she's fair," said Michael. "Very fair indeed."

"Then beat her. Not actually, of course, but beat her figuratively for a year. If you don't, she'll either be a shrew or a whiner. Both impossible to live with."

"Which did Captain Carthew do to you?" asked Michael twinkling.

"Neither, I ruled him with a rod of iron."

"But do you think I'm wise to wait like this before marrying her?" Michael asked.

"There's no wisdom in waiting to do an unwise thing."

"You're so sure it is unwise?"

"All marriages are unwise," said Mrs. Carthew sharply. "That's why everybody gets married. For most people it is the only imprudence they have an opportunity of committing. After that they're permanently cured of rashness, and settle down. There are exceptions of course : they take to drink. I must say I'm greatly pleased with these long-spurred columbines."

Michael thought she had finished the discussion of his marriage, but suddenly she said :

" I thought I told you to come and see me when you went down from Oxford."

" I ought to have come," Michael agreed rather humbly. He always felt inclined to propitiate the old lady.

" Here we have the lamentable result. Marriage at twenty-three."

" Alan married at twenty-three," he pointed out.

" Two fools don't make a wise man," said Mrs. Carthew.

" He's very happy."

" He would be satisfied with much less than you, and he has married a delightful girl."

" I'm going to marry a delightful girl."

The old lady made no reply. Nor did she comment again upon his prospect of happiness.

In mid May after a visit of nearly a month Michael left Cobble Place and went to stay at Plashers Mead. Guy Hazlewood was the only friend he still had who could not possibly have come into contact with Lily or her former surroundings. Moreover Guy was deep in love himself and he had been very sympathetic when he wrote to Michael about his engagement.

" Do I intrude upon your May idyll ? " Michael asked.

" My dear chap, don't be so absurd. But why aren't you married ? You're as bad as me."

" Why aren't *you* married ? "

" Oh, I don't know," Guy sighed. " Everybody seems to be conspiring to put it off."

They were sitting in Guy's green library. The windows

wide open let in across the sound of the burbling stream the warm air of the lucid May night, where bats and owls and evejars flew across the face of the decrescent moon.

"It's this dreamy country in which you live," said Michael.

"What about you? You've let people put off your marriage."

"Only for another two months," Michael explained.

"You see I'm down to £150 a year now," Guy muttered. "I can't marry on that, and I can't leave this place, and her people can't afford to make her an allowance. They think I ought to go away and work at journalism. However, I'm not going to worry you with my troubles."

Guy was a good deal with Pauline every day: Michael wrote long letters to Lily and read poetry.

"Browning?" asked Guy one afternoon, looking over Michael's shoulder.

"Yes, The Statue and The Bust."

"Oh, don't remind me of that poem. It haunts me," Guy declared.

A week passed. There was no moon now, and the nights grew warmer. It was weather to make lovers happy, but Guy seemed worried. He would not come for walks with Michael through the dark and scented water-meadows, and Michael used to think that often at night he was meeting Pauline. It made him jealous to imagine them lost in this amaranthine profundity. They were happy now, if through all their lives they should never be happy again. Yet Guy was obviously fretted: he was getting spoilt by good fortune. "And I have had about a fortnight of incomplete happiness," Michael said to himself. Supposing that a calamity fell upon him during this delay. He would never cease to regret his weakness in granting his mother's request: he would hate Stella for having interfered: his life would be miserable for ever. Yet what calamity did he fear ? In a sudden apprehension he struck a match and read her last letter.

1 ARARAT HOUSE,
ISLAND ROAD, W.

My dear,
It's getting awfully dull in London. Miss Harper asked me to call her " Mabel." Rather cheek, I thought, don't you think so ? But she's really awfully decent. I can't write a long letter because we're going to the Palace. I say, do buck up and come back to London, I'm getting bored. Love and kisses.
Lily.
What's the good of writing " kisses " ?

What indeed was the good of writing 'kisses'? Michael thought, as the match fizzed out in the dewy grass at his feet. It was not fair to treat Lily like this. He had captured her from life with Sylvia, because he had meant to marry her at once. Now he had left her alone in that flat with a woman he did not know at all. Whatever people might say against Lily, she was very patient and trustful. "She must love me a good deal," Michael said. "Or she wouldn't stand this casual treatment."

Pauline came to tea next day with her sisters Margaret and Monica. Michael had an idea that she did not like him very much. She talked shyly and breathlessly to him ; and he, embarrassed by her shyness, answered in monosyllables.

"Pauline is rather jealous of you," said Guy that evening, as they sat in the library.

" Jealous of me ? " Michael was amazed.

" She has some fantastic idea that you don't approve of our engagement. Of course I told her what nonsense she was thinking ; but she vowed that this afternoon you

3 z

showed quite plainly your disapproval of her. She insists that you are very cold and severe."

"I'm afraid I was very dull," Michael confessed apologetically. "But I was really envying you and her for being together in May."

"Together!" Guy repeated. "It's the object of everyone in Wychford to keep us apart!"

"Do tell her I'm not cold," Michael begged. "And say how lovely I think her; for really, Guy, she is very lovely and strange. She is a fairy's child."

"She is, she is," Guy said. "Sometimes I'm nearly off my head with the sense of responsibility I have for her happiness. I wonder and wonder until I'm nearly crazed."

"I'm feeling responsible just now about Lily. I've never told you, Guy, but you may hear from other people —that I've made what is called a mésalliance. Of course, Lily has been . . ." He stumbled. He could find no words that would not humiliate himself and her. "Guy, come up. with me to-morrow and meet her. It's not fair to leave her like this," he suddenly proclaimed.

"I don't think I can come away."

"Oh, yes, you can. Of course. You must," Michael urged.

"Pauline will be more jealous of you than ever, if I do."

"For one night," Michael pleaded. "I must see her. And you must meet her. Everyone has been so rotten about her, and Guy, you'll appreciate her. I won't bore you by describing her. You must meet her to-morrow. And the rooms in Ararat House. By Jove, you'll think them wonderful. You should see her in candlelight among the mirrors. Pauline won't mind your coming away with me for a night. We'll stay at Cheyne Walk."

"Well, as a matter of fact, I'm rather hard up just now . . ."

"Oh, what rot. This is my expedition. And when

you've seen her, you must talk to my mother about her. She's so prejudiced against Lily. You will come, won't you ? "

Guy nodded a promise, and Michael went off to bed on the excitement of to-morrow's joy.

Guy would not start before the afternoon, and Michael spent the morning under a willow beside the river. It was good to lie staring up at the boughs, and know that every fleecy cloud going by was a cloud nearer to his seeing Lily again.

Michael and Guy arrived at Paddington about five o'clock.

" We'll go straight round from here and surprize her," Michael said, laughing with excitement, as they got into a taxi. " She'll have had a letter from me this morning in which I was lamenting not seeing her for six weeks. My gad, supposing she isn't in ! Oh, well, we can wait. You'll love the room, and we'll all three sit out in the garden to-night, and you'll tell me as we walk home to Chelsea what you think of her. Guy, you've absolutely got to like her. And if you don't . . . oh, but you will. It isn't everybody who can appreciate beauty like hers. And there's an extra-ordinary subtlety about her. Of course she isn't at all subtle. She's simple. In fact that's one of the things Stella has got against her. What I call simplicity and absence of straining for effect Stella calls stupidity. My own belief is that you'll be quite content to look at her and not care whether she talks or not. I tell you she's like a Piero della Francesca angel. Cheer up, Guy. Why are you looking so depressed ? "

" Oh, I don't know," said Guy. " I'm thinking what a lucky chap you are. What's a little family opposition when you know you're going to be able to do what you want ? Who can stop you ? You're independent and you're in love."

" Of course they can't stop me," Michael cried, jumping up and down on the cushions of the taxi in his excitement. " Guy, you're great ! You really are. You're the only person who's seen the advantage of going right ahead. But don't look so sad yourself. You'll marry your Pauline."

" Yes, in about four years," Guy sighed.

" Oh, no, no, in about four months. Will Pauline like Lily ? She won't be jealous of me when I'm married, will she ? "

" No, but I think I shall be," Guy laughed.

" Laugh, you old devil, laugh," Michael shouted. " Here we are. Did you ever see such a house ? It hasn't quite the austerity of Plashers Mead, has it ? "

" It looks rather fun," Guy commented.

" You know," Michael said solemnly, pausing for a moment at the head of the steps going down to the front door. " You know, Guy, I believe that you'll be able to per- suade my mother to withdraw all her opposition to-night. I believe I'm going to marry Lily this week. And I shall be so glad—Guy, you don't know how glad I shall be."

He ran hurriedly down the steps and had pressed the bell of Number One before Guy had entered the main door.

" I say, you know, it will be really terrible if she's out after all my boasting," said Michael. " And Miss Harper too—that's the housekeeper—my housekeeper, you know. If they're both out, we'll have to go round and wait in the garden until they come in. Hark, there's somebody coming."

The door opened and Michael hurried in.

" Hullo, good afternoon, Miss Harper. You didn't ex- pect to see me, eh ? I've brought a friend. Is Miss Haden in the big room ? "

" Miss Haden is out, Mr. Fane," said the housekeeper.

" What's the matter ?   You're looking rather upset."

" Am I, Mr. Fane ? " she asked blankly.   " Am I ?   Oh, no, I'm very well.   Oh, yes, very well.   It's the funny light, I expect, Mr. Fane."

She seemed to be choking out all her words, and Michael looked at her sharply.

" Well, we'll wait in the big room."

" It's rather untidy.   You see, we—I wasn't expecting you, Mr. Fane."

" That's all right," said Michael.   " Hulloa . . . I say, Guy, go on into that room ahead.   I'll be with you in a minute."

Guy mistook the direction and turned the handle of Lily's bedroom door.

" No, no," Michael called.   " The double doors opposite."

" My mistake," said Guy cheerfully.   " But don't worry : the other door was locked.   So if you've got a Bluebeard's Closet, I've done no harm."

He disappeared into the big room, and the moment he was inside Michael turned fiercely to Miss Harper.

" Who's is this hat ? " he demanded, snatching it up.

" Hat ?   What hat ? " she choked out.

" Why is the door of her bedroom locked ?   Why is it locked—locked ? "

The stillness of the crepuscular hall seemed to palpitate with the woman's breath.

" Miss Haden must have locked it when she went out," she stammered.

" Is that the truth ? "   Michael demanded.   " It's not the truth.   It's a lie.   You wouldn't be panting like a fish in a basket, unless there was something wrong.   I'll break the door in."

" No, Mr. Fane, don't do that," the woman groaned out in a cracked expostulation.   " This is the first time since you've been away.   And it was an old friend."

"How dare you tell me anything about him ? Guy ! Guy ! "

Michael rushed into the big room and dragged Guy out.

"Come away, come away, come away. I've been sold."

"If you'd only listen a moment. I could——" Miss Harper began.

Michael pushed her out of their path.

"What on earth is it ? " Guy asked.

"Come on, don't hang about in this hell of a house. Come on, Guy."

Michael had flung the door back to slam into Miss Harper's face and, seizing Guy by the wrist, he dragged him up the steps, and had started to run down the road, when Guy shouted :

"Michael, the taxi ! The taxi's waiting with our bags."

"Oh, very well, in a taxi then, a taxi if you like," Michael chattered, and he plunged into it.

"Where to ? " the driver asked.

"Cheyne Walk. But drive quickly. Don't hang about up and down this road."

The driver looked round with an expression of injured dignity, shook his head in exclamation and drove off.

"What on earth has happened ? " Guy asked. "And why on earth are you holding a top-hat ? "

Michael burst into laughter.

"So I am. Look at it. A top-hat. I say, Guy, did you ever hear of anyone being cut out by a top-hat, cuckolded by a top-hat ? We'll present it to the driver. Driver ! Do you want a top-hat ? "

"Here, who are you having a game with ? " demanded the driver, pulling up the car.

"I'm not having a game with anybody," Michael said. "But two people and this top-hat have just been having a hell of a game with me. You'd much better take it as a present. I shall only throw it away. He refuses it," Michael went on. "He refuses a perfectly good top-hat. Who's the maker ? My god, his dirty greasy head has obliterated the name of the maker. Good-bye, hat ! Drive on, drive on," he shouted to the driver and hurled the hat spinning under an omnibus. Then he turned to Guy.

"I've been sold by the girl I was going to marry," he said. "I say, Guy, I've got some jolly good advice for you. Don't you marry a whore. Sorry, old chap !—I forgot you were engaged already. Besides, people don't marry whores, unless they're fools like me. Didn't you say just now that I was very lucky ? Do you know—I think I am lucky. I think it was a great piece of luck bringing you to see that girl to-day. Don't you ? Oh, Guy, I could go mad with disappointment. Will nothing in all the world ever be what it seems ? "

"Look here, Michael, are you sure you weren't too hasty ? You didn't wait to see if there was any explanation, did you ? "

"She was only going back to her old habits," said Michael bitterly. "I was a fool to think she wouldn't. And yet I adored her. Fancy, you've never seen her after all. Lovely, lovely animal ! "

"Oh, you knew what she was ? " exclaimed Guy.

"Knew ? yes, of course I knew, but I thought she loved me. I didn't care about anything when I was sure she loved me. She could only have gone such a little way down, I thought. She seemed so easy to bring out. Seeds of pomegranate. Seeds of pomegranate ! She's only eaten seeds of pomegranate, but they were enough to keep her behind. Where are we going ? Oh, yes, Cheyne Walk. My mother will be delighted when she hears my news, and so will everybody. That's what's amusing me. Everybody will clap their hands, and I'm wretched. But you are sorry for me, Guy ? You don't think I'm just a fool being shown his folly ? And at eighteen I was nearly off my head only because I saw someone kiss her ! There's one thing over which I score—the only person who can appreciate all the humour of this situation is myself."

Nearly all the way to Cheyne Walk Michael was laughing very loudly.

Chapter IX : *The Gate of Horn*

GUY thought it would be better if he went straight back to Plashers Mead; but Michael asked him to stay until the next day. He was in no mood, he said, for a solitary evening, and he could not bear the notion of visiting friends, or of talking to his mother without the restriction that somebody else's presence would produce.

So Guy agreed to spend the night in London, and they dined with Mrs. Fane. Michael in the sun-coloured Summer room felt smothered by a complete listlessness; and talking very little, he sat wondering at the swiftness with which a strong fabric of the imagination had tumbled down. The quiet of Cheyne Walk became a consciousness of boredom and futility, and he suggested on a sudden impulse that he and Guy should go and visit Maurice in the studio. It would be pleasant walking along the Embankment, he said.

"But I thought you wanted to keep quiet," Guy exclaimed.

"No, I've grown restless during dinner; and besides, I want to make a few arrangements about the flat, and then be done with that business—for ever."

They started off without waiting for coffee. It was a calm Summer evening of shadows blue and amethyst, of footfalls and murmurs, an evening plumy as a moth, warm and gentle as the throat of a pigeon. Nobody on any pavement was hurrying; and maidservants loitered in area gates, looking up and down the roads.

The big room at the top of 422 Grosvenor Road had never seemed so romantic. There were half a dozen people sitting at the open windows; and Cunningham was playing a sonata of Brahms, a sonata with a melody that was drawing the London night into this big room where the cigarettes dimmed and brightened like stars. The player sat at the piano for an hour, and Maurice unexpectedly made no attempt to disturb the occasion. Michael thought that perhaps he was wondering what had brought himself and Guy here, and for that reason did not rush to show Guy his studio by gaslight: Maurice was probably thinking how strange it was for Michael to revisit him suddenly like this after their quarrel.

When the room was lighted up, Michael and Guy were introduced to the men they did not know. Among them was Ronnie Walker, the painter whom Maurice had mentioned to Michael as an old lover of Lily. Michael knew now why Maurice had allowed the music to go on so long, and he was careful to talk as much as possible to Walker in order to embarrass Maurice, who could scarcely pay any attention to Guy, so nervously was he watching over his shoulder the progress of the conversation.

Later on Michael called Maurice aside, and they withdrew to the window-seat which looked out over the house-tops. A cat was yauling on a distant roof, and in the studio Cunningham had seated himself at the piano again.

"I say, I'm awfully sorry that Ronnie Walker should happen to be here to-night," Maurice began. "I have been rather cursing myself for telling you about him and . . ."

"It doesn't matter at all," Michael interrupted. "I'm not going to marry her."

"Oh, that's splendid," Maurice exclaimed. "I've been tremendously worried about you."

Michael looked at him; he was wondering if it were

possible that Maurice could be 'tremendously worried'
by anything.

"I want you to arrange matters," said Michael. "I
can't go near the place again. She will probably prefer to
go away from Ararat House. The rent is paid up to the
June quarter. The furniture you can do what you like
with. Bring some of it here. Sell the rest, and give her the
money. Get rid of the woman who's there—Miss Harper
her name is."

"But I shall feel rather awkward . . ."

"Oh, don't do it. Don't do it then," Michael broke in
fretfully. "I'll ask Guy."

"You're getting awfully irascible," Maurice complained.
. "Of course I'll do anything you want, if you won't always
jump down my throat at the first word I utter. What has
happened, though ?"

"What do you expect to happen when you're engaged
to a girl like that ?" Michael asked.

Maurice shrugged his shoulders.

"Oh, well, of course I should expect to be badly let
down. But then, you see, I'm not a very great believer in
women. What are you going to do yourself ?"

"I haven't settled yet. I've got to arrange one or two
things in town, and then I shall go abroad. Would you be
able to come with me in about a week ?"

"I daresay I might," Maurice answered looking vaguely
round the room. Already, Michael thought, the subject
was floating away from his facile comprehension.

The piano had stopped, and conversation became general
again.

"This is where you ought to be, if you want to write,"
Maurice proclaimed to Guy. "It's ridiculous for you to
bury yourself in the country. You'll expire of stagnation."

"Just at present I recommend you to stay where you are,"
said Castleton. "I'm almost expiring from the violence

with which I am being precipitated from one to another of Maurice's energies."

Soon afterwards Michael and Guy left the studio and walked home; and next morning Guy went back to Wychford.

Michael was astonished at his own calmness. After the first shock of the betrayal he had gone and talked to a lot of people; he had coldly made financial arrangements; he had even met and rather liked a man whom only yesterday morning he could not have regarded without hatred for the part he had played in Lily's life. Perhaps he had lost the power to feel anything deeply for long; perhaps he was become a sort of Maurice; already Lily seemed a shade of the underworld, merely more clearly remembered than the others. Yet in the moment that he was calling her a shade his present emotion proved that she was much more than that, for the conjured image of her was an icy pang to his heart. Then the indifference returned, but always underneath it the chill remained.

Mrs. Fane asked if he would care to go to the Opera in the evening: and they went to Bohême. Michael used to be wrung by the music, but he sat unmoved to-night. Afterwards at supper, he looked at his mother as if she were a person in a picture; he was saddened by the uselessness of all beauty, and by the number of times he would have to undress at night and dress again in the morning. He had no objection to life itself, but he felt an overwhelming despair at the thought of any activity in the conduct of it. He was sorry for the people sitting here at supper and for their footmen waiting outside. He felt that he was spiritually withered, because he was aware that he was surrendering to the notion of a debased material comfort as the only condition worth achieving for a body that remained perfectly well, grossly well it almost seemed.

" Michael, have you been bored to-night ? " his mother

asked, when they had come home and were sitting by the window in the drawing-room, while Michael finished a cigar.

He shook his head.

" You seemed to take no interest in the opera, and you usually enjoy Puccini, don't you ? Or is it Wagner you enjoy so much ? "

" I think summer in London is always tiring," he said.

She was in that rosy mist of clothes with which his earliest pictures of her were vivid. Suddenly he began to cry.

" Dear child, what is it ? " she whispered, with fluttering arms outstretched to comfort him.

" Oh, I've finished with all that. I've finished with all that. You'll be delighted—you mustn't be worried because I seem upset for the moment. I found out that Lily did not care anything about me. I'm not going to marry her or even see her again."

" Michael ! My dearest boy ! What is it ? "

" Finished. Finished. Finished," he sobbed.

" Nothing is finished at twenty-three," she murmured, leaning over to pet him.

" I do hate myself for having hurt your feelings the other day."

It was as if he seized upon a justification for grief so manifest. It seemed to him exquisitely sad that he should have wounded his mother on account of that broken toy of a girl. Soon he could control himself again ; and he went off to bed.

Next day Michael's depression was profound because he could perceive no reaction from himself on Lily. The sense of personal loss was merged in the reproach of failure ; he had simply been unable to influence her. She was the consummation of many minor failures. And what was to happen to her now ? What was to happen to all the people with whose lives he had lately been involved ? Must he

withdraw entirely and confess defeat ?   No doubt a cynic
would argue that Lily was hopeless, and indeed he knew that
from any point of view where marriage was concerned she
was hopeless.   He must leave her where he had found her,
in that pretty paradise of evil which now she well adorned.
If her destiny was to whirl downward through the labyrinths of the underworld, he could do no more. ·That
himself had issued with the false dreams through the ivory
gate was her fault, and she must pay the penalty of her
misdirection.   He would revisit Leppard Street, and from
the innermost circle where he had beheld Mrs. Smith he
would seek a way out through the gate of true dreams.   He
would be glad to see if the amount of security he had been
able to guarantee to Barnes had helped him at all.   He
had money and he could leave money behind in Leppard
Street, money that might preserve the people in the house
where he had lived.   Was this a quixotic notion, to leave
one set of people free from the necessity to hand themselves
over to evil ?   Michael's spirits began to rise as he looked
forward to what he could still effect in Leppard Street.
And for Lily what could he still do ?   He would visit
Sylvia and consult with her.   She was strong, and if she
had chosen harlotry, she was still strong.   She was not lazy
nor languid.   Lazy laughing languid Lily !   Lily did not
laugh much ; she was too lazy even for that.   How beautiful
she had been.   Her beauty stabbed him with the poignancy
of what was past.   How beautiful she had been.   When
Maurice went to tell her of the final ending of it all, she
would pout and shrug her shoulders.   That was all she
would do ; and she would be faintly resentful at having
been disturbed in her lazy life.   Perhaps Maurice would
fall in love with her, and it would be ironical and just that
she should fall violently in love with Maurice and be cast
off by him.   Maurice would never suffer ; as soon as a
woman showed a sign of upsetting his theories about

feminine behaviour he would be done with her. He would jilt her as easily as he jilted one Muse for another. Why was he being so hard on Maurice ?

" I believe that down in my heart, I still don't really like him," Michael said to himself. " Right back from the time I met him in Macrae's form at Randell's I've never really liked him."

It was curious how one could grow more and more intimate with a person, and all the time never really like him ; so intimate with him as to entrust him with the disposal of a wrecked love-affair, and all the while never really like him. Why then had he invited Maurice to go abroad ? Perhaps he wanted the company of someone he could faintly despise. Even friendship must pay tribute to human vanity. Life became a merciless business when one ceased to stand alone. The herding instinct of man was responsible for the corruption of civilization, and Michael thought of the bestiality of a crowd. How loathsome humanity was in the aggregate, but individually how rare, how wonderful.

Michael walked boldly enough towards Tinderbox Lane ; and when he rang the bell of Mulberry Cottage not a qualm of sentiment assailed him. He was definitely pleased with himself, as he stood outside the door in the wall, to think with what a serenity of indifference he was able to visit a place so much endeared to him a little time ago.

Mrs. Gainsborough answered the door and nearly fell upon Michael's neck.

" Good Land ! Here's a surprize."

" It's almost more of a surprize for me to see you, Mrs. Gainsborough."

" Why, who else should you see ? "

" I was beginning to think you never existed. Can I come in ? "

"Sylvia's indoors," she said warningly.

"I rather wanted to see her."

"She's been carrying on alarming about you ever since you stole her Lily. And she didn't take me on her knee and cuddle me, when she found you were gone off. How do you like me new frock ? "

Michael thought that in her chequered black and green gingham she looked like an old Summer number of an illustrated magazine, and he told her so.

"Well, there ! Did you ever ? I never did. There's a bouquet to hand a lady ! Back number ! Whatever next ? I wonder you hadn't the liberty to say I'd rose from the grave."

"Aren't I to see Sylvia ? " Michael asked, laughing.

"Well, don't blame me if she packs you off with a flea in your ear, as they say—well, she is a Miss Temper and no mistake. How do you like me garden ? "

Mulberry Cottage was just the bower of greenery that Michael had supposed he would find in early June.

"Actually roses," he exclaimed. "Or at least there will be very soon."

"Oh, yes. Glory de Die-Johns. That was always Pa's favourite. That and a good snooze of a Sunday afternoon was about what he cared most for in this world. But my Captain he used to like camellias, and gardenias of course— oh, he had a very soft corner in his heart for a nice gardenia. Ah dear, what a masher he was, to be sure."

Sylvia had evidently seen them walking up the garden path, for leaning over the railings of the balcony, she was waiting for them.

"Here's quite a stranger come to see you," said Mrs. Gainsborough with a propitiatory glance in Sylvia's direction.

"I rather want to have a talk with you," said Michael, and he too found himself rather annoyingly adopting a deprecating manner.

Sylvia came slowly down the balcony steps.

"I suppose you want my help," she said, and her underlip had a warning out-thrust.

"I'll get on with my fal-lals," Mrs. Gainsborough muttered, and she bundled herself quickly indoors.

Sylvia and Michael sat down on the garden-seat under the mulberry-tree whose leaves were scarcely yet uncurling. Michael found a great charm in sitting close to Sylvia like this: she and Stella both possessed a capacity for bracing him that he did not find in anyone else. Sylvia was really worth quarrelling with; but it would be very delightful to be friends with her. He had never liked a person so much whom he had so little reason to like. He could not help thinking that in her heart Sylvia must like him. It was a strangely provocative fancy.

"Lily and I have parted," he began at once.

"And why do you suppose that piece of information will interest me?" Sylvia asked.

Michael was rather taken aback. When he came to consider it, there did seem no good reason why Sylvia should any longer be interested after the way in which Lily had been snatched away from her. He was silent for a moment.

"But it would have interested you a short time ago," he said.

"No doubt," Sylvia agreed. "But luckily for me one of the benefits conferred by my temperament is an ability to throw aside things that have disappointed me, things that have ceased to be useful,—and what applies to things applies even more strongly to people."

"You mean to say you've put Lily right out of your life?" Michael exclaimed.

He was shocked by the notion, for he did not realize until this moment how much he had been depending upon Sylvia for peace of mind.

4 A

"Haven't you put her out of *your* life?" she asked looking round at him sharply. Until this question she had been staring sullenly down at the grass.

"Well, I had to," said Michael.

"You're bearing up very well under the sad necessity," she sneered.

"I don't know that I am bearing up very well. I don't think that coming to you to talk about it is a special sign of fortitude."

"What do you want me to do," Sylvia demanded. "Get her back into your life again? Isn't that the phrase you like?"

"Oh, no, that's unimaginable," said Michael. "You see it was really the second time. Once six years ago, and again now, very much more—more utterly. You said that your temperament enables you to throw off things and people. Mine makes me bow to what I fancy are irremediable strokes of fate."

"Unimaginable! irremediable! We're turning this interview into a Rossetti sonnet," Sylvia scoffed.

"I was thinking about that poem Jenny to-day. It's funny you should mention Rossetti."

"Impervious youth," she exclaimed.

"It's hopeless for you to try to wound me with words," Michael assured her with grave earnestness. "I was wounded the day before yesterday into complete immunity from small pains."

"I suppose you found her ."
Michael flushed and gripped her by the wrist.

"No, no, don't say something brutal and beastly," he stammered. "You know what happened. You prophesied it. Well, I thought you were wrong, and you were right. That's a victory for you. You couldn't wish for me to be more humbled than I am by having to admit that I wasn't strong enough to keep her faithful for six weeks. But we

did agree, I think, about one thing." He smiled sadly.
"We did agree that she was beautiful. You were as proud
of that as I was, and of course you had a great deal more
reason to be proud. You did own her. I never owned her,
and isn't that your great objection to the relation between
man and woman ? "

"What are you trying to make me do ? " Sylvia asked.

"I want you to have Lily to live with you again."

"To relieve yourself of all responsibility, I suppose," she
said bitterly.

"No, no, why will you persist in ascribing the worst
motive to everything I say ? Isn't your jealousy fed full
enough even yet ? "

Sylvia made the garden-seat quiver with an irritable
movement.

"You will persist in thinking that jealousy solves all
problems," she cried.

"Oh, don't let us turn aside into what isn't very important. You can't care whether I think you're jealous
or not."

"I don't care in so far as it is your opinion," Sylvia
admitted. "But I object to inaccurate thinking. If your
life was spent in a confusion of all moral values as mine is,
you would be anxious for a little straightforward computa-
tion for a change."

"Perhaps you are right," Michael admitted, "in thinking
that I'm asking you to look after Lily to relieve myself of
a responsibility. But it's only because I see no chance of
doing it in any other way. I mean—it's not laziness on my
part. It's a confession of absolute failure."

"In fact you're throwing yourself on my mercy," Sylvia
said.

"Yes, and also her," he added gently.

"Am I such a moral companion—such an ennobling
influence ? "

" I would sooner think of her under your influence than think of her drifting. What I want you to understand is that I'm not consigning her to you for sentimental reasons. I would sooner that Lily were dragged down by you at a gallop than that she should sink slowly and lazily of her own accord. You have a strong personality. You are well-read. You are quite out of the common, and in the life you have chosen, so far as I have had experience, you are unique."

Sylvia stared in front of her, and Michael waited anxiously for the reply.

" Have you ever read Petronius ? " she asked suddenly.

" Yes, but what an extraordinary girl you are—have you ever read Petronius ? "

" It's the only book in which anyone in my position with my brains could behold herself. Oh, it is such a nightmare. And life is a nightmare too. After all, what is life for me ? Strange doors in strange houses. Strange men and strange intimacies. Scenes incredibly grotesque and incredibly beastly. The secret vileness of human nature flung at me. Man revealing himself through individual after individual as utterly contemptible. What can I worship ? Not my own body soiled by my traffic in it. Not any religion I've ever heard of, for in all religions man is set up to be respected. I tell you, my dear eager fool, it is beyond my conception ever ever ever to regard a man as higher than a frog, as less repulsive than—ugh ! it makes me shudder—but oh, my son, doesn't it make me laugh. . . ." She rocked herself with extravagant mirth for a moment. Then she began again, staring out in front of her intensely, fiercely, speaking with the monotonous voice of a visionary. " So I worship woman, and in this nightmare city, in this nightmare life, Lily was always beautiful ; only beautiful, mind you. I don't want to worship anything but beauty. I don't care about purity or uprightness, but I must have beauty. And you came blundering along and kidnapped my lovely girl. You came along, thinking you were going to regenerate her, and you can't understand that I'm only able to see you in the shape of a frog. It does amuse me to hear you talking to me so solemnly and so earnestly and so nobly . . . and all the time I can only see a clumsy frog."

"But what has all this to do with Petronius ? There's nothing in that romance particularly complimentary to women," Michael argued.

"It's the nightmare effect of it that I adore," Sylvia exclaimed. " It's the sensation of being hopelessly plunged into a maze of streets from which there's no escape. I was plunged just like that into London. It is gloriously and sometimes horribly mad, and that's all I want in my reading now. I want to be given the sensation of other people having been mad before me . . . years ago in a nightmare. Besides, think of the truth, the truth of a work of art that seems ignorant of goodness. Not one moderately decent person all through."

" And you will take Lily back ? " Michael asked.

" Yes, yes, of course I will. But not because you ask me, mind. Don't, for heaven's sake, puff yourself up with the idea that I'm doing anything except gratify myself in this matter."

" I don't want you to do it for any other reason," he said. " I shall feel more secure with that pledge than with any you could think of. By the way, tell me about a man called Walker. Ronald Walker—a painter. He had an affair with Lily, didn't he ? "

" Ronnie Walker ? He painted her ; that was all. There was never anything more."

" And Lonsdale ? Arthur Lonsdale ? "

" Who ? The Honourable Arthur ? "

Michael nodded.

"Yes, we met him first at Covent Garden, and went to Brighton with him, and another boy—Clarehaven—Lord Clarehaven."

"Oh, I remember him at the House," said Michael.

"Money is necessary sometimes, you know," Sylvia laughed.

"Of course it is. Look here. Will you in future, whenever you feel you're in a nightmare—will you write to me and let me send money?" he asked. "I know you despise me and of course . . . I understand; but I can't bear to think of anyone being haunted as you must be haunted sometimes. Don't be proud about this, because *I've* got no pride left. I'm only terribly anxious to be of service to somebody. There's really no reason for you to be proud. You see I should always be so very much more anxious to help than you would to be helped. And it really isn't only because of Lily that I say this. I've got a good many books you'd enjoy, and I think I'll send them to you. Good-bye."

"Good-bye," she said, looking at him curiously.

Michael turned away from her down the gravel-path, and a moment later slammed the door. He had only gone a few steps away, when he heard Sylvia calling after him.

"You stupid," she said. "You never told me Lily's address."

"I'll give you a card."

Mr. Michael Fane, she read. 1 *Ararat House, Island Road*. She looked at him and raised her eyebrows.

"You see, I expected to live there myself," Michael explained. "I told a friend of mine, Maurice Avery, to clear up everything. The furniture can all be sold. If you want anything for here, take it of course; but I think most of the things will be too large for Mulberry Cottage."

"And what shall I say to Lily?" she asked.

"Oh, I don't think I should say anything about me."

"Who was the man ? "

"I never saw him," said Michael. "I only saw his hat."

She pulled him to her and kissed him.

"How many women have done that suddenly like that ? " she demanded.

"One—well, perhaps two." He was wondering if Mrs. Smith's kiss ought to count in the comparison.

"I. never have to any man," she said, and vanished through the door in the wall.

Michael hoped that Sylvia intended to imply by that kiss that his offer of help was accepted. Fancy her having read Petronius ! He could send her his Adlington's Apuleius. — She would enjoy reading that, and he would write in it : *I've eaten rose-leaves and I am no longer a golden ass.* Perhaps he would also send her his Shelton's Don Quixote. —

When Michael turned out of Tinderbox Lane into the Fulham Road, each person of humanity he passed upon the pavement seemed to him strange with unrevealed secrets. The people of London were somehow transfigured, and he longed to see their souls, if it were only in the lucid flashes of a nightmare. Yet for nearly a year he had been peering into the souls of people. Had he indeed ? Had he not rather been peering to see in their souls the reflection of his own ? He was moved by the thought of Sylvia in London, and suddenly he was swept from his feet by the surging against him of the thoughts of all the passers-by and, struggling in the trough of these thoughts, he was more and more conscious that unless he fought for himself he would be lost. The illusion fled on the instant of its creation ; and the people were themselves again, dull, quick, slow, ordinary, depressed, gay ; political busybodies, political fools, political slaves, political animals. How they huddled together, each one of them afraid to stand for himself. It was political passion that made them

animals, each dependent in turn on the mimicry of his
neighbour. Each was solicitous or jealous or fond or envious
of his neighbour's opinion. God was meaningless to the
political state : this herd cared only for idols. Michael
began to make a catalogue of the Golden Calves that the
Golden Asses of green England worshipped. They were
bowing down and braying to their Golden Calves, these
Golden Asses, and they could not see that there were rose-
trees growing everywhere, most prodigally of all in the
gutter, any one petal of which (what did the thorns matter ?)
would have given back to them their humanity. Yet even
then, Michael dismally concluded, they would continue
to bow down to the Golden Calves, because they would
fancy that it was the Calves who had planted and cultivated
the rose-trees. Then out of all the thronging thoughts
made visible he began to pursue the fancy of Sylvia in
London, and as he did so, she faded farther and farther from
his vision like a butterfly seen from a train, that keeps
pace, it seems for a moment, and is lost upon the flowery
embankment behind.

Meanwhile Michael was feeling sharpened for conflict
by that talk under the mulberry-tree : he realized what an
amount of determination he had stored up for the persuasion of Sylvia. Now there only remained Leppard Street,
and then he would go away from London. He walked on
through the Chelsea slums.

Leppard Street was more melancholy in the sunshine
than it had ever seemed in Winter, not so much because
the sun made more evident the corrosion and the foulness
as because of the stillness it shed. Not a breath of air
twitched the torn paper-bag on the doorstep of Number
One; and the five tall houses with their fifty windows
stared at the blank wall opposite.

Michael wondered if Barnes would be out of bed : it
was not yet one o'clock. He rang the front-door bell, or

rather he hoped that the creaking of the broken wire along the basement passage would attract Mrs. Cleghorne's attention. When he had tugged many times, she came out into the area and peered up to see who it was. The sudden sunlight must have dazzled her eyes, for she was shading them with her hand. With her fibrous neck working and with an old cap of her husband's pinned on a skimpy bun at the back of her head, she was horrible after Mrs. Gainsborough in the black and green gingham. Michael looked down at her over the railings; and she, recognizing him at last, pounced back to come up and open the door.

"I couldn't think who it was. We had a man round selling pots of musk this morning, and I didn't want to come trapesing upstairs for nothing."

Mrs. Cleghorne was receiving him so pleasantly that Michael scarcely knew what to say. No doubt his regular payment of rent had a good deal to do with it.

"Is Mr. Barnes up?" he asked.

"I don't know, I'm sure. I never go inside his door now. No."

"Oh, really? Why not?"

"I'm the last person to make mischief, Mr. Fane, but I don't consider he has treated us fair."

"Oh, really?"

"He's got a woman here living with him. Now of course that's a thing I should never allow, but seeing as you weren't here and was paying the rent regular I thought to myself that I'll just shut my eyes until you came back. It's really disgusting, and we has to be so particular with the other lodgers. It's quite upset me, it has; and *Mis*-ter Cleghorne has been intending to speak to him about it. Only his asthma's been so bad lately—it really seems to have knocked all the heart out of him."

This pity for her husband was very ominous, Michael thought. Evidently the landlady was defending herself against an abrupt forfeiture of rent for the ground-floor. Michael tapped at the door of his old room : it was locked.

" I'll get on down again to my oven," said Mrs. Cleghorne with a ratlike glance at the closed door. " I'm just cooking a bit of fish for my old man's dinner."

She fixed him with her eyes that were beady like the head of the hatpin in her cap, and sweeping her hand upwards over her nose, she vanished.

Michael rapped again and, as there was no answer, he went along the passage and tried the bedroom door. Barnes's voice called out to know who was there. Michael shouted his name, and heard Barnes whispering to somebody inside. Presently he opened the sitting-room door and invited Michael to come in.

It was extraordinary to see how with a few additions the character of the room had changed since Michael left it. The furniture was still there ; but what had seemed ascetic was now mean. Spangled picture-postcards were standing along the mantelpiece. The autotypes of St. George and the Knight in Armour were both askew : the shelves had novelettes interspersed among the books : a soiled petticoat of yellow moirette lay over Michael's narrow bed, which he was surprized to see in the sitting-room : a gas-stove had been fixed in the fireplace, and the old steel grate had been turned into a deposit for dirty plates and dishes : but what struck Michael most were the heavy curtains over the folding-doors between the two rooms. He looked at Barnes, waiting for him to explain the alterations.

" Looks a bit more homelike than it did, doesn't it ? " said Barnes, blinking round him.

A deterioration was visible even in Barnes himself. This was not merely the result of being without a collar or a shave, Michael decided : it was as hard to define as the evidence of death in a man's eyes ; but there clung to him an aura of corruption, and it seemed as if at a touch he would dissolve into a vile deliquescence.

"You look pretty pasty," said Michael severely.

"Worry, old man, worry," said Barnes. "Well, to put it straight, I fell in with a girl who was down on her luck, and I knew you'd be the very one to encourage a bit of charity. So I brought her here."

"Why are you sleeping in this room?" Michael asked.

"You're getting a Mr. Smart aren't you?" said Barnes. "Fancy you're noticing that. Oh, well, I suppose you've come to ask for your rooms back?"

Michael with the consciousness of the woman behind those curtained doors knew that he could discuss nothing at present. He felt that all the time her ear was at the keyhole and he went out suddenly, telling Barnes to meet him at the Orange that night.

Again the beerhall impressed him with its eternal sameness. It was as if a cinema film had broken when he last went out of the Café d'Orange, and had been set in action again at the moment of his return. He looked round to see if Daisy was there, and she was. Her hat which had formerly been black and trimmed with white daisies was now, to mark the season, white and trimmed with black daisies.

"Hullao, little stranger," she exclaimed. "Where have you been?"

So exactly the same was the Orange that Michael was almost surprized that she should have observed a passage of time.

"You never seem to come here now," she said reproachfully. "Come on. Sit down. Don't stand about like a man selling matches on the kerb."

"How's Bert?" Michael asked.

"Who?"

"Bert Saunders. The man you were living with in Little Quondam Street."

"Oh, him! Oh, I had to get rid of him double quick. What? Yes, when it came to asking me to go to Paris with a fighting fellow. Only fancy the cheek of it! It would help him, he said, with his business. Dirty Ecnop! I soon shoved him down the Apples-and-pears."

"I haven't understood a word of that last sentence," said Michael.

"Don't you know back-slang and rhyming-slang? Oh, it's grand! Here, I forgot, there's something I wanted to tell you. Do you remember you was in here with a fellow who you said his name was Burns?"

"Barnes, you mean, I expect. Yes, he's supposed to be meeting me here to-night, as a matter of fact."

"Well, you be careful of him. He'll get you into trouble."

Michael looked incredulous.

"It's true as I sit here," said Daisy earnestly. "Come over in the corner and let's have our drink there. I can't talk here with that blue-nosed —— behind me, squinting at us across his lager." She looked round indignantly at the man in question.

They moved across to one of the alcoves, and Daisy leant over and spoke quietly and rather tensely, so differently from the usual rollick of her voice that Michael began to feel a presentiment of dread.

"I was out on the Dilly one night soon after you'd been round to my place, and I was with a girl called Janie Filson. 'Oo-er,' she said to me. 'Did you see who that was passed?' I looked round and saw this fellow Burns."

"Barnes," Michael corrected.

"Oh, well, Barnes. His name doesn't matter, because it isn't his own, anyway. 'That's Harry Meats,' she said. And she called out after him. 'Hullao, Harry, where's Cissie?' He went as white as . . . . oh, he did go shocking white. He just turned to see who it was had called out after

him, and then he slid up Swallow Street like a bit of paper.
'Who's Cissie?' I said. 'Don't you remember Cissie
Cummings?' she said. 'That fair girl who always wore a
big purple hat and used to be in the Leicester Lounge and
always carried a box of chocolates for <u>swank</u>?' I did remember the girl when Janie spoke about her. Only I never
knew her, see? 'He wasn't very pleased when you mentioned her,' I said. 'Didn't he look awful?' said Janie, and
just then she got off with a fellow and I couldn't ask her
any more."

"I don't think that's enough to make me very much
afraid of Barnes," Michael commented.

"Wait a minute, I haven't finished yet. Don't be in
such a hurry. The other day I saw Janie Filson again.
She's been away to Italy—is there a place called Italy? Of
course there is. Well, as I was saying, she'd been to Italy
with her fellow who's a commercial traveller and that's why
I hadn't seen her. And Janie said to me, 'Do you know
what they're saying?' I said, 'No, what?' And she
said, 'Did you read nearly a year ago about a woman who
was found murdered in the Euston Road? A gay woman
it was,' she said. So I said, 'Lots of women is found
murdered, my dear, I can't remember every one I see the
picture of.' Well, anyone can't, can they?" Daisy broke off
to ask Michael in an injured voice. Then she resumed her
tale. "When I was with that fellow Bert I used to read
nothing else but murders all the time. Give anyone the
rats it would. 'Lots of women, my dear,' I said. And she
said, 'Well, there was one in particular who the police
never found out the name of, because there wasn't any
clothing or nothing found.' So I did remember about it,
and she said, 'Well, they're saying now it was Cissie Cummings.' And I said, 'Well, what of it, if it was?' And she
said, 'What of it?' she said. 'Well, if it was her,' she said,
'I know who done it.' 'Who done it?' I asked,—because,

you see, I'd forgotten about this fellow Burns. 'Why, Harry Meats,' she said. 'That fellow I saw on the Dilly the night when I was along with you.'"

"I don't think you have enough evidence for the police," Michael decided with half a smile. Yet nevertheless a malaise chilled him, and he looked over his shoulder at the mob in the beerhall.

"—— the police," Daisy exclaimed. "I don't care about them when I'm positive certain of something. I tell you, I know that fellow Burns, or Meats or whatever his name is, done it."

"But what am I to do about it ?" Michael asked.

"Well, you'll get into trouble, that's all," Daisy prophesied. "You'd look very funny if he was pinched for murder while you was out walking with him. Ugh! it gives me the creeps. Order me a gin, there's a good boy."

Michael obtained for Daisy her drink, and sat waiting for Barnes to appear.

"He won't come," Daisy scoffed. "If he's feeling funny about the neck, he won't come down here. He's never been down since that night he came down with you. Fancy, to go and do a poor girl in like that. I'd spit in his face, if I saw him."

"Daisy, you really mustn't assume such horrible things about a man. He's as innocent as you or me."

"Is he ?" Daisy retorted. "I don't think so then. You never saw how shocking white his face went when Janie asked him about Cissie."

"But, if there were any suspicion of him," Michael pointed out, "the police would have tackled him long ago."

"Oh, they aren't half artful the police aren't," said Daisy. "Nothing they'd like better than get waiting about and seeing if he didn't go and murder another poor girl, so as they could have him for the two and be all the more pleased about it."

"That's talking nonsense," Michael protested. "The police don't do that sort of thing."

"I don't know," Daisy argued. "One or two poor girls more or less wouldn't worry them. After all that's what we're for—to get pinched when they've got nothing better to do. Of course, I know it's part of the game, but there it is. If you steal my purse and I follow you round and tell a copper, what would he do? Why, pinch me for soliciting. No, my motto is; 'Keep out of the way of the police.' And if you take my advice, you'll do the same. If this fellow didn't do the girl in," Daisy asked earnestly, leaning forward over the table, "why doesn't he come down here and keep his appointment with you to-night? Don't you worry. He knows the word has gone round, and he's going to lie very low for a bit. I wouldn't say the tecs aren't watching out for him even now."

"My dear Daisy, you're getting absolutely fanciful," Michael declared.

"Oh, well, good luck to fanciful," said Daisy draining her glass. "Here, why don't you come home with me to-night?"

"What, and spend another three hours hiding in a cupboard?"

"No, properly, I mean, this time. Only we should have to go to a hotel, because the woman I'm living with's got her son come home from being a soldier and she wouldn't like for him to know anything. Well, it's better not. You're much more comfortable when you aren't in gay rooms, because they haven't got a hold over you. Are you coming?"

For a moment Michael was inclined to invite Daisy to go away with him. For a moment it seemed desirable to bury himself in a corner of the underworld: to pass his life there for as long as he could stand it. He could easily make this girl fond of him and he might be happy with her. No doubt, it would be ultimately a degrading happiness, but

yet not much more degrading than the prosperity of many
of his friends. He had always escaped so far and hidden
himself successfully. Why not again more completely?
What after all did he know of this underworld without
having lived of it as well as in it? Hitherto he had been a
spectator, intervening sometimes in the sudden tragedies
and comedies, but never intervening except as very essentially a spectator. He thought, as he sat opposite to Daisy
with her white dress and candid roguery, that it would be
amusing to become a rogue himself. There would be no
strain in living with Daisy. Love in the way that he had
loved Lily would be a joke to her. Why should not he take
her for what she was—shrewd, mirthful, kind, honest, the
natural light of love? He would do her no wrong by
accepting her as such. She was immemorial in the scheme
of the universe.

Michael was on the point of offering to Daisy his alliance,
when he remembered what Sylvia had said about men, and,
though he knew that Daisy could not possibly think in that
way about men, he had no courage to plunge with her into
deeper labyrinths not yet explored. He thought of the
contempt with which Sylvia would hail him, were they in
this nightmare of London to meet in such circumstances.
A few weeks ago, yesterday indeed, he might have joined
himself to Daisy under the pretext of helping her and
improving her. Now he must help himself: he must aim
at perfecting himself. Experiments, when at any moment
passion might enter, were too dangerous.

"No, I won't come home with you, dear Daisy," he said,
taking her hand over the puddly table. "You know, you
didn't kiss me that night in Quondam Street because you
thought I might one day come home with you, did you?"

She shrugged her shoulders.

"What's the good of asking me why I kissed you?" she
said embarrassed and almost made angry by his reminder.

"Perhaps I was twopence on the can. I can get very loving on a quartern of gin, I can. Oh, well, if you aren't coming home, you aren't, and I must get along. Sitting talking to you isn't paying my rent, is it?"

He longed to offer her money; but he could not, because it was seeming to him now indissolubly linked with hiring. However genuinely it was a token of exchange, money was eluding his capacity for idealization, and he was at a loss to find a symbol for service.

"Is there nothing I can do for you?"

"Yes, you can give me two quid in case I don't get off to-night."

He offered them to her eagerly.

"Go on, you silly thing," she said pushing the money away. "As if I meant it."

"If you didn't, I did," said Michael.

"Oh, all right," she replied with a wink, putting the money in her purse. "Well, chin-chin, Clive, don't be so long coming down here next time."

"Michael is my name," he said, for he was rather distressed to think that she would pass for ever from his life supposing him to be called Clive.

"As if I didn't know that," she said. "I remember, because it's a Jew name."

"But it isn't," Michael contradicted.

"Jews are called that."

"Very likely," he admitted.

"Oh, well, it'll be all the same in a hundred years."

She picked up her white gloves, and swaggered across the crowded beerhall. At the foot of the stairs she turned and waved them to him. Then she disappeared.

Michael sat on in the Café d'Orange, waiting for Barnes, but he did not arrive before closing-time; and when Michael was walking home, the tale of Daisy gathered import; and he had a dreary feeling that her suspicions

4 B

were true. He did not feel depressed so much because he was shocked by the notion of Barnes as a murderer (he thought that probably murder was by no means the greatest evil he had done), as because he feared the fancy of him in the hands of the police. It appalled him to imagine that material hell of the trial. The bandage dropped from the eyes of justice, and he saw her pig's-eyes mean, cowardly, revengeful ; and her scales were like a grocer's. He pitied Barnes in the clutches of anthropocracy. What a ridiculous word : it probably did not exist. After all, Daisy's story was ridiculous too. Barnes had objected to himself's hailing him as Meats : and there were plenty of reasons to account for his dislike of Janie Filson's salute without supposing murder. Nevertheless back again, as softly and coaxingly as the thought used to come to Michael when he was a small boy lying in bed, the thought of murder maintained an innuendo of probability. Yet it was absurd to think of murder on this Summer night, with all these jingling hansoms and all that fountainous sky of stars. Why then had Barnes not met him at the Orange to-night ? It was not like him to break an appointment when his pocket might be hurt. What rumour of Cissie Cummings had travelled even to Leppard Street ?

Michael had reached Buckingham Palace Road, and he took the direction for Pimlico ; it was not too late to get into the house. He changed his mind again and drove back to Cheyne Walk. Up in his bedroom, the curiosity to know why Barnes had not kept the appointment recurred with double force, and Michael after a search found the key of the house in Leppard Street and went out again. It was getting on for two o'clock, and without the lights of vehicles the night was more than ever brilliant. Under the plane-trees Michael was stabbed with one pang for Lily, and he repined at the waste of this warm June.

The clocks had struck two when he reached Leppard

Street, and the houses confronted him, their roofs and
chimneys prinked with stars. Several windows glimmered—
with a turbid orange light ; but these signals of habitation
only emphasized the unconsciousness of the sleepers
behind, and made the desolation of the rest more
positive. The windows of his old rooms were black, and
Michaël unlocked the front-door quietly and stood listening for a moment in the passage. He could hear a low
snarling in the bedroom, but from where he was standing
not a word was distinct and he could not bring himself to
the point of listening close to the keyhole. He shut the
front-door and waited in the blackness, fascinated by the rise
and fall of the low snarl that was seeming so sinister in this
house. It was incredible that a brief movement would open
the front-door again and let in the starlight ; for, as he stood
here, Leppard Street was under the earth deep down. He
moved a little farther into the hall and, putting out his
hand to feel for the balusters, drew back with a start, for
he might have clapped it down upon a cold bald head, so
much like that was the newel's wooden knob. Still the
snarling rose and fell : the darkness grew thicker and every
instant more atramental, beating upon him from the
steeps of the house like the filthy wings of a great bat : and
still the snarling rose and fell. It rose and fell like the
bubbling of a kettle, and then without warning the kettle
overflowed with spit and hiss and commotion. Every word
spoken by Barnes and the woman was now audible.

" I say he gave you thirty-shillings. Now then," Barnes
yapped.

" And I tell you he only gave me a sovereign, which you've
had."

" Don't I hear through the door what you get ...

Michael knew why Barnes had not been able to keep his
appointment to-night, and though he was outraged at the use
to which his rooms had been put, he was glad to be relieved

of the fear that this snarling was the prelude to the revelation of Barnes as a murderer. The recriminations with their
details of vileness were not worth hearing longer, and
Michael went quickly and quietly out into the Summer
night, which smelt so sweet after that passage.

He turned round by the lamp-post at the corner and
looked back at the five stark houses; he could not abandon
their contemplation; and he pored upon them as intensely
as he might have pored upon a tomb of black basalt rising
out of desert sand. He was immured in the speculation
of their blackness: he pondered hopelessly their meaning
and brooded upon the builders that built them and the
sphinx that commanded them to be built.

In his present mood Michael would have thought Stone-
henge rather prosaic; and he leaned against the wall in
the silence, thinking of brick upon brick, of brick upon
brick slabbed with mortar and chipped and tapped in
the past, of brick upon brick as the houses grew higher
and higher a railway-engine shrieked suddenly: the
door of Number One slammed: and a woman came hurrying down the steps. She looked for a moment to right and
left of her, and then she moved swiftly with a wild irregular
walk in Michael's direction. He had a sensation that she
had known he was standing here against this wall, that she
had watched him all the while and was hurrying now to ask
why he had been standing here against this wall. He could
not turn and walk away: he could not advance to meet her:
so he stood still leaning against the wall. Michael saw her
very plainly as she passed him in the lamplight. Her hat
was askew, and a black ostrich plume hung down over her
big chalky face: her lips were glistening as if they had
been smeared with jam. She was wearing a black satin
cloak, and she seemed, as her skirts swept past him, like an
overblown grotesque of tragedy being dragged by a wire
from the scene.

Michael shuddered at the monstrousness of her femininity; he seemed to have been given a glimpse of a mere mass of woman, a soft obscene primeval thing that demanded blows from a club, nothing else. He realized how in a moment men could become haters of femininity, could hate its animalism and wish to stamp upon it. The physical repulsion he had felt vanished when the sound of her footsteps had died away. In the reaction, Michael pitied her, and he went back quickly to Number One with the intention of turning Barnes into the street. He was rather startled as he walked up the steps to see Barnes' face pressed against the window-pane, for it seemed to him ludicrous that he should wave reassuringly to a mask like that.

Barnes hurried to open the front-door before Michael had taken the key from his pocket, and was not at all surprized to see him.

"Here, I couldn't get down to the Orange to-night. I've had a bit of trouble with this girl."

The gas was flaring in the sitting-room by now, and the night, which outside had been lightening for dawn, was black as ink upon the panes.

"Sit on the bed. The chairs are all full of her dirty clothes. I'll pull the blinds down. I'm going to leave here to-morrow, Fane. Did you see her going down the road? She must have passed you by. I tell you straight, Fane, half an hour back I was in two minds to do her in. I was, straight. And I would have, if . . . . Oh, well, I kept my temper and threw her out instead. Gratitude! It's my belief gratitude doesn't exist in this world. You sit down and have a smoke. He left some cigarettes behind."

"Who did?" Michael asked sharply.

"Who did what?"

"Left these cigarettes."

"Oh, they're some I bought yesterday," said Barnes.

"I think it's just as well for you that you are going to-morrow morning. I hope you quite realize that otherwise I should have turned you out."

"Well, don't look at me in that tone of voice," Barnes protested. "I've had quite enough to worry me without any nastiness between old friends to make it worse."

"You can't expect me to be pleased at the way you've treated my rooms," Michael said.

"Oh, the gas-stove, you mean?"

"It's not a question of gas-stoves. It's a question of living on a woman."

"Who did?"

"You!"

"If I'd had to live on her earnings, I should be very poorly off now," grumbled Barnes in an injured voice. Under Michael's attack he was regaining his old perkiness.

"At any rate, you must go to-morrow morning," Michael insisted.

"Don't I keep on telling you that I'm going? It's no good for you to nag at me, Fane."

"And what about the woman?"

"Her? Let her go to ——," said Barnes contemptuously. "She can't do me any harm. What if she does tell the coppers I've been living on her? They won't worry me unless they've nothing better to do, and I'll have hooked it by then."

"You're sure she can't do you any harm?" Michael asked gravely. "There's nothing else she could tell the police?"

"Here, what are you talking about?" asked Barnes, coming close to Michael and staring at him fixedly. Michael debated whether he should mention Cissie Cummings, but he lacked the courage either to frighten Barnes with the suggestion of his guilt or to preserve a superior attitude in the face of his enraged innocence.

"I shall come round to-morrow morning, or rather this

morning at nine," said Michael. "And I shall expect to find you ready to clear out of here for good."

"You're very short with a fellow, aren't you?" said Barnes. "What do you want to go away for? Why don't you stay so as you can see me off the premises?"

Michael thought that he could observe underneath all the assurance a sharp anxiety on Barnes' part not to be left alone.

"You can lay down and have a sleep in here. I'll get on into the bedroom."

Michael consented to stay, and Barnes was obviously relieved. He put out the gas and retired into the bedroom. The dawn was greying the room, and the sun would be up in less than an hour. Early sparrows were beginning to chirp. The woman who had burst out of the door and fled up the street seemed now a chimera of the night. Half-dozing Michael lay on the bed, half-dozing and faintly oppressed by the odour of patchouli coming from the clothes heaped upon the chairs. St. George was visible already, and even the outlines of The Knight in Armour were tremulously apparent. Michael wondered why he did not feel a greater resentment at the profanation of these rooms. And why did Barnes keep fidgeting on the other side of the folding doors? The sparrows were cheeping more loudly : the trains were more frequent. Michael woke from sleep with a start and saw that Barnes' was throwing the clothes from the chairs on the floor : stirred up thus in this clear light the scent of patchouli was even more noticeable. What on earth was Barnes doing? He was turning the whole room upside down.

"What the deuce are you looking for?" Michael yawned.

"That's all right, old man, you get on with your sleep. I'm just putting my things together," Barnes told him.

Michael turned over and was beginning to doze again,

when Barnes woke him by the noise he made in taking the dirty dishes out of the old grate.

"How on earth can I sleep, when you're continually fidgeting?" Michael demanded fretfully. "What's the time?"

"Just gone half-past five."

Barnes paid no more attention to Michael's rest, but began more feverishly than ever to rummage among all the things in the room.

Michael could not stand his activity any longer, and dry-mouthed from an uncomfortable sleep he sat up.

"What *are* you looking for?"

"Well, if you want to know, I'm looking for a watch-bracelet."

"It's not likely to be under the carpet," said Michael severely.

Barnes was wrenching out the tacks to Michael's annoyance.

"Perhaps it isn't," Barnes agreed. "But I've got to find this watch-bracelet. It's gold. I don't want to lose it."

"Was it a woman's?"

Barnes looked round at him like a small animal alarmed.

"Yes, it was a woman's. What makes you ask?"

"What's it like?"

"Gold. Gold, I keep telling you."

"When did you have it last?"

"Last night."

"Well, it can't have gone far."

"No, blast it, of course it can't," said Barnes, searching with renewed impatience. He was throwing the clothes about the room again, and the odour of staleness became nauseating.

"I'm going to wash," Michael announced, moving across to the bedroom.

"You'll excuse the untidiness," Barnes called out, after him in a tone of rather strained jocularity.

Of Michael's old room no vestige remained. A very large double-bed took up almost all the space, and all the furniture was new and tawdry. The walls were hung with studies of cocottes pretending to be naiads and dryads, — horrible women posed in the silvanity of a photographer's studio. The room was littered with clothes, and Michael could not move a step without entangling his feet in a petticoat or treading upon hidden shoes. He tried to splash his face, but the very washstand was sickly.

"Well, you've managed to debauch my bedroom quite successfully," he said to Barnes, when he came back to the sitting-room.

"That's all right. I'll get rid of all the new furniture. I can pop the lot. Well, it's mine. If I could find this bloody watch-bracelet, I could begin to make some arrangements."

"What about breakfast?" Michael began to look for something to eat. Every plate and knife was dirty, and there were three or four half-finished tins of condensed milk which had turned pistachio green and stank abominably.

"There's a couple of herrings somewhere," said Barnes. "Or there was. But everything seems upside down this morning. Where the hell is that watch? It can't have walked away on its own. If that mare took it! I've a very particular reason for not wanting to lose that watch. Oh, —— ——! wherever can it have got to?"

"Well, anyway shut up using such filthy language. When does the milkman come round?"

"I don't know when he comes round. Here, Fane, have you ever heard of anyone talking in their sleep?"

"Of course I've heard of people talking in their sleep," Michael answered. "It's not very unusual."

"Ah, hollering out, yes—but talking in a sensible sort

of a way, so that if you came in and listened to what they said, you'd think it was the truth ? Have you ever heard of that ?"

"I don't suppose I can give you an instance, but obviously it must often happen."

"Must it ?" said Barnes in a depressed voice. "You see, I set particular value by this watch-bracelet ; and I thought perhaps I might have talked about it in my sleep, and that mare just to spite me have gone and taken it. I wonder where it is now."

Michael also began to wonder where it was now, and Barnes' anxiety was transferred to him, so that he began to fancy the whole of this fine morning was tremendously bound up with exactly where the watch-bracelet now was. Barnes had begun to turn over everything for about the sixth time.

"If the watch is here," said Michael irritably, " it will be found when you move your things out, and if it's not here, it's useless to go on worrying about it."

"Ah, it's all very nice for you to be so calm. But what price its being my watch that's lost, not yours, old sport ?"

"I'm not going to talk about it any more," Michael declared. " I want to know what you're going to do when you leave here."

"Ah, that's it. What am I ?"

"Would you like to go to the Colonies ?"

"What, say good-bye to dear old Leicester-Square and pop off for good and all ? I wouldn't mind."

"I don't mind telling you," said Michael, " that if I'd discovered you here a week ago living like this, I should have had nothing more to do with you. As it is I've a good mind to sling you out to look after yourself. However, I'm willing to get you a ticket for wherever you think you'd like to go, and when I hear you've arrived, I'll send you enough money to keep you going for a time."

"Fane, I don't mind saying it. You've been a good pal to me."

"Hark, there's the milkman at last," Michael exclaimed. He went out into the sparkling air of the fine Summer morning and came back with plenty of milk for breakfast. After they had made a sort of meal, he suggested that Barnes ought to come with him and visit some of the Colonial Agencies. They walked down Victoria Street and across St. James' Park, and in the Strand he made Barnes have a shave. The visit to the barber took away some of his nocturnal raffishness, and Michael found him very amusing during the various discussions that took place in the Agencies.

"I think the walk has done you good."

"Yes," Barnes doubtfully admitted. "I don't think it has done me much harm."

They had lunch at Romano's, where Barnes drank a good deal of Chianti and became full of confidence in his future.

"That's where it is, Fane. A fellow like you is lucky. But that's no reason why I shouldn't be lucky in my turn. My life has been a failure so far. Yes, I'm not going to attempt to deny it. There are lots of things in my life that might have been different. You'll understand when I say different, I mean pleasanter for everybody all round, myself included. But that's all finished. With this fruit-farm—well, of course it's no good grumbling and running down good things—those apples we saw were big enough to make anybody's fortune! Cawdashit, Fane, I can see myself sitting under one of those apple-trees and counting the bloody fruit falling down at my feet and me popping them into baskets and selling them—where was it he said we sold them?" Barnes poured out more Chianti. "Really it seems a sin on a fine day like this to be hanging about in London. Well, I've had some sprees in old London, and that's a fact ; so I'm not going to start running it down now. If I hadn't lost that watch-bracelet, I wouldn't give a damn for anybody. "Good old London," he went on meditatively. "Yes, I've had some times—good times and bad times, and here I am."

He gradually became incoherent, and Michael thought it would be as well to escort him back to Leppard Street and impress on him once again that he must remove all his things immediately.

"You'll have to be quick with your packing-up. You ought to sail next week. I shall go and see about your passage to-morrow."

They drove back to Leppard Street in a taxi, and as they got out, Barnes said emphatically :

"You know what it is, Fane ? Cawdashit ! I feel like a marquis when I'm out with you, and if I hadn't have lost that watch-bracelet I'd feel like the bloody German Emperor. That's me. All up in the air one minute, and yet worry myself barmy over a little thing like a watch the next.

"Hullo !" he exclaimed, looking up the road as their taxi drove off. "Somebody else is playing at being a millionaire."

Another taxi was driving into Leppard Street.

Michael had already opened the front-door, and he told Barnes not to hang about on the steps. Barnes turned reluctantly from his inspection of the new taxi's approach. It pulled up at Number One, and three men jumped out.

"That's your man," Michael heard one of them say, and in another moment he heard, "Henry Meats . . . I hold a warrant . . . murder of Cissie . . . anything you say . . . used against you," all in the mumbo-jumbo of a nightmare.

Michael came down the steps again very quickly; and Barnes, now handcuffed, turned to him despairingly.

"Tell 'em my name isn't Meats, Fane. Tell 'em they've

made a mistake. Oh, my God, I never done it. I never done it."

The two men were pushing him, dead white, crumpled, sobbing, into the taxi; he seemed very small beside the big men with their square shoulders and bristly moustaches. Michael heard him still moaning as the taxi jangled and whirred abruptly forward. The third man watched it disappear between the two walls; then he strolled up the steps to enter the house. Mrs. Cleghorne was already in the hall, and over the balusters of each landing faces could be seen peering down. As if the word were uttered by the house itself, 'murder' floated in a whisper upon the air. The faces shifted; doors opened and shut far above; footsteps hurried to and fro; and still of all these sounds 'murder' was the most audible.

"This is the gentleman who rents the rooms," Mrs. Cleghorne was saying.

"But I've not been near them till yesterday evening for six months," Michael hurriedly explained.

"That's quite right," Mrs. Cleghorne echoed.

"Well, I'm afraid we must go through them," said the officer.

"Oh, of course."

"Let me see, is this your address?"

"Well, no—Cheyne Walk—173."

"We might want to have a little talk with you about this here Meats."

Michael was enraged with himself for not asseverating 'Barnes! Barnes! Barnes!' as he had been begged to do. He despised himself for not trying to save that white crumpled thing huddled between those big men with their bristly moustaches; yet all the while he felt violently afraid that the police officer would think him involved in these disgraceful rooms, that he would suppose the pictures and the tawdry furniture belonged to him, that he would imagine the petticoats and underlinen strewn about the floor had something to do with him.

"If you want me," he found himself saying, "you have my address."

Quickly he hurried away from Leppard Street, and travelled in a trance of shame to Hardingham. Alan was just going in to bat, when Michael walked across from the Hall to the cricket-field.

Stella came from her big basket chair to greet him, and for a while he sat with her in the buttercups, watching Alan at the wicket. Nothing had ever seemed so easy as the bowling of the opposite side on this fine June evening, and Michael tried to banish the thought of Barnes in the spaciousness of these level fields. Stella was evidently being very careful not to convey the impression that she had lately won a victory over him. It was really ridiculous, Michael thought, as he plucked idly the buttercups and made desultory observations to Stella about the merit of a stroke by Alan, it was more than ridiculous, it was deliberate folly to enmesh himself with such horrors as he had beheld at Leppard Street. There were doubtless very unpleasant events continually happening in this world, but wilfully to drag oneself into misery on account of them was merely to show an incapacity to appreciate the more fortunate surroundings of one's allotted niche. The avoidance of even the sight of evil was as justifiable as the avoidance of evil itself, and the moral economy of the world might suffer a dangerous displacement, if everyone were to involve themselves in such events as those in which himself had lately been involved. Duty was owing all the time to people nearer at hand than Barnes. No doubt the world would be better for being rid of him; diseases of the body must be fought, and the corruption of human society must be cleansed. Any pity for Barnes was a base senti-mentalism; it was merely a reaction of personal discom-

fort at having seen an unpleasant operation. The senti-
mentalism of that cry ' don't hurt him ' was really contemptible, and since it seemed that he was likely to be too
weak to bear the sight of the cleansing knife, he must in
future avoid the occasion of its use. Otherwise his intellectual outlook was going to be sapped, and he would find
himself in the ranks of the faddists.

" I think I shall stay down here the rest of the summer,
if I may," he said to Stella.

" My dear, of course you can. We'll have a wonderful
time. Hullo, Alan is retiring."

Alan came up and sat beside them in the buttercups.

" I thought I saw you just as I was going in," he said.
" Anything going on in town ? "

" No, nothing much," said Michael. " I saw a man
arrested for murder this afternoon."

" Did you really ? How beastly. Our team's just beginning to get into shape. I say, Stella. That youth
working on old Rundle's farm is going to be pret-ty good.
Did you see him lift their fast bowler twice running over
the pond ? "

Michael strolled away to take a solitary walk. It seemed
incredible now to think that he had brought Lily down
here, that he had wandered with her over this field. What
an infringement it must have seemed to Stella and Alan
of their already immemorial peace. They had really been
very good about his invasion. And here was the wood where
he and Stella had fought. Michael sat down in the glade
and listened to the busy flutterings of the birds. Why
had Stella objected to his marriage with Lily ? All the
superficial answers were ready at once ; but was not her
real objection only another facet of the diamond of selfishness ? Selfishness was a diamond. Precious, hard, and very
often beautiful—when seen by itself.

Michael spent a week at Hardingham during which he

managed to put out of his mind the thought of Barnes in prison awaiting his trial. Then one day the butler informed him of a person wishing to speak to him. In the library he found the detective who had asked for his address at Leppard Street.

"Sorry to have to trouble you, sir, but there was one or two little questions we wanted to ask."

Michael feared he would have to appear at the trial, and asked at once if that was going to be necessary.

"Oh, no, I don't think so. We've got it all marked out fair and square against Mr. Meats. He doesn't stand a chance of getting off. How did you come to be mixed up with him?"

Michael explained the circumstances which had led up to his knowing Meats.

"I see; and you just wanted to give him a bit of a helping hand. Oh, well, the feeling does you credit, I'm bound to say; but another time, sir, I should make a few enquiries first. We should probably have had him before, if he hadn't been helped by you. Of course I quite understand you knew nothing about this murder, but anyone can often do a lot of harm by helping undeserving people. We mightn't have nabbed him even now, if some woman hadn't brought us a nice little bit of evidence, and I found some more things myself after a search. Oh, yes, he doesn't stand an earthly. We knew for a moral cert who did it, straight away; but the police don't get a fair chance in England. We let all these blooming Radicals interfere too much. That's my opinion. Anyone would think the police was a lot of criminals by the way some people talk about them."

"Is anybody defending him?" Michael asked.

"Oh, he'll be awarded a counsel," said the detective indignantly. "For which you and me has to pay. That's a nice thing, isn't it? But he doesn't stand an earthly."

"Where will he be hanged?"

" Pentonville."

Michael thought how Mrs. Murdoch in Neptune Crescent would shudder some Tuesday morning in the near future.

" I'm sorry you should have had to come all this way to find me," Michael said. He hated himself for being polite to the inspector, but he could not help it. He rang the bell.

" Oh, Dawkins, will you give Inspector—what is your name, by the bye ? "

" Dawkins," said the inspector.

" How curious," Michael laughed.

" Yes, sir," the inspector laughed.

" Lunch in the gun room, Dawkins. You must be hungry."

" Well, sir, I could do with a snack, I daresay." He followed his namesake from the room, and outside Michael could hear them begin to chatter of the coincidence.

" But supposing I'd been in the same state of life as Meats," Michael said to himself. " What devil's web wouldn't they be trying to spin round me ? "

He was seized with fury at himself for his cowardice. He had thought of nothing but his own reputation ever since Meats had been arrested. He had worried over the opinion of a police inspector ; had been ashamed of the appearance of the rooms ; had actually been afraid that he would be implicated in the disgraceful affair. So long as it had been easy to flatter himself with the pleasure he was giving or the good he was doing to Meats, he had kept him with money. Now when Meats had been dragged away, he was anxious to disclaim the whole acquaintance-ship for fear of the criticism of a big man with a bristly moustache. The despair in Meats' last cry to him echoed round this library. He had seen society in action : not all the devils and fiends imagined by mediæval monks were so horrible as those big men with bristly moustaches. What did they know of Meats and his life ? What did they care,

4 C

but that they were paid by society to remove rubbish ? Justice had decreed that Meats should be arrested, and like a dead rat in the gutter he was swept-up by these scavengers. What compact had he broken that men should freeze to stones and crush him ? He had broken the laws of men and the laws of God ; he had committed murder. And were not murders as foul being committed every moment ? Murdered ambition, murdered love, murdered pity, murdered gratitude, murdered faith, did none of these cry out for vengeance ?

Society had seized the murderer, and it was useless to cry out. Himself was as impotent as the prisoner. Meats had sinned against the hive : this infernal hive, herd, pack, swarm, whichever word expressed what he felt to be the degradation of an interdependent existence. Mankind was become a great complication of machinery fed by gold and directed by fear. Something was needed to destroy this gregarious organism. War and pestilence must come ; but in the past these two had come often enough, and mankind was the same afterwards. This ant-hill of a globe had been ravaged often enough, but the ants were all busy again carrying their mean little burdens of food hither and thither in affright for the comfort of their mean little lives.

"And I'm as bad as any of them," said Michael to himself. "I know I have obligations in Leppard Street, and I've run away from them because I'm afraid of what people will think. Of course I always fail. I'm a coward!"

He could not stay any longer at Hardingham. He must go and see about Mrs. Smith now. Society would be seizing her soon and bringing her miserable life to an end in white-washed prison corridors. He must do something for Meats. Perhaps he would not be able to save him from death, but he must not sit here ringing bells for butlers called Dawkins to feed inspectors called Dawkins.

Stella came in with the first roses of the year.

"Aren't they beauties ?"

"Yes, splendid. I'm going up to town this afternoon."

"But not for long ? "

"I don't know. It depends. Do you know, Stella, it's an extraordinary thing, but ever since you've practically given up playing, I feel very much more alive. How do you account for that ? "

"Well, I haven't given up playing for one thing," Stella contradicted.

"Stella, do you ever feel inspired nowadays ?"

"Not so much as I did," she admitted.

"I feel now as if I were on the verge of an inspiration."

"Not another Lily," she said quickly with half a laugh.

"You've no right to sneer at me about that," he said fiercely. "You must be very careful, you know. *You'll* become flabby, if you aren't careful, here at Hardingham."

"Oh, Michael," she laughed. "Don't look at me as if you were a Major Prophet. I won't become flabby. I shall start composing at once."

"There you are," he cried triumphantly. "Never say again that I can't wake you up."

"You did not wake me up."

"I did. I did. And do you know I believe I've discovered that I'm an anarchist ? "

"Is that your inspiration ? "

"Who knows ? It may be."

"Well, don't come and be anarchical down here, because Alan is going to stand at the next election."

"What on earth good would Alan be in Parliament ?" Michael asked derisively. "He's much too happy."

"Michael, why are you so horrid about Alan nowadays ?"

He was penitent in a moment at the suggestion, but when he said good-bye to Stella he had a curious feeling that from henceforth he was going to be stronger than her.

On reaching London, Michael went to see Castleton at the Temple, and he found him in chambers at the top of dusty stairs in King's Bench Walk.

"Lucky to get these, wasn't I?" said Castleton. "By craning out of the window the river was visible.

"I suppose you've never had a murder case yet?" Michael asked.

"Not yet," said Castleton. "In fact, I'm going in for Chancery work. And I shall get my first brief in about five years with luck."

Michael enquired how one went to work to retain the greatest criminal advocate of the day, and Castleton said he would have to be approached through a solicitor.

"Well, will you get hold of him for me?"

Castleton looked rather blank.

"If you can't get him, get the next best, and so on. Tell him the man I want to defend hasn't a chance, and that's why I'm particularly anxious he should get off."

They discussed details for some time, and Castleton was astonished at Michael's wish to aid Meats.

"It seems very perverse," he said.

"Perverse!" Michael echoed. "And what about your profession? That is really the most perverse factor in modern life."

"But in this case," Castleton argued, "the victim seems so utterly worthless."

"Exactly," said Michael. "But as society never interfered when he was passively offensive, why, the moment he becomes actively offensive, should society have the right to put him out of the way? They never tried to cure him for his own good. Why should they kill him for their own?"

"You want to strike at the foundations of the legal system," said the barrister.

"Exactly," Michael agreed; and the argument came

to an end because there was obviously nothing more to be said.

Castleton promised to do all he could for Meats, and also to keep Michael's name out of the business. As Michael walked down the stairs, it gave him a splendid satisfaction to think how already the law was being set in motion against the law. A blow for Inspector Dawkins. And what about the murdered girl? " She won't be helped by Meats' death," said Michael to himself. " Society is not considering her protection now any more than it did when she was alive." *No slops must be emptied here:* and as Michael read the ascetic command above the tap on the stairs he wondered for a moment if he were, after all, a sentimentalist.

Mrs. Cleghorne was very voluble when he reached Leppard Street.

" A nice set-out and no mistake," she declared. " Half of the neighbourhood have been peeping over my area railings as if the murder had been done in here. Mr. Cleghorne's quite hoarse with hollering out to them to keep off. And it never rains but what it pours. There's a poor woman gone and died here now. However, a funeral's a little more lively than the police nosing round, though her not having a blessed halfpenny and owing me three weeks on the rent it certainly won't be anything better than a pauper's funeral."

" What woman ? " Michael asked.

" Oh, a invalid-dressmaker which I've been very good to —a Mrs. Smith."

" Dead ? " he echoed.

" Yes, dead, and laid out and got a clergyman sitting with her body. Well, clergyman ? Roman Catholic I *should* say. It quite worried Mr. Cleghorne. He said it gave him the rats to have a priest hanging around so close at hand. You see, being asthmatic, he's read a lot about these Roman Catholics, and he doesn't hold with them. They're that underhand, he says, it makes him nervous."

"Can I see this priest?" Michael asked.

"Well, it's hardly the room you're accustomed to. I've really looked at her more as a charity than an actual lodger. In fact my poor old mother has gone on at me something cruel for being so good to her."

"I think I should like to see this priest," Michael persisted.

Mrs. Cleghorne was with difficulty persuaded to show him the way, and she was evidently a little suspicious of the motive of his visit. They descended into the gloom of the basement, and the landlady pointed out to him the room that was down three steps and up another. She excused herself from coming too. The priest, a monkey-faced Irishman, was sitting on the pale blue chest, and as Michael entered, he did not look up from his Office.

"Is that you, Sister?" he asked. Then he perceived Michael and waited for him to explain his business.

"I wanted to ask about this poor woman."

Mrs. Smith lay under a sheet with candles winking at her head. Nothing was visible except her face still faintly rouged in the daylight.

"I was interested in her," Michael explained.

"Indeed!" said the priest, dryly. "I wouldn't have thought so."

"Is her cat here?"

"There was some sort of an animal, but the woman of the house took it off."

A silence followed, and Michael was aware of the priest's hostility.

"I suppose she didn't see her son before she died?" Michael went on. "Her son is with the Jesuits."

"You seem to know a great deal about the poor soul?"

"I thought I had managed to help her," said Michael in a sad voice.

"Indeed ?" commented the priest even more dryly.

"And there is nothing I can do now ?"

"Almighty God has taken her," said the priest. "There is nothing you can do."

"I could have some Masses said for her."

"Are you a Catholic ?" the priest asked.

"No ; but I fancy I shall be a Catholic," Michael said ; and as he spoke, it was like a rushing wind. He hurried out into the passage where a nun passed him in the gloom. "She will be praying," Michael thought, and looking back over his shoulder he said :

"Pray for me, Sister."

The nun was evidently startled by the voice, and went on quickly down the three steps and up the other into Mrs. Smith's den.

Michael climbed upstairs to interview the Solutionist. He found him lying in bed.

"Why wasn't that money paid regularly ?" he asked severely.

"Who is it ?" the Solutionist muttered in fuddled accents. "Wanted the money myself. Had a glorious time. The cat's all right; and the poor old rabbits are dead. Can't give everybody a good time. Somebody's got to suffer in this world."

Michael left him, and without entering his old rooms again went away from Leppard Street.

The moment had come to visit Rome, and remembering how he had once dissuaded Maurice from going there, he felt some compunction now in telling him that he wanted to travel alone. However, it would be impossible to visit Rome for the first time with Maurice. In the studio he led up to his backing out of the engagement.

"About this going abroad," he began.

"I say, Michael, I don't think I can come just now. The editor of The Point of View wants a series of articles on the ballet, and I'm going to start on them at once."

It was a relief to Michael, and he wished Maurice good luck.

"Yes, I think they're going to be rather good," he said confidently. "I'm going to begin with the Opera: then the Empire and the Alhambra: and in September there will be the new ballet at the Orient. Of course I've got a theory about English ballet."

"Is there anything about which you haven't got a theory?" Michael asked. "Hullo, you've got the Venetian mirror from Ararat House. I'm so glad."

"I've arranged all that," Maurice said. "Lily Haden has gone to live with a girl called Sylvia Scarlett. Rather a terror, I thought."

"Yes, I had an idea you'd find her a bit difficult."

"Oh, but I scored off her in the end," said Maurice quickly.

"Congratulations," said Michael. "Well, I'm going to Rome."

"I say, rather hot."

"So much the better."

"I used to be rather keen on Rome, but I've a theory it's generally a disappointment. However, I suppose I shall have to go one day."

"Yes, I don't think Rome ought to miss your patronage, Maurice."

They parted as intimate friends, but while Michael was going downstairs from the studio he thought that it might very easily be for the last time.

His mother was at home for tea; lots of women and a bishop were having a committee about something. When they had all rustled away into the mellow June evening, Michael asked what had been accomplished.

"It's this terrible state of the London streets," said Mrs. Fane. "Something has got to be done about these miserable women. The Bishop of Chelsea has promised to bring in some kind of a bill in Parliament. He feels so strongly about it."

"What does he feel ?" Michael asked.

"Why, of course, that they shouldn't be allowed."

"The remedy lies with him," Michael said. "He must take them the Sacraments."

"My dearest boy, what are you talking about ? He does his best. He's always picking them up and driving them home in his brougham. He can't do more than that. Really he quite thrilled us with some of his experiences."

Michael laughed and took hold of her hand.

"What would you say if I told you that I was thinking very seriously of being a priest ?"

"Oh, my dear Michael, and you look so particularly nice in tweeds."

Michael laughed and went upstairs to pack. He would leave London to-morrow morning.

Chapter X : *The Old World*

THE train crashed southward from Paris through the night; and when dawn was quivering upon the meadows near Chambéry Michael was sure with an almost violent elation that he had left behind him the worst hardships of thought. Waterfalls swayed from the mountains, and the grey torrents they fed plunged along beside the train. Down through Italy they travelled all day, past the cypresses, and the olive-trees wise and graceful in the sunlight. It was already dusk when they reached the Campagna, and through the ghostly light the ghostly flowers and grasses shimmered for a while and faded out. It was hot travelling after sunset; but when the lights of Rome broke in a sudden blaze and the train reached the station it was cool upon the platform. Michael let a porter carry his luggage to an hotel close at hand. Then he walked quickly down the Esquiline Hill. He wandered on past the restaurants and the barber-shops, caring for nothing but the sensation of walking down a wide street in Rome.

"There has been nothing like this," he said, "since I walked down the High. There will be nothing like this ever again."

Suddenly in a deserted square he was looking over a parapet at groups of ruined columns, and immediately afterwards he was gazing up at one mighty column jet black against the starshine. He saw that it was figured with innumerable horses and warriors.

"We must seek for truth in the past," he said.

How this great column affected him with the secrets of the past. It was only by that made so much mightier than the bars of his cot in Carlington Road, which had once seemed to hold passions, intrigues, rumours, ambitions and revenges. All that he had once dimly perceived as shadowed forth by them was here set forth absolutely. What was this column called? He looked round vaguely for an indication of the name. What did the name matter? There would be time to find a name in the morning. There would be time in the morning to begin again the conduct of his life. The old world held the secret; and he would accept this solitary and perdurable column as the symbol of that secret.

"All that I have done and experienced so far," Michael thought, "would not scratch this stone. I have been concerned for the happiness of other people without gratitude for the privilege of service. I have been given knowledge and I fancied I was given disillusion. If now I offer myself to God very humbly, I give myself to the service of man. Man for man standing in his own might is a blind and arrogant leader. The reason why the modern world is so critical of the fruits of Christianity after nineteen hundred years is because they have expected it from the beginning to be a social panacea. God has only offered to the individual the chance to perfect himself, but the individual is much more anxious about his neighbour. How in a moment our little herds are destroyed, whether in ships on the sea or in towns by earthquake, or by the great illusions of political experiment! Soon will come a great war, and everybody will discover it has come either because people are Christians or because they are not Christians. Nobody will think it is because each man wants to interfere with the conduct of his neighbour. That woman in Leppard Street who died in the peace of God, how much more was she a Christian than me, who without perceiving the beam in my own eye have trotted round operating on the motes of other people. And once I had to make an effort to kiss her in fellowship. Rome! Rome! how parochial you make my youth."

The last exclamation was uttered aloud.

"Meditating upon the decline and fall of the Roman Empire?" said a voice.

A man in a black cloak was speaking.

"No, I was thinking of the pettiness of youthful tragedies," said Michael.

"There is only one tragedy for youth."

"And that is?"

"Age," said the stranger.

"And what is the tragedy of age?"

"There is no tragedy of age," said the stranger.

THE END

Volume One
  Westminster
  Phillack
Volume Two
  Capri
  Iver   *July, 1912—October, 1914.*

Epilogical Letter

to

JOHN NICOLAS MAVROGORDATO

My dear John,

There is, I am inclined to think, a very obstinate shamelessness in prolonging this book with a letter to you. For that reason I append it thus as an epilogue: so that whoever wishes to read it will only have himself to blame, since he will already, as I hope, have finished the book.

You will remember that last year the first volume of Sinister Street obtained a great advertisement through the action of certain libraries. Whatever boom was thus effected will certainly be drowned this year in the roar of cannon, and the doctrine of compensation is in no danger of being disproved. I fancy, too, that the realities of war will obtain me a pardon in this volume for anything that might formerly have offended the sensitive or affronted the simple.

Much more important than libraries and outraged puritans is the question of the form of the English novel. There has lately been noticeable in the press a continuous suggestion that the modern novel is thinly disguised autobiography; and since the lives of most men are peculiarly formless this suggestion has been amplified into an attack upon the form of the novel. In my own case many critics have persisted in regarding Sinister Street merely as an achievement of memory, and I have felt sometimes that I ought to regard myself as a sort of literary Datas, rather than as a mask veiling the nature of a — novelist. You know from many hours of talk that if I were to set down all I could remember of my childhood, the book would not by this time have reached much beyond my fifth

i

year. Obviously in so far as I chose my own public school and my own college at Oxford there has been autobiography, but I fancy it would have been merely foolish to send Michael to Cambridge, a place of which I know absolutely nothing. Yourself assures me that nowadays it is a much better university than Oxford, and in thinking thus you are the only Oxford man who has ever held such a heresy. Obviously, too, it was unavoidable in writing about St. James' that I should draw certain characters from the life, and for doing this I have been attacked on grounds of good taste. I do not recognize the right of schoolmasters to be exempt from the privilege of public men to be sometimes caricatured. Therefore I offer no apology for doing so. With regard to the Oxford dons I felt it really would be unfair to apply to them what is after all much more likely to be a true impression of their virtues and follies than those formed by a schoolboy of his masters. Therefore in this second volume there is not a single portrait of a don. As a matter of fact dons are to the undergraduate a much less important factor than the schoolmaster is to the schoolboy, and the few shadows of dons which appear in this volume are as vital as most dons in the flesh seem to the normal undergraduate.

The theme of Sinister Street is the youth of a man who presumably will be a priest. I shall be grateful if my readers will accept it as such rather than as an idealized or debased presentation of my own existence up to the age of twenty-three. Whether or not it was worth writing at such length depends finally, I claim, upon the number of people who can bear to read about it. A work of art is bounded by the capacity of the spectator to apprehend it as a whole. This on your authority was said by Aristotle. "Art," says The Sydney Bulletin, a curious antipodean paper, "is selection." "It is time to protest," says an American paper, "against these long books. At this rate we shall soon be spending all our time with books." "The enormous length must make it formless," other critics have decided. Ultimately I believe Aristotle's remark to be the *truest guide, and I am tempted to hope that with the publication of the second volume many irrelevancies have established their relevancy.*

It is obvious that were I to continue the life of Michael Fane to the end of his seventy-second year, his story would run into twenty volumes as thick as Sinister Street. My intention, however, was not to write a life, but the prologue of a life. He is growing up on the last page, and for me his interest begins to fade. He may have before him a thousand new adventures: he may become a Benedictine monk: he may become a society preacher. I have given you as fully as I could the various influences that went to mould him. Your imagination of him as a man will be determined by your prejudice gathered from the narrative of these influences. I do not identify myself with his opinions: at the same time I may believe in all of them. He is to me an objective reality: he is not myself in a looking-glass.

I would like to detain you for a moment with a defence of my occasional use of archaic and obsolete words. This is not due to any ' preciousness,' but to efforts at finding the only word that will say what I mean. To take two examples. ' Reasty ' — signifies ' covered with a kind of rust and having a rancid taste,' and it seems to me exactly to describe the London air at certain seasons, and also by several suggestive assonances to convey a variety of subtler effects. ' Inquiline ' sounds a pompous word for lodgers, but it has not yet been sentimentalized like ' pilgrim ' ; it is not an Americanism like ' transients,' and it does give to me the sense of a fleeting stay ; whereas lodgers sound dreadfully permanent since they have been given votes.

We have in the English language the richest and noblest in the world, and perhaps after this war we shall hear less of the advocates of pure Saxon, an advocacy which personally I find rather like the attitude of the plain man who wants to assert himself on his first introduction to a duke.

There remains for me to apologize for the delay in the appearance of this volume. You who know how many weeks I have spent ill in bed this year will forgive me, and through you I make an apology to other readers who by their expressions of interest in the date of the second volume have encouraged me so greatly. Finally it strikes me that I have seemed above to be grumbling at criticism. This is not so. I believe there is nobody, certainly no young writer who is under such a debt of obligation as I am to the encouragement and the sympathy of his anonymous critics.

Accept this dedicatory epilogue, my dear John, as the pledge of our enduring friendship.

Yours ever

Compton Mackenzie.

Iver, October 18, 1914.

WILLIAM BRENDON AND SON, LTD.
PRINTERS, PLYMOUTH.

MARTIN SECKER
HIS COMPLETE CATALOGUE. MCMXIV

NOTE
The books in this Catalogue
marked * will be published
early next year.

The Books in this list should be obtainable from all Booksellers and Libraries, and if any difficulty is experienced the Publisher will be glad to be informed of the fact. He will also be glad if those interested in receiving from time to time Announcement Lists, Prospectuses, &c., of new and forthcoming books from Number Five John Street, will send their names and addresses to him for this purpose. Any book in this list may be obtained on approval through the booksellers, or direct from the Publisher, on remitting him the published price, plus the postage.

Telephone City 4779
Telegraphic Address:
Psophidian London

PART ONE
INDEX OF AUTHORS

ABERCROMBIE, LASCELLES
- SPECULATIVE DIALOGUES. *Wide Crown 8vo.* 5s. net.

THOMAS HARDY: A CRITICAL STUDY. *Demy 8vo.* 7s. 6d. net.

THE EPIC (*The Art and Craft of Letters*). *F'cap 8vo.* 1s. net.

AFLALO, F. G.
BEHIND THE RANGES. *Wide Demy 8vo.* 10s. 6d. net.

REGILDING THE CRESCENT. *Demy 8vo.* 10s. 6d. net.

BIRDS IN THE CALENDAR. *Crown 8vo.* 3s. 6d. net.

ALLSHORN, LIONEL
- STUPOR MUNDI. *Medium Octavo.* 16s. net.

APPERSON, G. L.
*THE SOCIAL HISTORY OF SMOKING. *Post 8vo.* 6s. net.

ARMSTRONG, DONALD
THE MARRIAGE OF QUIXOTE. *Crown 8vo.* 6s.

ARTZIBASHEF, MICHAEL
SANINE. *Preface by Gilbert Cannan. Crown 8vo.* 6s.

BARRINGTON, MICHAEL
GRAHAME OF CLAVERHOUSE. *Imperial 8vo.* 30s. net. Edition de Luxe 63s. net.

3

BENNETT, ARNOLD
>   THOSE UNITED STATES.   *Post 8vo.   2s. 6d. net.*

BLACK, CLEMENTINA
>   THE LINLEYS OF BATH.   *Medium 8vo.   16s. net.*
>   THE CUMBERLAND LETTERS.   *Medium 8vo.   16s. net.*

BOULGER, D. C.
>   THE BATTLE OF THE BOYNE.   *Med. 8vo.   21s. net.*
>   THE IRISH EXILES AT ST. GERMAINS.   *Med. 8vo. 21s. net.*

BOTTOME, PHYLLIS
>   THE COMMON CHORD.   *Crown 8vo.   6s.*

BROWN, IVOR
>   *YEARS OF PLENTY.   *Crown 8vo.   6s.*

BURROW, C. KENNETT
>   CARMINA VARIA.   *F'cap 8vo.   2s. 6d. net.*

CALDERON, GEORGE (With St. John Hankin)
>   THOMPSON : A Comedy.   *Sq. Cr. 8vo.   2s. net.*

CANNAN, GILBERT
>   ROUND THE CORNER.   *Crown 8vo.   6s.*
>   OLD MOLE.   *Crown 8vo.   6s.*
>   *YOUNG EARNEST.   *Crown 8vo.   6s.*
>   *SAMUEL BUTLER : A CRITICAL STUDY.   *Demy 8vo. 7s. 6d. net.*
>   SATIRE (*The Art and Craft of Letters*).   *F'cap 8vo. 1s. net.*

CHESTERTON, G. K.
>   MAGIC : A Fantastic Comedy.   *Sq. Cr. 8vo.   2s. net.*

CLAYTON, JOSEPH
>   THE UNDERMAN.   *Crown 8vo.   6s.*
>   LEADERS OF THE PEOPLE.   *Demy 8vo.   12s. 6d. net.*
>   ROBERT KETT AND THE NORFOLK RISING.   *Demy 8vo.   8s. 6d. net.*

COKE, DESMOND
THE ART OF SILHOUETTE. *Demy 8vo. 10s. 6d. net.*

CRAVEN, A. SCOTT
THE FOOL'S TRAGEDY. *F'cap 8vo. 6s.*

DE SELINCOURT, BASIL
WALT WHITMAN : A CRITICAL STUDY. *Demy 8vo. 7s. 6d. net.*
RHYME (*The Art and Craft of Letters*). *F'cap 8vo. 1s. net.*

DRINKWATER, JOHN
WILLIAM MORRIS : A CRITICAL STUDY. *Demy 8vo. 7s. 6d. net.*
*D. G. ROSSETTI : A CRITICAL STUDY. *Demy 8vo. 7s. 6d. net.*
*THE LYRIC (*The Art and Craft of Letters*). *F'cap 8vo. 1s. net.*

DOUGLAS, NORMAN
FOUNTAINS IN THE SAND. *Wide Demy 8vo. 7s. 6d. net.*
OLD CALABRIA. *Demy 8vo. 15s. net.*

DOUGLAS, THEO
WHITE WEBS. *Crown 8vo. 6s.*

FALLS, CYRIL
*RUDYARD KIPLING : A CRITICAL STUDY. *Demy 8vo. 7s. 6d. net.*

FEA, ALLAN
OLD ENGLISH HOUSES. *Demy 8vo. 10s. 6d. net.*
NOOKS AND CORNERS OF OLD ENGLAND. *Small Crown 8vo. 5s. net.*
THE REAL CAPTAIN CLEVELAND. *Demy 8vo. 8s. 6d. net.*

FRANCIS, RENE
EGYPTIAN ÆSTHETICS. *Wide Demy 8vo. 7s. 6d. net.*

FREEMAN, A. M.
THOMAS LOVE PEACOCK : A CRITICAL STUDY. *Demy 8vo. 7s. 6d. net.*

Martin Secker's Catalogue of Books Published at Number Five John Street Adelphi

*Martin
Secker's
Catalogue of
Books
Published at
Number
Five John
Street
Adelphi*

GRETTON, R. H.
HISTORY (*The Art and Craft of Letters*).   *F'cap 8vo.*
1s. net.

HANKIN, ST. JOHN
THE DRAMATIC WORKS, with an Introduction by
John Drinkwater. *Small 4to. Definitive Limited
Edition in Three Volumes.* 25s. *net.*
THE RETURN OF THE PRODIGAL. *Sq. Cr. 8vo.* 2s. *net.*
THE CASSILIS ENGAGEMENT. *Sq. Cr. 8vo.* 2s. *net.*
THE CHARITY THAT BEGAN AT HOME. *Sq. Cr.
8vo.* 2s. *net.*
THE CONSTANT LOVER, ETC. *Sq. Cr. 8vo.* 2s. *net.*

HAUPTMANN, GERHART
THE COMPLETE DRAMATIC WORKS. *6 vols. Crown
8vo.* 5s. *net per volume.*

HEWLETT, WILLIAM
TELLING THE TRUTH.   *Crown 8vo.*   6s.
UNCLE'S ADVICE: A NOVEL IN LETTERS. *Cr. 8vo.*   6s.
*THE CHILD AT THE WINDOW. *Crown 8vo.*   6s.

HORSNELL, HORACE
THE BANKRUPT.   *Crown 8vo.*   6s.

HOWE, P.P.
THE REPERTORY THEATRE.   *Cr. 8vo.*   2s. 6d. *net.*
DRAMATIC PORTRAITS.   *Crown 8vo.*   5s. *net.*
*BERNARD SHAW: A CRITICAL STUDY. *Demy 8vo.*
7s. 6d. *net.*
J. M. SYNGE: A CRITICAL STUDY. *Demy 8vo.*
7s. 6d. *net.*
CRITICISM (*The Art and Craft of Letters*). *F'cap
8vo.* 1s. *net.*

HUEFFER, FORD MADOX
HENRY JAMES: A CRITICAL STUDY. *Demy 8vo.*
7s. 6d. *net.*

6

IBSEN, HENRIK
  PEER GYNT. A New Translation by R. Ellis
  Roberts. *Wide Crown 8vo. 5s. net.*
JACOB, HAROLD
  PERFUMES OF ARABY. *Wide Demy 8vo. 7s. 6d. net.*
JAMES, HENRY
  *THE TURN OF THE SCREW. *F'cap 8vo. 2s. net.*
  *THE LESSON OF THE MASTER. *F'cap 8vo. 2s. net.*
  *THE ASPERN PAPERS. *F'cap 8vo. 2s. net.*
JOHNSON, OWEN
  THE SALAMANDER. *Crown 8vo. 6s.*
LAMONT, L. M.
  A CORONAL : AN ANTHOLOGY. *F'cap 8vo. 2s. 6d. net.*
  THOMAS ARMSTRONG, C.B. : A MEMOIR. *Demy 8vo. 10s. 6d. net.*
LLUELLYN, RICHARD
  THE IMPERFECT BRANCH. *Crown 8vo. 6s.*
LOW, IVY
  THE QUESTING BEAST. *Crown 8vo. 6s.*
MACHEN, ARTHUR
  HIEROGLYPHICS : A NOTE UPON ECSTASY IN LITERATURE. *F'cap 8vo. 2s. 6d. net.*
MACKENZIE, COMPTON
  CARNIVAL. *Crown 8vo. 6s. and 1s. net.*
  SINISTER STREET. Volume I. *Crown 8vo. 6s.*
  SINISTER STREET. Volume II. *Crown 8vo. 6s.*
  THE PASSIONATE ELOPEMENT. *Crown 8vo. 6s. and 2s. net.*
  *POEMS. *Crown 8vo. 5s. net.*
  KENSINGTON RHYMES. *Crown 4to. 5s. net.*
MAKOWER, S. V.
  THE OUTWARD APPEARANCE. *Crown 8vo. 6s.*
MAVROGORDATO, JOHN
  LETTERS FROM GREECE. *F'cap 8vo. 2s. net.*
  CASSANDRA IN TROY. *Small 4to. 5s. net.*

*Martin
Secker's
Catalogue of
Books
Published at
Number
Five John
Street
Adelphi*

MELVILLE, LEWIS

SOME ECCENTRICS AND A WOMAN. *Demy 8vo.* 10s. 6d. *net.*

METHLEY, VIOLET

CAMILLE DESMOULINS : A Biography.   *Demy 8vo.* 15s. *net.*

MEYNELL, VIOLA

LOT BARROW.	*Crown 8vo.*	6s.
MODERN LOVERS.	*Crown 8vo.*	6s.
*COLUMBINE.	*Crown 8vo.*	6s.

NIVEN, FREDERICK

A WILDERNESS OF MONKEYS.	*Crown 8vo.*	6s.
ABOVE YOUR HEADS.	*Crown 8vo.*	6s.
DEAD MEN'S BELLS.	*Crown 8vo.*	6s.
THE PORCELAIN LADY.	*Crown 8vo.*	6s.
HANDS UP !	*Crown 8vo.*	6s.

NORTH, LAURENCE

IMPATIENT GRISELDA.	*Crown 8vo.*	6s.
THE GOLIGHTLYS : FATHER AND SON.	*Cr. 8vo.*	6s.

ONIONS, OLIVER

WIDDERSHINS.	*Crown 8vo.*	6s.
IN ACCORDANCE WITH THE EVIDENCE.	*Cr. 8vo.*	6s.
THE DEBIT ACCOUNT.	*Crown 8vo.*	6s.
THE STORY OF LOUIE.	*Crown 8vo.*	6s.

PAIN, BARRY

ONE KIND AND ANOTHER.   *Crown 8vo.*   6s.
*THE SHORT STORY (*The Art and Craft of Letters*). *F'cap 8vo.*   1s. *net.*

PALMER, JOHN

*PETER PARAGON.   *Crown 8vo.*   6s.
COMEDY (*The Art and Craft of Letters*).   *F'cap 8vo.* 1s. *net.*

PERUGINI, MARK E.

*THE ART OF BALLET.   *Demy 8vo.*   15s. *net.*

PHILIPS, AUSTIN

*BATTLES OF LIFE.   *Crown 8vo.*   6s

8

PRESTON, ANNA
 The Record of a Silent Life. *Cr. 8vo.* 6s.

ROBERTS, R. ELLIS
 Henrik Ibsen : A Critical Study. *Demy 8vo.*
 7s. 6d. net.
 Peer Gynt : A New Translation. *Wide Crown*
 8vo. *5s. net.*

SABATINI, RAFAEL
 The Sea Hawk. *Crown 8vo.* 6s.

SAND, MAURICE
 The History of the Harlequinade. *Two*
 Volumes. *Med. 8vo.* *24s. net.*

SCOTT-JAMES, R. A.
 Personality in Literature. *Demy 8vo.* *7s. 6d.*
 net.

SIDGWICK, FRANK
 The Ballad (*The Art and Craft of Letters*). *F'cap*
 8vo. *1s. net.*

STONE, CHRISTOPHER
 The Burnt House. *Crown 8vo.* 6s.
 Parody (*The Art and Craft of Letters*). *F'cap 8vo.*
 1s. net.

STRAUS, RALPH
 Carriages and Coaches. *Med. 8vo.* *18s. net.*

STREET, G. S.
 People and Questions. *Wide Cr. 8vo.* *5s. net.*

SWINNERTON, FRANK
 George Gissing : A Critical Study. *Demy 8vo.*
 7s. 6d. net.
 R. L. Stevenson : A Critical Study. *Demy 8vo.*
 7s. 6d. net.

TAYLOR, G. R. STIRLING
 Mary Wollstonecraft : A Study in Economics
 and Romance. *Demy 8vo.* *7s. 6d. net.*

Martin Secker's Catalogue of Books Published at Number Five John Street Adelphi

*Martin
Secker's
Catalogue of
Books
Published at
Number
Five John
Street
Adelphi*

TAYLOR, UNA

MAURICE MAETERLINCK: A CRITICAL STUDY. *Demy 8vo. 7s. 6d. net.*

THOMAS, EDWARD

FEMININE INFLUENCE ON THE POETS. *Demy 8vo. 10s. 6d. net.*

A. C. SWINBURNE: A CRITICAL STUDY. *Demy 8vo. 7s. 6d. net.*

WALTER PATER: A CRITICAL STUDY. *Demy 8vo. 7s. 6d. net.*

THE TENTH MUSE. *F'cap 8vo. 2s. 6d. net.*

VAUGHAN, H. M.

AN AUSTRALASIAN WANDER-YEAR. *Demy 8vo. 10s. 6d. net.*

WALPOLE, HUGH

FORTITUDE. *Cr. 8vo. 6s. and 2s. net.*

THE DUCHESS OF WREXE. *Crown 8vo. 6s.*

WATT, L. M.

THE HOUSE OF SANDS. *Crown 8vo. 6s.*

WILLIAMS, ORLO

VIE DE BOHÈME. *Demy 8vo. 15s. net.*

GEORGE MEREDITH: A CRITICAL STUDY. *Demy 8vo. 7s. 6d. net.*

THE ESSAY (*The Art and Craft of Letters*). *F'cap 8vo. 1s. net.*

YOUNG, FILSON

*NEW LEAVES. *Wide Crown 8vo. 5s. net.*

A CHRISTMAS CARD. *Demy 16mo. 1s. net.*

*PUNCTUATION (*The Art and Craft of Letters*). *F'cap 8vo. 1s. net.*

YOUNG, FRANCIS BRETT

DEEP SEA. *Crown 8vo. 6s.*

*THE DARK TOWER. *Crown 8vo. 6s.*

YOUNG, F. & E. BRETT

UNDERGROWTH. *Crown 8vo. 6s.*

ROBERT BRIDGES: A CRITICAL STUDY. *Demy 8vo. 7s. 6d. net.*

PART TWO
INDEX OF TITLES

General Literature

*Martin
Secker's
Catalogue of
Books
Published at
Number
Five John
Street
Adelphi*

ARMSTRONG, THOMAS, C.B. A Memoir. Reminiscences of Du Maurier and Whistler. *Edited by L. M. Lamont.*

ART OF BALLET, THE. *By Mark E. Perugini.*

ART OF SILHOUETTE, THE. *By Desmond Coke.*

AUSTRALASIAN WANDER-YEAR, AN. *By H. M. Vaughan.*

BALLAD, THE. *By Frank Sidgwick.*

BATTLE OF THE BOYNE, THE. *By D. C. Boulger.*

BEHIND THE RANGES. *By F. G. Aflalo.*

BIRDS IN THE CALENDAR. *By F. G. Aflalo.*

BRIDGES : A CRITICAL STUDY. *By F. E. Brett Young.*

BUTLER : A CRITICAL STUDY. *By Gilbert Cannan.*

CAMILLE DESMOULINS. *By Violet Methley.*

CARMINA VARIA. *By C. Kennett Burrow.*

CARRIAGES AND COACHES : THEIR HISTORY AND THEIR EVOLUTION. *By Ralph Straus.*

CHRISTMAS CARD, A. *By Filson Young.*

COMEDY. *By John Palmer.*

CORONAL, A. A New Anthology. *By L. M. Lamont.*

CRITICISM. *By P. P. Howe.*

CUMBERLAND LETTERS, THE. *By Clementina Black.*

D'EON DE BEAUMONT. *Translated by Alfred Rieu.*

DRAMATIC PORTRAITS. *By P. P. Howe.*

DRAMATIC WORKS OF GERHART HAUPTMANN. *6 vols.*

Martin Secker's Catalogue of Books Published at Number Five John Street Adelphi

DRAMATIC WORKS OF ST. JOHN HANKIN. *Introduction by John Drinkwater.* 3 *vols.*

EGYPTIAN ÆSTHETICS. *By René Francis.*

EPIC, THE. *By Lascelles Abercrombie.*

ESSAY, THE. *By Orlo Williams.*

FEMININE INFLUENCE ON THE POETS. *By Edward Thomas.*

FOUNTAINS IN THE SAND. *By Norman Douglas.*

GISSING : A CRITICAL STUDY. *By Frank Swinnerton.*

GRAHAME OF CLAVERHOUSE. *By Michael Barrington.*

HARDY : A CRITICAL STUDY. *By Lascelles Abercrombie.*

HIEROGLYPHICS. *By Arthur Machen.*

HISTORY. *By R. H. Gretton.*

HISTORY OF THE HARLEQUINADE, THE. *By Maurice Sand.*

IBSEN : A CRITICAL STUDY. *By R. Ellis Roberts.*

IRISH EXILES AT ST. GERMAINS, THE. *By D. C. Boulger.*

JAMES : A CRITICAL STUDY. *By F. M. Hueffer.*

KENSINGTON RHYMES. *By Compton Mackenzie.*

LEADERS OF THE PEOPLE. *By Joseph Clayton.*

LETTERS FROM GREECE. *By John Mavrogordato.*

LINLEYS OF BATH, THE. *By Clementina Black.*

LYRIC, THE. *By John Drinkwater.*

MAETERLINCK : A CRITICAL STUDY. *By Una Taylor.*

MAGIC. *By G. K. Chèstèrton.*

MARY WOLLSTONECRAFT. *By G. R. Stirling Taylor.*

MEREDITH : A CRITICAL STUDY. *By Orlo Williams.*

MORRIS : A CRITICAL STUDY. *By John Drinkwater.*

NEW LEAVES. *By Filson Young.*

NOOKS AND CORNERS OF OLD ENGLAND. *By Allan Fea.*

OLD CALABRIA. *By Norman Douglas.*

OLD ENGLISH HOUSES. *By Allan Fea.*
PARODY. *By Christopher Stone.*
PATER : A CRITICAL STUDY. *By Edward Thomas.*
PEACOCK : A CRITICAL STUDY. *By A. Martin Freeman.*
PEER GYNT. *Translated by R. Ellis Roberts.*
PEOPLE AND QUESTIONS. *By G. S. Street.*
PERFUMES OF ARABY. *By Harold Jacob.*
PERSONALITY IN LITERATURE. *By R. A. Scott-James.*
POEMS. *By Compton Mackenzie.*
PUNCTUATION. *By Filson Young.*
REAL CAPTAIN CLEVELAND, THE. *By Allan Fea.*
REGILDING THE CRESCENT. *By F. G. Aflalo.*
REPERTORY THEATRE, THE. *By P. P. Howe.*
ROBERT KETT AND THE NORFOLK RISING. *By Joseph Clayton.*
ROSSETTI : A CRITICAL STUDY. *By John Drinkwater.*
SATIRE. *By Gilbert Cannan.*
SHAW : A CRITICAL STUDY. *By P. P. Howe.*
SHORT STORY, THE. *By Barry Pain.*
SOCIAL HISTORY OF SMOKING, THE. *By G. L. Apperson.*
SOME ECCENTRICS AND A WOMAN. *By Lewis Melville.*
SPECULATIVE DIALOGUES. *By Lascelles Abercrombie.*
STEVENSON : A CRITICAL STUDY. *By Frank Swinnerton.*
STUPOR MUNDI. *By Lionel Allshorn.*
SWINBURNE : A CRITICAL STUDY. *By Edward Thomas.*
SYNGE : A CRITICAL STUDY. *By P. P. Howe.*
TENTH MUSE, THE. *By Edward Thomas.*
THOSE UNITED STATES. *By Arnold Bennett.*
THOMPSON. *By St. John Hankin and G. Calderon.*
VIE DE BOHÈME. *By Orlo Williams.*
WHITMAN : A CRITICAL STUDY. *By Basil de Sélincourt.*

Martin Secker's Catalogue of Books Published at Number Five John Street Adelphi

13

Martin
Secker's
Catalogue of
Books
Published at
Number
Five John
Street
Adelphi

Fiction

ABOVE YOUR HEADS. *By Frederick Niven.*

ASPERN PAPERS, THE. *By Henry James.*

BANKRUPT, THE. *By Horace Horsnell.*

BATTLES OF LIFE. *By Austin Philips.*

BURNT HOUSE, THE. *By Christopher Stone.*

CARNIVAL. *By Compton Mackenzie.*

COLUMBINE. *By Viola Meynell.*

COMMON CHORD, THE. *By Phyllis Bottome.*

DEAD MEN'S BELLS. *By Frederick Niven.*

DEBIT ACCOUNT, THE. *By Oliver Onions.*

DEEP SEA. *By F. Brett Young.*

DUCHESS OF WREXE, THE. *By Hugh Walpole.*

FOOL'S TRAGEDY, THE. *By A. Scott Craven.*

FORTITUDE. *By Hugh Walpole.*

GOLIGHTLYS, THE. *By Laurence North.*

HANDS UP ! *By Frederick Niven.*

HOUSE OF SANDS, THE. *By L. M. Watt.*

IMPATIENT GRISELDA. *By Laurence North.*

IMPERFECT BRANCH, THE. *By Richard Lluellyn.*

IN ACCORDANCE WITH THE EVIDENCE. *By Oliver
Onions.*

LESSON OF THE MASTER, THE. *By Henry James.*

LOT BARROW. *By Viola Meynell.*

MARRIAGE OF QUIXOTE, THE. *By Donald Armstrong.*

MODERN LOVERS. *By Viola Meynell.*

14

OLD MOLE. *By Gilbert Cannan.*

ONE KIND AND ANOTHER. *By Barry Pain.*

OUTWARD APPEARANCE, THE. *By Stanley V. Makower.*

PASSIONATE ELOPEMENT, THE. *By Compton Mackenzie.*

PETER PARAGON. *By John Palmer.*

PORCELAIN LADY, THE. *By Frederick Niven.*

QUESTING BEAST, THE. *By Ivy Low.*

RECORD OF A SILENT LIFE, THE. *By Anna Preston.*

ROUND THE CORNER. *By Gilbert Cannan.*

SANINE. *By Michael Artzibashef.*

SEA HAWK, THE. *By Rafael Sabatini.*

SINISTER STREET. I. *By Compton Mackenzie.*

SINISTER STREET. II. *By Compton Mackenzie.*

STORY OF LOUIE, THE. *By Oliver Onions.*

TELLING THE TRUTH. *By William Hewlett.*

THE DARK TOWER. *By E. Brett Young.*

TURN OF THE SCREW, THE. *By Henry James.*

UNCLE'S ADVICE. *By William Hewlett.*

UNDERGROWTH. *By F. & E. Brett Young.*

UNDERMAN, THE. *By Joseph Clayton.*

WHITE WEBS. *By Theo Douglas.*

WIDDERSHINS. *By Oliver Onions.*

WILDERNESS OF MONKEYS, A. *By Frederick Niven.*

YEARS OF PLENTY. *By Ivor Brown.*

YOUNG EARNEST. *By Gilbert Cannan.*

Martin Secker's Catalogue of Books Published at Number Five John Street Adelphi

MARTIN SECKER

HIS COMPLETE CATALOGUE.   MCMXIV

BALLANTYNE
PRESS
LONDON

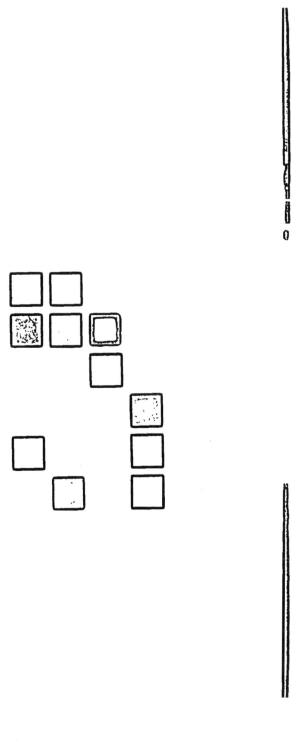

Lightning Source UK Ltd.
Milton Keynes UK
UKHW020629060820
367798UK00005B/601